Instructor's Resource Guide to Accompany

Organizational Behavior

SEVENTH EDITION

Don Hellriegel
Texas A & M University

John W. Slocum, Jr.
Southern Methodist University

Richard W. Woodman
Texas A & M University

Prepared by
Michael K. McCuddy
Valparaiso University

WEST PUBLISHING COMPANY
Minneapolis/St.Paul   New York   Los Angeles   San Francisco

WEST'S COMMITMENT TO THE ENVIRONMENT

In 1906, West Publishing Company began recycling materials left over from the production of books. This began a tradition of efficient and responsible use of resources. Today, up to 95% of our legal books and 70% of our college texts and school texts are printed on recycled, acid-free stock. West also recycles nearly 22 million pounds of scrap paper annually—the equivalent of 181,717 trees. Since the 1960s, West has devised ways to capture and recycle waste inks, solvents, oils, and vapors created in the printing process. We also recycle plastics of all kinds, wood, glass, corrugated cardboard, and batteries, and have eliminated the use of Styrofoam book packaging. We at West are proud of the longevity and the scope of our commitment to the environment.

Production, Prepress, Printing and Binding by West Publishing Company.

 TEXT IS PRINTED ON 10% POST CONSUMER RECYCLED PAPER  PRINTED WITH SOY INK

COPYRIGHT © 1995 by   WEST PUBLISHING CO.
610 Opperman Driv
P.O. Box 64526
St. Paul, MN 55164–0526

ISBN 0–314–05591–6

CONTENTS

PREFACE

This **Instructor's Resource Guide** accompanies the seventh edition of **Organizational Behavior** by Don Hellriegel, John W. Slocum, Jr., and Richard W. Woodman. The material contained in this guide is coordinated with and builds upon the text material.

Each chapter of the **Instructor's Resource Guide** is structured for ease of use. Each chapter contains the following sequentially ordered material:

- An overview of the chapter's content.

- A list of learning objectives for the chapter.

- An outline of the key topics discussed in the chapter.

- Definitions or descriptions of the key words and concepts that are used in the chapter.

- Detailed lecture notes in outline form. All the key words and concepts used in a chapter are underlined in the lecture notes. Transparencies are keyed to the lecture material and are highlighted in shaded boxes. Additionally, enrichment modules are provided in shaded boxes embedded within the lecture notes. The enrichment modules are intended to enhance and extend relevant concepts and ideas from the lecture notes.

- Suggested answers to the end-of-chapter discussion questions.

- Information on using the end-of-chapter self-diagnostic instrument.

- A descriptive overview of the end-of-chapter case and suggested answers for the case questions.

- A description of relevant video material that is available either in *West's Organizational Behavior Custom Video Series* or in various supplemental videos available from West. The video material is coordinated with the chapter content. A synopsis of each video is provided, along with suggested discussion questions and answers.

In addition to covering the 21 chapters of the text, the **Instructor's Resource Guide** contains instructional material related to the appendix and the integrating cases. Lecture notes are provided for the research methods material contained in the appendix. A descriptive overview of each integrating case acommpanies the detailed suggested answers for the case questions.

Supplemental materials are available from West Publishing Company for use with this **Instructor's Resource Guide**. These supplements include:

- A set of 266 transparency masters coordinated with the lecture notes for Chapters 1 through 21. The transparency masters reflect a mix of (1) figures and tables from the text, and (2) exhibits developed from the written text itself.

- A set of 50 color acetates which represent a subset of the 266 transparency masters. Most of the color acetates have been selected to enhance the presentation of figures from the text. All of the color acetates reflect major ideas and concepts presented in the text.

- A video package called *West's Organizational Behavior Custom Video Series*. This series contains videos for most but not all of the chapters. For those chapters where the custom video series does not have relevant material, supplementary videos are available from West.

- West's supplemental videos include tapes from the Association for Manufacturing Excellence and the Public Broadcasting System. Not only do these videos fill gaps in the custom video series, but they also supplement some chapters where a gap does not exist.

Additional information concerning these supplements is available from your local West representative.

When I agreed to develop this resource guide, I made a personal vow that it would be a guide worth being used. I hope I have accomplished that goal. You, the user, will be the ultimate judge.

The success of this project is due as much to others as it is to me, and I wish to thank them all. First, thanks are due to Don Hellriegel, John Slocum, and Dick Woodman. Working with them on this project has been a true pleasure; their support and encouragement were exceptional. Special thanks are due to Dick for recruiting me to write this resource guide, and to Don and John for generously supplying much of the material from which the enrichment modules were developed. I also wish to thank Professor Achilles A. Armenakis of Auburn University, whose written descriptions of the various videos provided the starting point for the video material that appears in this guide. A very special thanks is due to Esther Craig of West Educational Publishing, whose support, encouragement, and help contributed in many ways to the project's completion. Finally, though perhaps most importantly, I wish to express my deepest appreciation to Nancy, my wife and soulmate, and to Sean, Heather, and Ryan, our unmarried children. They sacrificed countless hours of family activities so I could work on this project—and to them, I dedicate this work.

Michael K. McCuddy
Valparaiso University

CHAPTER 1
INTRODUCTION TO ORGANIZATIONAL BEHAVIOR

CHAPTER OVERVIEW

Chapter 1 introduces the organizational behavior discipline by focusing on five specific, though not, unrelated themes. These themes have broad implications for how organizations function and how members of organizations behave. The themes are as follows:

1. Workplace diversity is increasing. Diversity contributes to differences in attitudes and behaviors. Diversity also creates pressure for people to change their behavior.

2. Seven issues are creating pressure for organizations to change during the 1990s. These issues include: downsizing, the lack of traditional promotional opportunities, expanding service organizations, total quality management, ethics, the global challenge, and use of technology.

3. Managerial skills which can help people respond to the challenges of workplace diversity and the issues facing organizations include: technical skills, interpersonal skills, conceptual skills, and communications skills.

4. To accomplish their work and use their skills, managers perform ten different roles (grouped into three categories). Interpersonal roles (*i.e.*, figurehead, leader, and liaison) enable managers to exercise their formal authority within the organizational system. Informational roles (*i.e.*, monitor, disseminator, and spokesperson) enable managers to establish and maintain a network of personal contacts, which is used to give and receive a wide range of information. Decisional roles (*i.e.*, entrepreneur, disturbance handler, resource allocator, and negotiator) enable managers to commit the organization or its subunits to specific courses of action.

5. A five-part conceptual model of organizational behavior is developed to promote understanding of how and why people behave as they do in organizational settings. The five major components of the conceptual model are: the environment, individual processes, interpersonal and group processes, organizational processes, and change processes. Each of the subsequent chapters in the text is linked into the conceptual model.

LEARNING OBJECTIVES

Upon completion of this chapter, the students should be able to:

1. Discuss diversity issues in organizations today.
2. Describe seven critical challenges facing organizations.
3. State the skills that employees need to develop to effectively work in a diverse organization.
4. Describe the roles that managers play.
5. Explain the fundamental concepts of organizational behavior.

CHAPTER OUTLINE

I. **Preview Case:** Cunningham Communications, Inc.

II. Diversity at Work

    A. The Workforce
    B. **Managing Diversity:** Hoechst-Celanese Diversity Programs
    C. Gender
    D. Race/Ethnicity
    E. Aging Workforce

III. Organizational Issues for the 1990s

    A. Downsizing
    B. Promotion
    C. Expanding Service Organizations
    D. Total Quality Management
    E. **Managing Quality:** USAA
    F. Ethics
    G. **Managing Ethics:** What To Do
    H. Global Challenge
    I. **Managing in Practice:** How Managers Learn Global Skills at Colgate-Palmolive Company
    J. Use of Technology
    K. Organizational Challenges

IV. Developing Skills

    A. Technical Skills
    B. Interpersonal Skills
    C. Conceptual Skills
    D. Communication Skills

V. Managerial Roles

    A. Interpersonal Roles
    B. Informational Roles
    C. Decisional Roles
    D. Summary of Roles

KEY WORDS AND CONCEPTS

Thirty-one key words and concepts are introduced in Chapter 1. The key words and concepts, along with definitions or appropriate descriptions, are as follows:

Communications skills: the abilities to send and receive information, and also to convey and understand thoughts, feelings, and attitudes.

Conceptual skills: the ability to view the organization as a whole and to apply one's planning and thinking abilities.

Decisional roles: the manager commits the organization or department to specific courses of action.

Disseminator role: the manager shares and distributes information to others in the organization.

Disturbance handler role: the manager resolves conflicts between subordinates or departments.

Diversity: a multi-dimensional mixture of people who vary by age, gender, race, religion, or life-style.

Downsizing: the process of letting people go in an attempt to improve efficiency and the organization's competitive position.

Empowerment: the employee's right to make decisions in their areas of responsibility.

Entrepreneurial role: the manager tries to improve the department and organization by identifying needed changes or by initiating projects.

Ethical dilemma: occurs when multiple competing values exist in a decision-making situation.

Ethics: the values and rules that define right and wrong.

Figurehead role: performing symbolic and ceremonial tasks for the department or organization.

Glass ceiling: a barrier so subtle that it is transparent, yet so strong that it prevents women and minorities from moving up in the management ranks.

Informational roles: managers build a network of contacts to enable them to receive and send large amounts of information.

Interpersonal roles: managers develop relationships with others and these relationships flow directly from the managers' formal authority.

Interpersonal skills: the abilities to lead, motivate, manage conflict, conduct group meetings, and work with others.

Leadership role: the manager directs and coordinates the tasks of subordinates in order to accomplish organizational goals.

Liaison role: the manager develops information sources, both inside and outside the organization.

Monitor role: the manager seeks and receives information.

Negotiator role: the manager represents a department or the company in negotiating with suppliers, customers, unions, and governments.

Organization design: a set of decisions about the shape and features of the organization's formal structure.

Organizational behavior: the study of human behavior, attitudes, and performance within organizational settings.

Outsourcing: the organization hires independent contractors and independent suppliers to do some of the firm's work rather than doing all of the work itself.

Process: how the tasks of the organization are carried out.

Resource allocator role: the manager decides who will get which resources and how much they will get.

Role: an organized set of behaviors associated with a particular job in an organization.

Skills: abilities which are performance-related and which can be learned.

Spokesperson role: the manager makes official statements to outsiders through the use of speeches, reports, television, and other media.

Technical skills: the ability to apply specific methods, procedures, and techniques in a specialized field.

Total Quality Management (TQM): an organizational philosophy and strategy for the long-term that makes continuous improvement a responsibility of all employees.

LECTURE NOTES

I.   Organizational behavior.

    A.   What is it?

        1.   <u>Organizational behavior</u> is the study of human behavior, attitudes, and performance within organizational settings.

        2.   Or alternatively, organizational behavior examines how and why people behave as they do in organizational settings.

    B.   Why should people study it?

        1.   By providing insights into how and why individuals and groups behave as they do, organizational behavior prepares people to become better employees and managers.

        2.   As current or future employees of organizations, organizational behavior helps people to understand what is happening in their organization and to them personally.

        3.   As future managers of organizations, organizational behavior helps to improve one's ability to deal effectively with individuals and groups in an organizational context.

    C.   An aid to understanding organizational behavior (see Transparency 1.1).

TRANSPARENCY 1.1
(FIGURE 1.1 IN THE TEXTBOOK)
ORGANIZATIONAL ICEBERG

---

        1.   Peoples' behavior is influenced by many factors—some overt and some covert.

        2.   Overt factors (easily seen or formal aspects of the organization) include goals, technology, structure, financial resources, and the skills and abilities of the organization's members.

        3.   Covert factors (hidden or behavioral aspects of the organization) include attitudes, communication patterns, team processes, personality, conflict, and problem-solving styles.

        4.   Together the overt factors and covert factors are like an organizational iceberg, with the overt factors being the tip of the iceberg showing above the water-line and the covert factors being the submerged part of the iceberg. To understand organizations and to function effectively in them, people must understand and utilize both parts of the iceberg. But all too often people focus primarily, if not solely, on the tip of the iceberg and discount or ignore the submerged portion of the organizational iceberg. And, like a real iceberg, it is the submerged potion that can sink the organization more easily than the visible portion.

II.   Understanding organizations and their effective functioning requires that one develop a comprehensive and systematic view of human behavior in the organizational context. One way of doing this is by examining important themes within the discipline of organizational behavior. Five specific themes are explored in the introductory chapter. These themes are: diversity at work, organizational issues for the 1990s, the skills needed to meet organizational challenges, the roles performed by managers, and the major components of organizational behavior. Transparency 1.2 summarizes these five themes.

TRANSPARENCY 1.2
(FROM TEXT MATERIAL IN THE TEXTBOOK)

FIVE ORGANIZATIONAL BEHAVIOR THEMES OF CHAPTER 1

III.   Theme 1: Diversity at work.

    A.   <u>Diversity</u> is defined as a multi-dimensional mixture of people who vary by age, gender, race, religion, or life-style.

        1.   Workplace diversity is increasing. Diversity contributes to differences in attitudes and behaviors, as well as creating pressure for people to change their behavior.

        2.   Diversity reflects some of the individual differences variables that affect how people behave. To adequately understand human behavior, therefore, one must appreciate these individual differences.

        3.   Race and gender have been the dominant diversity issues. However, other elements of diversity, such as age and beliefs, are becoming increasingly important.

    B.   Organizational and managerial implications of a more diverse workforce:

        1.   The changing composition of the workforce is affecting what people want and expect out of their work lives.

            a.   Increasingly, employees want their jobs to be challenging and to provide learning and growth opportunities. They also want to be <u>empowered</u>; that is, to be allowed to make decisions within their own areas of responsibility.

            b.   Views on promotions differ between older and younger workers. Older workers (over 40) value experience and have been willing to wait their turns in the promotional pipeline. Younger workers believe they should be promoted as quickly as competence permits, regardless of amount of experience.

        2.   Language differences may create communications barriers.

        3.   Ethnicity may influence the formation of informal groups within the organization. This, in turn, promotes teamwork and cohesiveness within the group but not between it and other groups.

        4.   Attitudinal and cultural differences may influence how people relate to their jobs and how they interact with other individuals and groups.

C.   Gender as a major diversity issue.

1.   Women constitute a significant segment of the workforce and will continue to be a significant segment in the foreseeable future. Some useful statistics for characterizing women in the workforce are as follows:

   a.   Since 1970, women have represented a large percentage of the growth in the U.S. workforce. This will continue.

   b.   About 35 percent of all women work in accounting/finance departments.

   c.   Women represent 35 percent of the managerial workforce but only one percent of top management.

   d.   Many female entrants to the workforce are better educated than in the past.

2.   With women becoming an increasingly large and significant component of the workforce, organizations are facing at least two major challenges in dealing with gender-related issues.

   a.   Women may encounter a <u>glass ceiling</u> in organizations—an invisible barrier that prevents them from advancing in the management ranks, thereby under-utilizing their managerial talents and skills. Organizations need to address the issue of ensuring full utilization of women's talents and skills.

   b.   Since women assume a disproportionate share of the responsibility for family care, organizations need to consider how they can contribute to the resolution of family-care problems. Sub-issues include provision of child-care facilities and arrangement of work and vacation schedules.

ENRICHMENT MODULE: MOMMY TRACK

What do you think of the idea to assist working mothers with small children—the establishment of a "mommy track" or an employment scheme that distinguishes between women who want to dedicate themselves to the job and those who want to combine career and children? Is it the answer to the growing number of women entering the workforce and management ranks or is it, as some contend, a "mommy trap"? Or is it an innovative program to attract and keep talented women, and aimed at increasing employee productivity , motivation, and satisfaction, while cutting down on absenteeism and turnover?

The "mommy track" concept was popularized by Felice Schwartz, a women's rights advocate who points out that too many employers give manager-moms only two options—full-time work or no work at all. Schwartz contends that instead, companies need to offer flexible working hours, part-time jobs, and job sharing for working mothers. For example, the accounting and consulting firm of Arthur Andersen & Company started a formal mommy track in 1989. A female worker can now work part-time for up to three years without leaving. The fast track to a partnership, however, has been delayed somewhat as a result—it may take eight years instead of six to become a partner. A major purpose of the Arthur Andersen program is to retain top female talent.

Could the mommy track approach be a danger signal for women? Will the mommy track concept be used by employers to perpetuate their "glass ceiling" philosophy? Some observers fear that a secondary track—one just for mothers—is a giant step backward for women. Some women are concerned that the mommy track can be used as an excuse for employers to not treat women as equally as they should be treated or to take mommy trackers less seriously than other employees.

Some opponents of the mommy track contend that a special track for women is illegal. An employer's attitude that "we didn't promote her because we felt she really cared about her kids more than the organization" is the same as any other discrimination. Companies may not even realize that what they are doing is sex discrimination. If the courts agree with this viewpoint, companies could be opening themselves up to a Title VII civil rights violation by "mommy tracking" certain employees.

A mommy track is likely to be a useful and welcome addition to a firm that enjoys a positive organizational culture. However, in an atmosphere of mistrust and suspicion, employees might perceive it as merely another management gimmick intended to perpetuate discriminatory policies.

This enrichment module is based on:

The mommy and daddy track. (1990, April 16). *Forbes*, 162-164.

    D.   Race/ethnicity as a major diversity issue.

          1.   Some useful statistics for characterizing minorities in the workforce are as follows:

               a.   During the rest of this decade minorities will account for about one-third of the growth in the U.S. workforce.

               b.   Less than 4 percent of top management positions are held by minority group members.

          2.   Organizations are facing at least two major challenges in dealing with race/ethnicity issues.

a.   Recruitment and retention of minority group workers will become increasingly important.

b.   Like women, minority group members may encounter a glass ceiling in organizations. More fully capitalizing on minority workers' abilities and skills will become more important.

ENRICHMENT MODULE: BLACK WOMEN AND MEN IN CORPORATE AMERICA

Black women seem to be rising through the corporate ranks more rapidly than black men. There are numerous reasons for this, including the following:

- Crime, drugs, and inadequate education sidetrack many black men from the corporate world.
- More and more African-American women and fewer and fewer African-American men are getting their educational credentials.
- Attitudes within corporate America seem to favor black women more than black men. Black women are seen as compliant and easier to get along with. Black men "are often seen by white supervisors as aggressive, suspicious or arrogant."
- To get ahead in corporate America one must understand the rules. Black males seem to take a much longer time to learn this than black females.
- Black women are viewed as "two-fers". With one person a company is getting both a woman and a minority group member.

This enrichment module is based on:

Gaiter, D.J. (1994, March 8). The gender divide: Black women's gains in corporate America outstrip black men's. *The Wall Street Journal*, A1 & A6.

TRANSPARENCY 1.3
(The above list of reasons for the more rapid advancement of black women
is contained in the transparency package.)

E.   Age as an emerging diversity issue.

1.   The number of middle-aged workers is increasing while the number of middle management jobs is decreasing. Displaced older workers may be unable to find jobs and salaries comparable to their previous employment.

2.   Older workers may need to be employed longer to provide adequate staffing levels in organizations.

IV.   Theme 2: Organizational issues for the 1990s.

A.   At least seven major issues will create pressure for organizations to change in the 1990s. These issues are: downsizing, the lack of traditional promotional opportunities, expanding service organizations, total quality management, ethics, the global challenge, and use of technology.

B.   Downsizing.

1.   <u>Downsizing</u> is the process of letting people go in an attempt to improve efficiency and the organization's competitive position.

2.   The main organizational challenge of downsizing is how to accomplish the reduction. Options include natural attrition, early retirements, shortened work weeks, and layoffs.

3.   While downsizing may accomplish its efficiency and competitiveness goals, it may also have detrimental psychological effects on the remaining workers.

4.   Downsizing also limits advancement opportunities because of the reduction in management positions.

ENRICHMENT MODULE: WALKING WOUNDED

Companies use downsizing to streamline their operations, thereby becoming more productive and more profitable. However, downsizing often produces results that are much less favorable than expected. An important reason for this is a phenomenon known as the "walking wounded"—the workers who are left after the others have been laid off. The walking wounded "can feel so distrustful, overworked and insecure that the businesses fail to achieve their projected gains in productivity and profitability." Moreover, the malaise of surviving employees can persist for months and may worsen over time.

A recent survey of 531 mostly large companies indicated that 85 percent expected corporate restructuring to improve profits, but only 46 percent of the companies had an earnings improvement within two fiscal years. The survey also indicated that 58 percent of the companies expected higher productivity, but only 34 percent achieved it within two fiscal years.

This enrichment module is based on:

Lublin, J.S. (1993, December 6). Walking wounded: Survivors of layoffs battle angst, anger, hurting productivity. *The Wall Street Journal*, A1 & A8.

C.   Lack of traditional promotional opportunities.

1.   Promotions have traditionally been used as an incentive to keep people working hard and to have them remain committed to the organization.

2.   However, traditional promotion opportunities will become much more limited because of increased competition due to considerable growth in the number of older workers in the workforce.

3.   Possible outcomes:

a.   Top management positions may be filled with increasingly talented people in the foreseeable future.

b.   Talented people may leave their employer and form their own businesses.

D.   Expanding service organizations.

1.   Service, not manufacturing, dominates the U.S. economy. Approximately two-thirds of U.S. gross national product and two-thirds of the employment are in the service sectors. For the past thirty years, about 90 percent of growth in nonagricultural employment has been in the service sector. Dominance of the service sector will continue in the future.

E.   Total quality management (TQM).

1.   <u>Total quality management</u> is an integrated approach for managing the various components and processes that affect the quality of a firm's products or services. TQM involves designing quality into products and services, preventing and correcting any product or service defects, and continuously improving the product or service as well as the process for delivering it.

2.   Businesses have become increasingly concerned about the quality of their products and/or services. In large part, this increased concern has grown out of the need to be competitive in both the domestic and global marketplaces.

F.   Ethics.

1.   <u>Ethics</u> is defined as the values and rules that define right and wrong. These values and rules derive from many different sources, including the law, organizational policies, behavioral norms, family background, religious beliefs, personal standards and needs.

2.   Conflicts among the different value sources may create problematic decision situations for people.   This causes <u>ethical dilemmas</u>. Additionally, many situations in organizations are not clearly black or white, right or wrong. There are lots of gray areas where potentially conflicting moral considerations might be involved. This also creates ethical dilemmas.

3.   The challenge to people in organizations is do what is morally right when there is not clear guidance on what is morally right.

G.   Global challenge.

1.   Increasingly, businesses operate and compete in a global environment. American firms operate overseas for a variety of reasons including cost advantages, market proximity, a favorable regulatory environment, etc. Sometimes firms conduct part of their business through <u>outsourcing</u>—that is, hiring independent contractors and suppliers rather than trying to do all the work themselves. Also, American firms, even if they do not produce products overseas, are increasingly interested in penetrating overseas markets. Likewise, foreign producers are increasingly interested in selling to Americans. Hence, significant global business competition has evolved and continues to evolve.

2.   The increasing globalization of business will require organizations having significant global operations to develop globally competent managers. This means recruiting, selecting and promoting people who can work effectively with people from different cultures.

H.   Use of technology.

    1.   Businesses are becoming more technologically oriented through the use of automation, robotics, and electronic information systems.

    2.   Technology can alter the way in which work is done, thereby helping the organization to operate more efficiently and effectively.

    3.   Technology also can alter the location in which work is accomplished, thereby permitting increased use of satellite business locations and telecommuting. Telecommuting poses a special challenge to management because of the absences of face-to-face contact with subordinates.

ENRICHMENT MODULE: WHAT WILL WORK BE LIKE IN THE YEAR 2000?

Fortune magazine identifies six trends will reshape the workplace by the year 2000. These trends are:

- "The average company will become smaller, employing fewer people."
- "The traditional hierarchical organization will give way to a variety of organizational forms, the network of specialists foremost among these."
- "Technicians, ranging from computer repairmen to radiation therapists, will replace manufacturing operatives as the worker elite."
- "The vertical division of labor will be replaced by a horizontal division."
- "The paradigm of doing business will shift from making a product to providing a service."
- "Work itself will be redefined: constant learning, more high-order thinking, less nine-to-five."

How will these trends affect the nature of managerial work in the future? First, managerial jobs will be changed. Managers will need to develop substantive expertise—a specialty in, say, finance, marketing, or computer systems, etc. Managers must possess skills at coordinating a team of specialists. Second, managerial jobs will be renamed. Rather than being called managers or facilitators or coaches or mentors, people in these jobs will likely be called coordinators. Third, "tomorrow's manager-replacements will have to excel at striking all kinds of deals." Fourth, these new coordinators must be able "to make others feel that they care."

This enrichment module is based on:

Kiechel III, W. (1993, May 17). How we will work in the year 2000. *Fortune*, 38+.

TRANSPARENCY 1.4
(The above description of future managerial work is contained in the transparency package.)

V.   Theme 3: Skills needed to meet organizational challenges.

    A.   All employees, but especially professional managerial employees, will need to respond to the challenges of workplace diversity and the issues facing organizations. Employees can do this by developing and utilizing their <u>skills</u> (*i.e.,* abilities which are performance-related and which can be learned) in each of the following areas: technical skills, interpersonal skills, conceptual skills, and communications skills.

B. <u>Technical skills</u> involve one's ability to apply the necessary methods, procedures, and techniques to work in a specialized field. Technical skills reflect either detailed or broader knowledge. Detailed knowledge refers to the hands-on skills necessary to perform a specific job. Broader knowledge refers to one's understanding of how the technical skills of many people combine to produce a given product or service.

C. <u>Interpersonal skills</u> involve one's abilities to deal with people as individuals or in groups. Interpersonal effectiveness is based upon mutual respect between oneself and others.

D. <u>Conceptual skills</u> involve one's abilities to think and plan, to see the "big picture" or overall organizational framework, and to relate variables to one another in the context of this big picture.

E. <u>Communications skills</u> include sending and receiving information in both oral and written forms, as well as being sensitive to and understanding of people's thoughts, feelings, and attitudes.

F. Communications skills provide the foundation for technical, interpersonal, and conceptual skills at all management levels (see Transparency 1.5). As one moves up the management hierarchy, detailed technical knowledge becomes less important for managerial success while broader technical knowledge, interpersonal skills, and conceptual skills become more important.

TRANSPARENCY 1.5
(FIGURE 1.2 IN THE TEXTBOOK)

SKILLS FOR EMPLOYEES

ENRICHMENT MODULE: ASSESSING AND DEVELOPING ENTRY-LEVEL JOB SKILLS
(*An Experiential Activity*)

This enrichment module is an experiential activity which relates to the material on technical, interpersonal, conceptual, and communication skills. The purpose of the exercise is to have students focus on these skills in relation to the jobs they expect to hold upon entering the workforce.

The procedure for using this exercise is as follows:

1.   Prior to conducting the exercise, generalized job descriptions are developed for typical entry level positions encountered by students in each of the academic majors (e.g., accounting, marketing, finance, human resources, etc.). *The Dictionary of Occupational Titles* is a reasonable source for brief but informative job descriptions. The job descriptions provide students with some background information so that they are not completely naive. Additionally, at least some of the students will have some personal knowledge of the nature of entry level jobs in their chosen field.

2.   Class members should be divided according to academic major and then subdivided into small groups of three to five within academic major.

3.   Each small group is given the following assignment:

   a.   Focusing on typical entry level jobs in your field, choose one that appeals to most, if not all, of the group members.
   b.   Identify the specific technical, interpersonal, conceptual, and communication skills which you believe will be needed to function effectively in that entry level job.
   c.   Discuss how these skills can be developed (or refined) through educational experiences and/or extracurricular activities.
   d.   Prepare a brief oral report of your discussion in order to share your ideas with the other class members.

4.   Small groups report out and the professor provides appropriate commentary and facilitates further discussion.

An alternative approach to the small group format is for the professor to choose two or three typical entry-level positions and then facilitate a class discussion focusing on items (3b) and (3c) above.

This enrichment module is adapted from an exercise developed by M.K. McCuddy.

VI.   Theme 4: Roles performed by managers.

   A.   Every organizational member has one or more roles to fulfill in performing his or her job. A <u>role</u> is defined as an organized set of behaviors associated with a particular job in an organization. Ten different roles are relevant to managers' jobs, and every manager's job consists of some combination of these roles. The particular combination of roles will influence which skills managers use in accomplishing their work and how they will use those skills.

   B.   The ten managerial roles are grouped into three broad categories: interpersonal roles, informational roles, and decisional roles (see Transparency 1.6).

TRANSPARENCY 1.6
(FIGURE 1.3 IN THE TEXTBOOK)

MANAGERIAL ROLES

---

1. Interpersonal roles derive from managers' formal authority and focus on managers developing relationships with other people rather than on collecting or sharing information or making decisions. Interpersonal roles include three specific sets of managerial behaviors: the figurehead role, the leadership role, and the liaison role. In the figurehead role, the manager performs various symbolic and ceremonial tasks on behalf of the organization. In the leadership role, the manager supervises and coordinates subordinates' work efforts in order to achieve organizational goals while satisfying employees' needs. In the liaison role, the manager develops information sources outside the organization or in other subunits within the organization.

2. Informational roles, which are created by enacting the interpersonal roles, are used to build a network of contacts inside and outside the organization. Informational roles consist of three sets of behaviors: the monitor role, the disseminator role, and the spokesperson role. In the monitor role, the manager searches for and gathers information that is relevant to the organization. In the disseminator role, the manager distributes information to others within the organization. In the spokesperson role, the manager distributes information to people outside the organization.

3. Decisional roles, which draw upon the interpersonal and informational roles, are used to commit the organization or its subunits to specific courses of action. Decisional roles include the following sets of managerial behaviors: the entrepreneurial role, the disturbance handler role, the resource allocator role, and the negotiator role. In the entrepreneurial role, the manager initiates projects or identifies changes in order to improve the organization or its subunits. In the disturbance handler role, the manager helps to resolve conflicts between organizational subunits or with outside organizations. In the resource allocator role, the manager decides upon the type and amount of resources to be distributed to different organizational subunits. In the negotiator role, the manager represents the organization or one of its subunits in dealing with customers, vendors, unions, and governmental agencies.

ENRICHMENT MODULE: MANAGERIAL ROLES
(*An Experiential Activity*)

This enrichment module is an experiential activity which pertains to the material on managerial roles. The purpose of the exercise is to have students explore how the roles are enacted in different managerial positions at different levels of the management hierarchy.

The procedure for using this exercise is as follows:

1. Class members should be divided into groups of three members each.

2. Each group decides on the type of business (e.g., financial services, manufacturing, utilities, retailing, etc.) in which to conduct interviews.

3. The group then assigns one of the members to interview a first-line supervisor or lower-level manager in the chosen business. A second group member is assigned to interview a middle-level manager in the business, and the third member will interview an upper-level manager in the business.

4. Each group member arranges for and conducts the assigned interview. The interview should focus on the following questions:

    a.   Which of the ten managerial roles exist in the interviewee's job?
    b.   How does the interviewee enact each of the managerial roles identified above?
    c.   What skills does the interviewee use in enacting the roles identified above?

5. Each member prepares an interview summary for the group.

6. During class-time four or five groups are selected at random to share their interview findings with the others members of the class.

This enrichment module is adapted from an exercise developed by M.K. McCuddy.

VII.   Several fundamental concepts of organizational behavior help to facilitate understanding of the conceptual model of organizational behavior which is developed as the fifth theme of this chapter.

   A.   People differ from one another. Managers can positively affect employees' performance by recognizing such differences and by treating people as individuals.

   B.   People's job behavior is a function of the interaction between internal and external factors. Internal factors include ability to learn, motivation, perception, attitudes, personality, and values. External factors include the organization's reward system, organizational politics, group behavior, managerial leadership styles, and the organization's design.

   C.   <u>Organization design</u> involves a set of decisions about the shape and features of the organization's formal structure.

   D.   Organizations consist of people interacting with and influencing one another in various ways and through various mechanisms; hence organizations are social systems.

E.   <u>Process</u> concerns how the tasks of the organization are carried out. Process includes decision making procedures, leadership styles and practices, communication channels, motivational methods, and conflict-resolution practices.

VIII.   Theme 5: The major components of organizational behavior.

A.   Managers' work affects and is affected by people. Therefore, managers should be knowledgeable about people and their behavior in an organizational context. This is why the discipline of organizational behavior is so valuable to current as well as future managers. Unfortunately, organizational behavior is not a precise discipline like chemistry or physics. Rather, it is a discipline that can be approached from many different perspectives.

B.   Many different factors affect the behavior of people in organizations. These factors may be psychological, sociological, political, economic, etc. They may be internal or external to the individual or the organization. They may interact with one another. Collectively, these factors represent a quite complex system—a system that is perhaps best represented with some sort of conceptual model.

1.   The conceptual model used in the textbook identifies five major categories of variables: the environment, individual processes, interpersonal and group processes, organizational processes, and change processes. Transparency 1.7 outlines the variables found within each category and shows how the variable categories are interrelated. Basically, individual processes, interpersonal and team processes, organizational processes, and change processes interact with each other and all operate within the context of the surrounding environment.

TRANSPARENCY 1.7
(FIGURE 1.4 IN THE TEXTBOOK)

FRAMEWORK FOR UNDERSTANDING ORGANIZATIONAL BEHAVIOR

---

2.   Individual processes explore how various factors affect individuals' job behavior and performance. Individual processes include: how personality and attitudes affect individuals' work behavior (Chapter 2); how perception influences individuals' capacity to learn behavior and their interpretation of behavior and situations within the organization (Chapter 3); how individuals make decisions (Chapter 4); how rewards influence work behavior (Chapter 5); how work behavior is stimulated, sustained, and stopped (Chapter 6); how work behavior can be influenced by goal-setting and performance enhancement techniques (Chapter 7); and how stress influences work behavior (Chapter 8).

3.   Interpersonal and team processes examine how different variables influence the behaviors of groups of people. These processes include: how individual work teams function (Chapter 9); how work teams interact with each other (Chapter 10); how leaders influence other people in order to achieve organizational goals (Chapter 11); how communications influences interpersonal and team effectiveness (Chapter 12); and how conflict arises and how its effective resolution can contribute to the effective functioning of work groups (Chapter 13).

4.   Organizational processes encompass the broader, organization-wide variables which

influence human behavior in the workplace. Organizational processes include: how the organization's culture influences the way in which the organization operates (Chapter 14); how power and political behavior influence the operations of the organization and its subunits (Chapter 15); how job design is used to help organize work tasks and work methods in order to carry out the organization's activities (Chapter 16); how various factors influence the features and shape of the organization as well as relationships among organizational subunits (Chapter 17); and how managerial decision making influences the organization's operations (Chapter 18).

5.   Change processes concern how organizations adapt to their respective environments and modify the work behaviors of organization members. Included among the key aspects of these change processes are the following: how the process of planned organizational change occurs (Chapter 19); how six basic strategies can be used to implement planned organizational change (Chapter 20); and how individuals' careers can be managed(Chapter 21).

IX.   Tying the five themes together.

A.   In performing their interpersonal, informational, and decisional roles, managers use their technical, interpersonal, conceptual, and communications skills to respond to the challenges posed by an increasingly diverse workforce and by various pressures for organizational change. Much of what managers do affects or is affected by people in one way or another. Therefore, to effectively perform their roles, utilize their skills, and respond to organizational challenges, managers must be knowledgeable about how and why people behave as they do. And how and why people behave as they do is what organizational behavior is all about.

DISCUSSION QUESTIONS: SUGGESTED ANSWERS

1.   *What types of diversity does your organization face today? How is your university or organization responding?*

Both work organizations and universities encounter diversity issues dealing with gender, race/ethnicity, age, physical abilities, and gender/sexual orientation. In work organizations, each of these diversity issues may be encountered in the recruitment, selection, and promotion of human resources. Additionally, some of these diversity issues reflect differing cultural values, which in turn influence peoples' job attitudes and behaviors. In the university environment, gender and race/ethnicity may influence decisions regarding admissions, financial aid, and faculty recruitment. Also, some universities have adopted policies regarding the use of "hate language"—often an outgrowth of race/ethnicity and/or gender/sexual orientation concerns.

The above examples should provide the basis for a more in-depth discussion focusing on the organization of interest. The key to this question is to determine how, if at all, the generic diversity issues of gender, race/ethnicity, age, physical abilities, and gender/sexual orientation manifest themselves in the organization of interest.

2.   *What roles did Andrea Cunningham play in her public relations firm? How effectively did she*

play these roles?

The evidence suggests that Cunningham enacted all ten managerial roles in her public relations firm. More solid evidence exists in support of some roles than others. Also, some specific incidents testify to more than one managerial role being enacted.

The managerial roles and specific activities by which those roles were enacted are as follows:

a.   Figurehead role: implied by Cunningham appearing to be the primary point of contact with clients.

b.   Leadership role: developing a mission statement, establishing account teams with profit-and-loss responsibility, setting goals for the account teams, and leaving a to-do list when she went on vacation.

c.   Liaison role: developing client contacts, using two key people to help run the firm, using account teams to facilitate the management process, and developing a trusting relationship with her secretary.

d.   Monitor role: getting information from prospective clients in the process of selling the firm's services; getting information from existing clients to effectively service accounts; and getting information internally from key management people, account teams, and the secretary.

e.   Disseminator role: setting goals for the account teams, and providing the vice president with a to-do list prior to leaving for vacation.

f.   Spokesperson role: personally delivering most of the firm's advice and insight to clients.

g.   Entrepreneurial role: instituting account teams, and then subsequently recognizing the need for change in the company's structure and operations (including the role played by the account teams).

h.   Disturbance handler role: attempting to make peace between two key people who were hired to help manage the company, but not appearing to do much to deal with account team rivalries and failure to cooperate with one another.

i.   Resource allocator role: assigning accounts to account teams.

j.   Negotiator role: attracting new clients.

Views will vary on how effectively Cunningham played each of these roles. Students, however, should consider that the leadership, liaison, monitor, disseminator, disturbance handler, and resource allocator roles probably were not enacted very well. Case evidence which supports this contention includes:

a.   Cunningham's own dissatisfaction because of her failure to delegate and to create a caring, growing organization.

b.   The vice president's mini-insurrection while Cunningham was on vacation, including his rejection of the company's mission and his failure to perform activities on the to-do list.

c.   The competition and rivalry that resulted from the account team structure.

d.   High turnover among the staff.

3.   *The most successful organizations will be those that recognize the challenge and opportunity for maintaining a diverse workforce. In light of the recent emphasis on downsizing, what potential problems do you see for maintaining a diverse workforce?*

Workforce diversity is a relatively recent concern in many companies. Consequently, there is the risk that a portion, perhaps a significant portion, of relatively recent hires reflect attempts to expand workforce diversity. If companies downsize on the basis of seniority, workforce diversity could be sacrificed.

Additionally, downsizing may limit promotional opportunities, which in turn may impact on workforce diversity in the higher managerial ranks. Women and minorities may encounter an more impenetrable glass ceiling with downsizing than without it because fewer managerial positions are needed in organizations.

4.   *If more people are entering the workforce and organizations are promoting people more slowly, what motivational challenges does this situation present for managers?*

Providing organizational members with challenging and stimulating work is the primary motivational challenge posed by an expanding workforce coupled with reduced promotional opportunities. As the workforce expands, many of the new entrants are looking for interesting and challenging jobs, where their training and skills will be utilized and where they can grow and develop. Sometimes new entrants are a bit too idealistic in terms of what they expect from their first job. Nonetheless, those expectations, idealistic or realistic, challenge managers to provide as stimulating a job experience as possible.

Traditionally, promotions have represented success and progress in the organization. Without adequate advancement opportunities, some organizational members are likely to become less motivated. Rather than continuing to perform well some employees may regress to minimally acceptable performance—essentially going through the motions and doing just enough to get by. Others may leave the organization to become entrepreneurs.

One reason for limited promotional opportunities is downsizing. Often, layers of middle management are eliminated through downsizing, thus creating fewer positions for possible advancement. If, however, elimination of layers of management is coupled with empowerment of lower level employees, work can still be made more challenging and stimulating even with fewer promotions.

5.   *What are some ethical dilemmas you have faced? How did you resolve them?*

Students could focus on ethical dilemmas which they have encountered in any area of their lives. Possible sources of ethical dilemmas are students' interpersonal relationships with family and/or friends, work experiences, educational experiences, etc. Perhaps the most salient ethical dilemmas for students are the ones they have encountered in the educational process. Recent wide-spread concerns about academic dishonesty in post-secondary education suggest the possibility of numerous ethical dilemmas. Whatever the focus of the ethical dilemmas, the key to this question is that each dilemma reflects multiple and competing ethical values. Additionally, the discussion should consider how the person's actions addressed these competing values.

6.   *How might organizations shape the behavior, attitudes, and values of their employees?*

Discussion of this question can revolve around the framework for understanding organizational behavior (Figure 1.4). Individual processes such as learning and reinforcement, work motivation, and the use of goal setting and reward systems can be utilized to shape behavior, attitudes, and values. Organizations can also utilize elements of interpersonal and team processes and organizational processes in shaping behavior, attitudes, and values. For example, the way in which leaders behave will influence employees' behavior, attitudes, and values. The design of specific jobs can influence the work behavior and attitudes of the job-holders. The design of the shape and features of the organization will also affect the organization's members. Other examples can be cited based upon the topics addressed in each of the chapters dealing with interpersonal and team processes or organizational processes. Perhaps one of the more obvious and dramatic ways in which organizations can shape employees' behavior, attitudes, and values is through planned organizational change and career planning and development.

7.   *How can you develop each of the four types of skills on your first job?*

This question focuses on technical, interpersonal, conceptual, and communications skills. Technical skills can be developed by learning specific job procedures and duties, by studying appropriate manuals or attending technically-targeted training sessions, and through on-the-job training regarding specific jobs elements. Interpersonal skills can be built through training in interviewing and counseling, and by actively participating on project teams. Conceptual skills can be developed by sharpening learning as much as possible about the organization, its products or services, and how one's department and job fit into the organization's plans and operations. Conceptual skills can also be built by enhancing analysis and planning abilities. Communications skills can be built by writing effective letters, memos, and reports, by making presentations, and by interacting with others on an individual or team basis. Communications skills can also be enhanced by learning to be a better listener.

The topic of this question can be addressed more fully by using the Enrichment Module: Assessing and Developing Entry-Level Job Skills.

8.   *What are some difficulties you might face in taking a managerial position in a foreign country?*

Three sections of the text provide information which is especially relevant to this question. The text sections are: **Managing in Practice:** How Managers Learn Global Skills at Colgate-Palmolive, **Managing Across Cultures:** Getting the Best From Managers in Different Cultures, and **Managing in Practice:** Cultural Influences on Behavior.

Among the difficulties identified in these sections are the following:

     a.   Understanding and appreciating the cultures of foreign countries.
     b.   Being willing to learn from people in other cultures.
     c.   Being able to work with people from other cultures as equals.
     d.   Being able to communicate with people who speak different languages.
     e.   Being able to understand business from a global perspective.
     f.   Recognizing that interpersonal, informational, and decisional roles may be enacted differently in different cultures.
     g.   Recognizing that differences in work behavior and attitudes in different countries are partly due to differences in cultural values.

9.   *What are some of the challenges that women and minority group members face in organizations?*

Both women and minority group members may encounter a glass ceiling in organizations. They will need to seek out ways, such as finding a mentor, to make sure that their talents and abilities are fully utilized by the organization.

Women and minority group members may encounter some form of attitudinal backlash simply because of their gender or minority group status. Rather than justly recognizing their abilities and performance, other organization members may attribute any successes to favorable treatment based upon gender or minority group status. This, in turn, could rachet up the pressure for women or minority group members to be exceptional performers.

Finally, women members of the workforce face a special challenge since they assume a disproportionate share of family care responsibilities. Meeting both work responsibilities and family care responsibilities can become a delicate balancing act which is physically and emotionally draining.

DEVELOPING SKILLS—
SELF DIAGNOSIS: HOW MUCH DO YOU VALUE DIVERSITY?

A 20-item self-assessment instrument permits students to determine the extent to which they value diversity. Responses to the 20 items are based on a five-point Likert-type response scale where SD (Strongly Disagree) = 1 and SA (Strongly Agree) = 5. A total score of 80 or above indicates the person can adapt easily to a multi-cultural work environment. A score lower than 50 indicates the person needs to improve their understanding of the need to value diversity.

Once students determine how much they value diversity, they could be encouraged to pursue one of two courses of action. Students whose scores indicate they can adapt to a multi-cultural environment, should determine the specific attitudinal and behavioral characteristics which can help them to function effectively in a multi-cultural environment. They should then consider what they can do to preserve and reinforce these characteristics. Students whose scores indicate they need to improve their understanding of the value of diversity, should look toward making some changes. They should determine the attitudinal and behavioral changes which they need to make in order to deal more effectively with people in a multi-cultural environment.

DEVELOPING SKILLS—
A CASE IN POINT: WANDA HILL AT TRUST CONSULTANTS

CASE OVERVIEW

Trust Consultants is a financial consulting and financial services firm. The case focuses on a luncheon meeting between Wanda Hill, a vice president at Trust Consultants in the Los Angeles, California office, and Jose Rodriquez, a subordinate completing his first year of employment with Trust Consultants. Rodriquez was hired to develop the Hispanic market. The purpose of the luncheon meeting was to review Rodriquez's performance. During the meeting Rodriquez requested a private office as a reward for his performance. He also threatened to resign if his request was not granted. His request, however, was in conflict with established organizational policy. Specifically, there were only six private offices for the 33 financial consultants in the Los Angeles office, and they were reserved for the most senior and experienced brokers. The case ends with Hill pondering a decision on Rodriquez's request.

CASE QUESTIONS

1.   *What are some diversity issues in this case?*

Ethnicity is evident in that Rodriquez, a Hispanic, was hired to develop the Hispanic market for Trust Consultants. Ethnicity is also evident in that Rodriquez spoke only Spanish with his clients when they met in the office. Rodriquez's observation of co-workers national and religious holidays also provides evidence for ethnicity as a diversity issue.

Age may be a critical diversity issue in this case. Rodriquez, as a younger or at least less senior employee, discounts the experience of the more senior workers. He seems to think that he has little, if anything, to learn from more experienced financial consultants. He also opposes organizational policies which benefit more senior workers. Overall, Rodriquez seems to be eager and impatient, a maverick rather than a team player—all of which may reflect the fairly common "young buck" phenomenon.

Gender does not appear to be much of a diversity issue. Hill, a woman, is a vice president; she has not encountered a glass ceiling, at least not yet. Also, Hill has male subordinates, including Rodriquez. No solid evidence exists to indicate that this relationship is problematic, though the potential does exist.

2.   *What roles did Hill play? How effective was she?*

The information in the case indicates that Hill played five specific managerial roles. These were: the leadership role, the liaison role, the monitor role, the disseminator role, and the resource allocator role.

In playing the leadership role, Hill conducted the performance appraisal meeting with Rodriquez; talked with financial consultants regarding job activities; engaged in informal coaching of employees; persuaded older employees to mentor younger employees; and persuaded younger employees, with the exception of Rodriquez, to take advantage of this mentoring. She also tried to build a high quality, professional team that would excel at matching clients with financial products. In general, Hill performed this role well except that she could not influence Rodriquez to access the knowledge and expertise of more experienced employees.

In the liaison role, she established personal contacts with the financial consultants. Hill appears to have played this role well with all the consultants except perhaps Rodriquez, who does not seem to be as open to sharing work-related information as the other consultants may be.

In the monitor role, Hill sought information from Rodriquez during the performance appraisal meeting and from the other financial consultants while helping them in their daily work activities. Hill seems to have performed this role effectively.

In the disseminator role, she distributed information through informal coaching of and daily contacts with the financial consultants. Hill also played the disseminator role during her discussion with Rodriquez regarding organizational policies on (a) recommending high risk investments to clients and (b) private offices for financial consultants. There is no evidence to indicate that Hill did not effectively fulfill the disseminator role in terms of informal coaching of and daily contacts with the financial consultants. However, in discussing organizational policies with Rodriquez, she appears to have been somewhat ineffective. She stated her views but Rodriquez seems to have dismissed them as being irrelevant to his work role at Trust Consultants.

In the resource allocator role, Hill had to make a decision regarding Rodriquez's request for a private office. The case ended with Hill contemplating this decision so no substantive evidence exists to indicate how effectively she played this role.

3.   *Should Hill give Rodriquez a private office? What factors influenced your decision?*

Students who answer this question with a **NO** are likely to cite one or more of the following reasons:

a.   It violates the established organizational policy of reserving private offices for the six most senior and experienced financial consultants.

b.   Hill should not be pressured by Rodriquez's threat to resign and seek employment elsewhere.

c.   Giving Rodriquez the office would not be fair to employees with more experience and greater seniority.

d.   Giving Rodriquez the private office could be perceived as giving him an undeserved reward. Even though he was a top performer, he did not assimilate himself very well into Trust Consultant's corporate culture.

Students who answer this question with a **YES** are likely to cite one or more of the following reasons:

a.   A private office will enhance Rodriquez's stature, which in turn will aid further development of the Hispanic market.

b.   If Rodriquez resigned his position at Trust Consultants, he would probably take his clients with him to his new employer. This could have a negative impact on Trust Consultant's penetration of the Hispanic market.

c.   Rodriquez is the top performing financial consultant in the Los Angeles office even though he has been employed for only a year.

d.   Performance rather than seniority or experience should be rewarded.

COURSE ENHANCEMENT—
WEST'S ORGANIZATIONAL BEHAVIOR CUSTOM VIDEO SERIES

Two videos from *West's Organizational Behavior Custom Video Series* can be used to enhance the material in Chapter 1. These videos are: *Scientech, Inc.* and *AT&T's Vision of the Future.*

VIDEO: *SCIENTECH, INC.*

Approximate Time: 4 minutes

Video Summary:

This video describes how Scientech, Inc.—an engineering and scientific organization devoted to finding solutions for problems associated with the world's most sophisticated technological systems such as nuclear power plants, commercial airliners, jet fighters, and computers—solved the organizational challenges it faced. Three main challenges are discussed: organizational growth, a changing market, and cash management. The challenge of growth was solved by focusing on leadership, shared ownership and profits, developing a corporate culture that empowers employees, providing incentives to exercise that empowerment, and stressing quality and integrity of work. The challenge of the changing market was met by being versatile in applying the company's expertise to different customers and by having employees with skills in multiple areas. The challenge of cash management was solved by hiring a financial manager, inserting penalty clauses into contracts, having advance approval for all expenditures exceeding $500, and the regular update and use of a cash flow model. As a result of these efforts, Scientech, Inc. experienced 900 percent growth in it sales and workforce over a three-year period. Additionally, all its expansion has been funded internally.

Discussion Questions and Suggested Answers for Video:

1.   *Scientech, Inc. seems to view its human resources as assets rather than as expenses. What implications does this have for how the organization operates?*

       When viewed as assets, human resources are treated as an investment. They are developed and nurtured because of the short-term and long-term contributions they can make to the company's operations. Scientech recruits talented people who are competent in multiple areas. Through shared ownership, empowerment, and proper incentives the company creates an environment that encourages them to fully utilize their talents.

2.   *Suppose that Scientech, Inc. viewed its human resources as expenses rather than assets. What differences would there be in how the organization operates?*

       When viewed as expenses, human resources are considered to be expendable commodities. People are not developed and nurtured. The corporate culture does not encourage empowerment. Rather, human resources are used for their immediate contribution, and when no longer needed for a specific purpose, they are "discarded" through terminations.

       Students should be encouraged to speculate about the possible organizational consequences of viewing employees as expenses. Impacts on productivity and profitability as well as employee satisfaction and commitment could be considered.

VIDEO: *AT&T'S VISION OF THE FUTURE*

Approximate Time: 14 minutes

Video Summary:

Telecommunications technology of the future will affect the ways organizational members communicate on and off the job. The concept of the "global village" and the role of telecommunications technology are dramatized in AT&T's Vision of the Future. This video segment concerns the life of a family in the future and the communications products they will use in their daily lives. The new products introduced by AT&T include televisions with communication capabilities, virtual reality video games with communication capabilities, and video conference calls with simultaneous foreign language translation capability. The possible ramifications of technology on organizational behaviors can be extrapolated from this video. For example, globalization is facilitated because language barriers are eliminated. The limitations of interpersonal interactions in geographically dispersed organizations are lessened. Tele-electronic organizational interfaces reduce travel cost, increase personal effectiveness, and eliminate health stress (*e.g.,* jet lag).

Discussion Questions and Suggested Answers for Video:

1. *What will people's jobs be like in the future if AT&T's vision become reality?*

    Responding to this question requires some speculation but that speculation can be grounded in logic and reason. For example, telecommuting would be facilitated. Vast information resources would be readily available for decision making. Global operations would be enhanced. Numerous other reasonable examples exist, and students should be encouraged to explore a wide range of possibilities.

2. *Given what people's jobs may be like in the future, what kinds of skills will they need? In turn, what are the implications for education and training?*

    Discussion of this question can be tied into the material on technical, interpersonal, conceptual, and communications skills. Each skill likely will be impacted, though in different ways. Technical skills will still be needed but perhaps at a much higher level of sophistication with regard to using the communications equipment of the future to the fullest extent possible. Interpersonal skills will need to be enhanced because more opportunities for interacting with people may be a natural outgrowth of machines taking over much of the "drudge work" of data management and analysis. Interpersonal skills may need enhancement as well because of the encounters made possible through video telecommunications equipment. Conceptual skills will need to be enhanced with regard to defining problems and formulating alternative solutions in order to capitalize on the full potential of the communication system. Communication skills—especially verbal—will need to be enhanced to fully and effectively utilize the system.

    Education and training will need to be altered so people come into the workplace with the requisite technical, interpersonal, conceptual, and communications skills. Exploration of needed educational and training changes should build upon the preceding discussion.

CHAPTER 2
PERSONALITY AND ATTITUDES

CHAPTER OVERVIEW

Chapter 2, as the initial chapter on individual processes, introduces two major individual differences variables: personality and attitudes. Personality is examined in terms of its basic nature and its sources (*i.e.*, heredity and various environmental factors). The key components of personality structure are introduced and related to specific personality traits (*i.e.*, self-esteem, locus of control, introversion and extraversion, dogmatism and authoritarianism) which have relevance for organizational behavior. The chapter also explores the basic nature of attitudes and the linkage between attitudes and behavior. Two major work attitudes—job satisfaction and organizational commitment—are considered as well.

Additionally, Chapter 2 promotes an understanding of the concept that human behavior involves a complex interaction of the person with events in the surrounding environment. Finally, individual differences are linked to ethical behavior.

LEARNING OBJECTIVES

Upon completion of this chapter, the students should be able to:

1. Define personality and describe the basic sources of personality differences.
2. Identify the "Big Five" personality factors and explain why these concepts are useful.
3. Provide some examples of specific personality traits that have important relationships to work behavior.
4. Explain the concept of attitudes and describe their components.
5. Describe the general relationship between attitudes and behavior.
6. Define job satisfaction and explain why it is important.
7. Explain the concept of organizational commitment and identify important work outcomes of commitment.

CHAPTER OUTLINE

KEY WORDS AND CONCEPTS

Twenty-six key words and concepts are introduced in Chapter 2. The key words and concepts, along with definitions or appropriate descriptions, are as follows:

Amoral management: reflects managerial behaviors that are indifferent to ethical considerations, as though different standards of conduct apply to business than to other aspects of life. Amoral mangers seem to lack awareness of ethical or moral issues and act with no thought for the impact that their actions might have on others.

Attitudes: relatively permanent feelings, beliefs, and behavioral tendencies directed toward specific persons, groups, ideas, issues, or objects.

Authoritarian personality: refers to people who rigidly adhere to conventional values, readily obey recognized authority, exhibit a negative view of society, are concerned with power and toughness, and oppose the use of subjective feelings.

Behavioral intentions model: a model which suggests that behavior is more predictable (and understandable) if we focus on a person's specific intentions to behave in a certain way. These specific intentions depend on both attitudes toward the behavior and perception of norms regarding the behavior.

"Big Five" personality factors: five distinct collections of related personality traits which describe an individual's personality structure in terms of adjustment, sociability, conscientiousness, agreeableness, and intellectual openness.

Cognitive moral development: refers to an individual's level of moral development. People pass through stages of moral reasoning as they mature. Higher levels of cognitive moral development are characterized by a more profound understanding of principles of justice, ethical behavior, and balancing individual versus social rights.

Culture: culture refers to the distinctive ways that different human populations or societies organize their lives.

Dogmatism: refers to the rigidity of a person's beliefs.

External locus of control: refers to an individual's belief that his/her life is controlled primarily by chance, fate, or other people.

Extraversion: the tendency to be oriented toward other people, events, and objects. Extraverts tend to be sociable, lively, impulsive, and emotionally expressive.

General theory of behavior: an attempt to understand or describe all behavior all the time.

Immoral management: refers to managerial behaviors that are devoid of any ethical principles. Immoral managers maximally exploit opportunities for personal or corporate gain to the exclusion of other considerations.

Individual differences: refers to the fact that people differ from one another in a variety of ways, including personality and attitudes.

Interactionist perspective: refers to the view that both the person and the situation in which the person is behaving must be examined in order to fully understand and explain the individual's behavior.

Internal locus of control: refers to an individual's beliefs that his/her life is controlled primarily by his/her own behavior and actions.

Introversion: the tendency to be directed inwardly and to have a greater sensitivity to abstract ideas and personal feelings. Introverts tend to be quiet, introspective, and emotionally unexpressive.

Locus of control: refers to the extent to which individuals believe that they can control events affecting them.

Moral management: managerial behaviors focus on and follow ethical norms, professional standards of conduct, and compliance with applicable regulations and laws. Moral managers will not pursue profits outside the boundaries of the law and sound ethical principles.

Nature-nurture controversy: a sharp disagreement within personality theory about the extent to which genetic factors influence personality. The nature position sides with heredity and the nurture position sides with a person's experiences with the environment.

Norms: rules of behavior, or proper ways of acting, which have been accepted as appropriate by members of a group or society.

Organizational commitment: refers to the strength of an employee's involvement in and identification with the organization.

Personality: a stable set of personal characteristics and tendencies that determine certain similarities and differences in the patterns of people's thoughts, feelings, and actions.

Personality trait: refers to the basic "units" or components of personality.

Reengineering: the radical redesign of business processes to achieve major gains in service or product quality, time, or cost. Reengineering is not fixing things that are broken. Rather, it is redesigning the organization with a view toward the future and unconstrained by existing methods, structures, or workforce availability.

Self-esteem: the evaluation people make of themselves in terms their own behavior, abilities, appearance, and worth.

LECTURE NOTES

I.   Each individual's behavior involves a complex interaction of the person with events in the surrounding environment. Part I of the text promotes understanding of the person variable through its focus on individual processes. Chapter 2 initiates the examination of the person by exploring personality and attitudes—two major individual differences variables (*i.e.*, the ways in which people differ from one another). Transparency 2.1 identifies the key ideas to be addressed in exploring personality and attitudes.

TRANSPARENCY 2.1
(FROM TEXT MATERIAL IN THE TEXTBOOK)

OVERVIEW OF PERSONALITY AND ATTITUDES AS MAJOR INDIVIDUAL DIFFERENCES

In addition to the primary focus on personality and attitudes, some attention is given to individual differences and ethical behavior.

II.   Personality as a major individual differences variable.

    A.   The basic nature of personality.

        1.   Personality represents personal characteristics that lead to consistent patterns of behavior.

        2.   Consistent with this general notion, Salvator Maddi, a personality theorist, has defined personality as "a stable set of characteristics and tendencies that determine certain commonalities and differences in the psychological behavior (thoughts, feelings, and actions) of people." These commonalities and differences "have continuity over time and may not be easily understood as the sole result of the social and biological pressures of the moment."

        3.   Three key ideas are embedded in Maddi's definition.

            a.   Personality theory is a general theory of behavior—it pertains to all behavior all the time.

            b.   Personality theory describes both what people have in common with one another and how they differ from one another.

            c.   Personality is relatively stable over time.

ENRICHMENT MODULE: STRAIGHTENING OUT MANAGERS' PERSONALITY DISORDERS

In the 1990s executive coaches are being used by companies in helping managers to correct their personality disorders. The reasoning behind this movement is quite simple: "If managers are battering and terrifying the talent around and beneath them, they're likely to be wounding the bottom line."

Managers who are in need of executive coaching do not lack technical skills. Rather, what they lack are the skills to lead and get along with others—skills which in part may be rooted in the behavioral characteristics and tendencies of people's personalities.

Most managers who need executive coaching fall into one of two categories. The first category consists of white men in their late 40s who have advanced rapidly because of outstanding technical ability—usually in engineering or finance. Typically, these men have been promoted recently to positions where their subordinates have much different technical backgrounds than they do. Shouting orders and taking names characterizes the management style used by people in this category. Managers in this category make people feel like idiots for asking questions, finish people's sentences, refuse to listen to others, and castigate both peers and subordinates. As a consequence, people in other departments often refuse to work with these managers' subordinates.

The second category of managers who need executive coaching typically includes women, not necessarily caucasian, in their late 30s. Women in this category have soared through the lower corporate ranks due to their brilliance and dedication to the job. However, they have now arrived at the point where they must work with equally talented peers, but they have not mastered the complex game of competition and cooperation played at the new managerial level. They perceive male chauvinism to be everywhere, whether it is real or imagined. Managers in this category tend to isolate themselves from people in their departments and from the rest of the organization.

This enrichment module is based on:

Smith, L. (1993, December 27). The executive's new coach. *Fortune,* 126-134.

B.   Sources of personality differences.

1.   The <u>nature-nurture controversy</u> is a sharp disagreement within personality theory about the relative impact of heredity and environment on personality. The nature position sides with heredity and the nurture position sides with a person's experiences with the environment. While some personality theorists have taken an extreme position which emphasized either heredity or environment, current thinking is that both heredity and environment are important determinants of personality.

2.   The sources of personality differences are summarized in Transparency 2.2 and are explained in more detail below.

TRANSPARENCY 2.2
(FIGURE 2.1 IN THE TEXTBOOK)

SOURCES OF PERSONALITY DIFFERENCES

3.   Heredity as a source of personality differences.

   a.   Research on twins raised apart indicates that heredity may play a larger role in personality formation than many experts had thought. About half the variance in personality has been attributed to heredity.

   b.   A currently popular view is that heredity may set limits on the development of personality characteristics; subject to these limitations, personality characteristics may then be determined by environmental forces.

4.   Environment as a source of personality differences.

   a.   Four environmental components—culture, family, group membership, and life experiences—contribute to personality differences.

   b.   Culture: <u>Culture</u> refers to the distinctive ways that different human populations or societies organize their lives. Culture contributes to both similarities and differences in behavioral patterns. Even though cultures are distinctive, they are not homogenous nor do all members of the culture respond to cultural characteristics in the same way. An example of this is provided by the tensions that exist between different generations in the American workforce (see Transparency 2.3).

TRANSPARENCY 2.3
(TABLE 2.1 IN THE TEXTBOOK)

TENSION BETWEEN THE "BABY BOOM" AND THE "BABY BUST" GENERATIONS

---

   c.   Family: One's family is the primary means for socializing an individual into a particular culture, thereby influencing personality formation. A variety of family-related variables influence personality development, including parental behavior, socioeconomic status, family size, birth order, race, religion, geographic location, parents' educational level, etc.

   d.   Group membership: The roles which people assume and the experiences they have as members of various groups are another source of personality similarities and differences. Personality similarities may arise among members of a given group, particularly if the group is a powerful force in the lives of long-term members. Personality differences may result from the multi-faceted influence of membership in many different groups, both past and present.

   e.   Life experiences: Each individual's life is unique in terms of specific events and experiences. In turn, these specific events and experiences may have an important impact on the development of one's personality.

C.   Personality structure and the "Big Five" personality factors.

   1.   An individual's personality may be described in terms of specific <u>personality traits</u>, which are the basic "units" or components of personality.

   2.   While thousands of personality traits exist, recent research has identified a small set

of key personality factors which can be used to describe the "structure" of an individual's personality. Five major personality factors—often called the "Big Five" personality factors—describe an individual's personality structure in terms of adjustment, sociability, conscientiousness, agreeableness, and intellectual openness (see Transparency 2.4).

TRANSPARENCY 2.4
(FIGURE 2.2 IN THE TEXTBOOK)

THE "BIG FIVE" PERSONALITY FACTORS

---

a.   Each factor is a collection of related personality traits.

b.   Each factor is represented on a continuum, with the endpoints of the continuum reflecting polar opposites on the personality factor. One end of the continuum has a positive connotation while the other has a negative connotation.

3.   An interesting example of negative aspects of personality—that is, traits that are not admired—is provided by the descriptions of America's toughest bosses (see Transparency 2.5).

TRANSPARENCY 2.5
(TABLE 2.2 IN THE TEXTBOOK)

FORTUNE MAGAZINE'S TOUGHEST BOSSES

ENRICHMENT MODULE: PSYCHO BOSSES FROM HELL

Jim Miller, CEO of Miller Business Systems, organized a national contest to find out just how bad a boss could be. In determining a contest winner Miller looked for the most gruesome description of a boss. Descriptions of criminal behavior and physical and sexual abuse were not eligible for the contest, however.

The winner's boss "wrote a memo threatening immediate dismissal for anyone adjusting the office thermostat." This boss "also demanded that employees taking time off for funerals show a copy of the obituary to verify their relationship to the deceased." Moreover, this boss "called a 900 number for psychic advice on key decisions."

The runners-up had equally interesting stories. A pregnant woman described the telephone call which her boss made to her when she was at home in labor. According to this woman, her boss continued the conversation for 20 minutes, even though she alerted him each time a new contraction was beginning. Her daughter was born an hour later, and her boss called her at the hospital first thing the following morning to discuss business. Another runner-up "described how his boss made him and his colleagues bark like dogs to receive their paychecks." Still another runner-up indicated that her supervisor's motto was "people are animals." Another runner-up's boss was an ex-military man who "liked to 'playfully' choke and bite employees."

This enrichment module is based on:

Psycho bosses from hell. (1993, October 18). *Fortune*, 44.

D. Specific personality traits associated with the "Big Five" and their linkages to behavior.

   1. Individual personality is important in the study of organizational behavior because of the linkage between personality and behavior. Thus, knowledge of personality differences helps managers and employees in diagnosing and understanding behavior in organizational settings.

   2. The linkage between a "Big Five" personality factor and specific behavior often is clearest when focusing on a single trait from the collection of traits that make up a single factor. Specific traits from each of the "Big Five" factors will be explored in the context of the personality/behavior linkage.

   3. Self-esteem.

      a. Self-esteem is the evaluation people make of themselves in terms their own behavior, abilities, appearance, and worth.

      b. Self-esteem most likely would be part of the adjustment factor of personality.

      c. People with high self-esteem, as compared to those with low self-esteem, will take more risks in job selection, may be more attracted to high-status occupations, are more likely to choose unconventional or nontraditional jobs, have more positive experiences in the job search process, are less easily influenced by others' opinions in the work setting, set higher goals for themselves and place more value on attaining those goals, and are less susceptible to adverse job conditions (*e.g.*, stress, conflict, ambiguity, poor supervision, poor working conditions, etc.).

4.   Locus of control.

a.   <u>Locus of control</u> refers to the extent to which individuals believe that they can control events affecting them. Locus of control may be internal or external. People with an <u>internal locus of control</u> believe that their lives are controlled primarily by their own behavior and actions. People with an <u>external locus of control</u> believe that their lives are controlled primarily by chance, fate, or other people.

b.   Locus of control is part of the conscientiousness factor of personality.

c.   Internals, as compared to externals, have better control over their own behavior, are more active politically and socially, search more actively for information about their situations, are more likely to attempt to influence others, are less likely to be influenced by others, may be more achievement oriented, dislike a directive style of supervision, and adjust more readily to personal changes such as international transfers.

d.   Job performance is also affected by locus of control. For instance, internals perform better in complex jobs where rewards are distributed contingently. On the other hand, externals perform better on routine, repetitive jobs lacking contingent rewards. More detailed information on the relationship between locus of control and job performance is provided in Transparency 2.6.

TRANSPARENCY 2.6
(FIGURE 2.3 IN THE TEXTBOOK)

THE EFFECTS OF LOCUS OF CONTROL ON PERFORMANCE

---

5.   Introversion and extraversion.

a.   <u>Introversion</u> is the tendency to be directed inwardly and to have a greater sensitivity to abstract ideas and personal feelings. Introverts tend to be quiet, introspective, and emotionally unexpressive.

b.   <u>Extraversion</u> is the tendency to be oriented toward other people, events, and objects. Extraverts tend to be sociable, lively, impulsive, and emotionally expressive.

c.   Most people are only moderately introverted or moderately extraverted, or are relatively balanced between introversion and extraversion. Both extreme introversion and extreme extraversion, while less commonly occurring, can interfere with a person's effectiveness in an organization.

d.   Introversion and extraversion are part of the sociability factor.

e.   Some extraversion is important for managerial success because of the manager's need to work through and with other people. Introverts perform better in a quiet environment while extraverts perform better in a environment with more sensory stimulation.

6.   Dogmatism and authoritarianism.

    a.   <u>Dogmatism</u> refers to the rigidity of a person's beliefs.

        (1)   Highly dogmatic people view the world as a threatening place, often regard legitimate authority as absolute, and accept or reject other people on the basis of their agreement or disagreement with accepted authority or doctrine.

        (2)   The highly dogmatic individual, as compared to the low dogmatic individual, is close-minded, depends more on authority figures for guidance and direction, is more easily influenced by authority figures, needs more group structure to work effectively with others, and limits the search for information in decision situations.

    b.   Authoritarianism is closely related to dogmatism but is narrower in scope. The <u>authoritarian personality</u> refers to people who rigidly adhere to conventional values, readily obey recognized authority, exhibit a negative view of society, are concerned with power and toughness, and oppose the use of subjective feelings.

        (1)   The authoritarian personality is subservient to authority figures and probably prefers highly directive, structured leadership.

    c.   Dogmatism and authoritarianism are part of the intellectual openness factor of personality.

ENRICHMENT MODULE: MATCHING PERSONALITY AND OCCUPATIONS

Should organizations try to match personality characteristics of employees with the requirements of the job? According to John Holland's personality-job fit theory, the answer is **YES**.

Holland's model is based on the concept of fit between a person's interests—interpreted to represent personality—and his or her occupation. According to this theory, there are six basic personality types. An individual's satisfaction and propensity to leave a job depend on the degree to which an individual's personality matches his or her occupation. That is, satisfaction is highest and turnover lowest where personality and occupation are in agreement. The key point of this model is that there do appear to be intrinsic differences in personality among individuals in different occupations. When individuals' personalities are congruent with their occupations, they are more satisfied and less likely to resign than people in incongruent occupations.

The following are examples of the six personality types, typical personality characteristics, and matching congruent occupations:

Personality Type	Personality Characteristics	Congruent Occupation
Artistic	Involves: Self-expression, creativity, emotional activities	Art, music, writing, design, architecture
Enterprising	Involves: Attaining power and status, verbal activities to influence and persuade	Law, small-business management, public relations
Social	Involves: Interpersonal and communication activities	Social work, teaching, counseling, foreign service
Investigative	Involves: Thinking, organizing, and understanding concepts	Mathematics, news reporting, biology, physical sciences
Realistic	Involves: Physical activities, skill, strength, coordination, assertive behaviors	Farming, forestry, training
Conventional	Involves: Rule-regulated activities, sublimation of personal need to organization or person of power and status	Accounting, finance, corporate management

This enrichment module is based on:

Holland, J. (1985). *Making vocational choices: A theory of vocational personalities and work environments*, 2nd ed. Englewood Cliffs, NJ: Prentice-Hall.

TRANSPARENCY 2.7
(The above table is contained in the transparency package.)

III.   The person and the situation.

A.   Personality is but one way, albeit a major way, of describing individual differences among people. Attitudes, perception, problem-solving styles, learning, motivation, and responses to stress (*i.e.,* the remainder of Part I of the text) also delineate individual differences among people. Taken together these variables define the similarities and differences which exist among people. In short, these variables define the person.

B.   However, behavior is not just a function of the person. Rather, behavior is always the result of a complex interaction between the person and the situation. This is known as an interactionist perspective—a perspective which is taken throughout the textbook.

IV.   Attitudes as a major individual differences variable.

A.   The basic nature of attitudes.

1.   Attitudes are relatively permanent feelings, beliefs, and behavioral tendencies directed toward specific persons, groups, ideas, issues, or objects.

2.   Like personality, attitudes are influenced by both heredity and person's background and life experiences.

3.   An attitude consists of three interactive components:

a.   An affective component, or the feelings, sentiments, moods, and emotions about someone or something.

b.   A cognitive component, or beliefs, opinions, knowledge, or information a individual has about someone or something.

c.   A behavioral component, or the predisposition to act on a favorable or unfavorable evaluation of someone or something.

B.   The linkage between attitudes and behavior.

1.   While attitudes are related to behavior, the relationship frequently is neither simple nor direct. The prediction of behavior from attitudes can be improved if general attitudes are used to predict general behaviors, if specific attitudes are used to predict specific behaviors, and if the time that elapses between attitude measurement and behavior is kept to a minimum.

2.   The behavioral intentions model, depicted in Transparency 2.8, provides a useful way to examine the relationship between attitudes and behavior.

TRANSPARENCY 2.8
(FIGURE 2.4 IN THE TEXTBOOK)

BEHAVIORAL INTENTIONS MODEL

---

a.   The model suggests that behavior is more predictable (and understandable) if we focus on a person's specific intentions to behave in a certain way. The model shows that behavioral intentions depend on both attitudes toward the behavior and perception of norms regarding the behavior. (<u>Norms</u> are rules of behavior, or proper ways of acting, which have been accepted as appropriate by members of a group or society.)

b. If both attitudes and perceptions of norms are positive, behavioral intentions will be strong. However, if the two are in conflict, behavioral intentions will be determined by the relative strength of attitudes and perceptions of norms.

c. Behavioral intentions will result in actual corresponding behavior when perceived situational or internal constraints—such as real or perceived skill deficiencies—are minimized.

3. Sometimes attitudes and behavior are so strongly linked that achieving successful behavioral change is difficult, if not impossible, unless supportive attitudes are in place. An example is provided by the attitudes which have hindered and helped various organizational efforts at <u>reengineering</u>—the radical redesign of business processes to achieve major gains in quality, time, or cost. The traditional work attitudes described in Transparency 2.9 reflect attitudes that hinder behavior change in reengineering efforts. The reengineered work attitudes in Transparency 2.9 are the attitudes which facilitate successful behavioral change in reengineering efforts.

TRANSPARENCY 2.9
(TABLE 2.3 IN THE TEXTBOOK)

TRADITIONAL VERSUS REENGINEERED WORK ATTITUDES

C. Job satisfaction as a major work attitude.

1. <u>Job satisfaction</u> refers to one's general attitude toward work or toward a job. Information about job satisfaction can be used to help determine actions that might be taken to improve people's lives at work, or to try to influence job performance.

2. The various sources of job satisfaction provide important clues regarding actions which can be taken to improve people's lives at work. Transparency 2.10 identifies several sources—called work factors—as well as the effects that those sources have on job satisfaction. A key idea here is that job satisfaction should be viewed primarily as an outcome of an individual's work experience.

TRANSPARENCY 2.10
(TABLE 2.5 IN THE TEXTBOOK)

EFFECTS OF VARIOUS WORK FACTORS ON JOB SATISFACTION

---

3. A clear and direct relationship between job satisfaction and job performance does not exist. In part, this is because job satisfaction is a general attitude and job performance is usually task specific. However, job satisfaction as a general measure appears to be directly related to overall organizational performance as a general measure.

4. Despite the absence of a clear satisfaction-performance relationship, the satisfaction

of organization members is important for two reasons:

   a.   Since satisfaction is an outcome of work, high levels of dissatisfaction help in identifying needed organizational changes.

   b.   Dissatisfied employees are more likely to be absent from work, have a higher turnover rate, and have more physical and mental health problems. In turn, absenteeism, turnover, and health problems are costly for organizations.

D.   Organizational commitment as a major work attitude.

   1.   <u>Organizational commitment</u> refers to the strength of an employee's involvement in and identification with the organization. High commitment is characterized by:

      a.   A strong belief in and acceptance of the organization's goals and values.

      b.   A willingness to exert considerable effort on behalf of the organization.

      c.   A strong desire to maintain membership in the organization.

   2.   People's initial commitment is determined by their individual characteristics and the degree of congruence between their expectations and organizational realities.

   3.   Subsequent commitment is influenced by job experiences—many of the same factors that influence satisfaction also influence commitment (again refer to Transparency 2.10).

   4.   Individuals with a higher level of organizational commitment are less likely to quit their jobs, are less likely to be absent from work, are more goal-directed in the pursuit of their work assignments, and waste less time at work. Because of these relationships, high levels of commitment prove less costly for the organization.

V.   Individual differences and ethics.

A.   Ethical behavior—an increasingly important consideration in all types of organizations—provides an excellent example of organizationally-relevant behavior that is influenced by individual differences. Some of the key individual differences in ethical behavior are as follows:

   1.   In making organizational decisions, people with a high internal locus of control exhibit more ethical behavior than people with a high external locus of control.

   2.   People with higher levels of <u>cognitive moral development</u>—or higher levels of moral judgment—are more likely to behave ethically.

   3.   Styles of managerial ethics:

      a.   <u>Immoral management</u> refers to managerial behaviors that are devoid of any ethical principles.

      b.   <u>Moral management</u> reflects managerial behaviors that are guided by ethical principles.

    c.   <u>Amoral management</u> refers to managerial behaviors that reflect an indifference toward ethical principles.

B.   Managers can cope with individual variations in ethical attitudes and behaviors by doing the following:

    1.   Identifying ethical attitudes which are crucial for the organization's operations, and developing these ethical attitudes through appropriate training programs.

    2.   Selecting employees with desired ethical attitudes.

    3.   Incorporating ethics into the performance review and evaluation process.

    4.   Establishing a work culture that reinforces ethical attitudes.

ENRICHMENT MODULE: ACADEMIC ETHICS

The ethical dilemmas which people encounter in business may be somewhat remote to business students with relatively little practical organizational experience. However, students commonly encounter ethical issues in academic activities. How students deal with issues of academic ethics provides experiences which may influence subsequent ethical (or unethical) behavior in business. In short, students are people at the beginning of the human resource pipeline for organizations. What students bring into that pipeline in terms of prior ethical experiences will have some, perhaps unknown, impact on their behavior in and movement through the pipeline.

Seven realistic ethical dilemmas which may be encountered in academia are presented below. Students should respond to each dilemma by completing the scales below each description. The scales assess whether the student himself or herself approves or disapproves of the behavior that is described, and the extent to which the student thinks most other students approve or disapprove of the same action. Student responses to these dilemmas can then be used to generate discussion regarding individual differences in ethical beliefs and the reasons for those differing beliefs. These dilemmas also can be used to help explore the impact of ethical behavior and unethical behavior on oneself, one's peers, and the organization at large.

Dilemma 1: John has heard through the grapevine that someone is selling a copy of the final exam in his statistics class and *everyone* has bought it. Rumor has it that the final is impossible, so if John doesn't get a copy, he will fail while everyone else does well, eliminating the possibility of a curve. John decides to buy a copy of the final exam.

Myself: Approve ___ ___ ___ ___ ___ ___ ___ Disapprove
Most Students: Approve ___ ___ ___ ___ ___ ___ ___ Disapprove

Dilemma 2: Laura's professor has decided to try something new—grading the class competitively. That means there are a set number of "A grades" given, a set number of "B grades" and so on. Laura really needs to get an "A" in this class in order to keep her scholarship, so when the professor gives an assignment with the reference material at the library, Laura is the first one there. After she finishes with the material, she decides to hide the book on another obscure shelf so no one else can use the material, thereby giving her an advantage over the rest of the class. She's not stealing the book, she says, just misplacing it.

Myself: Approve ___ ___ ___ ___ ___ ___ ___ Disapprove
Most Students: Approve ___ ___ ___ ___ ___ ___ ___ Disapprove

Dilemma 3: Mike's friend is a student aide for Mike's finance professor, and he confides to his friend how poorly he is doing in the class. He really is trying, but he cannot seem to grasp the material. Mike is worried about the final exam, which is comprehensive. So when Mike's friend offers to get a copy of the final for him if he promises not to tell anyone, Mike thinks he has found a solution to his problem.

Myself: Approve ___ ___ ___ ___ ___ ___ ___ Disapprove
Most Students: Approve ___ ___ ___ ___ ___ ___ ___ Disapprove

ENRICHMENT MODULE: ACADEMIC ETHICS
(Continued)

Dilemma 4: Alison has a major assignment in her communications class. The assignment is to interview someone in her field of study—public relations. She has been planning to interview the boss she had on her internship. But when Alison finally gets around to calling, her former boss is gone on vacation and won't be back until after the assignment's due date. Instead of trying to find someone else on such short notice, Alison decides to make up the interview, figuring she would probably know how her boss would answer anyway.

    Myself: Approve __ __ __ __ __ __ __ Disapprove
    Most Students: Approve __ __ __ __ __ __ __ Disapprove

Dilemma 5: Steve and his friend Dave are enrolled in the same class, a large lecture with required attendance. The professor lectures straight from the book and the material isn't very interesting. Steve and Dave work out a system where they trade off going to class and just sign each other's name as the roster goes around. This way they don't "waste" their time or get penalized for missing class.

    Myself: Approve __ __ __ __ __ __ __ Disapprove
    Most Students: Approve __ __ __ __ __ __ __ Disapprove

Dilemma 6: The professor has specified the exams to be "open book, open notes" because of their difficulty. Timothy looked through his fraternity files and found old exams for his class. Because he used them to study for the test, he classified them as "notes" and brought them to the exam. As it turned out, about one-third of the questions were the same, so Timothy just copied the answers from his "notes".

    Myself: Approve __ __ __ __ __ __ __ Disapprove
    Most Students: Approve __ __ __ __ __ __ __ Disapprove

Dilemma 7: Although Karen is a bright student and usually does well in school, she hates math. One day, while struggling on a quiz, she glances at her neighbor's test. Time is running out so she decides to copy one answer from her neighbor's paper. A few days later she learns that her neighbor has been accused of cheating—off Karen's quiz. This would be the other person's second offense, resulting in expulsion from school. Since Karen does not know the other person very well, she decides to keep silent and not blemish her record.

    Myself: Approve __ __ __ __ __ __ __ Disapprove
    Most Students: Approve __ __ __ __ __ __ __ Disapprove

This enrichment module is adapted from:

McCuddy, M.K., & Peery, B.L. (In press). Selected individual differences and collegians' ethical beliefs. *Journal of Business Ethics*.

> **TRANSPARENCIES 2.11 THROUGH 2.17**
> **(Each of the above ethical dilemmas is contained on a**
> **separate transparency in the transparency package.)**

VI.   Summing up: What's valuable about personality and attitudes?

   A.   Human behavior results from the complex interaction of variables related to the person and variables related to the situation. This chapter began the exploration of the variables related to the person by focusing on two key areas of individual differences: personality and attitudes. Knowledge of these individual differences is necessary in order to understand both the variability and consistency of people's work behavior in a variety of organizational settings.

DISCUSSION QUESTIONS: SUGGESTED ANSWERS

1.   *Describe the concept of personality and give some examples of how personality might affect employee behaviors at work.*

   In general, personality refers to personal characteristics that lead to consistent patterns of behavior. More specifically, personality may be defined as "a stable set of characteristics and tendencies that determine certain commonalities and differences in the psychological behavior (thoughts, feelings, and actions) of people." These commonalities and differences "have continuity over time and may not be easily understood as the sole result of the social and biological pressures of the moment."

   This specific definition of personality incorporates three key ideas. These ideas are:

   a.   Personality theory is a general theory of behavior—it pertains to all behavior all the time.
   b.   Personality theory describes both what people have in common with one another and how they differ from one another.
   c.   Personality is relatively stable over time.

   Personality can affect all areas of our lives, including behavior at work. Some examples of how personality can affect behavior at work include one's willingness and ability to work in groups, to assume leadership roles, or to tackle complex or challenging tasks. Personality influences job and career selection. Personality also can affect the way an individual makes decisions. In short, numerous examples can be generated and students should be encouraged to be both thorough and creative in providing examples.

2.   *Discuss the basic categories of factors that influence personality development.*

   Heredity and environment are the two broad categories of factors that influence personality development. Four subcategories exist within the environment category—culture, family, group membership, and life experiences.

   Heredity focuses on the genetic basis of personality. It emphasizes the behavioral characteristics and tendencies which appear to be passed on biologically from our parents. For example, whether a person is an introvert or an extravert appears to be based, at least partly, upon genetics. From the heredity viewpoint, commonalities and differences in personality probably would be due to the specific combinations of genes which people inherit.

Environment emphasizes situational events and experiences as contributors to personality. From the environment viewpoint, commonalities and differences in personality would be due to the influence of:

a.   The distinctive ways that different human populations or societies organize their lives.

b.   The nuclear and extended family, and a variety of family-related variables including parental behavior, socioeconomic status, family size, birth order, race, religion, geographic location, parents' educational level, etc.

c.   The roles which people assume and the experiences they have as members of various past and present groups.

d.   The specific events and experiences people have in their lives.

3.   *State the opposing positions in the nature-nurture controversy over personality formation. What influences on personality formation seem most important to you? Why?*

The nature-nurture controversy revolves around the question of which has the stronger influence on personality—heredity or experiences with the environment. On the one hand, the "extreme nature position" argues that an individual's personality is determined primarily by heredity. On the other hand, the "extreme nurture position" argues that an individual's personality is determined primarily by the environment. While this controversy has existed for years, the generally accepted current position is that both heredity and environment play roles in personality formation, and that the two interact in determining an individual's personality.

When students are asked about the relative importance of heredity and environment, three positions will likely emerge:

a.   One position is that personality is determined primarily by heredity. To support this position students will typically cite personality similarities between parents and their offspring. Students may also cite research on twins separated at birth or a very early age and then raised apart. One of the revelations of this stream of research is that twins raised apart are often quite similar in their personalities.

b.   A second position is that personality is determined primarily by the environment. Students will support this position by arguing for the influence of life experiences, particularly early childhood experiences, upon personality formation and development. Also cited in support of this position will be the influential roles of the nuclear and extended families in the early years of one's existence, and of peer group members in the late preteen and teenage years. The influences of religion, culture, or various group memberships may also be cited.

c.   A third position is that personality results from both heredity and the environment rather than being attributable primarily to one or the other. A common explanation is that heredity may provide some capacity for development of specific personality traits, but that the extent to which those traits are developed is a function of people's experiences with their own relatively unique environments.

4.   *Explain the "Big Five" personality factors. Use these factors to describe your perception of the*

President of the United States.

Five personality factors (or clusters of personality traits) are identified in the text. These five—known as the "Big Five" personality factors—are adjustment, sociability, conscientiousness, agreeableness, and intellectual openness.

Each factor exists on a continuum, with polar opposites defining the end points of the continuum. Therefore, the personality factors may be described as follows:

   a. Adjustment ranges from stable, confident, and effective to nervous, self-doubting, and moody.
   b. Sociability ranges from gregarious, energetic, and self-dramatizing to shy, unassertive, and withdrawn.
   c. Conscientiousness ranges from planful, neat, and dependable to impulsive, careless, and irresponsible.
   d. Agreeableness ranges from warm, tactful, and considerate to independent, cold, and rude.
   e. Intellectual openness ranges from imaginative, curious, and original to dull, unimaginative, and literal-minded.

Collectively, the "Big Five" personality factors can be used to describe or summarize an individual's personality structure.

In applying the "Big Five" to describe the President of the United States, students should focus on the trait labels at the ends of each continuum. Using these labels, students should describe their perceptions of the President and support their descriptions with actual examples of the President's behavior or expressed attitudes.

5.   *Compare and contrast self-esteem and locus of control.*

Both self-esteem and locus of control involve beliefs which people have about themselves. Self-esteem is the evaluation people make of themselves in terms their own behavior, abilities, appearance, and worth. Locus of control refers to the extent to which individuals believe that they can control events affecting them.

Self-esteem is one of the traits that is part of the adjustment factor of personality. Locus of control is a trait within the conscientiousness factor of personality.

Generally, individuals are characterized as having either low or high self-esteem. With locus of control, however, individuals are typically described as being either internals or externals. Internals believe that their lives are controlled primarily by their own behavior and actions. Externals, on the other hand, believe that their lives are controlled primarily by chance, fate, or other people.

High self-esteem and an internal locus of control share similar relationships with several behavioral variables. For instance, both groups are more likely to pursue challenging and complex jobs, are more goal-oriented, are more likely to influence others, and are less likely to be influenced by others. In contrast, both low self-esteem and an external locus of control are likely to be associated with the pursuit of less challenging jobs, a weaker goal-orientation, and a susceptibility to being influenced by others rather than influencing others.

6.   *Which of the personality dimensions discussed in the chapter seems most important for managerial behavior? Why?*

This question refers to the specific personality traits—self-esteem, locus of control, introversion and extraversion, dogmatism, and authoritarianism—that are cited as examples of some of the "Big Five" personality factors.

Each personality trait can be argued to be important for managerial behavior. This importance can be demonstrated by citing the relationships each trait has with various job behaviors and/or job performance.

In attempting to argue that one of these specific personality traits is the most important determinant of managerial behavior, students should be encouraged to consider how the related managerial behaviors impact upon the organization's operating effectiveness and efficiency.

7.   *Discuss the relationships among personality, situations, and behavior in terms of their interactions.*

The interactionist perspective argues that, in order to fully understand and explain behavior, both the person and the situation in which the person is behaving must be examined. Focusing only on one or the other discounts crucial information. The interaction between the two is essential for fully understanding and explaining behavior.

Both personality characteristics and situations play important roles in determining behavior. Which of the two is most important depends on the circumstances involved. The individual's personality will play an important—but varying—role in determining that person's behavior, subject to situational factors. If the situational factors are sufficiently powerful, individual differences may be overridden. Conversely, if the situational constraints are weak, individual personality will explain more of the variance in behavior. Students should understand that both personality and the situation have an impact on behavior, and that behavior at any point in time is always a complex interaction of the two.

There are many different ways of describing the person as well as the situation. Personality is one of the major ways for describing the person. Thus, one could also argue that personality variables and situational variables interact to determine people's behavior.

8.   *What are attitudes? Describe the basic components of attitudes.*

Attitudes are relatively permanent feelings, beliefs, and behavioral tendencies directed toward specific persons, groups, ideas, issues, or objects. An attitude consists of three interactive components:

   a.   An affective component, or the feelings, sentiments, moods, and emotions about someone or something.
   b.   A cognitive component, or beliefs, opinions, knowledge, or information an individual has about someone or something.
   c.   A behavioral component, or the predisposition to act on a favorable or unfavorable evaluation of someone or something.

9.   *How does the behavioral intentions model help explain that attitude-behavior relationships sometimes may appear to be weak and at other times may appear to be strong?*

The behavioral intentions model suggests that behavior is more predictable (and understandable) if we focus on a person's specific intentions to behave in a certain way. The model further shows that behavioral intentions depend on both attitudes toward the behavior and perception of norms regarding the behavior. If both attitudes toward the specific behavior and perceptions of norms regarding the specific behavior are consistent, behavioral intentions will be strong. In turn, the attitude-behavior relationship probably would be strong. However, if attitudes toward the specific behavior and perceptions of norms regarding the specific behavior are inconsistent, behavioral intentions will be determined by the relative strength of the two. In turn, the attitude-behavior relationship may be weakened.

The attitude-behavior relationship also may be strengthened or weakened due to perceived situational or internal constraints such as real or perceived skill deficiencies. The presence of constraints will weaken the attitude-behavior relationship.

10.   *What is the meaning of job satisfaction? Why is it important?*

Job satisfaction is a collection of attitudes one has toward a job or toward work. In other words, job satisfaction is a pleasurable or positive emotional state resulting from the individual's work experiences. If an individual's work is congruent with his or her needs, expectations, and values, job satisfaction should result.

Job satisfaction is important as a diagnostic tool in organizations. The various sources of job satisfaction provide important diagnostic clues regarding actions which can be taken to improve people's lives at work. Appropriate organizational changes are needed when there is a high level of dissatisfaction with one or more sources.

Additionally, job satisfaction is important because of its impact on certain crucial employee behaviors. Dissatisfied employees have a higher absenteeism rate, a higher turnover rate, and more physical and mental health problems than satisfied employees. Absenteeism, turnover, and health problems are costly for organizations.

11.   *Describe the concept of organizational commitment and explain why organizations seek strong employee commitment.*

Organizational commitment refers to the strength of an employee's involvement in and identification with the organization. High commitment is characterized by:

    a.   A strong belief in and acceptance of the organization's goals and values.
    b.   A willingness to exert considerable effort on behalf of the organization.
    c.   A strong desire to maintain membership in the organization.

The characteristics of individuals who are highly committed to the organization provide one argument for the utility of high employee commitment. Clearly, buying into the organization's goals and values, exerting great effort on behalf of the organization, and wanting to remain a member of the organization are valuable with respect to an organization's success.

High commitment also is useful to organizations because of its relationship to various job behaviors. Employees with a higher level of organizational commitment have lower absenteeism and turnover rates, are more goal-directed in the pursuit of their work assignments, and waste less time at work. Because of these relationships, high levels of commitment prove less costly for the organization.

12.   *Compare and contrast moral management, immoral management, and amoral management. Give an example of each.*

Moral management, immoral management, and amoral management refer to the extent to which ethics are incorporated into managerial behavior. With moral management, managerial behaviors are guided by ethical principles. In the pursuit of their activities, moral managers try to do what is just and right in balancing personal interests, corporate interests, and the interests of others. Moral managers follow sound ethical principles and norms, professional standards of conduct, and applicable laws and regulations.

With immoral management, managerial behaviors are not guided by ethical principles. Immoral managers deliberately try to challenge the limits of the law, sometimes even deliberately breaking it. Doing that which is just and right is the farthest thing from an immoral manager's mind. Instead, pursuing self- or corporate-interest with blatant disregard for the action's impact on others is characteristic of the immoral manager.

With amoral management, managerial behaviors reflect an indifference toward ethical principles. Amoral managers seem to be unaware of moral issues. They also pursue their managerial activities with no apparent consideration for the impact that their activities might have on other people.

To generate examples of each style of managerial ethics, students should be encouraged to draw upon current business events from publications such as *Business Week*, *Fortune*, or *The Wall Street Journal.*

13.   *Suggest some specific actions that organizations might take to encourage ethical behavior by managers and employees.*

Organizations can take the following specific actions to encourage ethical behavior by their members:

    a.   Identifying ethical attitudes which are crucial for the organization's operations, and developing these ethical attitudes through appropriate training programs.
    b.   Selecting employees with desired ethical attitudes.
    c.   Incorporating ethics into the performance review and evaluation process.
    d.   Establishing a work culture that reinforces ethical attitudes.

DEVELOPING SKILLS—
SELF DIAGNOSIS: MEASURING LOCUS OF CONTROL

This self-administered diagnostic instrument is a 30-item questionnaire which yields three locus of control scales, each consisting of ten items and ranging in value from 0 to 40. The three scales are: "I" or internal locus of control, "EO" or external locus of control (others), and "EC" or external locus of control (chance). The higher your "I" score, the more you tend to believe that you are generally responsible for what happens to you. The higher your "EO" score, the more you tend to believe that powerful other people determine what happens to you. The higher your "EC" score, the more you believe that chance plays a large role in what happens to you.

Scoring instructions are provided in the textbook along with summary data from over 300 managers who responded to the questionnaire.

DEVELOPING SKILLS—
A CASE IN POINT: CHUCK HOLEMAN—RETAIL SALES REPRESENTATIVE

CASE OVERVIEW

This case focuses on the attitudes and behavior of Chuck Holeman, a retail sales representative. During training Chuck seemed to be an eager, enthusiastic employee. Many of the company's sales managers expected him to progress rapidly once he was assigned his own sales territory. However, Chuck's job performance proved to be disappointing. In general, Chuck could be described as an employee who was dissatisfied with his job and not committed to his company. Additionally, he apparently felt that the company's policies required him to compromise his own ethical standards. Despite corrective efforts on the part of his supervisor, Chuck's performance continued to deteriorate.

CASE QUESTIONS

1.   *What attitudes contributed to Chuck Holeman's problems on the job? How did they manifest themselves?*

Chuck appears to have very strong attitudes regarding job situations that have ethical implications. If he does not believe that something is completely ethical, he will not do it. The apparent failure to follow the prescribed sales pitch because he did not believe it is one example of this. Another example is the belief that the company should not take advantage of customers by pushing high-priced products which were almost identical to lower-priced products. Still another example is rooted in the multiple observations of Chuck's belief in "complete openness and honesty."

Other attitudes also contributed to Chuck's job problems. He appeared to be unenthusiastic about his work, contrary to his attitude during training. He apparently believed that his sales job was merely that of being an order-taker. He tried to view things from the customer's viewpoint—which is admirable and could indicate a strong customer orientation—but apparently didn't adequately represent the company's viewpoint.

2.   *How would you describe Holeman's level of organizational commitment?*

Chuck's level of organizational commitment is quite low. He does not appear to have a strong belief in and acceptance of the company's goals and values. The specific examples cited for question 1 above could be used to support this assertion. Nor is there evidence that he is willing to exert considerable effort on behalf of the company. Chuck appears unenthusiastic to his customers, has failed to use prescribed promotional materials, has not pushed high-profit items, did not develop adequate skills in the financial end of sales, and failed to contact customers that had been lost by the company's previous sales representative. The strength of Chuck's desire to maintain his membership in the organization is uncertain. On the one hand, he said he would lick the problems in his sales territory—an indication of the desire to stay with the company. On the other hand, his work behavior up to that point did not indicate that he was willing to change and to behave in the manner necessary to keep his position with the company.

3.   *Would you find it difficult to follow the prescribed policies in this situation? What would you do if you were a salesperson in this company?*

Students should be encouraged to identify which specific policies would be more difficult to follow and which ones would be easier to follow. Reasons should be provided in either case.

Some of the policies (*e.g.,* pushing higher-priced products rather than lower-priced similar ones and using questionable promotional materials) have ethical implications. In addressing these particular policies, students should grapple with the issue of adhering to one's personal value structure when success in the organization appears to require sacrificing those values.

Students should also consider whether Chuck had realistic expectations regarding the company's policies and procedures. Perhaps the organization was being reasonable and Chuck was not. Also, Chuck's personality may have been incompatible with the situational demands of the company.

4.   *What would you do if you were Holeman's supervisor?*

Since this question asks students to speculate on their own likely managerial behavior, they should be very specific in their responses and should provide reasons for the actions they would take. Some students probably will recommend terminating Chuck because of the continuing problems even after the supervisor talked with him. Other students probably will recommend a "one last chance effort" wherein precise behavioral expectations, goals, timetables, and consequences are set forth.

COURSE ENHANCEMENT— *WEST'S ORGANIZATIONAL BEHAVIOR CUSTOM VIDEO SERIES*

Two videos from *West's Organizational Behavior Custom Video Series* can be used to enhance the material in Chapter 2. These videos are: *Microscope Magazine: AT&T's Walter Persons,* and *Arthur Andersen & Company: Ethics in Management.*

VIDEO: *MICROSCOPE MAGAZINE: AT&T'S WALTER PERSONS*

Approximate Time: 4 minutes

Video Summary:

Walter Persons, a production specialist at AT&T's Richmond Plant, is the focus of the video. The video demonstrates the positive effects of his personality on other employees and the managerial implications of personality. Mr. Person's varied roles at the plant include safety coordinator of the back panel shop, member of the medical emergency response team, and volunteer for other special projects. His outside interests include spending time with his family and performing as an actor at the local theater. Mr. Persons' supervisor and co-workers consider him to be an asset and enjoy his positive attitude and happy disposition. His fellow employees feel comfortable going to him for advice. The supervisor encourages all employees to develop outside interests and feels it helps the company's positive image. Viewers should recognize the importance of understanding personality characteristics and taking advantage of diversity in organizations. The video indicates how AT&T has taken advantage of diversity in its workforce to continue its mission.

Discussion Questions and Suggested Answers for Video:

1. *Which personality characteristics seem to best describe Walter Persons?*

    Discussion of this question could draw upon the "Big Five" personality factors—adjustment, sociability, conscientiousness, agreeableness, and intellectual openness. On the adjustment factor, Persons could be described as more stable, confident, and effective than nervous, self-doubting, and moody. On the sociability factor, he could be characterized as gregarious, energetic, and self-dramatizing rather than as shy, unassertive, and withdrawn. For the conscientiousness factor, Walter seems to be more planful, neat, and dependable than impulsive, careless, and irresponsible. On the agreeableness factor, he is warm, tactful, and considerate instead of independent, cold, and rude. Finally, for the intellectual openness factor, he could be described as imaginative, curious, and original rather than dull, unimaginative, and literal-minded.

2. *How would you characterize Walter Person's job satisfaction and organizational commitment?*

    Walter Person appears to be very satisfied with his job. A high level of congruency appears to exist between the nature of his work and his needs, expectations, and values.

    Person also appears to be highly committed to his employer. Based upon the facts presented in the video, one may conclude that he has a strong belief in and acceptance of the organization's goals and values, a willingness to exert considerable effort on behalf of the organization, and a strong desire to maintain membership in the organization.

VIDEO: *ARTHUR ANDERSEN & COMPANY: ETHICS IN MANAGEMENT*

Approximate Time: 11 minutes

Video Summary:

This video presents five vignettes revolving around different ethical issues that are commonly encountered in organizations. In the first vignette, two managers are discussing bids from competing suppliers. Both bids are equivalent in quality and service but one is lower in price. One manager wishes to follow company policy regarding use of the lowest-priced bid if the bids are essentially equivalent in other key aspects. The other manager argues for giving the business to a higher-priced bidder based on the argument of closer geographic location of that supplier. The higher-priced bidder also happens to be a friend of the second manager. As an inducement to acquiesce, the second manager offers to get the first manager invited to a party being given by his friend, the higher-priced bidder.

In the second vignette, a black women who works as a secretary complains to a co-worker about wage discrimination. She says that another co-worker, who started at the company at the same time she did and who does the same type of work, is paid 30¢ per hour more. When the first co-worker suggests that there might be an explanation other than wage discrimination, the black woman accuses her of sounding like management.

In the third vignette, one female worker complains to another female worker about being the target of unwanted verbal comments and physical contact from a male employee. She also is working on a project for the male employee so there is a supervisory relationship, at least with regard to the project.

In the fourth vignette, several managers are discussing a former employee. The terminated employee threatened a lawsuit but the company settled out of court because it was less costly than fighting a court battle. Subsequently, the former employee went into business for himself, competing for some of the same clients served by his former employer. Some of the managers seek to undermine their former employee and current business competitor by supplying clients with negative information about the former employee.

In the fifth vignette, two employees are compiling their expense reports from a recently completed business trip. One employee has lost his receipts and is seeking cost information from the other employee so that he can estimate his expenses and complete his report. Some items that should be supported by receipts are not, legitimate expenses are padded, and questionable expenses are added.

Discussion Questions and Suggested Answers for Video:

1.   *What are the ethical issues in the first vignette? What would you do?*

   One ethical issue concerns the trade-offs of business favors, company policy, and personal benefits. A related ethical issue involves channeling business to a personal friend when that friend is not the lowest bidder. Also, a bribery attempt, though of relatively small magnitude, is apparent in the second manager's offer to get the first manger invited to the higher bidder's party.

   An interesting discussion on what should be done will likely ensue. Some students will argue for adhering to company policy, no matter what. Others will argue that exchanging favors will benefit the company in the long-run. Whatever position the students take, they should be required to examine the economic, legal, and moral implications over both the short- and the long-term.

2.   *What are the ethical issues in the second vignette? What would you do?*

   At least two potential ethical issues exist in this vignette. One issue concerns the question of equal pay for equal work. The other issue concerns the implied racial basis for the discrimination. To resolve this ethical dilemma, the black women should discuss the situation with her supervisor and/or the company's human resource office in an open and honest fashion.

3.   *What are the ethical issues in the third vignette? What would you do?*

   The primary issue here is one of sexual harassment—both verbal and physical. Both forms are illegal. Perhaps the most effective way for the offended woman to handle the situation would be to assertively confront her immediate supervisor and/or the company's human resource office.

4.   *What are the ethical issues in the fourth vignette? What would you do?*

   A major ethical issue here concerns whether a company should compete fairly or should engage in morally, if not legally, questionable tactics. A related issue concerns whether one should deliberately undermine a competitor out of bitterness or spite. Also, the distribution of negative information about a former employee could be slanderous or libelous.

   The discussion of what to do could prove interesting. Some students may argue that "playing hard ball" is the only way to do business; thus, the proposed tactics are appropriate and should be implemented vigorously. Others will argue that competing vigorously and being ethical are not incompatible; therefore, they should cease all questionable activity and compete with their former employee on a fair basis. Hopefully, students taking the former position will be enlightened and influenced by a thorough discussion of the latter position.

5. *What are the ethical issues in the fifth vignette? What would you do?*

The primary ethical issue in this case concerns accuracy and honesty in filing expense reports. Specific examples include the following: some items that should be supported by receipts are not, legitimate expenses are padded, and questionable expenses are added. Related to this primary ethical issue is the justification that everybody does it—should unethical behavior be tolerated, perhaps even expected, because others engage in unethical behavior? Discussion of what should be done can focus on the justification aspect, then work back into the specifics of the situation.

CHAPTER 3
PERCEPTION AND ATTRIBUTION

CHAPTER OVERVIEW

Chapter 3 continues the exploration of individual processes by focusing on perception and attribution. The psychological process of perception is explored via a model which describes six sequential steps: environmental stimuli, observation, perceptual selection, perceptual organization, interpretation, and response. Three of the steps—perceptual selection, perceptual organization, and interpretation—are developed in considerable detail. The psychological process of attribution is examined in the context of an appropriate theoretical model for determining internal and external attributions of the causes of people's behavior.

LEARNING OBJECTIVES

Upon completion of this chapter, the students should be able to:

1. Describe the major elements of the perceptual process and explain why this process is important.
2. Define perceptual selection and perceptual organization.
3. Describe the factors that determine how one person perceives another.
4. Discuss the issue of accuracy in person perception.
5. Identify five kinds of perceptual errors.
6. Explain the process of attribution and how attributions influence behavior.
7. Describe important attributions that people make in the work setting.

CHAPTER OUTLINE

I.   **Preview Case:** Whom Should I Hire?

II.   The Perceptual Process

A.   **Managing in Practice:** The Icon Crisis

III.   Perceptual Selection

A.   External Factors
B.   Internal Factors
C.   **Managing Diversity:** Selective Perception of Managers
D.   **Managing Across Cultures:** Time Perception

IV.   Perceptual Organization

A.   **Managing in Practice:** Office Design, Layout, and Decor—What Do They Tell You?

V.   Person Perception

A.   Characteristics of the Person Perceived
B.   Characteristics of the Perceiver
C.   **Managing Across Cultures:** Perceptions of Japanese and American Business Associates
D.   The Situation
E.   Impression Management

VI.   Perceptual Errors

A.   **Managing Ethics:** Perceptions of Ethics in Organizations
B.   Accuracy of Judgment in Person Perception
C.   Perceptual Defense
D.   Stereotyping
E.   **Managing Diversity:** Sex Stereotypes in the Workplace
F.   Halo Effect
G.   Projection
H.   Expectancy Effects

VII.   Attributions: Perceiving the Causes of Behavior

A.   **Managing in Practice:** Searching for Causes of Job Applicant Behavior
B.   The Attribution Process
C.   Internal versus External Causes of Behavior
D.   Attributions of Success and Failure

VIII. Developing Skills

A.   **Self Diagnosis:** Measuring Perceptions of Women as Managers
B.   **A Case in Point:** The Internship

KEY WORDS AND CONCEPTS

Twenty-six key words and concepts are introduced in Chapter 3. The key words and concepts, along with definitions or appropriate descriptions, are as follows:

Attribution process: refers to the ways in which people attempt to understand the causes of others' (and their own) behavior.

Closure: the tendency to perceive an entire stimulus object as a constant, overall form even though only part of the object is evident.

Continuity: the tendency to perceive objects as continuous patterns.

Expectancy effects: the extent to which prior expectations bias how events, objects, and people are actually perceived.

Field dependence/independence: a personality characteristic wherein a field-dependent person tends to pay more attention to external environmental cues and a field-independent person relies mostly on bodily sensations.

Fundamental attribution error: the tendency people have for underestimating the impact of situational or external causes of behavior and overestimating the impact of personal or internal causes of behavior.

Halo effect: the process by which the perceiver evaluates all dimensions of another person based solely on one impression, either favorable or unfavorable.

Implicit personality theories: theories people have about how the physical characteristics, personality traits, and specific behaviors possessed by others are related.

Impression construction: refers to people consciously choosing the image they want to convey, and how they will go about conveying it.

Impression management: an attempt which people make to manipulate or control the impressions that others form about them.

Impression motivation: the degree to which people are motivated to actively manage the impressions they create.

Perception: the selection and organization of environmental stimuli to provide meaningful experiences for the perceiver. Through the perceptual process people search for, obtain, and process information in order to make sense of their surrounding environment.

Perceptual defense: the tendency for people to protect themselves against ideas, objects, or situations that are threatening.

Perceptual grouping: the tendency to form individual stimuli into a meaningful pattern by such means as continuity, closure, proximity, or similarity.

Perceptual organization: the process by which people group environmental stimuli into recognizable patterns.

Perceptual selection: the process by which people filter environmental stimuli so they can deal with the more important stimuli.

Perceptual set: an expectation of a perception based on past experience with the same or similar stimuli.

Person perception: the process by which individuals attribute characteristics or traits to other people. Person perception is closely related to the attribution process.

Pollyanna principle: pleasant stimuli are processed more efficiently and accurately than unpleasant stimuli.

Primacy effect: refers to the phenomenon where subsequent perceptions of a person are strongly influenced by the first impression of that individual.

Projection: the tendency for people to see their own traits in other people.

Proximity: a group of objects may be perceived as related because of their nearness to each other.

Self-fulfilling prophecy: expecting certain things to happen will shape the behavior of the perceiver in such a way that the expected is more likely to happen.

Self-serving bias: the strong tendency people have to attribute their successes to internal factors and their failures to external factors.

Similarity: the more alike stimuli are, the greater the tendency to perceive them as a common group.

Stereotyping: the tendency to assign attributes to someone solely on the basis of a category in which that person has been placed.

LECTURE NOTES

I.   Chapter 3 continues the exploration of individual differences by focusing on perception and attribution. Perception is important for understanding individual differences because people behave on the basis of their perceptions of reality rather than on the basis of what reality actually is. Attribution is important for understanding individual differences because it helps people in sorting out the causes of their own and others' behavior.

   A.   Transparency 3.1 summarizes the key ideas about perception and attribution that are presented in Chapter 3.

TRANSPARENCY 3.1
(FROM TEXT MATERIAL IN THE TEXTBOOK)

KEY IDEAS ABOUT PERCEPTION AND ATTRIBUTION

ENRICHMENT MODULE: WORK LIFE VERSUS FAMILY LIFE

Are employees perceived differently depending on whether or not they try to balance their work lives with their family lives? Faith Wohl, Director of Human-Resource Initiatives at DuPont, believes people who take advantage of the work-family options available at DuPont may be perceived as being less serious about their careers than other employees. Her challenge is to change DuPont's culture in order to support full use of work-family options such as a generous parental-leave policy, company-run day-care centers, funding for other high-quality child-care options within the community, after-school programs, summer camps for older children, time off to care for ill children, job sharing, counseling services for prospective adoptive parents, advice on school problems, and caring for disabled adult relatives. The cultural change is needed so that employees making use of these work-family options will not be perceived as less serious about their careers.

This enrichment module is based on:

Willis, C. (1993, December). The 10 most admired women managers in America. *Working Woman*, 55.

II.   Overview of the perceptual process.

    A.   Perception is the selection and organization of environmental stimuli to provide meaningful experiences for the perceiver. Through the perceptual process people search for, obtain, and process information in order to make sense of their surrounding environment.

    B.   The perceptual process, as presented in Transparency 3.2, consists of six basic elements arranged in a sequential fashion.   The elements, in step-by-step order, are: environmental stimuli, observation, perceptual selection, perceptual organization, interpretation, and response.

TRANSPARENCY 3.2
(FIGURE 3.1 IN THE TEXTBOOK)

BASIC ELEMENTS IN THE PERCEPTUAL PROCESS

III.   Detailed exploration of the selection and organization elements of the perceptual process.

    A.   Perceptual selection.

        1.   Perceptual selection is the process by which people filter environmental stimuli so they can deal with the more important stimuli.

        2.   Perceptual selection is influenced by external factors which are often stated as principles of perception. According to these various principles, an external factor (or stimulus) is more likely to be perceived when it is larger, more intense, stands out against the background or differs from what is expected, is in motion, is repeated, or is either familiar (in an unfamiliar situation) or novel (in a familiar situation).

3.   Perceptual selection also is influenced by internal factors which reflect various aspects or characteristics of the perceiver. Included among the important internal factors are personality, learning, and motivation.

    a.   Personality (a subject in Chapter 2) shapes and is shaped by perception. The personality characteristic of <u>field dependence/independence</u> provides an example of this shaping relationship. A field-dependent person tends to pay more attention to external environmental cues, while a field-independent person relies mostly on bodily sensations. By relying more heavily on their respective sources of information, each personality type strengthens its behavioral tendency in that direction.

    b.   Learning affects perception through the development of perceptual sets. A <u>perceptual set</u> is an expectation of a perception based on past experience with the same or similar stimuli. Learning also affects perception in that learning reflects a person's life experiences and the impact of culture on those experiences.

    c.   Motivation influences what a person perceives because people tend to perceive things that will satisfy their needs and that they have found to be rewarding in prior situations. The <u>pollyanna principle</u>—the notion that pleasant stimuli are processed more efficiently and accurately than unpleasant stimuli—provides a useful illustration of the impact of motivation on perception.

B.   Perceptual organization.

1.   <u>Perceptual organization</u> is the process by which people group environmental stimuli into recognizable patterns.

2.   One of the primary means by which perceptual organization takes place is perceptual grouping. <u>Perceptual grouping</u> is the tendency to form individual stimuli into a meaningful pattern by such means as continuity, closure, proximity, or similarity. People perceive meaningful patterns because of their tendency to perceive:

    a.   Stimuli as continuous patterns (<u>continuity</u>).

    b.   A stimulus object as a whole only though part of it is evident (<u>closure</u>).

    c.   Stimuli as related because of nearness to each other (<u>proximity</u>).

    d.   Stimuli as a group because of similar characteristics (<u>similarity</u>).

IV.   Person perception as a special case of the perceptual process.

ENRICHMENT MODULE: HOW DO YOU PERCEIVE YOUR CLASSMATES?
(An Experiential Activity)

An interesting discussion of person perception can be generated by using the following exercise:

> Organize students into four or five person groups. Working independently each group member writes down five things (e.g., perceived strengths and weaknesses, observations of classroom behavior, etc.) he/she perceives about each group member, including himself or herself. Additionally, each group member describes each of the others as well as themselves in terms of an animal, a food, or a musical instrument (these often provide insightful—and sometimes amusing—perspectives). Once the perceptions are written down, they are shared with the other members in a small group round-robin discussion format. Additionally, students should provide reasons for why they perceive people as they do.

This is an excellent way to get students to explore differences in the way people are perceived. It also helps to make them aware of similarities and differences in their self-perceptions versus the perceptions others have of them.

This enrichment module is adapted from an exercise developed by M.K. McCuddy.

A.   The perceptions that people have of one another are especially important for understanding behavior in organizational settings. These perceptions—known as person perceptions—represent a special case of the perceptual process. In particular, some of the key features of person perception are analogous to the processes of perceptual selection and perceptual organization.

B.   Linkages between person perception and perceptual selection.

1.   The primacy effect is one way in which person perception is like perceptual selection. The primacy effect refers to the phenomenon where subsequent perceptions of a person are strongly influenced by the first impression of that individual. Because of the primacy effect people tend to focus on stimuli which are consistent with their first impressions of others.

2.   Additionally, person perception is similar to perceptual selection because it is influenced by certain external and internal factors.

a.   The characteristics of the person being perceived (*i.e.,* facial expressions, general appearance, skin color, posture, age, gender, voice quality, personality traits, overt behaviors, etc.) represent an external factor affecting what people choose to perceive. Some of the stimuli will be more readily perceived because they fit with people's implicit personality theories about the physical characteristics, personality traits, and specific behaviors that are possessed by others. An interesting example of how implicit personality theory operates is provided in Transparency 3.3.

TRANSPARENCY 3.3
(TABLE 3.1 IN THE TEXTBOOK)

PERSONALITY JUDGMENTS ON THE BASIS OF VOICE QUALITY

---

b.   The characteristics of the perceiver—an internal factor in person perception—also influences what people choose to perceive. Perceivers' personality, learning, and motivation predispose them to focus on certain stimuli in person perception. As Transparency 3.4 shows, for instance, prior learning and enculturation will influence the perceptions people have of others from a different cultural background.

TRANSPARENCY 3.4
(TABLE 3.2 IN THE TEXTBOOK)

AMERICAN AND JAPANESE PERCEPTIONS OF THE OTHERS'
CHARACTERISTICS AND BUSINESS PRACTICES

---

c.   The situation or context within which the perception takes place—another external factor in person perception—affects what people choose to perceive about others. The situation may be particularly important with regard to first impressions or primacy effects.

C.   Linkages between person perception and perceptual organization.

1.   People also could use implicit personality theory as a way of organizing stimuli about other people into a meaningful whole.

2.   Additionally, the use of impression management may influence how stimuli are organized in person perception.

a.   Impression management refers to the attempt people make to manipulate or control the impressions that others form about them.

b.   Impression management consists of two related processes: impression motivation and impression construction. Impression motivation, the first process, concerns the degree to which individuals are motivated to actively manage their impressions. Impression construction, the second process, refers to individuals consciously choosing the image they want to convey, and how they will go about conveying it. Transparency 3.5 illustrates the processes which make up impression management.

TRANSPARENCY 3.5
(FIGURE 3.7 IN THE TEXTBOOK)

THE PROCESS OF IMPRESSION MANAGEMENT

ENRICHMENT MODULE: CREATING A POSITIVE FIRST IMPRESSION

Communication is an important concept in conveying positive first impressions. What sort of first impression do you believe you make? How aware are you of all the verbal and nonverbal signals you are sending? To project a positive impression you need to be a skilled communicator. Very simply, you need to communicate a positive first impression whether that message is written, spoken, or visual.

Communication is a complex skill and it takes a conscious effort to be effective. Surveys show that managers judge the ability to communicate effectively to be a critical characteristic of success.

Effective listening is one important aspect of communication. Listening involves careful attention and response to messages. Instead of evaluating the message or preparing a response, an effective listener tries to understand both direct and subtle meanings contained in messages. Give attention to the feelings of the sender as well as the verbal content. Observe people while they are speaking. Watch facial expressions, gestures, body movements, and eye contact. This will help you to understand the real content of the message. To be an effective listener, practice the following guidelines:

- Stop talking.
- Show the speaker you want to listen.
- Empathize with the speaker.
- Be patient—don't interrupt the speaker.
- Ask questions.
- Summarize, using the speaker's own words.
- Tolerate silence.
- Avoid judging.
- Give positive and reinforcing nonverbal messages.

Communicating is much more complex than selecting the right words. The messages you send nonverbally also communicate a lasting impression. In fact, nonverbal communication includes anything that sends a message. Body language is one type of nonverbal communication that includes facial expressions, vocal qualities, gestures, and posture.

What messages are you sending nonverbally? Are these messages consistent with your oral and/or written communications? With so much emphasis on the way a person moves his/her eyes, stands in a room in front of others, shakes hands, or touches another, it is imperative to take note of your own body language in an effort to determine if you are sending the message you desire.

In many cases people are unaware of the nonverbal signals they are sending. This often results in unexpected outcomes such as poorly perceived skills, a low evaluation, or no job offer. Pay special attention to your facial expressions, vocal quality, gestures, and posture, and practice the following guidelines:

- Smile. People who smile a lot are happier and the effect can become the cause. When the smile comes naturally, great. Otherwise, think of something pleasant or of a fun experience. Make eye contact and don't be afraid to look directly at the person you are speaking to.

- Vary your voice with pitch, intensity, and volume. Let your voice reflect your enthusiasm and interest. Inflect your voice down, never up. You shouldn't sound as if you are asking a question or seeking approval, but, rather, stating your objective.

ENRICHMENT MODULE: CREATING A POSITIVE FIRST IMPRESSION
(Continued)

●   Be aware of gestures. Don't put your hands in your pockets or lock them behind your back or grip them in your lap when sitting. Gestures should be relaxed and complement your message.

This enrichment module is based on:

Fandt, P. (1989). *Projecting the right image.* Orlando, FL: University of Central Florida Press.

TRANSPARENCY 3.6
(The above list of listening practices is reproduced in the transparency package.)

TRANSPARENCY 3.7
(The above guidelines are reproduced in the transparency package.)

V.   Detailed exploration of the interpretation element of the perceptual process.

     A.   The interpretation element of the perceptual process is concerned with perceptual errors and attributions.

     B.   Five common types of perceptual errors—perceptual defense, stereotyping, the halo effect, projection, and expectancy effects (see Transparency 3.8)—occur in the perceptual process in general and with person perception in particular. Minimizing the extent to which these errors occur is essential for accuracy in person perception.

TRANSPARENCY 3.8
(FROM TEXT MATERIAL IN THE TEXTBOOK)

COMMON PERCEPTUAL ERRORS

---

1.   <u>Perceptual defense</u> is the tendency for people to protect themselves against ideas, objects, or situations that are threatening.

2.   <u>Stereotyping</u> is the tendency to assign attributes to someone solely on the basis of a category in which that person has been placed.

3.   The <u>halo effect</u> is the process by which the perceiver evaluates all dimensions of another person based solely on one impression, either favorable or unfavorable.

4.   <u>Projection</u> is the tendency for people to see their own traits in other people.

5.   <u>Expectancy effects</u> refer to the extent to which prior expectations bias how events, objects, and people are actually perceived. An aspect of expectancy effects is the <u>self-fulfilling prophecy</u>—expecting certain things to happen will shape the behavior of the perceiver in such a way that the expected is more likely to happen.

ENRICHMENT MODULE: THE PYGMALION EFFECT

The pygmalion effect is the popularized term for the self-fulfilling prophecy, which describes the effect of the perceiver's expectations regarding the perceived. For example, if a manager expects a worker to do a good job, the worker is likely to perform well. This expectation affects not only the perception of the perceiver but the actual behavior of the perceived. The worker will actually perform better, not just be perceived as performing better.

A stimulating class discussion can center on how the pygmalion effect works both for and against students. Ask the students whether they have been guilty of this behavior or the victim of this behavior.

C. The <u>attribution process</u> refers to the ways in which people attempt to understand the causes of others' (and their own) behavior.

    1. Sometimes people make attributions consciously, but perhaps most often attributions are made unconsciously. Conscious causal attributions are most likely to be made when:

        a. The perceiver has been asked an explicit question about another's behavior.

        b. An unexpected event occurs.

        c. The perceiver depends on another person for a desired outcome.

        d. The perceiver experiences feelings of failure or loss of control.

    2. A model of the attribution process, shown in Transparency 3.9, indicates that information, beliefs, and motives held by the perceiver will influence the perceiver's attributions of internal and external cause of behavior. In turn, these attributions affect the perceiver's:

        a. Subsequent behavior in response to the behavior of others.

        b. Feeling or emotions about relevant events, people, and circumstances.

        c. Expectations of future events or behavior.

TRANSPARENCY 3.9
(FIGURE 3.8 IN THE TEXTBOOK)

THE ATTRIBUTION PROCESS

---

    3. Internal versus external causes of behavior.

        a. Causes of behavior may be classified as internal (*e.g.,* personality traits, emotions, motives, or abilities and skills) or external (*e.g.,* other people, the situation, or chance).

        b. The model presented in Transparency 3.10 attempts to explain how people assign causality to others' behavior. When consistency, distinctiveness and consensus are high, the perceiver tends to attribute others' behavior to external causes. However, when consistency is high but distinctiveness and consensus are low, the perceiver tends to attribute other's behavior to internal causes. When consistency is low, the perceiver may attribute others' behavior to either internal causes or external causes or to both.

> ```
> TRANSPARENCY 3.10
> (FIGURE 3.9 IN THE TEXTBOOK)
>
> KELLEY'S THEORY OF CAUSAL ATTRIBUTIONS
> ```

c.   Perceivers frequently make a fundamental attribution error in assigning behavioral causality. The fundamental attribution error refers to the tendency which people have to underestimate the impact of situational or external causes of behavior and to overestimate the impact of personal or internal causes of behavior.

4.   Individuals frequently attribute their own (and others') success or failure to ability, effort, task difficulty, or luck. Ability and effort are attributions of internal causation, whereas task difficulty and luck are attributions of external causation. People have a strong tendency to attribute their successes to internal factors and their failures to external factors—this is called a self-serving bias.

VI.   Pulling perception and attribution together: What are the implications for organizational behavior?

A.   People's behavior is influenced by their perceptions of the various environments in which they function. In part, perception is important for understanding the behavior of managers and non-supervisory employees because perception is a fundamental psychological process underlying all kinds of human behavior. In part, perception is important in understanding the behavior of organizational members because the organizational environment may be different (and perhaps even unique) relative to other environments in which people function.

B.   People's behavior is also influenced by the attributions they make about the causes of their own and others' behavior. Whether behavior is perceived to be due to environmental circumstances (external attributions) or to one's personality, attitudes, motivations, etc. (internal attributions), attributions have significant impacts on how people perceive and behave toward each other.

DISCUSSION QUESTIONS: SUGGESTED ANSWERS

1.   Explain the various "steps" in the process of perception.

The perceptual process is the psychological process by which an individual extracts or selects certain stimuli or information from the environment and arranges or organizes these stimuli in a way to make sense of the environment. This process involves several steps or elements. First, various environmental stimuli are observed through the five senses—taste, smell, hearing, sight, and touch. Next, external and internal factors interact to produce a filtering process that determines which particular stimulus will receive the most attention, or be perceived as most important. The sensory perceptions that have been selected are then organized into meaningful patterns through the application of figure-ground and various perceptual grouping mechanisms. At this point, the individual has selected and organized the environmental stimuli. The person then continues to process and interpret these stimuli. Perceptual errors and attributions play significant roles in interpreting the perceived stimuli. Ultimately, the perceived stimuli lead to covert responses (attitudes, motivations, and feelings) and overt responses (behavior). In summary, the individual observes, selects, organizes, interprets, and responds to environmental stimuli.

2.   *Identify the factors that determine the probability that some stimulus will be perceived.*

The likelihood of a stimulus being perceived is influenced by the external factors and internal factors of perceptual selection. The external factors are characteristics of stimuli which determine whether a given stimulus will be perceived. The internal factors reflect various aspects or characteristics of the perceiver.

External factors of perceptual selection include the following:

   a.   Size—the larger the size of a stimulus, the more likely it is to be perceived.
   b.   Intensity—the more intense a stimulus is, the more likely it is to be perceived.
   c.   Contrast—stimuli that stand out against the background or are unexpected are more likely to be perceived.
   d.   Motion—a moving stimulus is more likely to be perceived than a stationary one.
   e.   Repetition—a repeated stimulus is more likely to be perceived than a single one.
   f.   Novelty—a novel stimulus in a familiar situation is more likely to be perceived.
   g.   Familiarity—a familiar stimulus in an unfamiliar situation is more likely to be perceived.

Internal factors of perceptual selection include the following:

   a.   Personality—a person's defining behavioral characteristics and tendencies will influence what is perceived and how it is perceived. In turn, the stimuli that are perceived will influence a person's defining behavioral characteristics and tendencies.
   b.   Learning—affects perception through the development of perceptual sets and through its reflection of a person's life experiences and the impact of culture on those experiences.
   c.   Motivation—people tend to perceive things that will satisfy their needs and that they have found to be rewarding in prior situations.

3.   *Give an example from your own experience of when people seemed to interpret the same situation differently. Why did they do this?*

Differences in people's interpretation of the same environmental stimulus may be due to any one or some combination of the following factors:

   a.   The external factors and internal factors of perceptual selection.
   b.   The mechanisms of perceptual organization.
   c.   The occurrence of perceptual errors and attributions during the interpretation phase of the perceptual process.

In providing examples, students should focus on the specific aspects of the perceptual process that may be responsible for differing perceptions of the same stimulus. For instance, internal factors of perceptual selection may influence the differing perceptions that two students have of a large lecture course. One student may dislike a large class because it limits one's opportunity to ask a lot of questions and to receive frequent performance feedback. Another student may like a large lecture class because it permits a much greater degree of student anonymity. With each student there is a different perception of the same stimulus—a difference which is due to personality, learning, motivation, or some combination thereof.

4.   *Describe the key factors in person perception.*

Person perception is the process by which individuals attribute characteristics or traits to other people. The key factors are the characteristics of the person being perceived, the characteristics of the perceiver, and the situation or context within which the perception takes place.

5.   *Provide two examples of impression management from your own experiences.*

Impression management refers to an attempt that people make to manipulate or control the impressions that others form about them. Impression management may occur wherever and whenever people interact with one another. The likelihood of impression management occurring is a function of:

(a)   the degree to which individuals are motivated to actively manage their impressions, and

(b)   the extent to which individuals consciously choose the image they want to convey and how they will go about conveying that image.

Students' examples of impression management should consider both the motivation to manage impressions and the deliberate attempt to construct desired impressions.

6.   *Identify and explain the most common perceptual errors.*

The major perceptual errors discussed in the text are perceptual defense, stereotyping, halo effect, projection, and expectancy effects. Perceptual defense is the tendency to perceive stimuli that are supportive or satisfying and to ignore those stimuli that are unpleasant or disturbing. Stereo-typing is the process of assigning attributes to a person solely on the basis of a category to which that person belongs. The halo effect involves evaluating all dimensions of a person based solely on one impression or one dimension, either favorable or unfavorable. Projection is the tendency to for individuals to project their own feelings into their judgment of others. Expectancy effects in perception refer to the extent to which prior expectation bias how events, objects, and people are actually perceived.

7.   *From you own experience, which of the perceptual errors discussed seems most likely to occur? Give an example of a situation in which this error was made.*

Since this question asks for an opinion based on the student's experience, any of the perceptual errors—perceptual defense, stereotyping, halo effect, projection, and expectancy effects—might be chosen since they are quite common in everyday experience. Students are probably very familiar with stereotyping. Stereotypes regarding age, race, gender, and occupation can have significant effects on the processing and interpretation of social information, and thus should warrant discussion.

8.   *What perceptual errors by managers could create special problems in their evaluation of subordinates' job performance? In their evaluation of a job applicant?*

Any of the perceptual errors—perceptual defense, stereotyping, halo effect, projection, and expectancy effects—conceivably could cause errors in evaluating employees' job performance or applicants' job qualifications.

The halo effect is certainly one of the most obvious. For example, if a supervisor is favorably impressed with some aspect of an employee's behavior or character, this favorable impression may overshadow all other aspects of the employee's performance. This could lead to an inaccurate evaluation of overall job performance. The halo effect also could influence mangers' evaluations of job applicants. For instance, an interviewer may be so favorably impressed with an applicant's articulate responses to questions, that the applicant is viewed as having all the requisite job skills, even if some are lacking. Or the interviewer, based upon an applicant's impeccable business attire, may assume that applicant is a very knowledgeable and competent business person.

Projection could occur if a manager perceived some undesirable trait in an employee or in an applicant—a trait that the manager has but perhaps does not fully recognize—and assigns greater significance to this than is warranted. For instance, a domineering supervisor may complain about employees or applicants who seem to be pushy or overbearing.

Other examples could focus on perceptual defense, stereotyping, and/or expectancy effects.

9.   *Describe how a person determines whether someone else's behavior represents what he or she is truly like or simply reflects the circumstances of the situation.*

This discussion question focuses on the model of the attribution process shown in Figure 3.9 of the text.

The model presented in Figure 3.9 focuses on the concepts of consistency, distinctiveness, and consensus to explain internal versus external attributions. When consistency, distinctiveness and consensus are high, the perceiver tends to attribute others' behavior to external causes. However, when consistency is high but distinctiveness and consensus are low, the perceiver tends to attribute other's behavior to internal causes. When consistency is low, the perceiver may attribute others' behavior to either internal causes or external causes or to both.

10. *Explain the fundamental attribution error. Provide an example—either from your own experience or something you have read—of when an observer seemed to make the fundamental attribution error.*

The fundamental attribution error is the tendency to underestimate the impact of situational or external causes of behavior and to overestimate the impact of personal or internal causes of behavior when seeking to understand why people behave as they do.

Students' examples should illustrate the definition. While many possible examples exist, one which is probably familiar to many students involves the disproportionate work loads assumed by members of a project group. People who do not carry their fair share of the burden on the group project may be perceived to be lazy—perhaps an overestimate of an internal cause. Possible external causes—such as scheduling conflicts or other group members trying to exercise a high degree of control over the project—may be underestimated. On the other hand, people who carry far more than their fair share of the burden may be perceived to be pushy, bossy, aggressive, or wanting everything to go their own way—clearly internal attributions. Meanwhile, external factors—such as other group members not meeting deadlines or not producing quality output—may be underestimated.

11.   *From your own experience, give an example of attributions made following either success or failure on some task.*

Student examples should illustrate how perceivers determine whether the behavior of another person stems from internal causes or external causes, and the degree to which the conditions provide consensus, consistency, and distinctiveness. An example probably familiar to most students involves attributions made following performance on an exam. If the student performs poorly, he or she most likely will attribute the behavior to external causes—the exam was too difficult, the professor didn't explain the material, the student had two other exams on the same day, or other factors external to the individual. However, a strong performance on the exam most likely will be attributed to internal causes such as studying hard, being a good student, or just being smart.

12.   *Provide two real examples of the occurrence of a self-serving bias.*

The self-serving bias refers to a strong tendency which people have for attributing their successes to internal factors (such as ability and effort) and their failures to external factors (such as task difficulty or luck). Student examples should identify whether the factor(s) perceived to be responsible for the success or failure were internal or external. Subsequent class discussion could focus on examining the number and types internal factors and external factors cited in the success examples and in the failure examples.

DEVELOPING SKILLS—
SELF DIAGNOSIS: MEASURING PERCEPTIONS OF WOMEN AS MANAGERS

The self-diagnosis questionnaire entitled *Measuring Perceptions of Women as Managers* is designed for students to explore their attitudes toward women in managerial roles. The questionnaire consists of 12 sets of three items. In each set the respondent selects the item with which he/she most agrees and the item with which he/she least agrees. Scoring instructions are provided in the textbook immediately after the questionnaire. Possible total scores range from a low of 10 to a high of 70. A score in the range of 30 to 40 indicates a neutral position—neither positive nor negative attitudes about women as managers. The higher the score, the more an individual holds negative gender-role stereotypes about women as managers.

In discussing the results of the self diagnosis, emphasis should be placed upon perceptual errors that may occur when an individual holds negative gender-role stereotypes about women as managers. Discussion also should consider how negative gender-role stereotypes of women might influence attributions which are made about the causes of a woman employee's behavior. Also appropriate for consideration are suggested organizational and managerial actions to ensure that negative gender-role stereotypes do not harm the organization and its employees.

DEVELOPING SKILLS—
A CASE IN POINT: THE INTERNSHIP

CASE OVERVIEW

This case describes the chronological sequences of events which took place in a student's internship with ARC Corporation. The student, Ken Barrett, was supervised by Mr. Don Ahearn, industrial relations manager at ARC.

The internship project began with a lack of clarity and adequate direction despite Ken's attempts to get Mr. Ahearn to define the parameters of the project and his expectations for the project. The ill-defined nature of the project continued throughout the semester-long internship. Indeed, Ken was faced with defining the project parameters on his own, even to the extent of shifting the focus of the project in response to Ahearn's lack of interest in the work Ken had already done. Additionally, Ahearn repeatedly missed appointments with Ken and did not provide Ken with materials that he promised.

As the internship experience progressed, Ken became increasingly frustrated and dissatisfied. At the internship's conclusion, Ken had very negative perceptions of the experience while Mr. Ahearn apparently viewed it quite positively.

CASE QUESTIONS

1.   *Make a list of the possible differences in the way Ken and Mr. Ahearn perceived the internship.*

    Some of the possible differences include the different internal factors affecting perception such as motivation, perception of time, past experiences (learning), and personality. Students need to recognize that time availability, priorities, expectations, motivations, past work experience, etc. are very different for Ken and Mr. Ahearn, and that these differences form the basis of their differences in perceptions of the student internship.

    In addition, differences in interpretation of events and behaviors as well as their responses to events and behaviors could lead to differences in the way the internship was perceived by Ken and Mr. Ahearn. Students, such as Ken, typically may view an internship as one of their more important college experiences. Egos may be at stake because this may be the first real organizational responsibility for some individuals. The inclusion of the internship experience on a résumé may be quite important to the student. Also, the internship is very meaningful for Ken and is centered to his interests as a student. In contrast, the internship is much more peripheral to Ahearn and does not play a central role in his activities.

2.   *To what might Ken attribute Mr. Ahearn's behavior?*

    In making attributions about Ahearn's behavior, Ken might focus on consensus, consistency, and distinctiveness as suggested by Kelley's model of causal attributions. Based on this information, if consensus, consistency, and distinctiveness were all high, Ken might conclude that Ahearn's behavior stemmed from external causes. Ken might make a fundamental attribution error if he underestimated the impact of situational or external causes of Ahearn's behavior.

The interactions between Ken and Ahearn have ben limited enough that Ken may have some trouble making any attributions. For example, there needs to be enough interaction for the perceiver to judge consistency in the other person's behavior. On balance, however, Ken is probably likely to attribute Ahearn's behavior to internal causes, perceiving both low consensus and low distinctiveness in Ahearn's behavior. Ken was surprised when Ahearn dismissed or ignored something that he wanted to discuss. Ken may not believe that others would act in this manner (low consensus). Further, Ahearn acted this way just about every time they met (low distinctiveness). I would be easy for Ken to commit the "fundamental attribution error" since he may not be aware of external pressures that might cause Ahearn's behavior—time pressures, budgetary constraints, political concerns, etc.

3.   *To what would you expect Ken to attribute his "failure"?*

As presented in the text, there is a strong tendency for people to attribute their success with a task to internal factors and to attribute their failures to external factors. Certainly, we might expect this bias to be operating here. Ken might deny responsibility for his poor grade and attribute his unsuccessful internship to external factors such as the difficulty of the task, Ahearn's ambiguity about what he expected of the internship, Ahearn missing their meetings, or his bad luck in being assigned to ARC Corporation. This self-serving bias would prevent Ken from accurately assessing his performance and abilities and he might make the same mistakes again.

4.   *What were the main problems Ken faced during his internship? Why did these problems arise?*

The problems faced by Ken focus on his failure to get clear and specific guidelines from Mr. Ahearn at the first meeting, failure to get a commitment, and failure to discuss the parameters of the internship project. He left that first meeting feeling disappointed and with only a vague idea of what he was expected to do or what Ahearn wanted from a student intern. These issues became the basis of the interpretations and disappointments that followed. Any differences in expectations for and perceptions of the internship needed to be addressed—since they were not dealt with, the existence of later problems was predictable.

5.   *If you had been given this internship, what would you have done to improve the situation?*

To improve the situation, it would be necessary to establish clear guidelines and parameters before proceeding with the internship project. For example, the establishment of a psychological contract between Ken and Ahearn at the beginning of the internship would improve the situation. Agreement was needed concerning project parameters, responsibilities, support, availabilities of Mr. Ahearn and other personnel, timetables, and outcomes. Students might be reminded of how important it is to have performance and behavior expectations discussed prior to beginning any type of work project. Ideally, the criteria and/or guidelines will be in written form. Also, the professor, who supervises the internship on the academic side, needs to be more proactive in screening organizations and ensuring their understanding of and commitment to the internship program.

COURSE ENHANCEMENT—
WEST'S ORGANIZATIONAL BEHAVIOR CUSTOM VIDEO SERIES

One video from *West's Organizational Behavior Custom Video Series* can be used to enhance the material in Chapter 3. This video, which was relevant to Chapter 2 as well, is: *Microscope Magazine: AT&T's Walter Persons.*

VIDEO: *MICROSCOPE MAGAZINE: AT&T'S WALTER PERSONS*

Approximate Time: 4 minutes

Video Summary:

Walter Persons, a production specialist at AT&T's Richmond Plant, is the focus of the video. The video demonstrates the positive effects of his personality on other employees and the managerial implications of personality. Mr. Person's varied roles at the plant include safety coordinator of the back panel shop, member of the medical emergency response team, and volunteer for other special projects. His outside interests include spending time with his family and performing as an actor at the local theater. Mr. Persons' supervisor and co-workers consider him to be an asset and enjoy his positive attitude and happy disposition. His fellow employees feel comfortable going to him for advice. The supervisor encourages all employees to develop outside interests and feels it helps the company's positive image. Viewers should recognize the importance of understanding personality characteristics and taking advantage of diversity in organizations. The video indicates how AT&T has taken advantage of diversity in its workforce to continue its mission.

Discussion Questions for Video:

1. *How is Walter Persons perceived by his co-workers and boss? How do their perceptions of him influence their behavior toward him?*

    Person's co-workers and boss perceive him very positively. They describe him as an asset. They enjoy his positive attitude and happy disposition. His fellow employees feel comfortable going to him for advice. His supervisor commends his outside interests because it contributes to the company's positive image. Given the glowing statements made by his boss and co-workers, one might wonder if halo effects or expectancy effects are operating here.

2. *Do you think Walter's co-workers and boss attribute his behavior to internal or external causes?*

    Kelley's theory of causal attributions could be applied to this question. Based upon the criteria of consistency, distinctiveness, and consensus, the most likely attribution would be one of internal causation. Persons seems to be remarkably consistent and distinctive in his behavior—he is pleasant, outgoing, and helpful across a variety of different situations. Whether others behave similarly in these situations is indeterminate from the information provided.

CHAPTER 4
INDIVIDUAL PROBLEM-SOLVING STYLES

CHAPTER OVERVIEW

Chapter 4 continues the exploration of individual processes by focusing on individual problem-solving styles. A model of the individual problem-solving process is used to explain how people process information and make decisions. Next, four psychological functions of problem solving—sensation versus intuition in gathering information, and feeling versus and thinking in evaluating information—are developed as a foundation for the discussion of individual problem solving styles. Then four problem-solving styles (sensation-thinkers, intuitive-tinkers, sensation-feelers, and intuitive-feelers) are discussed in terms of their defining characteristics, impact on relationships with others, possible limitations, preferred occupations, and views of organizational effectiveness. Finally, there is a discussion of the implications of individual problem-solving styles for ethics, teamwork, and reengineering.

LEARNING OBJECTIVES

Upon completion of this chapter, the students should be able to:

1. Describe the four stages of the problem-solving model.
2. Explain two methods that individuals use to gather data.
3. State two methods that individuals use to evaluate information.
4. Identify their own problem-solving style.
5. List the strengths and weaknesses of four individual problem-solving styles.

CHAPTER OUTLINE

I.   **Preview Case:** Ben & Jerry's Homemade Ice Cream, Inc.

II.   Individual Problem-Solving Processes

III.   Psychological Functions in Problem Solving

   A.   Sensation Versus Intuition in Gathering Information
   B.   Feeling Versus Thinking in Evaluating Information
   C.   **Managing Across Cultures:** Problem Solving Styles of Canadian and Japanese Students

IV.   Individual Problem-Solving Styles

   A.   Sensation-Thinkers
   B.   **Managing in Practice:** Against the Grain
   C.   Intuitive-Thinkers
   D.   **Managing in Practice:** The CEO as Organizational Architect
   E.   Sensation-Feelers
   F.   **Managing in Practice:** Body Shop International
   G.   Intuitive-Feelers
   H.   **Managing in Practice:** Herb Kelleher of Southwest Airlines
   I.   Summary of Problem-Solving Styles

V.   Organizational Implications

   A.   **Managing Ethics:** What's Your Decision?
   B.   **Managing Diversity:** Reengineering at GTE

VI. Developing Skills

   A.   **Self Diagnosis:** Problem-Solving Style
   B.   **A Case in Point:** Whole Foods Market

KEY WORDS AND CONCEPTS

Fourteen key words and concepts are introduced in Chapter 4. One concept—reengineering—was originally introduced in Chapter 2 of the textbook. The key words and concepts, along with definitions or appropriate descriptions, are as follows:

Feeling: a psychological function in problem solving which refers to a tendency to base judgments more on personal values than on impersonal analysis and logic.

Feeling-type person: an individual who is aware of other people and their feelings, likes harmony, needs occasional praise, dislikes telling people unpleasant news, is sympathetic, and relates well to most people.

Intuition: a psychological function in problem solving which refers to a preference for looking for new possibilities rather than working with known possibilities or facts.

Intuitive-feeler (NF): refers to an individual problem-solving style which emphasize personal charisma and commitment to the people being lead.

Intuitive-thinker (NT): refers to an individual problem-solving style which emphasizes progress and ideas.

Intuitive-type person: an individual who looks first at ideas and possibilities rather than facts.

Problem-solving style: the way a person visualizes and thinks about situations.

Reengineering: the search for and implementation of changes in the organization's processes to achieve major gains in service or product quality, time, or cost.

Sensing: a psychological function in problem solving which refers to a preference for working with known possibilities and facts rather than looking for new possibilities.

Sensation-feeler (SF): refers to an individual problem-solving style which emphasizes the importance of interpersonal relations and of dealing with concrete problems in a methodical fashion.

Sensation-thinker (ST): refers to an individual problem-solving style which emphasizes order, control, and consistency.

Sensation-type person: an individual who wants, trusts, and remembers facts and would rather work with facts than look for possibilities and relationships.

Thinking: a psychological function in problem solving which refers to a tendency to base judgments more on impersonal analysis and logic than on personal values.

Thinking-type person: an individual who prefers impersonal principles and is not comfortable unless there is a logical or analytical basis for a decision.

LECTURE NOTES

I.   Chapter 4 continues the exploration of individual differences by focusing on individual problem-solving styles. A problem-solving style is the way a person visualizes and thinks about situations.

   A.   Different problem-solving styles are based upon how individuals gather and evaluate information. Do people gather information by their senses or by intuition? Do people evaluate information by using logical analysis or by using their instincts?

   B.   Differences in how people gather and evaluate information have important implications for organizational behavior, including ethics, teamwork, and reengineering efforts.

   C.   Transparency 4.1 provides an overview of the material contained in Chapter 4 of the textbook.

TRANSPARENCY 4.1
(FROM TEXT MATERIAL IN THE TEXTBOOK)
OVERVIEW OF MATERIAL ON INDIVIDUAL PROBLEM-SOLVING STYLES

II.   Individual problem-solving processes.

   A.   In making decisions, people rely on the problem-solving process which is shown in Transparency 4.2. Briefly, this model shows that two sources of environmental stimuli—external (outside the organization) and internal (inside the organization)—influence the decision maker's perceptions. The decision maker's personal frame of reference (*e.g.,* personal needs, personality characteristics, attitudes, etc.) and the perceptual filtering of information also influence the decision maker's perceptions of the decision situation. Perceptions of the decision situation reflect how the decision maker gathers information. The evaluation of available alternatives reflects how the decision maker evaluates information. Taken together, how one gathers information and how one evaluates information determines the decisions maker's problem-solving style. The decision-maker's problem-solving style then manifests itself in the various phases of the actual decision-making process.

TRANSPARENCY 4.2
(FIGURE 4.1 IN THE TEXTBOOK)

INDIVIDUAL PROBLEM-SOLVING PROCESS

III.   Psychological functions in problem solving.

A.   Problem solving is affected by the way in which one gathers information and the way in which one evaluates information.

1.   Sensing and intuition are two opposite ways of gathering information

a.   <u>Sensing</u> indicates a preference for working with known possibilities and facts rather than looking for new possibilities.

b.   <u>Intuition</u> indicates a preference for looking for new possibilities rather than working with known possibilities or facts.

2.   Thinking and feeling are opposite ways of evaluating information.

a.   <u>Feeling</u> reflects a tendency to base judgments more on personal values than on impersonal analysis and logic.

b.   <u>Thinking</u> reflects a tendency to base judgments more on impersonal analysis and logic than on personal values.

3.   Each individual has a preference for one way of gathering data and one way of evaluating it. Of the four psychological functions—sensing versus intuition and thinking versus feeling—one function will dominate and one function from the other set of paired opposites will play a supporting role. However, individuals tend to move toward a balance, or integration, of the four psychological functions as they mature in their careers.

ENRICHMENT MODULE: PROBLEM SOLVING AND WORKING RELATIONSHIPS

Awareness of differences in problem-solving styles can be very helpful in understanding work relationships with subordinates, peers, and superiors. For example, the individual who always seeks facts before acting (sensing) may easily view someone who acts more on intuitive insight as impulsive and as acting on mere whim without "doing their homework." In turn, the person who acts more on intuition might view the sensing person's care in getting all the facts before deciding as a case of worrying excessively about details and even as decision avoidance.

Thinkers are likely to see themselves as capable of making the hard decisions based upon a logical analysis of a situation and they see feelers as tenderhearted, given to irrational judgements, and too easily swayed by emotions and compassion. By contrast, feeling types will see themselves as sensitive, considerate, and responsive to people's needs, and will see thinking types as hard-nosed, distant, and insensitive.

People can learn to understand and even appreciate their differences and in doing so, it provides a way to look for improving their work relationships. Most situations call for a variety of managerial approaches, including the ability to use thought, feelings, intuition, judgment, and perceptions. Mutual adaptation among people can facilitate drawing on one another as sources of information.

B.   Characteristics of psychological functions when a given function is the dominant type.

    1.   Sensation versus intuition in gathering information.

        a.   A <u>sensation-type person</u> wants, trusts, and remembers facts and would rather work with facts than look for possibilities and relationships. Such an individual believes in experience and relies on the past in approaching current problems.

        b.   An <u>intuitive-type person</u> looks first at ideas and possibilities rather than facts. Such a person likes to solve new problems, dislikes repetitive work, may jump to conclusions, becomes impatient with routine details, and dislikes taking time to be precise.

        c.   As shown in Transparency 4.3, sensation-type people and intuitive-type people differ when compared on the following behavioral patterns and general characteristics: focus, time orientation, work environment, strengths, and possible weaknesses.

TRANSPARENCY 4.3
(TABLE 4.1 IN THE TEXTBOOK)

COMPARISONS OF SENSATION AND INTUITIVE TYPES OF PEOPLE

        d.   Sensation-type people and intuitive-type people also differ in terms of the characteristics of their problem-solving styles (see Transparency 4.4).

TRANSPARENCY 4.4
(FROM TEXT MATERIAL IN THE TEXTBOOK)

COMPARISONS OF PROBLEM-SOLVING CHARACTERISTICS OF
SENSATION AND INTUITIVE TYPES OF PEOPLE

(1)   The sensation-type person tends to:

(a)   Dislike new problems, unless there are standard ways to solve them.

(b)   Enjoy using skills already acquired more than learning new ones.

(c)   Work steadily with a realistic idea of how long a task will take.

(d)   Work through a task or problem to a conclusion.

(e)   Be impatient when details get complicated.

(f)   Distrust creative inspirations.

(2)   The intuitive-type person tends to:

(a)   Keep the total picture or overall problem continually in mind as problem solving proceeds.

(b)   Show a tendency, willingness, and openness to continually explore possibilities.

(c)   Rely on hunches and nonverbal cues.

(d)   Almost simultaneously consider a variety of alternatives and options and quickly discard those judged as unworkable.

(e)   Jump around among the usual sequence of steps in the problem-solving process and may even want to reassess whether the "real" has been identified.

2.   Feeling versus thinking in evaluating information.

a.   A feeling-type person is aware of other people and their feelings, likes harmony, needs occasional praise, dislikes telling people unpleasant news, is sympathetic, and relates well to most people. Such an individual bases decisions on how they will affect the emotional well-being of others, and looks to moral values for guidance.

b.   A thinking-type person prefers impersonal principles and is not comfortable unless there is a logical or analytical basis for a decision. Such a person's decisions are controlled by intellectual processes based on external data and generally accepted ideas and values.

c.　As shown in Transparency 4.5, feeling-type people and thinking-type people also differ when compared in terms of focus, time orientation, work environment, strengths, and possible weaknesses.

TRANSPARENCY 4.5
(TABLE 4.2 IN THE TEXTBOOK)

COMPARISONS OF FEELING AND THINKING TYPES OF PEOPLE

---

d.　Feeling-type people and thinking-type people also differ in terms of the characteristics of their problem-solving styles (see Transparency 4.6).

TRANSPARENCY 4.6
(FROM TEXT MATERIAL IN THE TEXTBOOK)

COMPARISONS OF PROBLEM-SOLVING CHARACTERISTICS OF
FEELING AND THINKING TYPES OF PEOPLE

---

(1)　The feeling-type person tends to:

(a)　Enjoy pleasing people, even in ways that others consider unimportant.

(b)　Dislike dealing with problems that require telling other people something unpleasant.

(c)　Be responsive and sympathetic to other people's problems.

(d)　Emphasize the human aspects in dealing with organizational problems and view the causes of inefficiency and ineffectiveness as interpersonal and other human problems.

(2)　The thinking-type person tends to:

(a)　Make a plan and look for a method to solve a problem.

(b)　Define carefully the specific constraints in a problem.

(c)　Proceed by increasingly refining an analysis.

(d)　Search for and obtain additional information in an orderly manner.

ENRICHMENT MODULE: HOW DIFFERENT STYLES SOLVE REAL PROBLEMS

The following chart shows how the four different problem-solving styles are typically used to solve real organizational problems. Also depicted is the time orientation and executive role that most closely fits with the problem-solving style.

Problem-Solving Style	Problem Stage	Time Orientation	Executive Role
Intuition	Vision --> Imagination	"What could be"	Leader
Feeling	Values --> Motivation	"What are we"	Champion
Thinking	Planning --> Objectives	"How to get it"	Administrator
Sensing	Actions --> Tasks	"Let it happen" "Do it"	Implementor

---

TRANSPARENCY 4.7
(The above chart is reproduced in the transparency package.)

---

3.   An excellent example of differences in problem-solving styles is provided by a comparative study of Canadian and Japanese students (see Transparency 4.8). Canadian students display a strong preference for the thinking style whereas Japanese students prefer the feeling style.

TRANSPARENCY 4.8
(FIGURE 4.2 IN THE TEXTBOOK)

COMPARISON OF STUDENT PROBLEM-SOLVING STYLES

III.   Individual problem-solving styles.

A.   The combination of preferences for information gathering and information evaluation produces an individual's problem-solving style, as shown in Transparency 4.10.

TRANSPARENCY 4.9
(FIGURE 4.3 IN THE TEXTBOOK)

INDIVIDUAL PROBLEM-SOLVING STYLES MODEL

ENRICHMENT MODULE: RELATING PROBLEM-SOLVING STYLES TO COLLEGE MAJOR

Students are usually very interested in whether there is a relationship between the major they have chosen and their problem-solving style. The following chart indicates how a student's problem-solving style may be related to his/her major by showing the percent of individuals in a specific major that have each style. Additionally, students might be asked to discuss how their problem-solving style affected their choice of a major. Emphasis should be placed upon the notion that each major can be performed by different styles but that there are some issues to consider. For example, if a student is an NF and desires to be an accountant, the student's mode of data gathering and data evaluation might generate considerable frustration for him/her. The typical accounting job requires an ST orientation.

MAJOR	Percent of ST	Percent of SF	Percent of NF	Percent of NT
Accounting	46	11	14	29
Artists	9	20	52	9
Education	13	42	39	6
Engineering	48	20	2	30
Finance	54	15	6	25
Journalism	15	23	42	20
Law	26	3	21	50
Liberal Arts	12	13	20	55
Management	25	15	20	40
Marketing	10	14	25	51
Nursing	11	49	32	8
Sales	11	81	8	0

TRANSPARENCY 4.10
(The above chart is reproduced in the transparency package.)

ENRICHMENT MODULE: CROSS-CULTURAL COMPARISONS
OF PROBLEM-SOLVING STYLES

The following chart indicates how managers' problem-solving styles vary in five different countries. An interesting discussion can be generated by fist examining the cultures of these countries and then relating these cultural differences to differences in the problem-solving style profiles.

PERCENTAGE FREQUENCIES OF MANAGEMENT STYLES

	GENERAL POPULATION	U.S.	Japan	MANAGERS U.K.	Mexico	Russia
ST	40	41	38	53	55	45
SF	15	13	20	15	16	6
NF	16	15	12	10	9	11
NT	29	31	30	22	20	38
	100%	100%	100%	100%	100%	100%

TRANSPARENCY 4.11
(The above chart is reproduced in the transparency package.)

B.   A <u>sensation-thinker (ST)</u> is concerned with establishing order, control, and consistency.

    1.   In relating to others, an ST responds positively to people sharing data in a highly organized fashion. They dislike using symbolic rewards but like to base verbal and monetary rewards on measurable performance standards.

    2.   An ST's possible limitations include: impatience, not noticing complications or new situations that arise, overemphasis on maintaining organizational stability, overlooking interpersonal events, and blaming others when things go wrong.

    3.   STs are interested in occupations—such as accounting, stock brokerage, computer programming, copy editing, engineering, etc.—that deal with the physical and impersonal side of organizations.

    4.   STs evaluate organizational effectiveness in terms of objective cost, volume, rate of return, and profitability measures.

C.   An <u>intuitive-thinker (NT)</u> is the architect of progress and ideas.

    1.   In relating to others, an NT responds positively to others' new ideas as well as to helping others to solve new problems. They are comfortable in organizations that focus on long-term results, rather than on procedures and rules. NTs respond to recognition of their accomplishments and of the influence of their work on others.

    2.   An NT's possible limitations include: leaving the implementation of creative ideas

to others, being insensitive to others' feelings, devaluing the input of people whose intellectual competence they question, and having high—and sometimes unreasonable—expectations for themselves and others.

3.   NTs are interested in occupations—such as entrepreneurial ventures, teaching in economics, business, philosophy or the physical sciences, architectural design, law, etc.—that deal with new possibilities and nonroutine tasks.

4.   NTs evaluate organizational effectiveness in terms of measures of growth and development (*e.g.*, growth in earning and profits, market share, rate of new product development, etc.).

D.   A <u>sensation-feeler (SF)</u> emphasizes the importance of interpersonal relations and of dealing with concrete problems in a methodical fashion.

1.   In relating to others, an NT responds positively to others' ideas if those ideas are concrete. They are easy to get along with. SFs involve others in a consensus-seeking decision-making process. They take calculated risks and encourage others to do the same. They are adaptable to new facts and new situations.

2.   An SF's possible limitations include: not accepting new theories and abstract ideas, promoting group discussion at the expense of solving the problem, seeking others' acceptance by promoting others' ideas, being adaptable to the point of breaking the system's rules and procedures, and not honoring prior commitments and decisions.

3.   SFs are interested in occupations—such as selling, counseling, negotiating, teaching, human resource management, etc.—that require personal contact with others in the organization or with customers.

4.   SFs evaluate organizational effectiveness in terms of employee loyalty, attitudes, turnover, and absenteeism.

F.   An <u>intuitive-feeler (NF)</u> relies on personal charisma and commitment to the people being lead.

1.   In relating to others, an NF responds positively to personal contact with other people. They are adventurous and risk-taking. They maintain close contact with their bosses. Their work organization is a source of social satisfaction.

2.   An NF's possible limitations include: making decisions on the basis of personal likes and dislikes, working in great burst of energy but needing frequent rest periods to recharge their energy levels, being overly dependent on the approval of others, and being vulnerable to other people's emotions.

3.   NFs are interested in occupations—such as public relations, politics, advertising, human resource management, etc.—that deal with the human side of the organization.

4.   NFs evaluate organizational effectiveness in terms of consumer and community satisfaction, identification of new problems or opportunities, social responsibility, and quality of life.

G.   The four problem-solving styles are summarized in Transparency 4.12.

TRANSPARENCY 4.12
(TABLE 4.3 IN THE TEXTBOOK)

SUMMARY OF PROBLEM-SOLVING STYLES

ENRICHMENT MODULE: A CLASH OF PROBLEM-SOLVING STYLES AT P&G

Sometimes people with different problem-solving styles can work effectively together, sometimes not. The problem-solving styles of John Pepper and Durk Jager—both senior executives at Proctor & Gamble Co. and candidates for the company's top job—definitely clash. The "gentlemanly manners and teamwork approach" of Mr. Pepper "don't mesh with...Mr. Jager's aggressive, quick-results style."

Mr. Pepper is known for his popular personal style. Employees give him "standing ovations at company meetings and rave about his small acts of generosity. One former P&G executive, Mr. McNamara, recalls the "emotional lift" he felt when Mr. Pepper remembered the name of McNamara's spouse. Another former P&G manager says, "John Pepper is a man who doesn't need to lead through fear or toughness." However, Pepper's critics say that he is plodding and indecisive. Despite admonitions from P&G's board of directors to be more decisive, Pepper "still constantly consults employees in an effort to build consensus. But he is often persuaded to agree with whoever has been in his office last."

Mr. Jager is known as a demanding taskmaster. He once "threatened—with a grin—to break employees' kneecaps if they didn't follow orders." According to a story that has circulated among P&G's employees, Mr. Jager, on a flight back to Cincinnati, "turned to a manager whom he had met for the first time and said, 'What do you do at P&G?' When the man tried to explain, Mr. Jager cut him off, saying, 'I'll let you know by the time we land whether you still have a job or not.' Even though Mr. Jager was kidding, the employee was a nervous wreck all the way back to Cincinnati."

This enrichment module is based on:

Stern, G. (1994, July 15). Two mismatched men compete for one big job. *The Wall Street Journal*, B1 & B6.

IV.   Individual problem-solving styles can influence organizations in a variety of ways. Among the likely organizational implications are the following:

    A.   Perceptions of ethical situations are likely to be influenced by a person's problem-solving style.

    B.   Individual problem-solving styles also affect the behavior of work teams. Difference in problem-solving styles can produce conflict. However, when individual differences are respected and appreciated, teamwork is often more effective when members with different problem-solving styles are combined into one team.

    C.   Reengineering—the search for and implementation of changes in the organization's processes to achieve major gains in service or product quality, time, or cost—also can be affected by individual problem-solving styles. Reengineering starts out with the fundamental question: "If we were to start a new organization, how should this place be run?" People will approach this question differently, based upon their own individual problem-solving styles.

V.   Summing up: What has been learned about individual problem-solving styles?

A.   Problem-solving styles represent another individual differences variable which influences people's behavior in organizational settings. Differences in problem-solving styles can affect how people relate to each other and the occupations they choose. Each problem-solving style has different strengths and weaknesses which in turn influence a variety of organizational behaviors.

B.   A summary comparison of the four different problem-solving styles vividly reinforces their potential behavioral implications. Sensation-thinkers (STs) use facts and logic to solve problems. Intuitive-thinkers (NTs) use abstract principles and logic to solve problems. Sensation-feelers (SFs) use facts and personal values to solve problems. Intuitive-feelers (NFs) use intuition and personal values to solve problems.

DISCUSSION QUESTIONS: SUGGESTED ANSWERS

1.   *Use the problem-solving chart shown in Figure 4.1 to describe how you chose the academic courses you are taking.*

Beginning on the left side of the figure, your perceptions of the decision situation would be influenced by two major sources of environmental stimuli—internal (such as degree requirements, course assignments, grading criteria, instructors, and/or course demands) and external (such as the job market or career aspirations). Your perceptions of the decision situation would also be influenced by your frame of reference (*e.g.,* past experiences with particular instructors, attitudes toward different fields of study, etc.) and your perceptual filtering of information (*e.g.,* stereotypes of different courses or professors, halo effect regarding particular professors, etc.). Your perception of the decision situation reflects how you gather information. Your evaluation of the available alternatives (such as various subjects or instructors) reflects how you evaluate information. How you gather information and how you evaluate information, in turn, define your problem-solving style. Given your individual problem-solving style, you then make a decision in light of the solvability of the problem and the risks and consequences of each of the alternatives. The results of the decision are the last in the process; yet through a feedback loop the model suggests it is the beginning of more decisions.

2.   *What is the likely influence of your problem-solving style on your selection of a job? Why do some people want to match the demands of the job with their preferred problem-solving style?*

Because people exhibit different problem-solving styles, they are usually better suited for certain jobs. The sensation-thinker is likely to be interested in occupations that deal with the details and the impersonal side of a company. This person may be attracted to jobs in fields such as accounting, production, computer programming, engineering, statistics, and financial analysis.

The intuitive-thinker is attracted to positions that deal with new possibilities and nonroutine tasks. Examples of occupations include systems analysis and design, attorneys, behavioral scientists, consultants, actors, and researchers.

The sensation-feeler is usually interested in jobs that require personal contact with others in the organization or with customers. Occupations would involve selling, counseling, teaching, preaching, nursing, and social work.

The intuitive-feeler usually prefers occupations that deal with the human side of the organization but unlike SFs, their jobs need not have as many personal and close contacts with others. This type of person excels in public relations, advertising, personnel, teaching, psychology, and journalism.

It is important that people match their preferred problem-solving style with the demands of their jobs. A good match will allow an individual to be more productive, may lead to him or her becoming satisfied, and avoid frustration from encountering a task in which their style is incompatible.

3.   *If an organization has managers with all four problem-solving styles, what diversity issues does this pose for employees?*

Diversity issues are usually conceptualized in terms of variables such as race, ethnicity, gender, or age. However, diversity, in its broadest sense, encompasses all individual differences variables, including problem-solving styles.

Sensation-thinkers (STs) are concerned with establishing order, control, and consistency, while intuitive-thinkers (NTs) are the architects of progress and ideas. Both sensation-feelers (SFs) and intuitive-feelers (NFs) are people oriented but SFs prefer to deal with concrete problems in a methodical fashion while NFs rely on personal charisma. These different problem-solving styles lead to different kinds of behaviors, and an organization having managers with all four problem-solving styles will need to deal with these different behaviors. Effective management of these different behaviors can lead to cooperation and effective teamwork. Ineffective management of these different behaviors could foster conflict.

Another diversity implication of having all four problem-solving styles in the same organization involves variations in how people gather information and evaluate information. Differences in how people gather and evaluate information will naturally lead to differing views on issues facing the organizations and to differing positions regarding how to best operate the organization.

4.   *Given the external environmental factors affecting Ben & Jerry's Homemade Ice Cream, why has it been so successful?*

Ben Cohen and Jerry Greenfield built a company around the philosophy of caring capitalism—certainly unique, if not revolutionary, in some quarters. This business philosophy was applied in their dealings with employees, customers, suppliers, and the community at large. However, they were more interested in maintaining the company's social mission than in managing the operating details of the business. These factors, perhaps more than any others, played significant roles in Ben & Jerry's success.

These success factors are related to Cohen and Greenfield's apparent problem-solving style. Both appear to be intuitive-feelers (NF). They seem to be insightful and mystical (they do not conduct market research), personal and idealistic. They are creators and originators. They have global ideas oriented toward people, and value the potential of human beings. Both are good at imagining and making new combinations. Both could be considered to have the goal of making things beautiful. In short, all the characteristics of intuitive-feelers that are listed in Table 4.3 of the textbook would apply in describing Ben Cohen and Jerry Greenfield.

5. *After fourteen years of legal battles, on October 2, 1990, a federal judge told Eastman Kodak to pay Polaroid $909.5 million for violating its instant-photography patents. After federal and state taxes, there is still some $600 million left. What kinds of arguments would I. McAllister Booth, CEO of Polaroid, present for spending the $600 million to the shareholders of Polaroid if he were either an NF or ST?*

A good way to approach this question is by considering how sensation-thinkers (STs) and intuitive-feelers (NFs) differ with regard to their views of organizational effectiveness. STs evaluate organizational effectiveness in terms of objective cost, volume, rate of return, and profitability measures. Thus, if Mr. Booth were a sensation-thinker, he would probably argue that the $600 million should be invested in making their business more productive and cost efficient. NFs evaluate organizational effectiveness in terms of consumer and community satisfaction, identification of new problems or opportunities, social responsibility, and quality of life. If Mr. Booth were an intuitive-feeler (NF), he would probably argue for investing in product improvement or product development, for investing in quality of work life improvements for Polaroid's employees, or for funding important and organizationally relevant social causes.

6. *The following stories were written by senior managers while attending an executive development program. Identify the problem-solving style of each and state the reasons for your choice.*

Story 1: *The organization I would like to work for would need to be highly attentive to the personal needs of the employees. Also, I would need to produce a good product—one that society thinks is important. The organization should have a fine service department to service the product it sells. To keep moving forward, the company would need to be innovative and able to stay in front of the competition. These factors all lead to a more profitable organization.*

Story 2: *Organizations that have the greatest success in reaching established goals and objectives are those that have a staff of people who know what they are doing. Ideally, the organization would have a unique product, be a medium size (less than a thousand employees), have formal lines of communication, and produce a return on investment of at least 12 percent on operating assets. The organization would be located in a single facility in the Sun Belt. The unique product line would have limited competition, and the competition would have relatively similar quality standards.*

The organization would consist of a chief executive officer with a staff of officers of marketing, finance, operations, human resources, and accounting. The structure below these officers would allow a hands-on management style that would capitalize on the ideas of all personnel.

Story 3: *Characteristics: (1) one product, (2) a highly centralized location, and (3) a small staff of professionals.*

My organization operates through the efforts of several groups. Each group is loosely organized to achieve its goals and objectives and has professional personnel with the various skills required to produce our product. Each group has an adviser or consultant who functions to help the group in its task. He or she does not function as the group leader but knows all aspects of the job.

The groups set their own goals, choose their own leaders, and discipline and reward their members. Their production rates and quality are closely monitored and reported to the leaders. To some extent, the group is rewarded for high profitability. Leaders are elected by the group and change from time to time.

Story 4:   *My ideal organization would consist of people who are all dedicated to achieving the goals of the organization and who are willing to do so in a friendly, cooperative way. To be effective, all the people must have a servant attitude toward one another (that is, they must think not of their own interests first, but of the interests of others). An attitude of humility would prevail, and the needs of others would be met before our own.*

I think of the New Testament church in its beginnings as an ideal organization. There was a structure, but it permitted everyone to share everything so no one was in need. As the organization grew and prospered, so did the people. People's needs come before the organization.

The problem-solving styles of the four stories are as follows:

Story 1:   This story was written by an intuitive-feeler because it emphasizes the human side of the organization by being attentive to the personal needs of the employees. The author is also concerned with consumer satisfaction with the product and the organization. The story reflects the author's desire for innovation and new opportunities to make the organization successful.

Story 2:   This story was written by an intuitive-thinking manager who is concerned with the principles on which the organization was built. The story discusses the relationships between various departments and the results desired for the organization. The story is creative and analytical but very impersonal. The author wants very structured authority with hands-on responsibility.

Story 3:   This story was written by a sensation-thinker. The author presents this story in a precise, factual, and rigidly ordered manner. This is characteristic of STs as they use precise facts and figures. The story shows an organization in a formal and impersonal way. Rewards and punishments are used as extreme behavioral outcomes. As in this story, ST managers are very efficient and get to the facts quickly.

Story 4:   This story was written by a sensation-feeler. The author is concerned about employee relationships to the company's success. The story discusses cooperation as an essential ingredient of effectiveness. This type of manager would work well within the status quo for harmonious and dedicated service. The author will excel in humanistic types of occupations such as a counselor, a teacher, a minister, or a personnel interviewer.

7.   *Should organizations attempt to select people for positions on the basis of their problem-solving styles? What would be the benefits? The dangers?*

In ideal circumstances, tasks and positions should determine the type of problem-solving person that might be best suited to carry out the task. The benefits would be that people are performing tasks for which they are most qualified. The dangers of this system are that people are not given the opportunity to learn new behaviors and they do not learn to respect and appreciate individual differences.

DEVELOPING SKILLS—
SELF DIAGNOSIS: PROBLEM-SOLVING STYLE

Students can diagnose their own problem-solving styles with a 20-item questionnaire. Each question consists of a pair of alternative items. The respondent is to indicate which item in the pair is more characteristic of him/her. While the process of responding to the questionnaire seems quite simple, the actual instructions for responding are a bit complicated. Therefore, students should be cautioned to read the instructions carefully and to follow them faithfully in responding. Instructions for scoring the questionnaire are provided also.

Four scores are generated from the questionnaire responses. Two of these scores indicate the student's relative tendencies toward sensing and intuition in information gathering. The other two scores reflect the student's relative tendencies toward thinking and feeling in the evaluation of information. Within each pair (sensing versus intuition and thinking versus feeling), scores can range from zero to 50 but the sum of the two scores must equal 50. For instance, if the sensing score is 21, the intuition score is 29. Or if the sensing score is zero, the intuition score is 50. For each pair, the higher score reflects the student's preference for gathering information or for evaluating information.

DEVELOPING SKILLS—
A CASE IN POINT: WHOLE FOODS MARKET

CASE OVERVIEW

This case describes the key management philosophies and procedures used at Whole Foods Market, a natural foods supermarket which was founded by John Mackey in 1980. Since its founding in Austin, Texas, Whole Foods Market has grown to a chain of 20 stores throughout Texas, Louisiana, California, Massachusetts, and Rhode Island. Each store employs between 60 and 140 people.

The key management philosophies and procedures are as follows:

1. Each store is organized into a variety of teams, each of which is responsible for its own work, selecting its new team members, and meeting regularly to discuss problems and make team decisions.
2. Recognizing and rewarding outstanding performance of individuals and teams.
3. Using organization-wide bonus plans and rewards for team profitability to practice the principle of shared fate—that is, having all team members share in the successes and the hard times experienced by the organization.
4. Practicing the principle of shared responsibility by locating authority and responsibility at the store and team levels rather than at corporate headquarters.
5. Encouraging creativity and experimentation at each store and on each team within a store.

6.   Encouraging and using participative management.

CASE QUESTIONS

1.   *What is John Mackey's problem-solving style? How is it demonstrated in the management of Whole Foods Market?*

Mackey most likely has an intuitive-feeler (NF) problem-solving style. Mackey's key management philosophies and procedures suggest that he relies on personal charisma and has a strong commitment to the people being lead.

Additionally, the summary material contained in Transparency 4.11 (Table 4.3 of the textbook), can be used to help identify Mackey's problem-solving style. The characteristics of the intuitive-feeler seem to be most compatible with the Mackey's key management philosophies and procedures.

2.   *What are some of the challenges that Mackey and his organization face as it expands into new regions?*

Some of the key challenges facing Mackey and his organization are:

a.   Imbuing each new store with the management philosophies, procedures, and corporate culture that has contributed significantly to Whole Foods' success.
b.   Recruiting people who can function effectively in a team environment.
c.   Recruiting or promoting and training people to serve as managers in a participative environment.
d.   Resisting the temptation to exercise more centralized control as operations become more far-flung and more difficult to monitor effectively.

COURSE ENHANCEMENT—
WEST'S ORGANIZATIONAL BEHAVIOR CUSTOM VIDEO SERIES

None of the videos from *West's Organizational Behavior Custom Video Series* are appropriate for use with material in Chapter 4.

CHAPTER 5
LEARNING AND REINFORCEMENT

CHAPTER OVERVIEW

Chapter 5 examines the individual process of learning. Three types of learning are explored: classical conditioning, operant conditioning, and social learning. Because of its practical utility for management, operant conditioning is explored in considerable detail. Emphasis is placed upon using the techniques of positive reinforcement, negative reinforcement, omission, and punishment to effectively manage the consequences of employees' behaviors. Attention also is given to the usage and effects of different schedules of reinforcement. Finally, the basic principles and procedures of behavioral modification—a practical application of the operant conditioning paradigm—is introduced. Also examined are the ethical considerations of behavioral modification.

LEARNING OBJECTIVES

Upon completion of this chapter, the students should be able to:

1. Discuss the differences among classical conditioning, operant conditioning, and social learning.
2. Describe the contingencies of reinforcement.
3. List the methods used to increase desired behaviors and reduce undesired behaviors.
4. Describe the principles and procedures of behavioral modification.
5. State two limitations of behavioral modification.

CHAPTER OUTLINE

I. **Preview Case:** Driver Behaviors at UPS

II. Types of Learning

A.   Classical Conditioning
B.   Operant Conditioning
C.   Social Learning
D.   **Managing Diversity:** Diversity at Coopers & Lybrand

III.   Contingencies of Reinforcement

A.   Positive Reinforcement
B.   **Managing Across Cultures:** Attracting Japan's Brightest
C.   Organizational Rewards
D.   **Managing in Practice:** Generating Ideas
E.   Negative Reinforcement
F.   **Managing Ethics:** Are You Sick or Well?
G.   Omission
H.   Punishment
I.   **Managing in Practice:** Positive Discipline at Tampa Electric
J.   Using Contingencies of Reinforcement

IV.   Schedules of Reinforcement

A.   Continuous and Intermittent Reinforcement
B.   Fixed Interval Schedule
C.   Variable Interval Schedule
D.   Fixed Ratio Schedule
E.   Variable Ratio Schedule
F.   Comparison of Intermittent Reinforcement Schedules
G.   **Managing Quality:** Diamond International's 100 Club

V.   Behavioral Modification

A.   Identifying Relevant Behaviors
B.   Charting Behavior
C.   Choosing a Contingency of Reinforcement
D.   Problem Solved?
E.   Limitations of Behavioral Modification
F.   **Managing in Practice:** Thin Promises
G.   Ethics of Behavioral Modification

VI.   Developing Skills

A.   **Case in Point:** Stonebriar Country Club
B.   **A Case in Point:** Synerdyne

KEY WORDS AND CONCEPTS

Thirty-seven key words and concepts are introduced in Chapter 5. The key words and concepts, along with definitions or appropriate descriptions, are as follows:

Antecedent: an environmental event which precedes and is a stimulus to a voluntary behavior.

Aversive events: consequences which are undesired by, or displeasing to, the individual.

Avoidance learning: a type of negative reinforcement which takes place when an individual prevents an unpleasant event from occurring by completing the proper behavior before the unpleasant event is presented.

Behavioral modification: refers to procedures and principles for changing behavior that are based on operant conditioning.

Charting: keeping track of employee behaviors by measuring them over time.

Classical conditioning: the process by which individuals learn reflex behavior.

Consequence: an environmental event which results from a voluntary behavior.

Contingency of reinforcement: the relationship between a behavior and the preceding and succeeding environmental events that influence that behavior.

Continuous reinforcement: the behavior is reinforced each time it occurs.

Escape learning: a type of negative reinforcement which takes place when an unpleasant event exists until an employee performs a behavior, or escape response, to terminate the unpleasant event.

Fixed interval schedule: a constant amount of time must pass before a reinforcer is provided, and reinforcement is applied to the first desired behavior to occur after the interval has passed.

Fixed ratio schedule: the desired behavior must occur a certain number of times before it is reinforced.

Intermittent reinforcement: a reinforcer is delivered after some, but not every occurrence of the desired behavior.

Interval schedule: reinforcers are delivered to the first desired behavior that occurs after a certain amount of time has elapsed.

Learning: a relatively permanent change in the frequency of occurrence of specific individual behavior.

Learning theory: an approach which stresses the assessment of behavior in objective, measurable (countable) terms.

Negative reinforcement: refers to the process whereby an unpleasant event is presented before the employee behavior occurs and then is removed after it occurs. Negative reinforcement increases the frequency of the target behavior.

Omission: occurs when all reinforcing events are stopped. Omission decreases the frequency of the target behavior.

Operant conditioning: a process wherein people operate on (or influence) the environment to produce a consequence, and because of the consequence they learn voluntary behavior.

Positive discipline: places emphasis on changing employee behaviors by reasoning rather than by imposing increasingly severe punishments.

Positive events: consequences which are desired by, or pleasing to, the individual.

Positive reinforcement: presenting a positive event contingent on the occurrence of a specific behavior. Positive reinforcement increases the frequency of the target behavior.

Primary reinforcer: an event—such as food, shelter, and water—for which the individual does not have to learn the value of the reinforcer.

Principle of contingent reinforcement: the reinforcer should be administered only if the desired behavior is performed.

Principle of immediate reinforcement: the reinforcer will have more effect if it is administered immediately after the desired behavior has occurred rather than being administered at some later time.

Principle of reinforcement deprivation: the more a person is deprived of the reinforcer, the greater the effect it will have on the future occurrence of the desired behavior.

Principle of reinforcement size: the larger the amount of reinforcer delivered after the desired behavior, the more effect the reinforcer will have on the rate of the desired behavior.

Punishment: takes place when an unpleasant event is presented after a behavior occurs. Punishment decreases the frequency of the target behavior.

Ratio schedule: reinforcers are delivered after a certain number of desired behaviors have been performed.

Reflex: an involuntary or automatic response that is not under an individual's conscious control.

Reinforcement: a behavioral contingency that increases the frequency of the particular behavior that it follows.

Reward: an event that a person finds desirable or pleasing.

Secondary reinforcer: an event—such as money or fringe benefits—that once had neutral value but has taken on some value (positive or negative) for an individual because of their past experience.

Self-efficacy: refers to the individual's belief that he/she can perform adequately in a situation.

Social learning: the process by which individuals learn voluntary behaviors by observing others and imitating their behaviors.

Variable interval schedule: the amount of time between reinforcers varies, and reinforcement is applied to the first desired behavior to occur after the variable time interval has elapsed.

Variable ratio schedule: a certain number of desired behaviors must occur before the reinforcer is delivered, but the number of behaviors varies about some average.

LECTURE NOTES

I.   Chapter 5 continues the exploration of individual processes by focusing on learning and the role of reinforcement in learning. The chapter is built around learning theory, an approach which stresses the assessment of behavior in objective (countable) terms. Emphasis is placed upon the development, maintenance, and change of employee behavior, using principles and procedures that are derived from learning theory. Effective managers should use these principles and procedures to promote desirable work behaviors (*i.e.*, behaviors which are consistent with and supportive of organizational standards and expectations) and to eliminate undesirable work behaviors (*i.e.*, behaviors which deviate from organizational standards and expectations). Transparency 5.1 provides an overview of the key ideas in Chapter 5.

TRANSPARENCY 5.1
(FROM TEXT MATERIAL IN THE TEXTBOOK)
KEY IDEAS ABOUT LEARNING AND REINFORCEMENT

ENRICHMENT MODULE: LEARNING EFFECTIVE WORK BEHAVIOR

ServiceMaster mops floors, washes laundry, scours toilets, and runs lunchrooms for institutions and businesses. Through its various subsidiaries, it cleans homes (Merry Maids), insures appliances (American Home Shield), fertilizes lawns (TruGreen), and kills pests (Terminix) for homeowners.

ServiceMaster has prospered while increasing service productivity and developing the potential of ordinary workers. ServiceMaster invests heavily in labor-saving tools. "But the company's major investment is in people, whom it trains meticulously." For example, "[m]oppers learn to stand straight, pull the mop toward them, and trace an S-shaped pattern on the floor." ServiceMaster emphasizes the development of observable, desirable work behaviors. Substantial rewards exist for good workers—ServiceMaster expects to draw 20 percent of its managers from the front lines.

This enrichment module is based on:

Henkoff, R. (1992, June 29). ServiceMaster: Piety, profits, and productivity. *Fortune*, 84.

II.   Overview of three different types of learning.

    A.   The basic nature of learning.

        1.   Learning is a relatively permanent change in the frequency of occurrence of specific individual behavior.

        2.   Since learning new work behaviors largely depends on environmental factors, the manager's goal is to provide an environment that will promote employee behaviors desired by the organization.

        3.   Learning can occur through classical conditioning, operant conditioning, and social learning. Operant conditioning and social learning are most important for understanding organizational behavior.

    B.   Classical conditioning.

        1.   Classical conditioning is the process by which individuals learn reflex behavior. A reflex is an involuntary or automatic response that is not under an individual's

conscious control.

2.   Transparency 5.2 provides examples of reflex behaviors.

TRANSPARENCY 5.2
(TABLE 5.1 IN THE TEXTBOOK)

EXAMPLES OF REFLEXIVE BEHAVIORS

---

3.   The basic classical conditioning process is as follows:

  a.   An unconditioned stimulus (environmental event) elicits a reflexive response.

  b.   If a neutral environmental event—called a conditioned stimulus—is paired with the unconditioned stimulus, the conditioned stimulus by itself will eventually elicit the reflexive behavior.

4.   The crucial factor in understanding classical conditioning is that a reflex response is controlled by the environmental event which precedes it—whether that event is an unconditioned stimulus or a conditioned stimulus.

5.   Reflex behaviors are not usually considered to be applicable to the work setting. Instead, managers are interested in employees' voluntary behaviors and in how those behaviors can be influenced.

C.   Operant conditioning.

1.   <u>Operant conditioning</u> is a process wherein people operate on (or influence) the environment to produce a consequence, and because of the consequence they learn voluntary behavior.

2.   Transparency 5.3 provides examples of operant behaviors and their consequences.

TRANSPARENCY 5.3
(TABLE 5.2 IN THE TEXTBOOK)

EXAMPLES OF OPERANT BEHAVIORS AND THEIR CONSEQUENCES

---

3.   The basic operant conditioning process consists of the following:

  a.   Behavior occurring in a particular situation will produce either a pleasant or an unpleasant consequence. If the consequence is pleasant, that behavior will be more likely to be repeated in the same (or similar) situation in the future. However, if the consequence is unpleasant, that behavior will be less likely to be repeated in the same (or similar) situation in the future.

  b.   This process is described in more detail in section III., A. because operant learning is a focal point of this chapter.

4.   The crucial factor in understanding operant conditioning is that an operant response

is controlled by the consequences following the behavior.

    5.   Managers are interested in operant behaviors because they can influence the strength and frequency of those behaviors by managing the consequences.

D.   Social learning.

    1.   <u>Social learning</u> is the process by which individuals learn voluntary behaviors by observing others and imitating their behaviors. Imitated behaviors which produce pleasant results will be repeated. Imitated behaviors that produce unpleasant results will not be repeated.

    2.   Transparency 5.4 shows the basic social learning process.

TRANSPARENCY 5.4
(FIGURE 5.2 IN THE TEXTBOOK)

A MODEL OF SOCIAL LEARNING

---

    a.   Through symbolic processes, mental images of observed behavior are formed. These mental images help guide and direct a person's behavior. The person models (or imitates) the observed behavior, thereby producing either a pleasant or an unpleasant result. Additionally, self-control influences the likelihood of behavior occurring—prior experience with negative results will decrease the likelihood of behavior and prior experience with positive results will increase the likelihood of behavior.

    b.   Self-efficacy is a central part of self-control and of social learning theory. <u>Self-efficacy</u> refers to the individual's belief that he/she can perform adequately in a situation. People with high self efficacy believe that:

        (1)   They have the ability needed to perform in the situation.

        (2)   They are capable of the effort required to achieve the goal.

        (3)   No outside events will prevent them from attaining a desired level of performance.

    3.   Managers can apply social learning theory by :

    a.   Identifying the behaviors that will lead to improved performance.

    b.   Selecting the appropriate model for employees to observe.

    c.   Making sure that employees are capable of meeting the new behaviors' required technical skills.

    d.   Creating a positive learning situation to increase the likelihood that employees will learn the new behaviors and act properly.

    e.   Providing positive feedback (praise or bonuses) for employees who have learned behavior and those who have served as models.

      f.   Developing organizational practices that maintain these newly learned behaviors.

III.   Contingencies of reinforcement.

    A.   A <u>contingency of reinforcement</u> is the relationship between a behavior and the preceding and succeeding environmental events that influence that behavior.

        1.   An <u>antecedent</u> is an environmental event which precedes and is a stimulus to a voluntary behavior. The probability of a particular behavior occurring can be increased or decreased by presenting or withdrawing a particular antecedent.

        2.   A <u>consequence</u> is an environmental event which results from a voluntary behavior. The probability of a particular behavior occurring is increased with pleasant consequences and decreased with unpleasant consequences.

        3.   Transparency 5.5 provides an example of the operant conditioning process.

TRANSPARENCY 5.5
(FIGURE 5.3 IN THE TEXTBOOK)

EXAMPLE OF CONTINGENT REINFORCEMENT

---

        4.   Consequences are categorized in two ways:

            a.   Consequences may be presented (applied) or withdrawn (removed).

            b.   Consequences may be positive or aversive. <u>Positive events</u> are desired by, or pleasing to, the individual. <u>Aversive events</u> are undesired by, or displeasing to, the individual.

This two-way categorization of consequences yields the four types of reinforcement contingencies shown in Transparency 5.6. <u>Reinforcement</u>, whether positive or negative, is a behavioral contingency that increases the frequency of the particular behavior that it follows. Omission and punishment are contingencies that decrease the frequency of the particular behavior that they follow.

TRANSPARENCY 5.6
(FIGURE 5.4 IN THE TEXTBOOK)

TYPES OF CONTINGENCIES OF REINFORCEMENT

    B.   Positive reinforcement.

        1.   <u>Positive reinforcement</u> presents a positive event contingent on the occurrence of a specific behavior. Positive reinforcement increases the frequency of the target behavior.   Thus, a manager's goal is to link positive outcomes to behavior that contributes to attaining the organization's goals.

        2.   Reinforcement versus reward.

a. A <u>reward</u> is an event that a person finds desirable or pleasing.

b. A reinforcer increases the frequency of the behavior that it follows.

c. A reward acts as a reinforcer if it increases the frequency of the behavior that it follows. If the reward does not increase the frequency of the behavior that it follows, it is not considered to be a reinforcer.

3. Primary and secondary reinforcers.

a. A <u>primary reinforcer</u> is an event—such as food, shelter, and water—for which the individual does not have to learn the value of the reinforcer.

b. A <u>secondary reinforcer</u> is an event—such as money or fringe benefits—that once had neutral value but has taken on some value (positive or negative) for an individual because of their past experience.

c. Most behavior is work settings is influenced by secondary reinforcers.

4. There are several factors which identify optimum reinforcement conditions—these are known as principles of positive reinforcement.

a. The <u>principle of contingent reinforcement</u> states that the reinforcer should be administered only if the desired behavior is performed.

b. The <u>principle of immediate reinforcement</u> states that the reinforcer will have more effect if it is administered immediately after the desired behavior has occurred rather than being administered at some later time.

c. The <u>principle of reinforcement size</u> states that the larger the amount of reinforcer delivered after the desired behavior, the more effect the reinforcer will have on the rate of the desired behavior.

d. The <u>principle of reinforcement deprivation</u> states that the more a person is deprived of the reinforcer, the greater the effect it will have on the future occurrence of the desired behavior.

5. Transparency 5.7 contains an extensive list of rewards that can be used by organizations. These rewards will act as reinforcers only if the individual receiving the reward finds it to be desirable and it increases the frequency of the behavior that it follows.

TRANSPARENCY 5.7
(TABLE 5.3 IN THE TEXTBOOK)

REWARDS USED BY ORGANIZATIONS

ENRICHMENT MODULE: LAVISH REWARDS AT IBM

Traditionally, International Business Machines, Inc. has lavishly rewarded employees, particularly its top performers. While IBM has cut back on some rewards and perks because of declining business fortunes, it has maintained other lavish rewards.

The "Golden Circle" is an annual gala celebration held for the best salespeople and their spouses. At a recent Golden Circle celebration held over an eight-day period at the Breakers resort in Palm Beach, Florida, "IBM flew in Bob Newhart for stand-up comedy. It hired Larry King to stage a mock talk show on current events. For evening entertainment, the money losing computer giant rented a museum and treated everybody to veal and salmon, a five-act circus, casino games, and Liza Minnelli, performing in person."

IBM also maintains three country clubs for its employees. "The clubs have evolved into vast playgrounds. The Poughkeepsie club also has an eight-lane bowling alley, a weight room and a shooting range. The Endicott club now has golf, swimming, tennis, bowling, indoor shooting and a skeet range. A third club in Sands Point, N.Y., has a private beach on Long Island Sound." Fees to belong to the clubs are very nominal—$17.12 a year at the Endicott club and $25 a year at the other two.

This enrichment module is based on:

Miller, M.W. (1993, October 27). Vestiges of success: As IBM losses mount, so do complaints about company perks. *The Wall Street Journal*, A1 & A14.

C.   Negative reinforcement.

   1.   <u>Negative reinforcement</u> refers to the process whereby an unpleasant event is presented before the employee behavior occurs and then is removed after it occurs. Negative reinforcement increases the frequency of the target behavior. Therefore, managers seek to link the removal of negative outcomes to behavior that contributes to attaining the organization's goals.

   2.   Two types of negative reinforcement:

      a.   <u>Escape learning</u> takes place when an unpleasant event exists until an employee performs a behavior, or escape response, to terminate the unpleasant event.

      b.   <u>Avoidance learning</u> takes place when an individual prevents an unpleasant event from occurring by completing the proper behavior before the unpleasant event is presented.

ENRICHMENT MODULE: CONSEQUENCES OF RENEGING ON LIFETIME EMPLOYMENT

Many large Japanese companies have had a policy of lifetime employment, keeping their employees on the payroll through good times and bad times. The lifetime employment policy has started to change at some large companies. Pioneer Electronics, for example, told 35 full-time middle managers, all in their 50s, that they would receive a hefty bonus if they retired—positive reinforcement of behavior deemed desirable by the organization. If they didn't accept the retirement offer, they would be fired eventually—a threat of punishment.

Pioneer's approach is a bit stricter than that of some other Japanese companies. Managers are asked to retire for the good of the company, but "they usually have the option of declining if they are willing to accept lower pay or a lesser job." Most, however, accept the offer of retirement. Doing so avoids the onset of aversive consequences.

This enrichment module is based on:

Japan reneging on lifetime guarantee: Firings at Pioneer Electronics send shock wave through nation. (1993, January 11). *The Dallas Morning News*, D-4.

D.   Omission.

    1.   <u>Omission</u> occurs when all reinforcing events are stopped. Omission results in a decrease in the frequency of behavior, and managers seek to link it to undesired work behavior.

    2.   The omission procedure consists of three steps:

        a.   Identifying the behavior that is to be reduced or eliminated.

        b.   Identifying the reinforcer that maintains the behavior.

        c.   Stopping the reinforcer.

    3.   Some possible pitfalls of omission:

        a.   Omission can occur accidentally if managers fail to reinforce desirable work behaviors.

        b.   While omission may effectively reduce undesired behavior, it does nothing to replace the undesired behavior with alternative desirable behaviors. Thus, omission should be used it conjunction with either positive or negative reinforcement to develop replacement behaviors.

E.   Punishment.

    1.   <u>Punishment</u> takes place when an unpleasant event is presented after a behavior occurs and the frequency of the behavior is decreased.

    2.   In order for unpleasant events to be punishers they must decrease the frequency of preceding behaviors. Otherwise, they are merely unpleasant events.

3.   There are several potential negative effects of punishment, as shown in Transparency 5.8.   The material in this transparency is self-explanatory.

TRANSPARENCY 5.8
(FIGURE 5.5 IN THE TEXTBOOK)

POTENTIAL NEGATIVE EFFECTS OF PUNISHMENT

---

4.   Punishment can be made effective by doing the following:

a.   With oral reprimands, follow the rule of thumb, "Praise in public; punish in private."

b.   Make punishment maximally effective by directly linking the punisher to the undesirable behavior (principle of contingent punishment), administering the punisher immediately (principle of immediate punishment), and using a greater amount of the punisher (principle of punishment size).

c.   Develop alternative desired behavior to replace the undesired behavior.

d.   Strike an appropriate balance between the use of pleasant and unpleasant events. Positive management procedures should dominate in any well-run organization.

e.   Use positive discipline which places emphasis on changing employee behaviors by reasoning rather than by imposing increasingly severe punishments. Management must make employees understand the organization's needs for certain standards of performance and behavior, and employees must exercise self-discipline in achieving those standards.

F.   Guidelines for using contingencies of reinforcement in the work setting (see Transparency 5.9):

TRANSPARENCY 5.9
(FROM TEXT MATERIAL IN THE TEXTBOOK)

GUIDELINES FOR USING CONTINGENCIES OF REINFORCEMENT

---

1.   Do not reward all employees the same.

2.   The failure to respond to behavior has reinforcing consequences; superiors are bound to shape the behavior of subordinates by their use or nonuse of rewards. Carefully examine the consequences of non-actions as well as actions.

3.   Let employees know which behaviors get reinforced.

4.   Let employees know what they are doing wrong.

5.   Do not punish employees in front of others.

6.   Make the response equal to the behavior by not cheating workers out of their just

rewards.

IV.   Schedules of reinforcement.

    A.   Schedules of reinforcement determine when reinforcers are applied.

    B.   Reinforcement can be classified as either continuous or intermittent.

       1.   In <u>continuous reinforcement</u>, the behavior is reinforced each time it occurs.

       2.   In <u>intermittent reinforcement</u>, a reinforcer is delivered after some, but not every occurrence of the desired behavior. Intermittent reinforcement can be further subdivided into interval schedules and ratio schedules.

          a.   An <u>interval schedule</u> means that reinforcers are delivered to the first desired behavior that occurs after a certain amount of time has elapsed.

          b.   A <u>ratio schedule</u> means that reinforcers are delivered after a certain number of desired behaviors have been performed.

          c.   Interval and ratio schedules can be further subdivided into fixed (not changing) and variable (constantly changing), thus yielding four major types of intermittent schedules.

             (1)   In a <u>fixed interval schedule</u>, a constant amount of time must pass before a reinforcer is provided. Reinforcement is applied to the first desired behavior to occur after the interval has passed.

             (2)   In a <u>variable interval schedule</u>, the amount of time between reinforcers varies. Reinforcement is applied to the first desired behavior to occur after the variable time interval has elapsed.

             (3)   In a <u>fixed ratio schedule</u>, the desired behavior must occur a certain number of times before it is reinforced.

             (4)   In a <u>variable ratio schedule</u>, a certain number of desired behaviors must occur before the reinforcer is delivered, but the number of behaviors varies about some average.

             (5)   The above four schedules are compared in Transparency 5.10; particular attention should be paid to the effects of each schedule on performance and behavior.

TRANSPARENCY 5.10
(TABLE 5.4 IN THE TEXTBOOK)
COMPARISON OF SCHEDULES OF REINFORCEMENT

V.   Behavioral modification.

A.   <u>Behavioral modification</u> refers to procedures and principles for changing behavior that are based on operant conditioning.

B.   Transparency 5.11 depicts a multi-step behavioral modification process. The primary steps in the process are:

1.   Pinpointing the relevant behaviors by observing the behaviors, measuring the behaviors, and describing the situation in which the behaviors occur.

2.   <u>Charting</u> behaviors or keeping track of employee behaviors by measuring them over time. Charting is done during a baseline period to determine the frequency of certain behavior and during an intervention period to determine if the intervention is working.

3.   Choosing a contingency of reinforcement that is appropriate for changing the behavior.

4.   Determining whether the problem has been solved by evaluating data charted during the intervention period.

TRANSPARENCY 5.11
(FIGURE 5.6 IN THE TEXTBOOK)

BEHAVIORAL MODIFICATION PROCEDURES AND PRINCIPLES

ENRICHMENT MODULE: PERSONAL BEHAVIORAL MODIFICATION
(An Experiential Activity)

An excellent way to reinforce the material on behavioral modification is to have the students develop and implement a personal behavioral modification program to change a personal habit which they dislike. Students may focus on changing certain study habits, mannerisms, eating or drinking behavior, exercise habits, etc. Have the students use the behavioral modification procedures and principles contained in Transparency 5.11 as a guide for their own behavioral modification program.

This enrichment module is adapted from an exercise developed by M.K. McCuddy.

C.   Limitations of behavioral modification.

1.   Behavioral modification often ignores individual differences in needs, values, abilities, and desires. Organizations can accommodate individual differences by trying to select and hire employees who value the rewards they offer, and by allowing employees to participate in determining their rewards.

2.   When workers feel that management is trying to exploit them, group norms emerge that aim to control the degree of cooperation with management. Organizations can deal with the power of group norms by building an atmosphere of trust prior to attempting any use of behavioral modification.

D.   The use of behavioral modification raises some ethical issues:

1. A major ethical issue concerns the freedom and dignity of people who are the targets of behavioral modification. Proponents of behavioral modification argue that individual freedom of choice with regard to behavior is inconsequential if rewards are administered so as to promote behaviors which are desirable from the organization's viewpoint. Opponents of behavioral modification argue that no one should be able to decide what behavior is beneficial for other people, let alone have enough power to manipulate people to change their behavior.

2. Employees may engage only in those behaviors that can be measured and ignore those that are not measured.

3. Many managers feel societal pressures to reinforce behaviors that they really do not desire themselves.

VI. Summing up: The role of learning in organizational behavior.

A. Like other individual processes—such as personality, attitudes, and problem-solving styles—learning has a significant impact on the ways in which people behave in organizational settings. Like the other processes, learning helps to explain the similarities and differences that exist in people's work behaviors.

B. Operant conditioning and social learning theory can be very helpful to managers. Operant conditioning provides managers with insights into managing environmental consequences so as to promote employee behaviors desired by the organization. For quite a long time it has served as the theoretical foundation for the management of organizations' reward and disciplinary systems. Social learning theory is emerging as a useful management tool for developing desirable employee behaviors through observation and modeling. Perhaps more importantly, the effective use of social learning theory fosters employee self-efficacy.

DISCUSSION QUESTIONS: SUGGESTED ANSWERS

1. *How can managers apply the principles of learning to improve employees' performance?*

A manager must understand that learning is a relatively permanent change in the frequency of occurrence of a specific individual behavior—whether the behavior is desirable or undesirable. The manager's goal is to exercise sufficient control over the consequences of behavior in order to increase the frequency of desirable work behaviors and decrease the frequency of undesirable work behaviors. Knowledge of the various principles of learning can help a manager to be more effective in controlling consequences, and thereby improving employees' performance.

2. *What ethical considerations should an organization consider before using a behavioral modification program?*

A major ethical consideration centers around a person's freedom and dignity. The question focuses on whether someone (*i.e.,* managers) should decide what is good or beneficial for other people and have enough power to manipulate them into changing their behavior. Another ethical consideration involves whether employees should engage only in those behaviors that can be measured and ignore those that are not measured. A third ethical consideration concerns whether managers should respond to societal pressures to reinforce behaviors that they really do not desire themselves.

3.   *How can team leaders use punishment effectively?*

To be effective in their use of punishment, team leaders should adhere to the following guidelines:

a.   Punishment should be connected immediately, directly, and obviously to the undesirable behavior.

b.   Punishment should be specifically targeted to the undesirable behavior and should take the form of a private reprimand which can be constructive and instructive.

c.   A alternative desired behavior should be developed to replace the undesired behavior.

d.   There should be a balanced use of pleasant and unpleasant events, with the emphasis being on positive management procedures.

e.   Team leaders should attempt to change team members' behaviors by reasoning rather than by imposing increasingly severe punishments.

4.   *Why do some people find gambling addictive? What types of reinforcement schedules do gambling casinos use?*

Gambling casinos rely upon the power of a variable ratio schedule of reinforcement. Gamblers win, but not on a regular basis. The prospect of winning—perhaps on the next bet, or the next, or the next...—is what sustains gambling behavior. Because the variable ratio schedule characteristically leads to very high performance and very slow extinction of behavior, some people can become addicted to gambling.

5.   *Which are the most effective reinforcement schedules for maintaining desirable behaviors over the long run?*

In the long run, the most effective reinforcement schedules appear to be the variable interval and variable ratio schedules. The variable interval schedule leads to moderately high and stable performance and results in a slow extinction of behavior. The variable ratio schedule leads to very high performance and results in very slow extinction of desired behaviors. The fixed ratio schedule, while leading quickly to very high and stable performance, results in moderately fast extinction of behavior; thus it is not as effective as either variable interval or variable ratio schedules over the long term. The continuous schedule—which is really a fixed ratio of 1:1—also leads quickly to high and stable performance but is subject to very rapid extinction of behavior. The fixed interval schedule leads to average and irregular performance and fast extinction of behavior.

6.   *Identify the types of reinforcement used by managers at Diamond International Corporation. Why are they effective?*

This question pertains to the "**Managing Quality:** The 100 Club" feature on pages 157-158 of the textbook.

By emphasizing teamwork and improving the quality of production, employees earn points which then can be traded for a company jacket and other merchandise. To operationalize this program of positive reinforcement, managers at Diamond International are using the fixed interval, fixed ratio, and continuous schedules of reinforcement.

Fixed interval scheduling is evident in the following: an employee earns 25 points a year for perfect attendance, 20 points for going through a year without formal disciplinary action, and 15 points for working a year without a lost-time injury accident. Fixed interval scheduling also is indicated by maintenance department employees receiving four points for keeping machine downtime under a specific time. Continuous scheduling is apparent in awarding points for employees supplying cost-savings ideas or for participating in community service activities. Fixed ratio scheduling is reflected in shipping department employees and production employees earning points for attaining their shipping or production targets, respectively.

7. *Describe the basic differences among classical conditioning, social learning, and operant conditioning. Which theory is most important for managers? Why?*

Classical conditioning is the process by which individuals learn reflexive (or involuntary) behavior. In classical conditioning, an unconditioned stimulus (environmental event) brings out a reflexive response.

Operant conditioning focuses on the learning of voluntary behavior. Operant conditioning emphasizes on the effects of consequences on desirable and undesirable behaviors. When a behavior is reinforced—either positively or negatively—it is repeated. When a behavior is or not reinforced, it is not repeated.

Social learning theory focuses on people learning new voluntary behaviors by observing another person and then modeling their own behavior after that person. A central part of the theory is a person's sense of self-efficacy, which influences how a person performs in a situation, how long they persist in doing a task, and how much effort will be expended.

An argument can be made that, for managers, the most important type of learning probably involves operant conditioning. Because of their control over positive and negative organizational events, managers can influence the behavioral consequences which employees experience. In turn, these behavioral consequences affect the frequencies with which desired and undesired behaviors are exhibited.

An argument also can be made that social learning is becoming increasingly important for managers. Use of models to facilitate training is an application of social learning theory. Creating organizational conditions which enhance employees' self-efficacy is also an application of social learning theory.

8. *What are some of the pitfalls in the rewards used in the health care system? How can they be overcome?*

This question pertains to the "**Managing Ethics:** Are you Sick or Well?" box on pages 149-150 of the textbook.

The United States health care system basically reinforces physicians for diagnosing well people as being sick. By pronouncing a well person sick, physicians get paid for doing diagnostic tests, office visits, etc. (positive reinforcement) and they have a lower probability of being sued (the avoidance form of negative reinforcement).

To overcome these pitfalls, the reinforcement contingencies need to be altered. Legislation could be enacted to limit the dollar amounts which could be awarded in medical malpractice suits. The medical insurance system could be restructured to emphasize wellness and preventive health care. For instance, many people do not get an annual physical because it is not covered by their medical insurance. If insurers were to cover the cost of annual physicals, the physicians focus could at least partly shift to preventive medicine and wellness.

9.   *Visit either a local health club or diet center and interview the manager. What types of rewards does it give members who achieve their targets? Does it use punishment?*

Students should not have a problem finding either a health club or a diet center manager eager to discuss his/her program. Typically, health clubs and diet centers use numerous positive reinforcement techniques to motivate and reward members. These rewards include T-shirts, photographs, posters, verbal support, newsletters, and personal notes to members who have reached targeted goals. The only type of punishment is cancellation of membership for not attending or not paying dues.

10.   *Can managers use positive discipline principles effectively in managing diversity in the workplace? What are some limitations to their use?*

Positive discipline places emphasis on changing employee behaviors by reasoning rather than by imposing increasingly severe punishments. In using positive discipline, managers must make their employees understand the organization's needs for certain standards of performance and behavior, and employees must exercise self-discipline in achieving those standards.

In applying positive discipline to managing diversity in the workplace, managers would try to get employees to understand the organization's expectations and requirements regarding all important aspects of relevant diversity issues. For instance, positive discipline could be used to deal with employees who make ethnic or racial slur toward their co-workers. Positive discipline could also be used to deal with an individual who makes suggestive and harassing remarks.

In part, diversity reflects people's attitudes, values, perceptions, and beliefs. Positive discipline might be used to change overt behavior regarding diversity issues, but it is questionable whether positive discipline can (or even should) effectively influence underlying attitudes, values, perceptions, and beliefs. Thus, the application of positive discipline to managing diversity could be somewhat limited.

The use of positive discipline may have limitations without regard to question of managing diversity. For example, since positive discipline is a multi-step procedure, it's use may be limited to instances where undesired behavior can be dealt with in a progressive fashion. Because some behavior may be so disruptive to the organization or so dangerous to oneself or to others, immediate and severe punitive action may be necessary. In such a case, trying to use positive discipline would probably have limited value.

11.   *How can you use social learning theory to improve your own performance?*

Social learning theory can be applied to improving your own performance as well as to improving others' performance. In applying it to improving your own performance, you could adapt the recommendations researchers have made to managers regarding their employees. Specifically, an individual can do the following things:

- Identify the behaviors that will lead to improved performance.
- Select an appropriate model to observe.
- Make sure that you are capable of meeting the technical skill requirements of the new behaviors.
- Structure a positive learning situation to increase the likelihood that you will learn the new behaviors.
- Provide positive consequences for engaging in proper modeling behaviors.
- Develop self-management practices that maintain these newly learned behaviors.

DEVELOPING SKILLS—
A CASE IN POINT: STONEBRIAR COUNTRY CLUB

CASE OVERVIEW

This case describes the reward system that Stonebriar Country Club uses with members who participate in their exercise and physical fitness program. The reward system is based on a point system that relates directly to cardiovascular fitness. Specific point values are assigned to different fitness activities.

In the context of the point structure, specific week-by-week goals are set for program participants. When participants reach a goal, a reward—such as a tote bag, sweatshirt, T-shirt, or jogging suit—is given. To keep track of points, members log in on a computer after they have completed an activity. This provides immediate feedback on total points earned to date. Additionally, monthly reports are mailed to members.

CASE QUESTIONS

1.   *What types of reinforcement does the Stonebriar Country Club use?*

   The major reinforcer used at Stonebriar is positive reinforcement. When members reach a goal, a reward is given. Rewards include merchandise such as a tote bag, sweatshirt, T-shirt, or jogging suit. Rewards also include recognition by getting one's name on the pound-lost list. Feedback on points accumulated is also a form of positive reinforcement used by Stonebriar.

2.   *What schedule of reinforcement does it use with its members?*

   Stonebriar primarily uses a fixed ratio schedule of reinforcement. A specified number of points is awarded for doing certain fitness-related behaviors a specified number of times.

DEVELOPING SKILLS—
A CASE IN POINT: SYNERDYNE

CASE OVERVIEW

This case describes an ethical dilemma facing Jan Perkins, a sales representative for Synerdyne. One of the customers in Jan's recently acquired sales territory asked for a financial kickback in order to retain the account. The customer insisted that Jan's predecessor provided this "special support" and that everybody in the industry did it. However, Synerdyne's corporate policy stresses high moral standards in dealing with customers and employees but does not have specific guidelines for dealing with the situation Jan faces. Losing the account would probably mean that Jan would not meet her sales quota for the year, would not get a bonus, and may be given a cheaper company car to drive.

CASE QUESTION

1.   *Be prepared to play the role of Jan Perkins in front of the class or some other small group. What would you say? How does Synerdyne's reward system affect your answer?*

The central focus of the role play should concern how Synerdyne's reward system may intentionally or unintentionally influence Jan to engage in unethical behavior in order to avoid negative consequences.

Jan should communicate with her boss regarding the situation. That way, everything is out in the open, and Jan does not have to risk compromising her personal ethical standards or losing her job. She still may lose out on the financial end given the way Synerdyne's reward system appears to be structured. If that happened, however, it would be useful information regarding the true nature of her employer.

If Jan chooses to not communicate with her boss regarding the situation and decides to follow the ethical course of action, she would be taking a short-term risk in terms of financial rewards and a long-term risk in terms both financial rewards and job security. On the other hand, if she decides to follow the unethical course of action, she may see a short-term financial gain. The unethical action, however, may come back to haunt her in terms of long-term job security and/or financial gain.

COURSE ENHANCEMENT—
WEST'S ORGANIZATIONAL BEHAVIOR CUSTOM VIDEO SERIES

Two videos from *West's Organizational Behavior Custom Video Series* can be used to enhance the material in Chapter 5. These videos are: *UPS: The Complete Package* and *Mary Kay Cosmetics: Spotlight on Success.*

VIDEO: UPS: *THE COMPLETE PACKAGE*

Approximate Time: 13 minutes

Video Summary:

This video is an excellent supplement to the preview case for Chapter 5.

The video provides an overview of the domestic and international operations of United Parcel Service. UPS provides the largest package distribution system in the United States and in the world. UPS delivers to every address in North America and can reach over four billion people world-wide—double the number reached by any telephone network.

UPS is noted for its friendly and efficient people, its reasonably priced shipping, and its clockwork delivery service. UPS lives by customer service—they want to do the right thing and do it well. The complete package of customer services at UPS includes a global network, information services, new technologies, and the flexibility to customize these services for each business need.

All of this is made possible by sophisticated technology and by employees who try harder and care more. According to UPS managers, people who try harder and care more, in turn, care more for the customers. UPS has developed a very dedicated work force by implementing "people policies" that emphasize respect for employees, giving employees satisfying work, and training employees properly. Ownership of shares in the company is also encouraged in order give people a greater stake in a high level of customer service.

Discussion Questions and Suggested Answers for Video:

1. *The preview case in Chapter 5 focused on the specific work behaviors that are expected of UPS drivers. What insights does the video provide regarding how UPS is able to make such detailed behavioral specifications?*

    Basically, these detailed specifications are possible because of the extensive data base UPS maintains through its sophisticated tracking, sorting, and electronic communications systems. UPS is able to plan its activities down to the minutest details as well as adapt rapidly to emerging circumstances.

2. *What are some of the key positive reinforcers that UPS provides its employees? How does the use of these positive reinforcers benefit the company?*

    Respecting employees, providing them with satisfying work, and ownership of company stock are key positive reinforcers. As a result, UPS has a dedicated work force that cares about what it does and how it does it.

VIDEO: *MARY KAY COSMETICS: SPOTLIGHT ON SUCCESS*

Approximate Time: 10 minutes

Video Summary:

The video is of the annual awards night sponsored by Mary Kay Cosmetics for the independent salespersons who sell the firm's products.

The video is an excellent demonstration of social learning theory in practice and the power recognition as a positive reinforcer. Everyone in the video is excited and "charged up." Those interviewed in the video reinforce the euphoria. Awardees are shown parading across the stage displaying their rewards of mink coats, roses, etc. Self-efficacy, a central element of social learning theory, is obvious through the interviews. According to some of the awardees, seeing and hearing others' success stories convinces them that they too can be winners.

Discussion Questions and Suggested Answers for Video:

1. *What are some of the possible benefits of recognition as a reinforcer? What are some of the limitations?*

    Recognition of success in front of one's peers can be a powerful reinforcer of behavior at a relatively low cost to the organization. Of course, the minimizing cost does not seem to be of particular concern at Mary Kay Cosmetics, given the lavish production of it "awards show." Recognition is also a means for satisfying higher order psychological needs—a subject of Chapter 6. Recognition also can spur others on through imitative behavior.

Like any reward, recognition must be able to increase the frequency of behavior for it to be considered a reinforcer. Recognition will not increase behavior rates unless it is valued by the recipient. Additionally, recognition which is not accompanied by corresponding tangible rewards—such as salary increases, bonuses, and/or promotions—may ring hollow for some people.

2.   *How do the key elements of social learning theory apply to Mary Kay Cosmetics?*

A good way to approach this question is by using the model of social learning which is depicted in Figure 5.2 of the textbook.

Symbolic processes, modeling, and self-control are evident in the video. The pomp and circumstance of the awards ceremonies and the testimonials of those in attendance provides powerful mental images to help guide people's behavior. Modeling—the acquisition of behavior by observing and imitating others—is present in the video. People wanting to be like others and taking aggressive action to do so is evidence of modeling. Self-control is evident in the aura of "I can do it too!" which emanates from the awards ceremonies. Indeed, an argument can be made that one effect of the awards show is to increase the sales representatives' self-efficacy by making them believe that (1) they have the ability needed, (2) they are capable of the effort required to achieve the goal, and (3) no outside events will prevent them from attaining their desired level of performance.

CHAPTER 6
WORK MOTIVATION

CHAPTER OVERVIEW

Chapter 6 continues the exploration of individual processes by focusing on work motivation. After developing information about the basic nature of motivation, the chapter focuses on two broad categories of work motivation theories: content theories and process theories. The content theories include the need hierarchy, ERG theory, achievement motivation theory, and the motivator-hygiene theory. These four content theories help managers to address the question: What drives behavior? The process theories developed in this chapter include expectancy theory and equity theory. Both process theories help managers in understanding the following motivational questions: Which direction does behavior take? How is behavior maintained? Additionally, practical managerial implications of each content theory and each process theory are discussed.

LEARNING OBJECTIVES

Upon completion of this chapter, the students should be able to:

1. Define motivation and the challenge of motivating others.
2. Explain and apply the needs hierarchy, ERG, achievement motivation, and motivator-hygiene content theories of motivation.
3. Describe and apply the expectancy and equity process theories of motivation.
4. State the organizational implications for each of the motivation theories.

CHAPTER OUTLINE

I. **Preview Case:** Bill Gates and Microsoft

II. Essentials of Motivation

KEY WORDS AND CONCEPTS

Forty-one key words and concepts are introduced in Chapter 6. The key words and concepts, along with definitions or appropriate descriptions, are as follows:

Ability: a person's talent for performing specific intellectual or manual tasks.

Achievement motivation theory: holds that people are motivated according to the strength of their desire either to perform in terms of a standard of excellence or to succeed in competitive situations.

Achievement motive: people who have a strong achievement motive exhibit long-term involvement, competition against some standard of excellence, and unique accomplishment. The achievement motive pertains to achievement motivation theory.

Affiliation motive: people who have a strong affiliation motive tend to establish, maintain, and restore close personal relationships with others. The affiliation motive is linked to McClelland's work on the achievement motivation theory.

Affiliation needs: needs for friendship, love, and a feeling of belonging. Affiliation needs pertain to the need hierarchy.

Cafeteria-style benefit plans: reward systems that permit employees to select their fringe benefits from a menu of alternatives.

Content theories: motivation theories which try to explain the specific factors that motivate people. Content theories seek to answer the following question: What drives behavior?

Deficiency needs: refers to the physiological, security, and affiliation needs categories of the need hierarchy.

Distributive justice: the extent to which someone perceives that rewards are related to performance.

Equity: in the equity theory of motivation, equity exists when the ratio of a person's outcomes to inputs equals the ratio of outcomes to inputs for similar others.

Equity theory: a process theory of motivation which focuses on an individual's feelings of how fairly he/she is treated in comparison with others.

ERG theory: a content theory of motivation which argues that the individual has three sets of basic needs: existence, relatedness, and growth.

Esteem needs: reflect personal feelings of achievement and self-worth and recognition or respect from others. Esteem needs pertain to the need hierarchy.

Existence needs: needs which are satisfied by food, air, water, pay, fringe benefits, and working conditions. Existence needs pertain to ERG theory.

Expectancy: a key expectancy theory variable which refers to the belief that a specific level of effort will be followed by a particular level of performance.

Expectancy theory: a process theory of motivation which states that people are motivated to work when they believe that they can get what they want from their jobs—whether what they want relates to the job itself or to the context (or environment) in which the job occurs.

Extrinsic factors: factors which are external to the job and are largely determined by the organization.

First-level outcomes: a key expectancy theory variable which refers to the results of behaviors associated with doing the job itself. These results include productivity, absenteeism, turnover, and quality of work.

Goal: a specific result an individual wants to achieve.

Growth needs: pertains to both the need hierarchy and ERG theory. With respect to the need hierarchy, growth needs refer to the esteem and self-actualization needs. With respect to the ERG theory, growth needs are satisfied through the opportunities for unique personal development which result from making creative or productive contributions at work.

Hygiene factors: a component of the motivator-hygiene theory which refers to company policy and administration, technical supervision, salary, working conditions, and interpersonal relations. Hygienes reflect an individual's negative feelings about the job and are related to the environment in which the job is performed.

Inequity: in the equity theory of motivation, inequity exists when the ratio of a person's outcomes to inputs does not equal the ratio of outcomes to inputs for similar others.

Inputs: an equity theory concept which refers to what an individual contributes to an exchange (interpersonal relationships are viewed as exchanges).

Instrumentality: a key expectancy theory variable which reflects the relationship between first-level outcomes and second-level outcomes.

Intrinsic factors: factors which are directly related to the job and reflect the personal reactions of individuals to the job.

Motivation: represents the forces acting on or within a person that cause the person to behave in a specific, goal-directed manner.

Motivator-hygiene theory: a controversial content theory of motivation which argues that: (1) Some job factors lead to satisfaction, whereas others may prevent dissatisfaction but are not sources of satisfaction. (2) Job satisfaction and dissatisfaction do not exist on a single continuum.

Motivator factors: a component of the motivator-hygiene theory which refers to work itself, recognition, advancement, and responsibility. Motivators reflect a person's positive feelings about the job and are related to the content of the job itself.

Needs: psychological, physiological, or social deficiencies that a person experiences at any particular time.

Needs hierarchy theory: a content theory of motivation which suggests that people have a complex set of exceptionally strong needs that can be arranged in a hierarchy.

Outcomes: an equity theory concept which refers to what an individual receives from an exchange (interpersonal relationships are viewed as exchanges).

Physiological needs: needs for food, water, air, and shelter. Physiological needs pertain to the need hierarchy.

Power motive: people who have a strong power motive take action that affects others' behavior and has a strong emotional impact on them. The power motive is linked to McClelland's work on the achievement motivation theory.

Procedural justice: refers to the notion that managers should be fair in applying rules and procedures and in involving employees in decisions that affect them.

Process theories: motivation theories which try to describe how factors internal to the person interact to produce certain kinds of behavior. Process theories seek to answer the following questions: Which direction does behavior take? How is behavior maintained?

Relatedness needs: needs which are satisfied by establishing and maintaining relationships with co-workers, superiors, subordinates, friends, and family. Relatedness needs pertain to ERG theory.

Second-level outcomes: a key expectancy theory variable which refers to the positive or negative events that first-level outcomes are likely to produce. Second-level outcomes include pay increases, promotions, acceptance by co-workers, and job security.

Security needs: needs for safety, stability, and absence of pain, threat, or illness. Security needs pertain to the need hierarchy.

Self-actualization needs: needs for self-fulfillment. Self-actualization needs pertain to the need hierarchy.

Thematic Apperception Test (TAT): a method for measuring the strength of a person's achievement motivation. The TAT is a projective method that emphasizes individual perceptions of stimuli, the meaning each individual gives to those stimuli, and how each individual organizes those stimuli.

Valence: a key expectancy theory variable which refers to the individual's preference for a particular second-level outcome.

LECTURE NOTES

I.   Chapter 6 examines individual processes from the perspective of motivation. Motivation represents the forces acting on or within a person that cause the person to behave in a specific, goal-directed manner.   Like the other individual processes studied thus far, motivation affects the similarities and differences that exist in organization members' behaviors. These behaviors, in turn, influence the organization's ability to achieve its goals.

   A.   Managers are interested in motivation because it addresses three questions: (1) What drives behavior? (2) Which direction does behavior take? (3) How is behavior maintained? Answers to these questions are provided through four content theories of motivation and two process theories of motivation. Transparency 6.1 summarizes the relationships between the questions and the theories that provide the answers.

TRANSPARENCY 6.1
(FROM TEXT MATERIAL IN THE TEXTBOOK)

KEY QUESTIONS AND ANSWERS ABOUT MOTIVATION

   B.   Managers are also interested in motivation because it helps their understanding of diversity in organizations. People want different things from their jobs (the saying "Different strokes for different folks!" applies here) and motivation helps to explain these differences. Transparency 6.2 provides an excellent illustration of work force diversity with regard to what people want from work.

TRANSPARENCY 6.2
(TABLE 6.1 IN THE TEXTBOOK)

DIVERSITY IN THE WORK FORCE: WHAT DO PEOPLE WANT?

ENRICHMENT MODULE: HOW WOULD PEOPLE LIKE TO SPEND THEIR TIME?

Just as people want different things from their work lives, they also want different things from their lives outside of work. This enrichment module provides some insight into how adults would like to spend their time. How people want (or don't want) to spend their time reflects their needs.

The top ten activities which individuals would like to spend **more** time doing are:

1. Short vacations (1-4 days)
2. Long vacations (5+ days)
3. Exercising
4. Spending leisure time with spouse/boyfriend/girlfriend
5. Having friends over
6. Reading books
7. Going out to movies
8. Going out to hear live music
9. Visiting in the homes of friends
10. Playing a sport

The top ten activities which individuals would like to spend **less** time doing are:

1. Attending to laundry/cleaning
2. Driving (to and from work and while running errands)
3. Doing housecleaning
4. Grocery shopping
5. Taking care of financial matters
6. Job
7. Doing/arranging for household repairs
8. Watching television
9. Preparing meals
10. Routine yardwork

This enrichment module is based on:

Flick, D. (1994, July 17). Americans feel conflict between the demands of work and the need for more leisure time. *The Dallas Morning News,* 1A & 22A.

    C.   Three organizational and work-setting factors are crucial in effectively creating and managing an organizational environment which arouses employee motivation.

        1.   Individuals must be attracted not only to join the organization but also to remain in it.

        2.   Individuals must be allowed to perform the task for which they were hired.

        3.   Individuals must go beyond routine performance and become creative and innovative in their work.

II.   Essentials of motivation.

A.   A key motivation principle states that performance is a function of both ability and motivation. <u>Ability</u> is a person's talent for performing specific intellectual or manual tasks. Exceptional ability alone will not ensure high performance. Exceptional ability accompanied by high motivation will produce high performance. To perform at a high level, a person must want to do the job and must able to do the job.

B.   As noted in the lecture introduction, motivation focuses on three questions: (1) What drives behavior? (2) Which direction does behavior take? (3) How is behavior maintained?

     1.   A generalized answer to these questions can be provided by examining the core motivational processes shown in Transparency 6.3. The motivational process begins with the employee identifying his/her needs and continues in a step-by-step pattern. The sequence of steps is essentially self-explanatory. However, two of the key motivational concepts which are embedded in the process need to be identified. <u>Needs</u> (see step 1) are psychological, physiological, or social deficiencies that a person experiences at any particular time. A <u>goal</u> (see step 3) is a specific result an individual wants to achieve.

TRANSPARENCY 6.3
(FIGURE 6.1 IN THE TEXTBOOK)

CORE MOTIVATIONAL PROCESS

---

     2.   The theoretical answers to these questions needs to be viewed in the context of three challenges of reality.

         a.   Motives can only be inferred; they cannot be seen.

         b.   Needs, desires, and expectations may change and may also conflict with each other.

         c.   Considerable differences exist in the way people select certain motives over others and in the energy with which they express these motives.

III.   Content theories of motivation.

A.   <u>Content theories</u> of motivation try to explain the specific factors that motivate people. Basically, content theories address the question: What drives behavior?

B.   Four content theories of motivation are discussed in this chapter: needs hierarchy theory, ERG theory, achievement motivation theory, and motivator-hygiene theory.

C.   Needs hierarchy theory.

     1.   <u>Needs hierarchy theory</u>, developed by Abraham Maslow, suggests that people have a complex set of exceptionally strong needs that can be arranged in a hierarchy, as shown in Transparency 6.4.

**TRANSPARENCY 6.4
(FIGURE 6.2 IN THE TEXTBOOK)**

MASLOW'S NEEDS HIERARCHY

---

2.   The needs hierarchy is based upon the following assumptions:

    a.   A satisfied need does not motivate. However, when one need is satisfied, another emerges to take its place, so people are always striving to satisfy some need.

    b.   The needs network for most people is complex, with several needs affecting the behavior of each person at any one time.

    c.   In general, lower level needs must be satisfied before higher level needs are activated sufficiently to drive behavior.

    d.   There are more ways to satisfy higher level needs than lower level needs.

3.   Definitions and managerial implications for the five needs categories.

    a.   <u>Physiological needs</u> are needs for food, water, air, and shelter. Managers who focus on physiological needs assume that people work primarily for money.

    b.   <u>Security needs</u> are needs for safety, stability, and absence of pain, threat, or illness. Managers who focus on physiological needs emphasize rules, job security, and fringe benefits.

    c.   <u>Affiliation needs</u> are needs for friendship, love, and a feeling of belonging. Managers who focus on affiliation needs are likely to act in supportive and permissive ways such as emphasizing employee acceptance of co-workers, extracurricular activities, and team-based norms.

    d.   <u>Esteem needs</u> reflect personal feelings of achievement and self-worth, and recognition or respect from others. Managers who focus on esteem needs emphasize public rewards and recognition for services.

    e.   <u>Self-actualization needs</u> are needs for self-fulfillment. Managers who focus on self-actualization needs may involve employees in designing jobs, make special assignments that capitalize on employees' unique skills, or give employee teams leeway in planning and implementing work procedures.

4. Significance of the needs hierarchy for the workplace (see Transparency 6.5).

**TRANSPARENCY 6.5
(FROM TEXT MATERIAL IN THE TEXTBOOK)**

NEEDS HIERARCHY: SIGNIFICANCE FOR THE WORKPLACE

---

    a.   Unless the <u>deficiency needs</u> (*i.e.*, physiological, security, and affiliation) are satisfied, an individual will fail to develop into a healthy person, both physically and psychologically.

b.   Satisfaction of growth needs (*i.e.*, esteem and self-actualization) will help a person grow and develop to his or her potential.

c.   Potentially, higher level needs are present in most people and will emerge and motivate behavior if conditions do not block them.

D.   ERG theory.

1.   ERG theory, developed by Clay Alderfer, argues that the individual has three sets of basic needs: existence, relatedness, and growth.

a.   Existence needs are satisfied by food, air, water, pay, fringe benefits, and working conditions.

b.   Relatedness needs are satisfied by establishing and maintaining relationships with co-workers, superiors, subordinates, friends, and family.

c.   Growth needs are satisfied through the opportunities for unique personal development which result from making creative or productive contributions at work.

ENRICHMENT MODULE: MOTIVATING CREATIVE PEOPLE

Developing an environment in which creative people will be motivated and satisfied is a challenge for management, but it is a challenge that can pay significant, broad-based dividends. The techniques which help to motivate creative people can be applied to every employee, thereby enhancing the creative efforts of everyone in the organization.

Here are some of the techniques that are particularly useful with creative people and may be applied more broadly to the entire work force:

1.   Accommodate creative people's idiosyncrasies.
2.   Stimulate creative people by doing whatever is necessary to facilitate idea generation.
3.   Recognize and reward creative people—not necessarily with money but with freedom, opportunity, and self-expression.
4.   Give creative people direction and feedback but do not hold the reigns of control too tightly.
5.   Protect creative people from others in the organization who don't understand what makes them tick.
6.   Be creative yourself.

This enrichment module is based on:

Farnham, A. (1994, January 10). How to nurture creative sparks. *Fortune*, 94-96+.

---

2.   ERG theory is similar to Maslow's need hierarchy in that:

a.   The three needs categories are arranged in a hierarchy of prepotency.

b.   There is a fulfillment-progression process wherein the next higher level need is activated once the preceding lower level need is satisfied.

3.   ERG theory differs from Maslow's need hierarchy by adding a frustration-regression process. As shown in Transparency 6.6, if a person is continually frustrated in attempts to satisfy growth needs, relatedness needs will reemerge as a significant motivating force. The individual will return to satisfying this lower level need instead of attempting to satisfy growth needs. In short, frustration leads to regression. The same behavior that had led to the frustration of growth needs now becomes the means for satisfying relatedness needs.

TRANSPARENCY 6.6
(FIGURE 6.3 IN THE TEXTBOOK)

ERG NEEDS MODEL

---

4.   Significance of the ERG theory for the workplace (see Transparency 6.7).

TRANSPARENCY 6.7
(FROM TEXT MATERIAL IN THE TEXTBOOK)

ERG THEORY: SIGNIFICANCE FOR THE WORKPLACE

---

a.   If an individual's effort to satisfy growth needs are blocked, managers or team leaders should try to redirect the employee's efforts toward satisfying relatedness or existence needs.

b.   Research tends to support the three broad categories of needs in ERG theory. The three categories probably are intuitively appealing to managers.

c.   ERG theory has been criticized by some managers because it doesn't help them understand what motivates employees.

E.   Achievement motivation theory.

1.   David McClelland argued that people have three important needs—power, affiliation, and achievement—which are rooted in culture.

a.   People who have a strong <u>power motive</u> take action that affects others' behavior and has a strong emotional impact on them.

b.   People who have a strong <u>affiliation motive</u> tend to establish, maintain, and restore close personal relationships with others.

c.   People who have a strong <u>achievement motive</u> exhibit long-term involvement, competition against some standard of excellence, and unique accomplishment.

2.   <u>Achievement motivation theory</u> holds that people are motivated according to the strength of their desire either to perform in terms of a standard of excellence or to succeed in competitive situations.

a.   The strength of people's achievement motivation depends on their personal childhood and adult experiences and the type of organization for which they work.

b.   The strength of a person's achievement motivation can be measured with the <u>Thematic Apperception Test (TAT)</u>. The TAT is a projective method that emphasizes individual perceptions of stimuli, the meaning each individual gives to those stimuli, and how each individual organizes those stimuli.

3.   High achievers share three major characteristics.

a.   They like to set their own goals.

b.   They prefer moderate goals that are neither so easy that attaining them provides no satisfaction nor so difficult that attaining them is more a matter of luck than ability.

c.   They prefer tasks that provide immediate feedback.

4.   The relationship between monetary incentives and achievement motivation.

a.   High achievers value their services very highly and therefore place a high price on them.

b.   High achievers value money as a strong symbol of achievement and adequacy, but money may create dissatisfaction if they believe it inadequately reflects their contributions.

5.   Significance of achievement motivation theory for the workplace (see Transparency 6.8).

TRANSPARENCY 6.8
(FROM TEXT MATERIAL IN THE TEXTBOOK)

ACHIEVEMENT MOTIVATION THEORY: SIGNIFICANCE FOR THE WORKPLACE

---

a.   Managers should arrange tasks so that employees receive periodic feedback about their performance so they can modify it when necessary.

b.   Managers should provide good role models of achievement.

c.   Managers should help employees modify self-images when necessary. High-achievement individuals accept themselves, seek job challenges and responsibilities, and are productive.

d.   Managers should help employees to learn how to set realistic goals and how to attain them.

e.   Successful managers rank higher in power motivation than in affiliation.

F.   Motivator-hygiene theory.

1.   <u>Motivator-hygiene theory</u> is a controversial content theory developed by Fred Herzberg. It is controversial because it argues that:

    a.   Some job factors lead to satisfaction, whereas others may prevent dissatisfaction but are not sources of satisfaction.

    b.   Job satisfaction and dissatisfaction do not exist on a single continuum (see Transparency 6.9).

TRANSPARENCY 6.9
(FIGURE 6.5 IN THE TEXTBOOK)

MOTIVATOR-HYGIENE SITUATIONS

---

2.   Motivator-hygiene theory revolves around two sets of factors.

    a.   <u>Motivator factors</u> include work itself, recognition, advancement, and responsibility. Motivators reflect a person's positive feelings about the job and are related to the content of the job itself. Motivators are <u>intrinsic factors</u>—they are directly related to the job and reflect the personal reactions of individuals to the job.

    b.   <u>Hygiene factors</u> include company policy and administration, technical supervision, salary, working conditions, and interpersonal relations. Hygienes reflect an individual's negative feelings about the job and are related to the environment in which the job is performed. Hygienes are <u>extrinsic factors</u>—they are external to the job and are largely determined by the organization.

ENRICHMENT MODULE: INTRINSIC AND EXTRINSIC FACTORS IN MOTIVATION

Corporations across the country are experimenting with numerous ways of using intrinsic and extrinsic factors to influence employee motivation. Here is an example of what one company—USAA (United Services Automobile Association)—is doing.

In San Antonio, in a building bigger than the Pentagon, USAA pampers its 13,000 employees with tennis courts, lighted softball fields, jogging trails, picnic groves, a lake stocked with trout and perch, a physical fitness center, and a subsidized cafeteria and food takeout service. The courtyards spaced throughout the three million square feet building come alive at lunchtime with art shows and folk dancers. There is a company store, a well-stocked library, and a clinic staffed by nine registered nurses. A subsidized van pool transports 1,700 riders a day from distances of up to 60 miles.

USAA spends $20 million a year on career training in order to promote from within the ranks. About 1,800 employees are enrolled in college courses given in 60 classrooms on the premises by area and local colleges. Employees doing graduate work have their tuition paid, including fees for CPA exams. Workers' ideas are welcomed, kept track of in a computer, and rewarded at recognition breakfasts with gifts of bicycles, cameras, and power tools.

This enrichment module is based on:

Battle, D., Canape, C., & Hencke, P. (1991). *Creating and motivating a superior loyal staff*. New York: National Institute of Business Management.

---

3.   Herzberg believes that, despite cultural differences, hygiene and motivator factors affect workers similarly around the world.

4.   Significance of motivator-hygiene theory for the workplace (see Transparency 6.10).

TRANSPARENCY 6.10
(FROM TEXT MATERIAL IN THE TEXTBOOK)
MOTIVATOR-HYGIENE THEORY: SIGNIFICANCE FOR THE WORKPLACE

---

a.   The theory appeals to managers because it uses common terms to explain motivation.

b.   Hygiene factors are easy to identify and have become targets of complaints by shareholders when share prices fall.

c.   Herzberg recommends focusing on motivators and not hygiene factors to motivate employees.

d.   The validity, and therefore the contribution, of motivator-hygiene theory has been challenged because:

       (1)   The theory was developed using a method-bound procedure.

       (2)   There is mixed research support for the notion that satisfaction and dissatisfaction are two separate dimensions.

G.   Transparency 6.11 highlights the basic relationships among the four content theories of motivation.

**TRANSPARENCY 6.11
(FIGURE 6.6 IN THE TEXTBOOK)
MATCHING CONTENT THEORIES**

---

1.   These comparisons may be summarized by saying that the content theories of motivation give managers an understanding of the particular work-related factors that start the motivational process. That is, content theories answer the question: What drives behavior?

IV.   Process theories of motivation.

A.   Process theories try to describe how factors internal to the person interact to produce certain kinds of behavior. Process theories seek to answer the following questions: Which direction does behavior take? How is behavior maintained?

B.   There are four major process theories of motivation:

1.   Expectancy theory and equity theory, which are presented in this chapter.

2.   Reinforcement theory, which was presented in Chapter 5.

3.   Goal-setting-theory, which will be presented in Chapter 7.

C.   Expectancy theory.

1.   Expectancy theory states that people are motivated to work when they believe that they can get what they want from their jobs—whether what they want relates to the job itself or to the context (or environment) in which the job occurs.

2.   Basic assumptions of expectancy theory.

a.   A combination of forces in the individual and the environment determines behavior.

b.   Individuals decide their own behaviors in organizations, although rules, technology, and work-group norms place many constraints on individual behavior. In deciding about their own behavior, people make membership decisions and job-performance decisions.

c.   Different individuals have different needs and goals and want different rewards from their work.

d.   Individuals decide among alternatives based on their perceptions of whether a certain behavior will lead to a desired outcome.

3.   The expectancy theory model.

a.   Expectancy theory is based upon five key variables:

    (1)   <u>First-level outcomes</u> are the results of behaviors associated with doing the job itself. These results include productivity, absenteeism, turnover, and quality of work.

    (2)   <u>Second-level outcomes</u> are the positive or negative events that first-level outcomes are likely to produce. Second-level outcomes include pay increases, promotions, acceptance by co-workers, job security, and social ostracism by peers.

    (3)   <u>Expectancy</u> is the belief that a specific level of effort will be followed by a particular level of performance. Expectancy values are probabilities ranging from 0 to +1. The closer the expectancy value is to 0, the less certain it is that a particular level of performance will follow a particular level of effort. The closer the expectancy value is to +1, the more certain it is that a particular level of performance will follow a particular level of effort.

    (4)   <u>Instrumentality</u> reflects the relationship between first-level outcomes and second-level outcomes. Instrumentality values are correlations ranging from -1 to +1. An instrumentality of -1 indicates that attaining second-level outcomes is inversely related to attaining first-level outcomes. An instrumentality of +1 indicates that attaining second-level outcomes is directly related to attaining first-level outcomes. An instrumentality of 0 indicates that attaining second-level outcomes is unrelated to attaining first-level outcomes.

    (5)   <u>Valence</u> refers to the individual's preference for a particular second-level outcome. A second-level outcome has a positive valence when the outcome is preferred, a negative valence when the outcome is not preferred or is to be avoided, and a zero valence when the individual is indifferent about the outcome.

b.   How these five key variables are put together to form the expectancy theory model is depicted in Transparency 6.12.

TRANSPARENCY 6.12
(FIGURE 6.7 IN THE TEXTBOOK)

EXPECTANCY THEORY IN ACTION

ENRICHMENT MODULE: DIAGNOSING MOTIVATION FROM THE PERSPECTIVE OF EXPECTANCY THEORY
(*An Experiential Activity*)

As suggested by Figure 6.7 in the textbook, an individual's motivation will be strong when (1) there is a high probability that putting forth effort will result in successful performance and (2) successful performance will lead to desired second-level outcomes. Motivation would be weakened if the expectancy probability is low, or if first-level and second-level outcomes are unrelated or inversely related, or if the second-level outcomes are negatively valent or neutral for the individual.

This exercise provides students with a opportunity to apply expectancy theory concepts in diagnosing the motivation of the individuals in the following scenarios.

Scenario 1: Arthur has been working for the same insurance firm for 20 years. He was recently transferred to a position where he supervises a group of young managers-in-training. As a senior employee he is well paid. Money, though, doesn't mean much to Arthur. His investments have done well and he has no family to support. Arthur's principal interest has always been the work itself. If he is diligent, Arthur is able to do a good job. But the transfer has taken him away from his previous work and he finds supervision uninteresting. In recognition of this, Arthur has been given a raise.

Expectancy theory diagnosis of scenario 1: Arthur probably has a relatively high expectancy; he has always been interested in the work, and with due diligence has performed well. Instrumentality appears to be high as well. Most likely, he was transferred to a training position because of his prior performance. At best, Arthur appears to be indifferent toward the available second-level outcomes. He's not particularly interested in money, but receives a raise. Moreover, he was transferred to a position where he found the work to be uninteresting. On balance, Arthur is at risk of becoming less motivated to perform his job well. In short, the effort he has put forth in the past has not resulted in positively-valenced outcomes.

Scenario 2: Diane works as a software designer for an innovative microcomputer manufacturer. She enjoys her job because it provides her with challenging and interesting work and it pays well. In her firm, bonuses are awarded every quarter on the basis of individual employee accomplishments. People who perform well are also given first choice of new project. As a well trained and competent worker Diane is able to do her job very well so long as she works hard.

Expectancy theory diagnosis of scenario 2: For Diane, expectancy appears to be high—her competency and hard work enable her to perform very well. A strong direct instrumentality appears to exist as well. Individual accomplishments are rewarded with quarterly bonuses; additionally, Diane is challenged by and is interested in her work, and it pays well. Finally, both the intrinsic and extrinsic second-level outcomes seem to have a strong positive valence for Diane. When all the expectancy theory variables are combined, Diane very clearly is a highly motivated employee.

This enrichment module is adapted from an exercise presented in:

Marcic, D. (1992). *Organizational behavior: Experiences and cases* (3rd ed.). St. Paul: West Publishing Company, 72-78.

---

4.   Some potential problems of the expectancy theory include:

a.   Accurate measurement of the choice (or effort) variable is difficult.

b.   The theory does not specify which second-level outcomes are important to a particular individual in a particular situation.

c.   The theory contains an implicit assumption that motivation is a conscious choice process.

5.   Significance of expectancy theory for the workplace (see Transparency 6.13).

TRANSPARENCY 6.13
(FROM TEXT MATERIAL IN THE TEXTBOOK)

EXPECTANCY THEORY: SIGNIFICANCE FOR THE WORKPLACE

---

a.   Managers should try to determine outcomes that each employee values.

b.   Managers should determine and state clearly the performance desired because employees need to understand what is expected of them.

c.   Managers should define good, adequate, and poor performance in terms that are observable and measurable.

d.   Managers should make sure that desired levels of performance set for employees can be attained.

e.   Managers should directly link the specific performance they desire to the outcomes employees desire.

f.   Managers should never forget that perceptions, not reality, determine motivation.

g.   Managers should analyze the entire situation, looking for factors (such as the informal work group or the organization's formal reward system) that conflict with the desired behaviors.

h.   Managers should make sure that changes in outcomes or rewards are large enough to motivate significant behavior.

D.   Equity theory.

1.   <u>Distributive justice</u>—the extent to which someone perceives that rewards are related to performance—underlies equity theory.

2.   <u>Equity theory</u> focuses on an individual's feelings of how fairly he/she is treated in comparison with others.

3.   The equity theory model.

a.   Equity theory views interpersonal relationships as exchanges in which individuals make contributions and expect certain results.

b.   In the context of this exchange, equity theory is based on the comparison of two variables:

(1)   <u>Inputs</u> represent what an individual contributes to an exchange.

(2)   <u>Outcomes</u> are what an individual receives from an exchange.

(3)   Transparency 6.14 provides examples of inputs and outcomes.

TRANSPARENCY 6.14
(TABLE 6.4 IN THE TEXTBOOK)

EXAMPLES OF INPUTS AND OUTCOMES IN ORGANIZATIONS

---

c.   Individuals assign weights to various inputs and outcomes according to their perceptions of the situation. After people balance the inputs and outcomes for themselves, they compare that with the perceived balance of inputs and outcomes of others in the same or a similar situation. <u>Equity</u> exists whenever the ratio of a person's outcomes to inputs equals the ratio of outcomes to inputs for similar others. <u>Inequity</u> exists when the ratios of outcomes to inputs are not equal. Inequity creates tension within an individual and among individuals. Since tension is not pleasurable, a person is motivated to reduce it to a tolerable level.

d.   Consequences of inequity.

(1)   People may increase or decrease their inputs to what they perceive to be an equitable level.

(2)   People may change their outcomes to restore equity.

(3)   People may mentally distort their own inputs and outcomes.

(4)   People may leave the organization or request a transfer to another department.

(5)   People may shift to a new reference group to reduce the source of an inequity.

(6)   People may mentally distort the inputs or outcomes of others.

ENRICHMENT MODULE: WHAT'S FAIR? WHAT'S NOT?
(*An Experiential Activity*)

People's perceptions of what is fair and unfair may change as companies alter their reward system practices. For instance, instead of regular pay raises, many companies are more often relying on rewards like one-time bonuses, shares of company stock, plaques, theater tickets, thank-you notes from the boss, etc. How will hard-working employees perceive and react to reward system changes like these?

Read the following story, then put yourself in the situation faced by Federal Express courier Mark Horton. How would you evaluate the outcomes in relation to the inputs? What about in relation to other couriers? What would you do if you perceived this to be an inequitable situation?

Here is what happened to Mr. Horton one afternoon on his rural courier route about 150 miles outside of Oklahoma City:

> "His truck broke down with no repair shop in sight. 'I had to make my deliveries by 4:30, and time was running out,' he says. So Horton, 35, strapped 18 packages to his back, hopped on a friend's bicycle, and pedaled for nine miles. 'I made every deadline,' he says. Horton's reward? A pin, a glass obelisk, an honorary dinner with some other world-beaters, and about $500 of company stock. He's pleased, he says, but 'naturally, I'd rather have a raise.'"

This enrichment module is based on:

Fierman, J. (1993, July 12). When will you get a raise? *Fortune*, 34-36.

4. Some potential problems of the equity theory of motivation include:

   a. The effects of changes in the comparison group or situation are unknown.

   b. The effects of long-term comparisons are unknown.

   c. Equity theory does not specify the particular course of action an individual would take to reduce inequity in a particular situation.

5. Significance of equity theory for the workplace (see Transparency 6.15).

TRANSPARENCY 6.15
(FROM TEXT MATERIAL IN THE TEXTBOOK)

EQUITY THEORY: SIGNIFICANCE FOR THE WORKPLACE

   a. Employees should be treated fairly.

   b. People make decisions concerning equity only after they compare their inputs and outcomes with those of comparable employees—either within or outside the organization.

   c. Managers should operate on the basis of both distributive justice and procedural justice. <u>Procedural justice</u> means that managers should be fair in applying rules and procedures and in involving employees in decisions that affect them.

d.   Employee assessments of procedural justice are related to their trust in management, intention to leave the organization, evaluation of their supervisor, employee theft, and job satisfaction.

E.   Comparisons between expectancy theory and equity theory.

1.   Expectancy theory emphasizes people's rational choices among alternative effort levels based upon how attainable the second-level outcomes are and how they value those outcomes. Motivation will be high when second-level outcomes are attainable and valued by the employee. Thus, managers need to make clear linkages between effort and performance and between performance and outcomes. Differences in how rewards are valued can be accommodated, at least partly, by the use of <u>cafeteria-style benefit plans</u> (*i.e.*, reward systems that permit employees to select their fringe benefits from a menu of alternatives).

2.   Equity theory stresses that people determine equity by comparing themselves to similar others. People are motivated to escape inequitable situations but are induced to stay on the job and perform at high levels in equitable situations.

3.   These comparisons may be summarized by saying that the process theories of motivation help managers to understand the role of rewards and decision-making in determining people's level of motivation. That is, process theories attempt to answer the questions: Which direction does behavior take? How is behavior maintained?

V.   Summing up: Why is motivation useful in organizational behavior?

A.   An understanding of work motivation revolves around the answers to three questions: (1) What drives behavior? (2) Which direction does behavior take? (3) How is behavior maintained? The content theories answer the first question by identifying the particular work-related factors that start the motivational process. The process theories answer the second and third questions by addressing the role of rewards and decision-making in determining people's level of motivation.

B.   Having motivated and capable employees is necessary for an organization to function effectively and efficiently.

DISCUSSION QUESTIONS: SUGGESTED ANSWERS

1.   *Think about the worst job you have ever had. What approach to motivation did that organization use? Now think about the best job you ever had. What approach to motivation did that organization use?*

Students can answer this question by referring to any of the content theories and/or process theories. For students who have not had any work experience, have them refer to a class they have taken (without mentioning the specific course or professor).

An example of a worst job may be in an organization that rewards employees based on their gender. Male employees are paid more than equally trained female employees because they are "the bread winners" of the family. Based on equity theory, female employees would feel that they are being treated unfairly since their pay, benefits, and other rewards are not equal to male employees.

An example of a best job may be in an organization that utilizes achievement motivation theory for employees. Employees receive periodic feedback on task performance and this feedback may enable them to modify their performance. Employees may also be given strong role models of achievement, and most may have mentors who encourage them to excel.

2.   *How does expectancy theory explain the behaviors of the employees who stole from their company after it announced that all employees would take a 15% pay cut for the next ten weeks?*

Expectancy theory would argue that an undesirable outcome—the temporary 15% pay cut—was received but was not linked to performance. Because a clear linkage between first-level outcomes and second-level outcomes was not established, little positive effect on motivation could be expected.

Expectancy theory could also argue that there was a net reduction in the sum of the valences associated with the second-level outcomes. The increase in employee theft may have been due to people's efforts to create a new package of second-level outcomes with a sum of valences that was essentially equivalent to the situation prior to the 15% pay cut.

3.   *Compare and contrast the role of financial incentives in the needs, ERG, and hygiene-motivator theories.*

Financial incentives would act as motivators of behavior in the need hierarchy and ERG theory but not in the motivator-hygiene theory. According to the needs hierarchy, financial incentives would provide the means for satisfying the physiological needs and to some extent the security needs. In ERG theory, financial incentives would be relevant to satisfying the existence needs. However, since financial incentives would be a hygiene factor in the motivator-hygiene theory, neither satisfaction nor motivation would be affected. Financial incentives would merely prevent dissatisfaction and would not contribute to motivating work behavior, according to the motivator-hygiene theory.

4.   *What lessons are to be learned from Motorola's motivational approach with its employees in its Guadalajara plant? Which of Maslow's categories of needs is Motorola trying to satisfy for its employees?*

This question pertains to the "**Managing Across Cultures:** Motorola's Guadalajara Employees" box on page 184 of the textbook.

Motorola had to address differences between the United States and Mexican cultures by adapting its motivational environment and programs to the priorities of its Guadalajara employees. Family, religion, and then work are the Mexican employees' priorities. Motorola has instituted motivational programs which have a family orientation such as hosting family dinners to celebrate the employment anniversaries of employees who have worked there 5, 10, 15, and 20 years; and permitting employees to borrow the company clubhouse for weddings, baptisms, and other family celebrations. The company bus picks up employees at central locations throughout the city. Motorola also provides a 70% subsidy for the costs of employees' mid-day meals which are served by managers. All of these elements primarily help to satisfy the affiliation needs.

5.   *How could a manager apply ERG theory to motivate employees?*

The manager would need to determine which need level—existence, relatedness, or growth—is unsatisfied for the employee and therefore has the capacity to serve as an energizer of his/her behavior. Then the manager would need to determine whether or not the employee has been frustrated in his/her attempts to satisfy the need level in question. If the employee has been frustrated at fulfilling a particular need level—say, growth needs or existence needs—managers could encourage the person to revert back to the next lower need level and work on satisfying it. However, if lower-level needs have been fulfilled, the manager could encourage the employee to work on satisfying the next higher need level. Managers could also try to remove obstacles—such as unclear performance expectations, inadequate training, or inappropriate job assignments—that may stand in the way of need satisfaction.

6.   *How can cafeteria-style benefits plans motivate employees?*

Cafeteria-style fringe benefits programs permit employees to select their fringe benefits from a menu of alternatives. The primary motivation effect of this is to enable employees to choose rewards that they value.

Discussion could center around how the benefit plans can satisfy the needs of the employee while providing what the employee values. For example, an employee with a family may need and value a comprehensive medical program. An older employee may need and value vacation time and/or an early retirement program but not need or value parental leave or child care.

7.   *What is the value of the motivator-hygiene theory?*

Despite criticisms about the validity of the motivator-hygiene theory, it does have some practical value for managers. First, the theory appeals to managers because it uses common terms to explain motivation. Second, hygiene factors are easy to identify and have become targets of complaints by shareholders when share prices fall. Third, the importance of the motivator factors in influencing employee motivation can't be denied. Fourth, despite cultural differences, hygiene and motivator factors may affect workers similarly around the world. This may be particularly valuable in managing a diverse work force in an increasingly global environment.

8.   *If high achievers are better performers, why don't organizations simply hire high achievers?*

High achievers like to set and pursue moderately challenging goals. They also prefer tasks that provide immediate feedback. Jobs which permit the pursuit of moderately challenging goals and provide immediate feedback will appeal to high achievers. However, not all jobs are designed like this. There are some jobs which are routine or repetitive in nature and/or provide little, if any, immediate feedback. These kinds of jobs would frustrate high achievers.

9.   *Discuss the organizational implications for overpayment and underpayment.*

Overpayment and underpayment represent inequity in an exchange relationship. Overpayment or underpayment occurs when the ratio of a person's outcomes to inputs is not equal to the outcomes to inputs ratio of a similar other. Overpayment can motivate an employee to work harder because of guilt or social pressure. Underpayment can demotivate an employee by placing a lower value on this/her output. This, in turn, may lead to actual lower output.

10.   *Evaluate the statement: "A satisfied worker is a productive worker." Under what conditions is the statement false? True?*

This statement reflects early views on the satisfaction-performance relationship. However, a review of research indicates that if there is a positive relationship between these variable, the correlations are consistently low. Other moderating variables such as job level, skills, work environment, rewards, etc. must be considered. An example of when this statement may be both true and false could occur with stockbrokers. When the stock market is moving up and volume is high, both satisfied and dissatisfied brokers are going to be productive. Conversely, when the market is down, the level of broker satisfaction is not likely to mean much to his or her productivity.

DEVELOPING SKILLS—
SELF DIAGNOSIS: WHAT DO YOU WANT FROM YOUR JOB?

This self-diagnostic instrument contains the 16 most mentioned characteristics that employees want from their jobs. Students are to rank order the 16 characteristics in terms of importance (1 = most important and 16 = least important) and satisfaction (1 = greatest satisfaction and 16 = least satisfaction). The rankings given by employees working in a wide variety of jobs and industries are provided in the text for comparative purposes.

The text poses two discussion questions relative to the diagnostic instrument:

1.   *Choose any theory of motivation and think about your answers. What situational factors (such as being in school, looking for a new job, wanting more responsibility, or desiring to work for a foreign organization) influenced your rankings of importance?*

The top four importance rankings given by employees in a variety of jobs were: (1) health insurance and other benefits, (2) interesting work, (3) work that is important to society, and (4) job security. Items (1) and (4) relate to lower level needs while items (2) and (3) pertain to higher level needs. In turn, lower level and higher level needs can be linked to each of the content theories of motivation. In terms of the expectancy theory of motivation, the items which are most important to have also would be the ones with a positive valence. In terms of the equity theory of motivation, these items would be outcomes that would factor into the determination of equity or inequity in an exchange relationship.

Students can do a similar analysis of their own importance rankings. They may be able to more easily identify with an application of one of the content theories than with an application of one of the process theories.

2.   *How do most of the managers who responded gain their job satisfaction? What theory of motivation helps you understand those rankings?*

The top four satisfaction rankings given by most of the responding mangers were: (1) working close to home, (2) contact with people, (3) working independently, and (4) interesting work. Perhaps the need hierarchy and ERG theory would be most applicable to answering this question. Interaction with family and people at work pertain to the need hierarchy's affiliation needs and to ERG theory's relatedness needs. Working independently and having interesting work relate to the need hierarchy's esteem and self-actualization levels and ERG theory's growth needs.

DEVELOPING SKILLS—
A CASE IN POINT: ROBERT PRINCETON

CASE OVERVIEW

This case describes the employment of Robert Princeton from the early fall of 1994 until January of 1995 as assistant manager for Falls Video, a family-owned chain of eight video rental outlets within a 25-mile radius of Glen Falls, New York. Princeton was hired to assist Mario Valencia, manager of the video store chain and son of the owners, "Momma and Poppa" Valencia.

Princeton's periodic attempts to make improvements in human resource policies and practices were rebuffed by Mario Valencia. Then in January of 1995, Robert met with Mario to discuss several proposals which he (Robert) had developed for improving business operations. Robert's proposals were met with Mario's outrage. The next morning Robert arrived at work to find a written reprimand on his desk. At 1:30 p.m. that same day Robert submitted his resignation.

The case ends with students being directed to write a memo to the faculty member teaching the course. The memo is to explain why Robert Princeton quit his job and how the situation could have been avoided or handled more effectively.

ELEMENTS TO BE ADDRESSED IN MEMO

Robert Princeton's decision to quit his job could be analyzed from the perspective of any of the four content or two process theories of motivation. The key elements of each such analysis are described below.

1. Application of the needs hierarchy would suggest that the physiological, security, and perhaps affiliation needs were reasonably well fulfilled, and therefore the esteem needs probably were the primary motivator of behavior. However, Princeton was unable to satisfy these needs.
2. From the perspective of ERG theory, one could argue that Princeton was repeatedly frustrated in trying to satisfy the growth needs. He chose to resign rather than regress to trying to satisfy the relatedness needs.
3. One also could argue that Princeton seems to have a strong achievement motive but that his boss prevented him from behaving in ways which would satisfy that motive.
4. Or motivator-hygiene theory could be used to argue that: (a) dissatisfaction was probably prevented because the relevant hygiene factors were reasonably fulfilled, but (b) the motivator factors were not really present in Princeton's job and he probably experienced no motivation or satisfaction.
5. From an expectancy theory viewpoint, Princeton probably perceived that the vigorous pursuit of meaningful activity had ultimately resulted in undesirable second-level

outcomes. Since he expected this to continue in the future, he chose to resign.

6. Or from an equity theory viewpoint, one could argue that Princeton felt he was underpaid. He probably compared himself to Mario Valencia, and he probably believed that his contributions were far greater than Mario's. This would contribute to a perceived underpayment situation. To deal with the tension created by underpayment, Robert chose to leave the organization.

Students may use whichever theoretical perspective they choose. However, they should develop it in detail and should recommend how to handle the situation more effectively given what the analysis has revealed.

COURSE ENHANCEMENT— *WEST'S ORGANIZATIONAL BEHAVIOR CUSTOM VIDEO SERIES*

One video from *West's Organizational Behavior Custom Video Series* can be used to enhance the material in Chapter 6. This video is: *Creative Apparel, Inc.*

VIDEO: *CREATIVE APPAREL, INC.*

Approximate Time: 4 minutes

Video Summary:

Creative Apparel, Inc. produces warm-up jackets for pro sports teams and clothes for the armed services. The company could not make products fast enough to satisfy customer demand. The company's owner responded to this challenge by:

1. Tapping into a new pool of labor by forming a partnership with the Passamaquoddy Indian tribe in the northeastern United States.
2. Developing basic job skills and a work ethic among the Passamaquoddy Indians.
3. Training a team of five employees who, in turn, became trainers of the other employees.
4. Hiring an outside consultant to assist with the process.
5. Having counselors help with substance abuse and personal problems.
6. Operating a child care center.
7. Providing medical insurance.
8. Instituting bonuses for high performance.
9. Hiring a bookkeeper and plant manager to handle daily operations.

The partnership has been a success. Sales have gone from $465,000 to $3.5 million. The company is profitable. The company has created 80 jobs in one of the poorest locales in America.

Discussion Questions and Suggested Answers for Video:

1. *From the general perspective of the content theories of motivation, what types of needs were satisfied by Creative Apparel's reward system?*

    Basically, the reward system at Creative Apparel attempted to satisfy the lower level needs. The emphasis was on money and fringe benefits which would provide for a more satisfying, more secure existence.

2.   *How might the expectancy theory of motivation be applied to explaining the work motivation of the Passamaquoddy Indian tribe?*

The Passamaquoddys' perceptions of effort-performance relationships (expectancies) were probably positively influenced by the owner's emphasis on training. Their perceptions of performance-outcome relationships (instrumentalities) were most likely affected by giving bonuses for high performance. Finally, the company's owner utilized outcomes—such as monetary bonuses, medical insurance, and child care facilities—that would have a strong positive valence for the Passamaquoddy Indians.

CHAPTER 7
MOTIVATING PERFORMANCE: GOAL SETTING AND REWARD SYSTEMS

CHAPTER OVERVIEW

Chapter 7 builds on the motivational materials presented in Chapters 5 and 6. This chapter continues the exploration of individual processes by examining goal setting and reward systems. The organizational context of goal setting and the basic nature of goals and goal setting are explored. Also considered is the potential organizational impact of conflicting stakeholder goals on the goal-setting process. A case is made for the customer being the most important stakeholder in terms of an organization's goal setting process and priorities. Additionally, Chapter 7 examines two major goal-setting approaches: (1) Locke and Latham's goal-setting model and (2) management by objectives (MBO). The chapter also explores four different reward systems—gain-sharing plans, flexible benefit plans, banking time off, and skill-based pay—which can be used separately or in combination to enhance people's job performance. The organizational and managerial implications of the different goal setting and reward systems are discussed as well.

LEARNING OBJECTIVES

Upon completion of this chapter, the students should be able to:

1. Explain the role of customers, suppliers, and others in the goal-setting process.
2. List the key factors in goal setting and performance and describe their relationships.
3. State how management by objectives (MBO) can be applied as a management philosophy and system.
4. Describe four reward systems for encouraging high performance.

CHAPTER OUTLINE

I.　**Preview Case:** One-Page Company Game Plan

II.　Essentials of Goal Setting

　　A.　Purposes of Goal Setting
　　B.　Impact of Stakeholders
　　C.　Customer Service Quality Goals
　　D.　**Managing Quality:** ISO 9000: Making the Grade

III.　Goal Setting and Performance

　　A.　Goal Setting Model
　　B.　**Managing in Practice:** Cheryl Womack
　　C.　**Managing Across Cultures:** Mexican Workers Get Raises
　　D.　Management by Objectives
　　E.　**Managing Ethics:** Churning Accounts
　　F.　**Managing Diversity:** Beyond Good Faith

IV.　Enhancing Performance Through Reward Systems

　　A.　Gain-Sharing Plans
　　B.　**Managing in Practice:** Long John Silver's Seafood
　　C.　Flexible Benefit Plans
　　D.　**Managing in Practice:** Playcare Development Center
　　E.　Banking Time Off
　　F.　Skill-Based Pay

V.　Developing Skills

　　A.　**Self Diagnosis:** Goal-Setting Questionnaire
　　B.　**A Case in Point:** Survival at Westinghouse Electronic Plant

KEY WORDS AND CONCEPTS

Fourteen key words and concepts are introduced in Chapter 7. The key words and concepts, along with definitions or appropriate descriptions, are as follows:

Code of ethics: refers to an organization's ethical guidelines for employee behavior.

Flexible benefit plans: a reward system which allows employees to choose the benefits they want, rather than having management choose benefits for them.

Gain-sharing plans: a reward system plan which provides regular cash bonuses to an organization's employees in return for higher productivity, cost reductions, or improved quality.

Goal clarity: a variable in Locke and Latham's goal-setting model which reflects the notion that a goal must be clear and specific if it is to useful for influencing motivation.

Goal commitment: a variable in Locke and Latham's goal-setting model which reflects the individual's determination to reach a goal, regardless of whether the goal was set by the person or by a manager.

Goal difficulty: a variable in Locke and Latham's goal-setting model which refers to the idea that a goal should be challenging but not too challenging.

Goal setting: a process intended to increase efficiency and effectiveness by specifying desired outcomes toward which individuals, departments, and organizations should work.

Goals: the future outcomes (results) that individuals, teams, and organizations desire and strive to achieve.

ISO 9000: a set of standards for quality, which is used widely in Europe and is taking hold in the rest of the world. The standards require the organization to prove that it is following its own procedures for inspecting production processes, updating engineering drawings, maintaining machinery, calibrating equipment, training employees, and dealing with customer complaints.

Management by Objectives (MBO): a philosophy and system of management that serves as both a planning aid and a method of working.

Profit-sharing plans: a reward system plan which gives employees a portion of the company's profits.

Scanlon plan: a popular method of gain-sharing whereby management shares with employees the benefits from improved productivity.

Skill-based pay: a reward system based on the number and level of job skills the employee has learned.

Stakeholders: groups having potential or real power to influence the organization's decisions.

LECTURE NOTES

I.   Chapter 7 continues the exploration of individual processes by focusing on goal setting and reward systems. Goal setting is an important determinant of individual work behavior because of its powerful effect on people's motivation. Reward systems also dramatically influence work behaviors because they can be tailored to satisfy individual needs while encouraging and reinforcing behaviors that contribute to the organization's effectiveness and efficiency. Transparency 7.1 summarizes the key ideas that are presented in Chapter 7.

> **TRANSPARENCY 7.1**
> **(FROM TEXT MATERIAL IN THE TEXTBOOK)**
>
> **KEY IDEAS ABOUT GOAL SETTING AND REWARD SYSTEMS**

II.   Essentials of goal setting.

A.   Basic concepts.

1.   <u>Goal setting</u> is a process intended to increase efficiency and effectiveness by specifying desired outcomes toward which individuals, departments, and

organizations should work.

    2.   <u>Goals</u> are the future outcomes (results) that individuals, teams, and organizations desire and strive to achieve.

B.   Purposes of goal setting.

    1.   Goals guide and direct behavior.

    2.   Goals provide challenges and standards against which individual, departmental, team, or organizational performance can be assessed.

    3.   Goals serve as a source of legitimacy.

    4.   Goals serve an organizing function.

    5.   Goals reflect what the goal setters consider important and thus provide a framework for planning and control activities.

C.   Impact of stakeholders on goal setting.

    1.   <u>Stakeholders</u> are groups having potential or real power to influence the organization's decisions. Stakeholders include customers or clients, employees, suppliers, shareholders, government agencies, unions, public interest groups, and lenders.

    2.   The goals of different stakeholder groups may or may not be compatible (see Transparency 7.2 for examples).

TRANSPARENCY 7.2
(TABLE 7.1 IN THE TEXTBOOK)

TYPICAL STAKEHOLDER GOALS

---

    3.   Competing stakeholder goals challenge management to create a unified and logical system of goal setting for the organization. This is difficult when:

        a.   Each stakeholder group has substantial power in relation to the organization.

        b.   Each stakeholder group pushes to maximize its own interests and perceives the interest of some or all other groups as incompatible with its own.

        c.   The stakeholders keep changing what they expect (want) from the organization.

        d.   The management team itself is divided into competing groups within the organization.

    4.   The most important stakeholders for any organization are the customers or clients.

D.   Customer service quality goals.

1.   Two key concerns need to be addressed in setting customer service quality goals.

   a.   Customers or clients are the sole judge of service quality. They assess it by comparing the service they receive to the service they desire.

   b.   Managers and other employees easily forget the first concern when competitors start vying for business.

2.   Categories of customer service quality goals.

   a.   Reliability—the ability to perform the promised service dependably and accurately.

   b.   Tangibles—the appearance of physical facilities, equipment, personnel, and communication materials.

   c.   Responsiveness—the willingness to help customers and to provide prompt service.

   d.   Assurance—the knowledge and courtesy of employees and their ability to convey trust and confidence.

   e.   Empathy—the provision of caring, individualized attention to customers or clients.

ENRICHMENT MODULE: WHAT M.B.A. IS RESPONSIBLE FOR WENDY'S SUCCESS?

As noted above, reliability, tangibles, responsiveness, assurance, and empathy are categories of customer service quality goals. The changes that were insituted at Wendy's Old Fashioned Hamburgers illustrate a suuccessful attempt to address these quality goals.

When James Near took over the presidency of Wendy's Old Fashioned Hamburgers in 1986, the company had lost its focus on customers and employees. Costs had soared; sales had dropped; the outlook was gloomy.

According to Mr. Near, what happened to Wendy's is typical "for service businesses that forget their business starts with people." He said, "managers weren't getting the respect they needed and were passing their frustration along to the crew. The crew, feeling unappreciated, made the customer feel the same. And the customers voted with their feet—as customers are wont to do."

How did Wendy's respond to this situation? First, they re-introduced the M.B.A., or "Mop Bucket Attitude." The "Mop Bucket Attitude says that all the business sophistication in the world pales before the 'wisdom' of a clean floor. Fancy price-cost tabulations or quarterly earnings have no meaning to the customer, but quality food, variety and atmosphere do."

Mr. Near figured that becoming the customers' preferred fast food restaurant depended upon becoming the preferred fast food employer. Therefore, Wendy's worked at developing the potential of its existing employees as well as at recruiting and retaining the best people it could find. Wendy's instituted extensive training, improved their basic compensation, offered an attractive fringe benefits package, paid quarterly cash bonuses, and created a stock option plan.

Wendy's also instituted goals and performance standards regarding quality, service, and cleanliness. And a new menu—including items to appeal to the cost-conscious consumer—was developed.

The customers began to come back and so did Wendy's growth in sales volume.

This enrichment module is based on:

Near, J.W. (1992, April 27). Wendy's successful 'mop bucket attitude.' *The Wall Street Journal*, A16.

---

3.   ISO 9000 is an example of customer service quality goals. ISO 9000 is a set of standards for quality, which is used widely in Europe and is taking hold in the rest of the world. The standards require the organization to prove that it is following its own procedures for inspecting production processes, updating engineering drawings, maintaining machinery, calibrating equipment, training employees, and dealing with customer complaints.

III.   Goal setting and performance.

A.   The goal-setting process is one of the most important tools for influencing employees' work motivation.

B.   The Locke and Latham model of individual goal-setting and performance, which is depicted in Transparency 7.3, consists of seven categories of variables.

> ### TRANSPARENCY 7.3
> ### (FIGURE 7.1 IN THE TEXTBOOK)
>
> ### GOAL-SETTING MODEL

1. The first category—"challenge"—consists of three variables: goal difficulty, goal clarity, and self-efficacy.

   a. <u>Goal difficulty</u> refers to the idea that a goal should be challenging but not too challenging.

   b. <u>Goal clarity</u> reflects the notion that a goal must be clear and specific if it is to useful for influencing motivation.

   c. Transparency 7.4 describes how goal difficulty and goal clarity are related to performance.

> ### TRANSPARENCY 7.4
> ### (TABLE 7.2 IN THE TEXTBOOK)
>
> ### IMPACT OF GOALS ON PERFORMANCE

   d. Self-efficacy (see Chapter 5)—an individual's belief about his/her ability to perform in a certain situation—is positively related to performance.

2. The second category—"moderators"—consists of four variables: ability, goal commitment, feedback, and task complexity.

   a. Ability limits an individual's capacity to respond to a challenge.

   b. <u>Goal commitment</u> reflects the individual's determination to reach a goal, regardless of whether the goal was set by the person or by a manager. Goal commitment is likely to be stronger when:

      (1) An individual makes a public commitment to achieve the goal.

      (2) An individual has a high need for achievement.

      (3) Individuals believe they can control the activities that will help in goal attainment.

      (4) Employees participate in goal setting unless the employees do not expect or want to participate.

      (5) Employees believe that positive outcomes are contingent on achieving goals.

      (6) Employees expect to be punished for not achieving goals (however, remember the side-effects of punishment from Chapter 5).

      (7) When expected and received rewards are the same.

c.   Feedback makes goal setting and individual responses to goal achievement a dynamic process.

d.   Task complexity—the effort encouraged by challenging goals leads directly to effective performance on simple tasks but not on complex tasks.

3.   The third category—"mediators"—consists of three variables: direction, effort, and persistence.

a.   Direction focuses behaviors on activities expected to result in goal achievement and simultaneously steers people away from activities irrelevant to achieving the goals.

b.   The effort a person exerts is positively related to increases in goal difficulty, assuming the person is trying to reach and is committed to the goal.

c.   Persistence reflects a person's willingness to work at a task over an extended period of time and overcome obstacles in order to achieve the goals.

4.   The fourth category consists of one variable—performance.

a.   Performance is likely to be high when challenging goals are set, moderators are present, and mediators are operating.

b.   Performance may be measured quantitatively or qualitatively. To facilitate the assessment of qualitative performance, organizations have often developed a <u>code of ethics</u> to guide employee behavior. An effective code of ethics should:

(1)   Help employees to identify what their organization recognizes as acceptable business practices.

(2)   Legitimize the consideration of ethics as part of decision making.

(3)   Avoid discussion among employees about what is right and wrong.

(4)   Avoid ambivalence in decision making caused by an organizational reward system that appears to reward unethical behavior.

5.   The fifth category consists of one variable—rewards.

a.   When a employee attains a high level of performance, rewards can be important inducements to maintain that level.

6.   The sixth category consists of one variable—satisfaction.

a.   The goal-setting model focuses on the employee's degree of satisfaction with having achieved goals.

b.   Since satisfaction is positively related to the number of successful goal attainment experiences, goal difficulty may need to be compromised to some degree in order for both satisfaction and performance to be maximized.

c.   The following enrichment module provides some additional insights about the relationship between goals and job satisfaction.

ENRICHMENT MODULE: GOALS HELP EMPLOYEES EXPERIENCE JOB SATISFACTION

Why are employees satisfied with their jobs? It seems that the best predictor of job satisfaction appears to be the perceived probability of attaining goals at work. Also, people are more satisfied when they perceive more positive and fewer negative goals in their work environment. Thus, it is important for managers to help employees distinguish between positive and negative goals, for not all goals affect satisfaction in the same way.

A recent study demonstrated that employees were satisfied with their jobs when they had high goal commitment, perceived high chances of success in attaining their goals, and had few negative goals in their job situation. The study further found that two indices of goal clarity—knowing the means for goal attainment and having specific deadlines for goal attainment—were also related to employees' satisfaction. The results of the study suggest that the goal dimensions which are important for performance and motivation may also be responsible for job satisfaction.

This enrichment module is based on:

Roberson, L. (1990). Prediction of job satisfaction from characteristics of personal work goals. *Journal of Organizational Behavior, 11*, 29-41.

---

7.   The seventh category consists of one variable—consequences.

    a.   Individuals who are both satisfied with and committed to the organization are more likely to stay with the organization and to accept the challenges that it presents than are individuals who are less satisfied and committed.

C.   Workplace significance of the Locke and Latham goal-setting model (see Transparency 7.5).

TRANSPARENCY 7.5
(FROM TEXT MATERIAL IN THE TEXTBOOK)

GOAL-SETTING MODEL: SIGNIFICANCE FOR THE WORKPLACE

---

1.   The goal-setting model provides an excellent framework to assist the manager or team in diagnosing the potential problems with low- or average-performing employees.

2.   The goal-setting model provides concrete advice on how to create a high-performance work environment.

3.   The goal-setting model portrays the system of interrelationships among the key factors affecting the achievement of high performance.

D.   <u>Management by objectives (MBO)</u> is a philosophy and system of management that serves as both a planning aid and a method of working. As shown in Transparency 7.5, the MBO process consists of four basic components, each with several dimensions. The arrows in Transparency 7.6 indicate that a strong interrelationship exists among the components and that all should operate simultaneously to make the MBO process effective.

TRANSPARENCY 7.6
(FIGURE 7.2 IN THE TEXTBOOK)

MANAGEMENT BY OBJECTIVES PROCESS

---

1.   The first component of the MBO process is goal setting.

    a.   Subordinates and superiors identify specific areas of job responsibility, develop performance standards in each area, and, possibly, formulate a work plan for achieving the goals.

    b.   In setting goals, managers and team leaders should:

        (1)   State what must be done.

        (2)   Specify how performance will be measured.

        (3)   Specify the performance standard.

        (4)   Set deadlines to reach goals.

        (5)   Rank goals in order of importance.

        (6)   Rate goals as to difficulty and importance.

2.   The second component of the MBO process is subordinate participation.

    a.   A moderate to high level of subordinate participation in goal setting seems to be effective, provided subordinates have some autonomy in their jobs or an increase in autonomy is planned as part of the process.

3.   The third component of the MBO process is implementation.

    a.   Implementation of the MBO process requires translating the outcomes from goal setting into actions that ultimately will lead to the attainment of the desired goals.

4.   The fourth component of the MBO process is performance appraisal and feedback.

    a.   Performance appraisal under MBO involves:

        (1)   Identifying specific goals and measurement factors.

        (2)   Measuring performance against those goals.

        (3)   Reviewing performance with the employee.

        (4)   Developing ways to improve future performance.

    b.   Feedback identifies the extent to which employees have attained their goals.

Feedback is essential for improving job performance and for encouraging personal development.

E.　Workplace significance of MBO (see Transparency 7.7).

TRANSPARENCY 7.7
(FROM TEXT MATERIAL IN THE TEXTBOOK)

MANAGEMENT BY OBJECTIVES: SIGNIFICANCE FOR THE WORKPLACE

1.　Certain criticisms apply to the way MBO is often actually used, rather than how MBO is supposed to be used. These criticisms are:

　a.　Too much emphasis is placed on reward-punishment psychology.

　b.　An excessive amount of paperwork and red tape develops, the very thing that MBO is supposed to reduce.

　c.　The process is really controlled and imposed from the top, allowing little opportunity for real employee participation.

　d.　The process turns into a zero-sum (win-lose) game between superior and subordinate.

　e.　Aspects of jobs that can be objectively rather than subjectively measured receive the most emphasis.

　f.　Too much emphasis on individual goals and performance drives out recognition of the need for collaborative teamwork and group goals.

IV.　Performance may be enhanced by using one or more of the following reward systems: gain-sharing, flexible benefits plans, banking time off, and skill-based pay. Transparency 7.8 summarizes the strengths and limitations of each reward system.

TRANSPARENCY 7.8
(TABLE 7.3 IN THE TEXTBOOK)

REWARD SYSTEMS THAT IMPROVE PRODUCTIVITY

ENRICHMENT MODULE: PAYING FOR TOP EXECUTIVE PERFORMANCE

At all levels of the organization, monetary compensation can be used to enhance performance. Executive pay has been criticized because CEOs often receive lavish compensation packages even when the company performs poorly. To make pay for performance work effectively at the top executive level, organizations should do the following:

1.   The CEO's annual base salary should be limited to $1 million. Anything beyond the base salary should be paid only when stringent performance goals are met.

2.   Boards of directors should have the latitude to reward improvements in quality, customer satisfaction, management development, and other key areas.

3.   Stock options should be charged against earnings.

4.   Large options should be priced at a premium in order to benefit shareholders before executives.

5.   Executives should be encouraged to own the company's stock.

This enrichment module is based on:

Byrne, J.A., Foust, D., & Therrien, L. (1992, March 30). Executive pay: Compensation at the top is out of control. Here's how to reform it. *Business Week*, 52-58.

A.   <u>Gain-sharing plans</u> provide regular cash bonuses to an organization's employees in return for higher productivity, cost reductions, or improved quality.

    1.   Gain-sharing plans differ from <u>profit-sharing plans</u> (*i.e*, plans which give employees a portion of the company's profits) in at least two ways.

        a.   Gain-sharing plans are tied to improvements at the plant, division, or department level rather than to company-wide profits.

        b.   Gain-sharing plans have a greater impact on individual performance because individuals have greater control over the factors that affect gain sharing than they do over the factors that affect company-wide profitability.

    2.   The <u>Scanlon plan</u>, a popular example of gain-sharing, is a system of rewards whereby management shares with employees the benefits from improved productivity. When actual labor costs are less than expected labor costs for a given sales volume, the difference goes into a gain-sharing bonus pool. The company and the employees share in the bonus pool.

ENRICHMENT MODULE: RAISING PRODUCTIVITY THROUGH GAIN-SHARING

A Whirlpool plant in Benton Harbor, Michigan had poor quality and productivity and was a candidate for closure when corporate headquarters told local management and labor that there was only one way of saving the plant—improve output.

The crisis was addressed by implementing a gain-sharing program which was designed "to rev up productivity as well as reward it." The gain-sharing plan was simple: The larger the gain in the quality of their output, the larger the pool of money shared by workers and the company.   The workers divide their share of the pool equally, which translated into an extra $2,700 in pay for each person in 1991. The company divides its share between shareholders and customers by balancing profits and prices.

Since 1988, productivity at the Benton Harbor plant increased by more than 19% and "the number of parts rejected has sunk to a world-class 10 per million from 837 per million."

This enrichment module is based on:

Wartzman, R. (1992, May 4). Sharing gains: A Whirlpool factory raises productivity—and pay of workers. *The Wall Street Journal*, A1 & A4.

B.   <u>Flexible benefit plans</u> allow employees to choose the benefits they want, rather than having management choose benefits for them. Employees tailor the benefit package to their needs by deciding what benefits they want and how much of their allotted benefit money to spend on each benefit.

     1.   Advantages of flexible benefit plans (see Transparency 7.9).

          a.   They allow employees to make important decisions about their personal finances.

          b.   The organization doesn't have to assume a paternalistic role of knowing what is best for each employee.

          c.   The economic value of employee benefits is highlighted.

     2.   Limitations of flexible benefit plans (see Transparency 7.9).

          a.   Record keeping becomes more complicated for the organization because of the different benefit choices available to employees.

          b.   Organizations can't accurately predict the number of employees who might choose each benefit. In turn, this could affect the costs of some benefits, such as insurance.

TRANSPARENCY 7.9
(FROM TEXT MATERIAL IN THE TEXTBOOK)

FLEXIBLE BENEFITS PLANS: ADVANTAGES AND LIMITATIONS

C.   Banking time off permits employees to accumulate days off with pay based on exceptional performance.

    1.   Potential issues associated with banking time off.

        a.   What happens if an employee wants to use banked time during a rush period?

        b.   What happens if an employee's extended absence could negatively affect productivity?

        c.   How long should a employee be permitted to retain banked time?

D.   <u>Skill-based pay</u> is a reward system based on the number and level of job skills the employee has learned.

    1.   Skill-based pay works particularly well with employees who set high but attainable goals and who want to manage themselves and participate in decisions that affect their performance.

    2.   Advantages of skill-based pay (see Transparency 7.10).

        a.   Flexibility in utilizing the work force, particularly in a production situation.

        b.   Increasing productivity while decreasing supervisory costs.

    3.   Limitations of skill-based pay (see Transparency 7.10).

        a.   Skill-based pay tends to produce high pay rates.

        b.   Learning multiple skills requires a large organizational investment in training and lost production time as employees learn new skills.

        c.   Employees may become frustrated when no job openings are available in areas for which they have learned these new skills.

TRANSPARENCY 7.10
(FROM TEXT MATERIAL IN THE TEXTBOOK)

SKILL-BASED PAY: ADVANTAGES AND LIMITATIONS

ENRICHMENT MODULE: REWARDING THE WRONG BEHAVIOR

Having reward systems which reward the wrong behavior can produce disastrous results. Consider, for instance, Sear's reward system which based auto mechanics' pay on the volume of repairs. Mechanics made unneeded repairs to meet their quotas and enhance their pay.

Motorola used a skill-based pay system to encourage individual development but expected employees to behave as team members. Employees figured that Motorola's management couldn't make up its mind about how it wanted employees to behave. Motorola replaced skill-based pay with an individual merit system.

This enrichment module is based on:

Fierman, J. (1994, June 13). The perilous new world of fair pay. *Fortune*, 57-64.

V.   Summing up: What are the implications for organizational behavior?

    A.   As part of their responsibilities, managers must create work environments which stimulate employees to perform at superior levels. One way of creating a stimulating work environment is through the effective use of goal setting. In fact, setting and achieving goals is one of the most powerful forces affecting employee motivation. Another way of creating a stimulating work environment is by using innovative reward systems which contingently link performance and the receipt of rewards, and which provide rewards that are tailored, as much as possible, to individual employees' needs.

DISCUSSION QUESTIONS: SUGGESTED ANSWERS

1.   *Imagine that you are establishing goal setting in an organization that you are familiar with. How might various stakeholders influence the goal-setting process?*

In answering this question, students should draw upon the material on typical stakeholder goals that is contained in Table 7.1 of the textbook. Given these typical stakeholder goals, students can make a reasonable assessment of which aspects of the referent organization's operations each stakeholder is likely to influence.

2.   *Think of an organization for which you currently work or have worked. How would you evaluate the organization and its employees in terms of the five service quality goals stated in the chapter?*

The five service quality goals are as follows:

    a.   Reliability—the ability to perform the promised service dependably and accurately.
    b.   Tangibles—the appearance of physical facilities, equipment, personnel, and communication materials.
    c.   Responsiveness—the willingness to help customers and to provide prompt service.

    d.   Assurance—the knowledge and courtesy of employees and their ability to convey trust and confidence.

    e.   Empathy—the provision of caring, individualized attention to customers or clients.

Students should examine the extent to which each of the service quality goals characterize the operations of their organization. Students without work experience should be encouraged to examine their college or university, a fraternity/sorority, or a service organization to which they belong.

3.   *List your five most important personal goals. Evaluate each for difficulty and clarity. What are the implications, if any, of this assessment for your behavior?*

Goal difficulty refers to the idea that a goal should be challenging but not too challenging. Goal clarity reflects the notion that a goal must be clear and specific if it is to useful for influencing motivation. Students should be encouraged to develop goals that are moderately challenging, specific, and clear.

An example of five common student goals might be: (1) to graduate as soon as possible; (2) to raise my GPA; (3) to get a good job; (4) to make a lot of money; and (5) to own my own business. Given the vague wording of each of these goals, a student probably would not be able to accurately asses either goal difficulty or goal clarity. These goals could be revised so that both goal difficulty and goal clarity could be more accurately determined. The revised goals might be as follows: (1) to graduate by Fall 1996; (2) to raise my GPA from 2.9 to 3.0 by Spring 1995; (3) to work for an organization that offer strong management training programs; (4) to earn a starting salary of $28,000; and (5) to own my own business within five years of graduating from college.

4.   *Think of a current or previous job. Evaluate your level of goal commitment. What factors influenced your level of goal commitment? Did your level of commitment affect your performance?*

Goal commitment refers to the individual's determination to reach a goal, regardless of whether the goal was set by the person or a manager. According to the text, goal commitment is likely to be stronger when:

    a.   An individual makes a public commitment to achieve the goal.
    b.   An individual has a high need for achievement.
    c.   An individual believes he/she can control the activities that will help in goal attainment.
    d.   Employees participate in goal setting unless the employees do not expect or want to participate.
    e.   Employees believe that positive outcomes are contingent on achieving goals.
    f.   Employees expect to be punished for not achieving goals.
    g.   When expected and received rewards are the same.

In discussing this question, students should explore the extent which each of the above factors was present in his or her job. If a student does not have previous work experience, he/she should be encouraged to examine work they have done with organizations such as a sorority or fraternity or service organization.

Also, performance is likely to be high when goal commitment is strong. Students should be encouraged to consider this relationship relative to the strength of goal commitment and the level of performance in their reference job (or other non-work situation).

5.   *In 1994, investigators revealed that researchers at St. Luc's Hospital in Montreal falsified data on breast cancer patients. Although the fabricated data didn't affect the results of the entire study, why do people engage in such behaviors?*

In the context of Chapter 7, a reasonable answer to this question is that researchers felt pressure to achieve some goal regarding the effectiveness of a cancer treatment procedure or program. The temptation to falsify data to demonstrate goal attainment may have been substantial, given the rewards (fame, revenues for the hospital, additional compensation for the physician-researchers, etc.) which could result from goal attainment.

Another reasonable answer in the context of this chapter's material is that St. Luc's Hospital may not have had a code of ethics to provide guidelines for employee behavior. Without adequate specification of behavioral expectations regarding acceptable practices within the organization, St. Luc's could have inadvertently encouraged the falsification of data.

6.   *What are the similarities and differences between gain-sharing and profit-sharing plans? Explain how each relates to goal-setting techniques.*

Gain-sharing plans and profit-sharing plans are similar in that:

  a.   They try to increase employee motivation and enhance employee performance by linking financial reward to performance standards.
  b.   They reward employees on the basis of some aggregate level of performance (*i.e.,* team, department, division, or entire organization).

Gain-sharing plans and profit-sharing plans are different in that:

  a.   Gain-sharing plans are tied to improvements at the plant, division, or department level rather than to company-wide profits.
  b.   Gain-sharing plans have a greater impact on individual performance because individuals have greater control over the factors that affect gain sharing than they do over the factors that affect company-wide profitability.

Key goal-setting variables—such as goal difficulty, goal clarity, and goal commitment—are related to both gain-sharing plans and profit-sharing plans. Effective use of either gain-sharing or profit-sharing could require the articulation of performance goals to which employees are willing to commit themselves, and that are moderately challenging, specific, and clear. Additionally, contingently rewarding goal attainment is an important linkage between the two reward system plans and goal setting.

7.   *What are some problems for employees working for an organization that has adopted skill-based pay?*

Skill-based pay works particularly well with employees who set high but attainable goals and who want to manage themselves and participate in decisions that affect their performance. Employees who do have these characteristics probably would not perform as well under a skill-based pay system. Also, they would probably be somewhat dissatisfied with the skill-based pay system. Whether or not employees have the previously mentioned characteristics, they may become frustrated when no job openings are available in areas for which they have learned new skills.

8.   *Can management equitably tie flexible benefits plans to employee performance? If so, what are the advantages of doing so? The disadvantages?*

Linking flexible benefit plans to employee performance implies either that receipt of benefits is contingent on performance, or that the dollar amount of benefits depends on the level of performance, or both. To convince employees that such a plan has both distributive justice and procedural justice, management, at a minimum should:

a.   Have a well-designed performance appraisal system.
b.   Clearly link benefit types and amounts to different performance levels.
c.   Clearly communicate performance appraisal and benefits information to employees, explaining both the mechanics of the plan and the reasoning behind it.
d.   Check for any tax code or other legal limitations regarding differences in fringe benefits for different classes of employees.
e.   Administer the plan consistently across people and across time.

Among the advantages of linking flexible benefit plans to employee performance are the following:

a.   Employees would no longer view benefits as an entitlement but rather as something to be received primarily, if not only, as a result of effective performance.
b.   Employees' job performance could be enhanced, thereby contributing to improved organizational effectiveness and efficiency.

Some of the disadvantages of linking flexible benefit plans to employee performance could include the following:

a.   An additional burden would be placed on the organization's record-keeping function.
b.   The costs of some benefits, like insurance, could be affected because they are based on the number of people covered.
c.   Some employees may react negatively to having the type and/or amount of their benefits tied to performance. This could create difficulties in hiring new employees and/or retaining existing employees.

DEVELOPING SKILLS—
SELF DIAGNOSIS: GOAL-SETTING QUESTIONNAIRE

This questionnaire consists of 30 statements for rating goal-setting in a current or previously-held job. Students are to indicate, on a five-point scale (1 = almost never and 5 = almost always), the extent to which each of the statements best describes goal-setting in the referent job.

The questionnaire is scored by totaling the responses for the 30 items.
Scores of 120-150 indicate a high-performing, highly satisfying work situation. Your goals are challenging, and you are committed to achieving them. When you achieve your goals, you are rewarded for attaining them. Scores of 80 -119 suggest a highly varied work situation with motivating and satisfying attributes on some dimensions and just the opposite on others. Scores of 30-79 suggest a low-

performing, dissatisfying work situation.

Questionnaire results could be used as the basis for a small group discussion. Participants should compare their scores and discuss what differences in those scores might mean in terms of goal setting within the students' employing organizations.

DEVELOPING SKILLS—
A CASE IN POINT: SURVIVAL AT WESTINGHOUSE ELECTRONIC PLANT

CASE OVERVIEW

This case describes the experiences of the Westinghouse Electronic Assembly in College Station, Texas with two different types of reward systems: skill-based pay and lump-sum bonuses. When the plant opened in 1983, a skill-based pay system—known as a "pay for knowledge" reward system—was instituted. Under this system employees received wages for each level of advanced training they completed successfully. While this system created a more flexible and knowledgeable work force, it also had the drawback of some employees' salaries eventually "topping out." In 1986, management faced the "top out" situation because about 64% of all employees would have achieved all possible levels of training by the end of the year. Employees were disgruntled about the prospects of no longer having a goal to strive for that, when attained, would result in a financial reward.

After considering several alternatives, the Westinghouse corporate human resource department instituted lump-sum payments to cope with the "topping out" problem. The lump-sum payments were based on a complex formula of labor indicators. Unfortunately, neither employees nor management at the College Station plant understood the formula very well. While everyone knew the lump sum payments were to be made for three years, the employees quickly learned to expect the year-end payments. Moreover, the lump-sum payments were available to technicians but not to managers, which resulted in managers resenting the payments.

As global competition increased in the electronic assembly industry, management faced another, more crucial problem—the College Station plant had to increase productivity and cut its labor costs. To achieve this, plant management decided to implement an MBO system.

CASE QUESTIONS

1. *What were some of the problems with the lump-sum payment plan?*

    Three basic problems existed with the lump-sum payment plan:

    a. The lump-sum payments were based on a complex formula of labor indicators which neither employees or management at the College Station plant understood very well.
    b. While everyone knew the lump sum payments were to be made for three years, the employees quickly learned to expect the year-end payments.
    c. The lump-sum payments were available to technicians but not to managers, which resulted in managers resenting the payments.

2. *If Westinghouse hired you as a consultant to advise them on developing an MBO process, what*

would you recommend?

In addressing this question, students should draw upon the following text material: (1) the four components of the MBO process, and (2) the problems with the way the MBO process is too often implemented.

The MBO process consists of four components: goal setting, subordinate participation, implementation, and performance appraisal and feedback. In making their recommendations, student should address each component in a reasonable level of detail.

Common criticisms of the way in which MBO is often implemented include:

    a.   Too much emphasis is placed on reward-punishment psychology.

    b.   An excessive amount of paperwork and red tape develops, the very thing that MBO is supposed to reduce.

    c.   The process is really controlled and imposed from the top, allowing little opportunity for real employee participation.

    d.   The process turns into a zero-sum (win-lose) game between superior and subordinate.

    e.   Aspects of jobs that can be objectively rather than subjectively measured receive the most emphasis.

    f.   Too much emphasis on individual goals and performance drives out recognition of the need for collaborative teamwork and group goals.

Students should develop their recommendations so as to minimize, if not eliminate, the possibility of these problems occurring with the implementation of an MBO program at the Westinghouse Electronic Assembly Plant.

3.   *Using the goal-setting model, diagnose the "pay for knowledge" system. What features of the goal-setting model are present in this system?*

The "pay for knowledge" reward system could be argued to be a generally effective implementation of the goal-setting model until the "topping out" situation arose. Goal difficulty, goal clarity, and self-efficacy—the crucial variables for creating challenge— seem to be present. Employees appear to have the necessary ability and strong goal commitment. However, no evidence exists to address the moderator variables of feedback and task complexity. The presence of the three mediator variables (*i.e.,* direction, effort, and persistence) could be implied because about 64% of all employees would have achieved all possible levels of training by the end of 1986. Performance does not appear to be a significant problem in 1986 although it would become a crucial issue shortly thereafter. Additionally, performance probably was high because challenging goals were set, moderators were present, and mediators were operating. Rewards appeared to be important inducements for maintaining performance. Finally, employees seemed to be satisfied with and committed to the company.

When the "topping out" situation occurred, most of the employees no longer had a goal to strive for. Thus the crucial goal setting variables of goal difficulty, goal clarity, and goal commitment were probably compromised to some extent. Moreover, since the "topped out" employees could no longer receive a financial reward for goal attainment, performance, satisfaction, and organizational commitment could be affected negatively.

COURSE ENHANCEMENT—
WEST'S ORGANIZATIONAL BEHAVIOR CUSTOM VIDEO SERIES

Two videos from *West's Organizational Behavior Custom Video Series* can be used to enhance the material in Chapter 7. One video, which was relevant to Chapter 5 as well, is: *Mary Kay Cosmetics: Spotlight on Success.* The other video is: *Motorola's Third Annual Total Customer Satisfaction Team Competition.*

VIDEO: *MARY KAY COSMETICS: SPOTLIGHT ON SUCCESS*

Approximate Time: 10 minutes

Video Summary:

The video is of the annual awards night sponsored by Mary Kay Cosmetics for the independent salespersons who sell the firm's products.

In the context of Chapter 7, the video provides insight into how Mary Kay Cosmetics encourages its independent salespersons to set challenging but attainable goals and then lavishly rewards them when the goals are achieved. A careful viewing of the video reveals that most of the elements of Locke and Latham's goal-setting model are present in the motivational system used by Mary Kay Cosmetics (see suggested answer to the discussion question below). Overt evidence exists for some of the elements, whereas other elements must be inferred from the comments made by the salespersons. The reward system is based on both tangibles (such as cars, mink coats, and other merchandise) and intangibles (such as self-pride, a sense of accomplishment, and recognition in front of one's peers).

Discussion Question and Suggested Answer for Video:

1. *How could the goal-setting model that was developed in Chapter 7 be applied to Mary Kay Cosmetics?*

    A detailed viewing of the video tape shows reveals overt and covert evidence which pertains to some, if not most, of the components of the goal-setting model. Among the key elements are the following:

    a. Goal difficulty is addressed through the emphasis on setting challenging but attainable goals.
    b. Goal clarity is implied through the specification of very specific sales objectives and timetables.
    c. Self-efficacy is evident in many salespersons' beliefs that they too have the ability to be highly successful.
    d. Goal commitment is evident in the statements made by many of the salespeople regarding intended future behavior.
    e. The mediators of direction, effort, and persistence can be inferred from the comments made by the salespeople.
    f. Performance is high, in part, because of the presence of the preceding factors.
    g. Meaningful rewards are provided to the salespeople as a result of their high performance.
    h. Both the salespeople who have been rewarded for their goal attainment and those who are still working toward their goals seem to be highly satisfied.
    i. The awardees appear to be highly committed to Mary Kay Cosmetics.

VIDEO: *MOTOROLA'S THIRD ANNUAL TOTAL CUSTOMER SATISFACTION TEAM COMPETITION*

Approximate Time: 18 minutes

Video Summary:

This video supplements the material on customer service quality goals.

The video describes Motorola's Third Annual Total Customer Satisfaction Team Competition. On January 20, 1993, 24 team finalists out of 3,700 problem-solving teams throughout Motorola's worldwide operations competed for gold and silver awards. The teams made a presentation on their efforts to increase total customer satisfaction. The presentations were made to a panel of judges selected from the top echelons of Motorola and the company's vendors. Each team was judged on seven criteria:

- Teamwork (10 points)
- Project selection (10 Points)
- Analysis techniques (20 points)
- Remedies (20 points)
- Results (20 points)
- Institutionalization (10 points)
- Presentation (10 points)

Discussion Question and Suggested Answer for Video:

1.   *Which of the customer service quality goals discussed in the text are illustrated in the video?*

Five categories of customer service quality goals were discussed in the text. These categories are:

a.   Reliability—the ability to perform the promised service dependably and accurately.

b.   Tangibles—the appearance of physical facilities, equipment, personnel, and communication materials.

c.   Responsiveness—the willingness to help customers and to provide prompt service.

d.   Assurance—the knowledge and courtesy of employees and their ability to convey trust and confidence.

e.   Empathy—the provision of caring, individualized attention to customers or clients.

Each of the projects presented in the video touches on one or more of the categories of customer service quality goals. Taken together, the projects illustrate all of the customer service quality goals.

CHAPTER 8
WORK STRESS

CHAPTER OVERVIEW

Chapter 8 concludes the exploration of individual processes with an examination of work stress, its causes, and its consequences. The chapter begins by describing the basic nature of stress, including definitions of fundamental concepts, an explanation of the fight-or-flight response, and a discussion of factors that influence whether an individual will experience stress in the workplace or in other situations. Next, the chapter explores sources of stress that exist within the workplace and in people's personal lives. Consideration is also given to three important effects of stress: health, job performance, and job burnout. Additionally, three personality types—the Type A personality, the Type B personality, and the hardy personality—are examined in terms of their ability to heighten or reduce people's reactions to stressful situations. Finally, there is a discussion of the methods that individuals and organizations can use to cope with stress.

LEARNING OBJECTIVES

Upon completion of this chapter, the students should be able to:

1. Define the concepts of stress and stressors.
2. Explain the general nature of the body's response to stressors.
3. Diagnose the sources of stress in organizations.
4. State the effects of stress on health.
5. Explain the relationship between stress and job performance.
6. Understand the nature and causes of job burnout.
7. Describe several methods for coping with stress.

CHAPTER OUTLINE

I.   **Preview Case:** Stress on the Job

II.   Nature of Stress

    A.   Fight-or-Flight Response
    B.   The Stress Experience
    C.   **Managing in Practice:** The Navy Pilot

III.   Sources of Stress

    A.   **Managing Across Cultures:** Siesta Sunset
    B.   Work Factors
    C.   **Managing Ethics:** Welcome to the Age of Overwork
    D.   **Managing Diversity:** Work and Family—Business as Usual
    E.   Life Stressors

IV.   Effects of Stress

    A.   Health and Stress
    B.   **Managing Across Cultures:** Karoushi, or Stress Death
    C.   Performance and Stress
    D.   **Managing in Practice:** "Just Enough but Not Too Much"
    E.   Job Burnout
    F.   **Managing Diversity:** The "New-Collar" Workers

V.   Personality and Stress

    A.   Type A and B Personalities
    B.   The Hardy Personality

VI.   Stress Management

    A.   Individual Stress Coping Methods
    B.   Organizational Stress Coping Methods
    C.   **Managing Quality:** AT&T's Wellness Program

VII.   Developing Skills

    A.   **Self Diagnosis:** Identifying Your Strategies for Coping with Stress
    B.   **A Case in Point:** The Stress of Shift Work

KEY WORDS AND CONCEPTS

Seventeen key words and concepts are introduced in Chapter 8. The key words and concepts, along with definitions or appropriate descriptions, are as follows:

Behavioral effects of stress: include decreased performance, absenteeism, higher accident rates, higher alcohol and other drug abuse rates, impulsive behavior, and difficulties in communication.

Depersonalization: refers to the treatment of people as objects.

Emotional effects of stress: include anger, anxiety, lowered self-esteem, poorer intellectual functioning (including an inability to concentrate and make decisions), nervousness, irritability, resentment of supervision, and job dissatisfaction.

Fight-or-flight response: refers to the biochemical and bodily changes that are a natural reaction to an environmental stressor.

Hardiness: refers to a cluster of personality characteristics that includes feeling a sense of commitment, responding to each difficulty as though it is a challenge and an opportunity rather than a threat, and having a sense over control over one's life. This collection of personality traits seems to act as a buffer for the negative effects of stress.

Job burnout: refers to the adverse effects of working conditions where stressors seem unavoidable and sources of job satisfaction and relief from stress seem unavailable.

Life stressors: refer to sources of stress that people have in their personal lives.

Physiological effects of stress: include increased blood pressure, increased heart rate, sweating, hot and cold spells, breathing difficulties, muscular tension, and increased gastrointestinal disorders.

Role ambiguity: occurs when the employee is uncertain about assigned jobs and responsibilities.

Role conflict: occurs when there are differing expectations of or demands placed on a person's role at work.

Role overload: occurs when role demands exceed a person's capacity to meet all of them adequately.

Stress: a consequence of or a general response to an action or situation that places special physical or psychological demands, or both, on a person.

Stress management: any program that reduces stress by understanding the stress response, recognizing stressors, and using coping techniques to minimize the negative consequences of stress.

Stressors: physical or psychological demands from the environment.

Type A personality: refers to people who are involved in a never-ending struggle to achieve more and more in less and less time.

Type B personality: the behavioral opposite of the Type A personality.

Wellness programs: activities that organizations sponsor to promote good health habits or to identify and correct health problems.

LECTURE NOTES

I.   Chapter 8 concludes the exploration of individual processes with an examination of work stress, its causes, and its consequences. Not everyone responds in the same way to the stressful situations that they encounter at work or in their personal lives. How individuals respond to stress will affect both themselves and the organization in profound ways. Transparency 8.1 provides an overview of the key ideas that organization members should learn in order to understand and effectively manage work stress.

TRANSPARENCY 8.1
(FROM TEXT MATERIAL IN THE TEXTBOOK)

KEY IDEAS ABOUT WORK STRESS

II.   Nature of stress.

A.   Stress and stressors are fundamental concepts.

1.   <u>Stress</u> is a consequence of or a general response to an action or situation that places special physical or psychological demands, or both, on a person.

2.   <u>Stressors</u> are the physical or psychological demands from the environment.

3.   Stressors create stress for a person when they are perceived as exceeding the individual's ability to respond.

B.   Fight-or-flight response.

1.   The <u>fight-or-flight response</u> refers to the biochemical and bodily changes that are a natural reaction to an environmental stressor.

2.   The fight-or-flight response is rooted in our ancestral heritage—the need to physically fight or flee in order to survive.

3.   The fight-or-flight response still has survival value in true emergencies but usually is not appropriate in work situations. Nonetheless, stress does occur in the workplace when stressors exceed the individual's ability to cope with the stressors.

C.   As shown in Transparency 8.2, four primary factors determine whether an individual will experience stress in the workplace or in other situations.

TRANSPARENCY 8.2
(FIGURE 8.1 IN THE TEXTBOOK)

THE RELATIONSHIP BETWEEN STRESSORS AND STRESS

---

1.   The person's perception of the situation.

a.   Employee perceptions of a situation can influence how (or whether) they experience stress.

2.   The person's past experiences.

a.   Positive reinforcement or previous success in a similar situation can reduce stress in the present situation.

b.   Punishment or past failure in a similar situation can increase stress in the present situation.

3. The presence or absence of social support.

     a. The presence of co-workers may enhance a person's self-confidence, thereby enabling the person to cope more effectively with stress.

     b. Or, the presence of co-workers may irritate people or make them anxious, thereby reducing their ability to cope with stress.

4. Individual differences with regard to stress reactions.

     a. Individual differences in personality (especially the adjustment factor from the Big Five personality factors discussed in Chapter 2), motivation, attitudes, and abilities will influence how people experience stress.

III. There are two major sources of stress: work stressors and life stressors. These stressors may affect behavior independently or interactively.

ENRICHMENT MODULE: WORK STRESSORS AND LIFE STRESSORS

Upper-middle class people face a lot of stressors, some of which are relatively unique to their socio-economic class. Upper-middle class people:

1. Routinely work 50- to 70-hour weeks because of financial commitments like costly mortgages, college tuition bills, and retirement savings.
2. Do not feel in control of their financial destiny because of corporate restructuring and rapidly changing technology.
3. Spend monetary resources on what they consider to be necessities of modern life (of course, these "necessities" would be considered unneeded luxuries by the less affluent).
4. Often experience pressures from operating their own small businesses.
5. Are pessimistic about their children's futures.
6. May experience marital strain because both husband and wife work in 75% of households with six-figure incomes.
7. May experience marital strain because their children feel neglected.

What methods do the experts recommend that upper-middle class people use to cope with stress? Here are some key suggestions:

1. Getting a grip on personal finances
2. Communicating with family members.
3. Having fun.
4. Managing work time more efficiently to cut the hours on the job.
5. Making sure that time at home is spent with the children.
6. Not letting resentments build.

This enrichment module is based on:

Spiers, J. (1993, December 27). Upper-middle-class woes. *Fortune*, 80-83+.

A.   Transparency 8.3 identifies six principal sources of work stress.

TRANSPARENCY 8.3
(FIGURE 8.2 IN THE TEXTBOOK)

SOURCES OF WORK STRESS

---

1.   Workload: <u>role overload</u> exists when role demands exceed a person's capacity to meet all of them adequately.

2.   Job conditions: poor working conditions (such as temperature extremes, loud noises, too much or too little light, radiation, air pollution, etc.), excessive travel, and long hours can be stressful.

3.   Role conflict and ambiguity can be stressful. <u>Role conflict</u> occurs when there are differing expectations of or demands placed on a person's role at work. <u>Role ambiguity</u> occurs when the employee is uncertain about assigned jobs and responsibilities. Being responsible for others and not being able to participate in important decisions affecting the job may also cause stress.

4.   Career development: job security (or lack thereof), promotions, transfers, and developmental opportunities can be very powerful stressors.

5.   Interpersonal relations in the organization can be either a source of stress or the social support that affects how people react to stress. Good working relationships diminish stress while poor working relationships increase stress.

6.   Conflict between work and other roles can be sources of stress.

ENRICHMENT MODULE: STRESS HAS GLOBAL DIFFERENCES

The prevalence of work stress usually does not surprise North American executives. They perceive work stress as an influence of the cultures that emphasize individualism , competitiveness, achievement, and material acquisitions. While North American executives are not alone in experiencing work stress, their stress does differ from executives in other parts of the world.

A recent study of stress experienced by executives around the world reported how work stress differs in mature industrialized countries versus developing and recently industrialized countries. For example, in mature industrialized countries such as Germany, Japan, Sweden, and the United States, managers perceived work stressors to be a lack of autonomy, poorly trained subordinates, losing their jobs, and family and social pressures. Managers in developing and recently industrialized countries such as Korea, Brazil, South Africa, and Egypt, focused on work stressors that included interpersonal relations, competition for promotion, lack of autonomy, and work overloads.

This enrichment module is based on:

Cooper, C. (1987, Winter). Executive stress around the world. *University of Wales Review of Business and Economics*, 3-8.

B.   Life stressors.

1.   The distinction between work and nonwork stressors isn't always clear. As shown in Transparency 8.4, both work and family stressors may contribute to work-family conflict because stress in one area can reduce a person's ability to cope with stress in the other. This conflict also is a source of stress, which leads to other problems.

TRANSPARENCY 8.4
(FIGURE 8.3 IN THE TEXTBOOK)

STRESSORS AND WORK-FAMILY CONFLICT

---

2.   Life stressors refer to sources of stress that people have in their personal lives. Included among life stressors are major changes such as divorce, marriage, or death of a family member. Transparency 8.5 provides an excellent example of life stressors that college students encounter. While life stressors often reflect negative events, they may reflect positive events as well. Marriage, taking a new job, and returning to school are usually positive events but they can be stressful.

TRANSPARENCY 8.5
(TABLE 8.1 IN THE TEXTBOOK)

STRESSFUL EVENTS FOR COLLEGE STUDENTS

IV.   Effects of stress.

A.   The effects of work stress may be positive or negative, but much of the research on stress focuses on its negative effects. The negative effects of stress occur in three main areas: physiological, emotional, and behavioral.

1.   The physiological effects of stress include increased blood pressure, increased heart rate, sweating, hot and cold spells, breathing difficulties, muscular tension, and increased gastrointestinal disorders.

2.   The emotional effects of stress include anger, anxiety, lowered self-esteem, poorer intellectual functioning (including an inability to concentrate and make decisions), nervousness, irritability, resentment of supervision, and job dissatisfaction.

3.   The behavioral effects of stress include decreased performance, absenteeism, higher accident rates, higher alcohol and other drug abuse rates, impulsive behavior, and difficulties in communication.

B.   Health and stress.

1.   Stress is linked to the following health problems: coronary heart disease, back pain, headaches, stomach and intestinal problems, various mental problems, and possibly cancer.

ENRICHMENT MODULE: THE WORKAHOLIC AND STRESS

Workaholic behavior can be stressful. Here's an example of a true workaholic who suffered a stroke, possibly as a result of his workaholic lifestyle.

Robert Lessin, the 39-year-old vice chairman of Smith Barney, a brokerage and investment banking firm, was a workaholic and one of Wall Street's most successful financial strategists. Lessin was often the point man, "visiting clients, attending conferences, and overseeing some 40 deals at a time."

Then one Saturday he had a stroke and was hospitalized. Initially, he was very accepting of everything that was happening around him, but by the following Monday he was anxious to return to work. He remained hospitalized yet took extraordinary measures to remain part of the working world. "He was too weak to read; and a breathing tube kept him from speaking, so his wife read memos and newspapers to him and translated his sign language." He made decisions "by giving a thumbs up or thumbs down with his usable left hand."

After spending seven weeks in the hospital, Mr. Lessin returned to work and "a blistering round of meetings from morning until evening." Despite the stroke, Mr. Lessin remained a workaholic. Perhaps his own words say it best:

> "My wife and my family have been incredible. But there is also only so much time in a day. I don't think things will be the same, but I don't think they will change much, either. This is the way I am."

This enrichment module is based on:

Rehfeld, B. (1994, June 19). Executive, interrupted: Wall St. star bounces back. *The New York Times*, F7.

---

2. Employees' stress-related illnesses also affect the organization.

   a. Increased premiums for health insurance and lost work days affect employers' costs of doing business.

   b. Over three-fourths of all industrial accidents are caused by a worker's inability to cope with emotional problems worsened by stress.

   c. Employers' legal problems, like stress-related workers' compensation claims, are growing.

C. Performance and stress.

   The positive and negative aspects of stress are most apparent in the inverted-U relationship between stress and performance, as shown in Transparency 8.6. At low levels of stress, employees may not be sufficiently alert, challenged, or involved to perform at their best. Increasing a low amount of stress may improve performance—up to the point where an optimum level of stress exists for a given task. Beyond this optimum point, performance begins to deteriorate. Then at excessive levels of stress, people are too agitated, aroused, or threatened to perform at their best.

> ### TRANSPARENCY 8.6
> ### (FIGURE 8.4 IN THE TEXTBOOK)
> ### TYPICAL RELATIONSHIP BETWEEN PERFORMANCE AND STRESS

    1.   The amount of stress which is too much, too little, or optimum will vary across people and across tasks.

    2.   As a practical matter, managers should be more concerned about their employees experiencing excessive stress than with how to increase the stress levels in their employees' work lives.

D.   Job burnout.

    1.   <u>Job burnout</u> refers to the adverse effects of working conditions where stressors seem unavoidable and sources of job satisfaction and relief from stress seem unavailable.

    2.   Burnout usually contains three components: a state of emotional exhaustion, <u>depersonalization</u> of individuals (*i.e.*, treating people as objects), and feelings of low personal accomplishment.

    3.   The probability of experiencing job burnout is highest with those people who have both a high frequency and high intensity of interpersonal contact.

    4.   Job burnout candidates share three characteristics.

        a.   They experience a great deal of stress as a result of job-related stressors.

        b.   They tend to be idealistic and self-motivating achievers.

        c.   They often seek unattainable goals.

    5.   In burnout the individual can no longer cope with job demands, and the willingness to even try drops dramatically.

V.   Personality and stress.

A.   Personality affects stress in two major ways.

    1.   Personality influences how individuals are likely to perceive situations and stressors.

    2.   Personality influences how individuals will react to environmental stressors.

B.   While many personality traits—like self-esteem and locus of control—can be related to stress, there are three personality traits that are of particular interest. These are the Type A personality, Type B personality, and the hardy personality.

    1.   Type A personality.

a.   People with a <u>Type A personality</u> are involved in a never-ending struggle to achieve more and more in less and less time.

b.   The Type A personality has four sets of behaviors and tendencies that cause stress or make stressful situations worse than they otherwise might be. The four sets of behaviors and tendencies include: time urgency, competitiveness and hostility, polyphasic behavior (*i.e.,* trying to do too many things at once), and a lack of advance planning.

c.   People with Type A behaviors are vulnerable to heart attacks. Recent research suggests that the anger, hostility, and aggression aspects of Type A behavior are most strongly related to stress reactions and heart disease.

2.   Type B personality.

a.   The <u>Type B personality</u> is considered to be the opposite of the Type A personality.

b.   Type B individuals tend to be more easy-going and relaxed, less concerned about time pressures, and less likely to overreact to situations in hostile or aggressive ways.

3.   The hardy personality.

a.   <u>Hardiness</u> is a cluster of personality characteristics that includes feeling a sense of commitment, responding to each difficulty as though it is a challenge and an opportunity rather than a threat, and having a sense of control over one's life.

b.   A high degree of hardiness reduces the negative effects of stressful events by altering the way those events are perceived.

VI.   Stress management.

A.   <u>Stress management</u> refers to any program that reduces stress by understanding the stress response, identifying and removing or reducing stressors, and using coping techniques to minimize the negative consequences of stress.

B.   Individual stress coping methods.

1.   Individual stress coping methods include activities and behaviors that are designed to:

a.   Eliminate or control the sources of stress.

b.   Make the person more resistant to stress or better able to cope with stress.

ENRICHMENT MODULE: SELF-TALK AND THE STRUGGLE INDEX

Rational Emotive Therapy (RET) can be used to reduce the amount of stress you experience by focusing on self-talk when you encounter stressful situations. Here's how it works. According to Rational Emotive Therapy, people have a three-phase response to stressful situations: (1) an activating event occurs; (2) the activating event is interpreted, thereby creating a belief or perception; and (3) as a consequence, stress is experienced. RET holds that it is the perception of the event, not the event itself produces the stress reaction. Perceptions of the event can be altered by changing negative self-talk to positive self-talk. The key to changing self-talk is becoming aware of what you say to yourself when you encounter stressful events.

One way of becoming aware of the dialogue you're having with yourself is to complete **The Struggle Index**, which is presented below.

Using the scale 4 = all the time, 3 = often, 2 = sometimes, and 1 = never, indicate how strongly you agree with each of the following statements.

- I am regularly exhausted by demands at work and home.
- My stress is caused by forces beyond my control.
- No matter how hard I work, I never feel caught up.
- I'm dissatisfied with my personal relationships.
- I don't know what I want out of life.
- If the people around me were more competent, I'd be happier.
- I "stew" in my anger rather than express it.
- I can't take criticism.
- I'm afraid I'll lose my job (or my house).
- I feel responsible for the happiness of people around me.

Scoring:

- 35-40: Life has become one crisis and struggle after another.
- 25-34: Your options are often clouded and you feel trapped.
- 15-24: You're aware that your life is in your hands.
- 10-14: You are your own best ally; you have a high degree of control and self-esteem.

This enrichment module is based on:

Eliot, R.S. (1994, May). Change your perceptions and lower your stress. *Soundview Executive Book Summaries, 16(5) Part 2, 6.*

2.   Individuals can cope with stress by (see Transparency 8.7):

TRANSPARENCY 8.7
(FROM TEXT MATERIAL IN THE TEXTBOOK)
INDIVIDUAL STRESS COPING METHODS

a.   Recognizing the stressors that are affecting one's life.

b.   Planning ahead and practicing good time management.

       c.   Getting plenty of exercise, eating a balanced diet, getting adequate rest, and taking care of oneself physically.

       d.   Developing a sound philosophy of life and maintaining a positive attitude.

       e.   Concentrating on balancing work life and personal life.

       f.   Learning a relaxation technique.

C.   Organizational stress coping methods.

    1.   Organizational stress coping methods are designed to reduce the harmful effects of stress in three ways (see Transparency 8.8).

       a.   Identifying and then modifying or eliminating work stressors (arrow 1 in Transparency 8.8).

       b.   Helping employees modify their perceptions and understanding of work stress (arrow 2 in Transparency 8.8).

       c.   Helping employees to cope more effectively with the consequences of stress (arrow 3 in Transparency 8.8).

TRANSPARENCY 8.8
(FIGURE 8.6 IN THE TEXTBOOK)

TARGETS OF ORGANIZATIONAL STRESS MANAGEMENT PROGRAMS

---

    2.   Stress management programs that eliminate or modify work stressors (arrow 1 in Transparency 8.8) include:

       a.   Improvements in the physical work environment.

       b.   Job redesign to eliminate stressors.

       c.   Changes in workloads and deadlines.

       d.   Structural reorganization.

       e.   Changes in work schedules, more flexible hours, and sabbaticals.

       f.   management by objectives or other goal-setting programs.

       g.   Greater levels of employee participation, particularly in planning changes that affect them.

       h.   Workshops dealing with role clarity and role analysis.

> ## TRANSPARENCY 8.9
> ### (FROM TEXT MATERIAL IN THE TEXTBOOK)
> ## ORGANIZATIONAL STRESS MANAGEMENT PROGRAMS THAT ELIMINATE OR MODIFY WORK STRESSORS

3. Stress management programs that target perceptions and experiences of stress and outcomes of stress (arrows 2 and 3 in Transparency 8.8) include:

   a. Team building.

   b. Behavior modification.

   c. Career counseling and other employee assistance programs.

   d. Workshops on time management.

   e. Workshops on job burnout to help employees understand its nature and symptoms.

   f. Training in relaxation techniques.

   g. Physical fitness or "wellness" programs. (<u>Wellness programs</u> are activities that organizations sponsor to promote good health habits or to identify and correct health problems.)

> ## TRANSPARENCY 8.10
> ### (FROM TEXT MATERIAL IN THE TEXTBOOK)
> ## ORGANIZATIONAL STRESS MANAGEMENT PROGRAMS THAT TARGET PERCEPTIONS AND EXPERIENCES OF STRESS AND OUTCOMES OF STRESS

4. Three major types of wellness programs exist.

   a. Programs that are aimed at raising awareness and providing information.

   b. Programs that involve employees in ongoing efforts to modify their life-styles.

   c. Programs that have the goal of creating an environment that will help employees maintain the healthy life-style developed in the other programs.

VII. Summing up: Why should managers be concerned about work stress?

A. A manager's primary concern in addressing work stress should be to deal with excessive stress rather than trying to find the optimum level of stress for each employee. By focusing on excessive levels of stress, managers can help to prevent significant physiological, emotional, and behavioral effects from occurring in their employees. Through such efforts, organizations may also realize improved performance and various cost savings. And, as managers try to minimize, if not eliminate, excessive levels of employee stress, they just might approach an optimum level of employee stress.

DISCUSSION QUESTIONS: SUGGESTED ANSWERS

1.   *Write a paragraph that summarizes the most important influences on how individuals experience stress.*

Students should refer to Figure 8.1 in answering this question. As shown in the figure, four primary factors determine whether an individual will experience stress in the workplace or in other situations. These factors are:

      a.   The person's perception of the situation.
      b.   The person's past experiences with reinforcement/success or punishment/failure in situations which are similar to the present situation.
      c.   The presence or absence of social support.
      d.   Individual differences with regard to stress reactions.

2.   *Explain the role of individual differences in experiencing stress.*

Individuals differ as to their personality characteristics, needs, values, attitudes, and abilities. As a result of these individual differences, what one person considers a major source of stress, another may hardly notice. Because of individual differences, the ways that individuals perceive work stressors and experience work stress will differ.

As explained in the text, personality influences how individuals are likely to perceive situations and stressors, and how they will react to these environmental stressors. According to current research, there are three major personality types that influence how an individual will experience work stress. These personality types are the Type A personality, the Type B personality, and the hardy personality. The probability that an individual might perceive a particular work situation as stressful is increased with the Type A personality but is reduced with the Type B personality and the hardy personality.

3.   *Describe some of the stressors in a job that you have held. Which were the most difficult ones to deal with? Why?*

Students should use Figure 8.2 in examining their referent job for the existence of stressors. The workload, job conditions, role conflict and ambiguity, career development, interpersonal relations in the organization, and conflict between work and other roles are the stressors which the students might consider. Also, the students should be encouraged to consider the moderating effects of perception, past experience, social support, and individual differences

4.   *Give an example of a time when the fight-or-flight response seemed particularly inappropriate for your own behavior.*

The fight-or-flight syndrome is a natural biological defense mechanism that was (and is) functional for survival. This survival reaction is composed of a series of biochemical changes which prepare an organism to deal with an environmental stressor by either confronting and fighting it or by fleeing and escaping from it. The biological changes allow the body to either fight or flee more effectively, thus increasing the chances for survival. While this response mechanism is critically important in a life-threatening situation, in many everyday work and personal situations it is generally less appropriate and contributes to the harmful effects of stress.

Most of the stressful situations which students have experienced are not life threatening and, while the body is prepared to take physical action, other behaviors are called for. Examples of situations when the fight-or-flight response is inappropriate could include the following: receiving a poor grade on an exam and yelling at the professor or a friend, or losing in a sports event and quitting the team in anger.

A sharing of individual experiences in response to this question could serve to generate class or small group discussion.

5.　*Identify the possible health consequences of excessive stress.*

Stress is linked to the following health problems: coronary heart disease, back pain, headaches, stomach and intestinal problems, various mental problems, and possibly cancer. Although it is difficult to determine the precise role stress plays in health in all individual cases, it is becoming increasingly clear that a great many illnesses are stress-related.

6.　*Describe the general relationship between performance and stress.*

The positive and negative aspects of stress are apparent in the relationship between stress and performance. The relationship is an inverted-U as can be seen in Figure 8.4. At low levels of stress, employees may not be sufficiently alert, challenged, or involved to perform at their best. Increasing amounts of stress can improve performance up to a point. An optimum level of stress probably exists for most tasks. Past this point, performance begins to deteriorate. At excessive levels of stress, employees are too agitated, aroused, or threatened to perform at their best.

7.　*Discuss the conditions and circumstances leading to job burnout.*

Job burnout refers to the adverse effects of working conditions where stressors seem unavoidable and sources of job satisfaction and relief from stress seem unavailable. In burnout the individual can no longer cope with job demands, and the willingness to even try drops dramatically.

The burnout phenomenon typically contains three components that include a state of emotional exhaustion, depersonalization of individuals being dealt with in the work setting, and feelings of low personal accomplishment. Job burnout candidates share three characteristics:

　　　　a.　　They experience a great deal of stress as a result of job-related stressors.
　　　　b.　　They tend to be idealistic and self-motivating achievers.
　　　　c.　　They often seek unattainable goals.

Most job-burnout research has focused on the human services sector of the economy called the "helping professions." Generally, burnout is thought to be more prevalent with those people who have both a high frequency and high intensity of interpersonal contact in their jobs. However, burnout may occur among any individuals who must deal extensively with other people as part of their job or who constantly face stressors with little relief.

8.   *Compare and contrast the hardy personality with the Type A personality.*

The Type A personality has four sets of behaviors and tendencies that cause stress or make stressful situations worse than they otherwise might be. The four sets of behaviors and tendencies include: time urgency, competitiveness and hostility, polyphasic behavior (*i.e.*, trying to do too many things at once), and a lack of advance planning.

The hardy personality refers to a cluster of personality characteristics that reduces the negative effects of stressful events by altering the way those events are perceived. These personality characteristics include feeling a sense of commitment, responding to each difficulty as though it is a challenge and an opportunity rather than a threat, and having a sense over control over one's life.

9.   *Design a stress management program for an organization. Justify the various components of your suggested program.*

The options which students can pursue in designing a stress management program fall into two broad categories: individual stress coping methods and organizational stress coping methods. Individual stress coping methods include:

   a.   Recognizing the stressors that are affecting one's life.
   b.   Planning ahead and practicing good time management.
   c.   Getting plenty of exercise, eating a balanced diet, getting adequate rest, and taking care of oneself physically.
   d.   Developing a sound philosophy of life and maintaining a positive attitude.
   e.   Concentrating on balancing work life and personal life.
   f.   Learning a relaxation technique.

Organizational stress coping methods include the following programs that eliminate or modify work stressors:

   a.   Improvements in the physical work environment.
   b.   Job redesign to eliminate stressors.
   c.   Changes in workloads and deadlines.
   d.   Structural reorganization.
   e.   Changes in work schedules, more flexible hours, and sabbaticals.
   f.   Management by objectives or other goal-setting programs.
   g.   Greater levels of employee participation, particularly in planning changes that affect them.
   h.   Workshops dealing with role clarity and role analysis.

Organizational stress coping methods also include programs that target perceptions and experiences of stress and outcomes of stress. Among these types of programs are the following:

   a.   Team building.
   b.   Behavior modification.
   c.   Career counseling and other employee assistance programs.
   d.   Workshops on time management.
   e.   Workshops on job burnout to help employees understand its nature and symptoms.
   f.   Training in relaxation techniques.
   g.   Physical fitness or "wellness" programs.

Students can select from this "menu" in designing a program but they should make their selections with the following goals in mind:

a.   Getting employees to understand the nature of stress and the stress response.
b.   Recognizing and then eliminating or reducing stressors in the workplace.
c.   Using appropriate coping techniques to minimize the negative consequences of stress.

DEVELOPING SKILLS—
SELF DIAGNOSIS: IDENTIFYING YOUR STRATEGIES FOR COPING WITH STRESS

This diagnostic exercise requires students to prepare essay responses to two sets of questions. One set of four questions requires students to explore a successful experience they had in coping with stress. A second set of four questions asks students to examine an unsuccessful experience they had in coping with stress. The written responses should then be analyzed in terms of how the student perceived and handled the two situations. The written responses could also be used as the basis for either a small or large group discussion.

DEVELOPING SKILLS—
A CASE IN POINT: THE STRESS OF SHIFT WORK

CASE OVERVIEW

This case focuses on stressful changes that occur when an individual switches from a daytime only work schedule to a shift work schedule. Carl Baker, a key player in this case, made such a change. His shift work at St. Regis Aluminum was based on the following cycle: two weeks of day shift (8:00 A.M. to 4:00 P.M.), two weeks of swing shift (4:00 P.M. to midnight), and two weeks of night shift (midnight to 8:00 A.M.). Then the whole cycle began again. The shift work cycle was disruptive to Carl's sleeping patterns, eating habits, family life, social relationships, and pursuit of personal interests. Carl's wife, Marilyn, and his ten-year-old son, Tom, were also negatively affected by his shift work. Marilyn was affected in terms of family and social relationships. Tom was affected by his father's absence from his Little League games.

CASE QUESTIONS

1.   *Identify the stressors that exist in this situation. Which do you think are the most important sources of stress?*

From the information given in the case, the major stressors come from the conflict between Carl's work and his personal roles (such as parent and spouse) and from life stressors such as changes in his job, eating and sleeping habits, social activities, and family life. Stresses affecting Marilyn are primarily from the conflict in her personal roles (such as parent and spouse) and from life stressors such as changes in family relationships, eating and sleeping routines, and social activities.

2.   *Can you predict other possible disruptions in the Bakers' family life that might stem from shift work?*

Other disruptions might include changes in the family's social and recreational activities, interactions and communications with each other, their roles and relationships, and the level of conflict and/or arguments they experience.

3.   *Suggest some things that St. Regis Aluminum might do to reduce stress for shift workers.*

St. Regis can target programs toward helping employees modify their perceptions and understanding of work stress and/or helping them to cope more effectively with the consequences of stress. Specifically, this might include workshops on coping with stress, training in relaxation techniques, and physical fitness or wellness programs.

4.   *Suggest some stress coping strategies that Marilyn and Carl Baker could use.*

Some suggestions for Marilyn and Carl include maintaining a positive attitude, considering the shift work to be a challenge for them to handle rather than a disaster, taking good care of themselves physically, planning ahead and practicing good time management, taking time off to enjoy themselves, and learning some relaxation techniques and exercises.

COURSE ENHANCEMENT— *WEST'S ORGANIZATIONAL BEHAVIOR CUSTOM VIDEO SERIES*

One video from *West's Organizational Behavior Custom Video Series* can be used to enhance the material in Chapter 8. This video is: *Southwest Airlines: 20th Anniversary.*

VIDEO: *SOUTHWEST AIRLINES: 20TH ANNIVERSARY*

Approximate Time: 17 minutes

Video Summary:

Southwest Airlines was founded in the early 1970s by Herb Kelleher. Mr. Kelleher's management philosophy and style is based on "having fun at work." Southwest Airlines is considered to be an innovative company with high employee morale and a strong competitive advantage. Although the airline is unionized, labor relations are among the best in the industry.

The video describes the 18-month celebration of the 20th anniversary of the airline. The video shows how the management philosophy and style of "having fun at work" permeates the organization. Southwest Airlines' employees do not seem to be having many negative work-related stressful experiences. Indeed, to the extent that stress exists, Southwest Airlines appears to be accentuating the positive. The activities sponsored by the airline are evidence of the lack of the negative aspects and the presence of the positive aspects of stress. For example, a party atmosphere is obvious at a function during which the Gatlin Brothers are entertaining employees. At another point employees are participating in a parade.

Mr. Kelleher emphasizes that he wants his employees "to have an affair of the heart with each other and with the airline customers." A symbol of this philosophy is the "Love Buck" that is printed and distributed throughout the company. Mr. Kelleher is seen as a father-figure hugging, kissing, and joking with employees and customers.

Discussion Questions and Suggested Answers for Video:

1. *What evidence exists to support the contention that Southwest Airlines' employees are able to cope effectively with whatever stressors they encounter?*

    Students can use Figure 8.1 of the text as an aid in discussing this question.

    As shown in the figure, four primary factors determine whether an individual will experience stress in the workplace or in other situations.

a.	The person's perception of the situation.
b.	The person's past experiences.
c.	The presence or absence of social support.
d.	Individual differences with regard to stress reactions.

    Based upon the video, one can surmise that Southwest's employees have positive perceptions of the situation and have had positive past experiences. Social support is definitely present and is clearly appreciated by employees throughout the organization. Insufficient data exist to comment on individual differences.

2. *Based upon the insights contained in the video, how can managers create an atmosphere that eliminates excessive stress in an organization while simultaneously capitalizing on the positive effects of stress in an organization?*

    Students could key off of Figure 8.4 in the text in answering this question. Students could argue that the philosophy of "having fun at work" keeps employees stimulated and interested while simultaneously avoiding excessive levels of stress with its associated deleterious effects. That is, stress may be at or near the optimum level for many, perhaps most, of Southwest's employees. The positive attitude which appears to be characteristic of Southwest's employees probably also contributes to experienced stress approaching, if not being in, the optimum range.

CHAPTER 9
DYNAMICS WITHIN GROUPS AND TEAMS

CHAPTER OVERVIEW

Chapter 9 begins the discussion of interpersonal and group processes by focusing on behavioral dynamics within groups or teams. The chapter begins by examining the relations between individuals and groups. Next, the chapter explores the basic nature of different types of groups as well as the stages of development these groups can go through. Then seven influences on group or team behaviors and outcomes are discussed. These influences include context, goals, size, member composition and roles, norms, cohesiveness, and leadership. Also considered is a six-phase model that can be used for improving team decision making. Finally, the nominal group technique and brainstorming are discussed as approaches for fostering team creativity.

LEARNING OBJECTIVES

Upon completion of this chapter, the students should be able to:

1. State the potential tensions between group and individual goals.
2. Define the most common types of groups and teams in organizations.
3. Express the evolving impact of groupware tools on groups and teams.
4. Describe the five-stages model of group development.
5. Discuss the key factors that influence group and team outcomes.
6. Explain the six-phase model of team decision making.
7. Apply the nominal group technique and electronic brainstorming to foster team creativity.

CHAPTER OUTLINE

I. **Preview Case:** Teams at MPI

II. Individual-Group Relations

      A.   Individualism and Collectivism
      B.   Individual and Team Goals

III.   Group Types and Development

      A.   Types of Task Groups
      B.   Types of Teams
      C.   **Managing Quality:** Teams at Mary T
      D.   Coalitions
      E.   Stages of Group Development

IV.   Influences on Groups and Teams

      A.   Context
      B.   **Managing in Practice:** Groupware at Westinghouse
      C.   **Managing Across Cultures:** Apple's Global Videoconferencing
      D.   Goals
      E.   **Managing Ethics:** Dateline Crashes
      F.   Size
      G.   Member Composition and Roles
      H.   **Managing Diversity:** United Nations at Tabra, Inc.
      I.   Norms
      J.   **Managing in Practice:** It's Only Fair
      K.   Cohesiveness
      L.   **Managing Ethics:** Beech-Nut's Groupthink
      M.   Leadership

V.   Improving Team Decision Making

      A.   Six-Phase Model
      B.   Assessment of Model
      C.   **Managing Across Cultures:** Group Meetings in China

VI.   Fostering Team Creativity

      A.   Nominal Group Technique
      B.   Brainstorming
      C.   **Managing in Practice:** Brainstorming to Action

VII.   Developing Skills

      A.   **Self Diagnosis:** People Are Electric
      B.   **A Case in Point:** Great Majestic Company

KEY WORDS AND CONCEPTS

Thirty-one key words and concepts are introduced in Chapter 9. One concept—norms—was originally introduced in Chapter 2 and is re-introduced here. The key words and concepts, along with definitions or appropriate descriptions, are as follows:

Brainstorming: a process, usually done with five to twelve people, in which individuals state as many ideas as possible during a 20 to 60-minute period.

Coacting group: a group in which the members perform their jobs relatively independently in the short run.

Coalition: a set of individuals (or organizations) who band together to pursue a specific goal.

Cohesiveness: the strength of the members' desire to remain in the group or team and their commitment to it.

Collectivism: refers to the ideas of being an integral part of the group, subordinating personal goals to group goals, showing deep concern for the welfare of the group, and showing intense emotional ties to the group.

Compliance conformity: a type of conformity that occurs when a person's behavior reflects the group's desired behavior because of real or imagined pressure.

Context: refers to the conditions and factors that represent givens for a team, including technology, physical working conditions, management practices, formal organizational rules, influences from higher management, and organizational rewards and punishments.

Counteracting group: a group in which the members interact to resolve some type of conflict, usually through negotiation and compromise.

Cross-functional teams: teams which bring together the knowledge and skills of people from various work areas to solve mutual problems.

Electronic brainstorming: makes use of computer technology to enter and automatically disseminate ideas in real time to all group members, each of whom may be stimulated to generate other ideas.

Free rider: a team member who obtains benefits from membership but does not bear a proportional share of the responsibility for generating the benefit.

Friendship group: a group that informally evolves to serve the goal of meeting its members' personal needs of security, esteem, and belonging.

Group: refers to people with shared goals who often communicate with one another over a period of time and are few enough so that each individual may communicate with all the others person-to-person.

Groupthink: refers to an agreement-at-any-cost mentality that results in ineffective team decision making and poor decisions.

Groupware: an approach to using specialized computer aids, communication tools, and designated physical facilities; thereby enabling teams to work faster, share information, make decisions, and achieve their goals.

Individualism: refers to the ideas of being distinct and separate from the group, emphasizing personal goals, and showing less concern and emotional attachment to groups, especially within work organizations.

Informal leader: an individual whose influence in the group grows over time.

Information technology: the means of assembling and electronically storing, transmitting, processing, and retrieving words, numbers, images, and sounds, as well as the electronic means for controlling machines of all kinds.

Interacting group: a group in which all members must complete their shares of the task in order for the group to accomplish its goal(s).

Nominal group technique: a structured process designed to foster creative team decision making where agreement is lacking or the members have incomplete knowledge of the nature of the problem.

Norms: are the rules and patterns of behaviors that are accepted and expected by members of a group or team.

Personal acceptance conformity: a type of conformity that occurs when the individual's behavior and attitudes are consistent with the group's norms and goals.

Problem-solving teams: teams which identify specific concerns in their areas of responsibility, develop potential solutions, and are often empowered to take action within defined limits.

Productivity: the relationship between the inputs consumed (labor hours and costs, raw materials, money, machines, and the like) and the outputs created (quantity and quality of goods and services).

Relations-oriented role: a group role that focuses on the members building team-centered tasks, sentiments, and viewpoints.

Self-managed teams: teams of employees who must work together and cooperate on a daily basis to produce an entire good (or major identifiable component) or service.

Self-oriented role: a group role that focuses only on members' individual needs, possibly at the expense of the group or team.

Task group: a group that is formally created by management to accomplish organizational goals.

Task-oriented role: a group role that focuses on members facilitating and coordinating decision-making tasks.

Team: a small number of people with complementary skills who are committed to a common purpose, set of performance goals, and approach for which they hold themselves mutually accountable.

Team goals: the end results desired for the team or group as a whole, not just those desired by the individual members.

LECTURE NOTES

I.   Chapter 9 begins the discussion of interpersonal and group processes by exploring behavioral dynamics within groups or teams. The focus of this chapter is twofold: diagnosing the functioning of groups/teams and—based upon the diagnosis—ways to improve the performance and effectiveness of groups/teams. Within this context, emphasis is placed on: relations between individuals and groups; the principal factors that affect group and team effectiveness; effective team decision-making processes; and ways to stimulate team creativity. Transparency 9.1 provides an overview of how the different chapter topics relate to the diagnosis and management of group and team dynamics.

**TRANSPARENCY 9.1
(FROM TEXT MATERIAL IN THE TEXTBOOK)**

KEY IDEAS ABOUT DIAGNOSING AND MANAGING GROUP/TEAM DYNAMICS

II.   Individual-group relations can be characterized in terms of individualism versus collectivism and individual versus group goals.

    A.   Individualism and collectivism are two cultural values that affect the use of groups and teams in organizations.

        1.   <u>Individualism</u> refers to the ideas of being distinct and separate from the group, emphasizing personal goals, and showing less concern and emotional attachment to groups, especially within work organizations.

        2.   <u>Collectivism</u> refers to the ideas of being an integral part of the group, subordinating personal goals to group goals, showing deep concern for the welfare of the group, and showing intense emotional ties to the group.

        3.   Subscribing to the cultural value of individualism does not preclude the use of groups or teams.

    B.   Individual and team goals.

        1.   Individual and team goals may be compatible or incompatible.

        2.   One type of goal incompatibility involves the <u>free rider</u>—that is, a team member who obtains benefits from membership but does not bear a proportional share of the responsibility for generating the benefit.

        3.   Free riding is most likely to occur with people who believe they should minimize their contributions in a team so long as they are not held individually accountable.

        4.   Most group members dislike free riding because it violates standards concerning equity, social responsibility, and reciprocity.

ENRICHMENT MODULE: UNDERSTANDING WORK GROUPS

According to Seth Allcorn, "A key to understanding how the organization works—or doesn't work—lies in understanding the kinds of groups that exist at work and how their dynamics influence behavior." Allcorn has developed a typology of four work groups—the homogenized group, the institutionalized group, the autocratic group, and the intentional group—that provides some interesting insights regarding group dynamics in the workplace.

From a psychological perspective, the homogenized group, the institutionalized group, and the autocratic group are "defensive"
regarding anxieties that arise from group membership. In contrast, the intentional group deals with group participation and membership in a nondefensive manner.

The following chart illustrates how members' status and roles (one of seven group culture variables considered by Allcorn) and the consequences of speaking out (one of five membership experiences variables) differ between the autocratic group and the intentional group.

	Autocratic Group	Intentional Group
Members' Status and Roles	Specific status and roles assigned; clear self-advancement guidelines not provided	Status and roles based on group and leader needs
Consequences of Speaking Out	Members fear the consequences when they can't forecast the leader's likely response	Members eagerly participate

This enrichment module is adapted from:

Allcorn, S. (1989, August). Understanding groups at work. *Personnel*, 28-36.

TRANSPARENCY 9.2
(The above chart is reproduced in the transparency package.)

III.   Types of groups and teams.

TRANSPARENCY 9.3
(FROM TEXT MATERIAL IN THE TEXTBOOK)

TYPES OF GROUPS AND TEAMS

A.   A group is comprised of people with shared goals who often communicate with one another over a period of time and are few enough so that each individual may communicate with all the others person-to-person.

B.   Groups can be classified as friendship groups or task groups.

    1.   A <u>friendship group</u> informally evolves to serve the goal of meeting its members' personal needs of security, esteem, and belonging.

    2.   A <u>task group</u> is formally created by management to accomplish organizational goals.

C.   Types of task groups.

    1.   Task groups can be classified on the basis of the relationships among group members.

    2.   A <u>counteracting group</u> exists when group members interact to resolve some type of conflict, usually through negotiation and compromise.

    3.   A <u>coacting group</u> exists when group members perform their jobs relatively independently in the short run.

    4.   An <u>interacting group</u> exists when all group members must complete their shares of the task in order for the group to accomplish its goal(s).

D.   Types of teams.

    1.   A <u>team</u> is a small number of people with complementary skills who are committed to a common purpose, set of performance goals, and approach for which they hold themselves mutually accountable. The essence of a team is the shared commitment by the members to their collective performance.

    2.   <u>Problem-solving teams</u> identify specific concerns in their areas of responsibility, develop potential solutions, and are often empowered to take action within defined limits.
        a.   Problem-solving teams fundamentally reorganize work or change the roles of managers.

    3.   <u>Cross-functional teams</u> bring together the knowledge and skills of people from various work areas to solve mutual problems.

        a.   Cross-functional teams differ from problem-solving teams in the following ways:

            (1)   Cross-functional teams have members from several departments or functions.

            (2)   Cross-functional teams deal with problems that cut across departments and functions.

            (3)   Cross-functional teams typically dissolve after the problem is solved.

    4.   <u>Self-managed teams</u> normally consist of employees who must work together and cooperate on a daily basis to produce an entire good (or major identifiable component) or service.

a.   Self-managed teams perform managerial tasks such as:

   (1)   Work and vacation scheduling.

   (2)   Rotation of job tasks and assignments among members.

   (3)   Ordering materials.

   (4)   Deciding on team leadership, which can rotate among members.

   (5)   Setting of key team goals.

   (6)   Budgeting.

   (7)   Hiring replacements for departing team members.

   (8)   Sometimes evaluating each other's performance.

b.   Self-managed teams typically eliminate one or more management levels because they are empowered to make decisions and they change how the work is organized.

ENRICHMENT MODULE: SELF-MANAGED TEAMS

Eric Gershman, president and founder of Published Image, a small financial newsletter publishing operation, revamped the organization and changed to self-managed teams to counter chronically high employee turnover, poor worker morale, poor product quality, and poor customer retention.

Now, Published Image's 26 employees are organized into four largely autonomous teams. Each team has a staff of sales, editorial, and production workers. Each team has its own clients. Each team member has specialized skills, but is capable of performing any of the team's functions. The team members determine their own work schedules, prepare budgets, and receive bonuses for team performance. Managers act in an advisory role rather than a supervisory role.

What are the effects? The customer loss rate is now less than 5% a year, compared to 33% before. Employee turnover is nonexistent.

This enrichment module is based on:

Selz, M. (1994, January 11). Testing self-managed teams, entrepreneur hopes to lose job. *The Wall Street Journal*, B1 & B2.

E.   Another type of group is the <u>coalition</u>—that is, a set of individuals (or organizations) who band together to pursue a specific goal.

   1.   Coalitions have four key features.

      a.   A coalition is deliberately created by its members.

      b.   A coalition operates independently of the formal organization.

      c.   A coalition is formed to achieve a specific and mutual goal(s).

      d.   A coalition requires united action by its members.

IV.   Stages of group development.

    A.   As shown in Transparency 9.4, groups and teams go through a five-stage developmental sequence: forming, storming, norming, performing, and adjourning.

TRANSPARENCY 9.4
(FIGURE 9.1 IN THE TEXTBOOK)

STAGES OF GROUP DEVELOPMENT

    B.   The types of task-oriented behaviors and relations-oriented behaviors differ from stage to stage (see Transparencies 9.5 and 9.6 for an overview of the behaviors at each stage).

TRANSPARENCY 9.5
(FROM TEXT MATERIAL IN THE TEXTBOOK)

TASK-ORIENTED BEHAVIORS THAT OCCUR AT EACH STAGE OF GROUP DEVELOPMENT

TRANSPARENCY 9.6
(FROM TEXT MATERIAL IN THE TEXTBOOK)

RELATIONS-ORIENTED BEHAVIORS THAT OCCUR AT EACH STAGE OF GROUP DEVELOPMENT

---

      1.   Forming.

          a.   Task-oriented behaviors focus on defining goals and developing procedures for performing their task.

          b.   Relations-oriented behaviors deal with member feelings and the tendency of most members to depend too much on one or two other members.

      2.   Storming.

          a.   Task-oriented behaviors revolve around conflicts concerning task behaviors, relative priorities of goals, who is to be responsible for what, and the task-related guidance and direction of the leader.

          b.   Relations-oriented behaviors are a mixture of expressions of hostility and strong feelings. The key is to manage conflict, not to suppress it or withdraw from it.

      3.   Norming.

          a.   Task-oriented behaviors evolve into a sharing of information, acceptance of different opinions, and positive attempts to compromise on decisions.

      b.   Relations-oriented behaviors focus on empathy, concern, and positive expressions of feelings leading to a sense of cohesion.

4.   Performing.

      a.   Task-oriented behaviors focus on the group or team showing how effectively it can achieve results.

      b.   Relations-oriented behaviors involve members understanding when they should work independently and when they should help each other.

      c.   Teams may differ after the performing stage (see the two dashed lines in Transparency 9.4). Some teams will continue to learn and develop, thereby further improving their effectiveness and efficiency. Other teams will perform only at the level needed for survival; this may be due to group norms not fully supporting the pursuit of effectiveness and efficiency, or to excessive self-oriented behavior by the group members.

5.   Adjourning.

      a.   Task-oriented behaviors are terminated.

      b.   Relations-oriented behavior are terminated.

IV.   Influences on group or team behaviors and effectiveness.

    A.   Transparency 9.7 identifies seven influences on group or team outcomes. As shown in the transparency, context and goals create the conditions within which group/team dynamics take place. Context and goals also influence group/team outcomes. Group size, member composition and roles, norms, cohesiveness, and leadership contribute to group/team behaviors and dynamics, and in turn to intergroup/team outcomes. Moreover, the seven influencing factors may also affect each other.

TRANSPARENCY 9.7
(FIGURE 9.2 IN THE TEXTBOOK)

KEY INFLUENCES ON GROUP AND TEAM OUTCOMES

    B.   Influence 1: context.

      1.   The context refers to the conditions and factors that represent givens for a team, including technology, physical working conditions, management practices, formal organizational rules, influences from higher management, and organizational rewards and punishments.

      2.   Information technology is an important contextual influence.

      3.   Information technology refers to the means of assembling and electronically storing, transmitting, processing, and retrieving words, numbers, images, and sounds, as well as the electronic means for controlling machines of all kinds.

4. Computer-based information technologies are part of <u>groupware</u>—an approach to using specialized computer aids, communication tools, and designated physical facilities, thereby enabling teams to work faster, share information, make decisions, and achieve their goals.

5. Groupware enables team members to work in the same or different locations and to perform their tasks at the same or different times. Transparency 9.8 provides examples of groupware for the following combinations of time and place: same time/same place, same time/different place, different time/same place, and different time/different place.

TRANSPARENCY 9.8
(FROM TEXT MATERIAL IN THE TEXTBOOK)

EXAMPLES OF GROUPWARE USED WITH TIME/SPACE COMBINATIONS

C. Influence 2: goals.

1. <u>Team goals</u> are the end results desired for the team or group as a whole, not just those desired by the individual members.

2. Both compatible and conflicting goals exist within a team.

D. Influence 3: size.

1. Normally, the effective size of a team ranges from two to 16 members. Twelve members is about the largest that is effective for complete person-to-person interaction.

2. Transparency 9.9, which is self-explanatory, summarizes some possible effects of size on teams.

TRANSPARENCY 9.9
(TABLE 9.2 IN THE TEXTBOOK)

SOME POSSIBLE EFFECTS OF SIZE ON TEAMS

E. Influence 4: member composition and roles.

1. Similarities and differences among individual members and their roles influence team behavior and dynamics as well as resulting outcomes.

2. Problem-solving styles influence decision making and other behaviors within groups and teams.

3. Group members can assume task-oriented, relations-oriented, and self-oriented roles (see Transparency 9.10). These roles influence members' behavior and group/team outcomes.

TRANSPARENCY 9.10
(FROM TEXT MATERIAL IN THE TEXTBOOK)

GROUP MEMBER ROLES AND SUBROLES

---

a.   The <u>task-oriented role</u> of members facilitates and coordinates decision-making tasks. This role can be divided into the following subroles: initiators, information seekers, information givers, coordinators, and evaluators.

b.   The <u>relations-oriented role</u> of members builds team-centered tasks, sentiments, and viewpoints. This role can be divided into the following subroles: encouragers, harmonizers, gatekeepers, standard setters, followers, and team observers.

c.   The <u>self-oriented role</u> focuses only on members' individual needs, possibly at the expense of the group or team. This role can be divided into the following subroles: blockers, recognition seekers, dominators, and avoiders.

d.   Effective problem-solving groups and teams have members who play both task-oriented and relations-oriented roles whereas ineffective groups and teams are likely to be dominated by individuals who primarily play self-oriented subroles.

**ENRICHMENT MODULE: DO YOU WANT TO BE THE
MICHAEL JORDAN OF BUSINESS?**

Can you become the Michael Jordan of business—an individual superstar, or will you need to be a team payer to succeed? The experts say that "to be a star among equals, be a team player." Your success will be determined by how effective you are as a team member, not by your individual accomplishments.

How can you become a more effective team member? Here are some suggestions:

- Learn how a group works and how a team goes through several stages of development before it matures.
- Learn the differences between destructive and healthy competition.
- Be recognized as a valuable resource to your team.
- Help your co-workers.
- Share information with your co-workers.
- Set personal goals which will also help your team.

This enrichment module is based on:

Schellhardt, T.D. (1994, April 20). Managing your career. *The Wall Street Journal*, B1.

---

4.   The growing diversity of the work force affects group behaviors and dynamics as well as group/team outcomes. Team effectiveness will be hampered to the extent that members have false stereotypes about each other in terms of such diversity.

F.   Influence 5: norms.

      1.   <u>Norms</u> are the rules and patterns of behaviors that are accepted and expected by members of a group or team.

      2.   Norms differ from organizational rules in that:

           a.   Rules are written, and, at times, may be unacceptable to and widely ignored by employees.

           b.   Norms may be unwritten, members must accept them and adhere to them before they can be said to exist.

      3.   Members should be aware of norms because doing so increases the potential for individual and group freedom and maturity, and norms can positively or negatively influence individual, group, and organizational effectiveness.

      4.   Teams often adopt norms to help them attain their goals.

      5.   The group's norms and goals may differ from management's standards and goals, and co-workers may have more influence than management in having employees follow certain norms and goals.

      6.   Groups and teams usually enforce norms that pertain to important behaviors such as aiding group survival and providing group benefits, simplifying or making predictable the behaviors expected of group members, and helping to avoid embarrassing interpersonal problems.

      7.   Pressures to adhere to norms may result in either compliance conformity or personal acceptance conformity.

           a.   <u>Compliance conformity</u> occurs when a person's behavior reflects the group's desired behavior because of real or imagined pressure.

           b.   <u>Personal acceptance conformity</u> occurs when the individual's behavior and attitudes are consistent with the group's norms and goals.

           c.   The individual is a true believer with personal acceptance conformity but not necessarily with compliance conformity.

G.   Influence 6: cohesiveness.

      1.   <u>Cohesiveness</u>—the strength of the members' desire to remain in the group or team and their commitment to it—is influenced by the degree of compatibility of group goals and individuals' goals.

           a.   Low cohesiveness is usually associated with low conformity while high cohesiveness may be associated with either high or low conformity.

      2.   When decision-making teams are both conforming and cohesive, groupthink may occur. <u>Groupthink</u> is an agreement-at-any-cost mentality that results in ineffective team decision making and poor decisions. Transparency 9.11 provides an excellent self-explanatory summary of the initial conditions that are likely to lead to

groupthink, the characteristics of groupthink, and the types of defective decision making that result from groupthink.

TRANSPARENCY 9.11
(FIGURE 9.3 IN THE TEXTBOOK)

MODEL OF GROUPTHINK

---

3.   The degree of cohesion is important because of its potential effects on team performance and <u>productivity</u> (*i.e.*, the relationship between the inputs consumed—labor hours and costs, raw materials, money, machines, and the like—and the outputs created—quantity and quality of goods and services).

     a.   If the team succeeds in reaching its performance goals, positive feedback on its successes may enhance cohesion.

     b.   Low cohesion may interfere with a team's ability to obtain its goals.

     c.   High cohesion may be associated with low efficiency if team goals and organizational goals are incompatible.

H.   Influence 7: leadership.

1.   Informal leaders are important in determining whether a group accomplishes its goals. An <u>informal leader</u> is an individual whose influence in the group grows over time.

2.   Multiple leaders may exist in a group or team because it has both relations-oriented and task-oriented goals.

3.   Effective team leaders influence virtually all the other factors that affect group or team behaviors (refer to Transparency 9.6).

ENRICHMENT MODULE: DYSFUNCTIONAL GROUP BEHAVIOR

When powerful individuals become committed to the achievement of predetermined goals at any cost, learning and feedback are discouraged by group members. One of the most famous examples of dysfunctional group performance is the case of the ill-fated space shuttle, Challenger.

The Challenger disaster was not the result of an unforeseeable freak hardware failure. Those capable of scrapping the Challenge launch knew beforehand of the problems that led to its ultimate destruction and loss of lives. In fact, one engineer wrote a memo that warned of a disaster if the rocket's safety seals were not fixed. Further, the investigation into the causes of the disaster was hampered by the management of Morton Thiokol Inc., the engineering company that made the boosters. Morton Thiokol's management punished and coerced those group members (engineers) who could and did give information to the presidential panel investigating the accident.

This enrichment module is based on:

Morgan, G. (1990). The Challenger disaster: A case of discouraged feedback. *Creative organization theory.* Newbury Park, CA: Sage.

V.   Improving team decision making.

    A.   Team decision making is likely to be superior to individual decision making when:

        1.   The greater diversity of information, experience, and approaches to be found in a team are important to the issues at hand.

        2.   The acceptance of the decisions arrived at is crucial for effective implementation by team members.

        3.   Participation is important for reinforcing the democratic values of representation versus authoritarianism, and for demonstrating respect for team members through team processes.

        4.   The team members rely on each other in performing their jobs.

    B.   Once the judgement has been made that team decision making is appropriate, a six-phase model (see Transparency 9.12) can be used to help the team become more effective in its decision making.

TRANSPARENCY 9.12
(FIGURE 9.4 IN THE TEXTBOOK)

TEAM DECISION-MAKING MODEL

---

    1.   Phase I: problem definition.

        a.   In this phase, the team should fully explore, clarify, and define the problem.

        b.   The generation and collection of information is a key part of Phase I.

c.   Another critical aspect of Phase I is recognizing the goals the team is trying to achieve by solving the problem.

2.   Phase II: solution generation.

a.   This phase prolongs the idea-generating process and discourages premature conclusions.

3.   Phase III: ideas to action.

a.   In this phase, the team evaluates ideas and comes up with a likely solution.

b.   Good parts of various ideas should be combined before carefully evaluating each alternative.

c.   The team should select the best alternatives and concentrate on them until everyone can agree on a solution or recognize there is a need to move on in the process.

4.   Phase IV: action planning.

a.   In this phase, the team anticipates implementation problems, makes plans to involve those whose support will be needed, and assigns and accepts action responsibilities.

5.   Phase V: evaluation planning.

a.   Teams may stop at this phase, losing the chance to learn from the experience.

b.   A team benefits from knowing why a solution worked so that it can be repeated, and why a solution didn't work so the same mistakes won't be made in the future.

c.   In order to take advantage of the potential for learning in this phase, a team must determine what kind of evaluation information is needed, who will obtain it, and when it must be collected.

6.   Phase VI: outcome evaluation.

a.   In this phase, the team can see the outcomes and whether the problem was solved. If the problem or some part of it remains, the team can recycle through the process.

b.   Phase VI also involves a review and evaluation of how well the team members worked together.

C.   Assessment of the six-phase model.

1.   Team decision making is usually messier than the neat, systematic progression of steps described in the six-phase model. Rather, teams often jump around or skip phases.

2. Following the model as closely as possible should improve the effectiveness of decision making in most teams.

3. Teams are probably more effective in Phases III, IV, and V than in Phases I, II, and VI.

VI. Fostering team creativity.

A. The nominal group technique and brainstorming are two approaches that can be used to foster creativity in Phase I, Phase II, and the initial part of Phase III of the six-phase team decision-making model.

B. Nominal group technique (NGT).

1. The <u>nominal group technique</u> is a structured process designed to foster creative team decision making where agreement is lacking or the members have incomplete knowledge of the nature of the problem.

2. The NGT is most useful for:

a. Identifying the critical variable in a specific situation.

b. Identifying the key elements of a plan designed to implement a particular solution to some problem.

c. Establishing priorities with regard to the problem to be addressed and goals to be attained.

3. The NGT is not very useful for:

a. Routine team meetings that focus primarily on task coordination or information exchange.

b. Negotiating that takes place in counteracting groups.

4. The NGT consists of four distinct stages.

a. Generating ideas: each participant, working alone, writes down ideas in response to a statement of a problem, a stimulus question, or some other central focus of the team.

b. Recording ideas: the ideas generated in stage 1 are recorded in a round-robin fashion.

c. Clarifying ideas: each idea on the listed generated in stage 2 is discussed to present the logic and thinking behind the ideas and to reduce misunderstanding.

d. Voting on ideas: some voting procedure is used to determine the outcome of the process—namely, a decision that incorporates the individual judgments of the participants.

5.   Assessment of the NGT.

    a.   Advantages include the emphasis on and attention to idea generation, increased attention that is paid to each idea, and the balanced participation and presentation by each member.

    b.   The NGT may be disadvantageous when problem identification is performed by people who are aware of existing problems and who are willing to communicate to others about them.

C.   Brainstorming.

1.   Traditionally, <u>brainstorming</u> is a process, usually done with five to twelve people, in which individuals state as many ideas as possible during a 20 to 60-minute period. Traditional brainstorming is done on a face-to-face basis.

    a.   The key guidelines for brainstorming include the following:

        (1)   The wilder the ideas the better.

        (2)   Don't be critical of any ideas.

        (3)   Hitchhike on or combine previously stated ideas.

    b.   Traditional brainstorming has not been exceptionally effective for generating ideas because of the cumbersome nature of the face-to-face process or people's inhibitions in the face-to-face process.

2.   <u>Electronic brainstorming</u> makes use of computer technology to enter and automatically disseminate ideas in real time to all group members, each of whom may be stimulated to generate other ideas.

    a.   Preliminary research indicates that electronic brainstorming is superior to traditional brainstorming in generating new ideas, perhaps because of the anonymity which electronic brainstorming permits.

VII.   Summing up: What are the practical organizational behavior implications of dynamics within groups and teams?

A.   People cannot escape groups in most work organizations. There are very few occupations where interaction with other people is nonexistent or almost so. Some jobs that might qualify for exceptionally limited human interaction include a forest ranger on fire-watch duty in a remote area or the sole night janitor at a restaurant. But for most of the work force, groups are an inevitable fact of occupational life. Because work groups are so pervasive in organizations, they can have very powerful effects on people's behavior. In turn, the ways in which people behave will affect how effectively and efficiently the organization will operate.

B.   By properly diagnosing and managing group/team dynamics, members of an organization can increase the likelihood that individuals, groups, and the entire organization will function more effectively.

DISCUSSION QUESTIONS: SUGGESTED ANSWERS

1. *Think about a team of which you have been a member. Was there any evidence of free riders on the team? Why were behaviors associated with free riding present or not present?*

A free rider is a team member who obtains benefits from membership but does not bear a proportional share of the responsibility for generating the benefit. Students probably will be very familiar with free riders from their experiences with groups that have been assembled for class projects. The students' answers should focus on the free rider's specific behaviors, the methods the group members used to cope with these behaviors, and the actions that could can prevent future occurrences of these behaviors.

In discussing the free rider phenomenon, students should consider the extent to which the group held its individual members accountable. They should also explore the extent to which the group's members disliked free riding because it violated standards concerning equity, social responsibility, and reciprocity.

2. *For the same team, was there any evidence that the team evolved according to the five-stage developmental sequence (see Figure 9.1)?*

Groups experiencing free riders have not progressed past the storming stage of development. In this stage, conflicts emerge over task behaviors and task responsibilities. Often the group suppresses conflict rather than learning to manage conflict. The suppressing of conflict is likely to create bitterness and resentment that leads to failure.

3. *What were the effects of the size of that team in terms of the dimensions shown in Table 9.2? Were these effects consistent with those predicted in Table 9.2?*

Table 9.2 identifies the following six dimensions which vary according to team size:

   a.   demands on the leader;
   b.   direction by the leader;
   c.   members' tolerance of direction from the leader;
   d.   inhibition in participation by ordinary members;
   e.   formalization of rules and procedures; and
   f.   the time required for reaching judgment decisions.

Three categories of team size are identified;

   a.   two to seven members;
   b.   eight to twelve members; and
   c.   thirteen to sixteen members.

The discussion should focus on how the predicted effects should change as team size increases, and whether the students' actual group experiences are consistent or inconsistent with these predicted effects.

4. *Was this a self-managed team? Use Table 9.1 to explain your answer.*

A self-managed team normally consists of five to fifteen members who work together on a daily basis to produce an entire good (or major identifiable component) or service. The typical classroom student group is not characterized by this type of working relationship. However, students with work experience may have encountered a self-managed team.

Table 9.1 contains a twelve-item questionnaire for assessing team or group autonomy. With this questionnaire, the students will be able to determine whether autonomy and responsibility on several issues and decisions resides with the team or with higher management. Autonomy and responsibility residing with the team constitutes evidence that it is a self-managed team.

5.   *Describe the context of another group or team of which you have been a member in terms of technology, organizational rules, influence of higher level management, and organizational rewards and punishments. In what ways did the context appear to affect the group's or team's dynamics or outcomes?*

Students' answers need to be directed toward conditions and factors outside the group that it cannot directly control. When responses are compared, students will be able to see how context differences can affect the group's behavior and effectiveness.

6.   *What were the formal and informal goals of this team or group? Were the informal goals consistent and supportive of the formal goals? Explain.*

Formal group goals could be labeled "team goals"—that is, they are the end results desired for the team or group as a whole, not just those desired by each individual member. Informal goals are more likely to reflect the end results desired by one person or a clique within the team. In their discussion, the students should differentiate between the goals of individuals or subgroups and the goals of the entire team.

The issue of conflicting goals is very familiar to those having experience with student project groups. Most likely, students will have excellent examples of being in a group where some members were striving for an "A" grade and were very task oriented while others were in the group for social reasons and were very relations oriented.

7.   *How would you describe this group or team as a whole in terms of task-oriented behaviors, relations-oriented behaviors, and self-oriented behaviors? Which of the behaviors seemed to contribute most to its performance? The least?*

Task-oriented behaviors include initiating, seeking information, giving information, coordinating, and evaluating. Relations-oriented behaviors include encouraging, harmonizing, gatekeeping, standard setting, following, and observing. Self-oriented behaviors include blocking, recognition seeking, dominating, and avoiding. These specific behaviors should be used in characterizing the referent group or team.

8.   *State three norms of a task group of which you have been a member. Did you or other members conform to these norms on the basis of compliance or personal acceptance? How did this conformity affect behavior? Explain.*

Norms are the rules and patterns of behaviors that are accepted and expected by members of a team or group. Examples from classroom task groups may involve issues such as attendance, shared leadership, equal division of responsibilities, suppression of disagreement and conflict, sitting together during class, and sharing information about common interests.

Compliance conformity occurs when a person's behavior becomes or remains similar to the group's desired behavior because of real or imagined group pressure. Personal acceptance conformity occurs when the individual's behavior and attitudes or beliefs are consistent with the group's norms and goals. These two types of conformity should be linked to the students' specific group experiences.

Students may be reluctant to discuss their conformity depending on whether norms of openness have been established in class.

9.   *The team decision-making model (see Figure 9.4) presents a phased sequence by which teams should proceed. How may the factors identified in Figure 9.2 help to work for or against the implementation of this model?*

The seven factors that influence group behaviors and effectiveness include context, goals, size, member composition and roles, norms, cohesiveness, and leadership.

Some examples of how these factors may work for the implementation of the decision-making model include the following:

    a.   Group norms may support nonjudgmental sharing of ideas in the problem definition and solution generation phases.

    b.   Group members may minimize their self-oriented behaviors throughout all phases of the decision-making process, thereby keeping the focus on the group's interests and goals.

    c.   Each phase could be helped if the group members tailor their task-oriented behaviors and relations-oriented behaviors to the demands of that particular phase.

A few examples of how these factors may work against the implementation of the decision-making model include the following:

    a.   The problem definition phase may be hindered if the group doesn't identify or recognize its goals.

    b.   Group size may impede problem generation in the problem definition phase. A very small group may not have the resources to generate a number of good ideas.

    c.   Group members who have very divergent problem-solving styles may impede the decision-making process at all stages.

10.   *What are the similarities and differences between the nominal group technique (NGT) and electronic brainstorming?*

Both NGT and electronic brainstorming are approaches for stimulating group creativity and are designed to help both group members and leaders become more effective. NGT is a structured process designed to stimulate creative group decision making where agreement is lacking or the members have incomplete knowledge concerning the nature of the problem. Electronic brainstorming makes use of computer technology to enter and automatically disseminate ideas in real time to all group members, each of whom may be stimulated to generate other ideas.

DEVELOPING SKILLS—
SELF DIAGNOSIS: PEOPLE ARE ELECTRIC

This self-diagnosis exercise focuses on how the members of a group make judgments or decisions. The activity has three primary goals: (1) to encourage the team participants to think creatively; (2) to help the participants to discover heuristics (rules of thumb) in their thinking patterns; and (3) to improve team effectiveness by uncovering judgmental thinking and biases.

To achieve these goals, the class is divided into small groups of approximately five members each. Working alone, the team members answer the following scenario questions:

> What if human beings were electrically powered rather than having their energy supplied through food, water, and rest? How would your personal life be affected? How would your professional life be affected? How would the following areas be changed: Employment? Education? Family? Leisure activities? Government programs? Global affairs? Other?

Then as a team, the members discuss the individual answers and try to reach a consensus. Finally, the team examines how it reached a consensus and how its decision-making process reflected the task-oriented, relations-oriented, and self-oriented behaviors that are described in Table 9.3 of the text.

DEVELOPING SKILLS—
A CASE IN POINT: GREAT MAJESTIC COMPANY

CASE OVERVIEW

This case focuses on the actions taken by seven bellmen at Great Majestic Lodge (GML) in response to the treatment they received from one of the tour operators who brought guests to the lodge. The key players in the case are: Susan Hoffman, manager of GML; Bob Tomblin, general manager of several recreational and lodging facilities in the area, including GML; the seven bellmen at GML; Mr. Sirkin, a tour director for the Jones Transportation Agency; and Mr. Grant Cole, president of the Jones Transportation Agency.

Like most of the employees at GML, the bellmen were college students. However, before being chosen to be bellmen, they must have worked for the company for three summers. Because of the importance of the bellmen to GML's guest relations, Mr. Tomblin chose the bellmen himself. He selected them on the basis of their past work performance, loyalty, efficiency, and ability to work with the public. The bellmen, a close-knit group, were paid $2.00 per hour plus tips. Tips, which constituted the biggest portion of the bellmen's pay, were pooled and divided equally among the seven bellmen at the end of each week.

Because of its size and accommodations, GML was a favorite spot for large, organized tours. The bellmen had the responsibility of placing the tour luggage in guest rooms as soon as the bus arrived, and retrieving the bags from guest rooms and loading the bus on the morning of departure. For this service, tour directors paid a standard gratuity of 75¢ per bag.

However, on one visit to GML Mr. Sirkin, a tour director, did not pay the gratuity, which would have amounted to approximately $90. GML's bellmen discovered from bellmen at other nearby resorts that Sirkin had not paid the standard gratuity there either. The GML bellmen decided that some action had to be taken but ruled out telling their boss, Susan Hoffman, because of her failure to deal with problems on prior occasions. Instead, they wrote a letter to Grant Cole, explaining the Sirkin incident. The bellmen reasoned that Mr. Cole would want to know about this because the Jones Transportation Agency had a reputation of being fair and equitable with their tips. Mr. Cole then informed Mr. Tomblin, a good personal friend, about the letter. Tomblin was enraged because the bellmen had violated company policy by not going through the chain of command. Tomblin demanded that Hoffman take some quick action in dealing with the seven bellmen.

CASE QUESTIONS

1. *What social influences and norms appear to have played a part in the behaviors of the bellmen?*

   A large number of social factors and norms appear to play a role in this case. Some of the more pertinent ones are as follows:

   a. The bellmen are college students working for the summer, thus they are temporary employees.
   b. The bellmen must have worked at the lodge for three summers and were chosen by Tomblin based on a number of factors.
   c. The bellmen had been especially productive and effective.
   d. There was a strong norm (expectation) of tips for good service.
   e. The bellmen were responding in terms of the norm of justice (equity) with a desire to "right" the "wrong" of the tour director.
   f. The bellmen lived and ate together in company facilities and were a highly cohesive group. They were well liked by other employees. In sum, the bellmen were a close-knit group from both task-oriented and relations-oriented perspectives.
   g. In the past, the bellmen had good relations with Tomblin.
   h. The role of the bellman was a highly prestigious position at the lodge.
   i. The bellmen felt they could apply pressure through the united act of sending a letter.
   j. They had access to outside information which enabled them, to collect data regarding Sirkin's behavior at other resorts.

2. *What contextual influences and goals are relevant in this situation to (1) the bellmen, (2) Hoffman, and (3) Tomblin?*

   From a task standpoint, the bellmen are in a critical role at the lodge. They help fulfill the following key tasks:

   a. They are key representatives of the lodge and are among the first individuals greeting guests; thus, impressions of the lodge are heavily influenced by the bellmen.
   b. They are an important public relations force for the lodge, not just a set of individuals who transfer luggage from one point to another.
   c. They have demonstrated the ability to provide prompt, professional service to the guests. Thus, from a task perspective, they have been effective and are viewed as such by higher management.
   d. They have shown flexibility in the tasks they perform by handling a wide range of special requests by the guests and the hotel management.

   Some of the organizational factors that appear to be relevant in this situation are as follows:

a.   The lodge is in a remote location and it is difficult to replace workers, especially those who are bellmen because long-term service is viewed as a prerequisite for effectiveness.

b.   The lodge serves many large, organized tours which represent good moneymakers for Great Majestic. Thus, management is sensitive in not wanting to upset representatives of these tours.

c.   The bellmen had a common set of interests by virtue of the organizational arrangement of pooling and dividing up tips. Thus, Sirkin's behavior represented a threat and cost to all of the bellmen. Moreover, there was the potential threat of other tour directors getting the idea that they could shirk on tips to the bellmen.

d.   From an organization standpoint, the bellmen skipped over their supervisor and made direct contact with an important outside customer with no knowledge of it by higher levels of management personnel.

e.   Hoffman's job is threatened by higher management.

f.   Hoffman is viewed as not evaluating the bellmen's problems.

g.   Tomblin is personally enraged and humiliated and is carrying the threat to his self-esteem into the threat of using formal organizational power, including dismissal, as a response.

3.   *What should Hoffman do? Why?*

Some of Hoffman's options include the following: demand an apology, reduce pay, fire and demote individuals, tell Tomblin to simply forget the incident, and so on. Some of the key issues, out of the many issues, that deserve particular attention include:

a.   The workers are in an isolated location, they are difficult to replace, they are experienced, and they had performed well.

b.   Hoffman had been viewed as not providing support in problem areas.

c.   Hoffman must share with Tomblin his decision regarding the action to be taken. At this point, it might be useful to ask the students how they feel about Tomblin. What do they think his reaction would be to a "soft" action?

The following is what actually happened. In a discussion with the bellmen, Hoffman decided to suspend each worker for one week without pay, but let each of them retain their share of the daily tips (the larger source of income anyway). Hoffman could thereby report back to Tomblin that the bellmen were each "laid off without pay for one week." This action helped Hoffman to establish a greater sense of trust with the bellmen.

The responses to the above questions have been expanded on from the notes provided in the following source: Baker, R.Z., Stout, M.K., Ulich, D., & Patterson, K. (1984). *Instructors manual to accompany Ritchie and Thompson's organization and people: Readings, cases, and exercises* (3rd ed.). St.Paul, West Publishing Company, 109-110.

COURSE ENHANCEMENT—
WEST'S ORGANIZATIONAL BEHAVIOR CUSTOM VIDEO SERIES

One video from *West's Organizational Behavior Custom Video Series* can be used to enhance the material in Chapter 9. This video is: *KL Spring and Stamping Company.*

VIDEO: KL SPRING AND STAMPING COMPANY

Approximate Time: 5 minutes

Video Summary:

KL Spring and Stamping Company, a supplier of springs to the auto industry, was losing business to imports. High prices, mediocre quality, and late deliveries plagued KL. Moreover, in the early 1980s the auto industry was changing significantly and rapidly, with increasing emphasis on price, quality, just-in-time delivery of inventory to the auto manufacturers, and technical support for the auto manufacturers. Also, springs were being replaced with electronic components, and KL forecast a 50-75% decline in demand for its product.

KL Spring and Stamping found that the solutions to its problems were on the factory floor—the production employees. According to the company's management, there was a library of knowledge out on the factory floor, just waiting to be accessed.

KL management re-oriented its thinking and developed a new mission statement to guide them in solving their problems as well as in future operations. The new mission statement—"We want to be known as a manufacturer of quality who produces springs as a by-product"—was an effective catalyst. The company implemented quality circles, getting production employees actively involved in the process. Since employees knew more about the production problems than management, they also had greater potential to solve them. Quality has improved immensely; among its various accolades, KL received the GM Mark of Excellence Award. KL no longer has a separate inspection department because all the employees are so highly committed to quality. Part of the cost savings that are achieved as a result of the quality circle efforts are shared with the employees in the form of monetary incentives.

Discussion Questions and Suggested Answers for Video:

1.　*What are some of the principal insights to be gained from the video?*

　　Some of the insights that students might suggest are:

　　　　a.　Employees possess much knowledge that could be very useful to the employer but which is all too often left untapped by the employer.
　　　　b.　Given a chance, most employees will respond with ideas that help the company.
　　　　c.　A clear vision and mission statement facilitates significant organizational changes.
　　　　d.　Quality must be paramount for a business to survive, let alone thrive, in a highly competitive industry.
　　　　e.　Using quality circles is an effective way to foster employee involvement.

2.　*Refer to the seven influences on group and team outcomes that are identified in Figure 9.2. Which of these influences enabled the quality circles to become effectively functioning groups?*

　　Management significantly altered the context for group behavior at KL Spring and Stamping. Context includes technology, physical working conditions, management practices, formal organizational rules, influences of higher management, and organizational rewards and punishments. In the case of KL Spring and Stamping, the following contextual features were changed:

　　　　a.　Management realized that it was not tapping the wealth of knowledge that existed among its employees.
　　　　b.　Quality products became paramount to compete effectively in the automotive

supply market.

c.   Management developed a new mission statement to guide the company's operations.

d.   Management implemented an incentive system which rewarded employees with a portion of the savings realized from the ideas generated by the quality circles.

Management also altered the company's goals. The company became customer-oriented, providing what the marketplace wanted. As reflected in the new mission statement, quality became the dominant goal.

COURSE ENHANCEMENT— *SUPPLEMENTAL VIDEOS AVAILABLE FROM WEST*

A video from the Association for Manufacturing Excellence and made available through West Publishing Company can be used to enhance the material in Chapter 9. This video is: *Self-Directed Work Teams—Passing the Baton.*

VIDEO: AME: SELF-DIRECTED WORK TEAMS—PASSING THE BATON

Approximate Time: 51 minutes

Video Summary:

Self-directed work teams provide a means for transferring authority, responsibility, and accountability from management to work teams. This video examines how self-directed work teams operate at four different companies: Northern Telecom, GM Delco, SCO (Santa Cruz Operations), and XEL Communications.

At Northern Telecom, work teams have provided a framework to act on ideas and improvements in achieving zero defects. In order to be successful, interpersonal skills training was needed to help teams learn to reach a decision. At one time employees were unaware of how their efforts impacted final product quality, but now employees receive meaningful daily feedback. Operators are now encouraged to ask any questions they feel are important, and communications between employees and management have improved greatly.

GM Delco is a union shop in Dayton, Ohio that makes components for anti-lock brake systems. The move toward self-directed work teams has changed the adversarial working relationships that typify a union environment. Employee work teams were empowered to make decisions. Advisors, the new title for supervisors, were consulted only if the work team could not reach a decision. Communications and relationships between hourly and salaried employees have improved. Also, employees are perceived as being more caring and committed to the company.

SCO, a publisher and distributor of software, is located in Santa Cruz, California and has a very diverse, transient work force. The company used self-directed work teams to stabilize the work force. The advantages of the teams at SCO have been improved communication, more caring employees, freedom to experiment, and the generation of new ideas. Employees are able to see the "whole picture" and operations have become more efficient as a result.

XEL Communications, an Aurora, California based manufacturer of voice and data transmission equipment, faced the competitive need to respond quickly to customer orders. XEL met this competitive challenge by instituting self-managed teams. This segment explains how self-directed work teams can create conflict and how conflict can be diagnosed and resolved. Conflict within and between self-directed work teams is to be expected, but it must be resolved. If it is not resolved, team spirit can be destroyed.

This video also contains a roundtable discussion, involving people from Northern Telecom, GM Delco, SCO, and XEL Communications. This discussion brings out some key points about self-managed work teams. Included among the key points are the following:

1. How self-directed teams operate is a function of the dynamics of leadership of a particular company.
2. Self-directed teams should evolve from the philosophy that the person doing the job knows the most about the job and should make most of the decisions regarding the job.
3. Generally, people who don't want teamwork will leave the organization voluntarily.
4. Some people don't want to participate; other people don't know how to participate. Some people may take a longer time before they want to participate.
5. Sometimes front-line managers fear that self-directed work teams will eliminate their jobs.
6. Front-line managers need to learn that their role is different with self-directed work teams—they cease being supervisors and become coaches and facilitators.
7. Letting go of authority and responsibility is as difficult for front-line managers as picking up authority and responsibility is for production employees.
8. Self-managed teams should be allowed to fail in order for them to learn and develop.
9. Just as managers in their new roles should guide team members, team members should help the managers stay with the new role behaviors.
10. Everyone should operate on the premise of helping each other.
11. Mutual trust between nonsupervisory employees and management is absolutely essential.
12. The leader must believe in the value of self-managed teams.
13. Boundaries and guidelines need to be set regarding the extent of the self-directed work team's authority and responsibility.
14. People need to be trained—especially in people skills—in order to participate effectively.
15. Team meetings should remain focused on improving the business.

Perhaps the narrator of the video provided the best summary of the important lessons to be gained from the four companies—trust, commitment, and enthusiasm must be maintained without slippage for self-managed work teams to take hold.

Discussion Questions and Suggested Answers for Video:

1. *Using the seven influences on group and team outcomes that are identified in Figure 9.2, analyze the functioning of the self-managing work teams at Northern Telecom, GM Delco, SCO (Santa Cruz Operations), and XEL Communications.*

The seven influences in Figure 9.2 are context, goals, group size, member composition and roles, norms, cohesiveness, and leadership. Listed below are some examples which students might cite in responding to this question.

   a. *At Northern Telecom:* context variable of management practices (*e.g.*, employees now receive daily feedback); and change in member composition and roles (*e.g.*, operators are now encouraged to ask any questions they feel are important, communications between employees and management have improved greatly).
   b. *At GM Delco:* member composition and roles (*e.g.*, employee work teams were empowered to make decisions, advisors were consulted only if the work team could not reach a decision); norms (*e.g.*, change in the adversarial working

relationships that typify a union environment); and cohesiveness (*e.g.,* employees are perceived as being more caring and committed to the company).

c.   *At SCO:* member composition and roles (*e.g.,* improved communication, freedom to experiment, employees are able to see the "whole picture"); and cohesiveness (*e.g.,* more caring employees).

d.   *At XEL Communications:* goals (*e.g.,* the need for resolving goal conflicts and other conflicts that occur between teams).

2.   *Discuss the different purposes for which self-directed work teams can be used.*

Self-directed work teams were used for a different purpose at each of the companies featured in the video. At Northern Telecom, self-directed work teams have provided a framework to act on ideas and improvements in achieving zero defects. At GM Delco, the move toward self-directed work teams has changed the adversarial working relationships that characterized the union environment. At SCO, self-directed work teams were used to stabilize a very diverse, transient work force. At XEL Communications, self-directed work teams were implemented to meet the competitive need to respond quickly to customer orders.

3.   *The roundtable discussion at the end of the video identifies numerous insights about the implementation and continuing operation of self-managed work teams. Which of these insights do you consider to be most important? Why?*

The 15 key points listed in the accompanying video summary identify the video's key insights about self-managed work teams. The class should bring up most, if not all, of these points prior to discussing which ones are most important.

CHAPTER 10
DYNAMICS BETWEEN GROUPS AND TEAMS

CHAPTER OVERVIEW

Chapter 10 continues the exploration of group dynamics but shifts the focus from dynamics within groups/teams to dynamics between groups/teams. Two major topics are considered in this chapter. The first major topic concerns the seven basic influences on outcomes between groups/teams. These influences are: uncertainty, goals, attitudinal sets, diversity, task relations, resource sharing, and substitutability. The second major topic involves seven approaches for fostering effective dynamics and outcomes between interdependent groups/teams. These approaches are: dialogue, superordinate group goals and rewards, plans and hierarchy, linking roles, cross-functional teams, integrating roles and teams, and groupware.

LEARNING OBJECTIVES

Upon completion of this chapter, the students should be able to:

1. State how the interactions between groups and teams impact their performance.
2. Explain how certain key influences affect the dynamics and outcomes between groups and teams.
3. Diagnose the cause of cooperative versus competitive relations between groups and teams.
4. Describe several approaches that can be used to foster effective outcomes between groups and teams.

CHAPTER OUTLINE

I.   **Preview Case:** Developing Aurora

II.   Key Influences on Outcomes

KEY WORDS AND CONCEPTS

Twenty-three key words and concepts are introduced in Chapter 10. The key words and concepts, along with definitions or appropriate descriptions, are as follows:

Attitudinal sets: the thoughts and feelings—either positive or negative—that members of two or more groups have toward each other.

Boundary-spanning roles: roles which provide specialized links to other teams or organizations and are often essential for facilitating information flow and decision making.

Dependent task relations: exist when one group has the ability and power to determine the behaviors and outputs of the other groups.

Dialogue: a process whereby people suspend their defensive exchanges to allow a free flow of inquiry into their own and others' assumptions and beliefs.

Effect uncertainty: the inability to predict the impact of a future state of the environment on the individual, team, or organization.

Goal conflict: occurs when one group's goals are viewed by one or more other groups as preventing them from attaining most or all of their goals.

Group identification: refers to the idea that one's own identity, and thus the perception of others' identity, is defined (at least in part) by reference to who is in or out of various groups/teams.

Hierarchy: allows the coordination of groups/teams through the participation of a common manager.

Independent task relations: exist when few, if any, interactions are needed between two groups or those that do occur take place at the discretion of the two groups.

Integrating roles: roles which are performed by employees who are permanently assigned to help teams work together.

Interdependent task relations: exist when collaboration, integration, and mutual decision making are necessary and desirable between groups in order for them to achieve their own goals.

Linking roles: roles which are performed by individuals in specialized positions who facilitate communication and problem solving between interdependent teams.

Loose coupling: occurs when groups affect each other occasionally (rather than constantly), negligibly (rather than significantly), and indirectly (rather than directly).

Planning: a process which develops an organization's, team's, or individual's destination (vision and goals), strategies for getting there, targets for achievement by specific dates, anticipated obstacles, and alternatives for dealing with those obstacles.

Positive multiculturalism: the condition in which an individual acquires new skills, perspectives, and attitudes that improve one's chances of relating effectively to members of other groups.

Resource sharing: the degree to which two or more groups must obtain needed goods or services from a common group and the degree to which these goods or services are adequate to meet the needs of all the groups.

Response uncertainty: the lack of knowledge of alternatives and/or the inability to predict the likely consequences of alternatives.

State uncertainty: an individual, team, or organization does not understand how factors in the environment might change.

Substitutability: the degree to which one group can obtain the services or goods provided by another group from alternative sources.

Superordinate group goals: ends that two or more groups might pursue but which can't be achieved without their cooperation.

Superordinate group rewards: the benefits received by members of the cooperating groups that are partially determined by the results of their joint efforts.

Uncertainty: the inability to predict something accurately.

Uncertainty absorption: occurs when one team makes particular decisions for another team or sets the decision-making guidelines for another team.

LECTURE NOTES

I.   Background on interteam dynamics.

    A.   The ability to diagnose and manage interteam relations is important for three reasons:

        1.   Teams must often work through and with other teams to accomplish their goals.

        2.   Teams within the organization often create problems for and demands on other teams.

        3.   The quality of interteam dynamics can affect an organization's effectiveness.

    B.   As shown in Transparency 10.1, two major topics are considered in the context of interteam dynamics. The first major topic concerns the seven basic influences on outcomes between groups/teams. The second major topic involves seven approaches for fostering effective dynamics and outcomes between interdependent groups/teams.

TRANSPARENCY 10.1
(FROM TEXT MATERIAL IN THE TEXTBOOK)

KEY IDEAS ABOUT DIAGNOSING AND MANAGING INTERTEAM DYNAMICS

ENRICHMENT MODULE: LIFE IN THE "SKUNK WORKS"

Ford Motor Company assembled a team of approximately 400 people to redesign the Ford Mustang, trying to create a product that would "stir the soul" but do so on a skinflint budget. To achieve their goal, "Team Mustang" broke many of the rules that had previously governed product development at Ford, a rigidly disciplined organization.

Prompted by federal legislation on passive restraints, a small group of Ford managers were given the assignment of redesigning the Mustang. But many skeptics at Ford didn't consider saving the Mustang to be worth the cost. Instead, they wanted to terminate production of the Mustang.

On a virtual crusade, that small group of managers formed a "skunk works" development team. They devised a new product development approach which focused on a highly integrated team. "The plan called for putting everyone involved under one roof—draftsmen sitting next to 'bean counters,' engineers one room away from stylists. That meant breaching the budgetary walls that divided departments and persuading department managers to cede some control over to their subordinates." Team Mustang also received the unprecedented freedom to make decisions without waiting for corporate headquarters' approval. Suppliers were selected from the best available and were asked to join the Mustang development process from the start.

According to Ford officials, "the Mustang was redone in three years for about $700 million. That is 25% less time and 30% less money than for any comparable new car program in Ford's recent history."

This enrichment module is based on:

White, J.B., & Suris, O. (1993, September 21). New pony: How a 'skunk works' kept Mustang alive—on a tight budget. *The Wall Street Journal*, A1 & A12.

II.   Key influences on outcomes between groups or teams.

   A.   Transparency 10.2 (Figure 10.1) identifies seven key influences on the outcomes of interacting groups or teams. As shown in the transparency, uncertainty and goals create the situational context within which intergroup/team dynamics take place. Uncertainty and goals also influence intergroup/team outcomes. Attitudinal sets, diversity, task relations, resource sharing, and substitutability contribute to intergroup/team behaviors and dynamics, and in turn to intergroup/team outcomes. Moreover, the seven influencing factors may also affect each other.

TRANSPARENCY 10.2
(FIGURE 10.1 IN THE TEXTBOOK)

KEY INFLUENCES ON OUTCOMES BETWEEN GROUPS AND TEAMS

   B.   Influence 1: uncertainty.

   1.   <u>Uncertainty</u> is the inability to predict something accurately.

   2.   Three types of uncertainty are relevant to individuals and teams in organizations.

a.   State uncertainty which means that an individual, team, or organization does not understand how factors in the environment might change.

b.   Effect uncertainty which is the inability to predict the impact of a future state of the environment on the individual, team, or organization.

c.   Response uncertainty which is the lack of knowledge of alternatives and/or the inability to predict the likely consequences of alternatives.

3.   Uncertainty can be managed through uncertainty absorption, which occurs when one team makes particular decisions for another team or sets the decision-making guidelines for another team.

4.   Uncertainty and uncertainty absorption affect the relative power of groups. Relative power is evaluated in terms of weight, domain, and scope.

a.   Weight refers to the degree to which a group can use its power to affect the behavior of another group.

b.   Domain refers to the number of other groups that a group can affect.

c.   Scope refers to the range of behaviors or decisions that a group can determine for another group.

5.   The technical expertise (expert power) of one group/team relative to other groups/teams strongly influences the process of uncertainty absorption. The greater the technical expertise in specific areas, the greater the degree of uncertainty absorption.

6.   Uncertainty absorption is significant because:

a.   It requires managers to decide which teams will have the authority to make decisions that affect others.

b.   It influences the relative power of groups and individuals within the groups.

c.   It requires managers to make sure that the uncertainties being absorbed by teams are consistent with their knowledge and expertise.

C.   Influence 2: goals.

1.   For an organization, an ideal state exists when each group views its goals, the goals of the entire organization, and the goals of other groups as compatible and mutually reinforcing.

2.   Goal conflict occurs when one group's goals are viewed by one or more other group's as preventing them from attaining most or all of their goals. At its extreme, goal conflict is a total win/lose situation. Frequently, however, goal conflict is mixed rather than a total win/lose situation. Mixed goal conflict may serve as a basis for creating coalitions in organizations.

3.   Goal conflict or mixed goal conflict is often manifested in various forms of intergroup competition. The results of such intergroup competition may be

summarized as follows:

a.   Within each competing team the members become more cohesive and focus more on task-oriented behaviors, and the leadership becomes more structured and directive.

b.   Each competing team may begin to see the other team as the enemy.

c.   The winning team often become more cohesive.

d.   The losing team may deny or distort the reality of losing. Over time, the losing team may reevaluate the situation which, in turn, could lead to reorganization, new leadership, and other changes.

ENRICHMENT MODULE: APPROACHES TO MANAGING INTERGROUP COMPETITION

In general, there are two different approaches to managing intergroup competition—taking action to prevent competition or dealing with the competition after it occurs. The strategies for taking action to prevent competition include:

- Rewarding groups on the basis of their contribution to the total organization rather than solely on individual group tasks.
- Rotating members among the various groups.
- Avoiding putting groups in positions of win-lose competition to obtain rewards.
- Emphasizing the sharing of resources.
- Rewarding groups for the help they extend to one another.
- Stimulating frequent interaction between groups.

The strategies for dealing with competition after it occurs include:

- Identifying a common enemy.
- Bringing representative subgroups into direct negotiations with one another.
- Training members of competing groups in group skills.
- Appealing to a common goal.

This enrichment module is based on:

Schein, E. (1988). *Process consultation.* Reading, MA: Addison-Wesley.

TRANSPARENCY 10.3
(The above lists are reproduced in the transparency package.)

D.   Influence 3: attitudinal sets.

1.   <u>Attitudinal sets</u> are the thoughts and feelings—either positive or negative—that members of two or more groups have toward each other.

2.   Attitudinal sets can be both a cause and a result of the dynamics and outcomes between groups. For instance, trust and cooperation can contribute to mutual goal attainment and can foster uncertainty reduction, which, in turn, can enhance trust

and cooperation further.

3.   The attitudinal sets that groups/teams hold about each other often become stereotypes that reinforce cooperation or competition.

4.   Attitudinal sets—whether cooperative or competitive—can influence the ability and willingness of teams to work together to achieve organizational goals. Cooperative attitudinal sets will facilitate goal attainment while competitive attitudinal sets will not.

E.   Influence 4: diversity.

1.   The way people act toward each other reflects, at least to some degree, the attitudes and behaviors developed from their respective group memberships, and the relations and possible stereotypes that exist among groups.

2.   Group identification refers to the idea that one's own identity, and thus the perception of others' identity, is defined (at least in part) by reference to who is in or out of various groups/teams.

3.   Diversity reflects any characteristics that is used identify another person or group as different.

4.   False diversity assumptions which are found in too many group and organizational cultures include:

a.   Otherness is a deficiency.

b.   Diversity poses a threat to the organization's effective functioning.

c.   Expressed discomfort with the dominant group's values is seen as oversensitivity by the minority groups.

d.   Members of all diverse groups want to become and should be more like the dominant group.

e.   Equal treatment means the same treatment.

f.   Managing diversity simply requires changing the people, not the organization culture.

5.   The collective research evidence supports the view that gender does not make a significant difference in managerial effectiveness.

6.   Diversity is significant because it creates unique challenges to make it work for rather than against the long-term interests of individuals, teams, and organizations. Effective management of diversity should encourage positive multiculturalism—the condition in which an individual acquires new skills, perspectives, and attitudes that improve one's chances of relating effectively to members of other groups.

F.   Influence 5: task relations.

1.   Three major types of task relations exist between groups/teams in organizations

(see Transparency 10.4).

TRANSPARENCY 10.4
(FIGURE 10.2 IN THE TEXTBOOK)

TASK RELATIONS BETWEEN TEAMS

---

a. Independent task relations exist when few, if any, interactions are needed between two groups or those that do occur take place at the discretion of the two groups.

   (1) Independent task relations reflects the notion of loose coupling. Loose coupling occurs when groups affect each other occasionally (rather than constantly), negligibly (rather than significantly), and indirectly (rather than directly).

b. Interdependent task relations exist when collaboration, integration, and mutual decision making are necessary and desirable between groups in order for them to achieve their own goals.

c. Dependent task relations exist when one group has the ability and power to determine the behaviors and outputs of the other groups.

   (1) Dependent task relations often occur when:

      (a) One group absorbs uncertainty for one or more other groups.

      (b) The services provided by a group are not easily substitutable.

      (c) One or more groups depend on a another group for needed resources.

2. Diagnosis of the nature and degree of task relations between teams and groups is essential to long-term effectiveness because:

   a. Task relations often influence the achievement of important organizational goals.

   b. Some degree of interdependent task relations is usually needed and must be managed.

   c. A wide range of task relations exists between groups within organizations.

G. Influence 6: resource sharing.

   1. Resource sharing refers to the degree to which two or more groups must obtain needed goods or services from a common group and the degree to which these goods or services are adequate to meet the needs of all the groups.

   2. The need for two or more groups or teams to share a common pool of resources can result in competition or cooperation between them.

H.   Influence 7: substitutability.

1.   <u>Substitutability</u> is the degree to which one group can obtain the services or goods provided by another group from alternative sources.

2.   The lower the substitutability of a group's or team's goods or services, the greater is its power within the organization. When substitutability is low, other groups may cope by providing extra rewards to the vital group, or by trying to eliminate the service group or its management by complaining to top management.

ENRICHMENT MODULE: GROUND RULES FOR INTERGROUP DECISION MAKING

Intergroup decision making provides fertile ground for the emergence of many different types of behavior. Some behaviors can inhibit the effective functioning of the decision-making process whereas other behaviors will contribute to the process being more effective.

When Baxter Healthcare Corporation implemented an employee advisory committee to deal with a problem that cut across several departments, some fundamental behavioral ground rules were established. The ground rules, to which all committee members had to pledge their commitment, included the following:

- Solving the pending work-related problem.
- Being a productive group member who is interested in teamwork and what it can achieve; not using team meetings as a personal gripe session.
- Listening to other members' reports for clues to solving the problem.
- Encouraging participation by all members.
- Consensus decision making.
- Having a positive attitude about the group and working to make it succeed.
- Offering ideas about issues to work on and being open to hearing about other people's concerns.
- Being honest in evaluating the group's process and program within the group or when asked outside.
- Accepting task assignments and reporting on time.
- Following a specific and accepted agenda.
- Obtaining and listening to outside experts.
- Being on time and supporting the group leader and facilitator in organizing and setting guidelines for group operation.
- Enforcing group rules as decided upon by all group members.
- Continuing active involvement through enthusiasm and commitment.
- Knowing why group participation is of interest and importance.

This enrichment module is based on:

"Group Decision Making at Baxter," by Lanny Blake, copyright January 1991. Reprinted with permission *Personnel Journal*, Costa, Mesa, CA. All rights reserved.

III.   Approaches for fostering effective dynamics and outcomes between interdependent groups/teams.

A.   Transparency 10.5 (Figure 10.3) identifies seven approaches for fostering effective dynamics and outcomes between interdependent groups/teams. As shown in the transparency, two of the approaches—dialogue and superordinate team goals and rewards—provide a foundation for using the other approaches. The other approaches include plans and hierarchy, linking roles, cross-functional teams, integrating roles and teams, and groupware.

TRANSPARENCY 10.5
(FIGURE 10.3 IN THE TEXTBOOK)

FOSTERING EFFECTIVE OUTCOMES BETWEEN GROUPS AND TEAMS

B. Dialogue.

    1. <u>Dialogue</u> is a process whereby people suspend their defensive exchanges to allow a free flow of inquiry into their own and others' assumptions and beliefs.

    2. Some of the basic guidelines for fostering dialogue between groups/teams are:

        a. Suspend your own assumptions and sense of certainty about others and the issues at hand.

        b. Listen to see if you are truly understanding or simply engaging in negative evaluation of the comments by others.

        c. Slow down the inquiry because dialogue requires time to develop.

        d. Reject polarization of views as acceptable.

    3. Through dialogue, mutual trust and common ground may be built, and false stereotypes and competitive relations may be resolved or reduced.

C. Superordinate group goals and rewards.

    1. <u>Superordinate group goals</u> are ends that two or more groups might pursue but which can't be achieved without their cooperation.

    2. Superordinate group goals probably will have a more powerful effect on the willingness of groups to cooperate if they are accompanied by superordinate group rewards.

    3. <u>Superordinate group rewards</u> are the benefits received by members of the cooperating groups that are partially determined by the results of their joint efforts.

D. Plans and hierarchy.

    1. <u>Planning</u> develops an organization's, team's, or individual's destination (vision and goals), strategies for getting there, targets for achievement by specific dates, anticipated obstacles, and alternatives for dealing with those obstacles.

    2. Plans involving the coordination of groups/teams often require the participation of a common manager. <u>Hierarchy</u> allows this to occur.

E. Linking roles.

1. <u>Linking roles</u> are performed by individuals in specialized positions who facilitate communication and problem solving between interdependent teams.

2. The creation of linking roles is important when the use of hierarchy, plans, or both becomes too slow or time-consuming.

3. <u>Boundary-spanning roles</u> provide specialized links to other teams or organizations and are often essential for facilitating information flow and decision making.

4. Four types of boundary-spanning roles and their functions are:

   a. The ambassador obtains personnel, funding, equipment, and legitimacy from higher management or other teams.

   b. The task coordinator facilitates integration and synchronization with other teams, typically those involved with a specific product or project.

   c. The scout engages in general scanning aimed at obtaining competitive, market, and technical ideas.

   d. The guard reduces dependence by controlling the information flow from the team.

F. Cross-functional teams.

1. Cross-functional teams temporarily bring together the knowledge and skills of people from different functional areas to solve joint problems.

G. Integrating roles and teams.

1. <u>Integrating roles</u> are performed by employees who are permanently assigned to help teams work together.

2. Integration activities may be performed by a single individual or by a team of employees.

3. Organizations use integrating teams when intergroup differences are large, the need for integration increases because of interdependent task relations, and the need to deal with nonroutine problems increases.

H. Groupware.

1. Originally introduced in Chapter 9, groupware is an approach to using specialized computer aids, communication tools, and designated facilities to enable groups/teams to work faster, share more information, communicate more accurately, and achieve their goals.

2. Four types of groupware that can facilitate interactions between groups/teams.

   a. Basic groupware which combines a messaging system with a database containing work records and memos.

   b. Workflow software which is designed to remake and streamline business processes and to route work automatically.

  c. Meeting software which allows participants in face-to-face or videoconference gatherings to communicate simultaneously by typing on PC keyboards.

  d. Scheduling software which uses a network to coordinate employee's electronic datebooks and determine when they can meet.

3. To be effective, groupware requires a change in both vertical and lateral power relationships, particularly in regard to information sharing.

ENRICHMENT MODULE: DEALING WITH INTERGROUP CONFLICT

Dealing with intergroup conflict is a task that managers continually face. Many methods exist for dealing with group conflict and these methods fall on a continuum from changing behavior to changing attitudes. The following intergroup conflict methods start with the behavioral change end of the continuum:

Physical separation is a method that is used to prevent more damage in groups or individuals that are not interdependent. Because the issues have not been resolved, it will require surveillance or another form of resolution that deals with attitudes.

Limited interaction is used in cases where superordinate goals exist and decision-making rules have been agreed to in advance. However, surveillance is still required to insure that the original conflict doesn't arise again. This type of interaction is useful when joint decisions are routine and interdependence is stable. This method does little to address attitudinal changes.

Integrators are individuals who have high legitimate status, high expertise, and attributes that are consistent with group ideals. These are people who represent each group and are able to keep the conflicting groups from interacting directly or at least limit interaction. Again, this does not attempt to change attitudes directly, but may have some attitudinal benefits.

Third-party consultants help to clarify assumptions and motives of the groups involved through facilitated discussion. It is the process of confronting differences and changing attitudes while maintaining some separation of the conflicting groups until the conflict is resolved.

Negotiations without consultants are used when the need to resolve the conflict is strong for both groups. Because this form of conflict resolution is so intense, the results may involve greater attitudinal change and acceptance. Another key is to make the losses great for those negotiating as well as for the group.

Exchanging members for a sufficient amount of time is used to let one group's members become familiar with how the other group operates. If this is done during the negotiations, the members will return without having to participate in the strain of the negotiations and will bring back a better understanding of the situation that can be explained to co-workers. This process will help attitudinal changes to occur within the organization.

Multilevel interaction refers to the intense interaction between many or all of the members of the opposing groups. This is at the end of the continuum that relies on attitudinal change. The key is that the opposing groups have a great deal to lose if they are unsuccessful in resolving the conflict.

This enrichment module is based on:

Morgan, G. (1991). *Creative organization theory.* Newbury Park, CA: Sage.

TRANSPARENCY 10.6
(A depiction of the continuum of methods for dealing with intergroup conflict
is contained in the transparency package.)

IV.   Summing up: Why should managers and other employees know about dynamics between groups/teams?

A.   Managers and other employees should understand interteam dynamics because behavior in organizations can be affected significantly by people who are not members of the immediate work group. Interteam dynamics can influence the effectiveness of the teams themselves as well as the individual members of the teams and the entire organization.

DISCUSSION QUESTIONS: SUGGESTED ANSWERS

1.   *Identify a group of which you are a member and another which is important to your group. How might this other group create state uncertainty, effect uncertainty, and response uncertainty for your group?*

In formulating their responses, students should use the following definitions:

   a.   State uncertainty means that an individual, group, or organization does not understand how factors in its environment might change.
   b.   Effect uncertainty is the inability to predict the impact of a future state of the environment on the individual, group, or organization.
   c.   Response uncertainty is a lack of knowledge of alternatives and/or the inability to predict the likely consequences of alternatives.

The students should consider how each of these relate to the groups cited in their examples. Student responses will vary depending on the nature of the groups they select as examples.

2.   *With respect to the other group identified, how does it affect the weight, domain, and scope of your group's power?*

The following definitions are relevant to answering this question:

   a.   The weight of a group's power is the degree to which it can affect the behavior of another group.
   b.   The domain of a group's power is the number of other groups it can affect.
   c.   The scope of a group's power is the range of behaviors or decisions that the group can determine for another group.

The discussion should be centered around these definitions. The students should identify the precise policies, procedures, and behaviors that affected the weight, domain, and scope of power in their example groups.

3.   *Consider the relationships between the student government and the administration of your college or university. Give an example of mutual goals, goal conflict, and mixed goal conflict for the two groups.*

Students' responses should reflect the following definitions:

   a.   <u>Mutual goals</u>. An ideal state exists in an organization when each group views its goals, the goals of the entire organization, and the goals of the other groups as compatible and mutually reinforcing. This is a win-win situation.

b.   <u>Goal conflict</u>. Goal conflict occurs when one group's goals are viewed by one or more other groups as preventing them from attaining most or all of their goals.

c.   <u>Mixed goal conflict</u>. Goal conflict between groups is more often mixed than a total win-lose situation. Mixed goal conflict often serves as a basis for creating coalitions in organizations.

4.   *How does the concept of substitutability apply to dormitories, food services, the copy center, and the book store on your campus? What policies or practices does your college or university pursue to limit the substitutability of these services? Are they effective? If so, how?*

Substitutability is the degree to which one group can obtain the services or goods provided by another group from alternative sources. If alternative services or goods are readily available, the power of the provider group is weaker than if no alternatives exist.

In addressing this question, the students should consider how the various campus services operate at your university. They should examine the types of alternative services (*e.g.*, off-campus housing, restaurants, and copy shops) that are provided to students. The students should also explore whether departments on campus are required to use services on campus or can contract with other organizations (*e.g.*, campus janitorial services versus contracting with an outside cleaning service).

5.   *In what ways can a human resources department absorb uncertainty for other departments in an organization?*

Uncertainty absorption occurs when one team makes particular decisions for another team or sets the decision-making guidelines for another team. There are a number of ways by which a human resources department, through its functions, could absorb uncertainty for another department. Some examples of uncertainty absorption by human resources included the following:

a.   Administration of governmental regulations and guidelines concerning equal employment opportunity, occupational safety and health, sexual harassment, etc.

b.   Performing or assisting with recruiting and selection of new employees.

c.   Conducting training programs and management development programs.

d.   Administering compensation and fringe benefits programs.

e.   Administering employee disciplinary procedures.

6.   *What are the types of task relations that probably exist between a purchasing department and a production department? Between purchasing and the human resources department? Between purchasing and the top management team? What factors probably influence the differences in these profiles of task relations?*

The discussion should draw on the text material regarding the following types of task relations:

a.   Independent task relations, which exist when few, if any, interactions are needed between two groups or those that do occur take place at the discretion of the two groups.

b.   Interdependent task relations, which exist when collaboration, integration, and mutual decision making are necessary and desirable between groups in order for them to achieve their own goals.

c.   Dependent task relations, which exist when one group has the ability and power to determine the behaviors and outputs of the other groups.

The relations between a purchasing department and a production department most likely would be interdependent if the organization were operating effectively. However, dependent task relations, where production is at the mercy of purchasing, could compromise the organization's effectiveness and efficiency.

Depending upon how the human resources department operates in a particular organization, the relations between purchasing and human resources may be independent, interdependent, or dependent. If human resources functions mostly as a personnel record-keeping function, then task relations would be relatively independent. If human resources and purchasing worked together in dealing with human resources issues as they affected the purchasing department, task relations would be interdependent. If human resources could dictate to purchasing on HR issues, then the task relations would be dependent.

Task relations would probably be dependent between purchasing and the top management team, with the former being dependent on the latter.

7.   *Is resource sharing becoming a smaller or larger problem in organizations? Why?*

Resource sharing refers to the degree to which two or more groups must obtain needed goods or services from a common group and the degree to which these goods or services are adequate to meet the needs of all groups. The need for two or more groups or teams to share a common pool of resources can result in competition or cooperation between them.

This is especially relevant to all the corporate restructuring and downsizing that has occurred during the last few years. Resource sharing can increase significantly as companies downsize. As a result, the prospect of destructive competition can increase unless resource sharing is managed effectively. Management must encourage collaborative problem solving among those groups that share resources, helping them to establish priorities to minimize unnecessary competition and destructive conflict.

8.   *Give examples of how attitudinal sets affect the relationships between any two groups or teams that are highly interdependent. Use the diagnostic questionnaire shown in Table 10.1 to develop the profile of the attitudinal sets between these two groups or teams.*

Attitudinal sets are the thoughts and feelings—either positive or negative—that members of two or more groups have toward each other. Groups that are interdependent must develop high levels of trust and cooperation since these attitudes will influence goals, uncertainty, substitutability, task relations, and resource sharing. If the interdependent groups trust each other, they will consider the other's point of view more, avoid blaming the other group when problems occur, and check with each other before making decisions that mutually affect them.

The diagnostic questionnaire shown in Table 10.1 will be useful in helping to determine whether the two groups are cooperative or competitive.

9.   *What aspects of intergroup relationships are likely to be aided by groupware technologies? Why?*

Groupware is an approach to using specialized computer aids, communication tools, and designated facilities to enable groups/teams to work faster, share more information, communicate more accurately, and achieve their goals. Communications are likely to be affected the most because of the ability of groupware technology to transcend time and place (see Chapter 9). To be effective, groupware requires a change in both vertical and lateral power relationships, particularly in regard to information sharing.

10. *Based on your experiences in organizations, have the methods they used for integrating groups worked well or poorly? Illustrate and explain your conclusion.*

The text discusses seven approaches for fostering effective dynamics and outcomes between interdependent groups/teams. These seven approaches are: dialogue, superordinate team goals and rewards, plans and hierarchy, linking roles, cross-functional teams, integrating roles and teams, and groupware. The students' examples should be linked to one or more of these seven approaches.

DEVELOPING SKILLS—
SELF DIAGNOSIS: INTERTEAM DYNAMICS QUESTIONNAIRE

This self-diagnostic instrument measures the dynamics that exists between two teams or groups. The responding student should be a member of one of the groups being diagnosed. Using a five-point Likert-type scale, the student indicates the extent of his/her agreement or disagreement with ten items pertaining to intergroup dynamics. Questionnaire scoring instructions are provided in the text.

The instrument yields a total score and three subscale scores. The subscales are: joint decision processes, openness of contact, and feelings about others. The total score can range from 10 to 50 while each of the subscale scores can range from 3 to 15.

The higher the total score, the more the interteam dynamics can be characterized as cooperative; and the lower the score, the more competitive. Any total score below 30 is a cause for concern.

On the subscales, lower scores also suggest competitive interteam dynamics. Any subscale score below 10 should be cause for concern.

Three discussion questions are provided to facilitate debriefing of the self-diagnostic activity.

1. *Is one of the three factors that comprise the interteam dynamics more important than the others? Which one? Why?*

Openness of contact is probably the most important of the three factors. Without sufficiently open contact, joint decision processes would be difficult, if not impossible, to have. Moreover, openness of contact provides information which is useful for developing positive feelings about others.

2. *What would you conclude if one of the three subscale scores is much higher than the other two? Much lower?*

Either case indicates that all is not well with the interteam dynamics. One very high score and two very low scores suggest that competitiveness is much more characteristic of the interteam dynamics but that there is some hope for becoming more cooperative. Of course, the two teams would have to work vigorously to overcome their competitive interactions. One very low score and two very high scores suggest that cooperativeness is much more characteristic of the interteam dynamics than is competitiveness. However, some improvement (perhaps just "fine tuning") is needed in the interteam dynamics in order for the groups to be highly cooperative.

3.   *Can high scores on one subscale make up for low scores on another?*

In light of the answer to question 1, students can argue that high scores on the joint decision processes and feelings about others subscales cannot compensate for lower scores on the openness of contact subscale.

DEVELOPING SKILLS—
A CASE IN POINT: MADISON ELECTRONICS COMPANY

CASE OVERVIEW

This case focuses on the relations between various departments that operate under a piece-rate incentive system. The piece-rate system was designed by outside consultants to help lower unit costs and increase efficiency. While there was initial resistance to implementing this system, most employees were happy because their earnings capability increased. The exception was the trimming department, which removed burrs and other irregular formations from the parts produced by casting. Specifications allowed the casting department to continue production without replacing worn dies, making it nearly impossible for employees in the next department in the sequence—trimming—to meet the standard production rate of 500 units per hour, let alone earn a bonus. On several occasions, the trimming department manager asked the casting department manager to replace the dies before they became so worn. The casting department manager was reluctant to do so because the downtime for casting employees would prevent them from achieving their own standard production rates. Moreover, management was reluctant to change a piece-rate incentive system that was designed by "experts."

CASE QUESTIONS

1.   *What are the major problems facing the managers and groups at MEC? Explain.*

Two major intergroup relations problems exist at MEC: dependency due to workflow and goal conflict. Each department in the production sequence has to complete its task before it can pass the product on to the next department. Therefore, each department is dependent on the preceding department in the sequence to meet its own production goals. The "loose" quality standards in casting allow inferior parts to proceed to trimming. While inferior parts are returned to casting for possible reworking, their all too frequent presence in the production sequence makes it difficult for trimming to achieve its production goals. This makes it relatively easy for casting to achieve their standard and bonus pay, while making it nearly impossible for trimming to make its standard, let alone earn bonus pay.

2.   *How would you advise the managers in this case to resolve the problems identified?*

By changing the type of task relations and establishing standards, some of the problems could be eliminated. The departments need to become more interdependent and develop agreement on standards so that they are rewarded for working together rather than independently. The two managers could also work toward a compromise. This would probably not occur without pressure on the casting department manager to force a change. Top management probably is not interested in changing the system because of the investment they made in the consultants who developed the plan. Also, top management probably is not interested in the trimming department's dissatisfaction with the incentive system because it is not affecting the goals of the entire organization.

3.   *What do you think of the individual piece-rate compensation system? Why?*

The piece-rate system works well where groups are involved in independent task relations. However, it does not work well with dependent or interdependent task relations. The piece-rate system does not encourage interdependent group behaviors even when they are needed for everyone's success. In the MEC case, the groups are not rewarded for working together to achieve organizational goals, but that is exactly the kind of behavior that is needed over the long term.

In addition, the piece-rate incentive system is based on a fixed ratio schedule of rewards (see Chapter 5). Therefore, barring the effects of other variables, the system should lead quickly to very high and stable performance but will also be subject to moderately fast extinction.

4.   *Evaluate the boundary-spanning roles of the managers of the casting and trimming departments in solving the problems identified.*

Boundary spanners are people who provide specialized links to other teams or organizations. Boundary spanners are often essential for facilitating information flow and decision making. The manager of the trimming department made a "feeble" attempt to perform the task coordinator type of boundary spanning role by asking the casting department manager to replace the dies before they became too worn. However, there was inadequate communication of information pertaining to the problem. The manager of the casting department did nothing to indicate even a feeble attempt at playing a boundary spanning role.

COURSE ENHANCEMENT—
WEST'S ORGANIZATIONAL BEHAVIOR CUSTOM VIDEO SERIES

One video from *West's Organizational Behavior Custom Video Series* can be used to enhance the material in Chapter 10. This video is: *AT&T's Microscope Magazine: Kittyhawk's Personal Storage Module.*

VIDEO: *AT&T'S MICROSCOPE VIDEO MAGAZINE: KITTYHAWK'S PERSONAL STORAGE MODULE*

Approximate Time: 5 minutes

Video Summary:

The video focuses on the development of Kittyhawk, a 1.3 inch diameter, 20 megabyte disk drive for small electronic devices such as calculators, palmtop computers, and video games. Hewlett-Packard had small electronic devices such as calculators, palmtop computers, and video games. Hewlett-Packard had expertise in disk drives but not in the integrated circuitry that was needed to control the Kittyhawk. Consequently, H-P formed a strategic business partnership with AT&T because AT&T had the skills that H-P needed. Moreover, the two companies had similar cultures: a focus on quality, a commitment to their customer bases, and an overall commitment to developing good products for key markets.

A skilled team was formed with members from both companies. The team, given a high degree of independence, was charged with developing the relevant technology to create the Kittyhawk. The team members were empowered to make decisions at the lowest levels. The team evolved into an effectively functioning, highly cohesive group. H-P members and AT&T members learned so much from one another and were so cohesive that it was hard to tell where the H-P team ended and the AT&T team began. In fact, one team member joked that "H-P members would get AT&T bonuses at the end of the year." H-P and AT&T essentially married the strengths and core competencies of each firm.

Discussion Questions and Suggested Answers for Video:

1. *The text discusses seven key influences on outcomes between groups or teams. Which of these influences are present in the partnership between Hewlett-Packard and AT&T?*

   Figure 10.1 of the text identifies seven key influences on the outcomes of interacting groups or teams. These key influences are: uncertainty, goals, attitudinal sets, diversity, task relations, resource sharing, and substitutability.

   The effectiveness of the team interactions of H-P and AT&T was affected by the following influences:

   a. Through their partnership, H-P and AT&T absorbed uncertainty for each other.
   b. H-P and AT&T had mutually compatible goals.
   c. H-P and AT&T members of the project team developed very trusting and positive attitudinal sets toward one another.
   d. Diversity in terms of skill variety was used to the partners' advantage on the Kittyhawk project.
   e. Task relations were interdependent.
   f. Extensive resource sharing occurred, particularly in technology.

2. *What did Hewlett-Packard and AT&T do to foster effective outcomes in their Kittyhawk partnership?*

   Figure 10.3 of the text identifies seven approaches for fostering effective dynamics and outcomes between interdependent groups/teams. These approaches include: dialogue, superordinate team goals and rewards, plans and hierarchy, linking roles, cross-functional teams, integrating roles and teams, and groupware.

   The Kittyhawk partnership definitely used superordinate goals, linking roles, cross-functional teams, and integrating roles and teams. They probably also used dialogue and groupware (given the nature of their respective businesses), but one must infer this from the overt data provided in the video.

COURSE ENHANCEMENT—
SUPPLEMENTAL VIDEOS AVAILABLE FROM WEST

Additionally, a video which is distributed by the Association for Manufacturing Excellence and is available through West Publishing Company can be used to enrich the material in Chapter 10. This video, is: *On the Road to Manufacturing Excellence—Hewlett-Packard.*

VIDEO: AME: ON THE ROAD TO MANUFACTURING EXCELLENCE—HEWLETT-PACKARD

Approximate Time: 7 minutes

Video Summary:

In 1985, falling sales in Hewlett-Packard's terminal division threatened their presence in the computer terminal business. In order to survive and remain competitive, management decided to develop a new terminal that would satisfy market demand for high quality, lower-cost computer products. In order to develop this new terminal, the "Frontier Team" was created. The Frontier Team faced several significant challenges including:

a.   Redesigning a product so that it had only one rather than four printed circuit boards.
b.   Reducing the parts count by 37%.
c.   Reducing the supplier base by 52%.
d.   Reducing manufacturing cycle time by 71%.
e.   Reducing manufacturing costs by 40%.
f.   Reducing labor costs by 33%.
g.   Increasing volume by 400%.

The Frontier Team was built across organizational functions encompassing employees from design, operations, purchasing, and marketing. When the team was formed there were some concerns about new roles and the fear of not succeeding. These fears disappeared as the team members worked together and the team proved to be successful and became more innovative and risk-taking in solving problems.

As a result of the Frontier Team's success, H-P was able to bring a high quality terminal to market at a per unit cost of about $1,000 less than its previously lowest-priced terminal.

Discussion Questions and Suggested Answers for Video:

1.   *Which approach did H-P use to foster effective dynamics and outcomes with the Frontier Team?*

      Seven approaches are discussed in the text: dialogue, superordinate team goals and rewards, plans and hierarchy, linking roles, cross-functional teams, integrating roles and teams, and groupware. H-P primarily used cross-functional teams encompassing employees from design, operations, purchasing, and marketing.

2.   *What problems did Hewlett-Packard encounter when first implementing the Frontier Team?*

      The principal problems that H-P encountered were the concern that people had about new roles and the fear of not succeeding. These problems can be related to the key factors that influence the outcomes of interacting groups or teams. Uncertainty (especially effect uncertainty and response uncertainty), goals, and task relations are particularly relevant.

3.   *What benefits accrued from implementing the Frontier Team?*

The basic benefits were becoming an industry leader with a low cost, high quality terminal.

CHAPTER 11
LEADERSHIP

CHAPTER OVERVIEW

Chapter 11 continues the exploration of interpersonal and group processes by focusing on leadership. The basic nature of leadership is explained by examining the linkage between leaders and their subordinates, by comparing the behaviors of managers and leaders, and by considering how a person's power affects leadership. Three leadership models are discussed. First, traditional leadership models—including trait models and behavioral models—are explored. Second, contingency leadership models are examined. The contingency models include: Fiedler's contingency model, Hersey and Blanchard's situational model, House's path-goal model, and the Vroom-Jago leadership model. Third, two emerging leadership models—the attribution model and the transformational model—are discussed. The limitations and practical implications of the various leadership models are examined as well.

LEARNING OBJECTIVES

Upon completion of this chapter, the students should be able to:

1. Identify the differences between leaders and managers.
2. List the skills and sources of power that leaders can use to influence subordinates.
3. Describe the traits model of leadership.
4. Define two key behavioral leadership dimensions.
5. Describe Fiedler's contingency model.
6. Explain the leadership and contingency variables in both Hersey and Blanchard's situational model and House's path-goal model.
7. Discuss the situational variables in the Vroom-Jago model.
8. Describe the attributional and charismatic models of leadership.

CHAPTER OUTLINE

KEY WORDS AND CONCEPTS

Thirty-nine key words and concepts are introduced in Chapter 11. Two of these concepts were originally introduced in earlier chapters (empowerment in Chapter 1 and impression management in Chapter 3). The key words and concepts, along with definitions or appropriate descriptions, are as follows:

Achievement-oriented leadership: a leader behavior variable in House's path-goal model that entails setting challenging goals, seeking improvement in performance, emphasizing excellence in performance, and showing confidence that members will perform well.

Attribution model: a leadership model which suggests that a leader's judgment about employees is influenced by a leader's attributions regarding employee performance.

Charismatic leaders: refers to leaders who concern themselves with developing a common vision of what could be, discovering or creating opportunities, and increasing peoples's desire to control their own behaviors.

Coercive power: a source of power that comes from the leader's ability to sanction or punish the team members.

Consideration: a variable in the behavioral leadership model that refers to the extent to which leaders are likely to have job relationships that are characterized by mutual trust, two-way communication, respect for employee's ideas, and consideration for their feelings.

Decision effectiveness: a leader effectiveness criterion in the Vroom-Jago leadership model which reflects decision quality, acceptance, and timeliness.

Delegating style: a leadership style that reflects the low task, low relationship combination of leader behavior variables in Hersey and Blanchard's situational model. The delegating style involves few leader task or relationship behaviors because subordinates are empowered to make decisions.

Directive leadership: a leader behavior variable in House's path-goal model that involves letting members know what they are expected to do, giving them specific guidance, asking them to follow rules and regulations, scheduling and coordinating their work, and setting standards of performance for them.

Empowerment: sharing influence and control with employees.

Expert power: a source of power that comes from the leader's special knowledge and expertise within a particular area.

Fiedler's contingency model: a leadership model which specifies that performance is contingent upon both the leader's motivational system and the degree to which the leader controls and influences the situation.

Follower readiness: a contingency behavior variable in Hersey and Blanchard's situational model that refers to subordinates' ability and willingness to perform the task.

Group atmosphere: a contingency variable in Fiedler's model that refers to a leader's acceptance by the team.

Hersey and Blanchard's situational model: a leadership model that is based on the amount of relationship (supportive) and task (directive) behavior that a leader provides in a situation. The amount of either relationship or task behavior is based on the readiness of the follower.

House's path-goal model: a leadership model which suggests that, to be effective, a leader must select a style that enhances employees' satisfaction with their jobs and increases their performance level. A leader can do this by clarifying the nature of the task, reducing roadblocks to successful task completion, and increasing opportunities for employees to feel worthwhile.

Impression management: refers to a leader's use of methods that enhance their attractiveness and appeal to others.

Initiating structure: a variable in the behavioral leadership model that refers to the extent to which mangers are likely to define and structure their roles and those of their employees.

Leader: a person who inspires employees with a vision and helps them cope with change.

Leader match: a self-teaching process utilizing a programmed learning text that instructs the individual on matching his or her least preferred co-workers (LPC) with the situation. Leader match pertains to Fiedler's contingency theory.

Leadership: the process whereby one person influences others to work toward a goal and helps them pursue a vision.

Least preferred co-worker: a leader behavior variable in Fiedler's contingency theory which refers to leadership style. Leaders who describe their least preferred co-workers in negative (low LPC) are task-oriented, and those who describe their least preferred co-workers in positive (high LPC) terms are relationship-oriented.

Legitimate power: a source of power that comes from the leader's position in the organization.

Manager: a person who directs the work of employees and is responsible for results.

Overall effectiveness: a leader effectiveness criterion in the Vroom-Jago leadership model which reflects decision effectiveness, the costs of time, and the benefits of employee development.

Participating style: a leadership style that reflects the low task, high relationship combination of leader behavior variables in Hersey and Blanchard's situational model. The participating styles relies on two-way communications and encourages and supports the skills the followers have developed.

Participative leadership: a leader behavior variable in House's path-goal model that includes consulting with others and evaluating their opinions and suggestions when making decisions.

Position power: a contingency variable in Fiedler's model that reflects the extent to which the leader has, reward, coercive, and legitimate power.

Referent power: a source of power that is associated with individuals who possess admired personal characteristics.

Relationship behavior: a leader behavior variable in Hersey and Blanchard's situational model which refers to the extent to which a leader listens, provides support and encouragement, and involves followers in the decision-making process.

Reward power: a source of power that comes from the leader's ability to provide something desired by team members in return for their desired behaviors.

Selling style: a leadership style that reflects the high task, high relationship combination of leader behavior variables in Hersey and Blanchard's situational model. The selling style encourages two-way communication between the leader and subordinates, and helps them to build self-confidence in performing the task.

Supportive leadership: a leader behavior variable in House's path-goal model that includes considering the needs of employees, displaying concern for their welfare, and creating a friendly climate in the work group.

Task behavior: a leader behavior variable in Hersey and Blanchard's situational model which refers to the extent to which a leader spells out to followers what to do, where to do it, and how to do it.

Task structure: a contingency variable in Fiedler's model that reflects the extent to which a task performed by employees is routine or nonroutine.

Telling style: a leadership style that reflects the high task, low relationship combination of leader behavior variables in Hersey and Blanchard's situational model. The telling style provides clear and specific instructions.

Traits model: a leadership model that is based on the observed characteristics which appear to differentiate between successful and unsuccessful leaders.

Transformational leaders: refers to leaders who rely on their referent and personal sources of power to arouse intense feelings and heighten employee motivation to follow them.

Vision: refers to a leader's ability to create and articulate a goal that binds people together, and to having a plan that energizes people to reach that goal.

Vroom-Jago leadership model: a leadership model which argues that different degrees of participation in decision making are appropriate for different problem situations.

LECTURE NOTES

I. Chapter 11 continues the exploration of interpersonal and group processes by focusing on leadership. Leadership is important for understanding behavior in work settings because it involves influencing others to pursue the organization's vision and to work toward its goals.

   A. Any reasonable discussion of leadership revolves around several very crucial questions, including the following: What is leadership? Do managers differ from leaders? How do leaders acquire their ability to influence? What characteristics do leaders have? How do leaders behave? How do situational factors influence leadership? How do perception and charisma affect leadership? Transparency 11.1 provides an overview of this chapter's answers to these questions.

TRANSPARENCY 11.1
(FROM TEXT MATERIAL IN THE TEXTBOOK)

KEY QUESTIONS AND ANSWERS ABOUT LEADERSHIP

II. Overview of leadership.

   A. What is a leader? What is a manager?

      1. Leadership is the process whereby one person influences others to work toward a goal and helps them pursue a vision. A leader inspires employees with a vision and helps them cope with change.

      2. A manager is a person who directs the work of employees and is responsible for results.

3.   Transparency 11.2 summarizes the differences in the leader's role and the manager's role.

TRANSPARENCY 11.2
(FIGURE 11.1 IN THE TEXTBOOK)

BEHAVIORS OF LEADERS AND MANAGERS

B.   Foundations of leadership.

1.   Leader-subordinate relationships.

a.   Subordinates value leadership, but leaders become valuable to an organization only after they have demonstrated their competence as leaders.

b.   Leadership grants people power over others.

c.   To retain a leadership position, a person must enable others to gain satisfactions that are otherwise beyond their reach.

2.   As shown in Transparency 11.3, successful leaders share several common skills.

TRANSPARENCY 11.3
(FIGURE 11.2 IN THE TEXTBOOK)

EFFECTIVE LEADERSHIP SKILLS

---

a.   Successful leaders attract employees by creating a vision.

b.   Successful leaders communicate effectively with their employees.

c.   Successful leaders share influence and control with employees—that is, they empower employees.

d.   Successful leaders understand their own strengths and weaknesses and tend to hire employees who can offset their weaknesses.

ENRICHMENT MODULE: DISCUSSION ACTIVITY—
WHO IS AN EFFECTIVE LEADER? AN INEFFECTIVE LEADER?

A good way to get students thinking about effective and ineffective leaders is to use the following discussion exercise. Organize the students into groups of 5-6 members. Drawing on their observations of people they have encountered in leadership positions have them:

- Identify who seemed to be **effective** leaders and discuss what they did that made them **effective**.
- Identify who seemed to be **ineffective** leaders and discuss what they did that made them **ineffective**.

ENRICHMENT MODULE: HOW TO BE A GREAT BOSS

Experts on employee productivity and satisfaction say that a person needs to learn seven skills in order to be a great boss. These skills are:

- Be a good and willing communicator. Great bosses share information and are good listeners.
- Specify job performance expectations. Great bosses provide positive performance feedback and tell employees about problems when they develop.
- Make daily contact with as many team members as possible. Great bosses regularly give employees information about company plans and performance. Great bosses also make eye contact in communicating with employees, and they are concerned about their employees personal lives but don't invade their privacy.
- Loosen the reins. Great bosses don't overcontrol their employees, and they give credit to those who deserve it.
- Have a sense of humor and admit mistakes. Great bosses enliven the work atmosphere while still having a seriousness of purpose.
- Provide direction and strive to be consistent. Great bosses have a clear vision and established priorities, both of which are shared with team members on a regular basis.
- Look for ways to improve and learn from others. Great bosses are open to change, and they try to learn from their own bosses—both good and bad.

This enrichment module is based on:

Maynard, R. (1991, December). How to be a great boss. *Nation's Business*, 44-45.

TRANSPARENCY 11.4
(The above list is reproduced in the transparency package.)

3. To influence others, leaders use one or more of the following sources of power:

    a. <u>Legitimate power</u>, which comes from the leader's position in the organization.

    b. <u>Reward power</u>, which comes from the leader's ability to provide something desired by team members in return for their desired behaviors.

    c. <u>Coercive power</u>, which comes from the leader's ability to sanction or punish the team members.

    d. <u>Referent power</u>, which is associated with individuals who possess admired personal characteristics.

    e. <u>Expert power</u>, which comes from the leader's special knowledge and expertise within a particular area.

4. Transparency 11.5 shows that wise and effective use of these powers in influencing others' behaviors, usually results in favorable outcomes for the organization and its employees.

TRANSPARENCY 11.5
(FIGURE 11.3 IN THE TEXTBOOK)

SOURCES OF A LEADER'S POWER AND EFFECTIVENESS

C.   There are five general approaches for assessing leadership: traits, behavioral, contingency, attributional, and charismatic. Two approaches—traits and behavioral—are considered to be traditional leadership models. Another two approaches—attributional and charismatic—are considered to be emerging leadership models.

III.   Traditional leadership models.

A.   Traditional leadership models include the traits and behavioral approaches.

B.   Traits model.

1.   The <u>traits model</u> is based on the observed characteristics which appear to differentiate between successful and unsuccessful leaders. Essentially, it tries to examine leadership from the perspective "who leaders are."

2.   The traits approach is inadequate for successfully predicting effective leadership performance.

a.   No consistent pattern of results has been found. However, the evidence suggests that many (but not all) successful leaders tend to share four traits.

(1)   They tend to be more intelligent than their subordinates.

(2)   They tend to be emotionally mature and have a broad range of interests.

(3)   They have strong inner motivation and a drive to achieve goals.

(4)   They are employee-centered.

b.   Most of the physical characteristics that have been linked to leadership probably are linked more closely to situational factors associated with the leader's position than to effective or ineffective leadership.

c.   Leadership is a far more complex phenomenon than the trait approach assumes.

C.   Behavioral models.

1.   Behavioral models of leadership address the questions: What do leaders do? How do they do it?

ENRICHMENT MODULE: LEADER BEHAVIOR AT SUNBEAM-OSTER CO.

How leaders behave can have very dramatic effects on their followers. Here is an example of how one leader's behavior affected his followers.

Paul Kazarian had the reputation of being "a hard-driving and demanding leader who rescued Sunbeam-Oster Co. from bankruptcy and made it profitable again." Turning Sunbeam-Oster around was achieved through a significant sacrifice of human resources. According to many Sunbeam-Oster employees,

> "Mr. Kazarian was an overbearing boss whose frequent harangues and erratic, autocratic behavior made their lives miserable. Mr. Kazarian...fired employees on a whim, stomped on telephones, shot BBs at empty chairs during meetings, made lewd suggestions to women in public (not Sunbeam employees), and routinely summoned top managers to 'crisis' meetings at odd hours, where he sometimes encouraged them to undercut fellow mangers whom they believe he perceived as a threat."

A group of employees banded together to undercut Mr. Kazarian. Six of his top subordinates initiated talks with the company's board of directors; these talks lead to Kazarian being fired.

This enrichment module is based on:

Suskind, R., & Alexander, S. (1993, January 14). Out of control: Fired Sunbeam chief harangued and hazed employees, they say. *The Wall Street Journal*, A1 & A8.

2.   The behavioral models of leadership identify two principal dimensions of leader behavior: consideration and initiating structure.

   a.   <u>Consideration</u> is the extent to which leaders are likely to have job relationships that are characterized by mutual trust, two-way communication, respect for employee's ideas, and consideration for their feelings. An emphasis on consideration tends to foster employee satisfaction, group harmony, and cohesion.

   b.   <u>Initiating structure</u> is the extent to which mangers are likely to define and structure their roles and those of their employees. An emphasis on initiating structure tends to improve performance, at least in the short run.

3.   Consideration has the most positive effects on group member's performance and satisfaction when (see Transparency 11.6):

TRANSPARENCY 11.6
(FROM TEXT MATERIAL IN THE TEXTBOOK)
WHEN IS CONSIDERATION EFFECTIVE?

   a.   The task is routine and denies employees any job satisfaction.

   b.   Employees are predisposed toward participative leadership.

   c. Team members must learn something new.

   d. Employees feel that their involvement in the decision-making process is legitimate and affects their job performance.

   e. Few status differences exist between leader and subordinate.

  4. Initiating structure has the most positive effects on group member's performance and satisfaction when (see Transparency 11.7):

TRANSPARENCY 11.7
(FROM TEXT MATERIAL IN THE TEXTBOOK)

WHEN IS INITIATING STRUCTURE EFFECTIVE?

---

   a. A high degree of pressure for output is imposed by someone other than the leader.

   b. The task satisfies employees.

   c. Employees depend on the leader for information and direction on how to complete the task.

   d. Employees are psychologically predisposed toward being told what to do and how to do it.

   e. No more than 12 employees report to the leader.

  5. Limitations of the behavioral model.

   a. The model pays little attention to the situation in which leader behavior occurs.

ENRICHMENT MODULE: LEADERSHIP STYLE DIFFERENCES—GENDER OR GENERATION?

The results of some surveys suggest that the leadership styles of women and men differ. Women are perceived as having a more participatively oriented, interactive style. Men are perceived as having a more autocratic, command and control style.

While the interactive style may occur more frequently among women than men, others argue that it is a generational phenomenon, not a gender phenomenon. Proponents of this argument say that the older generation is more likely to be behave autocratically and the younger generation is more likely to behave interactively.

So, is interactive leadership a gender phenomenon or a generational phenomenon? Perhaps it really doesn't matter since the behaviors of the interactive leader are probably the behaviors which future leaders—whether male or female, young or old—will need to exhibit to be successful. Successful future leaders, according to some experts, will:

- Value individual input and initiative.
- Value the employee as a human being, not just for his or her performance.
- Develop employees by mentoring and nurturing.
- Share information.
- Create new solutions rather than rely on the tried-and-true.
- Motivate workers rather than command them.
- Share power.

This enrichment module is based on:

Reprinted with permission from *Entrepreneur Magazine*, April 1992.

IV.   Contingency leadership models.

A.   Contingency leadership models focus on the variables that make certain leadership characteristics and behaviors effective in a specific situation.

1.   Transparency 11.8 identifies the principal contingency variables that affect leader behavior. These are: a leader's personal characteristics; employees' personal characteristics; the group's characteristics; and the structure of the group, department, or organization.

TRANSPARENCY 11.8
(FIGURE 11.4 IN THE TEXTBOOK)

CONTINGENCY VARIABLES THAT AFFECT LEADER BEHAVIOR

**ENRICHMENT MODULE: DISCUSSION ACTIVITY—
HOW DO SITUATIONAL VARIABLES AFFECT LEADERSHIP EFFECTIVENESS?**

This enrichment module extends the discussion of an earlier enrichment module "Discussion Activity: Who Is an Effective leader? An Ineffective Leader?" Have the student groups reassemble, focusing on the same effective and ineffective leaders they had discussed before. This time, however, have the students discuss the situational factors that may have influenced how effective the different leaders were.

---

2.   Contingency leadership models include Fiedler's contingency model, Hersey and Blanchard's situational leadership model, House's path-goal model, and the Vroom-Jago leadership model. Each of these models is explored in terms of leader behaviors, contingency variables, and leader effectiveness criteria.

B.   Fiedler's contingency model.

1.   <u>Fiedler's contingency model</u> specifies that performance is contingent upon both the leader's motivational system and the degree to which the leader controls and influences the situation.

2.   Key variables in Fiedler's contingency model.

   a.   Leader behaviors.

   (1)   The <u>least preferred co-worker</u> (LPC) scale is a measure of leadership style. It indicates whether leaders describe their least preferred co-workers in negative (low LPC) or positive (high LPC) terms.

   (2)   Low-LPC leaders tend to be task-oriented; they focus on improving relationships with subordinates only after they are assured that tasks are being completed.

   (3)   High-LPC leaders first concentrate on establishing good relationships with their subordinates, and then focus on task accomplishment.

   b.   Contingency variables.

   (1)   <u>Group atmosphere</u> refers to a leader's acceptance by the team. When a leader is accepted by the team, he/she does not have to "pull rank."

   (2)   <u>Task structure</u> reflects the extent to which a task performed by employees is routine or nonroutine.

   (3)   <u>Position power</u> is the extent to which the leader has reward, coercive, and legitimate power.

   c.   Leader effectiveness criteria.

   (1)   Group performance.

3.   As shown in Transparency 11.9, the three contingency variables combine to create

eight situations ranging from the most favorable for the leader to the least favorable for the leader. Task-motivated (low-LPC) leaders have the strongest positive effect on group performance in the three most favorable situations (1, 2, and 3) and in the least favorable situation (8). Relationship-motivated (high-LPC) leaders have the strongest positive effect on group performance under moderately favorable situations (4 to 7).

TRANSPARENCY 11.9
(FIGURE 11.6 IN THE TEXTBOOK)

CONTINUUM OF THE THREE BASIC LEADERSHIP VARIABLES

---

4. Limitations of Fiedler's contingency model (see Transparency 11.10).

    a. The LPC scale is a questionable measure of leader behavior. It implies that one must be either highly task-motivated or highly relationship-motivated; being both is precluded by the measurement system. The LPC score is also assumed to be constant over time.

    b. The leader can influence task structure and group atmosphere; therefore these two variables are not really contingency variables with respect to leadership.

5. Practical implications of Fiedler's contingency model (see Transparency 11.10).

    a. Both relationship-motivated and task-motivated leaders perform well in certain situations but not in others.

    b. Leaders' performance depends both on their motivational bases and the situation.

    c. Leaders can do something about their situations. They can be taught to become better leaders through <u>leader match</u>, a self-teaching process utilizing a programmed learning text that instructs the individual on matching his or her LPC with the situation.

TRANSPARENCY 11.10
(FROM TEXT MATERIAL IN THE TEXTBOOK)

LIMITATIONS AND IMPLICATIONS OF FIEDLER'S CONTINGENCY MODEL

C. Hersey and Blanchard's situational model.

1. <u>Hersey and Blanchard's model</u> is based on the amount of relationship (supportive) and task (directive) behaviors that a leader provides in a situation. The amount of either relationship or task behaviors is based on the readiness of the follower.

2. Key variables in Hersey and Blanchard's situational model.

    a. Leader behaviors.

        (1)   <u>Task behavior</u> is the extent to which a leader spells out to followers what to do, where to do it, and how to do it.

        (2)   <u>Relationship behavior</u> is the extent to which a leader listens, provides support and encouragement, and involves followers in the decision-making process.

    b.   Contingency variables.

        (1)   <u>Follower readiness</u> refers to subordinates' ability and willingness to perform the task.

    c.   Leader effectiveness criteria.

        (1)   Performance.

        (2)   Job satisfaction.

3.   According to the model shown in Transparency 11.11, the leader should use a different combination of relationship and task behaviors depending on the readiness of the followers.

TRANSPARENCY 11.11
(FIGURE 11.7 IN THE TEXTBOOK)

HERSEY AND BLANCHARD'S SITUATIONAL LEADERSHIP MODEL

---

    a.   A <u>telling style</u> (*i.e.*, high task, low relationship) provides clear and specific instructions. This style is appropriate when subordinates are either unable or unwilling to perform the task.

    b.   A <u>selling style</u> (*i.e.*, high task, high relationship) encourages two-way communication between the leader and subordinates, and helps them to build self-confidence in performing the task. The selling style is appropriate when subordinates lack the ability to do the task but are eager to do it.

    c.   A <u>participating style</u> (*i.e.*, low task, high relationship) relies on two-way communications and encourages and supports the skills the followers have developed. It works best when subordinates are able but not fully confident of their ability to perform.

    d.   A <u>delegating style</u> (*i.e.*, low task, low relationship) involves few leader task or relationship behaviors because subordinates are empowered to make decisions. This style is appropriate when subordinates are able, willing, and have the confidence to perform the task.

4.   Limitations of Hersey and Blanchard's situational model (see Transparency 11.12).

    a.   If each team member has a different readiness level, the leader will have difficulty deciding which leadership style is most appropriate.

    b.   The model relies only on one contingency variable—follower readiness.

c.   Contrary to the model, some leaders may not be able to adapt their leadership style to fit the situation.

d.   Mixed results have been found in studies which have attempted to validate the model.

5.   Practical implications of Hersey and Blanchard's situational model (see Transparency 11.12).

a.   Flexibility in choosing a leadership style is an appealing idea for many people.

b.   The model is easy to understand and its recommendations are straightforward.

c.   The leader must constantly monitor the readiness level of employees.

d.   Through the use of the appropriate style, the leader also can affect employees' readiness level and their progress in learning how to manage themselves.

TRANSPARENCY 11.12
(FROM TEXT MATERIAL IN THE TEXTBOOK)
LIMITATIONS AND IMPLICATIONS OF HERSEY AND BLANCHARD'S SITUATIONAL MODEL

D.   House's path-goal model.

1.   Based on the expectancy theory of motivation, House's path-goal model suggests that, to be effective, a leader must select a style that enhances employees' satisfaction with their jobs and increases their performance level. A leader can do this by clarifying the nature of the task, reducing roadblocks to successful task completion, and increasing opportunities for employees to feel worthwhile.

2.   Key variables in House's path-goal model.

a.   Leader behaviors.

(1)   Supportive leadership includes considering the needs of employees, displaying concern for their welfare, and creating a friendly climate in the in the work group.

(2)   Directive leadership involves letting members know what they are expected to do, giving them specific guidance, asking them to follow rules and regulations, scheduling and coordinating their work, and setting standards of performance for them.

(3)   Participative leadership includes consulting with others and evaluating their opinions and suggestions when making decisions.

(4)   Achievement-oriented leadership entails setting challenging goals, seeking improvement in performance, emphasizing excellence in

performance, and showing confidence that members will perform well.

    b.   Contingency variables.

        (1)   Employee characteristics such as safety, esteem, and affiliation needs; perceived ability; locus of control.

        (2)   Task characteristics (e.g., routine versus nonroutine tasks).

    c.   Leader effectiveness criteria.

        (1)   Employee job satisfaction.

        (2)   Job performance.

3.   House's path-goal model is shown in Transparency 11.13 and a self-explanatory application of the model is presented in Transparency 11.14

TRANSPARENCY 11.13
(FIGURE 11.8 IN THE TEXTBOOK)

HOUSE'S PATH-GOAL MODEL

TRANSPARENCY 11.14
(FIGURE 11.9 IN THE TEXTBOOK)

APPLYING HOUSE'S PATH-GOAL MODEL

---

4.   Limitations of House's path-goal model (see Transparency 11.15).

    a.   Research on the path-goal model has focused primarily on comparing the effects of supportive and directive leadership.

5.   Practical implications of House's path-goal model (see Transparency 11.15).

    a.   In comparing the supportive and directive leadership styles, employees who perform routine tasks are more productive and satisfied when their leader uses a supportive style. Employees who perform nonroutine tasks are more productive and satisfied when their leader uses a directive style.

    b.   Participative leadership increases employees' efforts if they are performing a nonroutine task, and has little effect on performance when they have a clear understanding of a routine task.

    c.   Achievement-oriented leadership has little impact on performance and satisfaction when employees perform routine tasks.

```
┌─────────────────────────────────────────────────────────────────┐
│                      TRANSPARENCY 11.15                           │
│               (FROM TEXT MATERIAL IN THE TEXTBOOK)                │
│                                                                   │
│       LIMITATIONS AND IMPLICATIONS OF HOUSE'S PATH-GOAL MODEL      │
└─────────────────────────────────────────────────────────────────┘
```

E.   Vroom-Jago leadership model.

  1.   The <u>Vroom-Jago leadership model</u> indicates that different degrees of participation in decision making are appropriate for different problem situations.

  2.   Key variables in the Vroom-Jago leadership model.

    a.   Leader behaviors.

      (1)   Transparency 11.16 identifies the five decision styles (or leader behaviors) in the Vroom-Jago leadership model.

```
┌─────────────────────────────────────────────────────────────────┐
│                      TRANSPARENCY 11.16                           │
│               (TABLE 11.2 IN THE TEXTBOOK)                        │
│                                                                   │
│             DECISION STYLES FOR LEADING A GROUP                   │
└─────────────────────────────────────────────────────────────────┘
```

      (2)   These leader behaviors vary on a continuum from highly autocratic to highly participative.

      (3)   The notation "A" means autocratic, and the roman numerals refer to degrees of autocracy. The notation "C" means consultation and the roman numerals refer to degrees of consultation. The notation "G" means group decision making with consensus as the goal.

    b.   Contingency variables.

      (1)   Eight problem attributes are used to describe differences among decision-making situations. These are: quality requirement, commitment requirement, leader's information, problem structure, commitment probability, goal congruence, subordinate conflict, and subordinate information.

    c.   Leader effectiveness criteria.

      (1)   Employee development.

      (2)   Time.

      (3)   <u>Decision effectiveness</u> depends on decision quality, acceptance, and timeliness.

      (4)   In turn, <u>overall effectiveness</u> depends on decision effectiveness, the costs of time, and the benefits of employee development.

  3.   The interrelationships between the contingency variables and leader behaviors is

depicted in the Vroom-Jago decision tree that is presented in Transparency 11.17.

TRANSPARENCY 11.17
(FIGURE 11.10 IN THE TEXTBOOK)

VROOM-JAGO DECISION TREE

---

4.   Limitations of the Vroom-Jago leadership model (see Transparency 11.18).

   a.   Most subordinates have a strong desire to participate in decisions affecting their jobs even though use of the model might suggest an autocratic decision-making approach.

   b.   Certain characteristics of the leader—such as conflict resolution skills—play a key role in determining the relative effectiveness of the different decision-making strategies suggested by the model.

   c.   The model is based on the premise that decisions go through a single process rather than multiple cycles or as part of broader considerations.

5.   Practical implications of the Vroom-Jago leadership model (see Transparency 11.18).

   a.   If leaders can diagnose situations correctly, choosing the best leadership style for those situations becomes easier, and they will be more likely to make high-quality, timely decisions.

TRANSPARENCY 11.18
(FROM TEXT MATERIAL IN THE TEXTBOOK)

LIMITATIONS AND IMPLICATIONS OF THE VROOM-JAGO LEADERSHIP MODEL

F.   A self-explanatory comparison of the four contingency models of leadership is provided in Transparency 11.19.

TRANSPARENCY 11.19
(TABLE 11.3 IN THE TEXTBOOK)

COMPARING THE FOUR CONTINGENCY LEADERSHIP MODELS

ENRICHMENT MODULE: BUILDER OR BLOODLETTER— WHAT KIND OF LEADER DOES KODAK NEED?

In general, contingency leadership models focus on the variables that make certain leadership characteristics and behaviors effective in a specific situation. Read the following account and discuss whether George Fisher is the right leader for Kodak, given his characteristics and behavior and the situation confronting him.

Here are some of the challenges facing Mr. Fisher: Net income has increased by only 11 cents a share over the past decade, yet Kodak continues to have a tremendous cash flow. Money and managerial resources have been haphazardly thrown at developing high-technology electronic products, many of which have failed miserably in the marketplace. Kodak's efforts in this area have been at the expense of its film products, yet it still dominates the consumer film market. Many Kodak employees remain excited about electronics but wonder how the company can make a profit from it.

Some 12 weeks before hiring George Fisher, Kodak's board of directors fired Chairman Kay R. Whitmore, complaining of a culture of liberal spending. The Kodak board assured analysts that Whitmore's "replacement would wield a sharp ax." Is George Fisher the person for the job? Did Kodak's board hire the bloodletter they promised, or did they hire a builder?

Fisher, a former CEO of Motorola, has been described as "the soft-spoken wizard who put Motorola, Inc. atop the evolving electronic world." Mr. Fisher "is a professorial type with no experience in, or appetite for, messy corporate retrenchment. Yet what he seems to have is an ability to conjure up a kind of Kodachrome image of Kodak's place—and treasured brand name—in a fast-moving multimedia revolution in which images and information merge."

This enrichment module is based on:

Rigdon, J.E., Hill, G.C., & Naik, G. (1993, October 29). New focus: Hiring Fisher, Kodak gambles on a future in multimedia world. *The Wall Street Journal*, A1 & A4.

V.   Emerging leadership models.

    A.   Emerging leadership models attempt to address issues—such as the effects of leaders' perceptions of their employees and leaders' charisma—that are not considered by contingency leadership models.

        1.   Two emerging models of leadership are examined: the attribution model and the transformational model.

    B.   The attribution model of leadership.

        1.   The <u>attribution model</u> (see Transparency 11.20) suggests that a leader's judgment about employees is influenced by the leaders' attributions regarding employee performance. A leader's attributions, as much as employee behaviors, determines how the leader responds to their performance.

TRANSPARENCY 11.20
(FIGURE 11.11 IN THE TEXTBOOK)
ATTRIBUTIONAL LEADERSHIP MODEL

---

a. The attribution of behavior to personal (internal) factors or situational (external) factors is critical for leader-follower relations. Leaders attempt to change an employee's behavior only when they make internal attributions.

b. Employees tend to attribute their team's or their personal performance problems to the leader's actions, rather than their own.

2. Limitations of the transformational model (see Transparency 11.21).

a. Leaders tend to be biased toward making internal attributions about poor employee performance, often leading to punitive actions.

3. Practical implications of the transformational model (see Transparency 11.21).

a. Leaders need to be careful, fair, and systematic about evaluating employee performance and making attributions regarding poor performance.

b. Leaders need to become more aware of the various options for dealing with different causes of poor performance.

TRANSPARENCY 11.21
(FROM TEXT MATERIAL IN THE TEXTBOOK)
LIMITATIONS AND IMPLICATIONS OF THE ATTRIBUTION MODEL

C. The transformational model of leadership.

1. Charismatics leaders and transformational leaders are closely linked.

a. Charismatic leaders concern themselves with developing a common vision of what could be, discovering or creating opportunities, and increasing peoples's desire to control their own behaviors.

b. Transformational leaders rely on their referent and personal sources of power to arouse intense feelings and heighten employee motivation to follow them.

c. Transformational leaders create a new vision—and through the use of their charismatic skills—excite, arouse, and inspire employees to greater efforts to achieve goals.

2. As shown in Transparency 11.22, transformational leaders exhibit three behaviors: vision, framing, and impression management.

TRANSPARENCY 11.22
(FIGURE 11.12 IN THE TEXTBOOK)

TRANSFORMATIONAL LEADERSHIP MODEL

---

a. <u>Vision</u> refers to a leader's ability to create and articulate a goal that binds people together, and to having a plan that energizes people to reach that goal.

b. Framing refers to a leader's ability to put the vision into context and to give it purpose and meaning.

c. <u>Impression management</u> refers to a leader's use of methods that enhance their attractiveness and appeal to others.

3. Limitations of the transformational model (see Transparency 11.23).

    a. Followers can be so zealous that they are blind to conditions surrounding the leader. At worst, transformational leaders emotionally manipulate followers and create visions for their own self-aggrandizement.

    b. Transformational leaders may lack communications and impression management skills.

    c. Some transformational leaders are known for their autocratic management style.

4. Practical implications of the transformational model (see Transparency 11.23).

    a. Transformational leaders may be most effective when an organization is new or when its survival is threatened.

TRANSPARENCY 11.23
(FROM TEXT MATERIAL IN THE TEXTBOOK)

LIMITATIONS AND IMPLICATIONS OF THE TRANSFORMATIONAL MODEL

ENRICHMENT MODULE: INSPIRING OTHERS—THE LANGUAGE OF LEADERSHIP

While strategic vision is considered an integral part of effective leadership, the leader's ability to communicate vision is crucial. The era of dictator management is being replaced by inspirational leadership. There are some important keys to being an effective transformational leader. The first element is to have a meaningful organizational vision. Next, the language of leadership must be able to generate acceptance and accomplishment of the mission.

Getting the message across requires a mission centered around intrinsically appealing goals with culturally important meanings. Four messages need to be communicated. These include the significance of the mission, why the mission exists, key antagonists, and why it will succeed. In describing the goals, important corporate values should be emphasized through the use of stories, analogies, and metaphors. The message should remain simple and the important tenets should be repeated. In all communications, genuine emotions should be used to emphasize importance. The leader must be perceived as being credible and having expertise on the subject. The language of leadership must not be used to screen out problems or make goals seem more possible than they really are.

This enrichment module is based on:

Conger, J. (1991). Inspiring others: The language of leadership. *Academy of Management Executive,* *5,* 31-45.

ENRICHMENT MODULE: TRANSFORMATIONAL OR POST-HEROIC LEADERSHIP

The nature of corporate leadership appears to be changing. In the future, corporate leaders will need to (1) develop and articulate a vision for the company, and (2) create an environment that enables employees to determine what needs to done and then permits them to do it well. In short, future corporate leaders will need to become transformational leaders.

No single avenue of success exists with transformational leadership. Robert Haas, CEO of Levi Strauss & Co., transformed a hierarchical, command and control company into a worldwide organization based on team management. In order to change the organization, leadership training is done throughout the company. One participant, Tommye Jo Daves, a sewing plant manager in Murphy, North Carolina, came out of the training with two principal lessons: "You can't lead a team by just barking orders, and you have to have a vision in your head of what you're trying to do." Haas tries to infuse these lessons throughout the organization by using "syndicate leadership." The company shares as much information as possible and expects its employees to develop business literacy. These radical changes have been accompanied by five consecutive years of record profits.

Wilbert Gore, founder of W.L. Gore & Associates, is another kind of transformational leader. A former research and development chemist for DuPont, Gore founded his company after failing to persuade Dupont management to manufacture a product for which Gore had developed a new production method while "fiddling around in his basement one night." Gore operated his company on the basis of Douglas McGregor's Theory Y concepts—at the time, visionary for a company to adopt. The company now operates on the basis of "un-management." There is no organizational structure. No one has titles except those that are required for legal incorporation. Associates must sponsor new hires. Each manufacturing team has a leader who has emerged from the group and has been approved by consensus within the group. Employees have to assume a lot of responsibility in order to function effectively. W.L. Gore & Associates has had 31 consecutive years of profitability, and has grown to 35 facilities and 5,600 associates worldwide.

While transformational leaders follow different paths, they all infuse their organizations with a common trait—"a clearly stated, oft-repeated set of core values that guide everyone's decisions."

This enrichment module is based on:

Huey, J. (1994, February 21). The new post-heroic leadership. *Fortune*, 42-50.

VI. Summing up: What are the major leadership implications for organizational behavior?

    A. As we pointed out at the beginning of our discussion, leadership is important for understanding behavior in work settings because it involves influencing others to pursue the organization's vision and to work toward its goals. Being an effective leader is not an easy task with simple answers; if anything, the proliferation of leadership models supports the observation that leadership is no simple matter. To be effective, leaders need to consider both their own and their followers' motivations, perceptions, abilities, and behaviors. Leaders also need to consider the various contextual variables that impact on their ability to function effectively. Leadership will be effective only to the extent that there is at least a reasonable level of "goodness-of-fit" among the variables that affect the leadership process.

DISCUSSION QUESTIONS: SUGGESTED ANSWERS

1.   *What skills must a person learn in order to lead?*

Successful leaders tend to be skilled in the following four areas:

    a.   They attract employees by creating a vision.
    b.   They communicate effectively with their employees.
    c.   They share influence and control with employees.
    d.   They understand their own strengths and weaknesses and tend to hire employees who can offset their weaknesses.

Developing competency in each of these areas would help an individual to become a more effective leader.

2.   *When someone once asked Bill Miller, president of EmCare, a leading emergency medical care management group, what it took to be an effective leader, his response was: "Great team members!" What does this response mean?*

Discussion of this question can be approached in at least two ways. First, an "acceptance of authority" line of reasoning can be used. This perspective argues that leaders can only become effective after proving their value to subordinates because they receive their authority only after being accepted by their subordinates. However, to be an effective leader an individual must have subordinates who are willing to be good followers or "great team members."

Second, a "leadership effectiveness criterion" argument can be offered. Since leader effectiveness is usually gauged in terms of the leader's effect on the followers, this line of reasoning argues that the followers must be doing a good job in order for the leader to be effective. Therefore, the leader is effective only when the followers are effective.

3.   *Under what conditions have you been a successful leader? Under what conditions have you failed? Were both situations similar? Explain the similarities or differences.*

The discussion could center around any of the contingency leadership models because those models focus on the variables that make certain leadership characteristics and behaviors effective in a specific situation. Students should focus on specific examples of their leadership style and the contingency variables that came into play. The contingency variables could include: a leader's personal characteristics; employees' personal characteristics; the group's characteristics; and the structure of the group, department, or organization. Emphasis should be placed on the specific contingency factors that enabled them to exercise effective leadership as well as those that contributed to ineffective leadership.

4.   *Suppose that a leader's style doesn't seem to match the situation. Can a leader's style change to produce a better match? What does Fiedler's theory say about that possibility?*

Hersey and Blanchard's situational model, House's path-goal model, and the Vroom-Jago leadership model all suggest that leader behavior is flexible and can be adjusted to different situations. Fiedler's contingency model, however, suggests that leader behavior is not flexible and therefore leaders must be matched with the situations in which they are more likely to function effectively.

5. *Are transformational leaders really different from other types of leaders? If so, in what ways? Under what situations are transformational leaders likely to be effective? Ineffective?*

Transformational leaders are charismatic. They rely on their referent and personal sources of power to arouse intense feelings and heighten employee motivation. These types of leaders almost have a magical appeal to employees. Transformational leaders create a new vision. Then by using their charismatic skills, they excite, arouse, and inspire employees to greater efforts to achieve goals.

In general, leaders inspire employees with a vision and help them cope with change. Transformational leaders go beyond the typical leader. When successful, transformational leaders are effective in creating a vision, framing that vision, and using impression management.

Figure 11.12 identifies, among other variables, the situational factors that impact on transformational leadership. Transformational leaders may be most effective when an organization needs to "pull" together to achieve a new vision or when its survival is threatened. Transformational leaders are not likely to be effective in the opposite conditions.

6. *Kathleen Manella, the director of housekeeping at a St. Paul hospital, discovered that she could get better performance from her staff by making the decisions autocratically rather than consultatively. Following the Vroom-Jago model, under what conditions would her leadership style be effective?*

In the Vroom-Jago model there are two autocratic styles of leadership: AI and AII. According to their model, Kathleen could use the AI style under the following problem attribute conditions:

a. Both the technical quality of the decision and subordinate commitment to the decision are very important, she has sufficient information to make a high quality decision, and she is reasonably certain that her subordinates would be committed to the decision even if she makes it herself.
b. The technical quality of the decision is very important but subordinate commitment to the decision is not important, and she has sufficient information to make a high-quality decision.
c. Both the technical quality of the decision and subordinate commitment to the decision are unimportant.
d. The technical quality of the decision is unimportant but subordinate commitment to the decision is important, and she is reasonably certain that her subordinates would be committed to the decision even if she makes it herself.

According to the Vroom-Jago model, Kathleen could use the AII style under the following problem attribute conditions:

a. Both the technical quality of the decision and subordinate commitment to the decision are important, she does not have sufficient information to make a high-quality decision, the problem is well structured, she is reasonably certain that her subordinates would be committed to the decision even if she makes it herself, and her subordinates do not share the organizational goals to be attained by solving the problem.
b. The technical quality of the decision is very important but subordinate commitment to the decision is not important, she does not have sufficient information to make a high-quality decision, the problem is well structured, and her subordinates do not share the organizational goals to be attained by solving the problem.
c. The technical quality of the decision is very important but subordinate commitment

to the decision is not important, she does not have sufficient information to make a high-quality decision, the problem is well structured, she is reasonably certain that her subordinates would be committed to the decision even if she makes it herself, and her subordinates do not share the organizational goals to be attained by solving the problem.

7.   *According to William Howell, president of J.C. Penney, "At Penney's, our philosophy is that the best ideas come from associates—employees—on the firing line rather than managers sitting in their offices." What style of leadership works most effectively in promoting this philosophy? Explain.*

Hersey and Blanchard's situational model could be used in discussing this question. In particular, the delegating style would seem appropriate to Mr. Howell's management philosophy. In practice, this style involves the exhibition of few leader task or relationship behaviors because subordinates are empowered to make decisions. This style is appropriate when subordinates are able, willing, and have the confidence to perform the task.

House's path-goal model of leadership also can be used in this discussion. This model identifies four distinct types of leader behavior: supportive, directive, participative, and achievement-oriented leadership. Mr. Howell's philosophy relates to the participative leadership style. Participative leadership—which includes consulting with others and evaluating their opinions and suggestions when making decisions—would be effective in promoting Mr. Howell's philosophy.

8.   *Ralph Stayer, CEO of Johnsonville Foods, says that a leader must develop a vision or employee job performance declines. Why is creating a vision so important?*

Creating a vision is what distinguishes leaders from managers. A leader inspires employees with a vision and helps them cope with change. In contrast, a manager directs the work of employees and is responsible for results.

A vision provides focus, binds people together in pursuit of a goal, and inspires people to work toward realizing that vision. Without this guiding beacon, employees will not remain focused on the job at hand, and therefore performance will decline.

9.   *What are some major differences between the four contingency models? Why do they exist?*

Major differences are found in the models' explanations of leader behaviors, contingency variables, and leader effectiveness criteria. These differences are summarized in Table 11.3.

Fiedler's contingency model uses the LPC to determine task-oriented and relationship-oriented leader behaviors. Hersey and Blanchard's situational model also uses task and relationship behaviors. House's path-goal model specifies four leader behaviors including supportive, directive, participative, and achievement-oriented. The Vroom-Jago model proposes a continuum of leader behaviors ranging from autocratic to participative.

The contingency variables also differ with each theory. Fiedler's model has three variables—group atmosphere, task structure, and leader position power. Hersey and Blanchard's model examines the readiness level of team members. House's model specifies employee characteristics and task characteristics. The Vroom-Jago model delineates eight problem attributes.

Each model uses different leader effectiveness criteria. Fiedler's model uses performance as the criterion measure of leader effectiveness. Both Hersey and Blanchard's model and House's model use performance and job satisfaction to measure leader effectiveness. The Vroom-Jago model examines employee development, time, decision effectiveness, and overall effectiveness.

10. *Assume that you are a student in a class and have been assigned to do a team project with five other classmates. How might Hersey and Blanchard's leadership model help you choose a leadership style? How might House's path-goal model help you choose a leadership style?*

According to Hersey and Blanchard's situational model, you would assess the follower readiness of other the project members. Based upon your assessment of their ability and willingness to perform the project's required tasks, you would choose the appropriate leadership style. This is the style that combines task behaviors and relationship behaviors in such a way as to provide the best fit with follower readiness.

In using House's path-goal model, you would assess the contingency variables of employee characteristics and task characteristics. Given these characteristics, you would then select a leadership style—supportive, directive, participative, or achievement-oriented—that most likely would enhance team member satisfaction and performance.

11. *What are some conditions under which leaders don't seem to make a difference?*

Data from numerous studies collectively demonstrate that, in many situations, whatever behaviors leaders exhibit are irrelevant. Certain individual, job and organizational variables can act as substitutes for leadership or neutralize the leaders' influence on employees.

Leadership substitutes act as a replacement for the leader's influence. For example, characteristics of employees such as their experience, training, professional orientation, or need for independence can neutralize the leaders' effect. Jobs that are inherently unambiguous and routine or that are intrinsically satisfying may place fewer demands on leaders than those that are novel or for which there is no clear answer. Organizational characteristics like explicit formalized goals, rigid rules and procedures, or cohesive work groups can act in place of formal leadership.

12. *Some managers believe that female leaders adopt a different style than male leaders: a style that shows more concern with interpersonal relations and encourages subordinates to participate in decisions. Do you agree? Why or why not?*

Discussion of this question can be related to the "Enrichment Module: Leadership Style Differences—Gender or Generation?"

Some evidence indicates that women and men are different in their leadership styles. Opponents of this viewpoint argue that any differences in leadership styles is more a function of generational differences than gender differences. Further, there is the argument that participatively-oriented behaviors will be crucial to leaders' success in the future, whether the leader is male or female, young or old.

In answering this question, students should be pressed to explain the reasoning behind their positions.

13.   *Consider all the men who have been president of the United States since you were born. How many of them would you classify as charismatic? How would you rate them as president?*

By definition, charismatic leaders concern themselves with developing a common vision of what could be, discovering or creating opportunities, and increasing peoples's desire to control their own behaviors. The discussion should be built around this definition. Students should compare and contrast recent presidents in terms of their abilities to create a common vision, to discover or create opportunities, and increase people's desire for self-control.

DEVELOPING SKILLS—
SELF DIAGNOSIS: WHAT'S YOUR LEADERSHIP STYLE?

This self-diagnosis instrument measures a person's leadership style in terms of consideration and initiating structure. Respondents indicate the extent to which each of 22 statements describes their leadership style.

Detailed scoring instructions are provided in the text. Two scores are produced: one for consideration, the other for initiating structure. A consideration score of greater than 40 indicates that you are a considerate leader—one who is concerned with the comfort, well-being, and contributions of others. An initiating structure score of greater than 47 indicates that you describe your leadership style as high on initiating structure—that is, you plan, organize, direct, and control the work of others.

DEVELOPING SKILLS—
A CASE IN POINT: SOUTHWESTERN MANUFACTURING COMPANY

CASE OVERVIEW

This case describes the leadership experiences of Ramona and Hector Ortega, owners of Southwestern Manufacturing Company, a producer of handmade Native American dolls. The Ortegas experienced considerable difficulty in getting their employees to cooperate with them. This failure to cooperate was evident in most, if not all, of the specific problems the Ortegas encountered. These specific problems include the following:

a.   Productivity did not meet the Ortegas' expectations.
b.   The Ortegas had planned to pay employees on a piece-rate basis but the employees bargained for a hourly wage.
c.   The employees' work habits were erratic.
d.   To counter the seasonal nature of demand for their existing product line, the Ortegas planned to expand the product line. However, the workers resisted because, from their viewpoint, they only knew how to make dolls.
e.   Interpersonal disputes among employees created tension in the workplace.
f.   The Ortegas attempted to implement a team approach but workers resisted it. The different teams were asked to generate ideas on how they could cooperate with each other. Not only did the teams not come up with any ideas, they didn't even meet.
g.   The Ortegas then appointed a leader for each group and again asked the groups to come up with ideas on how cooperate with each other. Still, none of the groups provided any

ideas on teamwork and cooperation.

CASE QUESTIONS

1.   *What are some of the leadership problems facing the Ortegas?*

All of the problems identified in the case summary are potential leadership problems for the Ortegas because they reflect the employees' unwillingness to cooperate.

2.   *If they decided to select a contingency model to help them choose a leadership style, which one might help the most?*

Reasonable arguments could be made for using Hersey and Blanchard's situational model or House's path-goal model. From the perspective of Hersey and Blanchard's model, the students can argue that follower readiness is very low. The followers appear to be unwilling and unable to perform the tasks associated with expanding the product line or implementing teamwork. Therefore, the Ortegas should use a "telling" leadership style,

From the perspective of House's path-goal model, supportive leadership would probably be called for. Research evidence shows that employees who perform routine tasks are more productive and satisfied when their leader uses a supportive style rather than a directive style. Clearly, the manufacture of hand-crafted dolls is more of a routine task than a nonroutine task. Supportive leadership includes considering the needs of employees, displaying concern for their welfare, and creating a friendly climate in the in the work group.

Also, discussion could focus on what a leader should do when different models give somewhat different signals as to how they should behave.

3.   *What specific transformational leadership behaviors might the Ortegas try in dealing with the workers?*

Creating a vision is the most important transformational leader behavior available to the Ortegas. Unless they are able to create and articulate a goal that binds people together and unless they have a plan that energizes people to reach that goal, little progress will likely be made. Currently, the Ortegas seem to be approaching their business from the perspective of "the latest management fad." They pick up ideas and try to implement them without consideration of how those ideas would help in realizing the corporate visions, were such a vision to exist.

The Ortegas also need to be concerned about framing their vision. Framing refers to a leader's ability to put the vision into context and to give it purpose and meaning. Without proper framing, the employees are unlikely to respond positively to the Ortegas' vision.

4.   *If the Ortegas hired you as a leadership consultant to advise them, which leadership style would you suggest to them? Why?*

In responding to this question, the students should link the facts of the case to the components of whichever leadership model they use as the basis of their answer. Special attention should be given to the likely effects the selected leadership style would have on the follower group.

COURSE ENHANCEMENT—
WEST'S ORGANIZATIONAL BEHAVIOR CUSTOM VIDEO SERIES

One video from *West's Organizational Behavior Custom Video Series* can be used to enhance the material in Chapter 11. This video is: *Tenneco's Leadership and Planning Conference (Leadership Segment).*

VIDEO: *TENNECO'S LEADERSHIP AND PLANNING CONFERENCE (LEADERSHIP SEGMENT)*

Approximate Time: 6 minutes

Video Summary:

This video segment of Tenneco's Leadership and Planning Conference features Dana Mead explaining Tenneco's leadership perspective to 300 Tenneco managers. Mr. Mead describes eight leader behaviors that are needed for Tenneco to transform itself into a world class corporation. These eight leader behaviors are:

1. Understand the purpose of what you are doing and how what you do contributes to achieving the corporation's objectives.
2. Motivate your people, communicate what your expectations are, and hold them accountable for results.
3. Initiate and manage continuous improvement. Become a risk taker.
4. Select excellent people.
5. Build teams unencumbered by functional or organizational boundaries.
6. Create an environment where people believe they are treated fairly.
7. Face and resolve conflict.
8. Lead by example. Exhibit high standards of performance, integrity, and ethics.

In short, Mr. Mead urged Tenneco's managers to become more than managers; he challenged them to become strong leaders of change.

Discussion Question and Suggested Answer for Video:

1. *Mr. Mead suggest that managers and leaders are not exactly the same thing. How do managers and leaders differ? Do the behaviors discussed by Mr. Mead relate more to managers or leaders? Explain.*

   Discussion of this question can be based on Figure 11.1 which summarizes the differences in the leader's role and the manager's role. Basically, leaders provide vision and direction, they align employees, and they inspire and motivate. Managers plan and budget, organize and staff, and exercise control. The eight behaviors cited by Mr. Mead relate more closely to leaders' behaviors than to managers' behaviors.

CHAPTER 12
INTERPERSONAL COMMUNICATION

CHAPTER OVERVIEW

Chapter 12 continues the discussion of interpersonal and group processes by examining interpersonal communication in dyads and in groups of three or more individuals. In the context of dyads, emphasis is placed on the basic elements of interpersonal communication, including senders and receivers; transmitters and receptors; messages and channels; meaning, encoding, decoding, and feedback; and potential interpersonal and cultural barriers. In the context of groups of three or more individuals, emphasis is placed on the variety, impacts, and implications of communications networks. Special attention is given to the five-person group. Attention is also given to various methods of fostering dialogue to improve interpersonal communications. Included among these methods are communication openness, constructive feedback, appropriate self-disclosure, active listening, and supportive nonverbal cues.

LEARNING OBJECTIVES

Upon completion of this chapter, the students should be able to:

1.   Describe the elements of interpersonal communication and their relationships to one another.
2.   State the potential interpersonal and cultural barriers to dialogue.
3.   Evaluate the effects of different types of communications networks.
4.   Describe how groupware aids support networking.
5.   Explain the skills and behaviors that are needed to foster dialogue.
6.   Give feedback, engage in self-disclosure, and actively listen.
7.   State how nonverbal cues may support dialogue between individuals.

CHAPTER OUTLINE

KEY WORDS AND CONCEPTS

Thirty-five key words and concepts are introduced in Chapter 12. One concept—impression management—was originally introduced in Chapter 3 and was reintroduced in Chapter 11. The key words and concepts, along with definitions or appropriate descriptions, are as follows:

Aggressive communication: expressing yourself in ways that intimidate, demean, or degrade another person and pursuing what you want in ways that violate the rights of another person.

Assertive communication: confidently expressing what you think, feel, and believe (values)—and standing up for your rights while respecting the rights of others.

Bypassing: an apparent agreement and understanding between two or more individuals that ultimately leads to expectations by each person about the near-term behavior of the other person.

Channels: the means by which messages travel from sender to receivers.

Cultural context: the conditions that surround and influence the life of an individual, group, or organization.

Data: the output of communication.

Decoding: the personal translation of received messages into interpreted meanings.

Distortion: a wide range of messages that a sender may use between the extremes of lying and complete honesty.

Electronic mail (E-mail): a computer-based system that enables participating individuals to exchange and store messages with their computers.

Encoding: the personal translation of meanings into messages that can be sent.

Ethnocentrism: occurs when a person believes that "only my culture makes sense, espouses the 'right' values, and represents the 'right' and logical way to behave."

Feedback: the receiver's response to the message.

High-context culture: refers to interpersonal communication that is characterized by: (1) the establishment of social trust before engaging in task-based discussions; (2) the value placed on personal relationships and goodwill; and (3) the importance of the surrounding circumstances during an interaction.

Honesty: the sender abides by consistent and rational ethical principles to respect the truth.

Impression management: the process by which a sender consciously attempts to influence the perceptions that the receivers form.

Intercultural communication: occurs whenever a message that must be understood by a member of one culture is received by a member of another culture.

Interpersonal communication: the transmission and reception of thoughts, facts, beliefs, attitudes, and feelings—through one or more information media—that produce a response.

Interpersonal communication network: refers to a pattern over time of communication flows between individuals.

Language routines: patterned responses to situations which often reflect the person's unique communication approach, or language choices that have become habits.

Listening: a process that integrates physical, emotional, and intellectual inputs in a search for meaning and understanding.

Low-context culture: refers to interpersonal communication that is characterized by: (1) directly and immediately addressing the tasks, issues, or problems at hand; (2) the high value placed on expertise and performance; and (3) the importance of clear, precise, and speedy interactions.

Lying: an extreme form of deception in which the sender states what is believed to be false in order to seriously mislead one or more receivers.

Meanings: a person's thoughts, feelings, beliefs (values), and attitudes.

Media richness: a medium's capacity for carrying multiple cues and providing rapid feedback

Messages: the transmitted data and the coded (verbal and nonverbal) symbols that give particular meanings to the data.

Meta-communication: refers to the (hidden) assumptions, inferences, and interpretations of the parties that form the basis of overt messages.

Noise: any interference with the intended message in the channel.

Nonassertive communication: the reluctance or inability to express consistently what you think, feel, and believe (values). Such action allows others to violate your rights without challenge.

Nonverbal communication: includes nonlanguage human responses (such as body motions and personal physical attributes) and environmental characteristics (such as a large or small office).

Receptors: refers to the means (media) that are available for receiving messages.

Self-disclosure: refers to any information that individuals communicate (verbally or nonverbally) about themselves to others.

Semantics: the special meaning assigned to words by different people.

Telecommuting: the practice of working at home while linked to the office or plant with groupware.

Transmitters: refers to the means (media) that are available for sending messages.

Voice mail: a computer-based messaging system that people access by telephone.

LECTURE NOTES

I.   Chapter 12 continues the discussion of interpersonal and group processes by focusing on interpersonal communication. Interaction between people, either on a one-on-one basis or within a group, revolves around communication. Therefore, understanding the nature of interpersonal communication, being able to diagnose communication problems, and having the necessary skills to communicate effectively are essential elements for understanding and managing behavior in organizational settings. Transparency 12.1 highlights the topics we will explore as we consider the role of interpersonal communication in organizational behavior.

TRANSPARENCY 12.1
(FROM TEXT MATERIAL IN THE TEXTBOOK)

KEY IDEAS ABOUT INTERPERSONAL COMMUNICATION

II.   Overview of interpersonal communication.

   A.   <u>Interpersonal communication</u> is the transmission and reception of thoughts, facts, beliefs, attitudes, and feelings—through one or more information media—that produce a response.

   B.   There are three basic interpersonal communication approaches.

      1.   <u>Assertive communication</u> means confidently expressing what you think, feel, and believe (values)—and standing up for your rights while respecting the rights of others.

      2.   <u>Nonassertive communication</u> is a reluctance or inability to express consistently what you think, feel, and believe (values) and allows others to violate your rights without challenge.

      3.   <u>Aggressive communication</u> means expressing yourself in ways that intimidate, demean, or degrade another person and pursuing what you want in ways that violate the rights of another person. A variant of this approach is called passive-aggressive communication and it involves some degree of subtle hostility and resentment.

II.   Elements of interpersonal communication—the basic dyadic (two person) model.

   A.   Accurate interpersonal communication takes place when the thoughts, facts, beliefs, attitudes, or feelings that the sender intended to transmit are the same as those understood and interpreted by the receiver.

ENRICHMENT MODULE: "I WANT TO KNOW WHAT YOU REALLY THINK"
(An Experiential Activity)

Suppose your boss (or a professor, a classmate, or a friend) says to you, "I want to know what you really think." Will you view this as the ideal opportunity to air your gripes? Or are you entering a minefield? Does the person really want to know what you think? How will he or she react if you are brutally honest? Must you use euphemisms and "walk on egg shells" because you're not sure if you can really trust this person to not retaliate in some way? Just what will you say and how will you say it?

What will you, as the sender of the interpersonal communication, do? How do you think the receiver of the interpersonal communication will react? This exercise will help you answer these questions and, in the process, begin to explore the nature of interpersonal communication within dyads.

The procedure for using this exercise is as follows:

1.   Each student selects a person with whom he or she has relatively frequent interpersonal communication and assumes that this focal person has said, "I want to know what you really think."

2.   Then working alone, the students develop two lists. One list should contain the student's candid thoughts, beliefs, attitudes, or feelings regarding his or her relationship with the selected focal person. The other list should contain the student's best estimate of how the focal person will perceive and react to the information on the first list.

3.   The students then review and reflect on the two lists, placing special emphasis on the reasons for any differences.

4.   Based upon the analysis in step (3), the students then prepare a list of four or five key insights which they have gained about interpersonal communication.

5.   In either a small-group or full-class format and without revealing the identity of the focal person, the students discuss their insights about interpersonal communication.

This enrichment module is based on an experiential activity developed by M.K. McCuddy.

B.   The basic dyadic interpersonal communication process is presented in Transparency 12.2. This process is explored in terms of sender and receiver; transmitters and receptors; messages and channels; meaning, encoding, decoding, and feedback; potential interpersonal barriers to interpersonal communication; and potential cultural barriers to interpersonal communication.

TRANSPARENCY 12.2
(FIGURE 12.1 IN THE TEXTBOOK)

ELEMENTS OF INTERPERSONAL COMMUNICATION

1.   Sender and receiver.

   a.   Because interpersonal communication is an exchange process, the roles of sender and receiver shift back and forth, depending upon where the two individuals are in the communication process.

b. More accurate communication between the sender and the receiver will occur as differences in their goals, attitudes, and beliefs diminish.

2. Transmitters and receptors.

   a. <u>Transmitters</u> (used by the sender) and <u>receptors</u> (used by the receiver) are the means (media) available for sending and receiving messages.

   b. Transmitters and receptors usually involve one or more of the senses, and can be verbal or nonverbal.

   c. The media that are available for transmitting and receiving messages vary in terms of <u>media richness</u> (*i.e.*, a medium's capacity for carrying multiple cues and providing rapid feedback).

      (1) The degree of media richness depends on:

         (a) The rapidity and use of feedback to correct and/or confirm intended meanings (range of slow to rapid).

         (b) The tailoring of messages to the personal circumstances of the receiver (range of low to high).

         (c) The ability to convey multiple cues simultaneously (range of single to multiple).

         (d) Language variety (range of standard to varied).

      (2) Transparency 12.3 shows how nine different media relate to the four media richness variables.

TRANSPARENCY 12.3
(FIGURE 12.2 IN THE TEXTBOOK)

EXAMPLES OF MEDIA RICHNESS FOR SENDING AND RECEIVING MESSAGES

---

   d. <u>Data</u> are the output of communication. Data become information when they reinforce or change the understanding of receivers with respect to their thoughts, feelings, attitudes, or beliefs.

3. Messages and channels.

   a. <u>Messages</u> include the transmitted data and the coded (verbal and nonverbal) symbols that give particular meanings to the data.

   b. <u>Channels</u> are the means by which messages travel from sender to receivers.

   c. Words and nonverbal symbols take on meaning because of the exchange between sender and receiver and the context in which that exchange occurs.

      d.   The greater the difference between the sent and the received message, the poorer the interpersonal communication.

4.   Meaning, encoding, decoding, and feedback.

      a.   <u>Meanings</u> represent a person's thoughts, feelings, beliefs (values), and attitudes.

      b.   <u>Encoding</u> is the personal translation of meanings into messages that can be sent.

      c.   <u>Decoding</u> is the personal translation of received messages into interpreted meanings.

      d.   <u>Feedback</u> is the receiver's response to the message. Feedback makes interpersonal communication a dynamic, two-way process.

      e.   Interpersonal communication is the most accurate when the sender's intended meaning matches the receiver's interpretation of them.

5.   Potential interpersonal barriers to interpersonal communication.

      a.   Many potential barriers to effective interpersonal communication exist. These barriers may be classified broadly as underlying barriers and direct barriers.

      b.   The potential underlying interpersonal communications barriers include the following (see Transparency 12.4):

TRANSPARENCY 12.4
(FROM TEXT MATERIAL IN THE TEXTBOOK)

POTENTIAL UNDERLYING INTERPERSONAL COMMUNICATION BARRIERS

---

      (1)   Individual personality traits such as low adjustment, low sociability, low agreeableness, low intellectual openness, and high dogmatism (see Chapter 2).

      (2)   Individuals with a low level of cognitive moral development (see Chapter 2).

      (3)   Individual perceptual errors such as perceptual defense, stereotyping, the halo effect, projection, expectancy effects, the fundamental attribution error, and the self-serving bias (see Chapter 3).

      (4)   Individual differences in problem-solving styles (see Chapter 4).

      c.   The potential direct interpersonal communications barriers include the following (see Transparency 12.5):

TRANSPARENCY 12.5
(FROM TEXT MATERIAL IN THE TEXTBOOK)

POTENTIAL DIRECT INTERPERSONAL COMMUNICATION BARRIERS

---

(1)   Nonassertive, passive-aggressive, and aggressive communication approaches.

(2)   <u>Noise</u> (*i.e.,* any interference with the intended message in the channel).

(3)   <u>Bypassing</u> (*i.e.,* an apparent agreement and understanding between two or more individuals that ultimately leads to expectations by each person about the near-term behavior of the other person).

(4)   <u>Semantics</u> (*i.e.,* the special meaning assigned to words by different people).

(5)   <u>Language routines</u> (*i.e.,* patterned responses to situations which often reflect the person's unique communication approach, or language choices that have become habits). Language routines can provide predictability with regard to the interpersonal communication or they can serve to discriminate against individuals or groups.

(6)   Lying and distortion.

    (a)   Lying and distortion take on meaning in relation to each other and in relation to honesty.

    (b)   <u>Lying</u> is an extreme form of deception in which the sender states what is believed to be false in order to seriously mislead one or more receivers.

    (c)   <u>Honesty</u> means that the sender abides by consistent and rational ethical principles to respect the truth.

    (d)   <u>Distortion</u> represents a wide range of messages that a sender may use between the extremes of lying and complete honesty.

    (e)   <u>Impression management</u>—the process by which a sender consciously attempts to influence the perceptions that the receivers form—is one type of personal distortion. Impression management usually occurs as ingratiation, self-promotion, or face-saving.

ENRICHMENT MODULE: ETHICS AND COMMUNICATION

In the past few years, many companies have adopted a code of ethics. Typically, the code is in written form and is placed in the employee handbook and/or displayed in prominent places throughout the office or plant.

A written code is one way of communicating an organization's ethics, but having a truly ethical organization goes beyond displaying a written code. People's actions and their perceived meanings are as important as, if not more important than, the actual written code in communicating an organization's ethics. These actions, and their perceived meanings, will influence the content of interpersonal communication. They may even become barriers to interpersonal communication or facilitators of interpersonal communication. As one observer indicated, "every organization is held together by communication" and "ethics must flow up and down, horizontally, vertically, and diagonally in corporate channels."

This enrichment module is based, in part, on:

Bush-Bacelis, J.L. (1988, April). Business ethics and communication: Separate or linked? In T.L. Keon & A.C. Bluedorn (Eds.), *Proceedings of the Midwest Academy of Management*, Toledo, OH, 19-22.

---

6.   Potential cultural barriers to interpersonal communication.

　　　a.   <u>Intercultural communication</u> occurs whenever a message that must be understood by a member of one culture is received by a member of another culture.

　　　b.   As cultural differences increase, the cultural barriers to effective intercultural communication increase.

　　　c.   <u>Cultural context</u>—the conditions that surround and influence the life of an individual, group, or organization—provides one perspective on potential barriers to intercultural communication.

　　　　　(1)   In a <u>high-context culture</u>, interpersonal communication is characterized by:

　　　　　　　(a)   The establishment of social trust before engaging in task-based discussions.

　　　　　　　(b)   The value placed on personal relationships and goodwill.

　　　　　　　(c)   The importance of the surrounding circumstances during an interaction.

　　　　　(2)   In a <u>low-context culture</u>, interpersonal communication is characterized by:

　　　　　　　(a)   Directly and immediately addressing the tasks, issues, or problems at hand.

      (b)   The high value placed on expertise and performance.

      (c)   The importance of clear, precise, and speedy interactions.

(3)   Interpersonal communication takes more time in a high-context culture than in a low-context culture.

(4)   A useful way to think about cultural context is relate it to the task-oriented and relations-oriented leader behaviors that were discussed in Chapter 11. Relations-oriented leader behaviors would relate to interpersonal communication in a high-context culture, whereas task-oriented leader behaviors would relate to interpersonal communication in a low-context culture.

(5)   Transparency 12.6 illustrates how the cultures of different nations vary on a cultural context continuum.

TRANSPARENCY 12.6
(FIGURE 12.3 IN THE TEXTBOOK)

EXAMPLES OF CULTURES ON THE CULTURAL CONTEXT CONTINUUM

---

    d.   <u>Ethnocentrism</u> is the greatest cultural barrier to interpersonal communication. It occurs when a person believes that "only my culture makes sense, espouses the 'right' values, and represents the 'right' and logical way to behave."

III.   Interpersonal communication networks—communication relationships beyond the basic dyad.

    A.   An <u>interpersonal communication network</u> refers to a pattern over time of communication flows between individuals. In other words, it reflects the communication relationships of individuals over time.

    B.   In organizations, an interpersonal communication network is based upon a combination of formally prescribed and informally developed relationships. For managers, this network extends vertically (to bosses and subordinates), laterally (to peers), and externally (to customers, suppliers, regulatory agencies, professional or trade associations, etc.).

    C.   As the size of the group expands, the communication network become increasingly complex.

    D.   The five-person group as an example of an interpersonal communication network.

        1.   Transparency 12.7 illustrates the types of interpersonal communication networks that can exist in a five-person group.

TRANSPARENCY 12.7
(FIGURE 12.4 IN THE TEXTBOOK)

FIVE ALTERNATIVE COMMUNICATION NETWORKS FOR A FIVE-PERSON GROUP

---

2.   Transparency 12.8 summarizes the effects of the different five-person networks on the degree of centralization, leadership predictability, average group satisfaction, and range in individual member satisfaction.

TRANSPARENCY 12.8
(TABLE 12.1 IN THE TEXTBOOK)

EFFECTS OF FIVE COMMUNICATION NETWORKS

E.   Implications of interpersonal communication networks (see Transparency 12.9).

TRANSPARENCY 12.9
(FROM TEXT MATERIAL IN THE TEXTBOOK)

IMPLICATIONS OF INTERPERSONAL COMMUNICATION NETWORKS

---

1.   Powerful individuals may limit others' access to information as one way of maintaining or increasing their power.

2.   Simple networks are often effective when the group members deal with simple problems or work on independent tasks.

3.   Complex networks are necessary for dealing with complex problems or interdependent tasks.

4.   No single network is likely to prove effective in all situations for a team with a variety of tasks and goals.

5.   Adequate sharing of information is crucial for dealing effectively with complex problems and interdependent tasks.

6.   A team must consider trade-offs and opportunity costs associated with the network it uses.

F.   Groupware-based networking.

1.   Some of the groupware aids that facilitate interpersonal communication include:

a.   Electronic mail (E-mail), which is a computer-based system that enables participating individuals to exchange and store messages with their computers.

b.   Voice mail, which is a computer-based messaging system that people access by telephone.

c.   Telecommuting, which is the practice of working at home while linked to the office or plant with groupware.

2.   Potential advantages of groupware for interpersonal communication.

a.   People can communicate with each other more easily, quickly, and less expensiv

3.   Potential limitations of groupware for interpersonal communication.

     a.   Groupware interferes with relationship building or complex group problem solving where face-to-face dialogue is crucial.

     b.   Groupware can blur the boundaries between work and nonwork time.

     c.   Groupware may erode the delegation of authority by creating too much and too frequent communication between superiors and subordinates.

     d.   Groupware creates the possibility of wasting time and effort due to dealing with increased volumes of meaningless data.

IV.   Fostering dialogue.

A.   The effectiveness of interpersonal communication relies, in part, upon developing mutual trust and a common ground between the sender(s) and receiver(s). Mutual trust and a common ground can be built through dialogue.

B.   True dialogue is based upon an interactive network of five sets of skills and behaviors, including communication openness, constructive feedback, appropriate self-disclosure, active listening, and supportive nonverbal cues.

C.   Communication openness.

1.   Transparency 12.10 depicts communication openness on a continuum ranging from closed, guarded, and defensive to open, candid, and nondefensive.

TRANSPARENCY 12.10
(FIGURE 12.6 IN THE TEXTBOOK)

THE COMMUNICATION OPENNESS CONTINUUM

---

     a.   When the communication is closed, guarded, and defensive, trust is low, hidden agendas exist, and there is an intent to conceal objectives. In short, meta-communication takes place. Meta-communication refers to the (hidden) assumptions, inferences, and interpretations of the parties that form the basis of overt messages.

     b.   When the communication is open, candid, and supportive, trust is high, agendas are shared, and there is an intent to reveal objectives. In short, direct communication takes place.

     c.   Communication openness usually is a matter of degree rather than an absolute.

ENRICHMENT MODULE: OPEN-BOOK VERSUS MUSHROOM APPROACHES TO INFORMATION MANAGEMENT

Some organizations are characterized as operating on the "mushroom theory of management." Employees are treated like mushrooms are raised. That is, the employees are kept in the dark and fed a diet of manure. Managers don't give employees "access to the information that is any business's lifeblood." The employees are kept in the dark about departmental (and sometimes personal) performance. They aren't familiar with the firm's financial statements or its strategic plans. And when any information is shared, it is probably vague and relatively useless.

Contrast the mushroom approach to information management with the open-book approach. Managers are beginning to recognize "that you cant' treat people like serfs and expect them to work like colleagues." These managers are providing the information that employees need to be effective, contributing members of the organization. Information that top managers take for granted is now routinely supplied to lower-level employees.

This enrichment module is based on:

Case, J. (1990, September). The open-book managers. *Inc.*, 104-113.

---

2. Implications of communication openness.

   a. The history of the interpersonal relationship will affect trust and risk taking in interpersonal communication.

   b. Guarded interpersonal communication is understandable and rational in adversarial relationships and win-lose situations but not in supportive relationships or win-win situations.

   c. Guarded communication is understandable and rational when you communicate with someone who has control over your fate.

D. Constructive feedback.

   1. Feedback refers to sharing our thoughts and feelings about others with them.

   2. To have effective dialogue, feedback should be supportive (*i.e.*, reinforcing ongoing behavior) or corrective (*i.e.*, indicating that a change in behavior is appropriate).

   3. Principles for making constructive feedback effective (see Transparency 12.11).

TRANSPARENCY 12.11
(FROM TEXT MATERIAL IN THE TEXTBOOK)

PRINCIPLES FOR MAKING CONSTRUCTIVE FEEDBACK EFFECTIVE

---

   a. Constructive feedback is based on a foundation of trust between sender and receiver.

   b. Constructive feedback is specific rather than general.

c.   Constructive feedback is given at a time when the receiver appears to be ready to accept it.

d.   Constructive feedback is checked with the receiver to determine whether it seems valid.

e.   Constructive feedback includes behaviors the receiver may be capable of doing something about.

f.   Constructive feedback doesn't include more than the receiver can handle at any particular time.

ENRICHMENT MODULE: THE VALUE OF GETTING AND USING FEEDBACK

Feedback and the skills to apply feedback effectively are keys to becoming a recognized leader in your field. However, many managers find the process of actively seeking feedback and using it—both positive and negative—to be difficult, if not impossible.

Robert Kaplan and his colleagues at the Center for Creative Leadership suggest that people do the following to develop their abilities in seeking and using feedback:

- Lower your defenses and take realistic stock of your strengths and weaknesses.
- Overcome the emotional barriers of getting feedback.
- Don't ask questions unless you are willing to hear the answers.
- Accept the validity of the comments about what you don't do well and take steps to improve.

When open communication is not the norm in an organization, it may be difficult to discover how you are perceived by others. Here is what Kaplan and his colleagues suggest doing in this situation:

- Ask peers for an informal, casual assessment. Make it clear that you will not resent feedback or punish anyone. What you really want to know is how other people perceive your strengths and weaknesses.
- Have peers complete questionnaires. Ask open-ended questions they can answer anonymously. Frame them carefully. Don't ask, "What do think of my work?" Instead, put them into a situational context such as "What are the things I do that help (or hurt) you in doing your job?"

This enrichment module is based on:

Kaplan, R., Drath, B., & Kofodimas, J. (1991). *Beyond ambition: How managers can lead better and live better.* San Francisco, CA: Jossey-Bass.

E.   Appropriate self-disclosure.

1.   <u>Self-disclosure</u> refers to any information that individuals communicate (verbally or nonverbally) about themselves to others.

2.   Nondisclosure individuals and total-disclosure individuals tend to function less effectively in organizations than do moderate-disclosure individuals.

3.　Individuals are likely to be less self-disclosing to people with higher formal power or to superiors who are not perceived as being trustworthy.

F.　Active listening.

1.　<u>Listening</u> is a process that integrates physical, emotional, and intellectual inputs in a search for meaning and understanding.

2.　Active listening is necessary to encourage maximum levels of openness and feedback.

3.　Guidelines for effective active listening include (see Transparency 12.12):

TRANSPARENCY 12.12
(FROM TEXT MATERIAL IN THE TEXTBOOK)
GUIDELINES FOR EFFECTIVE ACTIVE LISTENING

---

a.　Active listening involves having a reason or purpose for listening.

b.　Active listening involves suspending judgment, at least initially.

c.　Active listening involves resisting distractions, such as noises, sights, and other people, and focusing on the sender.

d.　Active listening involves pausing before responding to the sender.

e.　Active listening involves rephrasing in your own words the content and feelings of what the sender seems to be saying, especially when the message is emotional or unclear.

f.　Active listening seeks out the sender's important themes in terms of the overall content and feeling of the message.

g.　Active listening involves using the time differential between the rate of thought and the rate of speech to reflect on content and search for meaning.

G.　Supportive nonverbal cues.

1.　<u>Nonverbal communication</u> includes nonlanguage human responses (such as body motions and personal physical attributes) and environmental characteristics (such as a large or small office).

2.　The basic types of nonverbal cues are identified in Transparency 12.13, which is self-explanatory.

TRANSPARENCY 12.13
(TABLE 12.2 IN THE TEXTBOOK)
TYPES OF NONVERBAL CUES

ENRICHMENT MODULE: WHAT DOES BODY LANGUAGE MEAN?

Nonverbal cues often occur in the form of body language. Listed below are some examples of body language and the meanings commonly associated with them.

BODY LANGUAGE	COMMON INTERPRETATION
Facial Expressions	
Frown	Displeasure, unhappiness
Smile	Friendliness, happiness
Raised eyebrows	Disbelief, amazement
Narrow eyes, pursed lips	Anger
Biting lip	Nervousness
Gestures	
Pointing finger	Authority, displeasure, lecturing
Folded arms	Not open to change or communication
Arms at side	Open to suggestions, relaxed
Hands on hips	Anger, defensiveness
Hands lifted outward	Disbelief, uncertainty
Jiggling coins in pocket	Nervousness
Voice	
Shaky	Nervousness
Broken speech	Unprepared
Strong and clear	Confident
Body Postures	
Fidgeting, doodling	Boredom, nervousness
Shrugging shoulders	Indifference
Sitting on edge of chair	Listening, great interest
Slouching	Boredom, lack of interest
Shifting	Nervousness
Eye Contact	
Sideways glance	Suspicion
Steady	Active listening, interest
No eye contact	Disinterest

This enrichment module is based on:

Fandt, P.M. (1994). *Management skills: Practice and experience.* St. Paul, MN: West Publishing Company, 163.

TRANSPARENCY 12.14
(The above chart is reproduced in the transparency package.)

---

3.   Verbal and nonverbal cues may be related in that the nonverbal cue repeats, contradicts, substitutes for, or complements the verbal cues.

4.   Relationships between status and nonverbal cues include the following:

   a.   Employees of higher status typically have better offices than employees of lower status.

   b.   The offices of higher status employees are better protected from unwanted intrusions.

   c.   The higher the employee's status, the easier that employee finds it to invade the territory of lower status employees.

5.   While some of these patterns are changing and they do not apply universally, the typical relationships between gender and nonverbal cues include the following:

   a.   Women's use of space is more restricted than men's use of space.

   b.   Women tend to have more eye contact with other people than men do.

   c.   The nature of touching may indicate dominance, submissiveness, or intimacy.

V.   Summing up: How does an understanding of interpersonal communication benefit the members of an organization?

   A.   Communication is fundamental to the interaction of two or more people, and people are the essential building blocks of organizations. Without adequate communication, individual members of organizations would not be able to perform their jobs effectively, and teams could not function effectively. Indeed, as a wise sage once said, "Communication is the lifeblood of an organization."

   B.   Being an effective interpersonal communicator means that one understands the intricacies of the basic dyadic interpersonal communications process, appreciates the exponentially increasing complexity of interpersonal communications beyond the basic dyadic exchange, and has the necessary skills to build interpersonal trust and a common ground.

DISCUSSION QUESTIONS: SUGGESTED ANSWERS

1.   *What difficulties might most people have in trying to use the assertive communication approach consistently?*

Assertive communication means confidently expressing what you think, feel, and believe (values)—and standing up for your rights while respecting the rights of others.

Self-knowledge is fundamental to assertive communication. Therefore, to practice assertive communication consistently, one would need to have a high degree of self-knowledge. Self-knowledge would be diminished whenever people have "blind spots" about their own behavior.

Practicing assertive communication may be difficult when one person is in a low-power position and the other person is in a high-power position, particularly if the latter person can reward or punish the former person. Practicing assertive communication is also difficult when interacting with someone who practices aggressive communication.

2.   *Give two examples of how interpersonal classroom communication is likely to vary in a high-context culture and a low-context culture.*

Cultural context refers to the conditions that surround and influence the life of an individual, group, or organization. With respect to interpersonal communication, a high-context culture is characterized by:

    a.   The establishment of social trust before engaging in task-based discussions.
    b.   The value placed on personal relationships and goodwill.
    c.   The importance of the surrounding circumstances during an interaction.

In contrast, interpersonal communication in a low-context culture is characterized by:

    a.   Directly and immediately addressing the tasks, issues, or problems at hand.
    b.   The high value placed on expertise and performance.
    c.   The importance of clear, precise, and speedy interactions.

In a high-context culture, classroom communication would encourage the expression of opinions, foster consideration of alternative viewpoints, elicit involvement in nonthreatening or nonjudgmental ways, etc. In a low-context culture, classroom communication would be primarily from instructor to the students; discussion probably would be kept to a minimum, and certainly the expression of opinions would not be encouraged; etc.

3.   *Describe your communication network. Would you like to make any changes in it? Why or why not?*

The students could use Figure 12.4 to initiate discussion on this question. Figure 12.4 identifies different communications networks for a five-person group. The students should recognize that as group size increases, the communications network becomes more complex and the examples that are provided in Figure 12.4 would need to be adapted and extended.

Since people generally are involved with more than one communication network, the students should clearly identify the network they intend to describe. Descriptions should be detailed and, if possible, linked to the material in Figure 12.4.

4.   *What types of problems are less likely to be communicated effectively by E-mail than in face-to-face discussion? Explain.*

Complex group problems and relationship-building problems are more likely to be handled more effectively on a face-to-face basis than on an E-mail basis. Electronic communication cannot substitute effectively for personal contact in these types of situations.

5.   *Think of an organization or team of which you are a member. How would you assess it in terms of the continuum of communication openness? (See Figure 12.6).*

According Figure 12.6, closed, guarded, and defensive communication is accompanied by low trust, hidden agendas, and an intent to conceal objectives. On the other hand, open, candid, and supportive communication is accompanied by high trust, shared agendas, and an intent to reveal objectives.

This question encourages students to relate their own interpersonal communication experiences to the conceptual material in Figure 12.6. Students with work experience should base their examples on the work setting. Students without work experience should use college organizations or social groups that they belong to for examples.

6.   *What types of problems and limitations prevent meaningful self-disclosure between superiors and subordinates?*

Individuals are likely to be less self-disclosing to people with higher formal power or to superiors who are not perceived as being trustworthy. People may be somewhat reluctant to disclose to their superiors information about personal limitations or personal performance deficiencies. Such information could be used by the superior to make judgments about promotion or merit raises. Extreme self-disclosure can put the subordinate into a position of denying his or her own self interests. If the superior is perceived as untrustworthy, self-disclosure also could be detrimental to the person's self interest.

7.   *How are constructive feedback skills and active listening similar and different?*

Listening is a process that integrates physical, emotional, and intellectual inputs in a search for meaning and understanding. Active listening is necessary to encourage maximum feedback. Feedback refers to sharing our thoughts and feelings about others with them. In a sense, active listening provides meaningful input to the receiver, and constructive feedback provides meaningful output to the sender.

Active listening and constructive feedback are similar in the following ways: (1) both can be strongly influenced by individual differences and characteristics, such as degree of self-esteem; (2) both require an initial effort to be descriptive rather than evaluative; (3) both are influenced by the level of trust between the parties; and (4) both become more effective when there is specificity rather than vagueness in the message.

8.   *Describe the common nonverbal cues used by someone you have worked for or by someone you know well. Are they usually consistent or inconsistent with this person's verbal expressions? Explain.*

Students should select a familiar person to describe. The question is intended to encourage students to relate the materials presented in the text to their own experiences. Using familiar characters from a current movie and TV show would provide an alternative means of comparison and description.

Table 12.2 can be used to facilitate discussion on this question. For instance, the students could cite examples that pertain to the use of space (How does an individual have his or her office arranged?), eye contact (Do others look at you or beyond you?), touching (Do others pat you on the back? Do others use a firm grip or a soft grip in shaking hands?), body motion (How do others carry themselves? How do others gesture to get a point across?), or time (Are others punctual? Late? Early?).

9.   *If you take a job in a foreign culture, what communication practices must you be sensitive to?*

Discussion of this question can be based on the "Managing Across Cultures: Nonverbal Cues and Tips" segment of the text (pages 400-401) and/or "Managing Across Cultures: Nonverbal Expectations in Mexico" segment (pages 415-416).

In general, a person taking a job in a foreign culture must be sensitive to nonverbal cues. Cues regarding body language and personal space are particularly important.

10.   *If you are supervised by a person of a different gender, what nonverbal problems might you encounter?*

Some of the key nonverbal cues that appear to be gender related are the following:

   a.   Women's use of space is more restricted than men's use of space.
   b.   Women tend to have more eye contact with other people than men do.
   c.   The nature of touching may indicate dominance, submissiveness, or intimacy.

To the extent that these relationships are true and people have knowledge of them, people may have certain expectations of the opposite gender. Nonverbal cues which are consistent with these relationships would reinforce those expectations and vice versa.

Additional problems could be created because the above relationships do not apply to all people in all cultures, or to all subcultures within a given culture. Moreover, these relationships may be changing as more people begin adopting some of the nonverbal cues that traditionally have been associated with members of the opposite gender.

DEVELOPING SKILLS—
SELF DIAGNOSIS: PERSONAL COMMUNICATION PRACTICES

This 20-item self-diagnostic instrument measures interpersonal communication practices. Each survey item describes a scenario and two alternative responses to that scenario. By allocating 5 points between the two alternatives, the respondent indicates the extent to which each alternative characterizes his/her personal communication practices. The instructions for responding are a little complicated, so the students should be cautioned to follow the instructions carefully. Also, a scoring key is provided in the text.

The questionnaire yields two measures of personal communication practices: *receptivity to feedback* and *willingness to self-disclose*. The results are plotted on the chart contained in Figure 12.7. Higher scores on *receptivity to feedback* and *willingness to self-disclose* indicate a greater willingness to engage in personal openness in interpersonal communication.

DEVELOPING SKILLS—
A CASE IN POINT: XOGRAPHICS

CASE OVERVIEW

This is a three part case that focuses on communications within Xographics, a division of a large telecommunications company.

In **Part A**, we are introduced to Ellen Bohn, the new production superintendent, who inherited a situation of problem workers and poor performance. Three line managers, all with 20 more years' experience with Xographics, reported to Bohn. Bohn learned that many first-line supervisors were upset because all machine breakdowns had to be reported to higher management within 15 minutes of their occurrence. This prevented the workers from trying to make repairs themselves. Moreover, there was a rumor that five machine breakdown reports for a given worker would result in that worker being reassigned to a lower paying job.

In **Part B**, Bohn discovered that only about 40% of the scheduled maintenance jobs were ever performed and that the maintenance department was operating at 30% efficiency. Maintenance workers had staged a slowdown to try to force the company to increase wages. They also usually quit working an hour early in order to wash up. The head of the maintenance department attributed the inefficiency to the lack of qualified workers. Training of new hires was done by the more senior maintenance workers.

In **Part C**, Bohn had a revealing conversation with the personnel director, who cited some concrete examples of inadequate communication at Xographics. Xographics' style was characterized as the "mushroom style"—keep the workers in the dark and feed them a lot of manure.

CASE QUESTIONS: PART A

1.   *What should Bohn do?*

As a new manager, Bohn should meet with her supervisors. She can learn a lot from their experience by listening to their ideas about what problems exist and how they can be solved. If Ellen shows a sincere interest in the supervisor's opinions, a rapport can be developed and upward communication can be encouraged.

Although Ellen's ultimate goal is to increase productivity, there are some smaller steps she can takes toward that goal. Together with the supervisors, she can establish some guidelines on machine breakdowns and repairs. If these guidelines and their rationale are communicated to the workers, it would clear up a lot of immediate problems.

2.   *What other problems (unidentified by Bohn) might be present?*

There might not be much communication between supervisors and departments (horizontal channels), thus causing much confusion and inefficiency. In a production company like Xographics, it is especially important that horizontal channels are open. In order to coordinate so many specialized activities, good lines of communication are needed between departments. Another problem that might exist is the extensive use of the organizational grapevine. When the formal lines of communication do not adequately inform the workers, they rely on news from the grapevine, which may not always be accurate.

3.   *What additional steps might the supervisors take?*

Supervisors should serve as the link between management and the workers. One of their duties is to communicate information from management through the downward channels. Another responsibility is for them to convey information from the worker's level to management (upward communication). In order to avoid confusion or misinterpretation, supervisors should take steps toward transmitting these messages as accurately and efficiently as possible.

CASE QUESTIONS: PART B

4.   *How might Bohn approach the maintenance head?*

A face-to-face meeting with the maintenance head would provide a chance for two-way communication. Bohn might start by asking the maintenance head what assistance he needs from her in her role as production superintendent, and what some of the problems are that maintenance faces. Ellen should also ask for solutions from the maintenance head. She could then communicate to him her expectations of that department, and inquire about implementation dates for possible solutions.

5.   *Who else should Bohn talk to?*

Ellen should talk to some of the maintenance people to hear first-hand about the problems they are experiencing. Do they feel that they receive adequate training? Adequate work direction? Adequate wages? Ellen might also go back to the human resources department to determine if anything can be done in terms of hiring and training.

CASE QUESTIONS: PART C

6.   *What steps can Bohn take?*

Ellen should use the downward channels to communicate to the production workers. These workers have a real need for information concerning job descriptions, procedures and policies, and feedback about job performance. Together with the supervisors, Ellen needs to determine an efficient channel to keep her employees informed. Regular performance evaluations—at least on a yearly basis—should be initiated. If Ellen has a lot of production people under her, perhaps a weekly newsletter explaining policy and news about the job could be distributed.

Ellen could then work on establishing upward communication channels. Supervisors need to be encouraged to listen to the workers and to transmit relevant information back to Ellen. Even a simple approach like a suggestion box might facilitate the sharing of ideas. Workers could be rewarded for ideas that improve efficiency.

7.   *What does this conversation tell you about the company? What barriers to communication may exist?*

This conversation indicates that there is a serious lack of formal communication channels. Perhaps the company grew quickly, and management practices have not kept up with its growth. Whatever the cause, communication needs to be improved to increase productivity. However, some organizational barriers exist. The company consists of many levels and specialized tasks. This creates difficulty in accurately transmitting messages through the hierarchy. Different departments have different goals. In order to coordinate efforts, some common goals need to be established. Finally, everyone seems to have a title—something that may simply add to the communication barriers.

8.   *What role has the company's informal communication network played in this situation?*

Since formal channels are practically nonexistent, employees have created an informal communication channel to vent their anger and confusion. Managers hear about employees' feelings through this channel. However, because they hear only complaints, some useful information probably is being dismissed by managers.

COURSE ENHANCEMENT—
WEST'S ORGANIZATIONAL BEHAVIOR CUSTOM VIDEO SERIES

One video from *West's Organizational Behavior Custom Video Series* can be used to enhance the material in Chapter 12. This video is: *Tenneco's Leadership and Planning Conference (Communications Segment).*

VIDEO: *TENNECO'S LEADERSHIP AND PLANNING CONFERENCE (COMMUNICATIONS SEGMENT)*

Approximate Time: 10 minutes

Video Summary:

Oral persuasive communication is one of the skills needed by effective supervisors and managers. This skill is needed on a daily basis in challenging work group members to achieve lofty objectives. Sometimes oral persuasive communication skills must be applied to large collectives of employees, such as a CEO addressing all managers.

This video is an excellent example of Tenneco's CEO, Mike Walsh, addressing 300 managers at a planning conference. The conference was intended to outline the specific goals, strategies, and support processes needed to respond to Tenneco's environment. Mr. Walsh explained, with some audience participation, that Tenneco needed an operating cost leadership strategy that would be driven by quality initiatives and disciplined management processes, and supported by action plans, communication and a focus on results.

Mr. Walsh's communication style could be characterized as assertive, controlled, informative, realistic, and honest.

Discussion Question and Suggested Answer for Video:

1.   *How effective was Mr. Walsh as an interpersonal communicator? How was his level of effectiveness influenced through the use of dialogue?*

Mr. Walsh's effectiveness might be gauged from at least three different perspectives. First, Mr. Walsh appeared to be effective at getting his message across—the audience was attentive and somewhat responsive; he built on the audience's background and experience as he reviewed prior decisions and planning assumptions in relation to the current situation; and his communication could be described as assertive, controlled, informative, realistic, and honest. Second, one could argue that appearances are deceiving. While he appeared to be getting his message across and the audience was attentive, many of his attempts to generate audience participation were not very successful. Mr. Walsh ended up answering many of the questions he asked of the audience, and these were questions directed at prior decisions and planning assumptions. A third perspective revolves around the notion that the effectiveness of interpersonal communication relies, in part, upon developing mutual trust and a common ground between the sender(s) and receiver(s). Mr. Walsh seems to have done a good, if not excellent, job of fostering mutual trust and building a common ground. On balance, one might argue that Mr. Walsh was quite effective at communicating interpersonally.

Mutual trust and a common ground—the third perspective on effectiveness—can be built through dialogue. True dialogue is based on five sets of skills and behaviors: communication openness, constructive feedback, appropriate self-disclosure, active listening, and supportive nonverbal cues. For example, the video reveals a high level of communication openness. The interpersonal communication was open, candid, and supportive, and was linked to high trust, shared agendas, and the clear intent to reveal objectives.

CHAPTER 13
CONFLICT AND NEGOTIATION

CHAPTER OVERVIEW

Chapter 13 completes the discussion of interpersonal and group processes. The chapter begins by describing the nature of conflict and conflict management, giving special attention to different forms of conflict and different views of conflict. Next, the various levels of conflict are examined. Intrapersonal conflict, interpersonal conflict, intragroup conflict, and intergroup conflict are explored in terms of their basic nature and likely effects. Then five conflict-handling styles—avoiding, forcing, accommodating, collaborating, and compromising—are discussed. The situations in which each of these conflict-handling styles is appropriately utilized are considered as well. Finally, negotiation is explored as a means for resolving conflict. Emphasis is placed on integrative and distributive negotiations, and on the complexities associated with cross-cultural negotiations.

LEARNING OBJECTIVES

Upon completion of this chapter, the students should be able to:

1. Define four basic forms of conflict.
2. Explain the negative, positive, and balanced views of conflict.
3. Identify the principal levels of conflict within organizations.
4. Describe and apply five interpersonal conflict-handling styles.
5. Explain the basic types of negotiations.
6. Describe various negotiation strategies.

CHAPTER OUTLINE

I. **Preview Case:** Charlie Olcott

II. Conflict Management

KEY WORDS AND CONCEPTS

Thirty-seven key words and concepts are introduced in Chapter 13. Two concepts—role ambiguity and role conflict—were originally introduced in Chapter 8. The key words and concepts, along with definitions or appropriate descriptions, are as follows:

Accommodating style: a conflict-handling style that involves unassertive and cooperative behaviors.

Affective conflict: one of the four basic forms of conflict; it occurs when the feelings and emotions within an individual or between individuals are incompatible.

Approach-approach conflict: a type of intrapersonal conflict which occurs when an individual must choose among two or more alternatives, each of which is expected to have a positive outcome.

Approach-avoidance conflict: a type of intrapersonal conflict which occurs when an individual must decide whether to do something that is expected to have both positive and negative outcomes.

Attitudinal structuring: one of the four basic types of negotiations; attitudinal structuring is the process by which the conflicting parties seek to establish desired attitudes and relationships.

Avoidance-avoidance conflict: a type of intrapersonal conflict which occurs when an individual must choose among two or more alternatives, each of which is expected to have a negative outcome.

Avoiding style: a conflict-handling style that involves unassertive and uncooperative behaviors.

Cognitive conflict: one of the four basic forms of conflict; it occurs when the ideas and thoughts within an individual or between individuals are incompatible.

Cognitive dissonance: occurs when individuals recognize inconsistencies in their own thoughts and/or behaviors. Cognitive dissonance may produce intrapersonal conflict.

Collaborating style: a conflict-handling style that involves assertive and cooperative behaviors.

Collaboration: the process of sharing, examining, and assessing the reasons for the conflict, thereby leading to the development of an alternative that effectively resolves the conflict and is fully acceptable to everyone involved.

Compromising style: a conflict-handling style that involves an intermediate level of assertiveness and cooperativeness.

Conflict: the process that begins when one person perceives that another person has negatively affected, or is about to negatively affect, something that the first person, a group, or an organization cares about.

Conflict management: consists of diagnostic processes, interpersonal styles, negotiating strategies, and other interventions that are designed to avoid unnecessary conflict and reduce or resolve excessive conflict.

Distributive negotiations: one of the four basic types of negotiations; distributive negotiations involve win-lose, fixed amount situations where one party's gain is another party's loss.

Forcing style: a conflict-handling style that involves assertive and uncooperative behaviors.

Goal conflict: one of the four basic forms of conflict; it occurs when two or more desired or expected outcomes are incompatible.

Horizontal conflict: a type of intergroup conflict that occurs when there are clashes between groups of employees at the same hierarchical level in an organization.

Integrative negotiations: one of the four basic types of negotiations; integrative negotiations involve joint problem solving to achieve solutions by which both parties can gain.

Intergroup conflict: one of the levels of conflict; it involves opposition and clashes between groups.

Interpersonal conflict: one of the levels of conflict; it involves two or more individuals who believe that their attitudes, behaviors, or preferred goals are in opposition.

Interrole conflict: a type of role conflict that occurs when role pressures associated with membership in one group are incompatible with pressures stemming from membership in other groups.

Intersender role conflict: a type of role conflict that occurs when the messages and pressures from one role sender oppose messages and pressures from one or more other senders.

Intragroup conflict: one of the levels of conflict; it involves clashes among some or all of the group's members, which often affect the group's processes and effectiveness.

Intraorganizational negotiations: one of the four basic types of negotiations. Intraorganizational negotiations involve two or more sets of people representing two or more different organizations, and the negotiators within each set try to resolve intragroup conflict and build intragroup consensus prior to dealing with the other set(s) of negotiators.

Intrapersonal conflict: one of the levels of conflict; it occurs within an individual and often involves some form of goal, cognitive, or affective conflict.

Intrasender role conflict: a type of role conflict that occurs when different messages and pressures from a single member of the role set are incompatible.

Line-staff conflict: a type of intergroup conflict that involves clashes over authority relationships.

Negotiation: a process in which two or more people or groups, having both common and conflicting goals, state and discuss proposals for specific terms of a possible agreement.

Neurotic tendencies: irrational personality mechanisms that an individual uses—often unconsciously—which create inner conflict. Neurotic tendencies may contribute to intrapersonal conflict.

Person-role conflict: a type of role conflict that occurs when the role requirements are incompatible with the focal person's own attitudes, values, or views of acceptable behavior.

Procedural conflict: one of the four basic forms of conflict; it occurs when people differ over the process to use for resolving a matter.

Role: the cluster of tasks that others expect a person to perform in doing a job.

Role ambiguity: occurs when there is uncertainty or lack of clarity surrounding expectations about a single role.

Role conflict: occurs as a result of the incompatible messages and pressures from the role set.

Role set: the group of role senders that directly affect the focal person.

Vertical conflict: a type of intergroup conflict that occurs when there are clashes between employees at different levels in the organization.

LECTURE NOTES

I.   Chapter 13 completes the discussion of interpersonal and group processes through its focus on conflict and negotiation. <u>Conflict</u> is the process that begins when one person perceives that another person has negatively affected, or is about to negatively affect, something that the first person, a group, or an organization cares about. In an ideal world, conflict would not exist or all conflicts would have positive effects. But we don't live in an ideal world. Therefore we must learn how to mange conflict effectively. Effective conflict management is based upon the ability to understand and correctly diagnose conflict as well as having specific skills to deal with conflict situations. Transparency 13.1 outlines the various diagnostic tools and intervention techniques that we will be discussing as we explore conflict management in organizations.

TRANSPARENCY 13.1
(FROM TEXT MATERIAL IN THE TEXTBOOK)

KEY IDEAS ABOUT CONFLICT AND NEGOTIATION

II.   The nature of conflict management.

    A.   The ability to understand and diagnose conflict is essential to managing it.

    B.   <u>Conflict management</u> consists of diagnostic processes, interpersonal styles, negotiating strategies, and other interventions that are designed to avoid unnecessary conflict and reduce or resolve excessive conflict.

    C.   Conflict occurs in four basic forms: goal conflict, cognitive conflict, affective conflict, and procedural conflict.

        1.   <u>Goal conflict</u> occurs when two or more desired or expected outcomes are incompatible.

        2.   <u>Cognitive conflict</u> occurs when the ideas and thoughts within an individual or between individuals are incompatible.

        3.   <u>Affective conflict</u> occurs when the feelings and emotions within an individual or between individuals are incompatible.

        4.   <u>Procedural conflict</u> occurs when people differ over the process to use for resolving a matter.

    D.   Conflict may be viewed as being positive, negative, or balanced.

        1.   The positive view of conflict focuses on the constructive aspects of conflict. According to this view, conflict leads to constructive problem solving, provides a stimulus for positive change, helps make change more acceptable, encourages people to work out their differences, fosters participation in developing a fair and ethical organization, and challenges people to deal directly with injustices.

        2.   The negative view of conflict focuses on the destructive aspects of conflict. According to this view, conflict diverts effort away from goal attainment; depletes resources, especially time and money; negatively affects the psychological well-

being of employees; threatens important personal goals and beliefs; makes the establishment of supportive and trusting relationships difficult; and undermines performance.

3.   The balanced view of conflict holds that sometimes conflict is constructive and sometimes it is destructive. The balanced view acknowledges that conflict arises in organizations whenever interests collide, and is sensitive to the consequences of conflict.

ENRICHMENT MODULE: POSITIVE AND NEGATIVE EFFECTS OF CONFLICT

In a recent study, Robert Baron examined the perceived positive and negative effects of conflict and the conditions under which conflict is likely to result in negative effects or in positive effects. What did he find?

Baron's study identified seven negative effects of conflict and three positive effects. The negative effects were:

- Interferes with communication.
- Leads to or intensifies grudges and feuds.
- Interferes with cooperation and coordination.
- Diverts energies from major tasks or goals.
- Leads groups to stereotype each other.
- Leads to an increase in politics.
- Reduces the organization's capacity to compete in the marketplace.

The positive effects were:

- Brings important problems out into the open.
- Encourages consideration of new approaches and ideas; encourages innovation and change.
- Increases loyalty and performance within each of the groups in conflict.

Baron suggested that three cognitive factors influenced whether conflict would result in positive or negative effects. Strong negative emotions, an attributional bias, and stereotypical thinking increase the probability that a conflict situation will produce negative effects. Positive emotions, accurate attributions, and the absence of stereotypical thinking increase the likelihood that positive effects will result from the conflict situation.

This enrichment module is adapted from:

Baron, R.A. (1991). Positive effects of conflict: A cognitive perspective. *Employee Responsibilities and Rights Journal, 4(1)*, 25-35.

III.   Levels of conflict.

A.   Five major levels of conflict exist within organizations: intrapersonal (within an individual), interpersonal (between individuals), intragroup (within a group), intergroup (between groups), and interorganizational (between organizations.)

1.   The five levels are often interrelated.

2.   This chapter focuses primarily on the intrapersonal, interpersonal, intragroup, and intergroup levels.

B.   Intrapersonal conflict.

    1.   <u>Intrapersonal conflict</u> occurs within an individual and often involves some form of goal, cognitive, or affective conflict.

    2.   Intrapersonal conflict is triggered when a person's behavior will result in outcomes that are mutually exclusive.

    3.   Three basic types of intrapersonal conflict.

        a.   <u>Approach-approach conflict</u> occurs when an individual must choose among two or more alternatives, each of which is expected to have a positive outcome.

        b.   <u>Avoidance-avoidance conflict</u> occurs when an individual must choose among two or more alternatives, each of which is expected to have a negative outcome.

        c.   <u>Approach-avoidance conflict</u> occurs when an individual must decide whether to do something that is expected to have both positive and negative outcomes.

    4.   Intrapersonal conflict may also result from <u>cognitive dissonance</u>, which occurs when individuals recognize inconsistencies in their own thoughts and/or behaviors.

        a.   Dissonance may be reduced by changing thoughts and/or behaviors, or by obtaining more information about the dissonance-causing issue.

    5.   Neurotic tendencies can contribute to intrapersonal conflict.

        a.   <u>Neurotic tendencies</u> are irrational personality mechanisms that an individual uses—often unconsciously—and which create inner conflict.

        b.   People with neurotic tendencies have an excessive need to control, are very distrustful of others, may be fearful of uncertainty and risk, or may be excessively bold and impulsive.

        c.   Individuals with strong neurotic tendencies have difficulty resolving their personal conflict which, in turn, can trigger conflicts with other people.

    6.   With increasing frequency, the unresolved intrapersonal conflicts of employees or customers often trigger violent interpersonal conflict.

ENRICHMENT MODULE: VIOLENCE IN THE WORKPLACE

In 1992, the number of workplace homicides was 1,004. The vast majority of the killings—878—were due to robberies and miscellaneous crimes or were police killed in the line of duty. However, 87 of these workplace homicides were due to business disputes and another 39 workplace homicides involved personal disputes. Most often, the business disputes revolved around conflicts with current or former co-workers, or with customers or clients. Personal disputes usually involved a conflict with a relative of the victim or a current or ex-boyfriend.

From January 1, 1980 to December 31, 1988, 6,956 workplace homicides occurred. Approximately 54% of the victims were in sales or service occupations, or were executives, administrators, or managers. Often, the perpetrator was a disgruntled worker looking for revenge. For example, Robert Earl Mack wounded his supervisor and killed another manager after a termination hearing at a General Dynamics plant in San Diego. Another example is the kidnapping and murder of an Exxon Corp. executive. Investigators say that the person who is charged with these crimes was obsessed with retaliating against Exxon because he had been fired.

According to psychologists:

> "The most maliciously disgruntled share common histories of depression, paranoia, and violence. They generally have difficulty accepting authority and exhibit a fascination with weaponry. They also may be undergoing a private stress such as a divorce or death in the family that compounds feelings of insecurity at a time of job loss."

This enrichment module is adapted from:

O'Boyle, T.F. (1992, September 15). Disgruntled workers intent on revenge increasingly harm colleagues and bosses. *The Wall Street Journal*, B1 & B10.

Rigdon, J.E. (1994, April 12). Companies see more workplace violence. *The Wall Street Journal*, B1 & B6.

C.   Interpersonal conflict.

   1.   <u>Interpersonal conflict</u> involves two or more individuals who believe that their attitudes, behaviors, or preferred goals are in opposition.

   2.   Many interpersonal conflicts derive from role conflict or role ambiguity

   3.   Role conflict and role ambiguity are best understood in the context of the role episode model which is shown in Transparency 13.2.

TRANSPARENCY 13.2
(FIGURE 13.2 IN THE TEXTBOOK)

ROLE EPISODE MODEL

---

   a.   Key variables in the role episode model.

      (1)   A <u>role</u> is the cluster of tasks that others expect a person to perform

in doing a job.

(2)   The focal person is the role occupant.

(3)   Role senders are the individuals who hold expectations for the focal person's performance of his or her role.

(4)   A <u>role set</u> is the group of role senders that directly affect the focal person.

b.   How the role episode model works: Members of the role set have expectations, perceptions, and evaluations of the focal person's behaviors. These expectations, perceptions, and evaluations are communicated to the focal person. The focal person perceives and interprets these messages and responds to them. Incompatible messages and pressures from members of the role set cause the focal person to experience role conflict.

c.   Four types of role conflict may occur as a result of the incompatible messages and pressures from the role set.

(1)   <u>Intrasender role conflict</u> occurs when different messages and pressures from a single member of the role set are incompatible.

(2)   <u>Intersender role conflict</u> occurs when the messages and pressures from one role sender oppose messages and pressures from one or more other senders.

(3)   <u>Interrole conflict</u> occurs when role pressures associated with membership in one group are incompatible with pressures stemming from membership in other groups.

(4)   <u>Person-role conflict</u> occurs when the role requirements are incompatible with the focal person's own attitudes, values, or views of acceptable behavior.

d.   Role ambiguity also may result from the expectation, perceptions, and evaluations of members of the role set.

(1)   <u>Role ambiguity</u> occurs when there is uncertainty or lack of clarity surrounding expectations about a single role.

D.   Intragroup conflict.

1.   <u>Intragroup conflict</u> involves clashes among some or all of the group's members, which often affect the group's processes and effectiveness.

2.   Family-run businesses are especially susceptible to intragroup conflict.

E.   Intergroup conflict.

1.   <u>Intergroup conflict</u> involves opposition and clashes between groups.

2.   Intergroup conflict can produce distrust, rigidity, a focus only on self-interests, and

failure to listen.

3.   Four types of intergroup conflicts can occur within organizations: vertical conflict, horizontal conflict, line-staff conflict, and diversity-based conflict.

    a.   <u>Vertical conflict</u> occurs when there are clashes between employees at different levels in the organization. Vertical conflicts arise because of superiors' attempts to overcontrol, inadequate communication, goal conflict, or cognitive conflict.

    b.   <u>Horizontal conflict</u> occurs when there are clashes between groups of employees at the same hierarchical level in an organization. The clashes may arise from incompatible goals or attitudes.

    c.   <u>Line-staff conflict</u> involves clashes over authority relationships. Line managers often believe that staff managers reduce their authority over workers while their responsibility for the outcomes remains unchanged.

    d.   Diversity-based conflict in organizations is related to issues of race, gender, ethnicity, and religion.

IV.   Conflict-handling styles.

A.   The way in which a person manages interpersonal conflict is a function of two variables: concern for self and concern for others. Each variable can be dichotomized. Concern for self involves being either assertive or unassertive in pursuing personal goals. Concern for others involves being either cooperative or uncooperative relative to others' goals. Taken together, these two variables define five different conflict-handling styles, as shown in Transparency 13.3. The five conflict handling styles are the avoiding style, the forcing style, the accommodating style, the collaborating style, and the compromising style.

TRANSPARENCY 13.3
(FIGURE 13.3 IN THE TEXTBOOK)

INTERPERSONAL CONFLICT-HANDLING STYLES

---

1.   People have a natural tendency toward one or two of the conflict-handling styles.

2.   However, everyone is capable of using each style as the context and people change.

B.   The avoiding style.

1.   The <u>avoiding style</u> involves unassertive and uncooperative behaviors. People use this style to stay away from conflict, ignore disagreements, or remain neutral.

2.   The avoiding style can be used effectively in the following situations (see Transparency 13.4):

TRANSPARENCY 13.4
(FROM TEXT MATERIAL IN THE TEXTBOOK)

WHEN SHOULD YOU USE THE AVOIDING STYLE
TO HANDLE INTERPERSONAL CONFLICTS?

---

a.   When the issue is minor or only of passing importance and thus not worth the individual's time or energy to confront the conflict.

b.   When there isn't enough information available to the individual to effectively deal with the conflict at that time.

c.   When the individual's power is so low relative to the other person's such that there is little chance of causing change.

d.   When other individuals can more effectively resolve the conflict.

C.   The forcing style.

1.   The <u>forcing style</u> involves assertive and uncooperative behaviors. People use this style to achieve their own goals without consideration of others.

2.   The forcing style can be used effectively in the following situations (see Transparency 13.5):

TRANSPARENCY 13.5
(FROM TEXT MATERIAL IN THE TEXTBOOK)

WHEN SHOULD YOU USE THE FORCING STYLE
TO HANDLE INTERPERSONAL CONFLICTS?

---

a.   When emergencies require quick action.

b.   When unpopular courses of action must be taken for long-term organizational effectiveness and survival.

c.   When the person needs to take action for self-protection and to stop others from taking advantage of him or her.

D.   The accommodating style.

1.   The <u>accommodating style</u> involves unassertive and cooperative behaviors. People use this style as a representation of an unselfish act, a long-term strategy to encourage cooperation by others, or a submission to the wishes of others.

2.   The accommodating style can be used effectively in the following situations (see Transparency 13.6):

TRANSPARENCY 13.6
(FROM TEXT MATERIAL IN THE TEXTBOOK)

WHEN SHOULD YOU USE THE ACCOMMODATING STYLE
TO HANDLE INTERPERSONAL CONFLICTS?

---

a.   When the individuals are in a potentially explosive emotional conflict situation, and smoothing is used to defuse it.

b.   When keeping harmony and avoiding disruption are especially important in the short run.

c.   When the conflicts are based primarily on the personalities of the individuals and cannot be easily resolved.

E.   The collaborating style.

1.   The <u>collaborating style</u> involves assertive and cooperative behaviors. People use this style to maximize joint outcomes. <u>Collaboration</u> refers to the process of sharing, examining, and assessing the reasons for the conflict, thereby leading to the development of an alternative that effectively resolves the conflict and is fully acceptable to everyone involved.

2.   The collaborating style can be used effectively in the following situations (see Transparency 13.7):

TRANSPARENCY 13.7
(FROM TEXT MATERIAL IN THE TEXTBOOK)

WHEN SHOULD YOU USE THE COLLABORATING STYLE
TO HANDLE INTERPERSONAL CONFLICTS?

---

a.   When there is sufficient required interdependence so that spending the extra time and energy needed for working through individual differences makes sense.

b.   When there is sufficient parity in power among individuals so that they feel free to interact candidly, regardless of their formal superior/subordinate status.

c.   When there is potential for mutual benefits, especially over the long run.

d.   When there is sufficient organizational support for taking the time and energy to resolve disputes through collaboration.

F.   The compromising style.

1.   The <u>compromising style</u> involves an intermediate level of assertiveness and cooperativeness. People use this style as a pragmatic way for dealing with conflicts and to help maintain good interpersonal relations.

2.   The compromising style can be used effectively in the following situations (see Transparency 13.8):

TRANSPARENCY 13.8
(FROM TEXT MATERIAL IN THE TEXTBOOK)

WHEN SHOULD YOU USE THE COMPROMISING STYLE
TO HANDLE INTERPERSONAL CONFLICTS?

---

         a.   When agreement enables each person to be better off or at least not worse off than if no agreement were reached.

         b.   When achieving a total win/win agreement isn't possible.

         c.   When conflicting goals or opposing interests block agreement on one person's proposal.

3.   The compromising style may create several problems if used to early too resolve conflict. These problems include the following:

         a.   The people involved may be encouraging compromise on the stated issues rather than on the real issues.

         b.   Accepting the initial solution that is presented is easier than searching for alternatives that are more acceptable to everyone involved.

         c.   Compromise may be inappropriate to all or part of the situation because it may not be the best decision available.

G.   Key implications of the conflict-handling styles.

     1.   Successful people and high-performing organizations tend to use collaboration.

     2.   Collaboration is associated with the constructive use of conflict, positive feelings from others, and favorable evaluations of performance and abilities.

     3.   Forcing and avoiding tend to be associated with a less constructive use of conflict, negative feelings from others, and unfavorable evaluations of performance and abilities.

     4.   Accommodation and compromise have mixed effects in terms of feelings from others and evaluations of performance and abilities.

V.   Negotiation in conflict management.

A.   <u>Negotiation</u> is a process in which two or more people or groups, having both common and conflicting goals, state and discuss proposals for specific terms of a possible agreement.

B.   Four basic type of negotiations can be used by conflicting individuals or groups. The types of negotiations are: distributive, integrative, attitudinal structuring, and intraorganizational.

1.   <u>Distributive negotiations</u> involve win-lose, fixed amount situations where one party's gain is another party's loss.

2.   <u>Integrative negotiations</u> involve joint problem solving to achieve solutions by which both parties can gain.

3.   <u>Attitudinal structuring</u> is the process by which the conflicting parties seek to establish desired attitudes and relationships.

4.   <u>Intraorganizational negotiations</u> involve two or more sets of people representing two or more different organizations, and the negotiators within each set try to resolve intragroup conflict and build intragroup consensus prior to dealing with the other set(s) of negotiators.

C.   Guidelines for having successful integrative (win-win) negotiations:

1.   Separate the people from the problem.

2.   Focus on interests, not positions.

3.   Invent options for mutual gain.

4.   Insist on using objective criteria.

D.   Tactics to be cautious about in extreme distributive (win-lose) negotiations:

1.   I want it all.

2.   Time warp.

3.   Good cop, bad cop.

4.   Ultimatums.

E.   What happens when one of the conflicting parties uses a integrative (win-win) negotiating strategy and the other party uses a distributive (win-lose) negotiating strategy? The answer to this question is provided in Transparency 13.9, which is self-explanatory.

TRANSPARENCY 13.9
(FIGURE 13.4 IN THE TEXTBOOK)

MATRIX OF NEGOTIATED OUTCOMES

ENRICHMENT MODULE: WHAT NEGOTIATION STRATEGY SHOULD YOU USE?

In negotiating with another party, should you choose a unilateral strategy or an interactive strategy? A unilateral strategy is based only on your own perspective, whereas an interactive strategy also considers the perspective of the other party. There are times when an interactive strategy will work and times when a unilateral strategy will work. The SBS model of negotiation strategies provides a conceptual framework for determining when to use each strategy.

The SBS model specifies nine types of negotiating strategies, four of which are considered to be unilateral and the other five to be interactive. There are two types of collaboration (C1 and C2), two types of competition (P1 and P2), two types of subordination (S1 and S2), and three types of avoidance (A1, A2, and A3). The numeral "1" indicates a unilateral strategy while "2" and "3" indicate an interactive strategy.

- *Trusting collaboration* (C1) relies on trust, reciprocity, and openness to achieve a win-win outcome.
- *Principled collaboration* (C2) involves persuading the other party to conduct negotiations in the context of mutually agreed upon principles because mutual trust and reciprocity may be lacking.
- *Firm competition* (P1) uses highly aggressive tactics, bluffing, intimidation, misrepresentation of intentions, and "dirty tricks."
- *Soft competition* (P2) softens the directness of the firm approach and avoids using highly aggressive tactics or "dirty tricks."
- *Open subordination* (S1) involves yielding to the other party when one has little to lose by doing so, and thereby quells hostilities, enhances support, and fosters more interdependent relationships.
- *Focused subordination* (S2) involves discovering the outcomes that are important to the other party and then acquiescing to outcomes that are of interest only to the other party.
- *Active avoidance* (A1) is the refusal to negotiate.
- *Passive avoidance* (A2) involves delegating the negotiations to someone else in organization.
- *Responsive avoidance* (A3) involves the application of standard operating procedures or the development of new policies that address the other party's interests in order to avoid negotiations.

Determining which of the nine strategies to use is based on both negotiators' priorities regarding substantive outcomes (*i.e.*, the importance of the goals and issues at stake) and relationship outcomes (*i.e.*, the importance of feelings and attitudes between the parties). Transparency 13.10 presents a decision tree which shows when to use each negotiating strategy. Start at the left side, identifying first your priorities for substantive outcomes and relationship outcomes and then moving along the appropriate branch of the decision tree. Next, identify the other party's priorities for both outcomes, and proceed to the end of the appropriate branch. At the end of that branch you will discover the negotiation strategy that is most appropriate for that particular situation.

This enrichment module is adapted from:

Savage, G.T., Blair, J.D., & Sorenson, R.L. (1989, February). Consider both relationships and substance when negotiating strategically. *Academy of Management Executive, 3(1)*, 37-48.

TRANSPARENCY 13.10
FRAMEWORK OF NEGOTIATION STRATEGIES

F.   Negotiating across cultures.

1.   The issues and complexities involved in domestic negotiations are compounded in cross-cultural negotiations. This observation is illustrated with Transparency 13.11, which describes the traditional negotiating assumptions of three cultural groupings—Japan, U.S. and Canada, and Latin America. However, the traditional assumptions may not always apply when long-term and insider relationships have been established.

TRANSPARENCY 13.11
(TABLE 13.1 IN THE TEXTBOOK)

TRADITIONAL NEGOTIATING ASSUMPTIONS ACROSS THREE CULTURAL GROUPINGS

G.   Third-party facilitation.

1.   Third-party facilitation can be used help resolve conflict when the parties are locked into a win-lose situation.

2.   The key functions of the third-party facilitator include the following:

a.   Ensuring mutual motivation.

b.   Achieving a balance in situational power.

c.   Coordinating confrontation efforts.

d.   Promoting openness in dialogue.

e.   Maintaining an optimum level of tension.

VI.   Summing up: What are the key lessons for managing behavior in organizations?

A.   Conflict is inevitable in the workplace. It must be diagnosed, understood, and managed,

B.   Conflict can be managed destructively or constructively.

1.   Destructive handling of conflict will harm working relationships and negatively affect the performance of individuals, groups, and the entire organization. Destructive conflict should be minimized if it cannot be eliminated.

2.   Constructive handling of conflict will promote trust and cooperation, encourage the appropriate sharing of information and resources, and contribute to improved individual, group, and organization-wide effectiveness and efficiency. Constructive conflict resolution can be accomplished through the use of collaboration and integrative negotiations.

DISCUSSION QUESTIONS: SUGGESTED ANSWERS

1. *Would you have any difficulties in negotiating in Mexico or Latin America? Explain why or why not and identify the skills you possess or may need to develop to overcome any difficulties.*

    The students can base their responses to this question on the material contained in Table 13.1. From this table they can compare and contrast the traditional negotiating assumptions of people from the U.S. and Canada with the negotiating assumptions held by people from Latin America.

2. *Have you been involved in negotiations where the other party used or tried to use win-lose tactics? If yes, describe the situation. What did you do in response to these tactics? How did you feel? What was the outcome?*

    A response to this question could draw upon two sources of text material. One source covers the tactics that one might encounter in extreme distributive (win-lose) negotiations. These tactics include the following: I want it all; time warp; good cop, bad cop; and ultimatums. A second source is the matrix of negotiated outcomes shown in Figure 13.4.

    The students should relate the specific details of their negotiation experiences, if they have any, to either the win-lose negotiation tactics or the outcome matrix.

3. *Give four recommendations for reducing diversity-based conflicts in organizations. Explain the rationale for these recommendations.*

    In answering this question, the students could refer to the "Managing Diversity: Bridging Differences at General Computer, Inc." feature on page 440 of the text.

    Some of the ways for reducing diversity-based conflicts in organizations include the following:

    a. Diversity workshops which focus on exploring the diversity issues of race, gender, ethnicity, or religion.
    b. Group dynamics training programs which examine, among other things, the impact of race and gender on the functioning of work groups.
    c. Structuring the organization's performance appraisal and reward systems so that employees in general, and managers in particular, are evaluated and rewarded, at least in part, on how they handle diversity issues.
    d. Encouraging a climate of tolerance through sensitivity training.
    e. Establishing and developing work teams composed of members who are diverse with respect to race, gender, and/or ethnicity.
    f. Implementing a no-nonsense policy regarding sexual harassment.

    Many other examples could be cited. The students should be encouraged to be creative in their thinking.

4. *What is your personal view of conflict—positive, negative, or balanced? Cite two incidents from your personal experience to illustrate your view.*

    The positive view of conflict focuses on the constructive aspects of conflict. According to this view, conflict leads to constructive problem solving, provides a stimulus for positive change, helps make change more acceptable, encourages people to work out their differences, fosters participation in developing a fair and ethical organization, and challenges people to deal directly with injustices.

The negative view of conflict focuses on the destructive aspects of conflict. According to this view, conflict diverts effort away from goal attainment; depletes resources, especially time and money; negatively affects the psychological well-being of employees; threatens important personal goals and beliefs; makes the establishment of supportive and trusting relationships difficult; and undermines performance.

The balanced view of conflict holds that sometimes conflict is constructive and sometimes it is destructive. The balanced view acknowledges that conflict arises in organizations whenever interests collide, and is sensitive to the consequences of conflict.

Students usually are more inclined to support the negative view of conflict. They should be pushed to consider the potential utility of the positive view and the balanced view. The students should leave this discussion with the understanding that conflict, when properly diagnosed and managed, can facilitate change and strengthen interpersonal relations.

5.   *How might goal conflict, cognitive conflict, and affective conflict all come into play in a conflict situation? Illustrate your answer by referring to a personal conflict situation.*

Responses to this question should be based on the definitions of the three types of conflict. Goal conflict occurs when two or more desired or expected outcomes are incompatible. Cognitive conflict occurs when the ideas and thoughts within an individual or between individuals are incompatible. Affective conflict occurs when the feelings and emotions within an individual or between individuals are incompatible.

Possible examples of goal conflict could include:

a.   Some students in a project group work hard to achieve an "A" while other students in the group put forth only minimal effort.
b.   Working full- or part-time while going to school full- or part-time.
c.   Devoting time to a volunteer organization and spending time with one's children.
d.   Two individuals who car pool for an 8:00 A.M. class on campus may have different goals for arriving on campus. One likes to be in class 15 minutes before class starts and the other doesn't mind walking in 10 minutes late.

Some examples of cognitive conflict are:

a.   Two or more people have differing ideas regarding how to solve a problem.
b.   One person perceives a comment to be a genuine compliment while another person perceives the same comment to be a subtle jibe.
c.   An individual sees several possible ways—some positive and some negative—to interpret a superior's comment that "We sure need to take a look at performance around here!"

Affective conflict situations could include the following:

a.   Having both positive and negative feelings about someone (*i.e,* a love-hate relationship).

    b.   Being angry at your best friend.
    c.   Leaving home to go to college.

6.   *Give personal examples of your experience with approach-approach conflict, avoidance-avoidance conflict, and approach-avoidance conflict.*

Students should link their personal examples to the definitions of each type of intrapersonal conflict. Approach-approach conflict occurs when an individual must choose among two or more alternatives, each of which is expected to have a positive outcome. Avoidance-avoidance conflict occurs when an individual must choose among two or more alternatives, each of which is expected to have a negative outcome. Approach-avoidance conflict occurs when an individual must decide whether to do something that is expected to have both positive and negative outcomes.

Some possible examples of approach-approach conflict include:

    a.   Choosing between watching a critically acclaimed movie or visiting with friends.
    b.   Choosing between working at a good-paying summer job or taking some additional classes in order to complete the degree requirements a semester early.
    c.   Deciding which sorority or fraternity you will join.

Examples of avoidance-avoidance conflict situations include:

    a.   Turning in a poorly written report or not turning in the report at all.
    b.   Being the spokesperson for a group of students complaining to the college's dean about a particular professor or doing nothing about an intolerable situation.
    c.   Choosing between an invitation to a boring social event or spending Friday evening cleaning your dorm room.

Approach-avoidance conflict situations could include the following:

    a.   Spending the weekend studying for a Monday morning exam.
    b.   Working at a job where the supervisor yells a lot but the pay is good.
    c.   Embarking on a exercise program after being sedentary for a number of years.
    d.   Reporting a fellow student for cheating off of you on an exam.
    e.   Taking on a significant leadership role in a group project.

7.   *What are the similarities and differences among intrasender role conflict, intersender role conflict, and person-role conflict?*

Intrasender role conflict occurs when different messages and pressures from a single member of the role set are incompatible. Intersender role conflict occurs when the messages and pressures from one role sender oppose messages and pressures from one or more other senders. Person-role conflict occurs when the role requirements are incompatible with the focal person's own attitudes, values, or views of acceptable behavior.

The three types of role conflict are similar in that they all occur as a result of the incompatible messages and pressures from the role set. They are different with respect to which members of the role set constitute the specific source of the conflict. With intrasender role conflict, the source is a single individual. With intersender role conflict, the source is two of more other individuals. With person-role conflict, the source is the interaction of the focal person with the role requirements.

8.   *In which of your roles do you experience the most role ambiguity? Explain.*

Role ambiguity occurs when there is uncertainty or lack of clarity surrounding expectations about a single role. Since everyone plays multiple roles, the amount of ambiguity that is associated with each role will vary, probably considerably.

In discussing this question, the students should first identify the various roles they personally play (*e.g.*, student, employee, supervisor, spouse, son or daughter, volunteer, athlete, musician, etc.). The students should describe what is clear and what is ambiguous about the expectations, perceptions, and evaluations of the relevant role sets.

9.   *Why isn't the collaborative conflict-handling style used in all conflict situations?*

Each conflict-handling style can be used appropriately in certain situations (refer to Transparencies 13.4 through 13.8 for a summary of the situations in which each of the styles should be used).

The collaborating style can be used effectively in the following situations:

a.   When there is insufficient required interdependence so that spending the extra time and energy needed for working through individual differences makes sense.
b.   When there is sufficient parity in power among individuals so that they feel free to interact candidly, regardless of their formal superior/subordinate status.
c.   When there is potential for mutual benefits, especially over the long run.
d.   When there is sufficient organizational support for taking the time and energy to resolve disputes through collaboration.

Using the collaborative style in situations that are more appropriate for one of the other styles could waste resources, or even result in the conflict not being resolved effectively.

10.   *What difficulties might an individual encounter in trying to apply win-win tactics in negotiations?*

There are four principal guidelines for having successful win-win negotiations. These guidelines are:

a.   Separate the people from the problem.
b.   Focus on interests, not positions.
c.   Invent options for mutual gain.
d.   Insist on using objective criteria.

Difficulties would be created if an individual failed to follow these guidelines. For example, using subjective rather than objective criteria creates difficulty in applying a win-win approach.

Additionally, if an individual is using a win-win negotiating strategy and the other party to the conflict is using a win-lose strategy, the win-lose strategist will benefit at the expense of the win-win strategist.

DEVELOPING SKILLS—
SELF DIAGNOSIS: CONFLICT-HANDLING STYLES

This instrument measures an individual's preference for and use of each of the five conflict-handling styles. The instrument contains 30 pairs of statements, and the respondent distributes 5 points between each pair. How the points are distributed indicates the relative accuracy of the two statements in terms of describing how the respondent deals with conflict.

Detailed scoring instructions are provided in the text. A score is generated for each of the five conflict-handling styles. Each of the scores should interpreted using the following framework:

a.   A score from 36 to 45 indicates a strong preference for and use of that particular style.
b.   A score from 19 to 35 indicates a moderate preference for and use of that particular style.
c.   A score from 0 to 18 indicates little preference for and use of that particular style.

DEVELOPING SKILLS—
A CASE IN POINT: SUE'S DILEMMA

CASE OVERVIEW

This case describes an ethical dilemma faced by Sue, a recently hired employee of a national accounting firm. On an audit, she encountered a client who was paying a large number of employees as independent contractors, thereby avoiding applicable payroll taxes. Because Sue believed the practice to be improper as well as illegal, she reported it to her audit supervisor. The audit supervisor did not seem to be willing to do anything, but encouraged her to see the partner in charge if she was not satisfied. After reflecting on the situation and the accounting firm's professed ethical standards, Sue met with Paul, the partner in charge of the audit. Paul encouraged her to ignore the practice because many companies in the client's industry did the same thing. Additionally, Paul indicated that they would lose the client's account if an issue were made of the practice. Still feeling disturbed, Sue discussed the problem with two co-workers who had encountered the same problem the previous year and had ignored it. They admonished Sue to ignore the client's practice and be a "team player."

CASE QUESTIONS

1.   *Is there evidence of goal conflict, cognitive conflict, and affective conflict in this case? Explain.*

Goal conflict occurs when two or more desired or expected outcomes are incompatible. Goal conflict exists because of the problem that Sue encounters with the client's audit. She wants the client's questionable practice to be noted in the audit report but others in her firm (peers and superiors) wish to ignore the practice.

Cognitive conflict occurs when the ideas and thoughts within an individual or between individuals are incompatible. There is cognitive conflict because the practice that Sue wants to report is not perceived as wrong by others in her organization. In Sue's judgment, the practice was improper; however, the partner in charge of the audit perceived it differently and said many companies in the client's industry follow the same practice.

Affective conflict occurs when the feelings and emotions within an individual or between individuals are incompatible. Affective conflict would result because Sue's co-workers are likely to be angry if she pursues the issue. They encourage her to be a "team player." Affective conflict also could result from Sue being torn as to the course of action to take: Should she pursue the matter and have a clear conscience, or should she go along in order to get along?

2.   *What types of role conflict is Sue probably experiencing?*

She is most likely experiencing person-role conflict. This occurs when the role requirements are incompatible with the individual's own attitudes, values, or notions of acceptable behavior.

3.   *How would you use the concepts of approach-approach conflict, avoidance-avoidance conflict, and approach-avoidance conflict to diagnose this situation?*

Neither approach-approach conflict nor avoidance-avoidance conflict are particularly applicable in this case. However, approach-avoidance conflict is useful for diagnosing Sue's situation.

With the approach-avoidance concept, Sue would have to decide whether to do something that has both positive and negative outcomes. The decision concerning whether to go over the head of the partner in charge represents an approach-avoidance conflict for Sue. If she pursues it, she might be vindicated and have a clear conscience. However, doing so could harm relationships with co-workers and her superiors, and as a consequence she might have to change jobs.

4.   *State the role ambiguities that Sue is experiencing.*

Sue is experiencing role ambiguity because she does not have clear and consistent information about what is required in her job. For example, is it enough that she report her findings to the partner in charge? What responsibility does the firm have for the client's practice? What responsibilities does Sue have to the client firm or her organization? Is Sue expected to strictly adhere to the ethical standards which her employer emphasized in continuing education classes?

5.   *What should Sue do? Why?*

Sue needs to resolve the person-role conflict. She might start by trying to confirm whether the client's practice is illegal. If the practice is illegal, she has a responsibility to report the action even if it means going over the head of the partner in charge of the audit. This would enable her to have a clear conscience and remain faithful to her personal ethical standards. However, since her employer's practices might not change, she probably would also have to change jobs to completely eliminate the person-role conflict. In changing jobs, Sue should be sensitive to any information which could help her determine the likelihood of a good fit between herself and a prospective employer.

COURSE ENHANCEMENT—
WEST'S ORGANIZATIONAL BEHAVIOR CUSTOM VIDEO SERIES

One video from *West's Organizational Behavior Custom Video Series* can be used to enhance the material in Chapter 13. This video is: *Northwestern National Life Insurance Companies: Increasing Team Effectiveness Through Peer Feedback.*

VIDEO: *NORTHWESTERN NATIONAL LIFE INSURANCE COMPANIES: INCREASING TEAM EFFECTIVENESS THROUGH PEER FEEDBACK*

Approximate Time: 8 minutes

Video Summary:

This video explains how Northwestern National Life Insurance Company uses peer review to increase team effectiveness. The video does not deal with conflict specifically; however, the peer review process can be used to effectively address conflict in work teams and to improve the performance of team members.

The benefits of peer review are based on the question "Who knows associates better than those who work along side of them?" The video shows how the peer review of an associate takes place. The work team reviews the associate on five criteria: customer management, managing work objectives, self-management style, technical skills, and interpersonal effectiveness. The supervisor acts as a facilitator and coordinates the discussion of the focal associate. The work team assesses the focal associate in terms of being below, at, or above expected performance levels on the five criteria. They also discuss the focal associate's developmental needs.

Discussion Questions and Suggested Answers for Video:

1. *How would you react to being reviewed by your peers?*

   A good way to approach this question is to have the students assume that a significant part of their grade on a group project will be determined by peer review. The students should discuss the thoughts, attitudes, and feelings they think they would have in such a situation. They should also explore how they think they would behave in such a situation, particularly if they perceived the peer review to be unfair.

2. *What are some of the advantages and disadvantages of peer review with respect to managing conflict?*

   Some of the advantages which the students might cite include the following:

   a. Peer pressure may be more powerful than supervisory pressure in correcting problems that affect other members of the work team.
   b. Working relationships may be improved through honest, open communication.
   c. Conflicts can be openly and constructively confronted.

   Some of the disadvantages are:

   a. Individuals may try to ingratiate themselves with their peers in an attempt to receive a more favorable evaluation.
   b. Because peers may also be friends, there may be a reluctance to honestly deal with performance deficiencies.
   c. Because peers may also be friends, there may be a tendency to give credit when it is not justly due.
   d. The resolution of conflict may be avoided, thereby allowing it to worsen.

COURSE ENHANCEMENT—
SUPPLEMENTAL VIDEOS AVAILABLE FROM WEST

A segment of a video from the Association for Manufacturing Excellence and made available through West Publishing Company can be used to enhance the material in Chapter 13. This video segment, which was also relevant to Chapter 9, is: *Self-Directed Work Teams—Passing the Baton (XEL Communications).*

VIDEO: AME: SELF-DIRECTED WORK TEAMS—PASSING THE BATON (XEL COMMUNICATIONS)

Approximate Time: 5 minutes

Video Summary:

XEL Communications, an Aurora, California based manufacturer of voice and data transmission equipment, faced the competitive need to respond quickly to customer orders. XEL met this competitive challenge by instituting self-managed teams. This segment explains how self-directed work teams can create conflict and how conflict can be diagnosed and resolved. Conflict within and between self-directed work teams is to be expected, but it must be resolved. If it is not resolved, team spirit can be destroyed.

Discussion Question and Suggested Answer for Video:

1.   *How can self-directed work teams both foster and resolve conflict?*

Self-directed work teams can resolve conflict by establishing and working toward superordinate goals, by being open and honest with each other in their interpersonal communications, by being supportive and helpful of each other, by removing obstacles to effective interaction, by holding one another accountable and responsible for the team's outcomes, etc. Self-directed work teams can foster conflict if they are unwilling to engage in any or all of the activities identified above.

CHAPTER 14
ORGANIZATIONAL CULTURE

CHAPTER OVERVIEW

Chapter 14 introduces the section of the text that deals with organizational processes. Organizational culture is the first organizational process to be considered in this section.

The chapter begins by describing four types of organizational culture: the baseball team, club, academy, and fortress cultures. Then the basic nature of organizational culture is addressed—organizational culture is defined, six components of organizational culture are discussed, and different levels of organizational culture are identified. A major segment of the chapter focuses on how organizational culture is developed, maintained, and changed. Issues associated with (1) external adaptation and survival and (2) internal integration are examined in the context of developing an organizational culture. Six methods of maintaining and changing organizational cultures are explored. These methods include: what managers and teams pay attention to, measure, and control; the ways managers (particularly top managers) react to critical incidents and organizational crises; managerial and team role modeling, teaching, and coaching; criteria for allocating rewards and status; criteria for recruitment, selection, promotion, and removal from the organization; and organizational rites, ceremonies, and stories. Additional segments of the chapter address the relationships between culture and performance and culture and ethics. The issue of managing cultural diversity is discussed also. Finally, the chapter examines organizational socialization as a systematic process for bringing new employees into the organization's culture. Emphasis is placed on a typical seven step socialization process.

LEARNING OBJECTIVES

Upon completion of this chapter, the students should be able to:

1. Explain the concept of organizational culture.
2. Describe how organizational cultures are developed, maintained, and changed.
3. Understand the relationships between organizational culture and performance.
4. Discuss the implications of organizational culture for ethical behavior in organizations.
5. Explain the implications of effectively managing cultural diversity.

6.   Describe the process of organizational socialization and explain its relationship to organizational culture.

CHAPTER OUTLINE

I.   **Preview Case:** Bank of America

II.   Types of Organizational Culture

III.   Dynamics of Organizational Culture

A.   Developing Organizational Culture
B.   **Managing Across Cultures:** Effects of National Cultural Values on Organizations
C.   Maintaining Organizational Culture
D.   **Managing in Practice:** McKinsey & Co.—"The Firm"
E.   Changing Organizational Culture
F.   **Managing in Practice:** The Failed Courtship of Bell Atlantic and TCI

IV.   Performance and Organizational Culture

A.   **Managing Quality:** Gillette's Total Quality Culture
B.   Ethical Behavior and Organizational Culture
C.   **Managing Ethics:** Selling Auto Repair Service at Sears

V.   Managing Cultural Diversity

A.   **Managing Diversity:** Corporate Culture Versus Ethnic Culture

VI.   Organizational Socialization

A.   Socialization Process
B.   **Managing in Practice:** Herb Kelleher and Southwest Airlines
C.   Socialization Outcomes

VI.   Developing Skills

A.   **Self Diagnosis:** Assessing Ethical Culture
B.   **A Case in Point:** Procter & Gamble

KEY WORDS AND CONCEPTS

Twenty key words and concepts are introduced in Chapter 14. The key words and concepts, along with definitions or appropriate descriptions, are as follows:

Academy culture: a type of organizational culture that hires employees early in their careers but trains them to become expert in a particular function. The academy culture stresses continuity of service, functional expertise, and institutional wisdom.

Acculturation: refers to the methods by which cultural differences between a dominant culture and minority cultures or subcultures are resolved and managed.

Baseball team culture: a type of organizational culture that attracts entrepreneurs, innovators, and risk takers. In this type of culture, pay is directly linked to performance; considerable autonomy and financial rewards accrue to top performers; risks are high; and long-term security is virtually nonexistent.

Club culture: a type of organizational culture that values age and experience. Employees often start with the firm early in their careers and work at various jobs in different functions as they progress slowly but steadily up the corporate hierarchy. Organizations with this type of culture reward seniority, loyalty, commitment, and "fitting in." Such cultures provide stable, secure employment.

Cultural heroes: refers to people (alive or dead, real or imaginary) who possess characteristics highly valued by the culture and thus serve as role models.

Cultural symbols: the words (jargon or slang), gestures, and pictures or other physical objects that carry a particular meaning within a culture.

Cultural values: collective beliefs, assumptions, and feelings about what things are good, normal, rational, valuable, and so on.

External adaptation and survival: concerns how the organization will find a niche in and cope with its constantly changing external environment. External adaptation and survival is one of the two major organizational challenges that influence the formation of organizational culture.

Fortress culture: a type of organizational culture that is preoccupied with survival; this type of culture is typically associated with organizations that are in the process of downsizing or restructuring. Organizations with a fortress culture provide little job security and have difficulty rewarding employees for good performance.

High performance-high commitment work culture: a type of culture that is designed to foster high performance with high levels of employee involvement.

Internal integration: concerns the establishment and maintenance of effective working relationships among the members of the organization. Internal integration is one of the two major organizational challenges that influence the formation of organizational culture.

Organizational culture: a complex pattern of beliefs, expectations, ideas, values, attitudes, and behaviors shared by the members of an organization.

Organizational rites and ceremonies: organized, planned activities or rituals that have important cultural meaning.

Organizational socialization: the systematic process by which an organization brings new employees into its culture. Socialization involves the transmission of culture from senior to new employees, thereby providing the social knowledge and skills needed to perform organizational roles and tasks successfully.

Participative management: a process wherein managers share decision-making, goal-setting, and problem-solving activities with employees.

Principled organizational dissent: refers to individuals in an organization protesting, on ethical grounds, some practice or policy.

Strong culture: cultures where most mangers and employees share a set of consistent values and methods of doing business.

Subcultures: refers to distinctly different cultures existing in different corporate units of an organization.

Total quality culture: a type of culture that values customers, continuous improvement, and teamwork.

Whistle-blowing: a form of principled organizational dissent which refers to challenging the authority structure of an organization by exposing a practice that the organization's leaders or some of its members support.

LECTURE NOTES

I.   Chapter 14 introduces us to organizational processes by focusing on organizational culture. The chapter provides answers to many important questions about organizational culture, including the following: What types of organizational culture exist? What is organizational culture? How is it characterized? How does organizational culture develop? How is culture maintained? How can it be changed? How does organizational culture influence performance? How does it influence ethics? What can be done to effectively manage cultural diversity? What is organizational socialization and how is it related to organizational culture? The answers which Chapter 14 provides are summarized in Transparency 14.1.

TRANSPARENCY 14.1
(FROM TEXT MATERIAL IN THE TEXTBOOK)

KEY QUESTIONS AND ANSWERS ABOUT ORGANIZATIONAL CULTURE

II.   Types of organizational culture.

    A.   Four types of organizational cultures commonly exist in the business world. These cultures are labeled baseball team, club, academy, and fortress.

        1.   The baseball team culture attracts entrepreneurs, innovators, and risk takers. Pay is directly linked to performance. Considerable autonomy and financial rewards accrue to top performers. However, risks are high and long-term security is virtually nonexistent.

        2.   The club culture values age and experience; employees often start with the firm early in their careers and work at various jobs in different functions as they progress slowly but steadily up the corporate hierarchy. Organizations with this type of culture reward seniority, loyalty, commitment, and "fitting in." Club cultures provide stable, secure employment.

        3.   The academy culture hires employees early in their careers but trains them to become expert in a particular function. The academy culture stresses continuity of service, functional expertise, and institutional wisdom.

        4.   The fortress culture is preoccupied with survival; this type of culture is typically associated with organizations that are in the process of downsizing or restructuring.

Organizations with a fortress culture provide little job security and have difficulty rewarding employees for good performance.

B.   Most organizations are probably some blend of the four types of cultures rather then being purely one type of culture.

III.   Dynamics of organizational culture.

A.   What is organizational culture?

1.   <u>Organizational culture</u> represents a complex pattern of beliefs, expectations, ideas, values, attitudes, and behaviors shared by the members of an organization.

2.   Organizational culture reflects the collective impact of six components. These components are (see transparency 14.2):

TRANSPARENCY 14.2
(FROM TEXT MATERIAL IN THE TEXTBOOK)

COMPONENTS OF ORGANIZATIONAL CULTURE

---

a.   Routine behaviors such as organizational rituals and ceremonies and the language commonly used.

b.   The norms that are shared by work groups throughout the organization.

c.   The dominant values held by an organization.

d.   The philosophy that guides an organization's policy toward employees and customers.

e.   The rules of the game for getting along in the organization.

f.   The feeling or climate that is conveyed in an organization by the physical layout and the way in which members of the organization interact with customers or other outsiders.

ENRICHMENT MODULE: BILL HOBART'S TEN COMMANDMENTS

Sometimes the essence of a company's organizational culture can be distilled into a basic operating credo. William Hobart, CEO of the family-held Hobart Brothers Co., a manufacturer of equipment for a variety of industrial and commercial purposes, has developed such a credo. He calls it his "ten commandments."

Here are Bill Hobart's ten commandments, in paraphrased form:

- The company should stay focused on the customer in everything that it does; it should solve the customers' problems.
- The company should strive to be the best at what it does.
- Employees are the company's greatest asset.
- The company should remain financially sound—cash flow should be improved and debt should be reduced.
- The goals of shareholders and management should be coordinated.
- The company should remain privately held so that it can take a long-term view on investments and people.
- The company should grow profitably on a worldwide basis.
- The company should be ethical and fair in everything it does.
- The company and individuals within the company should put something back into the system.
- People should have fun with their work.

Bill Hobart's ten commandments certainly give us a feel for the company's norms and values, its philosophy, the rules governing how people behave toward one another, and its climate—all components of organizational culture.

This enrichment module is adapted from:

Sheridan, J.H. (1991, November 18). Managing by 'the golden rule.' *Industry Week*, 24+.

3.   Levels of organizational culture.

   a.   There are four levels of organizational culture—shared assumptions, cultural values, shared behaviors, and cultural symbols—which vary in terms of degree of visibility and ease of change (see Transparency 14.3).

TRANSPARENCY 14.3
(FIGURE 14.1 IN THE TEXTBOOK)
LEVELS OF ORGANIZATIONAL CULTURE

   (1)   Shared assumptions are the least visible and the most resistant to change. Shared assumptions represent beliefs about reality and human nature that are taken for granted.

   (2)   At the next level is cultural values, which represent collective beliefs, assumptions, and feelings about what things are good, normal, rational, valuable, and so on.

(3)   At the third level of visibility and ease of change are shared behaviors. At this level people may be unaware of the values that bind them together.

(4)   Cultural symbols represent the level of organizational culture that is most visible and least resistant to change. Cultural symbols are the words (jargon or slang), gestures, and pictures or other physical objects that carry a particular meaning within a culture.

     (a)   Important cultural symbols sometimes take the form of cultural heroes, or people (alive or dead, real or imaginary) who posses characteristics highly valued by the culture and thus serve as role models.

B.   How is organizational culture developed?

1.   Organizational culture forms in response to two major challenges that confront every organization: (a) external adaptation and survival; and (b) internal integration.

    a.   External adaptation and survival has to do with how the organization will find a niche in and cope with its constantly changing external environment. External adaptation and survival are concerned with the following issues (see Transparency 14.4):

TRANSPARENCY 14.4
(FROM TEXT MATERIAL IN THE TEXTBOOK)

ISSUES ASSOCIATED WITH EXTERNAL ADAPTATION AND SURVIVAL

---

(1)   Identifying the primary mission of the organization, and selecting strategies to pursue this mission.

(2)   Setting specific goals.

(3)   Determining how to pursue the goals, including selecting an organizational structure and reward system.

(4)   Establishing criteria to measure how well individuals and teams are accomplishing their goals.

    b.   Internal integration concerns the establishment and maintenance of effective working relationships among the members of the organization. Internal integration is concerned with the following issues (see Transparency 14.5):

TRANSPARENCY 14.5
(FROM TEXT MATERIAL IN THE TEXTBOOK)

ISSUES ASSOCIATED WITH INTERNAL INTEGRATION

---

(1)   Identifying methods of communication, and developing a shared

meaning for important concepts.

    (2)   Establishing criteria for membership in groups and teams.

    (3)   Determining rules for acquiring, maintaining, and losing power and status.

    (4)   Developing systems for encouraging desirable behaviors and discouraging undesirable behaviors.

2.   Organizational culture emerges as members discover or develop ways of coping with external adaptation and internal integration issues. One common pattern of the emergence of organizational culture is shown in Transparency 14.6.

TRANSPARENCY 14.6
(FIGURE 14.2 IN THE TEXTBOOK)

ONE COMMON PATTERN IN THE EMERGENCE OF CORPORATE CULTURES

---

3.   The culture, customs, and societal norms of the country in which an organization operates can influence the organization's culture. This is illustrated by the material contained in transparencies 14.7 and 14.8 regarding the effects of power distance and uncertainty avoidance on organizational cultures.

    (a)   Power distance refers to the extent to which a society encourages unequal distributions of power among people. In low power distance societies, more interaction takes place among people from different social classes, and individuals can move up in social status more easily.

TRANSPARENCY 14.7
(TABLE 14.1 IN THE TEXTBOOK)

SOME EFFECTS OF THE POWER DISTANCE DIMENSION ON ORGANIZATIONS

    (b)   Uncertainty avoidance refers to the extent to which individuals in a society feel threatened by ambiguous and unstable situations and try to avoid them. In high uncertainty avoidance societies, organizations tend to have many written rules and procedures, impose structure on employee activities, and reward managers for risk avoidance.

TRANSPARENCY 14.8
(TABLE 14.2 IN THE TEXTBOOK)

SOME EFFECTS OF THE UNCERTAINTY AVOIDANCE DIMENSION ON ORGANIZATIONS

C.   How is organizational culture maintained?

1.   Organizational culture is maintained by:

    a.   *What managers and teams pay attention to, measure, and control:* What managers and teams, notice, comment on, and deal with systematically send strong signals to organizational members about what is important and expected of them.

b.   *The ways managers (particularly top managers) react to critical incidents and organizational crises:* The manner in which a crisis is dealt with can either reinforce the existing culture or bring out new values and norms that change the culture in some way.

c.   *Managerial and team role modeling, teaching, and coaching:* Important messages about the organization's culture are transmitted to employees via the way managers fulfill their roles, the content and conduct of training programs, and day-to-day coaching on the job.

d.   *Criteria for allocating rewards and status:* The rewards and punishments attached to various behaviors convey to employees the priorities and values of both individual managers and the organization. The distribution of perks (status symbols) indicates which roles and behaviors are most valued by the organization.

e.   *Criteria for recruitment, selection, promotion, and removal from the organization:* Key elements of the human resource management function provide an important means for an organization to maintain its culture. Through its hiring practices an organization can select people who seem to provide a good fit with the organization's culture. Through job assignments and promotions, the organization can reward people who fit well with the organization's culture. This also provides an important message to other organizational members regarding what behaviors and activities are valued by the organization. Finally, through the termination process, an organization can remove people who cannot function within the constraints of its culture.

f.   *Organizational rites, ceremonies, and stories:* <u>Organizational rites and ceremonies</u> are organized, planned activities or rituals that have important cultural meaning.

   (1)   Transparency 14.9 contains some examples of organizational rites and ceremonies classified according to rites of passage, degradation, enhancement, and integration.

TRANSPARENCY 14.9
(TABLE 14.3 IN THE TEXTBOOK)

ORGANIZATIONAL RITES AND CEREMONIES

---

   (2)   Additionally, many of the underlying beliefs and values of an organization's culture are expressed as legends and stories that become part of its folklore.

D.   How is organizational culture changed?

1.   Organizational culture can be changed by using the methods for maintaining culture. Basically, culture can be changed by introducing change into any of the

methods that can be used for maintaining culture.

2.   Caution should be exercised in attempting to change culture for at least two reasons.

    a.   Focusing managerial efforts on changing ineffective behaviors and procedures may be more meaningful than attempting to change organizational culture.

    b.   Cultural change presumes the capability to accurately assess the existing organizational culture. This can be very difficult, particularly in most large, complex organizations which have distinctly different cultures in different corporate units (*i.e.,* subcultures).

ENRICHMENT MODULE: DOES YOUR ORGANIZATION'S CULTURE NEED TO BE CHANGED?

Diagnosing a company's corporate culture can be a difficult task. One relatively simple way of diagnosing an organization's culture is to look for signs of cultural health.

What are some of the signs that a company has an unhealthy corporate culture? According to Chaudron Associates, a consulting firm headquartered in San Diego, California, there are nine key signals. A company has a healthy culture if:

- The organization has a positive concern for its members.
- Management is dedicated to improving how they deal with employees.
- Management considers how organizational changes will affect employees.
- Employees are given the information they need in order to understand organizational changes.
- Employees are kept informed about daily events.
- Employees receive timely information about major changes.
- The organization empowers employees to make the decisions necessary to solve day-to-day work problems.
- Employee authority and responsibility are properly matched.
- Employee authority and responsibility are clearly defined.

This enrichment module is adapted from:

Copyright © 1992, Chaudron Associates. For permission to reprint, call 619/969-9531.

---

3.   Successfully changing the existing organizational culture requires the following (see Transparency 14.10):

TRANSPARENCY 14.10
(FROM TEXT MATERIAL IN THE TEXTBOOK)

REQUIREMENTS FOR SUCCESSFULLY CHANGING ORGANIZATIONAL CULTURE

---

    a.   Understanding the old culture first.

b. Providing support for employees and teams who have ideas for a better culture and are willing to act on their visions.

c. Finding the most effective subculture in the organization and using it as an example from which employees can learn.

d. Not attacking culture head on but finding ways to help employees and teams do their jobs more effectively.

e. Treating the vision of a new culture as a guiding principle for change.

f. Recognizing that significant organizationwide cultural change takes five to ten years.

g. Living the new culture because actions speak louder than words.

IV. Performance and organizational culture.

A. The rationale for attempting cultural change is to create a better performing, more effective organization—that is, a more successful organization.

B. Successful organizational cultures have been characterized in a number of ways, including the following: cultural strength, cultural type, participative management, employee involvement and commitment, and total quality.

1. Evidence suggests that strongly performing organizations also have <u>strong cultures</u> (*i.e.*, cultures where most mangers and employees share a set of consistent values and methods of doing business). Strong cultures tend to be associated with strong performance for three reasons.

a. A strong culture often provides a good fit between strategy and culture.

b. A strong culture may lead to the alignment of goals among employees.

c. A strong culture leads to employee commitment and motivation.

2. Some evidence indicates that performance may be affected more by cultural type than by cultural strength. For example, a large study of colleges and universities showed that those educational institutions that possessed a type of culture whose features matched their market niche and mission were more effective than institutions whose culture lacked such a match.

3. Some evidence suggests that the relationship between cultural attributes and performance should be viewed from a contingency perspective. Doing so can lead to the following conclusions:

a. Organizational culture can have a significant impact on a firm's long-term economic performance.

b. Organizational culture will probably be an even more important factor in determining success or failure of firms in the next decade.

c.   Organizational cultures that inhibit strong long-term financial performance are not rare; they develop easily, even in firms that are full of reasonable and intelligent people.

d.   Although tough to change, organizational cultures can be made more performance enhancing.

4.   <u>Participative management</u>—where managers share decision-making, goal-setting, and problem-solving activities with employees—tends to be associated with successful organizational cultures.

5.   Another characteristic of successful organizational culture is a <u>high performance-high commitment work culture</u>. This type of culture is designed to foster high performance with high levels of employee involvement.

6.   A <u>total quality culture</u>, which values customers, continuous improvement, and teamwork, is also associated with organizational effectiveness.

C.   The effects of organizational culture on employee behavior and performance can be summarized as follows (see Transparency 14.11):

TRANSPARENCY 14.11
(FROM TEXT MATERIAL IN THE TEXTBOOK)

EFFECTS OF ORGANIZATIONAL CULTURE ON EMPLOYEE BEHAVIOR AND PERFORMANCE

---

1.   Knowing the culture of an organization allows employees to understand the firm's history and current approach.

2.   Organizational culture can foster commitment to corporate philosophy and values.

3.   Organizational culture, through its norms, serves as a control mechanism to channel employees toward desired behaviors and away from undesired behaviors.

4.   Certain types of organizational cultures may produce greater effectiveness and productivity than others.

ENRICHMENT MODULE: SPEED! SIMPLICITY! SELF-CONFIDENCE?—
A RADICAL CHANGE IN THE CULTURE OF AMERICAN BUSINESS ORGANIZATIONS?

How important is the link between organizational culture and productivity? John Welch, Chairman and Chief Executive Officer of General Electric Company, believes the link is very crucial. He argues that productivity growth will determine not only the winners and losers in global competition but will significantly influence our standard of living and quality of life.

To Welch, the key to productivity growth is organizational culture. He argues that in the 1980s American corporations relied heavily on the hardware of business—technology, restructuring, downsizing, etc.—to produce productivity growth. "But hardware has it limits," says Welch. To have sustained productivity growth, American business needs to rely on software, like the Japanese have done. From Welch's perspective, the software of business is the organizational culture that drives business.

Welch argues that the culture of American business needs radical change in order to have sustained productivity growth and to compete effectively in the global economy. What is Welch's prescription for generating radical cultural change? He sums his prescription up in three words: speed, simplicity, and self-confidence.

- "Speed—in seeing what's happening in the world, in anticipating it, in responding to it—is of the essence."

- Speed results from simplicity. Organizations can simplify by articulating a clear and focused vision, revising sophisticated and cumbersome decision processes, designing products with fewer parts, revamping difficult-to-understand processes, eliminating ambiguous and deceptive marketing messages, communicating directly and honestly on an interpersonal basis, etc.

- Simplicity results from self-confidence. "It takes enormous self-confidence to be simple—particularly in large organizations." According to Welch, organizations must provide their members with ample opportunities to develop self-confidence. Organizations can accomplish this by ceasing to overcontrol people, and instead liberating and empowering them. Organizations should be enablers of innovation, boldness, and risk-taking.

Speed! Simplicity! Self-confidence! What will happen if this radical cultural change does not take place? According to John Welch:

> "The worst thing we can do is to stifle, to overcontrol our people. If we do, we will have none of the advantages of our competitors—their protectionism, their regimentation, their subsidies, their focused technology, their political support. All we'll have left are the bureaucratic encumbrances that burden them all."

This enrichment module is based on:

Welch, Jr., J.F. (1989, November). *Soft values for a hard decade: A view on winning in the '90s.* An Executive Speech Reprint, Corporate Publications Center, General Electric Company, Scotia, NY.

V.   Ethics and organizational culture.

    A.   Organizational culture appears to affect ethical behavior in the following ways:

        1.   A culture emphasizing ethical norms provides support for ethical behavior.

        2.   All authority figures—professionals and managers (especially top managers)—can encourage or discourage ethical behavior.

        3.   The presence or absence of ethical behavior in managerial actions both influences and reflects the prevailing culture.

        4.   <u>Principled organizational dissent</u> refers to individuals in an organization protesting, on ethical grounds, some practice or policy. Some organizational cultures permit and even encourage principled organizational dissent; other cultures punish it. <u>Whistle-blowing</u> is a form of principled organizational dissent which refers to challenging the authority structure of an organization by exposing a practice that the organization's leaders or some of its members support.

    B.   Much remains to be learned about creating cultures that encourage ethical behavior. Here are some of the actions organizations can take to develop an ethical culture, thereby encouraging ethical behavior on the part of organizational members (see Transparency 14.12):

TRANSPARENCY 14.12
(FROM TEXT MATERIAL IN THE TEXTBOOK)

ACTIONS ORGANIZATIONS CAN TAKE TO DEVELOP AN ETHICAL CULTURE

---

        1.   Be realistic in setting values and goals regarding employment relationships.

        2.   Encourage input from throughout the organization regarding appropriate values and practices for implementing the culture.

        3.   Do not automatically opt for a "strong" culture, which may suppress diversity and dissent.

        4.   Provide training programs for managers and teams on adopting and implementing the organization's values.

    C.   Without an ethical culture, an organization is unlikely to be effective and successful over the long-term.

ENRICHMENT MODULE: ORGANIZATIONAL CULTURE AND UNETHICAL BEHAVIOR

What type of organizational culture promotes unethical behavior? Perhaps we can find some clues to the norms and values that characterize an unethical culture by looking at the reasons people often cite for engaging in unethical behavior.

Individuals who pursue unethical actions often justify their behavior with one or more of the following reasons:

- The organization expects unethical behavior.
- Everybody else behaves unethically.
- Behaving unethically is the only way one can get ahead.
- The action is not truly immoral or illegal.
- The action is in the best interests of the individual and/or the company.
- The unethical actions will never be discovered.
- The company will condone the unethical behavior because it will help the company.

This enrichment module is adapted from:

McCuddy, M.K., Reichardt, K.E. & Schroeder, D.L. (1993). Ethical practices improve profitability: One step beyond the anecdotal. *1993 Proceedings: Decision Sciences Institute, 1,* 497-500.

VI.   Managing cultural diversity.

    A.   Because managing a cultural diverse work force is very challenging, successful organizations have to work vigorously at acculturation. <u>Acculturation</u> refers to the methods by which cultural differences between a dominant culture and minority cultures or subcultures are resolved and managed.

    B.   Managing cultural diversity can be aided by adhering to the following guidelines (see Transparency 14.13):

TRANSPARENCY 14.13
(FROM TEXT MATERIAL IN THE TEXTBOOK)

GUIDELINES FOR MANAGING CULTURAL DIVERSITY

---

1.   Bring the diversity issue out in the open and discuss it.

2.   Explore how all employees come to the workplace with a unique combination of background influences.

3.   Be an intercultural ambassador by making tact and respect the rule for discussions of ethnic, cultural, racial, or gender differences.

4.   Don't tolerate racist or sexist behaviors.

5.   Help employees balance personal and professional needs.

6.   Explain the unwritten rules of the organization to employees.

7.   Encourage employees to talk with co-workers about their concerns so they are exposed to a variety of viewpoints.

ENRICHMENT MODULE: WHEN CULTURES CLASH

When companies from different parts of the world enter into joint ventures, their employees often encounter difficulty in working together. These difficulties are usually rooted in cultural differences between the companies.

For example, when International Business Machines Corp. entered into a joint computer chip research project with Siemens AG of Germany and Toshiba Corp. of Japan, the project members experienced considerable culture clash. Since the joint project was conducted at IBM's facilities in East Fishkill, New York, Siemens and Toshiba tried to prepare their employees for living and working abroad. They weren't adequately prepared for what they encountered; nor were the IBMers.

The Toshiba employees were accustomed to everyone working in large open rooms, not the individualized offices common to IBM. Toshiba people believed the office structure inhibited the free flow of information. The Germans were horrified to find that most of the IBM offices were windowless, apparently fearful that the physical space would stifle their creativity.

Casual interaction, which often promotes information exchange in Japan, was very limited with the IBM contingent. This was most apparent at 7:00 or 8:00 o'clock in the evening when all the American engineers and most of the German engineers were gone but many of the Japanese engineers were still at work.

"Siemens scientists were shocked to find Toshiba colleagues closing their eyes and seeming to sleep during meetings (a common practice for Japanese managers when talk doesn't concern them)." IBM members of the project team complained that their Toshiba colleagues wouldn't make clear decisions and that the Siemens people planned too much.

This enrichment module is based on:

Browning, E.S. (1994, May 3). Side by side: Computer chip project brings rivals together, but cultures clash. *The Wall Street Journal*, A1 & A8.

ENRICHMENT MODULE: CULTURAL DIFFERENCES IN BUSINESS PRACTICES

As the preceding enrichment module demonstrated, Japanese and American business people are accustomed to quite different organizational cultures. These cultural differences are often reflected in business practices. Japanese business people seem to employ a different style and to talk a different language than their American counterparts.

The Japanese style emphasizes painstaking analysis and incremental movement. The American business style is faster-paced and often based on quantum leaps.

Language differences can be challenging as well. For instance, describing a project as difficult has very different meanings for American and Japanese business people. For Americans, difficult means "hard but doable." In contrast, for the Japanese, difficult means that the project is impossible.

This enrichment module is based on:

Impoco, J., Streisand, B., & Dentzer, S. (1992, July 6). The great divide: U.S.-Japanese business deals are often unable to bridge a vast culture gap. *U.S. News & World Report*, 52-54.

VII.   Organizational socialization.

A.   <u>Organizational socialization</u> is the systematic process by which an organization brings new employees into its culture. Socialization involves the transmission of culture from senior to new employees, thereby providing the social knowledge and skills needed to perform organizational roles and tasks successfully.

B.   Firms with strong organizational cultures frequently follow a seven step process for socializing new employees (see transparency 14.14. The seven steps are:

TRANSPARENCY 14.14
(FIGURE 14.4 IN THE TEXTBOOK)

AN EXAMPLE OF AN ORGANIZATIONAL SOCIALIZATION PROCESS

---

1.   Entry-level candidates are selected carefully.

2.   Humility-inducing experiences in the first months on the job cause employees to question their prior behaviors, beliefs, and values.

3.   In-the-trenches training leads to mastery of one of the core disciplines of the business.

4.   Careful attention is given to measuring operational results and rewarding individual performance.

5.   Adherence to the organization's values is emphasized.

6.   Reinforcing folklore provides legends and interpretations of important events in the organization's history that validate its culture and goals.

7.   Consistent role models and consistent traits are associated with those recognized as being on the fast track to promotion and success.

C.   Outcomes of the socialization process.

1.   Rapid socialization is advantageous for both the individual employee and the organization. For the individual, rapid socialization reduces the uncertainty and anxiety surrounding a new job. For the organization, rapid socialization helps the new employee become productive quickly.

2.   In an effective organizational culture, strong socialization contributes to organizational success. However, in an ineffective culture, strong socialization may hinder organizational success.

3.   Transparency 14.15, which is self-explanatory, lists some possible outcomes of successful and unsuccessful socialization.

TRANSPARENCY 14.15
(TABLE 14.5 IN THE TEXTBOOK)

POSSIBLE OUTCOMES OF SOCIALIZATION PROCESS

VIII.   Summing up: Why is organizational culture important to the study of organizational behavior?

A.   Organizational culture has many meanings. Some times it is considered to be the driving force behind the organization. Other times, culture is considered to be the force that binds the organization together. Still another view of culture is as the mechanism that uniquely links an organization to its environment. Culture is also the expression of that which is unique and characteristic of an organization. Culture is all of these—and probably more.

B.   Because of what it is, culture affects an organization and its members in profound ways. An organization's culture will influence how people perform their jobs; how they interact with customers, colleagues, bosses, and subordinates; how they will deal with those who are different from themselves; whether they will be ethical or unethical; etc. Culture influences how groups and teams interact—whether the will cooperate or compete, whether they will share resources, how they will resolve intergroup conflicts, etc. Culture also influences the organization's policies and procedures, its orientation toward customers, even its definition of who the customers are. In short, culture influences how effective or ineffective, efficient or inefficient individuals, groups and teams, and the entire organization will be.

C.   Because organizational culture can have such a pervasive influence, managers and employees must understand the nature of culture and its effects, and work vigorously to maintain an effective culture or to change an ineffective culture into an effective one.

DISCUSSION QUESTIONS: SUGGESTED ANSWERS

1.   *Provide three examples of how culture is manifested or revealed in an organization with which you are familiar.*

A good way to approach this question is by focusing on the six components of organizational culture discussed in the text. These components are:

a.   Routine behaviors such as organizational rituals and ceremonies and the language commonly used.

b.   The norms that are shared by work groups throughout the organization.

c.   The dominant values held by an organization.

d.   The philosophy that guides an organization's policy toward employees and customers.

e.   The rules of the game for getting along in the organization.

f.   The feeling or climate that is conveyed in an organization by the physical layout and the way in which members of the organization interact with customers or other outsiders.

Using these six components as guidelines, students can provide examples from their own experiences. If students do not have work experience, they can describe the cultures of their school, club, fraternity or sorority, or a social organization with which they are familiar.

2.   *What factors significantly influence the formation of organizational culture?*

The organizational challenges of (a) external adaptation and survival and (b) internal integration are the primary factors that influence the formation of organizational culture. External adaptation and survival concerns how the organization will find a niche in and cope with its constantly changing external environment. Internal integration concerns the establishment and maintenance of effective working relationships among the members of the organization.

External adaptation and survival involve the following specific issues:

a.   Identifying the primary mission of the organization, and selecting strategies to pursue this mission.

b.   Setting specific goals.

c.   Determining how to pursue the goals, including selecting an organizational structure and reward system.

d.   Establishing criteria to measure how well individuals and teams are accomplishing their goals.

Internal integration concerns the following issues:

a.   Identifying methods of communication, and developing a shared meaning for important concepts.

b.   Establishing criteria for membership in groups and teams.

c.   Determining rules for acquiring, maintaining, and losing power and status.

d.   Developing systems for encouraging desirable behaviors and discouraging undesirable behaviors.

Organizational culture develops as members work together in dealing with problems of external adaptation and survival and internal integration. As different methods and approaches are tried and found successful, they are shared and communicated throughout the organization.

Additionally, new organizations are often strongly influenced by the individual or individuals who were instrumental in their formation. Moreover, the culture of each organization reflects some aspects of the broader social culture.

3.   *Describe an organizational culture with which you are familiar. How did the organization develop its culture?*

The students should consider their answer to question 2 in addressing this discussion question. The primary focus should be on how the organization's culture developed in response to the challenges of external adaptation and survival and internal integration.

While the answer to question 2 provides a general framework for this question, the specific content of the answers will vary according to the examples cited by the students. Again, students can use either work or nonwork organizations to provide examples.

4.   *What are the primary methods used to maintain the organizational culture you identified in question 3?*

According to the text, the primary methods for maintaining and changing organizational culture are the following:

a.   What managers and teams pay attention to, measure, and control.
b.   The ways managers (particularly top managers) react to critical incidents and organizational crises.
c.   Managerial and team role modeling, teaching, and coaching.
d.   Criteria for allocating rewards and status.
e.   Criteria for recruitment, selection, promotion, and removal from the organization.
f.   Organizational rites, ceremonies, and stories.

These six methods provide the conceptual framework that students can draw upon in discussing examples taken from their own experiences.

5.   *Identify and discuss some constraints or limitations on changing the culture you selected in question 3.*

There are two perspectives regarding constraints on cultural change that can be used as conceptual background for discussing the students' examples.

The first perspective argues that although many organizations need to change deeply ingrained habits that are ineffective, the question really is whether the deep, core values of organizational culture are amenable to change. Accordingly, restricting managerial focus and efforts to changing ineffective behaviors and procedures may be more meaningful than attempting to change organizational culture.

A second perspective suggests that limitations stem from difficulties in accurately assessing organizational culture. Faced with differences in perceptions, researchers and managers may be hard pressed to identify the culture of an organization. Moreover, many large, complex organizations may have more than one culture. Having multiple subcultures increases the difficulty of accurately assessing organizational culture, let alone changing it.

6.   *How are organizational culture and performance related?*

The relationship between organizational culture and performance can be summarized into four key ideas. First, knowing the culture of an organization allows employees to understand the firm's history and current approach. Second, organizational culture can foster commitment to corporate philosophy and values. Third, organizational culture, through its norms, serves as a control mechanism to channel employees toward desired behaviors and away from undesired behaviors. Fourth, certain types of organizational cultures may produce greater effectiveness and productivity than others.

7.   *How might an organization use culture to increase the probability of ethical behavior and/or decrease the probability of unethical behavior by its members?*

An organization is more likely to increase ethical behavior and/or decrease unethical behavior by its members if it has:

     a.   A culture which values and supports ethical behavior with a code of ethics.
     b.   Mechanisms to reward or punish adherence to the code.
     c.   Authority figures who support and model ethical behavior.

Organizations can take some specific actions to facilitate the creation of a culture that encourages ethical behavior. The organization should:

     a.   Be realistic in setting values and goals regarding employment relationships.
     b.   Encourage input from throughout the organization regarding appropriate values and practices for implementing the culture.
     c.   Not automatically opt for a "strong" culture, which may suppress diversity and dissent.
     d.   Provide training programs for managers and teams on adopting and implementing the organization's values.

8.   *Discuss the issue of managing cultural diversity. How can organizations and managers deal with this challenge?*

Organizations are becoming increasingly diverse in terms of gender, race, ethnicity, and nationality. More than half the U.S. work force consists of women, minorities, and immigrants. The growing diversity of employees at many organizations can bring substantial benefits, such as more successful marketing strategies for different types of customers, improved decision making, and perhaps greater creativity and innovation. But there are costs and concerns as well, including communication difficulties, higher levels of organizational conflict, and the potential for higher turnover.

Effectively managing cultural diversity promises to be a significant challenge for organizations during the 1990s and beyond. Some guidelines for responding to this significant challenge include the following:

     a.   Bring the diversity issue out in the open and discuss it.
     b.   Explore how all employees come to the workplace with a unique combination of background influences.
     c.   Be an intercultural ambassador by making tact and respect the rule for discussions of ethnic, cultural, racial, or gender differences.
     d.   Don't tolerate racist or sexist behaviors.
     e.   Help employees balance personal and professional needs.

        f.   Explain the unwritten rules of the organization to employees.

        g.   Encourage employees to talk with co-workers about their concerns so they are exposed to a variety of viewpoints.

9.   *Describe the process of organizational socialization. Identify some key issues in organizational socialization.*

Students responses to this question should be based upon the seven step process for socializing new employees that firms with strong organizational cultures frequently follow. This process is depicted in Figure 14.4.

The seven steps in the process are:

        a.   Entry-level candidates are selected carefully.

        b.   Humility-inducing experiences in the first months on the job cause employees to question their prior behaviors, beliefs, and values.

        c.   In-the-trenches training leads to mastery of one of the core disciplines of the business.

        d.   Careful attention is given to measuring operational results and rewarding individual performance.

        e.   Adherence to the organization's values is emphasized.

        f.   Reinforcing folklore provides legends and interpretations of important events in the organization's history that validate its culture and goals.

        g.   Consistent role models and consistent traits are associated with those recognized as being on the fast track to promotion and success.

Some of the key issues in organizational socialization are:

        a.   How rapid should the socialization process be? Rapid socialization is advantageous for both the individual employee and the organization. For the individual, rapid socialization reduces the uncertainty and anxiety surrounding a new job. For the organization, rapid socialization helps the new employee become productive quickly. However, if rapid socialization takes places in an ineffective organizational culture, the results could be detrimental.

        b.   In an effective organizational culture, strong socialization contributes to organizational success. However, in an ineffective culture, strong socialization may hinder organizational success.

        c.   The socialization process can have successful and unsuccessful outcomes for both the individual and the organization (a list of possible socialization outcomes in contained in Table 14.5 of the text). Therefore, the socialization process should be managed so as to increase the likelihood of successful outcomes and decrease the likelihood of unsuccessful outcomes.

10.   *Describe the socialization process used by an organization with which you are familiar. What were the results of the socialization process?*

The students can use Figure 14.4 and Table 14.5 as the conceptual foundation for their answer. Figure 14.4 provides an example of how the socialization process frequently occurs. Table 14.5 contains a list of possible outcomes of the socialization process.

Using these two exhibits, the students should analyze a work or nonwork organization with which they are familiar. If the socialization process that they are familiar with deviates significantly from the one depicted in Figure 14.4, the students should discuss the differences and their potential implications. Additionally, the students should compare the socialization outcomes in their examples to those contained in Table 14.5. They should consider the possible reasons behind successful or unsuccessful socialization outcomes. Also, the students should consider how the culture of their example organizations contributed to the socialization process producing successful or unsuccessful outcomes.

DEVELOPING SKILLS—
SELF DIAGNOSIS: ASSESSING ETHICAL CULTURE

This diagnostic instrument contains nine statements about different ethical aspects of organizational culture. Drawing on their own work experience, the students indicate the extent to which each of the statements is true or false. A six-point response scale is used, thereby yielding a maximum score of 54. Four of the items are reverse scored; students should be reminded of this.

Scores can range from 9 to 54. Scores of 36 or above indicate a culture that tends to encourage or support ethical behavior. Scores of 28-35 indicate some ambivalence in regard to ethical issues. Scores of 27 or below represent a culture where unethical behavior is more likely to occur.

DEVELOPING SKILLS—
A CASE IN POINT: PROCTER & GAMBLE

CASE OVERVIEW

This case describes the key elements of Procter & Gamble's organizational culture. These key elements include:

a.   A highly rational, objective view of the world.
b.   The central goal of developing a technically superior product that will win in a blind taste test.
c.   Socialization of new employees through peer competition and cooperation, and new job assignments on a regularly scheduled basis.
d.   Requirements for high performance and conformity to the P&G way.
d.   A strong emphasis on written communication and use of a common language.
e.   Use of many systems to reinforce the notion that the organization, not any one individual, produces P&G's work.
f.   Giving P&G employees high levels of autonomy and responsibility.
g.   Encouraging high involvement through the overlap of individual and organizational interests.

Because of its culture, Procter & Gamble seldom makes big mistakes. However, P&G is slower to respond to environmental demands than are smaller, faster companies. While P&G' culture is suited to the consumer goods mass market where a methodical, objective approach pays off, their culture may not be adaptable to markets that are driven mainly by taste and fashion.

CASE QUESTIONS

1.   *List the major issues and ideas from this chapter that appear, in one form or another, in this case.*

Some of the ideas and issues from Chapter 14 that appear in the Procter and Gamble case include the following:

     a.   Types of organizational culture.
     b.   Components of organizational cultural.
     c.   Levels of organizational culture.
     d.   Development of organizational culture through (1) external adaptation and survival, and (2) internal integration.
     e.   Maintenance of culture, especially in terms of what managers and teams pay attention to, measure, and control; role modeling, teaching, and coaching; criteria for allocating rewards and status; and criteria for recruitment, selection, promotion and removal of organizational members.
     f.   Strong organizational cultures and their effects on performance.
     g.   High performance-high commitment work cultures.
     h.   Socialization of new employees in a strong organizational culture.
     i.   Outcomes of socialization in a strong culture.

2.   *Would you describe the P&G culture as most like a baseball team, club, academy, or fortress culture? Explain and defend your choice.*

Most likely, P&G has a club culture. Some of the signs that this is a club culture are:

     a.   The emphasis on new assignments in different areas.
     b.   Members continually move up in the company or they leave the company.
     c.   The emphasis on following the P&G way.
     d.   The emphasis on loyalty and commitment.

These P&G characteristics fit well with the definition of a club culture. As the text indicates, employees in a club culture often start with the firm early in their careers and work at various jobs in different functions as they progress slowly but steadily up the corporate hierarchy. Moreover, organizations with this type of culture reward seniority, loyalty, commitment, and "fitting in."

3.   *Using the culture of Procter and Gamble as an example, identify and discuss some of the positive and negative aspects of strong cultures.*

A strong culture is one where most managers and employees share a set of consistent values and methods of doing business. Based on the case description, Procter and Gamble definitely has a strong culture.

In general, a strong culture can be beneficial because it facilitates a good fit between strategy and culture, helps align goals among employees, and encourages employee commitment and motivation. All three of these beneficial factors appear to be present at P&G. Clearly, there is a good match between P&G's culture and its strategy. The strategy is to take a slow, methodical approach to developing and producing top quality products for mass consumption. The P&G culture supports this strategy. In fact, the argument can be made that P&G's congruent strategy and culture are grounded in their successful efforts at external adaptation and survival and internal integration. P&G's culture also facilitates goal alignment; the key to the employees' high involvement is the planned overlap between individual and organizational goals. Finally, P&G's emphasis on high performance and following the P&G way, on fitting in or moving on, are mechanisms for encouraging commitment and motivation.

One of the major detrimental aspects of a strong organizational culture is the encouragement and reinforcement of groupthink and the herd instinct. Additionally, a strong organizational culture can restrict creative thinking. Strong organizational cultures also discourage diversity, itself a potentially important source of creativity. Based on the case evidence, we cannot conclude that these detrimental effects are actually present at P&G, though the risk exists.

COURSE ENHANCEMENT— *WEST'S ORGANIZATIONAL BEHAVIOR CUSTOM VIDEO SERIES*

None of the videos from *West's Organizational Behavior Custom Video Series* are appropriate for use with the material in Chapter 14.

COURSE ENHANCEMENT— *SUPPLEMENTAL VIDEOS AVAILABLE FROM WEST*

A video from the Association for Manufacturing Excellence and made available through West Publishing Company can be used to enhance the material in Chapter 14. This video is: *We're Getting Closer: Cadillac.* It is a 12-minute segment of a video that also contains segments on Oregon Cutting Systems (used in Chapter 15) and Steelcase (used in Chapter 16).

VIDEO: *AME: WE'RE GETTING CLOSER: CADILLAC*

Approximate Time: 12 minutes

Video Summary:

This video describes Cadillac Motor Division's new organizational culture. The cultural transformation occurred as part of Cadillac's efforts to produce a better quality, more distinctive product and to better serve its customers.

At the beginning of the video, John Grettenberger, CEO of Cadillac, is shown addressing employees and making the announcement that Cadillac received the 1990 Malcolm Baldridge Quality Award. Receipt of this award provides external validation regarding the quality of Cadillac Motor Division's products and processes.

Much of the video is devoted to describing Cadillac's new organizational culture. A key element of the new culture is the definition of the customer. Cadillac does not confine the definition of the customer to the external entity that consumes an organization's products and services. For Cadillac, the customer includes both (1) external consumers of their products and services and (2) internal departments and individuals that utilize a subassembly from a previous process. Consistent with this definition of the customer, engineering, for example, includes the production workers in the plant among its customers.

According to Bob Dorn, chief engineer, "Our job is to make them (the production workers) more effective."

Cadillac's new culture is built around cooperation and mutual interest, unlike the adversarial ways of the old culture. Bill Bailey, a production operator, provides an interesting contrast of the old and new cultures. He describes the old Cadillac culture as a "mom and dad philosophy." "Mom and Dad tell you to do as you are told—if you don't, some disciplinary action will be taken. Now we communicate back and forth."

In developing the new culture, Cadillac's management realized "the union was not the enemy" and the union realized "management was not the enemy." Both realized that they had mutual and overlapping interests. This is reflected in a cornerstone of Cadillac's new culture—a concept known as "growing the green." This concept, which is both an artistic and an agricultural metaphor, uses colors to depict management's objectives, the union's objectives, and their common objectives. Management's objectives are depicted in blue, the union's objectives in yellow, and their overlapping objectives in green (which is derived by mixing blue and yellow). From this "green common ground" a sturdy tree (organization) grows.

Another key element of the new culture is symbolized with a three-legged stool. The legs represent engineering, suppliers, and process. Every leg must be in place for the stool to stand; without any one leg, the stool is dysfunctional. So it is with the Cadillac organization. Engineering, suppliers, and the production process have to be in place and work together in order for the organization to function effectively. One example of the coordination of the efforts of these three groups is having engineers and executives working for a day on the production line. Another example of the positive effects of simultaneous coordination and communication involves the improvements in the overhead system (*i.e.,* head liner, assist handles, map lights, visors, etc.) used in Cadillacs. This overhead system was reduced from 65 separate parts to one outsourced sub-assembly.

The new Cadillac culture also stresses employee involvement. Assembly operators are observed participating in a group discussion about quality improvement during their lunch break. One worker is shown calling an Eldorado owner to inquire about her satisfaction with the car she purchased. Having production employees contact car owners is strongly supported by both management and the production workers. Use of these various employee involvement mechanisms has helped Cadillac make dramatic improvements in product quality.

Discussion Questions and Suggested Answers for Video:

1.   *What components of organizational culture are evident in the video?*

The textbook identified several components of organizational culture, including the following:

   a.   Routine behaviors such as organizational rituals and ceremonies and the language commonly used.
   b.   The norms that are shared by work groups throughout the organization.
   c.   The dominant values held by an organization.
   d.   The philosophy that guides an organization's policy toward employees and customers.
   e.   The rules of the game for getting along in the organization.
   f.   The feeling or climate that is conveyed in an organization by the physical layout and the way in which members of the organization interact with customers or other outsiders.

The organization's dominant values (item c), philosophy (item d), and climate (item e) are most evident in the video. Cadillac's dominant values include a customer focus, management and union cooperation, and employee involvement. The company's philosophy is best captured through its definition of the customer and the symbolism of "growing the green" and the engineering, supplier, and production process legs of a stool. Cadillac's climate is evident in the internal and external customer focus, developing a common ground between management and the union, the development of close working relationships with suppliers, and the various employee involvement mechanisms.

2.   *Discuss how (a) external adaptation and survival and (b) internal integration are manifested in the development of Cadillac's new organizational culture.*

According to the text, external adaptation and survival involves the organization finding a niche in and coping with its constantly changing external environment. Issues that are associated with external adaptation and survival include:

   a.   Identifying the primary mission of the organization, and selecting strategies to pursue this mission.
   b.   Setting specific goals.
   c.   Determining how to pursue the goals, including selecting an organizational structure and reward system.
   d.   Establishing criteria to measure how well individuals and teams are accomplishing their goals.

Each of these issues is dealt with, either directly or indirectly, through Cadillac's concern with producing a better quality, more distinctive product and with doing a better job of serving its customers. In responding to its changing environment, Cadillac refocused it mission in terms of customer definition and service. It set quality goals and devised methods for achieving those goals. It also established appropriate criteria for measuring quality.

Internal integration involves establishing and maintaining effective working relationships among the members of the organization. Among the issues addressed in the context of internal integration are:

   a.   Identifying methods of communication, and developing a shared meaning for important concepts.
   b.   Establishing criteria for membership in groups and teams.
   c.   Determining rules for acquiring, maintaining, and losing power and status.
   d.   Developing systems for encouraging desirable behaviors and discouraging undesirable behaviors.

The internal integration issues identified in (a) and (d) are the most relevant to the information provided in the video. Both issues are manifested in the internal customer focus; the search for common ground between management and the union; the simultaneous coordination and communication among engineering, suppliers, and the process; and the various employee involvement mechanisms.

3.   *What has Cadillac done to maintain its new culture?*

The textbook discussed six methods for maintaining an organization's culture. Based on the information in the video, Cadillac appears to be using at least two of the of the six cultural maintenance methods. Insufficient evidence is provided in the video to make any conclusive statement about the other four cultural maintenance methods.

The methods which Cadillac seems to be using revolve around:

        a.   What managers and teams pay attention to, measure, and control.

        b.   Managerial and team role modeling, teaching, and coaching.

Quality appears to be foremost is terms of what managers and teams pay attention to, measure, and control. Cooperation and teamwork are modeled through the engineers and executives working for a day on the production line. Cooperation and teamwork are also encouraged through the various employee involvement mechanisms as well as through the symbolism of "growing the green" and the three-legged stool. More importantly, organizational members strive to put into practice the actions which these symbols suggest.

CHAPTER 15
POWER AND POLITICAL BEHAVIOR

CHAPTER OVERVIEW

Chapter 15 continues the exploration of organizational processes by focusing on power and political behavior. First, power and authority are defined. Then, five interpersonal sources of power—reward, coercive, legitimate, expert, and referent—are examined in terms of their basic nature, implications, and interrelationships. Next, four structural sources of power are considered. These are: knowledge as power, resources as power, decision making as power, and networks as power. Additionally, the chapter discusses how these structural sources of power affect the power possessed by lower-level employees in organizations. The effective use of power is discussed in the context of selecting an influence strategy and managing the exchange process. Chapter 15 also identifies the characteristics of people who use power effectively. Finally, the chapter examines the nature of organizational politics as well as the situational and personality factors that contribute to political behavior in organizations.

LEARNING OBJECTIVES

Upon completion of this chapter, the students should be able to:

1. Define the concepts of organizational power and organizational politics.
2. Describe the main interpersonal sources of power.
3. Identify and explain the primary categories of structural sources of power.
4. Discuss effective and ineffective uses of power.
5. Identify the personal and situational factors that contribute to the occurrence of political behavior.
6. Describe some personality dimensions that are related to political behavior.

CHAPTER OUTLINE

I.   **Preview Case:** The Politics of Innovation

II.   Power

    A.   **Managing in Practice:** The King is Dead

III.   Interpersonal Sources of Power

    A.   Reward Power
    B.   Coercive Power
    C.   Legitimate Power
    D.   Expert Power
    E.   **Managing Across Cultures:** Power and the Japanese CEO
    F.   Referent Power
    G.   Key Relationships

IV.   Structural Sources of Power

    A.   Knowledge as Power
    B.   **Managing Quality:** Computer Links Empower Employees
    C.   Resources as Power
    D.   Decision Making as Power
    E.   **Managing Across Cultures:** Power in Chinese and British Organizations
    F.   Networks as Power
    G.   **Managing Diversity:** African-American Business Networking
    H.   Lower-Level Employee Power

V.   The Effective Use of Power

VI.   Political Behavior

    A.   Organizational Politics
    B.   **Managing in Practice:** Picking a Successor at Booz, Allen, & Hamilton, Inc.
    C.   Forces Creating Political Behavior
    D.   **Managing Ethics:** The Politics of Employee Appraisal

VII.   Personality and Political Behavior

    A.   Need for Power
    B.   Machiavellianism
    C.   Locus of Control
    D.   Risk-Seeking Propensity

VIII.   Developing Skills

    A.   **Self Diagnosis:** How Much Power Do You Have in Your Group?
    B.   **A Case in Point:** The NASA Moonlander Monitor

KEY WORDS AND CONCEPTS

Twenty-three key words and concepts are introduced in Chapter 15. Seven of the key words and concepts were introduced in earlier chapters. Coercive power, expert power, legitimate power, referent power, and reward power were originally introduced in Chapter 11. Locus of control was contained in Chapter 2. The need for power was discussed as the power motive in Chapter 6. The key words and concepts, along with definitions or appropriate descriptions, are as follows:

Authority: refers to power that is legitimated by being (1) formally granted by the organization, and (2) accepted by employees as being right and proper.

Coercive power: an interpersonal source of power that refers to an individual's ability to influence other's behavior by punishing undesirable behavior.

Decision making as power: a structural source of power that refers to individuals or groups acquiring power to the extent that they can affect some part of the decision-making process.

Exchange process: refers to the "law of reciprocity" in power relationships. The law of reciprocity is the almost universal belief that people should be paid back for what they do.

Expert power: an interpersonal source of power that refers to an individual's ability to influence others' behavior because of recognized skills, talents, or specialized knowledge.

Influence strategies: the methods by which individuals or groups attempt to exert power or influence over others' behavior.

Intellectual capital: the knowledge, know-how, and skill that exist in the organization.

Knowledge as power: a structural source of power that refers to individuals, teams, groups, or departments having power because they possess knowledge crucial to attaining the organization's goals.

Legitimate power: an interpersonal source of power that refers to a manager's ability to influence subordinates' behavior because of the manager's position in the organizational hierarchy.

Locus of control: a personality variable that refers to the extent to which individuals believe they can control events that affect them.

Machiavellianism: a personality variable that refers to (1) the use of guile and deceit in interpersonal relationships, (2) a cynical view of the nature of other people, and (3) a lack of concern with conventional morality.

Machiavellians: people who view and manipulate others for their own purposes.

Need for power: a motive, or basic desire, to influence and lead others and to control the current environment.

Network analysis: a tool which managers and employees can use to diagram important relationship networks within the organization.

Networks as power: a structural source of power which implies that various affiliations, networks, and coalitions, both inside and outside, the organization, represent sources of power.

Organizational politics: involves actions by individuals or groups to acquire, develop, and use power and other resources in order to obtain preferred outcomes when there is uncertainty or disagreement about choices.

Political behavior: refers to individuals and groups attempting to influence the behavior of others and the course of events in the organization in order to protect their self-interests, meet their own needs, and advance their own goals.

Power: the capacity to influence the behavior of others.

Referent power: an interpersonal source of power that refers to an individual's ability to influence others' behavior as a result of being liked or admired.

Resources as power: a structural source of power that refers to departments, groups, or individuals acquiring power in the organization because they can provide essential or difficult-to-obtain resources.

Reward power: an interpersonal source of power that refers to an individual's ability to influence others' behavior by rewarding their desirable behavior.

Risk-seeking propensity: a personality variable that refers to differences in individuals' willingness to take risks.

Zone of indifference: refers to employees' reactions to managers' use of legitimate power. Influence attempts within a manager's specific responsibility area fall within the zone of indifference; and employees will accept managerial directives without questioning them. However, outside the zone of indifference, legitimate power disappears rapidly.

LECTURE NOTES

I.   Chapter 15 continues the exploration of organizational processes by addressing several important questions about power and political behavior. Among these questions are: What is power? Where does it come from? Who has power? Can power be used ineffectively? Can it be used effectively? What is political behavior in organizations? What factors create opportunities for political behavior to exist in organizations? Transparency 15.1 provides an overview of the chapter's answers to these questions.

TRANSPARENCY 15.1
(FROM TEXT MATERIAL IN THE TEXTBOOK)

KEY QUESTIONS AND ANSWERS ABOUT POWER AND POLITICAL BEHAVIOR

II.   The nature of power.

   A.   <u>Power</u> is the capacity to influence the behavior of others.

   B.   Power reflects interactions among people. An individual has power in relation to other people, a group has power in relation to other groups, etc.

   C.   Power and authority are closely related but not identical concepts.

      1.   Authority is narrower in scope than power and applies to fewer behaviors in an organization.

2. <u>Authority</u> is power legitimated by being:

    a.   Formally granted by the organization.

    b.   Accepted by employees as being right and proper.

D.   As shown in Transparency 15.2, there are two sources of power within organizations: interpersonal and structural.

TRANSPARENCY 15.2
(FIGURE 15.1 IN THE TEXTBOOK)

SOURCES OF POWER IN ORGANIZATIONS

III.   Interpersonal sources of power.

A.   Five interpersonal sources of power exist within organizations: reward power, coercive power, legitimate power, expert power, and referent power. These sources of power were introduced in Chapter 11 in the context of leadership. Now they are explored in a broader organizational context.

B.   Definitions of the interpersonal sources of power.

    1.   <u>Reward power</u> is an individual's ability to influence others' behavior by rewarding their desirable behavior.

    2.   <u>Coercive power</u> is an individual's ability to influence other's behavior by punishing undesirable behavior.

    3.   <u>Legitimate power</u> refers to a manager's ability to influence subordinates' behavior because of the manager's position in the organizational hierarchy.

    4.   <u>Expert power</u> is an individual's ability to influence others' behavior because of recognized skills, talents, or specialized knowledge.

    5.   <u>Referent power</u> is an individual's ability to influence others' behavior as a result of being liked or admired.

C.   Implications of the interpersonal sources of power.

    1.   Reward power.

        a.   Employees may comply with some influence attempts by managers because they expect to be rewarded for their compliance.

    2.   Coercive power.

        a.   Subordinates may comply with some influence attempts because they expect to be punished for failure to respond favorably to managerial directives.

    3.   Legitimate power.

a.   Employees have a <u>zone of indifference</u> with regard to the exercise of legitimate power. Influence attempts within a manager's specific responsibility area fall within this zone of indifference, and employees will accept managerial directives without questioning them. However, outside the zone of indifference, legitimate power disappears rapidly.

4.   Expert power.

    a.   Expert power is often relatively narrow in scope.

    b.   A lack of expert power often plagues new managers and employees.

    c.   Expert power is acquired as expertise as is demonstrated and applied over time.

5.   Referent power.

    a.   Referent power is usually associated with individuals who possess admired personality characteristics, charisma, or a good reputation.

D.   Key relationships among the interpersonal sources of power.

1.   The ways in which managers and other employees use one type of power can either enhance or limit the effectiveness of another source of power.

2.   The five sources of interpersonal power may be divided into two broad categories: organizational and personal.

    a.   The organizational category includes reward power, coercive power, and legitimate power. Top managers can grant or take away these types of power from lower level managers.

    b.   The personal category includes expert power and referent power. These types of power depend more on personal characteristics; top managers cannot grant or take away personal power.

    c.   Evidence suggests that, for influencing behavior, personal sources of power are more important than organizational sources of power.

IV.   Structural sources of power.

A.   Overview of structural sources of power.

1.   Situational variables—such as the design of the organization, access to powerful individuals and critical resources, the nature of the position a person holds, etc.—can influence who has power and how much power they have.

2.   An example of the situational determinants of power is provided in Transparency 15.3. This transparency identifies some position characteristics that determine relative power in an organization. These characteristics, and therefore the power associated with them, apply to both managerial and nonmanagerial positions.

3.   There are four important categories of structural sources of power. These categories are: knowledge as power, resources as power, decision making as power, and networks as power.

B.   Knowledge as power.

    1.   <u>Knowledge as power</u> means that individuals, teams, groups, or departments that possess knowledge crucial to attaining the organization's goals have power.

    2.   Control of information flows enhances the relative power of individuals and/or organizational units.

    3.   Computerization affects access to and use of information, which in turn can flatten the organizational hierarchy and alter power relationships.

    4.   Knowledge as power draws upon the <u>intellectual capital</u> of the organization (*i.e.,* the knowledge, know-how, and skill that exist in the organization).

C.   Resources as power.

    1.   <u>Resources as power</u> indicates that departments, groups, or individuals who can provide essential or difficult-to-obtain resources acquire power in the organization.

    2.   Which resources are most important depends on the situation, the organization's goals, the economic climate, and the goods or services being produced.

D.   Decision making as power.

    1.   <u>Decision making as power</u> means that individuals or groups acquire power to the extent that they can affect some part of the decision-making process.

    2.   Decision making as power may influence the goals being developed, premises being used in making a decision, alternatives being considered, outcomes being forecast, etc.

    3.   The ability to influence the decision-making process is a subtle and often overlooked source of power.

E.   Networks as power.

    1.   <u>Networks as power</u> implies that various affiliations, networks, and coalitions, both inside and outside the organization, represent sources of power.

    2.   Network linkages include traditional superior subordinate vertical relationships as well as horizontal linkages with co-workers and external contacts.

    3.   Within the overall context of vertical and horizontal linkages, power is provided by

information links, supply links, and support links.

4.   Power networks can be analyzed with a <u>network analysis</u>—a tool which managers and employees can use to diagram important relationship networks within the organization. By diagramming the *advice network,* the *trust network,* the *communication network,* etc., organizational members can diagnose power differences as well as how work actually gets done.

   a.   The advice network reveals employees that others depend on to solve problems and provide technical information.

   b.   The trust network shows which employees share delicate political information with each other.

   c.   The communication network indicates who talks to whom on a regular basis.

F.   Lower-level employee power.

1.   Lower-level employees in an organization's hierarchy may possess considerable power because of their access to information, resources, decision making and networks. Transparency 15.4 illustrates how lower-level employees acquire their power. The position characteristics listed in transparency 15.4 are taken from the material contained in Transparency 15.3. The expertise of management and employees reflects a source of interpersonal power—namely, expert power.

TRANSPARENCY 15.4
(FIGURE 15.4 IN THE TEXTBOOK)

MODEL OF LOWER-LEVEL EMPLOYEE POWER

ENRICHMENT MODULE: WHAT CONSTITUTES THE ABUSE OF POWER?
(*A Discussion Activity*)

Sometimes managers behave in ways that abuse their interpersonal and structural sources of power. Have the students read the following account of one executive's activities, then discuss whether he abused his power. Also, have the students identify the powers that were abused. They should also consider the individual and organizational implications of abusing power.

> After taking over the presidency of Paramount Communications, Inc., one of Mr. Stanley Jaffe's first moves was to terminate about 400 staff members. Simultaneously he indulged himself by having Paramount build a $1.5 million screening room on his New York estate. He also had the company buy a corporate jet to fly him between Hollywood and his New York estate, and to games played by professional athletic teams owned by Paramount subsidiaries.

> While the rest of the company was becoming more cost conscious and tightening its belt, Mr. Jaffe and his friends and relatives reaped considerable benefits. Jaffe collected substantial bonuses, stock, and stock options. His acquaintances and relatives began appearing on the payroll in key positions despite employment cutbacks in the company.

> Jaffe also tried to influence the operations of Paramount's Simon & Schuster publishing subsidiary and its New York Knicks and New York Rangers professional sports subsidiaries. At Simon & Schuster, he allegedly influenced the content and promotion of a book that contained material he disliked. In regard to the professional sports teams, one Madison Square Garden executive said, "Mr. Jaffe treated the sports operations more as a toy than as a business, and wanted a championship at any cost."

This enrichment module is based on:

Roberts, J.L. (1994, January 31). 'The blame game': Volatile Stanley Jaffe has scared Paramount but hasn't fixed it. *The Wall Street Journal*, A1 & A14.

V.   The effective use of power.

   A.   What is the effective use of power? The ineffective use of power?

      1.   The goal of the effective use of power is to influence the behavior of others in ways that are consistent with both the needs of the organization and its employees. If the use of power isn't carefully managed, powerful individuals may exploit those with less power and substitute their self-interests for the legitimate interests of the organization.

      2.   The effective use of power involves selecting the correct influence strategy and properly managing the exchange process.

      3.   The ineffective use of power involves choosing the wrong influence strategy and/or mismanaging the exchange process.

   B.   Selecting an influence strategy.

      1.   <u>Influence strategies</u> are the methods by which individuals or groups attempt to

exert power or influence over others' behavior.

2.   Transparency 15.5, which is self-explanatory, identifies different influence strategies that organization members can use in the workplace.

TRANSPARENCY 15.5
(TABLE 15.2 IN THE TEXTBOOK)

INFLUENCE STRATEGIES

---

a.   Rational persuasion, inspirational appeal, and consultation tend to be the most effective influence strategies.

b.   Coalition formation, legitimating, and pressure tend to be the least effective influence strategies.

c.   A contingency approach should be taken to the selection of an influence strategy. An individual must consider the available power sources, the direction of the influence attempt, and the goals being sought when selecting an influence strategy.

C.   Managing the exchange process.

1.   The <u>exchange process</u> in power relationships is based on the "law of reciprocity"—the almost universal belief that people should be paid back for what they do.

2.   The exchange process can be easily understood using the metaphor of *currencies,* as shown in Transparency 15.6.

TRANSPARENCY 15.6
(TABLE 15.3 IN THE TEXTBOOK)

ORGANIZATIONAL CURRENCIES TRADED IN THE EXCHANGE PROCESS

D.   Implications of the ineffective use of power (see Transparency 15.7).

TRANSPARENCY 15.7
(FROM TEXT MATERIAL IN THE TEXTBOOK)

IMPLICATIONS OF THE INEFFECTIVE USE OF POWER

---

1.   Ineffective users of power tend to rely too much on one or a few power bases or influence strategies.

2.   Ineffective users of power try to acquire enough power to simply order others around.

3.   Ineffective users of power tend to receive the lowest performance evaluations, earn less money, and experience the highest levels of job tension and stress.

E.   Implications of the effective use of power (see Transparency 15.8).

TRANSPARENCY 15.8
(FROM TEXT MATERIAL IN THE TEXTBOOK)
IMPLICATIONS OF THE EFFECTIVE USE OF POWER

---

1.   Effective users of power understand both the interpersonal and structural sources of power and the most effective methods of using them to influence people.

2.   Effective users of power understand the nature of the exchange process underlying many successful attempts to influence others.

3.   Effective users of power understand what is and what is not legitimate behavior in acquiring and using power.

4.   Effective users of power tend to seek positions that allow development and use of power. They choose jobs that immerse them in the crucial issues and concerns of an organization.

5.   Effective users of power exercise maturity and self-control.

ENRICHMENT MODULE: POWER AND MANAGERIAL INTEGRITY

Is the effective use of power related to managerial integrity? Or does being a person of integrity have nothing to do with how one uses power?

A reasonable argument can made that managerial integrity and the effective use of power go hand-in-hand. The argument would go something like this:

- The effective use of power involves a healthy dose of treating people humanely and fairly.

- Treating people humanely and fairly is an essential part of integrity.

- A person of integrity displays many behaviors that also reflect the effective use of power. These behaviors include, but are not limited to, the following: maintaining concern for the greater good, being truthful, fulfilling commitments, striving for fairness, developing others, and assisting others.

- The behaviors which reflect integrity also suggest sensitivity to the exchange relationship in the influence attempt.

The list of behaviors that characterize managerial integrity is adapted from:

Zauderer, D.G. (1992, Fall). Integrity—An essential executive quality. *Business Forum*, 12-16.

VI.   Political behavior.

    A.   <u>Political behavior</u> of individuals and groups consists of their attempts to influence the behavior of others and the course of events in the organization in order to protect their self-interests, meet their own needs, and advance their own goals.

        1.   In common use, political behavior usually implies that individuals or groups are gaining something at the expense of other employees, groups, or the organization. The text does not subscribe to that position.

    B.   <u>Organizational politics</u> involves actions by individuals or groups to acquire, develop, and use power and other resources in order to obtain preferred outcomes when there is uncertainty or disagreement about choices.

        1.   Political behavior may be either beneficial or detrimental to the organization and its members.

            a.   Beneficial effects can include career advancement, recognition and status for individuals looking after their legitimate interests, and achievement of organizational goals.

            b.   Detrimental effects can include demotions and loss of jobs for "losers" in the political process, a misuse of resources, and creation of an ineffective organizational culture.

        2.   Eliminating all political behavior isn't possible—it can only be managed.

    C.   Situational forces which create opportunities for political behavior.

        1.   The probability of political behavior increases when (see Transparency 15.9):

TRANSPARENCY 15.9
(FROM TEXT MATERIAL IN THE TEXTBOOK)

SITUATIONAL FACTORS THAT INFLUENCE THE LIKELIHOOD OF POLITICAL BEHAVIOR

---

        a.   Disagreements over goals exist.

        b.   Unclear goals exist.

        c.   There are differing ideas about the organization and its problems.

        d.   There is differing information about the situation.

        e.   Scare resources must be allocated.

        f.   Decision-making procedures and performance measures are highly uncertain and complex.

        g.   Competition among individuals and groups for scarce resources is strong.

        h.   Organizations provide few rules or policies.

      i.   Organizations reward political behavior.

      j.   Employee performance cannot be measured easily, and the performance appraisal process uses complex criteria to allocate scarce resources.

  2.   Even though many situational factors increase the probability of political behavior, there are strategies which can be pursued to better manage, if not avoid, organizational politics Transparency 15.10, which is self-explanatory, provides several examples of strategies that can be used to avoid organizational politics and the potential costs associated with each strategy.

TRANSPARENCY 15.10
(TABLE 15.4 IN THE TEXTBOOK)

STRATEGIES FOR AVOIDING THE USE OF POLITICAL BEHAVIOR IN DECISION MAKING AND THEIR POSSIBLE COSTS

---

  3.   The performance appraisal process can be made less political by (see Transparency 15.11):

TRANSPARENCY 15.11
(FROM TEXT MATERIAL IN THE TEXTBOOK)

METHODS FOR MAKING THE PERFORMANCE APPRAISAL PROCESS LESS POLITICAL

---

      a.   Articulating goals and standards as clearly and specifically as possible.

      b.   Linking specific actions and performance results to rewards.

      c.   Conducting structured, professional reviews, providing specific examples of observed performance and explanations for ratings given.

      d.   Offering performance feedback on an ongoing basis, rather than once a year.

      e.   Acknowledging that appraisal politics exist and making this topic a focus of ongoing discussion throughout the organization.

VII.   Personality and political behavior.

  A.   Four personality characteristics—the need for power, Machiavellianism, locus of control, and risk-seeking propensity—influence the likelihood that people will engage in political behavior.

  B.   Need for power.

    1.   The <u>need for power</u> is a motive, or basic desire, to influence and lead others and to control the current environment.

    2.   In general, individuals with a high need for power are more likely to engage in political behavior.

3.   The need for power may take two forms: personal power and institutional power.

   a.   People who emphasize personal power strive to dominate others; they want loyalty to themselves, rather than to the organization.

   b.   People who emphasize institutional power create a good climate or culture for effective work, and their subordinates develop an understanding of and loyalty to the organization.

   c.   An emphasis on personal power can be detrimental to the organization and its members, whereas as an emphasis on institutional power can be beneficial for an organization and its members.

C.   Machiavellianism.

1.   Machiavellianism is characterized by:

   a.   The use of guile and deceit in interpersonal relationships.

   b.   A cynical view of the nature of other people.

   c.   A lack of concern with conventional morality.

2.   Machiavellians are people who view and manipulate others for their own purposes.

3.   Machiavellians are likely to engage in political behavior.

D.   Locus of control.

1.   Locus of control refers to the extent to which individuals believe they can control events that affect them.

   a.   Internals believe that events result primarily from their own behavior.

   b.   Externals believe that powerful others, fate or chance are primarily in control of the events that affect them.

2.   Internals tend to exhibit more political behavior than externals and are more likely to attempt to influence other people.

ENRICHMENT MODULE: LOCUS OF CONTROL, ETHICS, AND POLITICAL BEHAVIOR

A recent study of college students compared the ethical standards of internal locus of control individuals with those of external locus of control people (McCuddy & Peery, in press). The results indicated that internals had higher ethical standards than externals. The textbook indicates that internals tend to exhibit more political behavior than externals. Taken together, the evidence suggests that internals have higher ethical standards but behave more politically, whereas externals have lower ethical standards yet exhibit fewer political behaviors.

Do these results seem counter-intuitive? Don't people normally expect lower ethical standards to go hand-in-hand with political behavior? Perhaps this is a misconception based on the viewpoint that ethical standards are good and desirable while political behavior is not.

What if we consider an alternative viewpoint: namely, both ethical standards and political behaviors can be good and desirable things to have in an organization. Based on this viewpoint, we could argue that internals, who believe they control their own destiny, may pursue their self-interest but do so in a just and fair manner.

What do you think? Have the students discuss their ideas concerning the possible linkages among locus of control, ethics, and political behavior.

Source for locus of control and ethical standards data: McCuddy, M.K., & Peery, B.L. (In Press). Selected individual differences and collegians' ethical beliefs. *Journal of Business Ethics.*

       E.   Risk-seeking propensity.

            1.   <u>Risk-seeking propensity</u> refers to differences in individuals' willingness to take risks. Some people are risk avoiders, and others are risk seekers.

            2.   Risk seekers are more willing to engage in political behavior.

       F.   The relationships between political behavior and the need for power, Machiavellianism, locus of control, and risk-seeking propensity are summarized in Transparency 15.12.

TRANSPARENCY 15.12
(FROM TEXT MATERIAL IN THE TEXTBOOK)

SUMMARY OF RELATIONSHIPS BETWEEN PERSONALITY AND POLITICAL BEHAVIOR

VIII.   Summing up: Why are power and political behavior important for understanding and managing organizational behavior?

       A.   Power is an essential element of the influence process. Without interpersonal or structural sources of power to draw upon, no one would be able to influence the behavior of someone else. Managers would not be able to influence their subordinates. Colleagues would be unable to influence one another. Lower-level employees would be unable to exert influence within the organization. Since any attempt to influence another person's behavior draws upon power, and since influencing others is part of what managers do, managers must understand power and utilize it effectively.

B.   Political behavior can never be eliminated from organizations because there will always be some people who try to advance their self-interests at the expense of others. However, by using their knowledge of political behavior, organization members can attempt to blunt its effects or to channel it to beneficial ends.

C.   Too often, power and political behavior seem to be viewed with a great deal of negativity. This is probably due to power being abused or political behavior being used in an exploitative manner. However, if power is used effectively and political behavior is managed appropriately, beneficial consequences can occur for the organization and its members.

D.   In the final analysis, power and political behavior are facts of organizational life. People must understand these facts of organizational life in order to diagnose organizations and to function as effectively as possible in them.

DISCUSSION QUESTIONS: SUGGESTED ANSWERS

1.   *Compare and contrast interpersonal and structural sources of power in organizations.*

Interpersonal sources of power focus on the influence potential that exists in interpersonal relationships between superiors and subordinates. Structural sources of power focus on situational factors within the organization that influence the relative power of individuals, groups, teams, and departments.

There are five interpersonal sources of power: reward power, coercive power, legitimate power, expert power, and referent power. Reward power, coercive power, and legitimate power are organizationally based—that is, they can be granted or taken away by top management. Expert power and referent power are personal in nature; they derive from the individual and cannot be granted or taken away by the organization.

The four sources of structural power are knowledge as power, resources as power, decision making as power, and networks as power. With structural sources of power, individuals, groups, teams, or departments have access to or control over something that is important to and desired by others. That something can be information (knowledge as power), essential or difficult-to-obtain resources (resources as power), the capability to affect some part of the decision-making process (decision making as power), or having access to various affiliations, networks, and coalitions, both inside and outside, the organization (networks as power). Having access to or control over one or more these items provides individuals and groups with power.

2.   *Were you ever in a situation in which you had the power to influence the behavior of others? If so, explain the source or sources of your power.*

The conceptual foundation for answering this question is provided in the response to question 1. The students should draw upon that conceptual foundation in analyzing whatever situation they use as a personal example.

3.   *Were you ever in a situation in which someone else had the power to influence your behavior? If so, explain the source or sources of your power.*

Like question 2, the conceptual foundation for answering this question is contained in the response to question 1. Again, the students should link this conceptual foundation with their personal example.

4. *Provide some suggestions for the effective use of power.*

Students can address this question in two different though related ways. First, they could focus on the goal of the effective use of power and then on the means by which that goal can be achieved. Using this perspective, one could argue that the goal of the effective use of power is to influence the behavior of others in ways that are consistent with both the needs of the organization and its employees. This goal can be achieved by selecting the correct influence strategy and properly managing the exchange process.

The second way in which this question could be answered is to cite the five characteristics that are shared by effective users of power. Specifically, effective users of power:

   a.   Understand both the interpersonal and structural sources of power and the most effective methods of using them to influence people.
   b.   Understand the nature of the exchange process underlying many successful attempts to influence others.
   c.   Understand what is and what is not legitimate behavior in acquiring and using power.
   d.   Tend to seek positions that allow development and use of power.
   e.   Exercise maturity and self-control.

5. *What is the nature of the exchange process in power relationships? Provide some examples of currencies that were commonly exchanged in an organization with which you are familiar.*

The exchange process in power relationships is based on the "law of reciprocity"—the almost universal belief that people should be paid back for what they do. The metaphor of currencies is a useful way to understand how the exchange process is used to influence behavior. Table 15.3 of the text provides examples of currencies that are commonly traded in organizations. These include: resources, assistance, cooperation, information, advancement, recognition, networks/contacts, and personal support.

6. *Based on your own experiences, give examples of both the effective and ineffective use of power. Explain why each outcome occurred.*

Much of the conceptual foundation for answering this question is provided in the suggested response for question 4. Additionally, the students should consider the following conceptual material in formulating their responses to this question:

   a.   If the use of power is not carefully managed, those individuals with power may exploit others in the organization who have less power.
   b.   Those with more power may also overvalue their own importance and confuse their self-interests with the interests of the organization.
   c.   Individuals who use power ineffectively are often those whose behavior is inconsistent with others' expectations.
   d.   Individuals who use power ineffectively may attempt to appear expert in an area where they do not have any real expertise.

e.   Ineffective users of power also tend to rely too heavily on one or a few sources of power.

The students should draw on this background material as they provide their personal examples and analyze them.

7.   *Define political behavior. What are some of the factors that can contribute to organizational politics?*

Political behavior is defined as the attempts of individuals and groups to influence the behavior of others and the course of events in the organization in order to protect their self-interests, meet their own needs, and advance their own goals. Political behavior usually implies that individuals or groups are gaining something at the expense of other employees, groups, or the organization.

Some of the situational forces which create opportunities for political behavior include the following:

a.   Disagreements exist over goals.
b.   Unclear goals exist.
c.   There are differing ideas about the organization and its problems.
d.   There is differing information regarding the decision situation.
e.   Allocation of scarce resources.
f.   There are highly uncertain and complex decision-making procedures and performance measures.
g.   Strong competition exists among individuals and groups for scarce resources.
h.   Organizations provide few rules or policies.
i.   Organizations reward political behavior.
j.   Employee performance cannot be measured easily.
k.   The performance appraisal process uses complex criteria for the allocation of scarce resources.

Individual differences among people also contribute to political behavior. Individuals tend to engage in political behavior more frequently when they have a strong need for power, an internal locus of control, a strong Machiavellian orientation, or a risk seeking propensity.

8.   *Based on your own experience, describe a situation in which political behavior seemed to be excessive. Why did it occur?*

In answering this question, the students should draw on the situational and personality factors that were identified in the suggested response to question 7. Each of the factors could contribute to excessive political behavior. "Real excess" would likely occur if several of the factors appear in combination. Also, Figure 15.5 could be useful in framing answer.

9.   *Why is the performance appraisal process prone to political abuse? How can the probability of political behavior be minimized in this process?*

The performance appraisal process is prone to political abuse when employee performance is not easily measured, and the performance appraisal process results in the allocation of scarce resources based on complex criteria.

The probability of political behavior can be minimized by adhering to the following guidelines:

    a.   Articulate goals and standards as clearly and specifically as possible.

    b.   Link specific actions and performance results to rewards.

    c.   Conduct structured, professional reviews, providing specific examples of observed performance and explanations for ratings given.

    d.   Offer performance feedback on an ongoing basis, rather than once a year.

    e.   Acknowledge that appraisal politics exist and make this topic a focus of ongoing discussion throughout the organization.

DEVELOPING SKILLS—
SELF DIAGNOSIS: HOW MUCH POWER DO YOU HAVE IN YOUR GROUP?

This diagnostic instrument enables students to determine the amount of power they have in a group of which they are a member. The instrument contains 20 items to which students respond on a seven-point Likert scale. The odd-numbered items form a visibility scale and the even-numbered items constitute an influence scale. Scores on each scale can range from 10 to 70, with higher scores indicating a greater degree of visibility or influence.

Using their scores on the two dimensions, students can determine their position on the visibility/influence matrix depicted in Figure 15.6 of the text. People in the high visibility/high influence quadrant may be upwardly mobile or "fast trackers." Those in the high visibility/low influence quadrant tend to hold positions that give them visibility but lack "clout" to get things done. Individuals in the low visibility/low influence quadrant have difficulty advancing in an organization. People in the low visibility/high influence quadrant often wield considerable "behind the scenes" influence but prefer to avoid the limelight.

The results of the self-diagnosis could be used as the basis for organizing a class discussion on power. Based on the students' visibility and influence scores, four discussion groups could be created—one corresponding to each of the quadrants. The discussion groups could then explore how they try to use power in a group and how others react to their use of power.

DEVELOPING SKILLS—
A CASE IN POINT: THE NASA MOONLANDER MONITOR

CASE OVERVIEW

This case describes the role which Chuck House, a young engineer at Hewlett-Packard (H-P), played in developing new applications for oscilloscope technology. House was part of a team that developed an improved airport control tower monitor. However, the FAA selected the design produced by another firm. Believing that his team's design represented a significant technological breakthrough, House set out to convince H-P to pursue development of the monitor even though H-P had lost the FAA contract.

In the process of ultimately convincing H-P management, House performed some interesting political maneuvers, including the following:

a.   He circumvented the marketing department and collected his own market research data. He took an unauthorized trip, during which he showed a prototype of the monitor to 40 computer manufacturers. Showing a prototype to customers violated H-P's security policies. However, based on the marketing information he generated he was able to convince senior H-P management to approve continued project development.

b.   During senior management's annual progress review, House encountered opposition from both the chief corporate engineer, who favored an alternative technology, and the marketing department. Based on data from existing customers, the marketing department projected a limited demand for the new monitor. House countered with his own marketing data, collected from potential customers through organizationally illegitimate means. He forecast a broader market. Because of the lack of corporate technological support and concern about insufficient market demand, the project was canceled. In canceling the project, David Packard said: "When I come back next year, I don't want to see that project in the lab."

c.   House interpreted Packard's statement as meaning the project should be out of the lab and in production in one year, not that the project should scrapped. House successfully enlisted the support of his boss and members of the project team. He also convinced potential customers to contact senior management and express interest in the monitor.

When senior management returned for the next annual review, the monitor was on the market. Being both angered and amused, Packard nonetheless chose to support the monitor project and approved the research on additional applications for the monitor. Numerous applications were subsequently developed including the oscilloscope monitor used on NASA's moon missions.

CASE QUESTIONS

1.   *List and explain the sources of power that House used.*

In terms of interpersonal sources of power, Chuck House primarily used expert and referent power. In developing the technology and its potential product applications, House drew upon his specialized knowledge, skills, and ability. In short, House used a healthy dose of expert power in bringing the project to fruition. Also, House apparently was liked and respected—he was able to convince others on his team and his boss to work on the project even after it was "canceled." This suggests that he used referent power.

House used all four structural sources of power in getting the monitor into the marketplace. He used knowledge as power, drawing on his engineering expertise as well as the marketing information he generated through organizationally illegitimate means. He used resources as power because significant amounts of money and time went into development of the monitor. Additionally, after it was "canceled," resources for the monitor project were hidden under other budgetary items. House used decision making as power because he was able to influence the decision-making process through his activities. Finally, he used networks as power by developing an important external network with potential customers as well as a crucial internal network with his boss and co-workers. However, he neglected developing an internal network with the marketing department or the chief engineer.

2.   *Identify and explain the factors that increased political behavior in Hewlett-Packard during this time.*

Several situational factors could have increased the likelihood of political behavior at H-P. Goals regarding the monitor project were somewhat ambiguous, particularly in its earlier stages. There were differing ideas about the value of the project and its potential in the marketplace. House and the marketing department had different information about the market viability of the oscilloscope monitor. The criteria for evaluating project progress appeared to be uncertain and perhaps complex as well. H-P's rules and policies regarding product development may have been somewhat ambiguous; however, there were some clearly delineated policies that he violated more than once.

In addition, some of Chuck's personality characteristics may have been a factor in the occurrence of political behavior. Specifically, Chuck's behavior can be characterized as reflecting a strong need for power, an internal locus of control, and a risk seeking propensity. All three personality characteristics tend to be associated with more frequent occurrence of political behavior.

3. *Did House use power effectively or ineffectively? Defend your answer.*

The text presents five characteristics of people who use power effectively. Effective users of power:

      a.   Understand both the interpersonal and structural sources of power and the most effective methods of using them to influence people.

      b.   Understand the nature of the exchange process underlying many successful attempts to influence others.

      c.   Understand what is and what is not legitimate behavior in acquiring and using power.

      d.   Tend to seek positions that allow development and use of power.

      e.   Exercise maturity and self-control.

A reasonable argument can be made that House was effective with regard to items a and d, somewhat effective with regard to items b and e, and ineffective in terms of item c.

House was effective with regard to understanding the sources and uses of power. The suggested response to question 1 clearly demonstrates this. In addition, House put himself in a position which allowed the development and use of power.

House was somewhat effective in understanding the nature of the exchange process and in exercising maturity and self-control. He seems to have understood the exchange process relative to his boss, co-workers on the project team, and potential customers. However, he was insensitive to the exchange process regarding the marketing department. Also, House was only somewhat effective in using maturity and self-control in influencing others. On the positive side, he persisted because he believed strongly in the project and the potential it offered the organization (rather than to himself personally). On the negative side, he used organizationally illegitimate means on several occasions to further the project.

By violating certain organizational policies, and circumventing the marketing department, House shows that he may not have truly understood what was and was not a legitimate use of power. Of course, he may have clearly understood the difference but chose to ignore it.

4. *Suggest some strategies that House might have utilized to reduce the political resistance to this innovation.*

Students could base their answers to this question on the material contained in Table 15.4 of the text. Specifically, House could have tried to find slack resources to be used in pursuing the project. He could have argued that employing the resources on a project that might have some payoff would be better than not using the resources at all. Additionally, House could have enlisted the support of the marketing department and the chief engineer when he first sought to go ahead with the project. Having their support could have made the decision appear less important. Their support also could have reduced system complexity and uncertainty.

COURSE ENHANCEMENT— *WEST'S ORGANIZATIONAL BEHAVIOR CUSTOM VIDEO SERIES*

None of the videos from *West's Organizational Behavior Custom Video Series* is appropriate for use with the material contained in Chapter 15.

COURSE ENHANCEMENT— *SUPPLEMENTAL VIDEOS AVAILABLE FROM WEST*

A video from the Association for Manufacturing Excellence and made available through West Publishing Company can be used to enhance the material in Chapter 15. This video is a 16-minute segment of *We're Getting Closer* that focuses on *Oregon Cutting Systems*.

VIDEO: *AME: WE'RE GETTING CLOSER: OREGON CUTTING SYSTEMS*

Approximate Time: 16 minutes

Video Summary:

Oregon Cutting Systems, a major producer of blades and chains for chain saws, had a history of ignoring customer complaints. The CEO remarked that they used to have the view the customers' problems were not the company's problems. OCS has changed that view—now the customers' problems are the company's problems and OCS works very hard at trying to solve them.

OCS changed the way it operated. In an effort to improve efficiency and product quality, Oregon Cutting Systems implemented just-in-time (JIT) manufacturing and statistical process control (SPC) procedures. Underlying these, however, was OCS's initiative at employee empowerment.

Part of the OCS's approach to employee empowerment can be seen through their application of SPC. At Oregon Cutting Systems, SPC is considered an operator tool, not a management tool. Operators are encouraged to identify problems and solve them without management input. Thus, operators spend 5-10% of their time collecting data, using control charts, analyzing data, identifying problems, and acting on those problems.

Another perspective on OCS's approach to employee empowerment is reflected in attitude of top management. The CEO advocates that employees should make decisions and then ask for forgiveness if they are wrong, rather than not making any decisions or asking for permission to make decisions. A consequence of this top management attitude is that it eliminates the separation between management and production employees.

Other organizational members also have had positive reactions to employee empowerment at OCS. According to Charlie Clough, OCS's manager of industrial engineering, "the best experts you can hire are on the floor already." One operator observes that "if you let the person building the product have input on the product, they are going to feel closer to it and strive to produce a better product." A supervisor claims that decision making has improved as a result of employee empowerment. The supervisor isn't responsible for making all of the decisions; instead, she feels like a coach and trainer.

Discussion Questions and Suggested Answers for Video:

1. *Discuss how the structural sources of power are used by Oregon Cutting Systems to empower lower-level employees?*

   The textbook identifies four sources of structural power: knowledge as power, resources as power, decision making as power, and networks as power. At OCS, lower-level employees clearly have three of the four structural sources of power available to them. Knowledge as power is evidenced through the use of SPC to deal with production problems. Decision-making as power is manifested in the attitudes of top management and the daily activities of all organizational members. Networks as power is manifested in the closer linkages between managers and production workers, and the coaching/training roles being assumed by supervisors.

   Students might wish to refer to Figure 15.4 in the text when discussing this question.

2. *Which interpersonal sources of power seem to be used by OCS's lower-level employees?*

   Expert power is the one interpersonal source of power that clearly exists for OCS's lower-level employees. In part, their expert power derives from their knowledge of the process used to produce the company's products. As the manager of industrial engineering said, "the best experts you can hire are on the floor already." The expert power of lower-level employees is also based upon their knowledge of SPC and their ability to use it effectively.

CHAPTER 16
JOB DESIGN

CHAPTER OVERVIEW

Chapter 16 examines the job design component of organizational processes. First, the chapter discusses the nature of job design and its relationship to reengineering. Next, a framework for comparing five common approaches to job design is introduced. The five approaches—job rotation, job engineering, job enlargement, job enrichment, and the sociotechnical systems model—are then reviewed. Technology's role in job design is considered, with emphasis being placed on the dimensions of work-flow uncertainty, task uncertainty, and task interdependence. The chapter then explores the job characteristics enrichment model as an in-depth application of the job enrichment approach to job design. The components of the model are discussed and two ways of diagnosing the need for job enrichment are explained. Several methods for implementing job enrichment by changing the core job characteristics are introduced. The sociotechnical systems approach to job design is also discussed in some detail. Environmental forces, the social system, the technological system, and moderator variables—the four key components of the sociotechnical systems model—are examined. Principles for effective sociotechnical systems design are presented too.

LEARNING OBJECTIVES

Upon completion of this chapter, the students should be able to:

1.   Describe five approaches to job design and indicate the differences between them.
2.   Discuss the relationship between reengineering and job design.
3.   Indicate the problems caused by poorly designed jobs.
4.   Discuss the linkages between technology and job design.
5.   Describe the job characteristics enrichment model and explain how it may affect performance, work motivation, and satisfaction.
6.   Explain the primary components of the sociotechnical systems approach to job design.

CHAPTER OUTLINE

KEY WORDS AND CONCEPTS

Twenty-nine key words and concepts are introduced in Chapter 16. One concept—reengineering—has already been mentioned in both Chapters 2 and 4. The key words and concepts, along with definitions or appropriate descriptions, are as follows:

Autonomy: a core job characteristic that refers to the degree to which the job provides freedom, independence, and discretion to the employee in scheduling tasks and in determining procedures to be used in carrying out the tasks.

Flextime: a technique that allows employees, within certain limits, to vary their arrival and departure times to suit their individual needs and desires, and helps in self-scheduling of work.

Growth-need strength: an individual differences variable in the job characteristics enrichment model that refers to the degree to which an individual desires the opportunity for self-direction, learning, and personal accomplishment at work.

Human factor approach: an approach to job design that focuses on minimizing the physical demands and biological risks at work. This approach is sometimes referred to as *ergonomics*.

Job characteristics enrichment model: focuses on increasing the amounts of skill variety, task identity, task significance, autonomy, and feedback in a job. In turn, these job characteristics influence three critical psychological states; and when all three critical psychological states are positive, a cycle of strong work motivation is activated.

Job design: the specification of tasks that are to be performed by employees, including expected interpersonal and task relationships.

Job diagnostic survey: a survey method of job diagnosis that is designed to measure the job characteristics in Hackman and Oldham's job characteristics enrichment model and the likely outcomes of job redesign.

Job engineering: one of the five common job design approaches; it focuses on the tasks to be performed, methods to be used, work flow between employees, layout of the workplace, performance standards, and interdependencies between people and machines.

Job enlargement: one of the five common job design approaches; it expands the number of different tasks performed by an employee, usually at the same basic level of responsibility.

Job enrichment: one of the five common job design approaches; it adds tasks to employees' jobs by allowing them to assume more responsibility and accountability for planning, organizing, controlling, and evaluating their own work.

Job feedback: a core job characteristic that refers to the degree to which carrying out the job-related tasks provides the individual with direct and clear information about the effectiveness of his or her performance.

Job rotation: one of the five common job design approaches; it involves moving employees from job to job, thereby giving them an opportunity to perform a greater variety of tasks.

Motivating potential score: an overall measure of the job enrichment potential that exists in a particular job. The motivating potential score reflects core job characteristics of skill variety, task identity, task significance, autonomy, and job feedback.

Pooled interdependence: a type of task interdependence that occurs when an employee is not required to communicate extensively with other individuals in the organization to complete their tasks.

Reciprocal interdependence: a type of task interdependence that occurs when outputs from one individual (or group) become the inputs for others and vice versa.

Reengineering: refers to radically new ways of thinking about organizations, including breaking away from the outdated rules and assumptions that underlie how tasks have been performed in the past.

Sequential interdependence: a type of task interdependence that occurs when one employee must complete certain tasks before other employees can perform their tasks.

Skill variety: a core job characteristic that refers to the degree to which a job requires a range of personal competencies and abilities to carry out the work.

Social information: refers to comments, observations, and similar cues provided by people whose view of the job an employee values.

Social information processing model: a job design model which specifies that the individual's social environment may provide cues as to which dimensions might be used to characterize the work environment, what the relative importance of the dimensions should be, how others evaluate each of the dimensions, and how the work setting in general should be evaluated.

Sociotechnical systems model: one of the five common job design approaches; it considers every organization to be made up of people (the social system) using tools, techniques, and knowledge (the technical system) to produce goods or services valued by customers.

Task identity: a core job characteristic that refers to the degree to which a job requires completion of a whole and identifiable piece of work, that is, doing a task from beginning to end with a visible outcome.

Task interdependence: a technology dimension that refers to the degree to which decision making and cooperation between two or more employees is necessary for them to perform their jobs.

Task significance: a core job characteristic that refers to the degree to which the employee perceives the job as having a substantial impact on the lives of other people, whether these people are within or outside the organization.

Task uncertainty: a technology dimension that refers to the degree of knowledge that an employee has about how to perform the job and when it needs to be done.

Technical system: refers to the tools, techniques, methods, procedures, and knowledge used by an organization's employees to acquire inputs, transform inputs into outputs, and provide goods or services to clients and customers.

Technology: the application of science to invent techniques and machines to transform objects (material, information, and people) in support of desired goals.

Vertical loading: delegating to employees responsibilities that were formerly reserved for management or staff specialists.

Work-flow uncertainty: a technology dimension that refers to the degree of knowledge that an employee has concerning when inputs will be received and require processing.

LECTURE NOTES

I.   Chapter 16 focuses on several key questions concerning the effective design of jobs in organizations. Among these important questions are: What is job design? Why should job design be? How, if at all, is job design related to other important approaches for changing people's work done? How can different approaches to job design be compared? What are the commonly used approaches to job design? How is job design affected by technology? Given the increasing complexity facing many organizations, what job design approaches are likely to have the greatest impact? How can they be implemented? Transparency 16.1 summarizes the answers that Chapter 16 provides for these questions.

> **TRANSPARENCY 16.1**
> **(FROM TEXT MATERIAL IN THE TEXTBOOK)**
>
> **KEY QUESTIONS AND ANSWERS ABOUT JOB DESIGN**

II.   Introduction to job design.

   A.   <u>Job design</u> is the specification of tasks that are to be performed by employees, including expected interpersonal and task relationships.

   B.   Job design occurs every time individuals are assigned work, given instructions, or empowered to perform tasks and pursue goals.

   C.   Relationship between job deign and reengineering.

   1.   Job design is one of the cornerstones of reengineering efforts in organizations.

   2.   <u>Reengineering</u> refers to radically new ways of thinking about organizations, including breaking away from the outdated rules and assumptions that underlie how tasks have been performed in the past.

   3.   The objective of reengineering is to eliminate—or prevent—the erection of barriers between employees and consumers.

   4.   Reengineering involves three separate but related phases.

      a.   *Rethinking,* or evaluating the organization's current goals and underlying assumptions in terms of a commitment to customer satisfaction.

      b.   *Redesigning,* or analyzing the organization's process for producing its products or services and determining which elements in the process need to be changed to increase job satisfaction and customer focus.

      c.   *Retooling,* or evaluating the current use of advanced technologies to identify opportunities for improving the quality of services and products and customer satisfaction.

D.   A comparative framework for five common approaches to job design.

    1.   Five of the most common approaches to job design are: job rotation, job engineering, job enlargement, job enrichment, and sociotechnical systems.

    2.   These five approaches to job design can be compared in terms of two criteria: impact and complexity.

        a.   Impact refers to the extent to which a job design approach is likely to be linked to factors beyond the immediate job (*e.g.*, reward systems, leadership practices, organization structure, etc.) as well as its likely effects on productivity and quality.

        b.   Complexity refers to the extent to which a job design approach is likely to require:

            (1)   Changes in many factors.

            (2)   The involvement of individuals with diverse skills at various organizational levels.

            (3)   High levels of decision-making skills for successful implementation.

        c.   As shown in Transparency 16.2, job rotation has the least impact and complexity while sociotechnical systems has the most. Job engineering and job enlargement possess moderate degrees of impact and complexity, whereas job enrichment has somewhat greater impact and complexity than either of these two.

TRANSPARENCY 16.2
(FIGURE 16.1 IN THE TEXTBOOK)

COMPARISON OF FIVE JOB DESIGN APPROACHES

---

        d.   These five job design approaches are described in more detail in the next section of the lecture outline. Two of the approaches—job enrichment and sociotechnical systems—are developed in considerable depth after an overview of the five different approaches is provided and the role of technology in job design is discussed.

        e.   The five job design approaches discussed in this chapter do not include all of the important job design approaches. For example, the <u>human factor approach</u> (sometimes labeled *ergonomics*) focuses on minimizing the physical demands and biological risks at work.

III.   Overview of common job design approaches.

    A.   Job rotation.

        1.   <u>Job rotation</u> involves moving employees from job to job, thereby giving them an opportunity to perform a greater variety of tasks.

2. Task variety is added in order to reduce employee boredom. However, if all the tasks are similar and routine, the intended effect may not be achieved.

3. Job rotation may be beneficial as part of a larger redesign effort and/or as a training technique to improve the skills and flexibility of employees.

B. Job engineering.

1. Job engineering focuses on the tasks to be performed, methods to be used, work flow between employees, layout of the workplace, performance standards, and interdependencies between people and machines.

2. Job engineering emphasizes specialization of labor, which is intended to:

a. Allow workers to learn a task rapidly.

b. Permit short work cycles so performance can be almost automatic and involve little or no mental effort.

c. Make hiring easier because low-skilled people can be easily trained and paid relatively low wages.

D. Reduce the need for supervision because of work simplification and standardization.

3. Because of its emphasis on specialization, job engineering can create boring jobs. However, job engineering remains an important job design approach because it results in production efficiencies.

4. Job engineering tends to be more successful when it is combined with a concern for the social context in which jobs are performed.

5. Some of the concepts and tools of job engineering are used in reengineering efforts.

C. Job enlargement.

1. Job enlargement expands the number of different tasks performed by an employee, usually at the same basic level of responsibility.

2. By adding similar tasks to the job, some task variety is introduced and the job may become more interesting for the worker.

3. If an enlarged job requires more careful attention and concentration, some employees may find it interesting, but others may view it negatively.

D. Job enrichment.

1. Job enrichment adds task to employees' jobs by allowing them to assume more responsibility and accountability for planning, organizing, controlling, and evaluating their own work.

E. Sociotechnical systems.

1.   The <u>sociotechnical systems model</u> considers every organization to be made up of people (the social system) using tools, techniques, and knowledge (the technical system) to produce goods or services valued by customers.

2.   The social and technical systems need to be congruent with each other and fit with the organization's external environment.

F.   Transparency 16.3, which is self-explanatory, summarizes the focus of the five job design approaches.

TRANSPARENCY 16.3
(FROM TEXT MATERIAL IN THE TEXTBOOK)

FOCUS OF FIVE JOB DESIGN APPROACHES

ENRICHMENT MODULE: EFFECTS OF GENERIC APPROACHES TO JOB DESIGN

Two researchers analyzed numerous job design approaches and determined that they could be grouped into four generic categories: mechanistic, motivational, biological and perceptual/motor. The mechanistic approach stresses work simplification and task specialization (*e.g.,* job engineering). The motivational approach focuses on how the characteristics of jobs affect people's motivation (*e.g.,* job enlargement and job enrichment). The biological approach considers body movements, body measurements, work physiology, and occupational medicine (*e.g.,* the human factor approach or ergonomics). The perceptual/motor approach emphasizes motor skills and mental processing of information.

What are the positive and negative effects of these generic approaches to job design? The positive effects for the motivational approach—satisfaction, motivation, and absenteeism rate—are also the negative effects for the mechanistic and perceptual/motor approaches. Conversely, the positive effects for the mechanistic and perceptual/motor approaches—training times, utilization levels, and error rates—are the negative effects for the motivational approach. For the biological approach, the positive outcomes include beneficial physical and health effects while the primary negative outcome is the costs of changes in equipment or the job environment.

This enrichment module is based on:

Campion, M.A., & Thayer, P.W. (1987, Winter). Job design: Approaches, outcomes, and trade-offs. *Organizational Dynamics*, 66-79.

IV.   Technology and job design.

A.   <u>Technology</u> is the application of science to invent techniques and machines to transform objects (material, information, and people) in support of desired goals.

B.   An organization's <u>technical system</u> comprises the tools, techniques, methods, procedures, and knowledge used by employees to acquire inputs, transform inputs into outputs, and provide goods or services to clients and customers.

C.   Three technology dimensions—work-flow uncertainty, task uncertainty, and task interdependence—can have an important impact on job design.

1. Work-flow uncertainty is the degree of knowledge that an employee has concerning when inputs will be received and require processing. Low work-flow uncertainty indicates that the employee most likely has little autonomy concerning which tasks will be performed or when or where they will be performed. High work-flow uncertainty reflects a high degree of discretion in making these task decisions.

2. Task uncertainty is the degree of knowledge that an employee has about how to perform the job and when it needs to be done. Low task uncertainty implies that an employee is knowledgeable about prespecified ways of producing the desired results. High task uncertainty indicates that there are few (if any) prespecified ways of doing some or many of the job's tasks, and therefore the employee needs to draw on experience, judgment, intuition and problem-solving ability.

3. Transparency 16.4 provides some examples of the types of jobs that fit with the four combinations of low versus high work-flow uncertainty and task uncertainty.

TRANSPARENCY 16.4
(FIGURE 16.2 IN THE TEXTBOOK)

TECHNOLOGY FRAMEWORK AND JOB DESIGN

---

4. Job redesign efforts often modify the levels of work-flow and task uncertainty that exist in jobs. Job engineering for example, tends to decrease work-flow and task uncertainty whereas job enrichment generally increases both.

5. Task interdependence is the degree to which decision making and cooperation between two or more employees is necessary for them to perform their jobs.

    a. Pooled interdependence occurs when an employee is not required to communicate extensively with other individuals in the organization to complete their tasks. Increasing pooled interdependence decreases the amount of required coordination between jobs.

    b. Sequential interdependence occurs when one employee must complete certain tasks before other employees can perform their tasks. Increasing sequential interdependence increases the need for coordination between jobs.

    c. Reciprocal interdependence occurs when outputs from one individual (or group) become the inputs for others and vice versa. Reciprocal interdependence usually requires a high degree of collaboration, communication, and team decision making.

ENRICHMENT MODULE: TECHNOLOGY'S IMPACT: NEW JOBS! NEW LIFE STYLES!

Dramatic changes in information technologies are having far-reaching effects on how people do their jobs and live their lives. For example, information technologies, such as desktop and laptop computers, E-mail, fax/modems, portable phones, beepers, etc., have made telecommuting a reality for increasing numbers of workers. Mobile offices—which may be in the employees' home or car, the customers' offices, an airport, etc.—also have been made possible through the application of information technologies.

Both telecommuting and mobile offices give workers greater autonomy and control with respect to both their work lives and personal lives. As a result, employees may be more highly motivated and productive, thereby benefitting the organization. The company's costs may be reduced as well. But telecommuting and mobile offices have their downside too. Relationships with colleagues and bosses, as well as customers or clients, can be affected. Employee morale may suffer. People must be self-starters; if they're not, telecommuting and mobile offices won't be effective. Employees must be skilled problem solvers; if they're not, the looser supervision could be disastrous.

Advanced information technologies have enabled perpetual motion executives (PMXs) to travel frequently (or almost constantly in some cases) and still perform many of their job tasks in hotels, in airports, and on airplanes. How PMXs perform their jobs has a significant impact on how their subordinates' jobs are designed. The successful PMXs empower subordinates to an exceptional degree—in short, their subordinates have highly enriched jobs.

Whether a person is working at home, in a mobile office, or jetting around the world, their lifestyles may be affected. Personal and family relationships may be affected, either positively or negatively. Too much time may be spent performing job tasks and too little time on rest and recreation.

This enrichment module is based on:

Malone, M.S. (1994, April 11). Perpetual motion executives (call them PMXs). *Forbes ASAP*, 93-97.

Shellenbarger, S. (1993, December 16). I'm still here! Home workers worry they're invisible. *The Wall Street Journal*, B1 & B2.

Shellenbarger, S. (1994, August 17). Overwork, low morale vex the mobile office. *The Wall Street Journal*, B1 & B7.

Shellenbarger, S. (1993, December 14). Some thrive, but many wilt working at home. *The Wall Street Journal*, B1 & B10.

V.   Job characteristics enrichment model.

    A.   One of the best known approaches to job enrichment is the job characteristics enrichment model developed by Richard Hackman and Greg Oldham. We will use this model as the basis for a more detailed examination of job enrichment.

    B.   The job characteristics enrichment model focuses on increasing the amounts of skill variety, task identity, task significance, autonomy, and feedback in a job. In turn, these job characteristics influence three critical psychological states; and when all three critical psychological states are positive, a cycle of strong work motivation is activated.

C.   Transparency 16.5 presents the job characteristics enrichment model, identifying the variables and their interrelationships.

TRANSPARENCY 16.5
(FIGURE 16.3 IN THE TEXTBOOK)

JOB CHARACTERISTICS ENRICHMENT MODEL

---

1.   The model specifies five core job characteristics that are important to job enrichment. These job characteristics are: skill variety, task identity, task significance, autonomy, and job feedback (see Transparency 16.6).

TRANSPARENCY 16.6
(FROM TEXT MATERIAL IN THE TEXTBOOK)

MEANINGS OF THE FIVE CORE JOB CHARACTERISTICS

---

a.   Skill variety is the degree to which a job requires a range of personal competencies and abilities to carry out the work.

b.   Task identity is the degree to which a job requires completion of a whole and identifiable piece of work, that is, doing a task from beginning to end with a visible outcome.

c.   Task significance is the degree to which the employee perceives the job as having a substantial impact on the lives of other people, whether these people are within or outside the organization.

d.   Autonomy is the degree to which the job provides freedom, independence, and discretion to the employee in scheduling tasks and in determining procedures to be used in carrying out the tasks.

e.   Job feedback is the degree to which carrying out the job-related tasks provides the individual with direct and clear information about the effectiveness of his or her performance.

ENRICHMENT MODULE: DIAGNOSING THE JOB OF BEING A STUDENT
(*An Experiential Activity*)

The work that students do may be conceptualized as a job (also see discussion questions 5 and 8). Using the job characteristics inventory that is contained in Table 16.1 of the textbook, have the students analyze their job from two different perspectives: (1) a lecture mode of teaching and learning, and (2) an experiential approach to teaching and learning. The results are likely to show that, with a lecture approach, the job of being a student is perceived as relatively unenriched. However, with an experiential approach, the student's job most likely will be perceived as being highly enriched by most students.

---

2.   The model specifies three critical psychological states that result from the core job characteristics.

a.   Skill variety, task identity, and task significance affect the employees' *experienced meaningfulness of work.*

b.   Autonomy influences the employees' *experienced responsibility for work outcomes.*

c.   Job feedback affects the employees' *knowledge of the actual results of work.*

3.   The job characteristics enrichment model identifies four personal and work outcomes: high internal work motivation, high-quality work performance, high satisfaction with the work, and low absenteeism and turnover.

a.   These personal and work outcomes will occur when the three critical psychological states are positive.

4.   The model also contains three major individual differences variables that affect how employees respond to enriched jobs. These individual differences variables are: knowledge and skill, strength of growth needs, and satisfaction with contextual factors.

a.   Employees are more likely to react positively to job enrichment when:

(1)   They have the knowledge and skills needed to perform an enriched job.

(2)   They have high growth-need strength (*i.e*, the degree to which an individual desires the opportunity for self-direction, learning, and personal accomplishment at work.)

(3)   They are satisfied with contextual factors at work such as organizational policies and administration, technical supervision, salary and benefit programs, interpersonal relations, working conditions, electronic monitoring of employees' work, etc.).

D.   Determining whether job enrichment is needed.

1.   Job diagnosis is used to determine whether job design problems exist and to estimate the potential for job enrichment success.

2.   Two methods of job diagnosis are: structural clues and the survey.

3.   Structural clues method of job diagnosis.

a.   The structural clues method involves checking for contextual factors that are often associated with deficiencies in job design.

b.   Five structural clues are typically used to diagnose potential job design problems and the potential for employee acceptance of job enrichment. These clues and their implications are described below.

(1)   Autonomy is usually much lower when *inspectors or checkers,* rather than the employees themselves, examine work.

(2)   The existence of *troubleshooters* usually means that the exciting and challenging parts of a job have been taken away from employees.

(3)   *Communications and customer relations departments* usually cut the link between employees who do the job and customers or clients.

(4)   *Labor pools* are appealing because they seem to increase both efficiency and flexibility. However, such pools may destroy workers' feelings of ownership and task identity.

(5)   A *narrow span of control* may result in centralization of decision making and overcontrol, thereby reducing autonomy.

4.   Survey method of job diagnosis.

a.   With this method, employees complete some type of questionnaire that is designed to assess job design problems and the potential for job enrichment success.

b.   One important survey method is the job diagnostic survey (JDS); it is designed to measure the job characteristics in Hackman and Oldham's job characteristics enrichment model and the likely outcomes of job redesign.

c.   The JDS provides an overall measure of job enrichment potential which is called the motivating potential score (MPS). MPS is determined as follows:

$$MPS = \frac{Skill\ Variety + Task\ Identity + Task\ Significance}{3} \times Autonomy \times Job\ Feedback$$

(1)   The combination of skill variety, task identity, and task significance has the same weight as autonomy and job feedback in the MPS score because of the different linkages to the three critical psychological states, all three of which must be present for high internal work motivation to occur.

E.   Five approaches are typically used to implement a job enrichment program within the context of the job characteristics enrichment model. These approaches are vertical loading, the formation of natural work teams, establishment of customer relationships, employee ownership of the product, and employee receipt of direct feedback (see Transparency 16.7). The first two are the main implementation approaches while the latter three approaches are often used in conjunction with vertical loading or forming natural work teams.

TRANSPARENCY 16.7
(FROM TEXT MATERIAL IN THE TEXTBOOK)

FIVE APPROACHES FOR IMPLEMENTING JOB ENRICHMENT

---

1.   Vertical loading.

a. <u>Vertical loading</u> refers to delegating to employees responsibilities that were formerly reserved for management or staff specialists.

b. Vertical loading includes giving employees responsibilities for setting production schedules, determining work methods, checking work quality, determining individual work schedules, assigning priorities to tasks and projects, and solving problems on their own.

c. Flextime provides an example of how vertical loading can be accomplished. <u>Flextime</u> allows employees, within certain limits, to vary their arrival and departure times to suit their individual needs and desires and helps in self-scheduling of work.

ENRICHMENT MODULE: HOW TO MAKE FLEXTIME EFFECTIVE

Flextime can help employees to balance the demands of their work lives and their personal lives. As a result, the employees may be more satisfied and productive, and feel less stressed. However, some managers fear that they will lose control because employees may be unsupervised for part of their working hours. To overcome such fears and to make flextime effective, clear work goals and performance criteria should be established, responsibility for results should be shifted to employees, and issues concerning home/work conflicts should be openly and constructively addressed.

This enrichment module is based on:

Shellenbarger, S. (1994, January 13). More companies experiment with workers' schedules. *The Wall Street Journal*, B1 & B6.

Shellenbarger, S. (1994, January 13). The keys to successful flexibility. *The Wall Street Journal*, B1 & B6.

---

2. Formation of natural work teams.

a. The formation of natural work teams combines individual jobs into a formally recognized unit on the basis of logical and meaningful work relationships.

b. The criteria for forming natural work units include: geographic territories, types of businesses, organizational functions, alphabetic or numeric categories, or customer groups.

3. Establishment of customer relationships.

a. One of the most important concepts of job enrichment is putting employees in touch with the users of their output.

b. The establishment of customer relationships often is a logical outcome of forming natural work units.

4. Employee ownership of the product.

a. Allowing employees to build an entire product or complete an entire task cycle is likely to generate a sense of pride and achievement, thereby resulting in a sense of ownership.

    b.   Being responsible for a specific geographic territory can also create a sense of ownership.

    5.   Employee receipt of direct feedback.

        a.   Job enrichment stresses feedback to employees directly from the performance of the task.

        b.   This may be accomplished by sending reports or computer output directly to employees rather than to their supervisors, by letting employees perform their own quality checks, or by having employees communicate directly with clients or customers.

F.   Technology and job characteristics.

    1.   Changing one or more of the five core job characteristics usually means changing one or more of the three technological dimensions.

    2.   Transparency 16.8 provides an example of the technological changes that will probably accompany a job enrichment program involving vertical loading and the formation of natural work teams.

TRANSPARENCY 16.8
(FIGURE 16.4 IN THE TEXTBOOK)

SAMPLE JOB CHARACTERISTICS AND TECHNOLOGICAL LINKS

G.   Social information processing.

    1.   Employees' perceptions of job characteristics may be influenced by <u>social information</u>, which refers to comments, observations, and similar cues provided by people whose view of the job an employee values. Social information may be provided by people within or outside the organization.

    2.   According to the <u>social information processing model</u>, the individual's social environment may provide cues as to which dimensions might be used to characterize the work environment, what the relative importance of the dimensions should be, how others evaluate each of the dimensions, and how the work setting in general should be evaluated.

    3.   Job characteristics and social information (cues) probably combine to affect employees' reactions to their jobs.

VI.   Sociotechnical systems model.

    A.   The sociotechnical systems model can be used to design work that integrates people with technology and optimizes the fit between the organization's technological and social systems and with the external environment.

B.   The sociotechnical systems model, which consists of four major parts, is depicted in Transparency 16.9. The four components are: environmental forces, social system, technological system, and moderators.

TRANSPARENCY 16.9
(FIGURE 16.5 IN THE TEXTBOOK)

SOCIOTECHNICAL SYSTEMS MODEL

---

1.   Environmental forces.

   a.   Environmental forces reflect events and pressures that occur in an organization's external environment.

   b.   The influence of an organization's various external stakeholders (*e.g.*, customers, suppliers, the local community, etc.) are key elements of the environment.

2.   Social system.

   a.   The social system includes those aspects of the organization's "human side" that can influence how individuals and teams perform tasks as well as people's attitudes toward work and the organization.

   b.   The primary elements of an organization's social system were discussed in previous chapters. Included among the social system's elements are dynamics within groups and teams (Chapter 9), leadership (Chapter 11), and organizational culture (Chapter 14).

3.   Technological system.

   a.   The technological system includes the following:

      (1)   The three technological dimensions of work-flow uncertainty, task uncertainty, and task interdependence.

      (2)   The type and complexity of the production process, and the time pressure inherent in the process.

      (3)   The physical work setting.

      (4)   The nature of raw materials used in production

4.   Moderators.

   a.   In the sociotechnical systems model, moderators are variables that affect the relationships between the social system and the technological system.

   b.   Work roles, goals, and skills and abilities of the employees are key moderators in the sociotechnical systems models. In other words, these three variables can influence the "goodness of fit" between the social system and the technological system.

C. Transparency 16.10 identifies six key principles of sociotechnical systems design.

TRANSPARENCY 16.10
(FROM TEXT MATERIAL IN THE TEXTBOOK)

KEY PRINCIPLES OF SOCIOTECHNICAL SYSTEMS DESIGN

---

1. *Innovativeness:* organization leaders and members should maintain a futuristic rather than historical orientation, including a propensity for risk taking and provision of rewards for innovation.

2. *Human resource development:* the talents, knowledge, skills, and abilities of organization members should be developed and tapped through work design, supervisory roles, organizational structure, and the work-flow process.

3. *Environmental agility:* the organization should remain aware of it external environment and should respond appropriately by recognizing customer importance; proactivity versus reactivity; and structural, technical, and product or service flexibility.

4. *Cooperation:* Individuals and departments should work together to accomplish common goals through teamwork, mutual support, shared values, and common rewards.

5. *Commitment/energy:* Employees should be dedicated to accomplishing organizational goals and should be prepared to expend energy in doing so.

6. *Joint optimization:* the organization should use both its social and technical resources effectively, including the design of technology to support teamwork and flexibility.

D. Organizational significance of using the sociotechnical system approach to job design.

   1. The basic issue to be confronted in using the sociotechnical systems model concerns the management philosophy and values that define an organization's culture. Managers who are interested only in production and efficiency won't benefit from using the sociotechnical systems approach to job design. Those who are interested in organizational effectiveness and efficiency as well as improving the social system, however, will benefit from using the sociotechnical systems model.

   2. Some jobs cannot be enriched without redesigning the entire operation. When changing a job is technologically impossible, other techniques (such as flextime) may soften the impact of otherwise boring jobs.

VI. Summing up: What does job design contribute to the understanding and management of organizational behavior?

   A. At its most fundamental level, the manner in which jobs are designed represents the packaging of work requirements, expectations, and tasks for each member of the organization. How these requirements, expectations, and tasks are "packaged" will influence people's motivation, satisfaction, and performance. The design of work will also affect how and when organizational members interact with each other. In addition, It will be a major determinant of the organizations's effectiveness and efficiency.

B.   Because of its pervasive influence on people's behavior in organizational settings, managers must develop at least three specific competencies regarding job design.

    1.   Managers must be able to diagnose the need for changes in the ways existing jobs are designed.

    2.   Managers must be able to use job design principles in planning for the operation of a new facility.

    3.   Whether they are redesigning existing jobs or designing new ones, managers must be able to "package" jobs in such a way that the organization can effectively and efficiently produce its products or services while simultaneously providing stimulating work for the employees.

DISCUSSION QUESTIONS: SUGGESTED ANSWERS

1.   *Why should job design be an important area of concern for organizations?*

At its most basic level, job design reflect how specific tasks are grouped into specific clusters known as jobs. The nature of jobs will affect:

    a.   How employees perform the tasks that are needed to achieve the organization's goals.
    b.   People's work motivation.
    c.   Interpersonal relationships at work.
    d.   Which employees interact with external stakeholders and how those employees will interact with those stakeholders.
    e.   Relationships among tasks.
    f.   Who will participate in decision making.
    g.   The development and functioning of work teams.
    h.   The flow of communications within the organization.

2.   *Why is job design important to reengineering?*

Quite simply, job design is important to reengineering because it is one of the cornerstones of reengineering efforts in organizations. Through job design, tasks can be packaged so that organization members can work together more effectively and serve the organization's customers more effectively. Eliminating or preventing the erection of barriers between employees and customers is the fundamental objective of reengineering.

3.   *What are the similarities and differences between job rotation and job enlargement?*

Both job rotation and job enlargement try to increase task variety in people's jobs in order to reduce boredom and enhance motivation. However, the two techniques differ concerning how to increase task variety. Job rotation increases task variety by moving employees from job to job.

Job enlargement increases task variety by expanding the number of different tasks performed by an employee, usually at the same basic level of responsibility.

4.   *How do the assumptions of job engineering differ from those of job enrichment?*

Job engineering focuses on the tasks to be performed, methods to be used, work flow between employees, layout of the workplace, performance standards, and interdependencies between people and machines. Job engineering assumes that jobs should be simplified and highly specialized so little mental effort is required to perform them proficiently. In contrast, job enrichment adds tasks to employees' jobs by allowing them to assume more responsibility and accountability for planning, organizing, controlling, and evaluating their own work. Job enrichment encourages the development of jobs which are more complex, challenging, and stimulating as a means for improving performance.

5.   *Think about your role as a student as though it were a job. Analyze your student job in terms of task uncertainty, work-flow uncertainty, and task interdependence. Can this analysis vary by specific course and instructor? Explain.*

Task uncertainty, work-flow uncertainty, and task interdependence can be used to describe the nature of an organization's technical system in the following manner:

    a.   When task uncertainty is low, organization members know how to produce desired results in a prespecified way. When task uncertainty is high, members do not have many (if any) prespecified ways to produce desired results on the job's tasks, and therefore they need to draw on their experience, judgment, intuition and problem-solving ability.

    b.   When work-flow uncertainty is low, organization members have little autonomy concerning which tasks will be performed or when or where they will be performed. When work-flow uncertainty is high, organization members have a high degree of discretion in deciding which tasks will be performed or when or where they will be performed.

    c.   Increasing pooled interdependence decreases the amount of required coordination between jobs. Increasing the sequential interdependence of tasks increases the need for coordination between jobs. Reciprocal interdependence usually requires a high degree of collaboration, communication, and team decision making.

As the question implies, these technology concepts can be used to analyze the job of being a student. For example, let's consider a large lecture course where specific topics are scheduled for instructor presentation on each day, student questions are limited essentially to points of clarification regarding the lecture material, and the sole means of evaluation of learning are exams with objective types of questions. Here the task uncertainty and work-flow uncertainty are probably quite low and a great deal of pooled interdependence exists.

Now contrast this example with a seminar where small groups of students choose, within a broad framework, research topics to pursue, work together in developing those topics, and then share the results of their research efforts with other members of the class in an open discussion format. In this example, task uncertainty and work-flow uncertainty are high and a substantial level of reciprocal interdependence exists.

The students' responses should reflect knowledge of these three technology dimensions. However, their responses will vary depending on the pedagogical approach and requirements of the specific course they choose as an example.

6.   *Why does technology often need to be changed as a first step in changing job characteristics?*

Three technology dimensions—work-flow uncertainty, task uncertainty, and task interdependence—can influence job design and may need to be changed as the first step in job design. The levels of work-flow uncertainty and task uncertainty may need to be altered to accommodate a particular approach to job design. For example, both types of uncertainty might need to be decreased to accommodate job engineering but increased to accommodate job enrichment. In addition, the nature of task interdependence might need to be changed to facilitate implementation of a particular job deign approach. For instance, sequential or reciprocal task interdependence facilitates job design approaches—such as job enrichment and sociotechnical systems—that emphasize teamwork.

7.   *Does electronic monitoring of workers create any ethical dilemmas for you? Explain.*

In responding to this question, the students can refer to the "Managing Ethics: Electronic Monitoring of Work" feature on page 545-546 of the text.

Electronic monitoring of work can occur through the use of various information technologies. These technologies provide opportunities for excessive invasion of employees' privacy. An ethical dilemma arises from the tension between management's need to know how employees are performing their jobs and the employees' right to privacy.

Another ethical dilemma is posed when information technologies are used as part of a job design program. Often jobs are redesigned to give employees more autonomy and responsibility. Granting someone else autonomy and responsibility implies that a certain level of trust exists. However, electronic surveillance is a signal that people are not really trusted.

8.   *How would you compare each of the job characteristics in your instructor's job with those in your job as a student? Discuss their similarities and differences.*

To answer this question, the students should refer to the definitions of the core job characteristics that are identified in Figure 16.3. The students should then analyze both jobs with respect to their relative amounts of skill variety, task identity, task significance, autonomy, and job feedback. The students may need some assistance in analyzing the instructor's job since they may not be aware of all the things a professor does outside the classroom.

This question could also be answered with the aid of the job characteristics inventory contained in Table 16.1 of the textbook. The students could complete this inventory for their own jobs as students and their instructors' jobs. Scoring of the job characteristics inventory yields information on each of the core job characteristics. These results could then be used in comparing the two jobs.

9.   *What clues might you look for in determining whether the manager's job of a local sports shoe store needs to be redesigned?*

Students can base their responses to this question on the material pertaining to the two methods of job diagnosis—structural clues and the survey method.

The structural clues method of job diagnosis involves checking for contextual factors that are often associated with deficiencies in job design. To determine whether a manager's job needs to be redesigned, the diagnostician should examine the context regarding the existence of inspectors or checkers, troubleshooters, communications and customer relations departments, labor pools and a narrow span of control. Eliminating one or more of the contextual factors, if they are present, would help enrich the manager's job.

The survey method of job diagnosis could use the job diagnostic survey (JDS). With this method, the diagnostician would use employees' questionnaire response to determine the motivating potential score (MPS). The MPS is an overall measure of job enrichment potential.

10. *Why might some managers and employees welcome the sociotechnical systems approach to job design and others oppose it?*

The sociotechnical systems model emphasizes designing jobs so as to help optimize the fit between the organization's technological and social systems and with the external environment. In practice, this usually means grouping jobs into work teams having a high degree of reciprocal and/or sequential interdependence among jobs. Work roles are deliberately designed to integrate people with technology.

Support for or opposition to the sociotechnical systems approach is perhaps best discussed in the context of variables that moderate the relationship between an organization's technological system and its social system. People's work roles, goals, and skills and abilities are key moderator variables. A sociotechnical systems approach to job design is more likely to be supported by those who: (a) agree with the work roles and goals of a team environment, and (b) have the abilities and skills to function in such an environment.

Another factor which could influence support for or opposition to the sociotechnical systems approach is organizational culture. Different subcultures may exist within the organization, and some subcultures may buy into teamwork while other subcultures may not.

A final factor that could explain differences in opinions regarding this approach involves the potential limitations of technology. Some jobs cannot be enriched without redesigning the technology of the entire operation. When this situation confronts an organization, both support for and resistance to change may be substantial.

DEVELOPING SKILLS—
SELF DIAGNOSIS: REDESIGN OF THE DATA ENTRY OPERATOR JOB

Use of this self-diagnostic instrument exposes students to the survey method of job diagnosis. The instrument provides (1) a description of the Data Entry Operator's job, and (2) 12 diagnostic questions to be used in analyzing the job. Each of the 12 diagnostic questions contains a proposal that might result in improving work performance. Students are to indicate whether they would or would not implement the proposal. They also must rank order the actions which they would take. Finally, the students should relate each of the changes they would make to an appropriate concept in the job characteristics enrichment model. They should also use concepts from the job characteristics enrichment model to justify each of the proposals they would not pursue.

Presented below are some possible explanations for each of the proposed actions (listed by question number):

1. Decreases autonomy.
2. Increases autonomy.
3. Decreases autonomy.
4. Decreases autonomy and task significance.
5. Forming natural work teams, thereby increasing skill variety, task identity, task significance, autonomy, and job feedback.
6. Using vertical loading to enhance autonomy.
7. Enhances job feedback.
8. Enhances autonomy and job feedback.
9. Increases task identity.
10. Establishing customer relationships to increase skill variety, autonomy, and job feedback.
11. Using vertical loading to enhance autonomy.
12. Establishing customer relationships to increase task identity, task significance, autonomy, and job feedback.

DEVELOPING SKILLS— A CASE IN POINT: MCGUIRE INDUSTRY

CASE OVERVIEW

This brief case describes the problematic repair process at a modern $30 million Department of Defense facility that overhauls engines for military vehicles. The overhaul operation consists of highly specialized work groups performing routine repetitive tasks through most, if not all, of the overhaul operation. Employees are tightly controlled and status differences between the line workers and managers are accentuated.

CASE QUESTIONS

1. *Is the technical system compatible with the social system? Explain.*

    The technical system reflects sequential interdependence of tasks, thereby necessitating at least a moderate degree of communication and coordination. No evidence exists to indicate that such coordination and communication, if they exist, are effective. Work groups are used, but not necessarily to support a sequentially interdependent production process. On balance, joint optimization of the technological and social systems has not occurred.

2. *How might the skill variety, task identity, and task significance of the production employees be increased?*

    Skill variety, task identity, and task significance could be increased by restructuring the existing work groups into natural work units. In engine overhaul operations, natural work units could be formed around the various engine subassemblies. Workers in these units could then be responsible for cleaning, repairing, and testing all components in their subassembly and then reassembling the subassembly. Final assembly and operational testing could constitute another set of natural work units.

3. *How might the autonomy and job feedback of the production employees be increased?*

Autonomy could be increased by transforming the work groups into self-managed teams. Team members could assume scheduling and quality control (*i.e.*, testing) responsibilities. Job feedback can be enhanced by having the people who repair the components test them also.

4. *Should the production jobs be enriched? Explain.*

A job diagnosis would need to be conducted in order to realistically respond to this question. The students could attempt to apply the structural clues method of job diagnosis to the case even though the case facts are quite limited.

Three structural clues seem especially relevant. The uses of testers (*i.e.*, inspectors or checkers) indicates less autonomy in the production jobs. The work groups may in fact be labor pools rather than true work teams. Labor pools tend to destroy workers' feelings of ownership and task identity. The span of control ranged from 10-15 workers, and the supervisor exercised tight control; thus, autonomy was diminished. The presence of these three structural clues suggest that there is at least a reasonable degree of potential for enriching the production jobs.

COURSE ENHANCEMENT— *WEST'S ORGANIZATIONAL BEHAVIOR CUSTOM VIDEO SERIES*

None of the videos from *West's Organizational Behavior Custom Video Series* are appropriate for use with the material in Chapter 16.

COURSE ENHANCEMENT— *SUPPLEMENTAL VIDEOS AVAILABLE FROM WEST*

Two videos from the Association for Manufacturing Excellence, which are made available through West Publishing Company, can be used to enhance the material in Chapter 16. One video is the *Allen-Bradley* segment of the tape *On the Road to Manufacturing Excellence*. The other video is the *Steelcase* segment of *We're Getting Closer*.

VIDEO: AME: ON THE ROAD TO MANUFACTURING EXCELLENCE—ALLEN-BRADLEY

Approximate Time: 8 minutes

Video Summary:

This video focuses on Allen-Bradley's fully automated assembly operation which imposes a tightly integrated information system on top of a manufacturing process. Statistical process control (SPC) is a critical component of the system with statistical quality checks being performed at 3,500 different points in the assembly process.

The video shows how routine and repetitive production tasks can be relegated to technology, and how human resources interface with that technology. A good deal of the interface is on the engineering and design side of the company's operations. Still, interfaces do exist for the operators (known as equipment attendants). In comparison to a conventional factory, the operators are far fewer in number and they have different duties. The equipment attendants have two primary responsibilities: feeding component parts into the machines and solving problems that arise. The cellular design of the automated assembly process is intended to facilitate teamwork among the equipment attendants in support of the sequential interdependence of the fully automated assembly process.

Discussion Question and Suggested Answer for Video:

1.   *Analyze Allen-Bradley's fully automated assembly process from a job engineering perspective.*

Allen-Bradley's technical system is a fully automated assembly operation that is sequentially interdependent. Low work-flow uncertainty and low task uncertainty also characterize the process. The job tasks that equipment handlers perform are designed to fit with an supplement the automated assembly operation. Teamwork among the equipment handlers is expected and encouraged so the all the cellular units in the sequentially interdependent design can operate at peak efficiency.

VIDEO: *AME: WE'RE GETTING CLOSER: STEELCASE*

Approximate Time: 11 minutes

Video Summary:

Steelcase, a leading designer and manufacturer of office furniture, is featured in this video. The relatively recent shift in customers' needs toward customized furniture has brought about a significant redesign of the manufacturing process at Steelcase.

The new manufacturing process, which is arranged according to product rather than function, divides the work force into work cells. Essentially, these work cells are self-managing teams where decision making and problem solving have been pushed down to production workers. The work cell design also takes a broad view of who the customers are. In addition to purchasers or end users, customers include the next cell in the production process.

Simplified and highly specialized tasks have been replaced by more complex tasks that have enhanced skill variety, task identity, etc. The redesigned manufacturing process requires workers who are more flexible and well-trained. A very revealing segment of the video features a three-person team that replaced 12 workers who produced a specific chair subassembly. The three-person team maintained output quantity while increasing output quality and absolutely eliminating scrap.

Steelcase's supervisors appear to be having more difficulty with the changes than the workers. Because they were asked to adopt a new philosophy of management, some of the supervisors perceived a loss of control, power, and decision-making authority.

Discussion Questions and Suggested Answers for Video:

1. *Analyze the job design changes at Steelcase from the perspective of the job characteristics enrichment model.*

    Briefly, the job characteristics enrichment model focuses on increasing the amounts of skill variety, task identity, task significance, autonomy, and feedback in a job. By enriching jobs, particularly for those who will respond positively to such efforts, certain critical psychological states can be activated. As a result, beneficial personal and work outcomes will occur.

    Steelcase probably increased all five core job characteristics through their redesign of the manufacturing process. The newly designed process required people to use a greater variety of skills than before. The three-person team that replaced 12 workers is a good example of this. Another example is the creation of self-managed units which required people to go beyond performing routine, repetitive tasks. Also, the use of self-managed teams probably increased task identity, task significance, autonomy, and job feedback. Reorganizing the manufacturing process according to product rather than function probably had a positive effect on both task identity and task significance. Self-inspection on quality also increased job feedback.

    No direct evidence exists to validate the activation of the three critical psychological states. However, their presence can be inferred from some of the results—improved productivity and quality as well as having satisfied employees.

    It appears that Steelcase's employees possessed the individual differences characteristics which facilitate a positive reaction to job enrichment efforts. They had the knowledge and skills necessary to perform the redesigned jobs. There seemed to be an appropriate level of growth-need strength. They appeared to be satisfied with the contextual factors.

2. *Analyze the job design changes at Steelcase from the perspective of the sociotechnical systems model.*

    In general, the sociotechnical systems model emphasizes designing work so as to optimize the fit between the organization's technological and social systems and with its external environment. Steelcase redesigned its manufacturing process in order to better respond to its customer's needs—thus, the company was seeking a good fit between the organization and its environment. An integral part of the redesigned manufacturing process was the creation of work cells. These work cells were basically self-managed work teams that were supported by appropriate alterations in Steelcase's technical system.

    The sociotechnical systems perspective could also be discussed in terms of the principles of sociotechnical systems design. The text identified six sociotechnical design principles: innovativeness, human resource development, environmental agility, cooperation, commitment/energy, and joint optimization. The evidence in the video suggests that Steelcase utilized each of these principles, at least to some extent. By responding to its customers' needs and redesigning its manufacturing process so that it could better respond to those needs indicates use of the innovativeness and environmental agility principles. The use of the self-managed team concept reflects usage of the human resource development and cooperation principles. Usage of these two principles is also supported by the three-person team that replaced 12 workers on one manufacturing operation. The three-person team produced as much as the 12 workers together and with much higher quality. This latter point also demonstrates usage of the commitment/energy principle. Finally, through the redesign of it manufacturing process, Steelcase appears to have jointly optimized usage of its social and technical resources.

3.   *Discuss some of the positive and negative results of redesigning jobs in the manner Steelcase did.*

Some of the positive effects are: improved productivity, improved quality, lower scrap rate, better cost control, enhanced job satisfaction for employees, development of employees' decision-making and problem-solving skills, and having a better trained and more flexible work force. Some of the negative effects include the supervisors' perceived loss of control, power, and decision-making authority.

CHAPTER 17
ORGANIZATION DESIGN

CHAPTER OVERVIEW

Chapter 17 continues the discussion of organization processes by focusing on organization design. Initially, the chapter defines organization design, identifies its objectives, and links organization design to other group and organizational processes. Next, environmental forces, strategic choices, and technological capabilities—the three primary factors that influence organization design decisions—are discussed. These three primary factors are then incorporated into a comparative framework for determining the conditions under which different organization design approaches will be effective. Next, the relationship between organization design and reengineering is examined and the strategic choice of mechanistic versus organic systems is considered. Seven organizational design approaches—functional design, place design, product design, horizontal design, matrix design, multinational design, and network design—are then linked to the comparative framework. Finally, each of the seven approaches is explored in depth, with emphasis being placed on the conditions of use or implications that are associated with them.

LEARNING OBJECTIVES

Upon completion of this chapter, the students should be able to:

1. Explain the influence of environmental forces, strategic choices, and technological factors on the design of organizations.
2. Indicate the relationship between reengineering and organization design.
3. Point out the key differences and relationships in seven organization designs and the nature of mechanistic and organic systems.
4. Describe functional, place, product, horizontal, and matrix designs and the conditions for their use.
5. Discuss multidivisional, multinational, and network designs and conditions for their use.

CHAPTER OUTLINE

I.   **Preview Case:** Xerox's New Design

II.   Key Factors in Design

      A.   Environmental Forces
      B.   Strategic Choices
      C.   Technological Factors
      D.   **Managing in Practice:** Fannie Mae
      E.   Comparative Framework
      F.   Relation to Reengineering
      G.   **Managing Quality:** Ford Reengineers Accounts Payable

III.   Mechanistic Versus Organic Systems

      A.   Hierarchy of Authority
      B.   Division of Labor
      C.   **Managing in Practice:** Gore's Organic System
      D.   Rules and Procedures
      E.   Impersonality
      F.   **Managing Diversity:** Sexual Harassment Complaint Procedures

IV.   Functional Design

      A.   Line and Staff Functions
      B.   Link to Task Environment
      C.   Chain of Command
      D.   Span of Control
      E.   **Managing Ethics:** Ethics Positions and Offices
      F.   Conditions for Use

V.   Place Design

      A.   Link to Internationalization
      B.   Conditions for Use

VI.   Product Design

      A.   Typical Evolution
      B.   Multidivisional Design
      C.   **Managing in Practice:** Johnson & Johnson's Multidivisional Design
      D.   Conditions for Use

VII.   Integration of Units

      A.   Horizontal Design
      B.   **Managing Quality:** NCR's U.S. Group Quality Improvement Design
      C.   Matrix Design

VIII.   Multinational Design

A. Basic Options
B. Conditions for Use
C. **Managing Across Cultures:** Ford's New Global Design

IX. Network Design

A. **Managing in Practice:** Eastman Chemical's Network Design
B. Key Characteristics
C. Role of Information Technologies
D. External Networking
E. **Managing Across Cultures:** Procter & Gamble's New Network Design

X. Developing Skills

A. **Self Diagnosis:** Inventory of Effective Design
B. **A Case in Point:** Aquarius Advertising Agency

KEY WORDS AND CONCEPTS

Twenty-nine key words and concepts are introduced in Chapter 17. One concept—organization design—was originally introduced in Chapter 1. The key words and concepts, along with definitions or appropriate descriptions, are as follows:

Bureaucracy: a form of organization that is essentially the same as a mechanistic system. Bureaucracy has the following characteristics: (1) The organization operates according to a set of rules that are intended to tightly control employees' behavior. (2) All employees must strictly follow rules and procedures in making decisions. (3) Each employee's job involves a specified area of expertise, with strictly defined obligations, authority, and powers to compel obedience. (4) Each lower-level position is under the tight control and direction of a higher one. (5) Candidates for jobs are selected on the basis of "technical" qualifications. (6) The organization has a career ladder; promotion is by seniority or achievement, and depends on the judgment of superiors.

Centralization: all major, and oftentimes many minor, decisions are made only at the top levels of the organization.

Complexity dimension: refers to whether the environmental characteristics are few and similar (homogeneous) or many and different (heterogeneous).

Differentiation: the degree to which units differ in structure (low to high), members' orientation to a time horizon (short to long), managers' orientation to other people (permissive to authoritarian), and members' views of the task environment (certain to uncertain).

Division of labor: refers to the various ways of dividing up tasks and labor to achieve goals.

Dynamism dimension: relates to whether environmental characteristics remain basically the same (are stable) or change (are unstable), and to the need for speed in responding to stakeholders' demands.

Functional design: an organization design approach that creates positions and units on the basis of specialized activities.

Hierarchy of authority: represents the extent to which decision-making processes are prescribed and formal power is allocated.

Horizontal design: an organization design approach that emphasizes the processes and mechanisms for linking units that are in lateral relationships to each other, such as marketing and manufacturing departments.

Impersonality: refers to the extent to which organizations treat their employees, as well as outsiders, according to objective, detached, and rigid characteristics.

Integration: the degree of collaboration and mutual understanding required among units to achieve their goals, for which the division of labor and task interdependencies create the need.

Line functions: those jobs that directly affect the principal work flow in an organization.

Matrix design: an organization design approach that is based on multiple support systems and authority relationships in which some employees report to two superiors rather than one.

Mechanistic system: a form of organization that is characterized by reliance on formal rules and regulations, centralization of decision making, narrowly defined job responsibilities, and a rigid hierarchy of authority.

Multidivisional design: a type of product organization design that organizes tasks into divisions on the basis of the product or geographic markets in which their goods or services are sold.

Multinational design: an organization design approach that attempts to maintain three-way organization perspectives and capabilities among products, functions, and geographic areas.

Network design: an organization design approach that is intended to facilitate managing highly diverse, complex, and dynamic factors involving multiple units and many people, both within and external to the organization. The network design sometimes is called a spiderweb or cluster organization.

Organic system: a form of organization that is characterized by low-to-moderate use of formal rules and regulations, decentralized and shared decision making, broadly defined job responsibilities, and a flexible authority structure with fewer levels in the hierarchy.

Organization design: the process of diagnosing and selecting the structure and formal system of communication, division of labor, coordination, control, authority, and responsibility necessary to achieve the organization's goals.

Place design: an organization design approach that involves establishing an organization's primary units geographically while retaining significant aspects of functional design.

Procedures: the preset sequences of steps the managers and employees must follow in performing tasks and dealing with problems.

Product design: an organization design approach that involves the establishment of self-contained units, each capable of developing, producing, and marketing its own goods or services.

Rules: formal, written statements specifying acceptable and unacceptable behaviors and decisions by organization members.

Scalar chain of command: refers to the flow of authority and responsibility in a clear, unbroken vertical line from the top to the bottom of the organization hierarchy.

Span of control: the number of employees supervised by a superior.

Staff functions: the support jobs that provide service and advice to line departments.

Task environment: refers to the external stakeholders and forces that directly affect the organization.

Uncertainty: the gap between what is known and what needs to be known to make effective decisions and perform tasks effectively.

Unity of command: no subordinate should receive orders from more than one superior.

LECTURE NOTES

I.   Chapter 17 focuses on issues that concern how to structure relationships among groups, teams, departments, and divisions so that organizations can achieve their goals and satisfy the demands of customers and other stakeholders. Several key issues are addressed in the chapter, including the following: What is the basic nature of organization design? What are the primary factors that influence organization design decisions? How do these factors influence organization design decisions? In selecting an organization design, what options are available? How does each option work? When should each option be used? Transparency 17.1 highlights these questions as well as the answers that the chapter provides.

TRANSPARENCY 17.1
(FROM TEXT MATERIAL IN THE TEXTBOOK)
KEY QUESTIONS AND ANSWERS ABOUT ORGANIZATION DESIGN

II.   Overview of organization design.

     A.   <u>Organization design</u> is the process of diagnosing and selecting the structure and formal system of communication, division of labor, coordination, control, authority, and responsibility necessary to achieve the organization's goals.

     B.   Organizational design decisions are influenced by environmental forces, technological factors, and strategic choices.

     C.   The objectives of organizational design include:

         1.   Facilitating information flow and decision making in satisfying the demands of customers, suppliers, and regulatory agencies.

         2.   Delineating authority and responsibility relationships among organizational units.

         3.   Providing for necessary integration (or coordination) among organizational units.

     D.   The cornerstones of organizational design include:

1.   The design of individual jobs.

2.   The formation and use of teams.

3.   The design of interteam relations.

4.   Organizational culture and power and political behavior.

ENRICHMENT MODULE: CREATING THE HORIZONTAL ORGANIZATION

Many authorities suggest that new, and sometimes radically different, organization designs, will be needed if corporations are to be successful in the future world of hyper-change. One approach companies can take is to create a horizontal organization. Frank Ostroff and Doug Smith, consultants at McKinsey & Co., developed the following ten-point plan for creating a horizontal organization:

- Organize primarily around process, not task.
- Flatten the hierarchy.
- Put senior leaders in charge of processes and resulting performance.
- Let performance objectives and operational activities be customer driven.
- Use teams as the building blocks of the organization's design.
- Combine nonmanagerial and managerial activities wherever possible.
- Stress the development of multiple competencies by every employee.
- Inform and train organization members to be problem solvers.
- Maximize supplier and customer contact with organization members.
- Reward both team performance and individual skill development.

This enrichment module is based on:

Byrne, J.A. (1993, December 20). The horizontal corporation. *Business Week,* 76-81.

Stewart, T.A. (1992, May 18). The search for the organization of tomorrow. *Fortune,* 92-98.

III.   Key factors in organizational design.

A.   Perfect, flawless organization designs do not exist. Therefore, the key to selecting an organization design is to make design choices that minimize operational problems, given the organization's particular situation.

B.   Organization design decisions are influenced by three primary factors: environmental forces, strategic choices, and technological capabilities. Transparency 17.2 illustrates some of the variables that managers must deal with under each of these three factors.

TRANSPARENCY 17.2
(TABLE 17.1 IN THE TEXTBOOK)

KEY FACTORS IN ORGANIZATION DESIGN DECISIONS

C.   Environmental forces.

1.   In making organizational design decisions, managers need to consider the characteristics of the present and future environments and the demands those environments place or will place on the organization.

2.   The characteristics and demands of the environment can be described in terms of the complexity and dynamism of the organization's task environment.

   a.   The <u>task environment</u> includes the external stakeholders and forces that directly affect the organization.

   b.   Task environments are classified on the basis of complexity and dynamism.

      (1)   <u>Complexity</u> refers to whether the environmental characteristics are few and similar (homogeneous) or many and different (heterogeneous). Homogeneity and heterogeneity depend on the number of factors and number of subenvironments that are involved.

      (1)   <u>Dynamism</u> relates to whether environmental characteristics remain basically the same (are stable) or change (are unstable), and to the need for speed in responding to stakeholders' demands.

   c.   As shown in Transparency 17.3, four "pure" types of task environments can be generated from the complexity and dynamism dimensions. These four task environments are: homogeneous-stable (box 1 in Transparency 17.3), heterogeneous-stable (box 2), homogeneous-unstable (box 3), and heterogeneous-unstable (box 4). Transparency 17.3 also provides some detail regarding the nature of each type of task environment.

TRANSPARENCY 17.3
(FIGURE 17.1 IN THE TEXTBOOK)

BASIC TYPES OF TASK ENVIRONMENTS

---

      (1)   Taken together, the degree of complexity and the degree of dynamism determine the amount of environmental uncertainty an organization faces.

      (2)   Environmental uncertainty is related to the skills and abilities that organization members must have in order to operate successfully.

         (a)   When environmental uncertainty is low, organizational members need relatively less skills, formal training , and experience.

         (b)   When environmental uncertainty is high, organizational members need to have far more sophisticated skills, insight, judgment, and problem-solving abilities.

D.   Strategic choices.

   1.   While many of top management's strategic choices affect organization design decisions, four key ones are:

a.   Top management's philosophy regarding mechanistic versus organic organization forms. (Ideas about mechanistic and organic forms of organization are developed more fully under item "H" of part "III" of the lecture notes.)

b.   The types of customers to be served by the company.

c.   The location in which to produce and market goods and services.

d.   The organization's commitment to the pursuit of total quality.

E.   Technological factors.

1.   Work-flow uncertainty, task uncertainty, and task interdependence affect organization design as well as job design. In the context of job design, these concepts referred to relationships among jobs. In the context of organization design, however, they refer to relationships among teams or departments.

2.   In terms of organization design, the technological factors are defined as follows:

a.   Work-flow uncertainty is the degree of knowledge in a department (or other unit) about when inputs will be received for processing. With low work-flow uncertainty, organizational units have little autonomy in deciding which tasks will be performed or when or where they will be performed. With high work-flow uncertainty, departments or teams have a great deal of autonomy in making these work-flow decisions.

b.   Task uncertainty is the degree of knowledge in a department with respect to performing the tasks assigned to it. When task uncertainty is low, the organizational units have prespecified ways of dealing with assigned tasks. When task uncertainty is high, members of organizational units have few (if any) prespecified ways for dealing with assigned tasks.

c.   Task interdependence may be pooled, sequential, or reciprocal.

(1)   Pooled interdependence occurs when departments or teams are relatively autonomous and make an identifiable contribution to the organization.

(2)   Sequential interdependence occurs when one department or team must complete certain tasks before one or more other departments or teams can perform their tasks.

(3)   Reciprocal interdependence occurs when the outputs from one department or team become the inputs for another department or team and vice versa.

(4)   Transparency 17.4 arrays the three types of interdependencies on a continuum ranging from simple to complex. In general, the more complex the interdependency of departments and teams, the greater the need for integration.

```
┌─────────────────────────────────────────────────────────────────┐
│                      TRANSPARENCY 17.4                             │
│                 (FIGURE 17.3 IN THE TEXTBOOK)                      │
│                                                                    │
│     TYPES OF TASK INTERDEPENDENCE IN ORGANIZATION DESIGN           │
└─────────────────────────────────────────────────────────────────┘
```

F. Environmental forces, strategic choices, and technological factors can be combined into a comparative framework for determining the conditions under which different organization design approaches will be effective (see Transparency 17.5). When the pattern of environmental forces, technological factors, and strategic choices is *simple, certain, and uniform*, a functional form of organization design is likely to be most appropriate. As the pattern of these three factors, becomes increasingly *complex, uncertain, and diverse*, different organization design become appropriate.

```
┌─────────────────────────────────────────────────────────────────┐
│                      TRANSPARENCY 17.5                             │
│                 (FIGURE 17.4 IN THE TEXTBOOK)                      │
│                                                                    │
│      FACTORS AND KEY OPTIONS IN ORGANIZATION DESIGN               │
└─────────────────────────────────────────────────────────────────┘
```

G. Relationship of organization design to reengineering.

   1. Reengineering—a concept which was introduced in previous chapters—refers to radically new ways of thinking about organizing and breaking away from outdated assumptions, rules, and procedures.

   2. Diagnosing environmental forces, strategic choices, and technological factors is consistent with the thrust of reengineering.

   3. While reengineering advocates "staring over from scratch," such a radical approach isn't always necessary or feasible in changing an organization's design. In some situations, an evolutionary approach may be more effective and feasible.

   4. Both reengineering and effective organization design stress organizing in a way that is likely to deliver value to customers and other stakeholders.

H. Mechanistic versus organic systems.

   1. What is a mechanistic system? What is an organic system?

      a. A <u>mechanistic system</u> is characterized by reliance on formal rules and regulations, centralization of decision making, narrowly defined job responsibilities, and a rigid hierarchy of authority.

      b. An <u>organic system</u> is characterized by low-to-moderate use of formal rules and regulations, decentralized and shared decision making, broadly defined job responsibilities, and a flexible authority structure with fewer levels in the hierarchy.

ENRICHMENT MODULE: ALCO STANDARD'S ORGANIC SYSTEM

Alco Standard, a conglomerate with annual revenue of $4.9 billion, operates differently than most conglomerates. Its approach embodies the philosophy of an organic system. Currently, Alco is organized into two operating division: paper products distribution and office products sales/service. Within each division are dozen of autonomous businesses. None of the operating units are forced into a "one-size-fits-all" corporate mold. Yet, while they remain independent, the various operating units have access to timely corporate market and financial information. Alco's business units seem to have the best of both world's—the support of a large corporation and the greater freedom of a small business. As Coley Evans, Jr. president of a business unit acquired by Alco in 1991 says, "If you can't own the business yourself, working for Alco is as close to having your own business as you can get."

This enrichment module is based on:

Lubove, S. (1992, December 7). How to grow big yet stay small. *Forbes*, 64+.

---

2.   Top management typically makes strategic and philosophical choices that determine the extent to which an organization will operate as a mechanistic system or an organic system.

3.   These systems range on a continuum from pure mechanistic to pure organic.

4.   A mechanistic type of system is essentially a bureaucracy and an organic system is basically the opposite of a bureaucracy. A <u>bureaucracy</u> has the following characteristics:

    a.   The organization operates according to a set of rules that are intended to tightly control employees' behavior.

    b.   All employees must strictly follow rules and procedures in making decisions.

    c.   Each employee's job involves a specified area of expertise, with strictly defined obligations, authority, and powers to compel obedience.

    d.   Each lower-level position is under the tight control and direction of a higher one.

    e.   Candidates for jobs are selected on the basis of "technical" qualifications.

    f.   The organization has a career ladder; promotion is by seniority or achievement, and depends on the judgment of superiors.

5.   Transparency 17.6 compares mechanistic and organic systems on six dimensions: hierarchy of authority, centralization, division of labor, rules, procedural specifications, and impersonality.

TRANSPARENCY 17.6
(FIGURE 17.5 IN THE TEXTBOOK)

GENERAL CHARACTERISTICS OF MECHANISTIC AND ORGANIC SYSTEMS

---

a.   <u>Hierarchy of authority</u> represents the extent to which decision-making processes are prescribed and formal power is allocated. Mechanistic systems use many hierarchical levels to achieve tight control, while organic systems use fewer levels to foster goal attainment and innovation.

b.   <u>Centralization</u> means that all major, and oftentimes many minor, decisions are made only at the top levels of the organization. Mechanistic systems emphasize centralization and organic systems stress decentralization.

c.   <u>Division of labor</u> refers to the various ways of dividing up tasks and labor to achieve goals. Mechanistic systems place greater emphasis on division of labor.

   (1)   Division of labor will increase efficiency but only up to a certain point. Beyond that point quality and productivity may suffer, employees may be absent more frequently or quit, and costs of coordination may rise because the jobs are very routine and boring.

d.   <u>Rules</u> are formal, written statements specifying acceptable and unacceptable behaviors and decisions by organization members. In a mechanistic system, rules are created whenever possible; whereas in an organic system, rules are developed only when necessary.

e.   <u>Procedures</u> are the preset sequences of steps the managers and employees must follow in performing tasks and dealing with problems. Procedures often comprise rules that are to be used in a particular sequence. Numerous procedures, many of which are developed at the top levels of the organization and passed downward through written communications, exist in a mechanistic system. Fewer procedures exist in an organic system, and employees have input into the development of those procedures.

f.   <u>Impersonality</u> is the extent to which organizations treat their employees, as well as outsiders, according to objective, detached, and rigid characteristics. A mechanistic system relies on these characteristics more than an organic system does.

IV.   Organization design approaches.

   A.   Seven approaches to organizational design are examined. These approaches include: functional design, place design, product design, horizontal design, matrix design, multinational design, and network design.

   B.   Functional design.

      1.   A <u>functional design</u> creates positions and units on the basis of specialized activities.

2.   In a functional design, tasks can be grouped by *function* or *process* used. Transparency 17.7 provides an example of an organization that uses both function and process in its functional organization design.

**TRANSPARENCY 17.7
(FIGURE 17.6 IN THE TEXTBOOK)**

CALLAWAY GOLF'S DESIGN BY FUNCTION AND PROCESS

---

3.   Variables to be considered in creating a functional organization design.

   a.   Line versus staff functions.

      (1)   <u>Line functions</u> are those jobs that directly affect the principal work flow in an organization.

      (2)   <u>Staff functions</u> are support jobs that provide service and advice to line departments.

      (3)   Transparency 17.8 illustrates Con Edison's use of a line and staff design.

**TRANSPARENCY 17.8
(FIGURE 17.7 IN THE TEXTBOOK)**

CON EDISON'S DESIGN FOR LINE AND STAFF FUNCTIONS

---

   b.   Linkages of various functions with the task environment.

      (1)   Transparency 17.9, which is self-explanatory, shows how different functions are linked to various external stakeholders in an organization's task environment.

**TRANSPARENCY 17.9
(TABLE 17.2 IN THE TEXTBOOK)**

FUNCTIONAL FORM OF ORGANIZATION AND THE TASK ENVIRONMENT

---

   c.   Chain of command.

      (1)   The <u>scalar chain of command</u> refers to the flow of authority and responsibility in a clear, unbroken vertical line from the top to the bottom of the organization hierarchy.

      (2)   The <u>unity of command</u> principle states that no subordinate should receive orders from more than one superior.

   d.   Span of control.

      (1)   <u>Span of control</u> refers to the number of employees supervised by a superior.

(2)   As illustrated in Transparency 17.10, the number of levels in an organization's hierarchy tends to increase as the span of control deceases.

TRANSPARENCY 17.10
(FIGURE 17.8 IN THE TEXTBOOK)

SPAN OF CONTROL AND ORGANIZATION SHAPE

---

4.   Conditions for using a functional design (see Transparency 17.11).

TRANSPARENCY 17.11
(FROM TEXT MATERIAL IN THE TEXTBOOK)

CONDITIONS FOR USING A FUNCTIONAL DESIGN

---

a.   Advantages of a functional design.

    (1)   It permits clear identification and assignment of responsibilities.

    (2)   Employees easily understand the design.

    (3)   May be effective when the organization has a narrow product line and does not serve different geographic areas or different types of customers.

    (4)   The addition of specialized staff departments may enable the organization to deal more effectively with environmental complexity and dynamism.

b.   Disadvantages of a functional design.

    (1)   It fosters a limited point of view that focuses on a narrow set of tasks.

    (2)   Horizontal integration across functional departments often becomes difficult as the organization expands it geographic coverage or line of products or services.

    (3)   With the exception of marketing, most employees have no direct contact with customers and may lose sight of the need to meet or exceed customer expectations.

c.   Other implications.

    (1)   The addition of horizontal design mechanisms, such as linking roles and task forces, may facilitate the use of the functional design.

C.   Place design.

1.   A <u>place design</u> involves establishing an organization's primary units geographically

while retaining significant aspects of functional design.

2. Place design can be used to address cultural or legal differences that exist in different countries or the lack of uniformity among customers in different geographic regions.

3. Conditions for using a place design (see Transparency 17.12).

TRANSPARENCY 17.12
(FROM TEXT MATERIAL IN THE TEXTBOOK)

CONDITIONS FOR USING A PLACE DESIGN

---

a. Advantages of a place design.

(1) It promotes direct contact between the different organizational units and customers or other stakeholders, thereby permitting greater adaptability to the stakeholders' demands.

(2) Lower costs for materials, freight, labor, etc. may result.

b. Disadvantages of a place design.

(1) Control and coordination problems increase.

D. Product design.

1. A product design involves the establishment of self-contained units, each capable of developing, producing, and marketing its own goods or services.

2. A product design often evolves from a functional design or place design as the organization encounters greater environmental complexity and dynamism. The functional or place designs may not be discarded altogether. Instead, the product design may incorporate features of functional designs into the organization of each product division.

3. The multidivisional design, sometimes referred to as the *M-form*, is a variation of the product design. The multidivisional design organizes tasks into divisions on the basis of the product or geographic markets in which their goods or services are sold. Divisional managers are primarily responsible for day-to-day operations, and top corporate level managers concentrate on strategic issues.

4. Conditions for using a product design (see Transparency 17.13).

TRANSPARENCY 17.13
(FROM TEXT MATERIAL IN THE TEXTBOOK)

CONDITIONS FOR USING A PRODUCT DESIGN

---

a. Advantages of a product design.

(1)   It eases problems of integration by focusing functional expertise and knowledge on specific goods or services.

(2)   It often reduces the environmental complexity facing any one team, department, or division.

b.   Disadvantages of a product design.

(1)   A firm must have a large number of managerial personnel to oversee all the product lines.

(2)   Higher costs result from the duplication of various functions.

c.   Other implications.

(1)   The addition of horizontal design mechanisms, such as linking roles, task forces, integrating roles, and cross-functional teams, may facilitate use of the product design.

E.   Horizontal design.

1.   A horizontal design is one of two approaches for integrating units that are discussed in Chapter 17.

2.   Horizontal design refers to the processes and mechanisms for linking units that are in lateral relationships to each other, such as marketing and manufacturing departments.

3.   Horizontal design decisions should consider:

a.   The degree of differentiation between units.

b.   The degree of required integration between units.

c.   The degree of uncertainty (including task, work-flow, and environmental) confronting each unit.

4.   Transparency 17.14 depicts how the differentiation, integration, and uncertainty dimensions vary.

TRANSPARENCY 17.14
(FIGURE 17.10 IN THE TEXTBOOK)

VARIABLES THAT AFFECT HORIZONTAL RELATIONS BETWEEN UNITS

---

5.   Differentiation is the degree to which units differ in structure (low to high), members' orientation to a time horizon (short to long), managers' orientation to other people (permissive to authoritarian), and members' views of the task environment (certain to uncertain).

6.   Integration is the degree of collaboration and mutual understanding required among units to achieve their goals, for which the division of labor and task

interdependencies create the need.

a.   Too little horizontal integration will lead to lower quality decisions and the misuse of resources because each unit will "do its own thing."

b.   Too much horizontal integration results in units getting in the way of each other.

c.   Horizontal integration can be accomplished by using the seven approaches that were discussed in Chapter 10 regarding how to foster effective dynamics and outcomes between groups and teams. These seven methods are: dialogue, superordinate group goals and rewards, plans and hierarchy, linking roles, cross-functional teams, integrating roles and teams, and groupware.

7.   <u>Uncertainty</u> is the gap between what is known and what needs to be known to make decisions effectively and perform tasks effectively.

a.   The following factors should be considered in determining the degree of uncertainty:

(1)   The completeness of information and guidelines available to help employees perform their tasks.

(2)   The frequency with which units can be expected to face problems that they have to solve jointly.

(3)   The amount of actual thinking time required before units can try to implement solutions to mutual problems.

(4)   The probability that units can be reasonably certain of the results of their independent and mutual efforts.

8.   Conditions for using a horizontal design (see Transparency 17.15).

TRANSPARENCY 17.15
(FROM TEXT MATERIAL IN THE TEXTBOOK)

CONDITIONS FOR USING A HORIZONTAL DESIGN

---

a.   Under conditions of low differentiation, low required integration, and low uncertainty, organizational units are practically independent of each other. Therefore, the organization does not need to expend many (if any) resources to foster integration. Few (if any) formal horizontal integration mechanisms are needed.

b.   As the degree of differentiation, required integration, and uncertainty increase, an organization must expend more resources, increase its use of formal horizontal integration mechanisms, and use appropriate behavioral processes to obtain integration.

c.   With high differentiation, high required integration, and high uncertainty, an organization must expend considerable resources and use a wide variety of formal horizontal mechanisms and behavioral processes.

F.   Matrix design.

1.   Matrix design is the other approach for integrating units that is discussed in Chapter 17.

2.   <u>Matrix design</u> is based on multiple support systems and authority relationships in which some employees report to two superiors rather than one.

3.   Transparency 17.16 shows how a matrix design usually combines functional and product designs through the use of dual authority, information, and reporting relationships, and systems.

TRANSPARENCY 17.16
(FIGURE 17.11 IN THE TEXTBOOK)

PARTIAL ILLUSTRATION OF A BASIC MATRIX DESIGN

---

4.   Every matrix design contains three unique sets of role relationships:

   a.   The top manager who heads up and balances the dual chains of command.

   b.   The managers of functional and product departments who share subordinates.

   c.   The managers (or specialists) who report to both a functional manager and a product manager.

5.   The matrix design typically evolves through several stages.

   a.   The first stage usually is a temporary task force composed of representatives of different departments or divisions of the organization. The task force is created to study a specific problem and make recommendations.

   b.   The second stage usually involves the creation of a permanent team to address a specified need or problem. The team consists of representatives from different areas, with each representing the view of their home area.

   c.   The third stage occurs when a project manager is appointed and held accountable for integrating the team's inputs and activities in producing its final output.

   d.   With the appointment of project managers, an organization is well on the way toward a matrix design.

6.   Conditions for using a matrix design (see Transparency 17.17).

```
┌─────────────────────────────────────────────────────────────────┐
│ ┌───────────────────────────────────────────────────────────────┐ │
│ │                    TRANSPARENCY 17.17                          │ │
│ │           (FROM TEXT MATERIAL IN THE TEXTBOOK)                 │ │
│ │          CONDITIONS FOR USING A MATRIX DESIGN                  │ │
│ └───────────────────────────────────────────────────────────────┘ │
└─────────────────────────────────────────────────────────────────┘
```

    a.   Advantages of a matrix design.

        (1)   It makes specialized knowledge available to all projects.

        (2)   It uses people flexibly.

    b.   Disadvantages of a matrix design.

        (1)   Demands substantial managerial resources while employees learn how to function in the new organization.

        (2)   Learning may require two or three years because significant attitude change may need to occur.

        (3)   Special training programs in interpersonal communication, conflict resolution, and negotiation skills may be needed.

    c.   Other implications.

        (1)   The matrix design may be appropriate when organization members must be highly responsive to both function or product line (or place) concerns.

        (2)   The matrix design may be appropriate when an organization faces a complex, dynamic task environment coupled with a complex and uncertain technology that requires employees to process lots of information.

        (3)   The matrix design may be appropriate when an organization has multiple products and limited resources.

G.   Multinational design.

    1.   A <u>multinational design</u> attempts to maintain three-way organization perspectives and capabilities among products, functions, and geographic areas.

    2.   Most multinational designs focus on the relative emphasis that should be given to place and product organization designs. Transparency 17.18 shows the likely effect of choosing a design based primarily on place or product line. Placing greater relative emphasis on a product organization is appropriate for integrated global business operations. On the other hand, relative dominance of the place organization would be more effective for tailoring the firm's business to the unique markets of many different countries.

TRANSPARENCY 17.18
(FIGURE 17.12 IN THE TEXTBOOK)

BASIC OPTIONS IN MULTINATIONAL DESIGN

---

3.   Conditions for using a multinational design (see Transparency 17.19).

TRANSPARENCY 17.19
(FROM TEXT MATERIAL IN THE TEXTBOOK)

CONDITIONS FOR USING A MULTINATIONAL DESIGN

---

  a.   Worldwide product-line divisions will be more dominant than geographically based divisions when an organization is faced with:

  (1)   The growing presence and importance of global competitors and customers.

  (2)   A rise in global market demand for products.

  (3)   New information technologies.

  (4)   Efficient factories that can manufacture goods for customers throughout the world.

  b.   A worldwide product-line division may not be as effective at opening up new territories as a geographically organized division.

G.   Network design.

1.   The six organization designs discussed thus far have limitations that often hinder them in coping effectively and efficiently with turbulent environments and technologies. The <u>network design</u>—sometimes called a spiderweb or cluster organization—is intended to facilitate managing highly diverse, complex, and dynamic factors involving multiple units and many people, both internal and external to the organization.

2.   The network design focuses on sharing authority, responsibility, and control among people and units that must cooperate and communicate frequently to achieve common goals.

3.   A network design exists only when most of the following factors operate in support of each other (see Transparency 17.20):

TRANSPARENCY 17.20
(FROM TEXT MATERIAL IN THE TEXTBOOK)

KEY ELEMENTS OF A NETWORK DESIGN

---

  a.   The organization maintains superiority through innovation and adaptation by combining resources in novel ways.

b.   People who must collaborate to perform their tasks share responsibility.

c.   Common goals linked to satisfying the needs of one or more important external stakeholders are formulated.

d.   All channel communication networks are used both internally and externally, and the emphasis is on lateral rather than vertical communication.

e.   Information technologies assist organization members in networking internally and externally.

f.   Interdependent organization members are primarily cooperative rather than competitive.

g.   The organization's culture focuses both on problems of external adaptation and internal integration.

h.   Teams, departments, and divisions view themselves in relation to others with common superordinate goals and rewards.

4.   Four key developments in information technology have enabled organizations to utilize both internal and external networking. These developments are as follows:

a.   The shift from organizational units having their own unique computing capability to a network of linked business processes.

b.   The shift from limited access central computing to network computing where information is widely available.

c.   Real-time data collection and updating of data bases, thus permitting real-time decision making.

d.   Global networking which permits real-time communication and access to electronically stored information at will from anywhere in the world.

ENRICHMENT MODULE: GROUPWARE NETWORKS AND ORGANIZATION DESIGN

In part, organization design facilitates information flow within the organization and between the organization and its external environment. Groupware networks have begun to have very dramatic effects on these information flows. Information which once was available to only a select few, can now be simultaneously available to numerous people both within and outside the organization. Within the organization, groupware networks help to flatten the organizational hierarchy and serve as a vehicle for empowerment. Outside the firm, groupware networks facilitate the development of closer working relationships with suppliers and distributors.

This enrichment module is based on:

Wilke, J.R. (1993, December 9). Computer links erode hierarchical nature of workplace culture. *The Wall Street Journal*, A1 & A7.

5.   Implications of a network design (see Transparency 17.21).

TRANSPARENCY 17.21
(FROM TEXT MATERIAL IN THE TEXTBOOK)

IMPLICATIONS OF A NETWORK DESIGN

---

a.   The network design is particularly effective in creating alliances with other organizations.

b.   The network design is intended to create successful external relationships by: making those relationships important; promoting long-term investments and commitments; establishing interdependent relationships, thus keeping power balanced; integrating relationships in order to maintain contact and communication; keeping each other informed; and establishing a framework for institutionalizing the relationships.

ENRICHMENT MODULE: THE VIRTUAL CORPORATION

Is the virtual corporation just a "business buzz word" or is it something real? The electronics industry describes the *virtual* concept as "an entity or experience that perpetually adapts to the needs of the user." If a corporation perpetually adapts to the needs of its stakeholders, both external and internal, then the virtual organization would be a reality.

Consistent with this notion of perpetual flexibility, the dominant characteristic of a virtual corporation is its boundaryless nature. The distinctions between "what is inside" and "what is outside" the organization become blurred in the virtual corporation. Co-destiny is the operating philosophy of virtual corporations. Very close working relationships with suppliers and distributors are forged through shared plans and information, sole sourcing, joint venturing, cross investment, joint training, shared infrastructure, point-of-sale data tracking and electronic data exchange, and so on.

This enrichment module is based on:

Byrne, J.A. (1993, February 8). The virtual corporation. *Business Week*, 98-102.

Malone, M.M., & Davidow, W. (1992, December 7). Virtual corporation. *Forbes ASAP*, 103-107.

V.   Summing up: What does organization design contribute to the understanding and management of organizational behavior?

A.   In order to achieve its goals and respond effectively to the demands of customers and other stakeholders, an organization must perform a lot of different activities. Performing these activities effectively and efficiently is determined, in part, by: (1) how the activities are subdivided; (2) how the activities are coordinated, once they are subdivided; and (3) how dividing and coordinating the organization's activities influences its communications and decision-making processes. This, of course, is the domain of organization design.

B.   In dividing up work and coordinating it, managers must be cognizant of the factors that influence organization design decisions. Managers must also be able to link these organization design factors to available organization design options. An appropriate fit between design factors and design options can facilitate the effective functioning of the organization.

DISCUSSION QUESTIONS: SUGGESTED ANSWERS

1.   *What are two similarities between functional and product organization design?*

Functional organization design creates positions and units on the basis of specialized activities, such as engineering, marketing, and manufacturing. Product organization design involves the establishment of self-contained units, each capable of developing, producing, and marketing its own goods or services. A product design may evolve from a functional design as the organization encounters greater environmental complexity and dynamism. Consequently, the functional design and the product design have similarities, some of which are the following:

a.   Line and staff functions may be similar with both approaches to organization design. With both approaches, staff departments provide the line departments with the expert advice they need to make decisions about complex problems. Moreover, with both approaches, the addition of specialized staff departments may enable the organization to deal more effectively with environmental complexity and dynamism.

b.   The chain of command and the span of control may be similar with both types of organization design.

c.   Both approaches provide for clear delineation of responsibilities.

d.   Both design approaches can integrate activities by adding horizontal design mechanisms, such as linking roles, task forces, integrating roles, and cross-functional teams.

2.   *What are two differences between functional and product organization design?*

Some of the differences between a functional organization design and a product organization design probably occur because organizations may adopt the product design in order to improve upon the functional design. Some of the differences between the two approaches are as follows:

a.   The functional design is more likely to be effective when the organization has a narrow product line and does not serve different geographic regions or different types of customers. Product organization design is likely to be more appropriate for responding to the demands of different types of customers.

b.   In the functional design, employees who do similar work—and therefore face similar problems—are grouped together. This facilitates interaction and mutual support. In the product organization design, grouping of employees is according to product line rather than type of function. Thus, employees will interact with people engaged in many different activities and who experience many different problems.

c.   Integration occurs more easily in the product design than in the functional design because functional expertise and knowledge is focused on specific goods or services.

d.   With a product organization design, a company must have a large number of managerial personnel to oversee all the product lines.

e.   A product organization design results in higher costs because of the duplication of various functions.

3.   *Why do information technologies affect organization design?*

Basically, information technologies affect organization design through their impact on how people in different teams, departments, divisions, and organizations interact. Information technologies can have many specific effects on relationship patterns, including the following:

a.   Information technologies help organization members to network and communicate internally and externally.
b.   Information technologies provide more people with access to more information.
c.   Information technologies can provide real-time data access and support real-time decision making.
d.   Information technologies can help push decisions down to lower levels in the organization.
e.   Information technologies can encourage shared decision making.
f.   Information technologies can help organizations in monitoring the external environment, and in coping more effectively with a rapidly changing environment.
g.   Information technologies can influence work-flow uncertainty and task uncertainty.

All of these information technology effects could produce changes in authority and responsibility relationships, the chain of command, span of control, etc., thereby affecting the organization's design.

4.   *Which organization design is used the college in which you are enrolled?*

In responding to this question, the students should draw upon the conceptual descriptions of the seven approaches to organizational design that are discussed in Chapter 17. The students should select the functional design, place design, product design, horizontal design, matrix design, multinational design, or network design to apply to their institution. Discussion should consider why a particular design appropriately describes the organization design approach used at the student's university.

5.   *Which other organization design could be used for the college in which you are enrolled? What might be the advantages and disadvantages of this alternative design?*

A decision about an alternative design should be based upon a diagnosis of key aspects of the organization and external environment. Using Figure 17.4 for guidance, students can perform a diagnosis of the college they attend. They should analyze the environmental forces, strategic choices, technological factors, and the foundation influences that exist for the college. Then, in light of their analysis, they should determine which of the seven organization design approaches would be appropriate. To explore the advantages and disadvantages of an alternative design, the students could draw upon the relevant "conditions for use" discussions in the chapter.

6.   *Describe the mechanistic or organic characteristics of an organization of which you are a member. Are any changes needed? Explain.*

Figure 17.5 provides a conceptual foundation for responding to this question. This figure compares mechanistic and organic systems in terms of hierarchy of authority, centralization, division of labor, rules, procedural specifications, and impersonality. The students should use these six dimensions in describing their example organizations. In addition, the students should discuss whether their example organization needs to become more mechanistic or more organic. Discussing why such a change is needed and how such a change could be implemented would further enhance the students understanding of the managerial and organizational implications that are associated with the strategic choice between mechanistic and organic systems.

7.   *Give three personal experiences with organizational rules that seemed to be either helpful or counterproductive in terms of organizational effectiveness.*

Conceptually, this question focuses on the functional and dysfunctional effects of rules—in short, the dual character of rules. The dual character of rules is manifested in several ways, including the following:

      a.   Rules protect as well as restrict.
      b.   Rules coordinate as well as block.
      c.   Rules channel effort as well as limit it.
      d.   Rules permit universalism as well as provide sanctuary for the inept.
      e.   Rules maintain stability as well as retard change.
      f.   Rules permit diversity as well as restrict it.

In discussing their personal experiences with organizational rules, the students may tend to emphasize the dysfunctional effects of rules without recognizing that some rules that are desirable for the organization as a whole may be interpreted as undesirable from the standpoint of an individual organization member. Moreover, the students should recognize that rules which are viewed as bad today may have been desirable when they were first developed. Finally, some consideration should be given as to why people become frustrated with organizational rules. Does their frustration result from simply having certain behaviors and decisions regulated, or is it rooted in the substance of the rules?

8.   *How might top managers' philosophy and the organization's culture influence organization design decisions?*

Top management's philosophy can affect the organization's strategic choices. One important way in which management philosophy has an impact is the strategic choice between a mechanistic form of organization and an organic form of organization. Top management's philosophy also affects the organization's culture. Indeed, management's philosophy regarding the relationships with employees and customers is a key element of organizational culture.

As we noted in Chapter 14, an organization's culture consists of the following elements:

      a.   Routine behaviors such as organizational rituals and ceremonies and the language commonly used.
      b.   The norms that are shared by work groups throughout the organization.
      c.   The dominant values held by an organization.
      d.   The philosophy that guides an organization's policy toward employees and customers.
      e.   The rules of the game for getting along in the organization.
      f.   The feeling or climate that is conveyed in an organization by the physical layout and the way in which members of the organization interact with

customers or other outsiders.

All of these elements influence the ways in which people relate to one another in the organizational context. How people relate to one another—in terms of teams, departments, and divisions—is a major concern of organization design.

In summary, management's philosophy and strategic choices as well as the organization's culture will dramatically influence the pattern of working relationships that exist among various organizational units. These three factors will also affect how various organizational units relate to the external environment.

9. *What difficulties are associated with the matrix design? Would you like to work in an organization that utilizes a matrix design? Why or why not?*

The major difficulty with a matrix design is that it relies on dual authority, information, and reporting relationships and systems. This duality can be complex and difficult for organization members to understand. The duality of the matrix design also can generate role conflict and role ambiguity for organization members.

Another difficulty is that the matrix design often requires substantial managerial resources while employees learn how to operate within the system. Moreover, learning may require two or three years because significant changes in the employees' attitudes may need to occur. Finally, special training programs in interpersonal communication, conflict resolution, and negotiation skills may be needed.

Many students may indicate that they would not like to work in an organization with a matrix design because of the ambiguity and confusion in authority and responsibility relationships that it could create for them. However, students who have a high tolerance for ambiguity could function adequately, if not thrive, in such an organization.

10. *What forces work for and against the establishment of a network design?*

The following list identifies forces that facilitate the establishment of a network design:

a. The organization maintains superiority through innovation and adaptation by combining resources in novel ways.
b. People who must collaborate to perform their tasks share responsibility.
c. Common goals linked to satisfying the needs of one or more important external stakeholders are formulated.
d. All channel communication networks are used both internally and externally, and the emphasis is on lateral rather than vertical communication.
e. Information technologies assist organization members in networking internally and externally.
f. Interdependent organization members are primarily cooperative rather than competitive.
g. The organization's culture focuses both on problems of external adaptation and internal integration.
h. Teams, departments, and divisions view themselves in relation to others with common superordinate goals and rewards.

The absence of the forces identified above would be detrimental to the establishment of a network design. The viability of a network design would diminish in relation to the number of critical forces that are absent.

DEVELOPING SKILLS—
SELF DIAGNOSIS: INVENTORY OF EFFECTIVE DESIGN

This self-diagnostic instrument contains 15 statements that describe an effective organization design. Students can use this questionnaire to assess the design of an organization for which they currently work or have worked in the past. The students evaluate the organization by indicating, on a seven-point Likert scale, the strength of their agreement or disagreement with each statement. Scoring is accomplished by summing the numerical responses to the 15 items. Scores can range from 15 to 105. In general, the higher the score the more effective the organization design.

DEVELOPING SKILLS—
A CASE IN POINT: AQUARIUS ADVERTISING AGENCY

CASE OVERVIEW

This case describes the organization design of Aquarius Advertising Agency. Figure 17.4 and Table 17.14 contain important diagnostic data. Figure 17.4 contains the organization chart. Table 17.14 presents the results of a sociometric study of formal and informal communication patterns.

Analysis of these data indicate that the organization is hierarchical in nature and is functionally designed. Most communication goes through the account executives. Some lateral communication takes place among the various specialists within the agency and between some specialists and clients.

CASE QUESTIONS

1.   *How would you characterize the organization design that exists at the Aquarius Advertising Agency?*

     The Aquarius Advertising Agency uses a functional organization design. Activities and tasks are grouped according to specialization. Specific line functions (*e.g.,* accounts, operations, and marketing) and staff functions (*e.g.,* legal, financial, traffic, and personnel) have been delineated. The organization is very hierarchical; little lateral interaction takes place (see Table 17.3). The account executives' role appears to be the principal mechanism for horizontal integration.

2.   *What are the advantages and disadvantages of the organization design at Aquarius?*

     The advantages of the functional design used at Aquarius seem to be the following:

     a.   Responsibilities are clearly identified and assigned.
     b.   People easily understand the chain of command and authority and responsibility relationships.

The disadvantages of the functional design, which appear to be more numerous, are as follows:

    a.   It inhibits needed interaction among departments.

    b.   It fosters tunnel vision with respect to the organization's goals.

    c.   People tend to focus on a narrow set of tasks.

    d.   The hierarchical structure can be slow and cumbersome, thereby inhibiting flexibility and responsiveness.

    e.   Horizontal integration may be problematic.

3.   *Design an organization that could eliminate the disadvantages of the Aquarius organization design.*

Either a horizontal design or a matrix design would probably be appropriate for the Aquarius Advertising Agency. Using cross-functional teams would be a reasonable possibility for horizontal integration. With a matrix design, account executives could become project managers and team members could be drawn from each of the functional departments to collectively focus their talents on specific accounts.

COURSE ENHANCEMENT—
WEST'S ORGANIZATIONAL BEHAVIOR CUSTOM VIDEO SERIES

One video from *West's Organizational Behavior Custom Video Series* can be used to enhance the material in Chapter 17. This video is: *Microscope Video Magazine: AT&T Microelectronics.*

VIDEO: *MICROSCOPE VIDEO MAGAZINE: AT&T MICROELECTRONICS*

Approximate Time: 4 minutes

Video Summary:

This video describes how AT&T Microelectronics of Berkeley Heights, New Jersey has restructured the office of the chief executive officer. The president, Bill Warwick, and the vice president, Curtis Crawford, are sharing CEO responsibilities so that AT&T Microelectronics can be more responsive to customers, strategic business units (SBUs), and AT&T employees.

Mr. Warwick is responsible for three SBUs—Advanced Integrated Modules, Metal Oxide Semiconductors, and High Performance Integrated Circuits. Mr. Crawford is responsible for the other three SBUs—Lightwave, Power Systems, and Interconnection Technologies. With this structure, each executive can devote more time to their areas of primary responsibility yet still act for the other executive. This shared workload results in quicker decisions and makes AT&T a more agile and responsive organization.

Discussion Questions and Suggested Answers for Video:

1.   *What advantages may occur when executive responsibilities are shared as they are at AT&T Microelectronics?*

There are several advantages of such an arrangement. First, each SBU gets more top executive support. Second, customers and employees within each SBU also get more top executive attention. Third, decisions can be made more quickly. Fourth, each executive has back-up coverage from the other executive. Fifth, the company becomes a more flexible and responsive organization. Sixth, a synergy of talents can be created. Seventh, the executives' work lives and personal lives can be kept in better balance.

2.   *What disadvantages may occur when executive responsibilities are shared as they are at AT&T Microelectronics?*

The primary disadvantage of this arrangement is that it may introduce some ambiguity due to violation of the unity of command principe. However, any ambiguity would be more than offset by the many advantages identified in question 1.

COURSE ENHANCEMENT—
SUPPLEMENTAL VIDEOS AVAILABLE FROM WEST

One video from the Association for Manufacturing Excellence and made available through West Publishing Company can be used to enhance the material in Chapter 17. This video is a segment of the tape *On the Road to Manufacturing Excellence* that pertains to *Xerox*.

VIDEO: AME: ON THE ROAD TO MANUFACTURING EXCELLENCE—XEROX

Approximate Time: 8 minutes

Video Summary:

This video describes how Xerox went from an industry leader in the 1960s to an also-ran in the 1980s. Since the mid-1970s Xerox had been attacked viciously by Japanese competition—Japanese copier manufacturers could sell their products for what it cost Xerox to make them. Xerox profits in 1981 fell to $600 million from $1.149 billion. Individual functional areas were doing well, but the company as a whole was not. The Japanese were capturing a large share of the market. Xerox had become complacent and had lost its customer focus.

Xerox's solutions to these problems were multi-faceted. The company initiated benchmarking in order to better understand their competitor's products. Xerox employees were encouraged to learn as much about their competitors as possible. The company encouraged employees to work together, eliminate internal competition, and begin horizontal integration. Xerox also worked closely with suppliers to increase their product quality. Top management learned to be vigilant and involved in order to regain and retain a position of industry leadership.

Discussion Questions and Suggested Answers for Video:

1.   *Referring to the "Enrichment Module: Creating the Horizontal Organization" on page 400, discuss whether Xerox did anything that was compatible with the action steps needed to develop a horizontal organization.*

This enrichment module describes a ten-point plan for creating a horizontal organization. Four of the elements in the ten-point plan were either directly evident or implied in the video. These points were:

   a.   *Let performance objectives and operational activities be customer driven*—Xerox regained customer focus and benchmarked its products against competitor's products.

   b.   *Maximize supplier and customer contact with organization members*—Xerox worked closely with suppliers to increase product quality.

   c.   *Put senior leaders in charge of processes and resulting performance*—Xerox's top management realized that they had to be vigilant and involved.

   d.   *Inform and train organization members to be problem solvers*—Xerox's functional groups ceased competing and began cooperating and working together to solve problems.

We must emphasize, however, that Xerox's use of these elements was not necessarily a deliberate application of the horizontal organization concept. Rather, Xerox took some steps that also happened to be compatible with part of the methodology for creating a horizontal organization.

2.   *Chapter 10 of the text discussed seven methods for fostering effective dynamics and outcomes between groups and teams. Chapter 17 indicates that these methods also can be used to facilitate horizontal integration. Which methods could Xerox use to improve its own horizontal integration? Why should they be used?*

The seven methods that can be used to facilitate horizontal integration are: dialogue, superordinate group goals and rewards, plans and hierarchy, linking roles, cross-functional teams, integrating roles and teams, and groupware. Xerox probably could use any of the seven, either singly or in combination. One possible combination is the use of dialogue, cross-functional teams, and superordinate group goals and rewards.

Dialogue is fundamental to integration; communication is essential for cooperation. The use of cross-functional teams could capitalize on the Xerox's initiatives to eliminate internal competition and foster cooperation across functions. Also, since the separate functions were doing well but the company as a whole was not, superordinate goals and rewards could be used to foster cooperation.

CHAPTER 18
ORGANIZATIONAL DECISION MAKING

CHAPTER OVERVIEW

Chapter 18 completes the discussion of organizational processes through its examination of organizational decision making. The chapter's initial focus is on ethics in decision making, with special emphasis being placed on the nature of ethical decision making, ethical dilemmas that may be encountered in business, and issues to be considered in improving ethical decision making. Next, three decision making models—the rational model, the bounded rationality model, and the political model—are explained. Attention is given to the defining characteristics of each model and how, if at all, each model considers ethics. A five-phase model of managerial decision making is explored next. The five phases include: problem recognition, problem interpretation, attention to problems, courses of action, and aftermath. The nature of each phase is described and implications of the phases are discussed. Finally, the topic of stimulating creativity is considered, with emphasis being placed on the lateral thinking method and the devil's advocate method.

LEARNING OBJECTIVES

Upon completion of this chapter, the students should be able to:

1. Identify the core issues in ethical decision making.
2. Explain three basic models of organizational decision making.
3. Describe the phases of managerial decision making.
4. Explain the common human biases in decision making.
5. Describe two methods for stimulating creativity.

CHAPTER OUTLINE

I. **Preview Case:** Rules to Decide By

II.   Ethical Decision Making

       A.   Ethical Intensity
       B.   **Managing Diversity:** Denny's Errors and Recovery
       C.   Decision Principles and Rules
       D.   **Managing Ethics:** Designing an Effective Code
       E.   Affected Individuals
       F.   Benefits and Costs
       G.   Determination of Rights

III.   Decision-Making Models

       A.   Rational Model
       B.   **Managing Quality:** Providing Reliable Service
       C.   Bounded Rationality Model
       D.   Political Model

IV.   Phases of Managerial Decision Making

       A.   Problem Recognition
       B.   **Managing in Practice:** The Challenger Disaster
       C.   Problem Interpretation
       D.   Attention to Problems
       E.   **Managing in Practice:** Challenger Flashback
       F.   Courses of Action
       G.   Aftermath
       H.   **Managing Across Cultures:** Royal Dutch/Shell's Decision Making

V.   Stimulating Creativity

       A.   Lateral Thinking Method
       B.   Devil's Advocate Method

VI.   Developing Skills

       A.   **Self Diagnosis:** Individual Ethics Profile
       B.   **A Case in Point:** Olson Medical Systems

KEY WORDS AND CONCEPTS

Twenty-eight key words and concepts are introduced in Chapter 18. Two concepts were originally introduced in earlier chapters. Ethics was identified in Chapter 1 and risk propensity was explained in Chapter 15 under the label of risk-seeking propensity. The key words and concepts, along with definitions or appropriate descriptions, are as follows:

Aftermath: involves an evaluation of the results of the actions that were taken.

Availability bias: refers to the tendency to recall specific instances of an event and therefore overestimating how often such an event occurs (or failing to recall specific instances of an event and underestimating how frequently it occurs).

Bounded rationality model: a decision-making model that recognizes the limitations of the individual's rationality and reveals the day-to-day decision-making processes used by individuals.

Confirmation bias: refers to the natural tendency to seek support for an initial view of a situation rather than to look for disconfirming evidence.

Devil's advocate method: a person or small task force develops a systematic critique of a recommended course of action.

Dictionary rule: a decision-making rule that ranks items in the same way a dictionary does: one criterion (*i.e.*, letter) at a time, with the greatest importance going to the first criterion, and so on.

Distributive justice principle: treating individuals differently should not be based on arbitrarily defined characteristics; employees who are similar in relevant respects should be treated similarly and those who are different in relevant respects should be treated differently in proportion to their differences.

Employment at will: a doctrine which holds that parties to an employment agreement have equal bargaining power and therefore the right to fire is absolute and creates very little cost to either party.

Escalating commitment: a process of continuing or increasing the commitment of resources to a course of action, even though a substantial amount of feedback indicates that the action is wrong.

Ethical intensity: refers to the degree of importance given an issue-related moral imperative.

Ethics: deals with right or wrong in the actions and decisions of individuals and the organizations of which they are a part.

Lateral thinking method: a deliberate process for the generation of new ideas through a change in the individual's or team's typical logical pattern for processing and storing information.

Law of small numbers bias: refers to the tendency to consider small samples as representative of the larger population, even when they are not.

Managerial decision making: a multi-phase process that begins with a recognition or awareness of problems and concludes with an assessment of the results of actions taken to solve those problems.

Organizational creativity: the production of novel and useful ideas by an individual or team of individuals working together.

Organizational innovation: the implementation of creative and useful ideas through unplanned or planned organizational change.

Political model: a decision-making model which suggests that organizational decisions reflect the desire of individuals to satisfy their own interests.

Problem framing: refers to whether a situation is presented or viewed in positive or negative terms.

Problem interpretation: refers to the process of giving meaning and definition to problems that have been recognized.

Rational model: a decision-making model which holds that decision making involves intentionally choosing among alternatives to maximize benefits to the organization.

Risk propensity: the general tendency of the decision maker to take or avoid risks.

Satisficing: the practice of selecting an acceptable goal or solution.

Selective perception bias: refers to the tendency to see what a person expects to see.

Structured problems: have clear-cut decision parameters which make problem recognition straight-forward.

Unstructured problems: have ambiguous decision parameters which create difficulty in actually recognizing the problem.

Utilitarianism: emphasizes the provision of the greatest good for the greatest number in judging the ethics of decision making.

Values: the relatively permanent and deeply held desires of individuals.

Vertical thinking method: the logical step-by-step process of developing ideas by proceeding on a continuous path from one bit of information to the next.

LECTURE NOTES

I.   Overview of organizational decision making.

      A.   Sometimes rules are used to make decisions easily and quickly. For example, individuals and organizations can use the <u>dictionary rule</u> to make decisions. This rule ranks items in the same way a dictionary does: one criterion (*i.e.,* letter) at a time, with the greatest importance going to the first criterion, and so on.

      B.   Sometimes decision rules are misapplied. Moreover, many decisions cannot be made through the application of decision rules. Therefore, managers must be knowledgeable about organizational decision making.

      C.   Chapter 18 considers various issues regarding organizational decision making. Among the key questions being examined in this chapter are the following: What is ethical decision making? How can ethical decision making be improved? What models can be used to describe the nature of decision making in organizations? How do mangers go about making decisions? How can creativity be stimulated in order to improve organizational decision making? These questions and the chapters's answers to them are summarized in Transparency 18.1.

TRANSPARENCY 18.1
(FROM TEXT MATERIAL IN THE TEXTBOOK)

KEY QUESTIONS AND ANSWERS ABOUT ORGANIZATIONAL DECISION MAKING

II.   Ethical decision making.

      A.   An overview of ethical decision making.

1. Organizational decisions reflect underlying ethical principles and rules.

2. <u>Ethics</u> deals with right or wrong in the actions and decisions of individuals and the organizations of which they are a part.

ENRICHMENT MODULE: ETHICS—DOING IT RIGHT!

Can an organization operate ethically and still succeed financially? Many managers argue that the only road to long-term success is through ethical activity. Unfortunately, research on the linkage between ethics (or a related concept—corporate social responsibility) and financial performance has proven to be inconclusive. However, anecdotal data concerning the connection is often quite powerful.

Consider, for example, Ben & Jerry's Homemade, Inc., a producer of gourmet ice creams and frozen yogurt. Ben & Jerry's is noted for its corporate social conscience. It supports numerous social causes, including preservation of the rain forest; helping the homeless; saving family farms; eliminating poverty, particularly as it impacts on children; improving automobile fuel efficiency; and so forth. Plus, the company's social conscience is evident in its day-to-day operations, which Ben Cohen, one of the founders, calls *Caring Capitalism*. For instance, the company purchases milk from family-owned farms in Vermont; nuts from natives of the Brazilian rain forest; brownies made by unemployed and homeless people in Yonkers, New York; and blueberries from the Passamaquoddy Indians in Maine. Moreover, Ben & Jerry's Homemade, Inc. enjoys continued growth in sales, net income, and earnings per share.

ENRICHMENT MODULE: ETHICS—DOING IT WRONG!
(*An Experiential Activity*)

There is no evidence to clearly indicate that unethical actions are more prevalent than ethical actions in business organizations. However, unethical actions receive much more media attention. Indeed, rarely a week goes by without one or more scandals being reported in such publications as *The Wall Street Journal*, *The New York Times*, *Business Week*, *Newsweek*, etc. For instance, here is a sampling four recent media reports of unethical activities:

- Some key executives at Kidder, Peabody, & Co., a brokerage firm, allegedly covered up very substantial financial losses that were incurred in its bond trading activities.
- Top executives at Phar-Mor, Inc., a discount retailer, committed financial fraud of sufficient magnitude to force the company into bankruptcy.
- Some operators of grain elevators allegedly were watering grain in order to make it weigh and cost more.
- Various health care professionals allegedly have submitted fraudulent claims to Medicare for payment.

Many other instances of unethical activity are regularly reported in the media. To enhance students' understanding of the importance of ethical behavior in business, have them review several issues of an appropriate magazine or newspaper for examples of unethical actions that have taken place. The students should give special attention to both (1) the individual, group, and/or organizational consequences of the unethical activities, and (2) what companies are doing to deal with these unethical activities.

---

3. Ethical dilemmas are often encountered in making decisions that involve ethical issues. Transparency 18.2 identifies 26 ethical issues that may be encountered in

business organizations.

> ## TRANSPARENCY 18.2
> ## (TABLE 18.1 IN THE TEXTBOOK)
>
> ## MAJOR ETHICAL ISSUES FACING U.S. INDUSTRIES:
> ## IN RANK ORDER OF IMPORTANCE

B.   Ethical decision-making can be improved with a knowledge of five core ethical issues. These core ethical issues involve ethical intensity, decision principles and rules, affected individuals, benefits and costs, and determination of rights.

   1.   Ethical intensity.

      a.   <u>Ethical intensity</u> refers to the degree of importance given an issue-related moral imperative.

      b.   Ethical intensity is determined by the combined impact of the decision maker's interpretation of the following six components:

         (1)   *Magnitude of the consequences* involves the total harm or benefits that occur for the individuals who are affected by the ethical issue.

         (2)   The *probability of effect* is a joint result of the probability that the decision will be implemented and that it will cause the harm or benefit predicted.

         (3)   *Social consensus* is the degree of public agreement that a proposed decision is evil or good.

         (4)   *Temporal immediacy* concerns the amount of time until the onset of the consequences of the decision.

         (5)   *Proximity* of the ethical issue involves the feeling of nearness (social, cultural, psychological, or physical) that the decision maker has for victims or beneficiaries of the decision.

         (6)   *Concentration of effect* is an inverse function of the number of people affected by the decision.

      c.   Ethical intensity increases or decreases as its components increase or decrease.

   2.   Decision principles and rules.

      a.   As shown in Transparency 18.3, various principles and rules can be used to guide decision making. These guidelines range from those that justify extremely self-serving decisions to those that require careful consideration of others' rights and costs.

TRANSPARENCY 18.3
(TABLE 18.2 IN THE TEXTBOOK)

STATED PRINCIPLES OF BEHAVIOR

---

b.   The <u>distributive justice principle</u> is one important guideline for organizational decision making. This principle means that treating individuals differently should not be based on arbitrarily defined characteristics. Employees who are similar in relevant respects should be treated similarly and those who are different in relevant respects should be treated differently in proportion to their differences.

c.   The likelihood of ethical decision making can be increased with certain rules and principles, including the following (see Transparency 18.4):

TRANSPARENCY 18.4
(FROM TEXT MATERIAL IN THE TEXTBOOK)

GUIDELINES FOR IMPROVING ETHICAL DECISION MAKING

---

(1)   Develop and follow a clear code of ethics.

(2)   Establish and follow a procedure for organization members to report unethical behavior.

(3)   Involve employees in the identification of ethical problems to achieve a shared understanding and resolution of them.

(4)   Monitor performance regarding ethical issues.

(5)   Include ethical decision making as a critical element of the performance appraisal process.

(6)   Publicize the organizational priorities and efforts related to ethical issues.

3.   Affected individuals.

a.   The essence of ethics involves the effects that a decision has on identifiable individuals, groups, and organizations. Thus, ethical decision making should consider who will experience benefits or costs as a result of a particular decision.

b.   The ethical interpretation of the effects of decisions on identifiable parties can change over time. One example of such a change is provided by changing viewpoints of the <u>employment at will</u> doctrine. This doctrine holds that parties to an employment agreement have equal bargaining power and therefore the right to fire is absolute and creates very little cost to either party. Whereas companies once could fire employees for any reason and without explanation, they now may be subject to wrongful discharge lawsuits.

4.   Benefits and costs.

    a.   Judging the benefits and costs of a proposed decision requires a determination of the interests and values of those affected.

    b.   <u>Values</u> are the relatively permanent and deeply held desires of individuals.

    c.   Conflicting values between stakeholders can lead to different interpretations of ethical responsibilities.

    d.   Utilitarianism is a commonly used approach for assessing the benefits and costs of a decision. <u>Utilitarianism</u> emphasizes the provision of the greatest good for the greatest number in judging the ethics of decision making.

5.   Determination of rights.

    a.   Who has rights and who doesn't, and what those rights are have changed over time. For example, employees now have rights that they didn't have a few decades ago—equal employment opportunity and freedom from sexual harassment are but two of these rights.

    b.   An important aspect of rights focuses on who is entitled to benefits or to participation in the decision to change the allocation of benefits and costs.

    c.   The determination of rights often involves balancing the rights of the individual, the needs and rights of the employer, and the interests of the community at large.

III.   Decision-making models.

    A.   Three decision-making models are used to illustrate the complexity and variety of decision-making situations in an organization. These models are: the rational model, the bounded rationality model, and the political model.

    B.   The rational model of decision making.

        1.   The <u>rational model</u> holds that decision making involves intentionally choosing among alternatives to maximize benefits to the organization.

        2.   Key assumptions of the rational model:

            a.   Complete information concerning alternatives is available.

            b.   These alternatives can be ranked according to objective criteria.

            c.   The alternative selected will provide the maximum gain possible for the organization (or decision makers).

            d.   Ethical dilemmas do not exist.

        3.   Transparency 18.5 illustrates how the rational model is used at Xerox.

TRANSPARENCY 18.5
(TABLE 18.3 IN THE TEXTBOOK)

PORTION OF XEROX'S RATIONAL DECISION-MAKING PROCESS

C.   The bounded rationality model of decision making.

    1.   The <u>bounded rationality model</u> recognizes the limitations of the individual's rationality and reveals the day-to-day decision-making processes used by individuals.

    2.   The bounded rationality model is characterized by the following attributes:

        a.   Individuals tend to make <u>satisficing</u> decisions, which is the practice of selecting an acceptable goal or solution. Acceptable may mean easier to identify and achieve, less controversial, or otherwise safer than the best available alternative.

        b.   Individuals usually make a limited search for possible goals or solutions to a problem, considering alternatives only until they find one that seems adequate.

        c.   Individuals often have inadequate information about problems and they face environmental forces that they cannot control.

    3.   Implications of the bounded rationality model.

        a.   It provides insights into the limitations of organizational decision making.

        b.   It recognizes the potential for ethical dilemmas in decision making, but offers no guidance on how to resolve them.

D.   The political model of decision making.

    1.   The <u>political model</u> suggests that organizational decisions reflect the desire of individuals to satisfy their own interests.

    2.   In the political model, all aspects of the decision making process are merely methods to tilt decision outcomes in someone's favor.

    3.   Decision outcomes are affected by the distribution of power in the organization and the effectiveness of the tactics used by participants in the decision-making process.

    4.   While the political model doesn't explicitly consider ethical dilemmas, it does draw on some of the principles of behavior that were identified in Transparency 18.3. These are the hedonistic principle, the might-equals-right principle, and the conventionalist principle—all of which relate to making self-serving decisions.

ENRICHMENT MODULE: HOW CAN CUSTOMERS AFFECT ORGANIZATIONAL DECISION MAKING?

Focusing on the customers has almost become a "religion" in many companies—and probably rightfully so. Customers can have significant effects on how an organization operates, including its decision-making processes.

How can customers influence an organization's decision making? Answer—they can be good consumers! Experts suggest that consumers should use the following five strategies to get the service they deserve:

- They should vote with their feet if they don't get good service.
- They should ignore advertising about the quality of customer service.
- They should listen to their friends' recommendations.
- They should get an ally within the organization (*e.g.,* customer service agents or customer advocates).
- They should complain if they are not satisfied with quality of customer service, even if the complaint is only about something small.

Not only can consumers can use these five strategies to get better service, but in the process they may have some significant impact on organizational decision making. New problems may be identified. Problems may be interpreted differently. New courses of action may be identified and initiated.

The consumer strategies that are identified in this enrichment module are based on:

Davis, K. (1992, February). How to get the service you deserve. *Kiplinger's Personal Finance Magazine,* 47-51.

IV.   Phases of managerial decision making.

    A.   <u>Managerial decision making</u> is a multi-phase process that begins with a recognition or awareness of problems and concludes with an assessment of the results of actions taken to solve those problems.

    B.   As depicted in Transparency 18.6, the phases of managerial decision making are: problem recognition, problem interpretation, attention to problems, courses of action, and aftermath.

TRANSPARENCY 18.6
(FIGURE 18.2 IN THE TEXTBOOK)

PHASES OF MANAGERIAL DECISION MAKING

    C.   Problem recognition.

        1.   Previous decisions and decision-making experiences, new information, and individual problem-solving styles may influence whether a manager recognizes a problem.

        2.   <u>Structured problems</u> have clear-cut decision parameters which make problem

recognition straight-forward.

3.   <u>Unstructured problems</u> have ambiguous decision parameters which create difficulty in actually recognizing the problem.

4.   The recognition of a problem usually triggers activities that may either lead to a quick solution or be part of a long, drawn-out process.

5.   Major disasters or accidents often occur because a number of events signaling danger have been unrecognized or misinterpreted and have accumulated over time.

6.   The likelihood of incorrect problem recognition and formulation can be increased when (see Transparency 18.7):

TRANSPARENCY 18.7
(FROM TEXT MATERIAL IN THE TEXTBOOK)

PROBLEMS WITH PROBLEM RECOGNITION AND FORMULATION

---

a.   Someone else gives you a problem they have defined.

b.   A quick solution is desired.

c.   A low-quality solution is acceptable.

d.   The problem seems familiar.

e.   Emotions are high.

f.   People do not have previous experience in challenging problem definitions.

g.   The problem is complex.

**ENRICHMENT MODULE: THE PROSPECTS OF A PAPERLESS SOCIETY—
IMPENDING DOOM OR CREATIVE OPPORTUNITY**

Once a problem has been recognized, it must be interpreted or given meaning and definition. The following account describes how one decision maker interpreted the problem (or challenge) facing his company.

Faced with predictions of a paperless society, R.R. Donnelley & Sons, the world's largest commercial printer, chose to interpret the problem differently. Donnelley, under the leadership of John Walter, has interpreted the prospect of a paperless society in a beneficial way. According to Mr. Walter, "Donnelley isn't primarily in the business of slapping ink on paper. Rather, it's in the business of delivering information from publishers to consumers in many different forms." These forms could include traditional high-volume, mass printing; low-volume customized printing; compact disks; data bases; and so forth. In short, any potential threat to Donnelley's traditional printing business is being blunted, in part, through a creative interpretation and definition of the prospective impact of a paperless society.

This enrichment module is based on:

Samuels, G. (1994, May 9). Covering the bases. *Forbes*, 44-45.

D.   Problem interpretation.

1.   Problem interpretation refers to the process of giving meaning and definition to problems that have been recognized.

2.   A manager may choose to not act on a problem when he or she:

a.   Has to deal with too many high-priority problems

b.   Believes the problem will go away with time.

c.   Believes that attempting to do something about the problem will only worsen the situation.

3.   Six types of biases can affect problem interpretation (see Transparency 18.8).

**TRANSPARENCY 18.8
(FROM TEXT MATERIAL IN THE TEXTBOOK)**

BIASES THAT CAN AFFECT PROBLEM INTERPRETATION

---

a.   Risk propensity is the general tendency of the decision maker to take or avoid risks.

(1)   Risk avoiders focus on potential negative outcomes and tend to overestimate the probability of loss relative to the probability of gain.

(2)   Risk avoiders focus on potential positive outcomes and tend to overestimate the probability of gain relative to the probability of loss.

b. <u>Problem framing</u> refers to whether a situation is presented or viewed in positive or negative terms.

    (1)   When a situation is presented in favorable terms, people tend to be more risk averse because they believe they have more to lose.

    (2)   When a situation is presented in unfavorable terms, people tend to be risk seeking because they believe they have little to lose.

c. The <u>availability bias</u> refers to the tendency to recall specific instances of an event and therefore overestimating how often such an event occurs (or failing to recall specific instances of an event and underestimating how frequently it occurs).

d. The <u>confirmation bias</u> refers to the natural tendency to seek support for an initial view of a situation rather than to look for disconfirming evidence.

e. The <u>selective perception bias</u> refers to the tendency to see what a person expects to see.

f. The <u>law of small numbers bias</u> refers to the tendency to consider small samples as representative of the larger population, even when they are not.

    (1)   A related bias concerns occupational specialization, which can create tunnel vision.

E. Attention to problems.

1. After problems have been recognized and interpreted, judgments need to be made regarding which problems will receive attention, how much, and in what order.

2. Problems receiving the greatest attention are likely to:

a. Be supported by strong external pressure.

b. Be supported by the necessary resources to take action.

c. Represent an irresistible opportunity.

3. The number and variety of recognized problems needing attention almost always exceed the manager's capacity for addressing and solving all of them within the desired time frame.

F. Courses of action.

1. The development and evaluation of courses of action (alternatives) and the implementation of the selected alternative can range from a *quick-action process* to a *convoluted-action process.*

2. A quick-action process is appropriate when (see Transparency 18.9):

a. The nature of the problem is well structured.

b.   A single manager is clearly recognized as having the authority and responsibility to solve the problem.

c.   The search for information about the problem and alternatives is quite limited.

3.   A convoluted-action process is appropriate when (see Transparency 18.9):

a.   The problem is unstructured.

b.   A long period of time is required.

c.   Many vested interests and power relationships are involved.

d.   Many people are involved in an extensive search for solutions.

TRANSPARENCY 18.9
(FROM TEXT MATERIAL IN THE TEXTBOOK)

CONDITIONS FOR USING QUICK-ACTION OR CONVOLUTED-ACTION PROCESSES

G.   Aftermath.

1.   The aftermath of the decision involves an evaluation of the results of the actions that were taken.

2.   With structured problems, the costs and benefits associated with the actions can be easily calculated.

3.   With unstructured problems, assessment of the action may be problematic because a considerable period of time may elapse before the outcomes are known and their consequences can be determined.

4.   As part of the aftermath, decision makers should learn both from successes that were achieved and any mistakes that were made.

5.   Sometimes escalating commitment will occur as part of the aftermath. Escalating commitment is a process of continuing or increasing the commitment of resources to a course of action, even though a substantial amount of feedback indicates that the action is wrong.

a.   People may escalate commitment to a course of action if they wish to justify previous decisions or they believe that consistency of action is desirable.

V.   Stimulating creativity.

A.   Organizational creativity and organizational innovation.

1.   Organizational creativity is the production of novel and useful ideas by an individual or team of individuals working together.

    2.   <u>Organizational innovation</u> is the implementation of creative and useful ideas through unplanned or planned organizational change.

B.   Creativity helps organization members to recognize problems, identify opportunities, and undertake novel courses of action to solve problems.

ENRICHMENT MODULE: THE LINKED CONCEPTS OF EMPOWERMENT AND CREATIVITY

Empowerment and creativity are related phenomena. Empowered and creative people share similar characteristics regarding their cognitive styles and behaviors. Both empowerment and creativity emphasize cognitive variables such as imagination, optimism, self-awareness, self-efficacy, etc.; and behavioral variables including independence, involvement, and persistence. The environments that enable empowerment and creativity are similar as well. For instance, trust, choice, information sharing, risk taking, etc. are defining environmental features for both.

To be beneficial for organizations, empowerment and creativity should be congruent. By failing to empower people, an organization can stifle creativity. Without creative people, the opportunities conferred by empowerment may not be recognized and/or developed. However, an organization can reap substantial benefits from empowering already creative people or using empowerment to help people become more creative.

This enrichment module is based on:

Velthouse, B.A. (1990, Fall). Creativity and empowerment: A complementary relationships. *Review of Business*, 13-18.

C.   Barriers to creative thought and innovative action include the following:

    1.   *Perceptual blocks*—the failure to use all the senses in observing, failure to investigate the obvious, difficulty in seeing remote relationships, and failure to distinguish between facets of cause-and-effect relationships.

    2.   *Cultural blocks*—a desire to conform to established norms, overemphasis on a particular style for handling conflict, the drive to be practical and to economize, and a disbelief in the value of open-ended exploration.

    3.   *Emotional blocks*—fear of making a mistake, fear and distrust of others, and latching on to the first idea that comes along.

**ENRICHMENT MODULE: BECOMING MORE CREATIVE—LEARNING TO THINK
LIKE CHILDREN RATHER THAN ADULTS**

As people grow older they often seem to lose the creative perspectives of their childhood. You don't believe this? Give most any adult a box, and that adult will tell you it's a box. Give the same box to a typical child and the child has a fort, a play house, a spaceship, a tunnel, a downhill racer, and so on.

Perhaps adults need to relearn how to see the world through the eyes of children; and in the process, they just might become more creative. Brian Honess, who knows a lot about the creative bent of children, suggests that adults can become more creative by using any one of seven techniques that work well in fostering creativity in children.

One of these techniques—alternative analysis—could be especially useful in developing creative solutions in the managerial decision making process. Alternative analysis is a three-step process. At the first step, all the attributes of a product or service are listed. Then at the second step, possible alternatives to each of the several product or service attributes are listed in a column format—one column of alternatives for each of the original attributes. At the third step, a new product or service is created by selecting one alternative from each of the columns.

This enrichment module is based on:

Honess, C.B. (1993, January-March). Kids are us. *B&E Review*, 14-18.

    D.   Methods for stimulating creativity.

          1.   Lateral thinking method.

                a.   The <u>lateral thinking method</u> is a deliberate process for the generation of new ideas through a change in the individual's or team's typical logical pattern for processing and storing information.

                b.   In contrast, the <u>vertical thinking method</u> is the logical step-by-step process of developing ideas by proceeding on a continuous path from one bit of information to the next.

                c.   Transparency 18.10 summarizes the major differences between lateral thinking and vertical thinking.

**TRANSPARENCY 18.10
(TABLE 18.4 IN THE TEXTBOOK)**

CHARACTERISTICS OF LATERAL VERSUS VERTICAL THINKING

---

                d.   Lateral thinking and vertical thinking are complementary, not contradictory. Lateral thinking is useful for generating ideas and vertical thinking is useful for developing them.

                e.   Four lateral thinking techniques can be used to help develop new ideas (see Transparency 18.11).

TRANSPARENCY 18.11
(FROM TEXT MATERIAL IN THE TEXTBOOK)

USEFUL LATERAL THINKING TECHNIQUES

---

(1)   The *reversal technique* allows new ideas to be suggested by examining the current problem and turning it completely around, inside out, or upside down.

(2)   The *cross-fertilization technique* involves asking experts from other disciplines (preferably far afield from the problem) to view the problem and suggest methods for solving it from their own areas.

(3)   The *analogy technique* involves translating the problem into an analogy, refining and developing the analogy, and then retranslating to the problem to judge the suitability of the analogy.

(4)   The *random-word stimulation technique* involves selecting a word from a dictionary or specially prepared word list, and then seeking to discover a link between the word and the problem.

2.   Devil's advocate method.

a.   The <u>devil's advocate method</u> calls for a person or small task force to develop a systematic critique of a recommended course of action.

b.   Transparency 18.12 illustrates how the decision-making process works when the devil's advocate method is used.

TRANSPARENCY 18.12
(FIGURE 18.3 IN THE TEXTBOOK)

DECISION MAKING WITH A DEVIL'S ADVOCATE

---

c.   Benefits of the devil's advocate method.

(1)   The organization avoids costly mistakes by hearing viewpoints that identify potential pitfalls.

(2)   The probability of groupthink may be reduced and the probability of creative solutions to problems may be increased.

VI.   Summing up: Why is decision making important in understanding and managing organizational behavior?

A.   Decision making is important for understanding and managing organizational behavior because much of what mangers do revolves around making decisions. Their decisions can positively or negatively affect individuals, groups, and other organizations; consequently, effective managerial decision making must consider relevant ethical implications. Every decision cannot be made in the same way; different decision problems may call for different approaches. The effective decision maker should be knowledgeable about and capable of using different decision-making approaches or models. Effective decision makers also should be knowledgeable about the steps or phases they go through in making a decision, and they should try to make each phase contribute as much as possible to making an effective decision. Effective decision-making also hinges upon the decision makers' ability to be creative in identifying and interpreting problems and in developing solutions to those problems.

DISCUSSION QUESTIONS: SUGGESTED ANSWERS

1.   *Think of an issue that created an ethical dilemma for you. How would you evaluate this dilemma in terms of each of the six components of ethical intensity?*

The six ethical intensity components are:

a.   *Magnitude of the consequences*—which involves the total harm or benefits that occur for the individuals who are affected by the ethical issue.

b.   The *probability of effect*—which is the joint result of the probability that the decision will be implemented and that it will cause the harm or benefit predicted.

c.   *Social consensus*—which is the degree of public agreement that a proposed decision is evil or good.

d.   *Temporal immediacy*—which concerns the amount of time until the onset of the consequences of the decision.

e.   *Proximity*—which involves the feeling of nearness (social, cultural, psychological, or physical) that the decision maker has for victims or beneficiaries of the decision.

f.   *Concentration of effect*—which is an inverse function of the number of people affected by the decision.

The students should describe their example ethical dilemmas in sufficient detail to permit analysis in terms of the six components of ethical intensity. This discussion can then be used as a lead-in to question 2.

2.   *Of the six ethical intensity components, which two are likely to be the most important in the majority of situations? Explain.*

Because individuals place different values on the six ethical intensity components, there isn't a stock answer about which components are most important. The components that are perceived to be most important will vary across the students. The discussion should explore why the students rate the components as they do.

3.   *What are the similarities and differences between the distributive justice principle and utilitarianism?*

The distributive justice principle means that treating individuals differently should not be based on arbitrarily defined characteristics. Employees who are similar in relevant respects should be treated similarly and those who are different in relevant respects should be treated differently in proportion to their differences. Utilitarianism emphasizes the provision of the greatest good for the greatest number in judging the ethics of decision making.

Both principles are similar in terms of emphasizing fair treatment. However, they differ with regard to focus of fair treatment. With the distributive justice principle the focus is on the individual. With utilitarianism, the focus is on the group level, at minimum.

4. *Rearrange the ethical principles in Table 18.2 in rank order from your most-preferred to least-preferred principle. What does this ranking tell you about how you are likely to interpret situations involving ethical dilemmas?*

The current ordering of the ethical principles in Table 18.2 is from most self-serving (item number 1) to greatest consideration of others' rights and costs (item number 12). Reordering these from most-preferred to least-preferred should provide the students with some insight regarding how self-serving or considerate of others they are. Part of the discussion should focus on the attributions people make when others engage in self-serving versus altruistic behavior.

5. *What are the three potential ethical dilemmas that managers may experience when conducting performance appraisals?*

The process and content of performance appraisal has implications for:

    a. The individual's sense of self-esteem.
    b. The economic rewards that the organization is able and willing to make available to the individual.
    c. The individual's current and long-term potential in the organization.

Each of these areas can present ethical dilemmas as managers grapple with what is appropriate and what is inappropriate in appraising people's performance. What is perceived to be right or wrong will be influenced by attributions, perceptions, and perceptual biases.

6. *At which managerial level—first-line, middle, and top—is a manager most likely to use each of the decision-making models (rational model, bounded rationality model, and political model)?*

All three models may be used at each managerial level, but the degree of emphasis may differ. One rationale for differing degrees of emphasis concerns the occurrence of programmed and nonprogrammed decisions. Programmed decisions occur with a decreasing frequency and nonprogrammed decisions occur with an increasing frequency as one ascends the management hierarchy, and vice versa. First-line supervisors, who make mostly programmed decisions, are more likely to emphasize the rational model. Middle managers, who encounter a mixture of programmed and nonprogrammed decisions, probably will use the bounded rationality model most frequently. Top managers, who deal mostly with nonprogrammed decisions, probably will rely more heavily on the political model.

7. *How is the decision-making process for professionals likely to differ from that of nonprofessional employees?*

In general, professional employees are more likely to have a central role in the problem recognition and problem interpretation phases of decision making. Moreover, professionals are more likely to set the agenda regarding which problems will receive attention from nonprofessional employees. Nonprofessional employees will generally give attention to those problems that have been recognized, at least partially interpreted, and assigned priorities by professionals.

8.   *What are the most common problems in achieving effective problem recognition?*

The most common impediments to effective problem recognition are the following:

  a.   Someone else gives you a problem they have defined.
  b.   A quick solution is desired.
  c.   A low-quality solution is acceptable.
  d.   The problem seems familiar.
  e.   Emotions are high.
  f.   People do not have previous experience in challenging problem definitions.
  g.   The problem is complex.

9.   *How might creativity help employees who experience difficulties in problem identification and interpretation?*

Difficulties in problem identification and interpretation may result from people inappropriately using habitual patterns of thinking. Individuals may tend to recognize only those problems that are familiar. Or they may interpret most, if not all, problems in a familiar way. Creativity can help employees break these habitual patterns of thinking by getting people to approach problem situations in novel ways.

10.   *What are two differences between the lateral thinking method and the devil's advocate method?*

A good way to approach this question is to use the six characteristics of lateral thinking presented in Table 18.4 of the text as a basis of comparison with the devil's advocate method. In using lateral thinking, the decision maker characteristically:

  a.   Tries to find new ways for looking at things, and is concerned with change and movement.
  b.   Avoids looking for what is "right" or "wrong," and instead tries to find what is different.
  c.   Analyzes ideas to determine how they might be used to generate new ideas.
  d.   Attempts to introduce discontinuity by making "illogical" (free association) jumps from one step to another.
  e.   Welcomes chance intrusions of information to use in generating new ideas; considers the irrelevant.
  f.   Progresses by avoiding the obvious.

The devil's advocate method—which calls for a systematic critique of a recommended course of action—differs particularly with respect to items b, d, and f. The devil's advocate method does look for right and wrong in developing a critique. The method also is intended to progress logically, not with illogical jumps. A systematic critique looks at the obvious as well as nonobvious, avoiding neither one.

DEVELOPING SKILLS—
SELF DIAGNOSIS: INDIVIDUAL ETHICS PROFILE

The Individual Ethics Profile (IEP) is designed to measure a person's preference among three major ethical concepts: utilitarianism, moral rights, and justice. Utilitarianism refers to the greatest good for the greatest number. The moral rights concept is based on the idea that an individual's personal rights must not be violated. The justice concept suggests that benefits and burdens should be allocated fairly.

To determine preferences among the three ethical concepts, students react to twelve pairs of statements. The students indicate which statement out of each pair they agree with most. Or if they don't really agree with either statement in the pair, they indicate which statement they disagree with the least. Instructions are provided for scoring the instrument, and the students should be cautioned to follow them carefully. The results provide a numerical rating of the strength of an individual's preferences for each of the ethical perspectives.

DEVELOPING SKILLS—
A CASE IN POINT: OLSON MEDICAL SYSTEMS

CASE OVERVIEW

This case describes a portion of the monthly meeting of the executive team at Olson Medical Systems, a producer and distributor of computer-based financial systems for hospitals and nursing homes throughout the United States. The participants in the meeting include T.G. Olson, the founder and CEO, and executives from marketing, operations, systems development, finance/accounting, and systems analysis. The monthly meetings focus on plans, problems, and opportunities for the company.

The case provides detailed dialogue of the discussion of one agenda item at a recent meeting. The agenda item concerned maintenance contracts. The discussion focused on various issues associated with maintenance contracts for the company's Medicalc software package. Many different problem perspectives were brought out during the discussion. These various perspectives are identified in the suggested answer to case question 1.

CASE QUESTIONS

1. *What problem statements were offered (explicitly or implicitly) during this meeting?*

    The following list identifies the implicit and explicit problem statements:

a.	Remaining a successful organization.
b.	Getting a good return on investment for software maintenance contracts.
c.	Determining how much to increase the price of maintenance contracts.
d.	Not losing business.
e.	Making fewer software changes.
f.	Replacing Stan Freedson.
g.	Better marketing of the maintenance agreements.
h.	Determining how to sell service contracts.
i.	Finding out more about client's needs.

j.   Determining the cost of keeping the software current.
k.   Finding out projected changes in the schedules for the next couple of years.

2.   *How are these statements related to each other (i.e., which statements are the means of solving others)?*

The interrelationships of the above problem statements may be summarized as follows:

- *Finding out more about the client's needs* provides the means for *better marketing of the maintenance agreements* and *determining how to sell service contracts*, which in turn provide the means for *not losing business*. In other words, solving item I leads to solving G and H, both of which lead to solving D.
- *Replacing Stan Freedson* leads to *making fewer software changes*, which in turn leads to *getting a good return on investment for the software maintenance contracts*. Item F leads to E, then E leads to B.
- *Finding out the projected changes in the schedules for the next couple of years* leads to *determining the cost of keeping the software current*, which leads to *determining how much to increase the price of maintenance contracts*, which in turn leads to *getting a good return on investment for software maintenance contracts*. Item K leads to J, J leads to C, and C leads to B.
- Both *not losing business* and *getting a good return on investment for software maintenance contracts* provide the means for *remaining a successful organization*. Items B and D lead to A.

3.   *What different purposes do problem statements serve (e.g., to keep people involved in the process, to avoid blame, etc.)? For what purposes were the statements offered in this case, in your opinion?*

Problem statements are offered for many reasons. Some of the purposes include the following: to serve as a starting point, to narrow the problem (*i.e.*, to make it more manageable), to identify allies, to keep people involved in the process, to rearrange priorities, to generate solutions, to obscure or eliminate certain solutions, to suggest causal relationships, to protect someone's turf, and so forth. Generally, these purposes relate to managing the decision making process, promoting group outcomes, and/or serving self-interests.

With regard to the case, determining the purpose(s) behind the various statements can be quite difficult without some knowledge of the people involved. At best, speculative observations can be offered. For example, self-interest might play a role, or some of the individuals may simply be doing a credible job of representing their area of expertise. In discussing possible purposes, the students should be asked to logically justify their speculations.

4.   *What other problem perspectives can you think of that might be useful to this team?*

Other problem perspectives that might be useful include:

a.   How to maintain goodwill with clients.
b.   How to reduce the cost of software maintenance.
c.   How to get out of the software maintenance business.
d.   How to compete with other software companies.
e.   How to remain solvent.

5. *Which model of decision making (i.e., rational, bounded rationality, or political) best describes the decision-making process in this case? Explain and justify your answer.*

To answer this question, the students should look first to the definitional basis of each decision-making model and then compare the case facts to the definitional elements.

The rational model holds that decision making involves intentionally choosing among alternatives to maximize benefits to the organization. The rational model assumes the availability of complete information and the objective ranking of alternatives. Neither assumption characterizes the decision-making process at Olson Medical Systems; therefore, the rational model does not provide a good description of their decision-making process.

The bounded rationality model of decision making recognizes the limitations of the individual's rationality and reveals the day-to-day decision-making processes used by individuals. With this model, people tend to make satisficing decisions, conduct a limited search for possible solutions, and often have inadequate information or face environmental forces that they cannot control. The case evidence suggests that all these conditions were present, at least to a moderate extent; therefore, the bounded rationality model provides a credible description of Olson Medical System's decision-making process.

The political model of decision making suggests that organizational decisions reflect the desire of individuals to satisfy their own interests. In the political model, all aspects of the decision making process are merely methods to tilt decision outcomes in someone's favor. Further, decision outcomes are affected by both the distribution of power in the organization and the effectiveness of the decision participants' tactics. There is little evidence to support the use of power to influence decision outcomes, nor does the evidence strongly suggest that the decision-making process was being manipulated in any substantial way to tilt the outcome in someone's favor. Thus, little evidence exists to support characterizing Olson Medical Systems' organizational decision making as political.

COURSE ENHANCEMENT—
WEST'S ORGANIZATIONAL BEHAVIOR CUSTOM VIDEO SERIES

None of the videos from *West's Organizational Behavior Custom Video Series* are appropriate for use with the material in Chapter 18.

COURSE ENHANCEMENT—
SUPPLEMENTAL VIDEOS AVAILABLE FROM WEST

A PBS Video that is available through West Publishing Company can be used to enhance the material in Chapter 18. This video is: *Ethics and Work with Joanne Ciulla.*

VIDEO: *PBS: ETHICS AND WORK WITH JOANNE CIULLA*

Approximate Time: 30 minutes

Video Summary:

In this video, Bill Moyers, a Public Broadcasting System reporter, interviews Joanne Ciulla, a business professor at the Wharton School. The discussion topic focuses on ethics in business.

According to Professor Ciulla, ethics became an important and popular topic when American businesses began losing their competitive edge. In order to regain their competitive advantage, and to do so quickly, businesses often took on a "short-term-boom-town" atmosphere. Moyers adds the clichés of "rules are for fools," "greed is good," and "he who dies with the most toys, wins" to further characterize this short-term orientation.

Professor Ciulla argues that businesses must build a "sustainable" competitive advantage if they are going to survive and be successful. She further suggests that in developing a sustainable competitive advantage, companies must grapple with relevant ethical issues.

One example of relevant ethical issues concerns the global economy and the differing business practices throughout the world. Business practices in one country can influence those in other countries. Interpretations of business practices in other countries may differ from those in the U.S. (*e.g.*, insider trading in Hong Kong is different than in the U.S.); consequently, ethics may be violated inadvertently. Professor Ciulla suggests that global norms are necessary.

Ciulla also points out that companies expect employees to be loyal, yet employees don't really trust companies. She questions whether the expectation of company loyalty is ethical when mergers, acquisitions, and downsizing are undermining the trust employees place in organizations.

Ciulla believes that a moral crisis is developing between people's work lives and nonwork lives. She argues that people want meaningful work, wealth, and leisure. Ciulla questions the ethics of people sacrificing their nonwork lives for their work lives.

She also contends that ethical issues are a source of stress. An individual has one set of values and beliefs but sees them violated at work, which results in stress. Inequity at work causes stress as well, and Ciulla questions whether inequity/injustice at work should be considered to be unethical. Ciulla also wonders about the ethics of making work more meaningful as opposed to more comfortable.

Discussion Questions and Suggested Answers for Video:

1.   *What ethical issues does Professor Ciulla raise?*

The ethical issues raised by Professor Ciulla include the following:

a.   Since business practices are interpreted differently in different countries, should a set of global norms be developed?

b.   Can businesses really act ethically for the sake of ethics? Or are ethical actions merely avenues to enhanced profitability?

c.   In terms of trust and loyalty, should there be a reciprocal relationship between the company and its employees?

d.   Is there any moral crisis involved in people trying to strike a balance between their work and nonwork lives?

f.   What, if anything, should businesses do to avoid violating the personal moral values of its employees?

g.   What are the ethical implications of inequity and injustice in the workplace?

h.   What can (or should) businesses do to make things better for their employees?

2.   *In your opinion, how should business organizations deal with these ethical issues?*

This question should generate an interesting and lively discussion. However, the key to gaining insight from the discussion is to have the students explore the reasons behind their statements regarding how organizations should deal with these issues. Additionally, the students should be encouraged to consider the likely consequences of their recommended actions.

CHAPTER 19
NATURE OF PLANNED ORGANIZATIONAL CHANGE

CHAPTER OVERVIEW

Chapter 19 introduces the discussion of change processes in Part IV of the textbook. In particular, Chapter 19 focuses on the nature of planned organizational change. First, planned organizational change is defined and its goals are described. Next, four dramatic pressures for organizational change are explored. These pressures include globalization, information technology and computers, the changing nature of management, and the changing nature of the work force. The phenomenon of resistance to change is explained, with consideration being given to overt and covert resistance, the various sources of resistance, and how to overcome resistance. The various sources of resistance include six individual sources (*i.e.*, perceptions, personality, habit, threats to power and influence, fear of the unknown, and economic reasons) and five organizational sources (*i.e,* organization design, organizational culture, resource limitations, fixed investments, and interorganizational agreements). Overcoming resistance to change is examined in the context of force field analysis. Next, organizational diagnosis is discussed, with emphasis on the basic steps in the diagnostic process, the need to assess readiness for change, and principles of organizational change. Finally, the chapter explains four approaches for diagnosing and initiating planned organizational changes. These approaches are: the systems approach, the innovation approach, the action research approach, and the organization development approach.

LEARNING OBJECTIVES

Upon completion of this chapter, the students should be able to:

1. Identify the goals of planned organizational change.
2. Discuss the "revolutions" that are creating pressures on organizations to change.
3. Describe individual and organizational resistance to change.
4. Diagnose the pressures for and resistance to change in a work setting.
5. Provide suggestions for overcoming resistance to change.
6. Explain the importance of an accurate diagnosis of organizational functioning and problems.
7. Describe some general models or approaches for organizational change.

CHAPTER OUTLINE

I.   **Preview Case:** Managing in the Midst of Chaos

II.   Goals of Planned Change

    A.   Improving Organizational Adaptability
    B.   Changing Individual Behaviors

III. Pressures for Change

    A.   Globalization
    B.   **Managing Across Cultures:** Arvin Industries
    C.   Information Technology and Computers
    D.   Changing Nature of Management
    E.   **Managing Quality:** The Non-manager Managers
    F.   Changing Nature of the Work Force
    G.   **Managing Across Cultures:** 12,000 World Managers View Change

IV.   Resistance to Change

    A.   Individual Resistance to Change
    B.   **Managing Diversity:** Ineffective Training Increases Resistance
    C.   Organizational Resistance to Change
    D.   Overcoming Resistance to Change
    E.   **Managing Ethics:** Overcoming Resistance to Integrity

V.   Organizational Diagnosis

    A.   **Managing in Practice:** The Chairman's Rice Pudding
    B.   Readiness for Change
    C.   Principles of Change

VI.   Changing Organizations

    A.   A Systems Approach to Change
    B.   Innovation
    C.   **Managing in Practice:** The Nuts and Bolts of Innovation
    D.   Action Research
    E.   Organization Development

VII. Developing Skills

    A.   **Self Diagnosis:** Rate Your Readiness for Change
    B.   **A Case in Point:** Planned Change at the Piedmont Corporation

KEY WORDS AND CONCEPTS

Twenty-six key words and concepts are introduced in Chapter 19. Two of these concepts were introduced in earlier chapters. Information technology appeared in Chapter 9 and innovation was introduced in Chapter 18 as organizational innovation. The key words and concepts, along with definitions or appropriate descriptions, are as follows:

Action research: a data-based, problem-solving process of organizational change that closely follows the steps involved in the scientific method.

Business revolutions: sudden radical and complete reorientations of the way business is done.

Computer-integrated manufacturing: a type of information technology that uses computer networks to link sales, production, and shipping.

Contingency work force: refers to part-time employees, free-lancers, subcontractors, and independent professionals hired by companies to cope with unexpected or temporary challenges.

Culture variable: a variable in the systems model of change that reflects the shared beliefs, values, expectations, and norms of organizational members.

Design variable: a variable in the systems model of change that refers to the formal organizational structure and its systems of communication, control, authority, and responsibility.

Electronic data interchange: a type of information technology that links an organization to its suppliers and customers electronically.

Force field analysis: suggests that any situation can be considered to be in a state of equilibrium resulting from a balance of forces constantly pushing against each other—that is, forces for change and forces for maintaining the status quo.

Globalization: business organizations are redesigning and internationalizing to compete effectively in both the domestic and international market places. Globalization results from the economic impact of Germany and Japan, the emergence of "newly industrialized" countries, the dramatic shift from planned economies to market economies occurring in the former communist block countries, and the emergence of new "power blocks" of international traders.

Information technology: comprises complex networks of computers, telecommunications systems, and remote-controlled devices.

Innovation: the initiation or adoption of new products, services, processes, procedures, or ideas by an organization.

Moving: the second step in the Lewinian model of change; this step shifts the behaviors of the organization or one of its subunits to a new level.

Organization development: a planned, systematic process of organizational change based on behavioral science research and theory.

Organizational diagnosis: refers to a multi-step process of: (1) recognizing and interpreting the problem and assessing the need for change; (2) determining the organization's readiness and capability for change; (3) identifying managerial and work-force resources and motivations for change; and (4) determining a change strategy and goals.

People variable: a variable in the systems model of change that applies to the individuals working for the organization, including their individual differences—personalities, attitudes, perceptions, attributions, problem-solving styles, needs, and motives.

Planned organizational change: the intentional attempt by managers and employees to improve the functioning of groups, teams, departments, divisions, or an entire organization in some important way.

Pressures for change: the dramatic forces that profoundly affect all organizations and societies.

Quality of work life: the degree to which people are able to satisfy important personal needs through their work.

Refreezing: the third step in the Lewinian model of change; this step stabilizes the organization at a new state of equilibrium.

Resistance to change: may be manifested overtly in strikes, reduced productivity, shoddy work, and even sabotage; or covertly in the forms of increased tardiness and absenteeism, requests for transfers, resignations, loss of motivation, lower morale, higher accident or error rates, or lack of participation when there is an opportunity to participate.

Strategy variable: a variable in the systems model of change that comprises the organization's planning process, including activities undertaken to identify appropriate goals and prepare specific plans to acquire, allocate, and use resources in order to accomplish those goals.

Systems model of change: describes the organization as six interacting variables that could serve as the focus of planned change: people, culture, task, technology, design, and strategy.

Task variable: a variable in the systems model of change that involves the nature of work itself—whether the job is simple or complex, novel or repetitive, standardized or unique.

Technology variable: a variable in the systems model of change that encompasses the problem-solving methods and techniques used and the application of knowledge to various organizational processes.

Unfreezing: the first step in the Lewinian model of change; this step usually involves reducing those forces maintaining the organization's behavior at its present level.

Virtual reality: a type of information technology that is created by a display and control technology that surrounds the user with an artificial environment that mimics real life.

LECTURE NOTES

I.   Chapter 19 introduces the discussion of change processes in Part IV of the textbook by focusing on the nature of planned organizational change. Chapter 19 addresses some important questions about planned organizational change, including the following: What is planned organizational change, and what are its goals? Why is there a need for planned organizational change? Do people and organizations resist change, and if so, how and why? Can resistance to change be overcome? How can the need for organizational change be determined? How can organizations be changed? These questions, along with the accompanying answers, are highlighted in Transparency 19.1.

TRANSPARENCY 19.1
(FROM TEXT MATERIAL IN THE TEXTBOOK)

KEY QUESTIONS AND ANSWERS ABOUT PLANNED ORGANIZATIONAL CHANGE

II. Goals of planned change.

    A. <u>Planned organizational change</u>—which is the focus of this chapter—represents the intentional attempt by managers and employees to improve the functioning of groups, teams, departments, divisions, or an entire organization in some important way.

    B. Organizations change in response to environmental pressures, and in some cases, in anticipation of them.

ENRICHMENT MODULE: HOW TWO COMPANIES REACTED TO THEIR ENVIRONMENTS

Motorola is known for having a corporate culture that anticipates and adapts to external environmental changes. Motorola has an "intelligence department" that scours conferences, journals, etc. for information on the latest technological developments. Then it develops detailed "technology road maps" that help in identifying likely technology breakthroughs, how and when those breakthroughs might be incorporated into new products, at what cost, and what the competition is doing.

Gillette Co., a manufacturer of shaving equipment, provides an example of what can happen when an organization does not pay attention to its external environment. When Wilkinson Sword Ltd. took a significant chunk of Gillette's market share with its introduction of the first coated stainless steel razor blade, Gillette learned some powerful lessons about its business environment. The lessons: "Never take a rival for granted, no matter how small. Don't concede market niches to competitors, because niches have a way of growing. And don't dally in bringing out new products for fear of cannibalizing old ones; if you don't bring them out, a competitor may."

This enrichment module is based on:

Hill, G.C., & Yamada, K. (1992, December 9). Staying power: Motorola illustrates how an aged giant can remain vibrant. *The Wall Street Journal*, A1 & A14.

Ingrassia, L. (1992, December 10). Keeping sharp: Gillette holds its edge by endlessly searching for a better shave. *The Wall Street Journal*, A1 & A6.

    C. Planned change efforts are based on two general objectives:

        1. Improving the capacity or ability of the organization to adapt to changes in its environment.

        2. Changing patterns of employee behaviors.

    D. Improving organizational adaptability.

        1. Traditionally, an organization's concern with change has by handled primarily, if

not solely, by specialized departments. In today's business environment, managing change is the concern of all parts of the organization. Transparency 19.2 provides an example of how basic business functions throughout the organization are changing in order to adapt to the environment.

TRANSPARENCY 19.2
(TABLE 19.1 IN THE TEXTBOOK)

CHANGES IN BASIC BUSINESS FUNCTIONS

E.   Changing individual behaviors.

　　1.   An organization may not be able to change its strategy for adapting to its environment unless its members behave differently in their relationships with one another and their jobs.

　　2.   Behavior should be a primary target for planned organizational change. Change programs must have an effect on employee roles, responsibilities, and working relationships.

III.   Pressures for change.

A.   Around the world, organizations are undergoing several <u>business revolutions</u>—sudden radical and complete reorientations of the way business is done.

　　1.   The revolutions include:

　　　　a.   The globalization of markets.

　　　　b.   The spread of information technology and computer networks.

　　　　c.   The dismantling of organizational hierarchies which fundamentally alters management's tasks.

　　　　d.   Changes in the nature of the work force.

　　2.   These revolutions result from <u>pressures for change</u>—the dramatic forces that profoundly affect all organizations and societies—in the same four domains.

B.   Globalization.

　　1.   The emergence of international and multinational corporations creates pressure on domestic corporations to redesign and internationalize their operations.

　　2.   The pressure of <u>globalization</u> results from:

　　　　a.   The economic recoveries of Germany and Japan after their defeat in World War II.

　　　　b.   The emergence of "newly industrialized" countries.

      c.   The dramatic shift from planned economies to market economies occurring in the former communist block countries.

      d.   The emergence of new "power blocks" of international traders, such as the economic unification of Europe and the Pacific Rim countries.

C.   Information technology and computers.

    1.   Information technology permits organizations to develop the flexibility that is needed to adapt to their environments.

    2.   Information technology (IT) comprises complex networks of computers, telecommunications systems, and remote-controlled devices.

      a.   Transparency 19.3 provides examples of information technologies that will be common in organizations of the future.

TRANSPARENCY 19.3
(TABLE 19.2 IN THE TEXTBOOK)

INFORMATION TECHNOLOGY OF THE FUTURE

---

      b.   Some of the cutting-edge information technologies include the following:

         (1)   Virtual reality is created by a display and control technology which surrounds the user with an artificial environment that mimics real life.

         (2)   Electronic data interchange (EDI) links an organization to its suppliers and customers electronically.

         (3)   A version of EDI, know as computer-integrated manufacturing (CIM), uses computer networks to link sales, production, and shipping. Transparency 19.4 provides an example of computer-integrated manufacturing.

TRANSPARENCY 19.4
(FIGURE 19.1 IN THE TEXTBOOK)

COMPUTER-INTEGRATED MANUFACTURING

D.   Changing nature of management.

    1.   As shown in Transparency 19.5, the roles and practices of managers are being reconceptualized in adaptive, flexible organizations.

TRANSPARENCY 19.5
(TABLE 19.3 IN THE TEXTBOOK)

CONTRAST BETWEEN OLD-STYLE AND NEW-STYLE MANAGERS

---

    2.   New style managers may still be relatively rare but corporate America is definitely moving in this direction.

  E.   Changing nature of the work force.

    1.   The following list identifies some the primary changes that are occurring in the work force (see Transparency 19.6).

TRANSPARENCY 19.6
(FROM TEXT MATERIAL IN THE TEXTBOOK)

PRIMARY CHANGES IN THE NATURE OF THE WORK FORCE

---

    a.   Increasing diversity in terms of gender and race.

    b.   Dual-career families are becoming the norm rather than the exception.

    c.   Continued growth in the <u>contingency work force</u>, which includes part-time employees, free-lancers, subcontractors, and independent professionals hired by companies to cope with unexpected or temporary challenges.

    d.   The work force is becoming better educated.

    e.   The work force is becoming less unionized.

    f.   The values and expectations of the work force are changing with respect to the rewards people seek from work and the balance they seek between work and other aspects of their lives.

        (1)   One manifestation of changing values and expectations is employees' concern with the <u>quality of work life</u>—the degree to which people are able to satisfy important personal needs through their work.

    g.   People's interorganizational and international mobility will increase.

    2.   Global organizations face similar changes in the nature of their work forces worldwide.

IV.   Resistance to change.

  A.   <u>Resistance to change</u> may be overt or covert.

    1.   Overt resistance to change may be manifested in strikes, reduced productivity, shoddy work, and even sabotage.

    2.   Covert resistance may occur in the forms of increased tardiness and absenteeism, requests for transfers, resignations, loss of motivation, lower morale, higher accident or error rates, or lack of participation when there is an opportunity to participate.

  B.   As shown in Transparency 19.7, the sources of resistance to change can be either individual or organizational in nature.

**TRANSPARENCY 19.7
(FIGURE 19.4 IN THE TEXTBOOK)
SOURCES OF RESISTANCE TO CHANGE**

---

1.   Six important sources of individual resistance to change.

   a.   *Perceptions*: this source of resistance includes perceptual defense (*i.e.*, people selectively perceiving those things that fit most comfortably with their current view of the world) and stereotyping (*i.e.*, characterizing people solely on the basis of some category to which they belong).

   b.   *Personality*: this source of resistance includes dogmatism (*i.e.*, the rigidity of a person's beliefs) and dependency on others.

      (1)   Personality is seldom the most important factor in individual resistance to change.

   c.   *Habit*: individuals tend to continue responding to stimuli in their accustomed ways.

   d.   *Threats to power and influence*: individuals or groups often resist changes that they perceive as reducing their power and influence.

   e.   *Fear of the unknown*: uncertainty about the nature of change or the potential consequences of change causes resistance.

   f.   *Economic reasons*: people resist changes which could threaten their economic security.

2.   Five important sources of organizational resistance to change.

   a.   *Organization design*: organizations need stability and continuity in order to function effectively, yet this legitimate need for structure may lead to resistance to change.

   b.   *Organizational culture*: ineffective organizational cultures inhibit adaptability and tend to rigidly socialize people to the existing culture even in the face of evidence that it no longer works.

   c.   *Resource limitations*: changes that could or should be made, may be deferred or abandoned because of insufficient capital, time, and/or skilled people.

   d.   *Fixed investments*: organizations may be unable to change because of investments in physical assets (*e.g.*, equipment, buildings, and land) or human assets (*e.g.*, unproductive employees with a great deal of seniority) that they can't easily alter.

   e.   *Interorganizational agreements*: agreements between organizations usually impose obligations on people that can restrain their behaviors.

ENRICHMENT MODULE: RESISTANCE TO CHANGE AT TENNECO

When Michael Walsh was hired as CEO of Tenneco after completing a corporate turnaround of the Union Pacific Railroad, he faced powerful forces resisting change. For years, Tenneco's profitable divisions subsidized its losing divisions, so there was little motivation to turn the losers into profit makers or to make the winners more profitable. The company produced products with little regard for what was actually being sold. There were stifling layers of management, wide spread acceptance of the status quo, and considerable cynicism about efforts to change.

Walsh initiated several actions to counter these forces for resisting change, including the following:

- He eliminated inefficiencies, like "the 179-mile routes that some parts used to travel inside factories."
- He eliminated a lot of the procedures that separate top management and lower-level employees.
- He set specific performance targets for which the responsible people were held accountable—and there was no tolerance for missing them.
- Rather than firing existing managers, he retained them but changed their roles. For example, divisional managers now had to operate in a group context where "they are encouraged to openly question and criticize one another's performances."
- He encouraged employee involvement at the lower levels of the organization as well. According to one rank and file worker, Tenneco's view of lower-level employees was "We hired you from the neck down." Now the worker says, "Walsh treats us like we have minds."

Walsh's efforts have enabled Tenneco to begin transforming itself into a more viable, competitive company.

This enrichment module is a useful supplement to the video on *Tenneco's Leadership and Planning Conference* which is described at the end of this chapter.

This enrichment module is based on:

Johnson, R. (1993, March 29). New blood: Tenneco hired a CEO from outside, and he is refocusing the firm. *The Wall Street Journal*, A1 & A14.

    C.   Overcoming resistance to change.

           1.   Force field analysis provides a useful way for understanding change. <u>Force field analysis</u> suggests that any situation can be considered to be in a state of equilibrium resulting from a balance of forces constantly pushing against each other—that is, forces for change and forces for maintaining the status quo. The various sources of resistance to change are forces for maintaining the status quo.

                        a.   The combined effects of the forces for change and resistance to change are depicted in Transparency 19.8.

TRANSPARENCY 19.8
(FIGURE 19.5 IN THE TEXTBOOK)

FORCE FIELD ANALYSIS

---

2. To initiate change, the current equilibrium of forces must be modified by doing one or more of the following:

   a. Increasing the strength of pressure for change.

   b. Reducing the strength of resisting forces or removing them completely.

   c. Changing a resistance into a pressure for change.

3. Benefits of force field analysis:

   a. By becoming skillful at diagnosing the forces pressing for and resisting change, individuals should have an improved understanding of the relevant aspects of any change situation.

   b. Force field analysis highlights the factors that can be changed and those that can't.

4. Based on force field analysis, change can be managed using a three-step process.

   a. Unfreezing usually involves reducing those forces maintaining the organization's behavior at its present level.

   b. Moving shifts the behaviors of the organization or one of its subunits to a new level.

   c. Refreezing stabilizes the organization at a new state of equilibrium.

5. Successful methods for overcoming resistance to change often include the following components:

   a. *Empathy and support* to aid in understanding how employees are experiencing change.

   b. *Communication* to reduce gossip and unfounded fears, thereby reducing uncertainty about the potential consequences of change.

   c. *Participation and involvement* to increase employee ownership of and commitment to the change.

ENRICHMENT MODULE: HOW OUTSIDERS OVERCOME RESISTANCE TO CHANGE
(*The Basis for a Class Debate*)

Sometimes an executive from outside the company (or even industry) is appointed as CEO with the expectation that she or he will initiate profound changes. Initiating change is not problem-free, and these executives sometimes encounter resistance. How they try to overcome resistance is an interesting study of influence tactics.

For example, Gerald Grinstein, CEO of the railroad carrier Burlington Northern, Inc., tried to overcome union resistance to changes the company wanted to make by building personal relationships with the workers. He rode with locomotive crews, visited repair shops, and provided personal financial assistance (*i.e.*, checks of $50 or $100) to employees with problems like family illnesses, house fires, etc.

Or consider the quite different approach used by Mr. Michael Armstrong, the CEO brought in to head Hughes Aircraft Co. Armstrong assured his top executives that he respected their talents and that he wanted them to remain as part of the management team. Then he gave the executives "a week to decide to join his efforts or else clear out their desks."

These two contrasting approaches for overcoming resistance to change could provide the basis for a stimulating class debate concerning the merits of different approaches to overcoming resistance to change.

This enrichment module is based on:

Cole, J. (1993, March 30). Gentle persuasion: New CEO at Hughes studied its managers, got them on his side. *The Wall Street Journal*, A1 & A8.

Machalaba, D. (1993, April 6). Learning curve: Burlington Northern shows risks of hiring an outsider as CEO. *The Wall Street Journal*, A1 & A4.

V.   Organizational diagnosis.

   A.   An accurate diagnosis of organizational problems is absolutely essential as a starting point for planned organizational change.

   B.   Four basic steps should be undertaken in <u>organizational diagnosis</u>:

      1.   Recognizing and interpreting the problem and assessing the need for change.

      2.   Determining the organization's readiness and capability for change.

      3.   Identifying managerial and work-force resources and motivations for change.

      4.   Determining a change strategy and goals.

   C.   Typically, diagnostic information is gathered using one or more of the following methods: questionnaires, interviews, observation, or the company's records.

   D.   Assessing readiness for change.

1.   Two important aspects of individual readiness for change are the degree of employee satisfaction with the status quo and the perceived personal risk from possible changes. Transparency 19.9 shows that when dissatisfaction with the current situation is high and the perceived personal risk is low, readiness for change will be high, and vice versa.

TRANSPARENCY 19.9
(FIGURE 19.6 IN THE TEXTBOOK)

EMPLOYEE READINESS FOR CHANGE

---

2.   Another important aspect of employees' readiness for change involves their expectations. Ideally, expectations regarding change should be positive yet realistic.

E.   Principles of change.

1.   Two crucial factors should be recognized when conducting an organizational diagnosis.

a.   Since organizational behavior is the product of many interacting forces, whatever is diagnosed has multiple causes and should be recognized as such. Otherwise, simplistic and ineffective change strategies might be implemented.

b.   Much of the diagnostic information that is generated will reflect symptoms rather than causes of problems. To be effective, change strategies must be focused on the causes of problems.

2.   Among other things, the following principles of organizational change, emphasize the importance of diagnosis (see Transparency 19.10).

TRANSPARENCY 19.10
(FROM TEXT MATERIAL IN THE TEXTBOOK)

PRINCIPLES OF ORGANIZATIONAL CHANGE

---

a.   You must understand something thoroughly before you try to change it.

b.   You cannot change just one element of a system.

c.   People resist anything they feel is punishment.

d.   People are reluctant to endure discomfort, even for the sake of possible gains.

e.   Change always generates stress.

f.   Participation in setting goals and devising strategies reduces resistance to change and increases commitment.

g.   Behavioral change comes in small steps.

VI.   Changing organizations.

    A.   Four of the most important and widely used approaches for diagnosing and initiating organizational change are: a systems approach, innovation, action research, and organizational development.

    B.   A systems approach to change.

        1.   The systems model of change describes the organization as six interacting variables that could serve as the focus of planned change: people, culture, task, technology, design, and strategy.

            a.   The people variable applies to the individuals working for the organization, including their individual differences—personalities, attitudes, perceptions, attributions, problem-solving styles, needs, and motives.

            b.   The culture variable reflects the shared beliefs, values, expectations, and norms of organizational members.

            c.   The task variable involves the nature of work itself—whether the job is simple or complex, novel or repetitive, standardized or unique.

            d.   The technology variable encompasses the problem-solving methods and techniques used and the application of knowledge to various organizational processes.

            e.   The design variable is the formal organizational structure and its systems of communication, control, authority, and responsibility.

            f.   The strategy variable comprises the organization's planning process, including activities undertaken to identify appropriate goals and prepare specific plans to acquire, allocate, and use resources in order to accomplish those goals.

        2.   The interdependent nature of the six variables in the systems model of change is illustrated in Transparency 19.11. A change in any one variable usually results in a change in one or more of the others. The model shown in this transparency also provides the conceptual framework for examining specific approaches and techniques of organizational change in Chapter 20.

TRANSPARENCY 19.11
(FIGURE 19.7 IN THE TEXTBOOK)

A SYSTEMS MODEL OF CHANGE

---

        3.   Implications of the systems model of change.

            a.   It helps managers and employees think through interrelationships among the six variables.

            b.   Organizational change can be introduced by altering these variables singly or in combination.

C.   Innovation as an approach to change.

    1.   <u>Innovation</u> is the initiation or adoption of new products, services, processes, procedures, or ideas by an organization.

    2.   While critics of U.S. industry cite numerous impediments to innovation (*e.g.,* an overemphasis on short-term profits, government regulation, reward structures that punish creativity and risk taking, etc.), the central issues appear to involve management philosophy, practices, and culture.

    3.   Organizations that are effective at innovation can be characterized as follows (see Transparency 19.12):

TRANSPARENCY 19.12
(FROM TEXT MATERIAL IN THE TEXTBOOK)
CHARACTERISTICS OF INNOVATIVE ORGANIZATIONS

---

    a.   The organization continuously "reinvents" itself and its products or services.

    b.   Innovation in work practices is as important as innovation in new product development and manufacture.

    c.   Innovation is everywhere in the organization, not just in research and development labs and research centers.

    d.   Organizations need to learn how to identify these many innovations and share them throughout the system.

    e.   Large numbers of employees must share a vision of the importance of innovation in order for change to occur and be disseminated throughout the organization.

    f.   Innovation, like everything else the organization does, must allow the organization to meet customer needs.

D.   Action research as an approach to change.

    1.   <u>Action research</u> is a data-based, problem-solving process of organizational change that closely follows the steps involved in the scientific method.

    2.   Action research consists of three essential steps:

        a.   Gathering information about problems, concerns, and needed changes from members of an organization.

        b.   Organizing this information in some meaningful way and sharing it with the employees involved in the change effort.

        c.   Planning and carrying out specific actions to correct identified problems.

3.   Action research is useful for two reasons:

  a.   The current situation in the organization is diagnosed carefully.

  b.   Employees are involved in the change process.

    (1)   People are more likely to implement and support a change they have helped create.

    (2)   Once managers and employees have identified the need for change and have widely shared this information, the need becomes difficult for people to ignore.

E.   Organization development as an approach to change.

  1.   <u>Organization development</u> (OD) is a planned, systematic process of organizational change based on behavioral science research and theory.

  2.   The goal of OD is to create adaptive organizations capable of repeatedly transforming and reinventing themselves as needed to remain effective.

  3.   OD is based on many of the concepts that were presented in preceding chapters of the textbook.

  4.   Certain characteristics distinguish OD from other approaches to organizational change, including the following (see Transparency 19.13):

TRANSPARENCY 19.13
(FROM TEXT MATERIAL IN THE TEXTBOOK)

DEFINING CHARACTERISTICS OF ORGANIZATION DEVELOPMENT

---

  a.   OD seeks to create self-directed change to which people are committed.

  b.   OD is a systemwide change effort.

  c.   OD typically places equal emphasis on solving immediate problems and the long-term development of an adaptive organization.

  d.   OD places more emphasis than other approaches on a collaborative process of data collection, diagnosis, and action for arriving at solutions to problems.

  e.   OD has a dual emphasis on organizational effectiveness and human fulfillment through the work experience.

VI.   Summing up: What are the organizational and managerial implications of planned change?

A.   Change in the business world is a pervasive phenomenon. The external business environment can change rapidly and dramatically. Organizations can adapt to these environmental changes by engaging in planned organizational change.

B.   Unfortunately, however, planned change may be resisted even though it is needed. Effective managers should be able to diagnose and deal with resistance to change so that the organization can effectively adapt to its environment. More fundamentally, effective managers need to overcome resistance to change in order to develop the employee behaviors which are necessary to support environmental adaptation.

C.   Effective managers also must be able to diagnose the need for organizational change and be able to either initiate appropriate changes or bring together the people who have the requisite competencies to implement needed changes.

DISCUSSION QUESTIONS: SUGGESTED ANSWERS

1.   *What are the basic objectives of planned organizational change? Which one seems most fundamental to you? Defend your answer.*

Planned change efforts have two basic objectives:

    a.   Improving the capacity or ability of the organization to adapt to changes in its environment.
    b.   Changing patterns of employee behaviors.

Changing patterns of employee behavior is the most fundamental objective because any planned organizational change program will be effective only to the extent that employee behaviors are changed so as to be congruent with and supportive of the planned change.

2.   *What are some of the external and internal pressures for change at your college or university? Explain. (You might consider funding, student life, curriculum development, or similar types of pressures.)*

A reasonable way to approach this question is by drawing on the chapter's discussion of different pressures for change. Each of the four types of pressures that were identified—globalization, information technology and computers, the changing nature of management, and the changing nature of the work force—could create pressure for change in higher education.

Globalization is creating pressure for higher education in terms of curriculum development, overseas study opportunities, and faculty competence. Increasingly, students in general, and business students in particular, need to have an understanding of and appreciation for people from different cultures. Successful competition in the global marketplace depends upon understanding different cultural practices, norms, etc. Not only must students be increasingly global in their thinking, but faculty must lead the way in the global orientation of higher education.

Information technology and computers places tremendous demands on students, faculty, and institutions to remain on the cutting edge of information in a field. Fortunately, information technology and computers facilitate getting on the cutting edge and remaining there. Information technology also influences how an education, or at least parts of it, can be delivered. Distance learning, which is made possible through sophisticated telecommunications technology, is one example. Another example is the use of the **Internet** to create student project teams composed of members from different universities around the nation or even around the world.

The changing nature of management can create pressure on curriculum development for business education. Students will need to have the requisite skills to begin functioning successfully in a different managerial world, and curricula will need to respond to those demands.

The changing nature of the work force may affect the recruiting process at many colleges and universities as well as the composition of students in the classroom. For example, the proportion of traditional to nontraditional students has had dramatic effects on when and where degree programs are offered, and even to some extent on the types of degree programs offered. The changing nature of the work force also has contributed to the demand for non-credit continuing education programs.

While a particular college or university may not be experiencing all of these pressures, they are suggestive of the examples students can develop in responding to this question.

3. *Identify the primary sources of individual resistance to change. Which have you had the most experience with? Describe a personal experience with individual resistance to change.*

There are six primary sources of individual resistance to change. These sources are: perceptions, personality factors, habit, threats to power and influence, fear of the unknown, and economic reasons. Most likely, the students will provide a variety of examples that illustrate most, if not all, of the sources of individual resistance.

4. *Identify the major sources of organizational resistance to change. Which have you had the most experience with? Describe a personal experience with organizational resistance to change.*

The five primary sources of organizational resistance to change are: organization design, organizational culture, resource limitations, fixed investments, and interorganizational agreements. Like question 3, the students will have a variety of responses, but it is less likely that all five organizational sources will be illustrated with student examples.

5. *Based on your own work experience, use force field analysis to analyze a situation that needed changing. Start by describing the setting and situation. What were the main pressures and resistances to change operating in the situation?*

The following conceptual background should be used in answering this question. Force field analysis is a useful diagnostic technique for examining situations needing or undergoing change. In any situation, pressures for change act in opposition to forces for maintaining the status quo. Force field analysis requires the diagnostician to fully analyze the current situation, determining those factors that can and cannot be changed. Change can be initiated by doing one or more of the following:

    a.   Increasing the strength of pressure for change.
    b.   Reducing the strength of resisting forces or removing them completely.
    c.   Changing a resistance into a pressure for change.

Based on this conceptual foundation, question 5 is designed to give students an opportunity to practice using the force field method of diagnosis. The students should provide sufficient detail in their examples so others can easily understand the nature of the forces at work in the situation.

6. *Use the three-step process of unfreezing, moving, and refreezing to describe some major behavioral change from your own experience.*

    In discussing their personal behavioral change experiences, the students should provide an appropriately detailed description of what happened during each of the three steps. These detailed descriptions should capture the following critical features of each step:

    a. Unfreezing occurs when the individual becomes aware that the existing behavioral pattern is no longer acceptable or no longer gets the job done.
    b. The moving phase then occurs as the individual learns a new behavioral pattern that is appropriate for the situation.
    c. Finally, the newly acquired behavioral pattern must be refrozen by being supported by the environment, friends, co-workers, and so forth.

7. *Based on your own work experience, analyze a change situation in terms of the readiness for change on the part of individuals involved.*

    Individuals' readiness for change is affected by the degree of their satisfaction with the status quo and the perceived personal risk from possible changes. Figure 19.6 of the text shows that when dissatisfaction with the current situation is high and the perceived personal risk is low, readiness for change will be high, and vice versa. Individuals' readiness for change also is influenced by their expectations. Ideally, expectations regarding change should be positive yet realistic.

    The students should analyze their example situations in light of the above material.

8. *What are six major systems variables that affect an organization's ability to change? Describe them and give an example to show how they are interrelated.*

    The six major variables in the systems model of change are: people, culture, task, technology, design, and strategy. The *people variable* applies to the individuals working for the organization, including their individual differences—personalities, attitudes, perceptions, attributions, problem-solving styles, needs, and motives. The *culture variable* reflects the shared beliefs, values, expectations, and norms of organizational members. The *task variable* involves the nature of work itself—whether the job is simple or complex, novel or repetitive, standardized or unique. The *technology variable* encompasses the problem-solving methods and techniques used and the application of knowledge to various organizational processes. The *design variable* is the formal organizational structure and its systems of communication, control, authority, and responsibility. The *strategy variable* comprises the organization's planning process, including activities undertaken to identify appropriate goals and prepare specific plans to acquire, allocate, and use resources in order to accomplish those goals.

    The interrelated nature of the six variables can be illustrated using Figure 19.7 in the text. Viewing the organization from the systems perspective means that a change in any one variable usually results in a change in one or more of the others. For example, a change in strategy could affect the culture that is needed to successfully implement the strategy, the type of design that the organization needs, the tasks to be performed, the technology needed to perform these tasks, and the types of skills people need to perform the tasks.

9. *Why might innovation be low in an organization? Explain why innovation is crucial in effective organizations.*

By their very nature, organizations tend to resist change and hamper innovation. Many critics of U.S. industry argue that the lack of innovation is a serious shortcoming in the face of increased global competition. The reasons for an inability to generate sufficient innovation include: (1) an overemphasis on short-term profits; (2) an unwillingness to invest due to the high cost of capital; (3) government regulation; (4) resistance to change; (5) rigid organizational design and procedures that stifle new ideas; (6) reward structures that punish creativity and risk taking; and (7) perhaps most importantly, problems that involve management philosophy, practices, and culture.

Organizations must innovate in order to adapt to changing environments. Without innovation, an organization probably will not be successful or remain competitive. Moreover, innovation is imperative for stability and growth.

10.   *What does the process of action research involve? Suggest a situation in which it might be used effectively.*

Action research is a data-based, problem-solving process of organizational change that closely follows the steps involved in the scientific method. The process of action research consists of three essential steps:

a.   Gathering information about problems, concerns, and needed changes from members of an organization.

b.   Organizing this information in some meaningful way and sharing it with the employees involved in the change effort.

c.   Planning and carrying out specific actions to correct identified problems.

Action research can be used effectively when:

a.   The current situation in the organization is diagnosed carefully.

b.   Employees are involved in the change process.

DEVELOPING SKILLS—
SELF DIAGNOSIS: RATE YOUR READINESS FOR CHANGE

This instrument enables students to determine the likelihood of change being successfully implemented in an organization where they currently work or used to work. The students rate their organizations on 10 dimensions that contribute to successful organizational change. These dimensions are: leadership, motivation, direction, customer focus, rewards, organizational structure, communication, prior change experience, morale, and decision making.

A three-point rating scale indicates the readiness of the organization for change: 1 = we're good at this; 2 = we could use some improvement on this; and 3 = we have a problem with this. The points assigned to the various dimensions are added to generate a readiness score. Readiness scores of 24-30 indicate that implementing change is likely to be successful. Scores of 17-23 suggest that change is possible, but may be difficult. Scores of 10-16 indicate that implementing meaningful change is unlikely.

DEVELOPING SKILLS—
A CASE IN POINT: PLANNED CHANGE AT THE PIEDMONT CORPORATION

CASE OVERVIEW

Piedmont Corporation, which produces and markets a variety of computer products for the global market, uses special task forces to develop, produce, and sell major new products. One new product in development is the Omega word processor. This case describes the efforts made by the Omega task force to deal with their lack of substantive progress in team meetings.

Being frustrated with the lack of progress, the team leader, Stan Ledford, contacted Sue Srebla, an internal organization development consultant for Piedmont. After hearing Ledford's view of the situation, Srebla proposed a team building intervention for the Omega task force. Ledford agreed to put the proposal on the agenda for the team's next meeting and asked Sue to attend to answer questions and to begin establishing relations with team members. A spirited discussion of the proposal occurred at the meeting, ending in its unanimous approval by the task force.

During the following week Sue interviewed each team member, seeking information in three major areas: things the team did well, things that impeded task performance, and suggestions for improvement. Sue briefed Stan on the interview results prior to the feedback meeting with the team so he would be prepared to lead the meeting and help group members address important issues. The feedback identified several strengths and weaknesses. The strengths were: the members' expertise, willingness to work hard, and fierce loyalty to the product. The impediments to team performance were: members' lack of input into the agenda for meetings, Stan's laissez-faire leadership style, and one or two members' domination of meetings. Team members engaged in an open discussion of the feedback and made several concrete suggestions for improvement. Subsequently, most of these suggestions were successfully implemented. Sue continued to work with the team on an occasional basis but they required her assistance with decreasing frequency.

CASE QUESTIONS

1. *Using the force field analysis techniques discussed in the chapter, analyze this case. Be specific about the pressures for change and the resistance to change that seem to be operating in this situation. Identify which types of pressure and resistance are likely to be the strongest.*

    The major pressures for change were: (a) the dissatisfaction of both Stan and the other team members with their task force meetings, and (b) their willingness to do something about this dissatisfaction. Other pressures for change could be the team's strengths—namely, the members' expertise, willingness to work hard, and fierce loyalty to the product. Essentially, the forces for maintaining the status quo were the following impediments to team performance: members' lack of input into the agenda for meetings, Stan's laissez-faire leadership style, and one or two members' domination of meetings.

    One or two member's domination of meetings may be the strongest resistance to change. However, this resistance can be more than overcome by the team's general level of dissatisfaction with their meetings and their motivation to have good task interactions among the members.

2. *Use the systems model of change to identify key variables that might be changed in order to increase the overall effectiveness of Piedmont Corporation.*

The systems model of change identifies people, culture, task, technology, design, and strategy as potential targets of change. Based on the case evidence, Piedmont clearly needs to focus on the people and perhaps the culture variable. Effective working relationships are extremely important to Piedmont's success. Improving these relationships will impact on the people variable and foster the cultural change that supports improved working relationships.

3.   *Describe the readiness for change that seems to be exhibited by individuals in this case.*

Both the team leader and the team members seem to be quite ready for change as is evidenced by how enthusiastically they embraced the team building effort. This observation also is supported by a more analytical approach to the situation. The text indicates that when dissatisfaction with the status quo is high and the perceived personal risk is low, readiness for change will be high, and vice versa. The case facts suggest that dissatisfaction with the team meetings is relatively high and that personal risk is relatively low. Also, the team members seem to have positive yet realistic expectations regarding the prospects of change. Therefore, the Omega task force should be ready for change.

4.   *Would you describe the change approach in use as action research? Why or why not?*

Action research is a data-based, problem-solving process of organizational change that closely follows the steps involved in the scientific method. The action research process consists of:

   a.   Gathering information about problems, concerns, and needed changes from members of an organization.
   b.   Organizing this information in some meaningful way and sharing it with the employees involved in the change effort.
   c.   Planning and carrying out specific actions to correct identified problems.

The change approach that was used with the Omega task force definitely could be described as an application of action research. Each of the three stages of action research took place, and in the prescribed order.

COURSE ENHANCEMENT—
WEST'S ORGANIZATIONAL BEHAVIOR CUSTOM VIDEO SERIES

One video from *West's Organizational Behavior Custom Video Series* can be used to enhance the material in Chapter 19. This video is: *Tenneco's Leadership and Planning Conference (Change Segments)*. There are three sequential segments to this video. The first segment runs for approximately seven minutes, the second segment for about 13 minutes, and the third segment for five minutes.

VIDEO: *TENNECO'S LEADERSHIP AND PLANNING CONFERENCE (CHANGE SEGMENTS)*

Approximate Time: 25 minutes

Video Summary:

The video contains three segments of Tenneco's Leadership and Planning Conference with the company's managers. This video was intended for viewing by the various levels of employees throughout Tenneco who were not among those attending the conference. The purpose of showing the video to employees throughout the company was to create readiness for and mobilize support for strategic change.

In segment 1, Mike Walsh, Tenneco's CEO, talks about the company's crisis response to external environmental changes. To adapt to its environment, Tenneco needs to institute an operating cost leadership strategy. Walsh explains that this is different from the crisis responses Tenneco was accustomed to. It would also be more difficult since Tenneco had no experience upon which to rely.

Segment 2 features Dana Mead, a top Walsh assistant, explaining how the operating cost leadership strategy will be implemented. He explains two matrices that illustrate the timing and interfacing of strategic reviews, capital reviews, budget reviews, human resource reviews, and risk management. In his closing remarks, Mr. Mead emphasizes the need for change by saying that the operating cost leadership strategy is not a voluntary choice; rather it is a management necessity if Tenneco is to continue to succeed. He admits the change process will be difficult when he says, "Incremental change may seem less painful but as Sears, IBM, GM, and Westinghouse can attest, the comfortable route isn't going to get us there. It is difficult but liberating; it is stressful but it is the way modern organizations succeed."

Segment 3 features Mike Walsh in a wrap-up session where he is attempting to rally the managers' support for embracing the operating cost leadership strategy. He points out that Tenneco's approach is different from other large corporations experiencing change. For example, rather than initiating change by replacing or eliminating operating managers, Tenneco elected to rely on existing managers in implementing the changes. Walsh also tries to mobilize support for the strategic change by emphasizing that the organization will help those in attendance to become better managers and leaders; that they must continue to get positive results if they are to retain their credibility; and that the outcomes for all will be self-satisfaction, security, opportunity, and fun.

Discussion Questions and Suggested Answers for Video:

1. *Using the Lewinian model of change, how would you explain the behavior of Mr. Walsh and Mr. Mead?*

   The Lewinian model of change is a three-step process of unfreezing, moving, and refreezing. Walsh and Mead were operating essentially in the unfreezing step. Unfreezing usually involves reducing those forces maintaining the organization's behavior at its present level. Walsh and Mead were trying to create a readiness for change and mobilize support for change. They did this by focusing on the environmental forces necessitating change, what the change would be like, and the organizational and personal consequences of successfully making the change as well as the consequences of failing to change or failing to change successfully.

2. *What individual sources of resistance to change were Walsh and Mead trying to overcome?*

   Six sources of individual resistance to change were identified in the text. These sources were: perceptions, certain personality characteristics, habit, threats to power and influence, fear of the unknown, and economic reasons. Most likely, Walsh and Mead were trying to overcome resistance from perceptions, habit, fear of the unknown, and economic reasons.

   Changing to an operating cost leadership strategy would require Tenneco to operate much differently than it previously had, and with no experience to draw on. Therefore, Walsh and Mead may have expected fear of the unknown to be a very dominant source of individual resistance to change. Additionally, the new strategy required that managers break old habits, and learn how to be better managers and leaders. Thus, habit could be a powerful source of resistance. Perceptions could also be an important source of resistance since the proposed strategic change and the methods of implementation were not only different from existing strategy and implementation methods but quite complex. Finally, Walsh's comments in the third segment can be linked to economic reasons for resistance to change. He emphasized the crucial need for positive results and the individual outcomes of self-satisfaction, security, opportunity, and fun that would be associated with success.

3.   *What organizational sources of resistance to change were Walsh and Mead trying to overcome?*

Five sources of organizational resistance to change were identified in the text. These were: organization design, organizational culture, resource limitations, fixed investments, and interorganizational agreements. Based on the evidence in the video, the most likely organizational source of resistance would be culture. Changing to an operating cost leadership strategy appears to be a drastic reorientation of Tenneco's strategy. The matrix design that would be used for implementing this strategy also represented a dramatic change. Both of these items point to culture. Recall from Chapter 14 that culture is developed through (a) external adaptation and survival, and (b) internal integration. Tenneco's switch to an operating cost leadership strategy reflects external adaptation and survival. Its methods for implementing that strategy are an example of internal integration.

CHAPTER 20
APPROACHES TO PLANNED ORGANIZATIONAL CHANGE

CHAPTER OVERVIEW

Chapter 20 continues the exploration of the topic of organizational change by focusing on the implementation of planned organizational changes. The chapter begins by examining the challenge of planned change. The need for adaptive, flexible organizations and for organizationwide change is considered. With appropriate emphasis on the necessity for a contingency perspective, the systems model of change that was developed in Chapter 19 is reintroduced to provide the structure for most the remainder of the chapter.

Using this systems model, the various methods for implementing planned organizational change are categorized according to people- and culture-focused approaches to change, task- and technology-focused approaches to change, and design- and strategy-focused approaches to change. Each of the three categories of approaches is introduced with an assessment of the relative direct impact of the different methods on the six variables in the systems model of change. Five people- and culture-focused approaches to change are discussed: survey feedback, team building, process consultation, quality-of-work-life (QWL) programs, and high-performance-high-commitment (HP-HC) work systems. Five task- and technology-focused approaches are explained: job design, sociotechnical systems (STS), quality circles, reengineering, and total quality management (TQM). Two design- and strategy-focused approaches to change are explored: adaptive organization designs and strategic change, with special emphasis on the open systems planning model.

Finally, the chapter examines potential ethical issues in planned organizational change. Ethical issues are considered in four main areas: selection of a change approach, selection of a change target, managerial responsibilities, and manipulation.

LEARNING OBJECTIVES

Upon completion of this chapter, the students should be able to:

1. Identify and describe five people- and culture-focused approaches to organizational change.
2. Explain some key issues in changing organizational culture.
3. List and explain the approaches to organizational change that focus on task and technology.
4. Describe the design- and strategy-focused approaches to organizational change.
5. Discuss ethical issues in organizational change.

CHAPTER OUTLINE

I.   **Preview Case:** A Grim Fairy Tale

II.   The Challenge of Change

    A.   Organizationwide Change
    B   Contingency Perspective

III. People- and Culture-Focused Approaches

    A.   Survey Feedback
    B.   Team Building
    C.   Process Consultation
    D.   Quality-of-Work-Life Programs
    E.   **Managing Diversity:** Workplace Flexibility at Corning
    F.   Changing Cultures
    G.   **Managing in Practice:** Changing Big Blue's Culture
    H.   High Performance-High Commitment Work Systems

IV.   Task- and Technology-Focused Approaches

    A.   Job Design
    B.   Sociotechnical Systems
    C.   Quality Circles
    D.   **Managing Across Cultures:** Quality Circles in Japan
    E.   Reengineering
    F.   Total Quality Management
    G.   **Managing Quality:** Quality at AT&T Universal Card Services

V.   Design- and Strategy-Focused Approaches

    A.   Adaptive Organization Designs
    B.   **Managing in Practice:** The Adaptive Organization
    C.   Strategic Change

VI.   Ethical Issues in Organizational Change

    A.   **Managing Ethics:** The Tyranny of Change

VII. Developing Skills

A.   **Self Diagnosis:** Attitudes Toward Change
B.   **A Case in Point:** Understanding Quality Systems—The Westinghouse Corporation

KEY WORDS AND CONCEPTS

Twenty-three key words and concepts are introduced in Chapter 20. Several of these concepts have been introduced in earlier chapters. Reengineering has appeared in Chapters 2, 4, and 16. Self-managed teams occurred in Chapter 9. Visioning was introduced in Chapter 11. The high-performance-high-commitment work system was in Chapter 14. Flextime, job design, and sociotechnical systems appeared in Chapter 16. Finally, the concepts of matrix organization and network organization were in Chapter 17 under the labels matrix design and network design. The key words and concepts that appear in this chapter, along with definitions or appropriate descriptions, are as follows:

Adaptive organizations: a design-focused approach to change that is temporary and highly flexible; has ever-changing networks of teams, projects, alliances, and coalitions; encourages employees to rely less on guidance from their manager; and expects organization members to continuously examine and improve the work process, even if this means going outside the boundaries of their regular job.

Alternative work schedule: a program that includes the use of part-time employment, job sharing, or work at home. An alternative work schedule program frequently is used as a component of a quality-of-work-life program.

Autonomous groups: work groups that plan their work, control its pace and quality, and make many of the decisions traditionally reserved to management (synonymous with self-managed teams).

Collateral organization: a type of adaptive organization wherein a parallel, coexisting organization can be used to supplement an existing formal organization.

Continuous improvement: refers to the continual emphasis in total quality management of improving products or services and the processes for delivering them. One-time programs or quick-fixes are unacceptable with continuous improvement.

Flextime: a program that gives employees some control over their own work schedules. Flextime frequently is used as a component of a quality-of-work-life program.

High-performance-high-commitment (HP-HC) work system: a culture-focused approach to change wherein technology and teamwork are blended to create a sense of ownership among employees while utilizing the most sophisticated work practices and technologies.

Job design: an approach to organization change that focuses on both task and technology; job design is a deliberate, planned restructuring of the way work is performed in order to increase employee motivation, involvement, and efficiency—and ultimately to improve performance.

Matrix organization: a type of adaptive organization that represents a balance between organizing resources according to products or functions.

Network organization: a type of adaptive organization that is a complex mosaic of lateral communication, decision-making, and control processes.

Open systems planning: a method for implementing strategic change; it is designed to help an organization systematically assess its environment and develop an appropriate strategic response.

Process consultation: a people-focused approach to change wherein guidance is provided by a consultant to help members of an organization perceive, understand, and act on process events that occur in the work environment.

Quality circles: an approach to organization change that focuses on both task and technology; quality circles are work groups, generally containing less than a dozen volunteers from the same work area, who meet regularly to monitor and solve job-related quality and/or production problems.

Quality-of-work-life (QWL) programs: a people-focused approach to change that includes activities undertaken by an organization to improve conditions that affect an employee's experience with an organization.

Reengineering: an approach to organization change that focuses on both task and technology; it is a fundamental rethinking and radical redesign of business practices to reduce costs and improve quality, service, and speed.

Self-managed teams: work groups that plan their work, control its pace and quality, and make many of the decisions traditionally reserved to management (synonymous with autonomous groups).

Sociotechnical systems: an approach to organization change that focuses on both task and technology; it simultaneously focuses on changing both the technical and social aspects of the organization to optimize their relationship and thus increase organizational effectiveness.

Strategic change: a strategy-focused approach to planned organizational change that is designed to alter the organization's intended courses of action to attain its goals.

Survey feedback: a people-focused approach to change that consists of (1) collecting information (usually by questionnaire) from members of an organization or work group); (2) organizing the data into an understandable and useful form; and (3) feeding it back to the employees who generated the data.

Team building: a people-focused approach to change by which members of a work group or team diagnose how they work together and plan changes to improve their effectiveness.

Total quality management: an approach to organization change that focuses on both task and technology; it emphasizes meeting or exceeding customer expectations. When an organization achieves "total quality," all activities and processes are designed and carried out to meet all customer requirements while reducing both the time and cost required to provide them.

Virtual corporation: a temporary network of independent companies linked by information technology to share skills, costs, and access to customers. A virtual corporation is similar to an adaptive organization.

Visioning: a central concept in many approaches to strategic change that refers to choosing a desired future state or condition for the organization. It includes identifying and articulating the organization's core mission and its goals, and specifying, at least broadly, how the goals and mission are to be achieved.

LECTURE NOTES

I.   Implementing planned change presents a significant challenge to organizations. Using the systems model of change that was introduced in Chapter 19, we will examine various approaches for implementing planned organizational change. We will also consider some ethical issues that occur in conducting planned change. Transparency 20.1 summarizes the key ideas to be presented concerning the implementation of planned organizational change.

TRANSPARENCY 20.1
(FROM TEXT MATERIAL IN THE TEXTBOOK)

KEY IDEAS ABOUT IMPLEMENTING PLANNED ORGANIZATIONAL CHANGE

II.   The challenge of change.

    A.   Since adaptive, flexible organizations have a competitive advantage over rigid, static ones, managing change has become a central focus of effective organizations worldwide.

        1.   Transparency 20.2 illustrates this widespread interest in managing change as manifested in some currently popular management concepts.

TRANSPARENCY 20.2
(TABLE 20.1 IN THE TEXTBOOK)

THE LANGUAGE OF ORGANIZATIONAL CHANGE

---

        2.   Managing change effectively requires the understanding and use of many of the principles and concepts of organizational behavior that have been developed in previous chapters.

    B.   Organizationwide change.

        1.   To be successful, change usually must be organizationwide.

        2.   An excellent example of organizationwide change is the revolution that has taken place during the past quarter-century in the design and management of manufacturing facilities. Known by a variety of names such as high-performance-high-commitment work systems, high-involvement plants, etc., these revolutionary facilities share some important characteristics, including the following (see Transparency 20.3):

TRANSPARENCY 20.3
(FROM TEXT MATERIAL IN THE TEXTBOOK)

CHARACTERISTICS OF REVOLUTIONARY MANUFACTURING FACILITIES

---

           a.   *Selection*: job applicants are provided with a great deal of information regarding the jobs they are applying for; and there is a high degree of self-selection out of a culture and work environment that might not be a good fit for an individual.

  b. *Pay system*: skill-based pay is emphasized.

  c. *Plant physical layout*: there are few barriers or status differences between managerial and nonmanagerial employees.

  d. *Job design*: employees typically have enriched jobs.

  e. *Organization design*: these plants have flat structures, wide spans of control, and relatively small central office staffs because many activities are handled directly by work teams.

  f. *Plant culture*: participative management is emphasized and decision-making responsibility is pushed as low in the organization as possible.

C. Contingency perspective.

  1. The contingency perspective recognizes no single best approach to managing change and holds that no approach is likely to be effective in all circumstances. This is the perspective being emphasized in the text.

  2. The systems model of change that was developed in Chapter 19 is compatible with a contingency perspective. The variables in this systems model can be used to organize approaches to change into three major categories: people- and culture-focused approaches, task- and technology-focused approaches, and design- and strategy-focused approaches.

ENRICHMENT MODULE: CHANGE IN ACTION—AN EXAMPLE OF USING MULTIPLE SYSTEM VARIABLES

Programs of planned organizational change often use a combination of approaches to affect several of the system variables simultaneously. For example, Supradur Cos., Inc. used three system variables—task, technology, and culture—as action levers for change. Supradur used automation, statistical process control, and union-management cooperation to change the way its manufacturing facility operated, thereby impacting on the task and technology variables. The company also revamped its culture from one that emphasized hierarchical decision making and control to one that encouraged employee involvement.

This enrichment module is based on:

Burck, C. (1994, January 24). Reinventing under fire. *Fortune*, 106.

III. People- and culture-focused approaches to change.

  A. People- and culture-focused approaches to change rely on active involvement and participation by many employees.

    1. People-focused approaches can improve such individual and group processes as decision making, communications, and working relationships.

2.   Culture-focused approaches can affect the shared values, expectations, attitudes, and behaviors of organizational members.

B.   This chapter explores four people-focused approaches to change—survey feedback, team building, process consultation, and quality-of-work-life (QWL) programs—and one culture-focused approach—namely, high-performance-high-commitment work systems.

1.   Transparency 20.4 summarizes the five people- and culture-focused change approaches in terms of the relative impact each approach has on the six major systems variables (*i.e.*, people, culture, task, technology, design, and strategy).

TRANSPARENCY 20.4
(TABLE 20.2 IN THE TEXTBOOK)

COMPARISON OF RELATIVE DIRECT IMPACT OF PEOPLE- AND CULTURE-FOCUSED APPROACHES ON SYSTEM VARIABLES

---

a.   While the direct impacts identified in Transparency 20.4 represent the initial target of the change effort, successful change ultimately will affect all six major system variables.

C.   Survey feedback as a people-focused approach to change.

1.   <u>Survey feedback</u> consists of:

a.   Collecting information (usually by questionnaire) from members of an organization or work group.

b.   Organizing the data into an understandable and useful form.

c.   Feeding it back to the employees who generated the data.

2.   Objectives of survey feedback.

a.   To improve relationships among members of groups or teams or between departments through the discussion of common problems.

b.   To identify team, department, and organizational problems.

3.   Feedback of data.

a.   Typically, all employees receive a summary of the responses from the entire organization, department, or team, as well as their individual responses.

b.   Feedback is provided in one of three ways:

(1)   Almost simultaneously.

(2)   Team meetings held at the highest organizational level first, followed by team meetings at each succeeding lower level.

(3)   Team meetings held first at the lowest participating organizational

level, followed by team meetings at each succeeding higher level.

4. Implications of survey feedback.

    a. It deals with organizational members in the context of their own jobs, problems, and work relationships.

    b. It can effectively meet both organizational goals and individual and group needs.

    c. It helps identify problems and clarify issues, which in turn may indicate the need for changes in the other five system variables.

D. Team building as a people-focused approach to change.

1. Team building is a process by which members of a work group or team diagnose how they work together and plan changes to improve their effectiveness.

2. In team building, the members focus on one or more of the following:

    a. Setting goals or priorities for the team.

    b. Analyzing or allocating the way work is performed.

    c. Examining the way the team is working.

    d. Examining relationships among the people doing the work.

3. Traditional work groups operate differently than effective teams do in modern, adaptive, high performance organizations. Transparency 20.5 contrasts the functioning of traditional work groups with that of modern teams.

TRANSPARENCY 20.5
(TABLE 20.3 IN THE TEXTBOOK)

CONTRASTS BETWEEN TRADITIONAL WORK GROUPS AND NEW WORK TEAMS

---

    a. To help build effective teams, organizations should (see Transparency 20.6):

TRANSPARENCY 20.6
(FROM TEXT MATERIAL IN THE TEXTBOOK)

SUGGESTIONS FOR DEVELOPING EFFECTIVE TEAMS

---

    (1) Help team members develop an understanding of the importance of what they are doing and a shared vision of where they are going.

    (2) Select team members based on skills and potential rather than personality.

    (3) Set some performance goals that are attainable to build success and

confidence.

    (4)   Bring new challenges and information to the team regularly to maintain momentum and enthusiasm.

    (5)   Use positive feedback, recognition, and rewards.

4.   Implications of team building.

    a.   It addresses immediate group problems and helps team members to learn how to deal with new problems.

    b.   It can produce various positive organizational outcomes, such as improved employee attitudes, increased involvement and participation, improved problem-solving skills, etc.

    c.   It increases the likelihood that the group will become a high-performance work team.

    d.   It moves the team up the performance curve that is depicted in Transparency 20.7

TRANSPARENCY 20.7
(FIGURE 20.1 IN THE TEXTBOOK)

THE TEAM PERFORMANCE CURVE

---

    e.   It can provide a useful way to involve employees in an organizational change program and to increase collaborative efforts.

E.   Process consultation as a people-focused approach to change.

1.   <u>Process consultation</u> is guidance provided by a consultant to help members of an organization perceive, understand, and act on process events that occur in the work environment.

    a.   Transparency 20.8 illustrates the nature of process events and contrasts them with content.

TRANSPARENCY 20.8
(FIGURE 20.2 IN THE TEXTBOOK)

SOME EXAMPLES OF DIFFERENCES BETWEEN CONTENT AND PROCESS

---

2.   Process consultation usually addresses one or more of the following concerns (see Transparency 20.9):

TRANSPARENCY 20.9
(FROM TEXT MATERIAL IN THE TEXTBOOK)

CONCERNS ADDRESSED BY PROCESS CONSULTATION

---

        a.   *Communication*—organization members must understand the nature and style of the organization's communication process.

        b.   *Leadership*—team members must understand leadership styles and how individuals can adjust their styles to improve the fit with different situations.

        c.   *Decision making and problem solving*—efficient decision-making and problem-solving processes are crucial for individual and group effectiveness in organizations.

        d.   *Norms and roles*—organization members should be aware of role-taking processes and should consciously examine, and if necessary, change the norms.

        e.   *Conflict resolution*—organization members should be able to diagnose, understand, and resolve conflicts between individuals, teams, and departments

    3.   Implications of process consultation.

        a.   It often is effective in changing attitudes and norms, improving interpersonal and decision-making skills, and increasing group cohesiveness and teamwork.

F.   Quality-of-work-life programs as a people-focused approach to change.

    1.   <u>Quality-of-work-life (QWL) programs</u> are activities undertaken by an organization to improve conditions that affect an employee's experience with an organization.

    2.   QWL programs use various techniques to improve employees' work experiences, such as team building, job redesign, participative management, quality circles, work-environment improvement, and flextime or other alternative work schedule programs.

        a.   <u>Flextime</u> programs give employees some control over their own work schedules.

        b.   <u>Alternative work schedule</u> programs include the use of part-time employment, job sharing, or work at home.

    3.   QWL programs usually have two objectives:

        a.   Improving the quality of work life for employees.

        b.   Improving group, team, and/or organizational productivity.

    4.   Implications of QWL programs.

        a.   They increase employee involvement, improve working conditions, change organizational culture, and improve work attitudes.

        b.   They can improve productivity but the relationship between QWL programs and productivity changes is complex, often indirect, and not easily measured.

    c.   They have the potential for improving communication, coordination, motivation, and performance capabilities, which in turn could increase productivity.

    d.   Middle managers and first-line supervisors may resist QWL programs because of a perceived threat to their power and right to make decisions.

ENRICHMENT MODULE: PRODUCTIVITY IMPROVEMENT AT FORD MOTOR CO.

Ford Motor Co. executives say the increased cooperation of their work force is the most important reason for their improved productivity. But the improved cooperation and team spirit in trying to lower costs didn't come easily. Early on, employees who offered suggestions for cost savings were ridiculed by co-workers. Lower-level managers also had negative attitudes toward employee involvement. However, trust between management and labor gradually developed—to the benefit of both parties.

Peter Pestillo, a Ford executive who handles labor relations, encapsulates the essence of Ford's approach to improving productivity by contrasting it with General Motor's approach. He says, "GM was determined to minimize the role of the hourly people" whereas "Our goal was to maximize the contribution of the hourly people."

This enrichment module is based on:

Templin, N. (1992, December 15). Team spirit: A decisive response to crisis brought Ford enhanced productivity. *The Wall Street Journal*, A1 & A13.

    G.   High-performance-high-commitment work systems as a culture-focused approach to change.

        1.   While it is difficult to accurately assess and change organizational culture, the probability of success can be increased by attending to the following issues (see Transparency 20.10):

TRANSPARENCY 20.10
(FROM TEXT MATERIAL IN THE TEXTBOOK)

ISSUES TO ADDRESS IN CHANGING ORGANIZATIONAL CULTURE

---

    a.   *Capitalize on dramatic opportunities*—organizations need to take advantage of opportunities for cultural change.

    b.   *Combine caution with optimism*—organization members need to be optimistic about the advantages of cultural change yet the organization needs to proceed with caution.

    c.   *Understand resistance to cultural change*—identifying and reducing the sources of resistance to cultural change is valuable.

> d.   *Change many elements, but maintain some continuity*—institute necessary changes, but recognize and retain that which is of value.
>
> e.   *Recognize the importance of implementation*—planned changes must be carried through.
>
> f.   *Modify socialization tactics*—since socialization is the primary way that people learn the organization's culture, changing socialization processes can be effective for changing the culture.
>
> g.   *Find and cultivate innovative leadership*—cultural change must begin at the top of the organization, and good leadership is crucial.

ENRICHMENT MODULE: THE CULTURE OF ORGANIZATIONAL DINOSAURS

Giant, bureaucratic organizations like IBM, General Motors and Sears Roebuck may be organizational dinosaurs that are burdened by (1) the weight of their hierarchical structures and cumbersome, slow-moving processes; and (2) their seeming inability to adapt to their environment. The existing culture of these organizations is the primary impediment to change, according to the experts. The corporate culture of organizational dinosaurs emphasizes past successes; maintaining the status quo; looking backward and inward, rather than forward and outward; being caretakers rather than innovators; denying competitors' abilities to produce superior products or services; and being risk averse.

Without significantly changing their cultures, can these organizational dinosaurs survive? Because of their size and resources, companies like IBM, Sears, and General Motors will probably be around in some form in the foreseeable future, but not as highly competitive and successful firms—unless they change their cultures. The highly successful and competitive businesses will be those that are able to adapt quickly to the demands of their environments. The organizational dinosaurs that don't learn to adapt quickly may face a slow, painful death on their way to extinction.

This enrichment module is based on:

Gleckman, H. (1993). Meet the giant-killers. *Business Week/Enterprise*, 68-73.

Loomis, C.J. (1993, May 3). Dinosaurs? *Fortune*, 36-42.

> 2.   The <u>high-performance-high-commitment work system</u> is a primary way of introducing cultural change. These systems blend technology and teamwork to create a sense of ownership among employees while utilizing the most sophisticated work practices and technologies.
>
> 3.   HP-HC work systems are characterized by delegation, teamwork across boundaries, empowerment, integration of people and technology, and a shared sense of purpose.
>
> 4.   HP-HC work systems are designed to manage human, technological, and financial resources efficiently and to more fully engage the talents and capacities of employees.

IV.   Task- and technology-focused approaches to change.

A. Emphasis of task- and technology-focused approaches.

    1. The task-focused approach to change emphasizes making changes in the work of individuals, groups, and teams.

    2. The technology-focused approach concentrates on the technological processes and tools used to perform the work.

B. This chapter explores five approaches that focus on both task and technology: job design, sociotechnical systems, quality circles, reengineering, and total quality management. (Although job design and sociotechnical systems were examined in Chapter 16, they are explored here as approaches to organizational change.)

    1. Transparency 20.11 summarizes the five task- and technology-focused change approaches in terms of the relative impact each approach has on the six major systems variables (*i.e.*, people, culture, task, technology, design, and strategy).

TRANSPARENCY 20.11
(TABLE 20.4 IN THE TEXTBOOK)

COMPARISON OF RELATIVE DIRECT IMPACT OF TASK- AND TECHNOLOGY-FOCUSED APPROACHES ON SYSTEM VARIABLES

C. Job design as both a task- and technology-focused approach to change.

    1. Job design represents a deliberate, planned restructuring of the way work is performed in order to increase employee motivation, involvement, and efficiency—and ultimately to improve performance.

    2. Each of the job design techniques discussed in Chapter 16 can be used as a method of implementing organizational change.

    3. Job design is most successful in the context of a comprehensive planned change program that examines the complex fit among the tasks to be performed, the types of technology used, the design and culture of the organization or team, and the nature and characteristics of the people doing the work.

D. Sociotechnical systems as both a task- and technology-focused approach to change.

    1. The sociotechnical systems (STS) approach simultaneously focuses on changing both the technical and social aspects of the organization to optimize their relationship and thus increase organizational effectiveness.

    2. Job redesign is often a part of the STS approach to change (see Chapter 16).

    3. Autonomous groups or self-managed teams are often used to implement change from a STS perspective. These are work groups that plan their work, control its pace and quality, and make many of the decisions traditionally reserved to management. The role of management in the STS approach is to ensure that teams have sufficient resources to accomplish their tasks.

E. Quality circles as both a task- and technology-focused approach to change.

1.   <u>Quality circles</u> are work groups, generally containing less than a dozen volunteers from the same work area, who meet regularly to monitor and solve job-related quality and/or production problems. Quality circles also may be used to improve working conditions, increase employee involvement and commitment, and encourage employee self-development.

2.   In contrast to many other change approaches, quality circles typically have a narrower focus and management retains more control.

3.   Implications of quality circles.

   a.   Quality circles can generate productivity and quality gains.

   b.   Quality circles can foster greater employee involvement.

   c.   Maintaining initial successes over a period of time requires the expenditure of considerable energy and the maintenance of employee interest.

   d.   Quality circles may not fit with an organization's culture, and are unlikely to foster a participative culture unless other changes are made simultaneously.

   e.   Quality circles appear to work well with only a limited range of problems.

F.   Reengineering as both a task- and technology-focused approach to change.

1.   <u>Reengineering</u>, sometimes called process redesign, is a fundamental rethinking and radical redesign of business practices to reduce costs and improve quality, service, and speed.

2.   Reengineering is a more radical approach to planned organizational change in that the most fundamental ideas and assumptions of the organization are challenged.

3.   Reengineering usually involves the following types of changes (see Transparency 20.12):

TRANSPARENCY 20.12
(FROM TEXT MATERIAL IN THE TEXTBOOK)

TYPICAL CHANGES PRODUCED BY REENGINEERING

---

   a.   Work units change from functional departments to process teams.

   b.   Individual jobs change from simple to multidimensional tasks.

   c.   People's roles change from being controlled to being empowered to make decisions.

   d.   Performance appraisal changes from measuring activities to measuring results.

   e.   Managers change from supervisors to coaches.

f.   Organization designs change from tall to flat hierarchies.

G.   Total quality management as both a task- and technology-focused approach to change.

    1.   <u>Total quality management</u> (TQM) focuses on meeting or exceeding customer expectations. When an organization achieves "total quality," all activities and processes are designed and carried out to meet all customer requirements while reducing both the time and cost required to provide them.

    2.   TQM is partly technical and partly cultural.

        a.   The technical part of TQM involves the use, among other things, of just-in-time (JIT) inventory systems.

        b.   The cultural part of TQM involves shared values emphasizing quality, empowerment, and continuous improvement. <u>Continuous improvement</u> refers to the continual emphasis on improving products or services and the processes for delivering them. One-time programs or quick-fixes are unacceptable with continuous improvement.

    3.   Transparency 20.13 identifies the important elements of TQM.

TRANSPARENCY 20.13
(TABLE 20.6 IN THE TEXTBOOK)

ELEMENTS OF TOTAL QUALITY MANAGEMENT

---

    4.   A focus on quality and continuous improvement is essential to competing effectively in the global economy. One way in which quality is encouraged and rewarded in the United States is with the Malcom Baldrige National Quality Award. The criteria for this award are compatible with the elements of TQM that are described in Transparency 20.13.

V.   Design- and strategy-focused approaches to change.

A.   Emphasis of design- and strategy-focused approaches.

    1.   Design-focused approaches to change involve redefining positions or roles and relationships among positions, and redesigning department, division, and/or organization structure.

    2.   Strategy-focused approaches involve a reexamination of the organization's basic mission or goals and the specific plans or strategies for attaining those goals.

B.   This chapter examines adaptive organization designs as a design-focused approach to organization change and strategic change as a strategy-focused approach.

    1.   Transparency 20.14 summarizes adaptive designs and strategic change approaches in terms of their relative impact on the six major systems variables (*i.e.*, people, culture, task, technology, design, and strategy).

> **TRANSPARENCY 20.14**
> **(TABLE 20.7 IN THE TEXTBOOK)**
>
> **COMPARISON OF RELATIVE DIRECT IMPACT OF DESIGN- AND
> STRATEGY-FOCUSED APPROACHES ON SYSTEM VARIABLES**

C.   Adaptive designs as a design-focused approach to change.

    1.   <u>Adaptive organizations</u> have the following characteristics (see Transparency 20.15):

> **TRANSPARENCY 20.15**
> **(FROM TEXT MATERIAL IN THE TEXTBOOK)**
>
> **CHARACTERISTICS OF ADAPTIVE ORGANIZATIONS**

        a.   The objective of the adaptive organization is to eliminate the traditional bureaucratic organization in favor of ever-changing networks of teams, projects, alliances, and coalitions.

        b.   Employees rely less on guidance from their manager.

        c.   Organization members continuously examine the work process and have responsibility for improving it, even if this means going outside the boundaries of their regular job.

        d.   Much of the structure of adaptive organizations will be temporary and flexible, determined more by what needs to be done than by traditional boundaries between functions, products, and levels of the hierarchy.

> **ENRICHMENT MODULE: THE IRONY OF BEING ADAPTIVE**
>
> McKinsey & Co., a large management consulting firm, at one time had characteristics that were remarkably similar to those of adaptive organizations. McKinsey's cherished organizational traditions included collaborative working relationships among consultants, a non-hierarchical organizational structure, and putting a client's interests ahead of the firm's interests. However, as the firm has grown rapidly, its adaptive nature has been challenged. How has McKinsey & Co. responded to this challenge? One former senior partner says, "You have to have more structure, more layers, committees, regions, and spheres." Indeed, the consulting firm now is organized by industry specialties, functional groups, and geographic territories. The firm which prided itself on its flexible, egalitarian nature seems to have become less adaptive.
>
> This enrichment module is based on:
>
> Milbank, D. (1993, September 8). Management job: McKinsey confronts challenge of its own: The burdens of size. *The Wall Street Journal*, A1 & A8.

    2.   The virtual corporation is related to the adaptive organization. A <u>virtual corporation</u> is a temporary network of independent companies linked by information technology to share skills, costs, and access to customers.

3.   Both adaptive organizations and virtual corporations require managers to build relationships, negotiate win-win deals, find competent venture partners, and provide the temporary organization with a balance of freedom and control.

4.   Three types of organization design characterize flexible, adaptive organizations. These are: the collateral organization, the matrix organization, and the network organization. (Matrix and network designs were discussed in Chapter 17).

5.   The collateral organization as an adaptive design.

   a.   A <u>collateral organization</u> is a parallel, coexisting organization that can be used to supplement an existing formal organization.

   b.   Collateral organizations have the following characteristics (see Transparency 20.16):

TRANSPARENCY 20.16
(FROM TEXT MATERIAL IN THE TEXTBOOK)

CHARACTERISTICS OF COLLATERAL ORGANIZATIONS

---

   (1)   All communication channels are open and connected.

   (2)   There is rapid and complete exchange of relevant information on problems and issues.

   (3)   The norms in use encourage careful questioning and analysis of goals, assumptions, methods, alternatives, and criteria for evaluation.

   (4)   Managers are not restricted to their formal subordinates.

   (5)   Mechanisms are developed to link the collateral and formal organization.

   c.   Implications of the collateral organization.

   (1)   It gives managers a way to match problems with the organizational structures best suited to solve them.

   (2)   It creates more complex roles for employees, thereby providing significant motivational opportunities.

   (3)   It may help develop managerial skills, may foster organizational innovation, and may help in coping with crises requiring decentralized decision making.

6.   The matrix organization as an adaptive design.

   a.   A <u>matrix organization</u> represents a balance between organizing resources according to products or functions.

   b.   Like other organization development methods, the matrix organization emphasizes collaborative behavior and the effective use of teams.

  c. Implications of the matrix organization.

    (1) It helps to create a culture that is receptive to organizational change.

    (2) It may be superior to other organization designs when an organization uses complex technology, faces rapidly changing market conditions, and needs a high degree of cooperation among projects and functions.

    (3) It is costly to implement and maintain and can be extremely difficult to manage effectively.

 7. The network organization as an adaptive design.

  a. The <u>network organization</u> is a complex mosaic of lateral communication, decision-making, and control processes.

  b. Three basic types of network organizations are illustrated in Transparency 20.17.

TRANSPARENCY 20.17
(FIGURE 20.4 IN THE TEXTBOOK)

EXAMPLES OF NETWORK DESIGNS

---

  c. Implications of a network organization.

    (1) It emphasizes the use of sophisticated information technologies to coordinate activities and perform work.

    (2) Managers can assemble temporary teams of employees to bring expertise to bear on projects and concerns as needed.

 D. Strategic-change as a strategy-focused approach to change.

  1. <u>Strategic change</u> is planned organizational change designed to alter the organization's intended courses of action to attain its goals.

  2. <u>Open systems planning</u>—a method for implementing strategic change—is designed to help an organization systematically assess its environment and develop an appropriate strategic response.

  3. Open systems planning proceeds according to the following steps (see Transparency 20.18):

TRANSPARENCY 20.18
(FROM TEXT MATERIAL IN THE TEXTBOOK)

STEPS IN OPEN SYSTEMS PLANNING

---

a.   Assess the external environment in terms of its expectations and demands on the organization's behavior.

b.   Assess the organization's current response to these environmental demands.

c.   Identify the organization's core mission.

d.   Create a realistic scenario of future environmental demands and organizational responses.

e.   Create an ideal scenario of future environmental demands and organizational responses.

f.   Compare the present with the ideal future and prepare an action plan for reducing the discrepancy.

4.   <u>Visioning</u>—a central concept in many approaches to strategic change—refers to choosing a desired future state or condition for the organization. It includes identifying and articulating the organization's core mission and its goals, and specifying, at least broadly, how the goals and mission are to be achieved.

ENRICHMENT MODULE: VISIONING AT IBM

Lou Gerstner, who became the CEO of International Business Machines in 1993, has a vision for the company that consists of the following key elements:

- IBM will not be split up; instead its component parts will be even more closely linked.
- IBM will reassert its identity as the primary computing resource for customers.
- IBM will be the dominant supplier of technology in the computer industry.
- The centerpiece of IBM's technology will a new microprocessor design that will run a wide array of standard software and will sharply cut manufacturing costs.
- While IBM will still make mainframe computers, they are no longer central to the company's strategy.
- IBM is its own worst enemy. Opportunities must not be wasted, bureaucracy must be minimized, and the good of the company must come before the good of the divisions.

This enrichment module is based on:

Kirkpatrick, D. (1993, November 15). Gerstner's new vision for IBM. *Fortune*, 119-126.

VI.   Ethical issues in organizational change.

A.   Ethical issues regarding organizational change can arise in four primary areas: selection of a change approach, selection of a change target, managerial responsibilities, and manipulation. Two examples of relevant ethical questions in each area are provided below.

1.   Selection of a change approach.

a.   Does the manager or change agent have a vested interest in using a particular technique so that other alternatives might not receive a fair hearing?

b.   Do individuals involved in the diagnosis have biases that might predetermine the problems identified and thus influence the change approach chosen?

2.   Selection of a change target.

a.   Which individuals, teams, or departments of the organization will the change program focus on?

b.   Which members of the organization will participate in diagnosing, planning, and implementing the change and to what degree?

3.   Managerial responsibilities.

a.   Whose vision will guide the change effort?

b.   Whose values influence the adoption of goals and methods chosen to accomplish them?

4.   Manipulation.

a.   To what extent should the organization disclose all aspects of the change in advance?

b.   To what extent do employees have the right to participate in, or at least be aware of, changes that affect them, even indirectly?

ENRICHMENT MODULE: THE ETHICS OF DOWNSIZING

Companies frequently use downsizing as a way to produce organizational change. For instance, downsizing can be used to help improve productivity or efficiency by reducing personnel costs. Downsizing also can be used to deal with changes that are precipitated by mergers and acquisitions. Additionally, downsizing may be a response to changing market demand for a company's products or services.

Whatever the reason for downsizing, it usually eliminates people and has potentially detrimental effects on the survivors. The survivors are expected to be productive and make significant contributions to improving the organization. Yet they may be less productive due to anxiety and uncertainty about their futures with the company.

Partly because of its effects on survivors, downsizing as a way to introduce organizational change is fraught with ethical issues. Among two of the more important ethical issues are the following:

- How can management expect employees to be committed to the future of the organization, if it can't offer them job security?
- How can management be serious about empowering employees when, at any time, employees may lose their jobs?

These two questions could provide the foundation for an interesting discussion of the ethical considerations, not only of downsizing but also other methods of implementing change.

This enrichment module is based on:

Henkoff, R. (1994, January 10). Getting beyond downsizing. *Fortune*, 58-64.

Monistere, D.J. (1994, May). Downsizing: A practical application. *NBDC Report*, No. 162.

VII. Summing up: What are the key managerial lessons regarding the implementation of planned organizational change?

     A. The environment in which businesses operate may change dramatically and frequently. Therefore, to remain competitive and to be effective, organizations must adapt to their environments. Implementing planned organizational change is a major way for organizations to adapt to their environments.

     B. To be effective, managers must be able to implement needed changes in the organization. By understanding the various approaches to planned organizational change, managers have an appropriate knowledge base for initiating needed changes. This chapter has provided a foundation for future and more in-depth learning abut how to implement planned organizational change. Managers should continue to develop their knowledge-base regarding planned organizational change. Managers who don't continue to learn about managing change will less valuable to their organizations. They will be less adaptive when increasing numbers of organizations need them to be more adaptive so that the organizations themselves can be more adaptive.

DISCUSSION QUESTIONS: SUGGESTED ANSWERS

1.   *Describe an ideal "adaptive organization" and then describe an organization with which you are familiar. Compare the two descriptions and suggest how the real organization could become more like your ideal of an adaptive organization.*

The ideal adaptive organization might be described as follows:

      a.   The objective is to eliminate the traditional bureaucratic organization in favor of ever-changing networks of teams, projects, alliances, and coalitions.

      b.   Employees rely less on guidance from their manager.

      c.   Organization members continuously examine the work process and have responsibility for improving it, even if this means going outside the boundaries of their regular job.

      d.   Much of the organizational structure will be temporary and flexible, determined more by what needs to be done than by traditional boundaries between functions, products, and levels of the hierarchy.

The students could use these characteristics as the basis for comparison with their example organizations. In addition to describing how the organizations differ, the students should be encouraged to consider why those differences might exist.

To address the part of the question concerning how to make the example organization more like an adaptive organizations, the students could focus on one of the three types of adaptive organizations discussed in the text: collateral organizations, matrix organizations, and network organizations. In short, the students could describe how their example organization could be transformed into, say, a network organization.

2.   *Can employees always have a high level of participation in organizational change programs? Why or why not?*

While it is often desirable, it is not always possible to have a high degree of employee involvement in change programs. For example, employees may not have the necessary level of expertise or knowledge to make a significant contribution to the change program. In other instances, time constraints may prevent the active involvement of large numbers of people. Additionally, there may be technological or task constraints that prevent high levels of participation. However, a great deal of empirical evidence indicates that low levels of employee participation in change programs should be management's last resort rather than their first choice. Change is more likely to be effectively implemented and sustained when there is high participation and involvement on the part of those who must do the changing.

3.   *Write a brief summary description of each of the five people- and culture-focused change approaches presented in the chapter.*

Survey feedback consists of (a) collecting information (usually by questionnaire) from members of an organization or work group; (b) organizing the data into an understandable and useful form; and (c) feeding it back to the employees who generated the data. Some or all employees use this information as the basis for planning actions to deal with specific issues and problems.

Team building is a process by which members of a work group or team diagnose how they work together and plan changes to improve their effectiveness. Many different work groups comprise an organization, and much of an organization's success depends on how effectively people can work together as a team.

Process consultation is guidance provided by a consultant to help members of an organization perceive, understand, and act on process events that occur in the work environment. Process events are the ways in which individuals do their work. Process event include the behaviors of people at meetings; formal and informal encounters among people at work; and, in general, any of the behaviors involved in performing a task.

Quality-of-work-life (QWL) programs are activities undertaken by an organization to improve conditions that affect an employee's experience with an organization. QWL programs usually have two objectives: (a) improving the quality of work life for employees; and (b) improving group, team, and/or organizational productivity.

The *high-performance-high-commitment work system* is a primary way of introducing cultural change. These systems blend technology and teamwork to create a sense of ownership among employees while utilizing the most sophisticated work practices and technologies. HP-HC work systems are characterized by delegation, teamwork across boundaries, empowerment, integration of people and technology, and a shared sense of purpose. HP-HC work systems are designed to manage human, technological, and financial resources efficiently and to more fully engage the talents and capacities of employees.

4. *Write a brief summary description of each of the five task- and technology-focused change approaches presented in the chapter.*

Job design represents a deliberate, planned restructuring of the way work is performed in order to increase employee motivation, involvement, and efficiency—and ultimately to improve performance. Each of the job design techniques discussed in Chapter 16 can be used as a method of implementing organizational change.

The *sociotechnical systems* (STS) approach simultaneously focuses on changing both the technical and social aspects of the organization to optimize their relationship and thus increase organizational effectiveness. Job redesign and autonomous groups or self-managed teams often are part of the STS approach to change.

Quality circles are work groups, generally containing less than a dozen volunteers from the same work area, who meet regularly to monitor and solve job-related quality and/or production problems. Quality circles also may be used to improve working conditions, increase employee involvement and commitment, and encourage employee self-development.

Reengineering, sometimes called process redesign, is a fundamental rethinking and radical redesign of business practices to reduce costs and improve quality, service, and speed. Reengineering is a more radical approach to planned organizational change in that the most fundamental ideas and assumptions of the organization are challenged.

Total quality management (TQM) focuses on meeting or exceeding customer expectations. When an organization achieves "total quality," all activities and processes are designed and carried out to meet all customer requirements while reducing both the time and cost required to provide them.

5.   *What are the similarities and differences between survey feedback and team building?*

Both survey feedback and team building focus on group problems in a constructive manner. Survey feedback seeks to improve relationships among members of groups or between departments through the discussion of common problems. Team building attempts to improve the effectiveness of work groups by having group members focus on setting goals, analyzing the way work is done, examining the way the group is working, and evaluating relationships among the people doing the work.

One major difference between survey feedback and team building is found in their initiating conditions. Survey feedback usually begins with the commitment and endorsement of top management. Team building begins when group members recognize a problem in group functioning for which this approach seems appropriate. In some cases, a survey is used during the team building process.

Another major difference between survey feedback and team building is the breadth of their focus. Team building focuses on team problems, whereas survey feedback has a much broader focus—often the entire organization or a major subunit of the organization.

6.   *Compare and contrast quality-of-work-life programs and high-performance-high-commitment work systems.*

Both quality-of-work-life programs and high-performance-high-commitment work systems address the need to provide a quality working environment. QWL's purpose is to improve important conditions that affect employees' experiences with the organization, whereas HP-HC work systems are intended to foster a positive organizational culture. QWL emphasizes that productivity is a result of improving employee attitudes, increasing levels of employee involvement, improving working conditions, and changing the work group and/or organizational culture. An underlying assumption of the HP-HC work system is that superior technology, efficient task design, congruent structure and processes, good planning, and the like are necessary, but not sufficient, conditions for high performance. Individuals and work teams must be committed to make technology, task design, structure, and strategy work.

7.   *Explain why both HP-HC work systems and total quality management may require significant changes in organizational culture to be effective.*

By definition, high-performance-high-commitment work systems blend technology and teamwork to create a sense of ownership among employees while utilizing the most sophisticated work practices and technologies. Such systems are characterized by delegation, teamwork across boundaries, empowerment, integration of people and technology, and a shared sense of purpose. Each of these HP-HC characteristics may challenge the core values and beliefs of an organization's culture. Thus, the core values and beliefs would need to be changed in order for an HP-HC work system to be effective. Fortunately, the HP-HC work system may actually facilitate changes in an organization's core values and beliefs.

Total quality management (TQM) focuses on meeting or exceeding customer expectations. When an organization achieves "total quality," all activities and processes are designed and carried out to meet all customer requirements while reducing both the time and cost required to provide them. TQM impacts on an organization's culture in that TQM involves shared values emphasizing quality, empowerment, and continuous improvement. If an organization's culture does not have these core values, they would need to be developed in order for TQM to be effective.

8.   *Compare and contrast reengineering and TQM.*

Reengineering is a fundamental rethinking and radical redesign of business practices to reduce costs and improve quality, service, and speed. TQM focuses on achieving "total quality" by designing and implementing activities and processes to meet all customer requirements while reducing both the time and cost required to provide them.

Both reengineering and TQM are similar in their focus on quality, cost, and the customer. Both may require significant cultural changes in order to be effective. Both focus on empowering employees.

Reengineering and TQM differ in terms of the scope of change. Reengineering is broader in scope. It is a is a more radical approach to planned organizational change in that the most fundamental ideas and assumptions of the organization are challenged. TQM does not necessarily challenge an organization's fundamental assumptions and ideas.

9.   *Based on your own experience, describe an organization, group, or team that needed change. Which of the change approaches presented would you use? Why?*

This question provides students with an opportunity to diagnose a work situation from the perspective of their own work experience and attempt to apply their judgement regarding which approach or combination of approaches would effectively improve their situation. A good answer should contain a careful diagnosis and a clear rationale that links this diagnosis with the proposed change program.

A useful way to approach this question would be to use the tables (see Tables 20.2, 20.4, and 20.7) that identify the relative direct impacts of the various change methods on the six system variables—people, culture, task, technology, design, and strategy. In diagnosing their example situation, the students can identify which system variables created problems. Then they could select a planned change approach based on which method or combination of methods would likely have the greatest impact on the problematic system variables.

DEVELOPING SKILLS—
SELF DIAGNOSIS: ATTITUDES TOWARD CHANGE

This diagnostic instrument provides 14 questions that students can use to assess their attitudes toward change. Using a current or past job as a reference point, the students respond to each question on a 7-point Likert scale. Instructions for scoring the instrument are included in the text, and students should be reminded that several of the items are reverse scored. Scores can range from 14 to 98. Scores from 70 to 98 reflect very positive attitudes toward change while scores of 42 or below indicate negative attitudes. Scores of 43 to 69 suggest ambivalence toward change.

DEVELOPING SKILLS—
A CASE IN POINT: UNDERSTANDING QUALITY SYSTEMS—THE WESTINGHOUSE CORPORATION

CASE OVERVIEW

This case focuses on the quality improvement efforts of the Westinghouse Defense and Electronics Group at its College Station, Texas facility. The facility, known as the Westinghouse Electronic Assembly Plant (EAP) was built in response to a growing market in high technology wiring assemblies and to provide a competitive advantage for Westinghouse. The plant design called for a state-of-the-art assembly system that included modern management practices, advanced information systems, and the latest in engineering technologies.

When W-EAP opened in 1983, it began producing printed "circuit board" assemblies—a part of a larger component that the parent plant supplied to external customers for use in land-based and airborne radar systems. In late 1984, a U.S. government audit of a major competitor resulted in more rigorous standards for product- and process-quality being imposed on all defense contractors. Although W-EAP was producing "good" quality (roughly 90% of the parts met standard the first time through), the new defense contractor compliance standards required substantial changes and improvements in work processes and procedures.

To initiate the change process, the W-EAP management team asked each member to answer the question, "If you owned this business, how would you fix it?" Using the responses to this question, a committee was formed under the direction of Keith Hudspeth, then product line manager, to develop an action plan for solving the quality problems at W-EAP. After extensive discussion with people throughout the plant, Hudspeth's committee identified three key issues that needed to be addressed in the action plan. These issues were:

1. A need existed for a system to allow W-EAP to relay the vision and goals of the customer requirements to all employees.
2. A need existed for a system to change the current internal measures and allow W-EAP employees to measure the important aspects of the business from the customer's viewpoint.
3. The plant needed a system that would allow employees to assume responsibility for their own destiny, and W-EAP must reward and recognize employee efforts in this direction.

Three task teams were then formed to develop the action plan, with each team focusing on one of the three issues.

CASE QUESTIONS

1. *List the ideas and concepts from this chapter that appear, in one form or another, in this case.*

   The key concepts that appear in the case are as follows:

   a. Westinghouse-EAP is part of the revolution that has taken place during the past quarter-century in the design and management of manufacturing facilities. This type of plant is known by a variety of names such as high-performance-high-commitment work systems, high-involvement plants, new design plants, quality-of-work-life organizations, and productive workplaces.

b. Based on part a of the answer, HP-HC work systems characterize W-EAP.

c. The sociotechnical systems approach appears in the plant design which called for a state-of-the-art assembly system that included modern management practices, advanced information systems, and the latest in engineering technologies.

d. Total quality management is implied in the orientation taken toward changing organizational procedures and processes to improve quality.

e. The quality-of-work-life concept is implied in the issue that dealt with W-EAP employees exercising self-control and being rewarded for their efforts at doing so.

f. Strategic change is reflected both in the reasons for opening the W-EAP facility and in its revamping of procedures and processes to better meet customer quality requirements.

2. *Assume that you are part of the Westinghouse team responsible for developing a comprehensive plan to resolve these issues. Ask yourself, "If I owned this business, how would I fix it?" Explain and defend your plan.*

The Westinghouse Solution: In September of 1985, the Hudspeth Committee proposed to the W-EAP management team a performance management system called the Quality Yield Enhancement System (Q-YES). Through the cumulative efforts of the task teams coupled with the creativity of Hudspeth's committee, a management system evolved that was based on setting goals, measuring goal progress, and providing rewards for goal achievement.

Setting Goals. Q-YES requires the establishment of goals for the basic business measures of quality (actual first time through yields), productivity (actual board production), and attendance levels (for both teams and individuals). Having specific, measurable goals was important for creating awareness of the plant's situation. Having employees aware of the plant's goals, their team's goals, and their own individual goals allowed for a clear understanding of what was necessary to survive and become competitive in the electronic components business.

Measuring Progress. Each team now records their own progress and reports their information regularly to their supervisor. In addition, all team goals and measurements are visibly displayed at their respective work stations for all plant personnel to observe. If a problem is observed internally by a team member or brought to the team's attention by an external source, the team can meet and decide how to resolve the concern. This type of problem-solving behavior seems to occur naturally as a result of having (a) progress data immediately available and (b) the responsibility for acting on the information.

Regulation and Rewards. The plan formally recognizes team goal achievement on a monthly and quarterly basis. All teams that meet monthly quality and productivity goals earn a stripe on their team Q-YES flag. If the overall plant achieves its monthly goal, coffee and doughnuts are provided for all employees. At the end of each quarter, the team from each functional group that exceeds its monthly quality, productivity, and attendance goals by the highest margin is named Outstanding Quarterly Goal Achiever. The award winners receive a plaque, their names and pictures appear in the plant and local newspaper, and the team is invited to a luncheon sponsored by the plant manager.

Conclusion and Summary. Q-YES, a simple, "back to the basics" approach to improvements, has yielded very impressive benefits for W-EAP. The first time through quality level went from 91.5% in 1985 to 100% in 1988. Product line outputs have increased over 100% in the first four years of the program. The hours of technician time per circuit board have decreased by approximately 50%. This increase in quality yields and work force productivity has saved W-EAP's primary customer well over $100 million in product costs in just four years of continuous improvement.

While the quality and productivity results have been important for meeting the plant's goals, the Q-YES process itself creates the real potential for future growth. The new cooperative problem-solving abilities, a sense of individual and team accountability for performance goals, and a successful recognition process promises continued performance results in the future. From a W-EAP perspective, the results of Q-YES demonstrate the impact that a sense of clear accountability and recognition for goal achievement can have on the productivity and commitment of a work force.

In 1986, *Business Week* called Westinghouse-EAP the "factory of the future" with its highly technical equipment and modern team approach to management. In 1987, W-EAP was selected as the "Electronics Plant of the Year" by the National Electronics Packaging and Production Conference. Then in 1988, Westinghouse-EAP was one of five companies honored by the Instructional Systems Association as an example of "distinguished achievements in quality and productivity through human resource development."

The current environment of the electronics defense business is still extremely competitive. However, Westinghouse-EAP continues to be a very aggressive domestic assembly operation.

Source: This case teaching note was prepared by G.C. McMahan during his tenure as Westinghouse Manufacturing Fellow, Department of Management, Texas A & M University, January 1990. Reprinted with permission.

COURSE ENHANCEMENT—
WEST'S ORGANIZATIONAL BEHAVIOR CUSTOM VIDEO SERIES

None of the videos from *West's Organizational Behavior Custom Video Series* are appropriate for use with the material in Chapter 20.

COURSE ENHANCEMENT—
SUPPLEMENTAL VIDEOS AVAILABLE FROM WEST

A video from the Association for Manufacturing Excellence, which is available through West Publishing Company, can be used to enhance the material in Chapter 20. This video is the 10-minute segment of *On the Road to Manufacturing Excellence* that deals with *Motorola*.

VIDEO: *AME: ON THE ROAD TO MANUFACTURING EXCELLENCE—MOTOROLA*

Approximate Time: 10 minutes

Video Summary:

This video describes the challenge facing Motorola in terms of its need to change and how it responded to that challenge by implementing significant organizational changes. Motorola's survival as a leading manufacturer of cellular telephones was threatened by at least two dozen off-shore companies, including several Japanese firms. To remain a viable competitor in the global marketplace for cellar telephones,

Motorola had to transform its highly structured, functionally specialized, mechanistic organization to a more adaptive type of organization.

At Motorola, new products traditionally had been created and brought to the marketplace in a sequentially interdependent fashion; however, the process was inefficient and became a competitive disadvantage. Motorola embraced a new system wherein members from different functions in the organization (*e.g.*, design, operations, and purchasing) and outside suppliers worked together in close coordination to develop new products. The new system permitted new products to be created more quickly and less expensively. Motorola considers change to be an important component of its strategy for success.

Some of the key elements of Motorola's change include the following:

1.   Products and manufacturing processes are designed simultaneously.
2.   Effecting meaningful change is, in part, a matter of educating employees about the need for change.
3.   Operations engineers were placed on the factory floor for rapid response to problem situations.
4.   The layers of management were pared from seven to three, and decision-making responsibilities were pushed down. This streamlining has improved communication between employees.
5.   Suppliers came to be viewed as business partners. Now, fewer suppliers are used but they provide quality, price, and delivery in return for a bigger share of Motorola's supply business.
6.   Motorola's operational philosophy emphasizes a continuous process of renewal.

Discussion Questions and Suggested Answers for Video:

1.   *What system variables—people, culture, task, technology, design, and strategy—did Motorola focus on in instituting change in its cellular telephone business?*

The primary system variables that Motorola seems to be attacking are task, technology, and design. The above list of key elements in Motorola's change program suggests that design is the primary variable of interest, while task and technology are supporting variables.

2.   *What change methods did Motorola appear to be using? Were these change methods appropriate, given the systems variables they were trying to affect?*

Motorola's primary intervention appeared to be some form of adaptive organization design, perhaps a network organization or a matrix organization although there is insufficient evidence to tell which one. Items 1, 3, 4, and 5 from the list of key elements in Motorola's change program support the notion of an adaptive organization design.

Motorola's primary change approach may be supported by the use of sociotechnical systems—one of the task-and technology-focused approaches to change. Although not explicitly stated in the video, there appears to be an effort to jointly optimize the organization's social and technological systems (see items 1, 3, and 4 from the above list of key elements for inferential support). Also, Motorola's belief that change is a continuous process of renewal is suggestive of the continuous improvement aspect of total quality management—another of the task- and technology-focused approaches to change.

Answers to the second part of this question could draw on the tables (see Tables 20.2, 20.4, and 20.7, especially the latter two) that identify the relative direct impact of the various change methods on the six system variables. Basically, Motorola seems to be having the desired effects on the design, task, and technology variables.

CHAPTER 21
CAREER PLANNING AND DEVELOPMENT

CHAPTER OVERVIEW

Chapter 21, with its focus on career planning and development, concludes the discussion of change processes in organizations. First, the chapter examines the various forces that impact on careers. Next, three stages of socialization—anticipatory socialization, encounter, and change and acquisition—that have important implications for careers are considered. Then, career changes are explored in terms of (1) matching individual and organizational needs through career planning and development, and (2) career, occupational, and organizational choices. Next, career stages are explained both from the perspective of career movement within an organization and the perspective of working-life career stages. Emphasis is placed on vertical, horizontal, and inclusion career movements within an organization; and on the establishment, advancement, maintenance, and withdrawal career stages that people move through during their working lives. Finally, the chapter discusses four important career planning issues: dual-career couples, child care, women in management, and outplacement.

LEARNING OBJECTIVES

Upon completion of this chapter, the students should be able to:

1. Describe the socialization process.
2. Define career and describe its components.
3. Explain the factors that influence a person's choices of career and occupation.
4. Describe the four career stages that most people pass through.
5. Identify the central activities and career concerns associated with each career stage.
6. Discuss the factors that affect career planning.
7. List the problems facing dual-career couples, women managers, and employees who have been outplaced.

CHAPTER OUTLINE

I.   **Preview Case:** Winning the Career Game

II.   Organizational Socialization: The Process of Joining Up

    A.   Anticipatory Socialization Stage
    B.   **Managing Quality:** Realistic Job Previews at Nissan
    C.   Encounter Stage
    D.   **Managing Diversity:** Pepsi-Cola's Designate Program
    E.   Change and Acquisition Stage

III. Career Changes

    A.   **Managing Across Cultures:** Speed Bumps on a Career Path
    B.   Matching Organizational and Individual Needs
    C.   Career Choice
    D.   **Managing in Practice:** Cross Colours
    E.   Occupational Choice
    F.   Organizational Choice

IV.   Career Stages

    A.   Career Movement Within an Organization
    B.   Working-Life Career Stages

V.   Career Planning Issues

    A.   Effects of Career Planning
    B.   Dual-Career Couples
    C.   **Managing Across Cultures:** 3M
    D.   Child Care
    E.   Women in Management
    F.   Outplacement
    G.   **Managing in Practice:** Coping with Job Loss

VI.   Developing Skills

    A.   **Self Diagnosis:** Life Success Scale
    B.   **A Case in Point:** Tradeoffs

KEY WORDS AND CONCEPTS

Twenty-three key words and concepts are introduced in Chapter 21. One concept—the glass ceiling—has already appeared in Chapter 1. The key words and concepts, along with definitions or appropriate descriptions, are as follows:

Advancement career stage: a career stage in a person's working life that often involves new experiences: special assignments, transfers, promotions, offers from other organizations, and doing tasks that increase the employee's visibility to higher management.

Anticipatory socialization: the process of accepting the beliefs and values of an organization before an individual actually joins it.

Career: a sequence of work-related positions occupied by a person during a lifetime.

Career development: involves making decisions about occupation and engaging in activities to attain career goals.

Career plan: the individual's choice of occupation, organization, and career path.

Career plateau: a level at which the likelihood of promotions is very low.

Career stage: is a period of time in a person's life that is characterized by distinctive and fairly predictable developmental tasks, concerns, needs, values, and activities.

Decliners: one of three paths that typically are taken during the maintenance career stage of a person's working life. Decliners have little chance for promotion and are often given staff positions that managers view as dead-end jobs.

Dual careers: refers to both partners working outside the home.

Establishment career stage: a career stage in a person's working life that involves fairly routine tasks which are parts of larger projects being directed by more senior employees or managers. In this stage, employees gain experience and learn how to effectively handle the superior-subordinate relationship as well as assigned tasks.

Glass ceiling: refers to artificial, invisible barriers based on attitudes and organization folklore that women and members of minorities face that prevent them from rising above a certain level in an organization.

Golden handcuffs: refers to the salary, perks (*e.g.,* country club memberships, plush office, and company car), and fringe benefits (*e.g.,* deferred compensation plans and stock options) that organizations use to tie employees to them.

Horizontal career movement: a lateral change to another functional or technical area within a given organization.

Inclusion career movement: a movement toward the inner circle, or core, of the organization.

Maintenance career stage: a career stage in a person's working life that is often associated with various personal changes, including changes in physical appearance and stamina and the possibility of experiencing a mid-life crisis.

Mentor: typically refers to an older and more experienced employee who will sponsor and speak to other's about the newcomer's accomplishments.

Mid-life crisis: results in radical changes in a person's behavior and usually occurs between the ages of 39 and 44.

Outplacement firms: organizations that assist laid-off managers in career planning and job hunting.

Realistic job preview: provides applicants with an accurate description of the job they will perform and the department they will work in.

Solid citizens: one of three paths that typically are taken during the maintenance career stage of a person's working life. Solid citizens are reliable and do good work but have little chance of promotion because they lack technical skills or interpersonal skills, have little desire for further promotions, or are too valuable in their present positions.

Stars: one of three paths that typically are taken during the maintenance career stage of a person's working life. Stars will continue to receive promotions, new job assignments, greater responsibility, and higher status.

Vertical career movement: a change up or down formal organizational levels within a given organization.

Withdrawal career stage: a career stage in a person's working life that occurs for most people when they reach about 60 years of age. Even though people are still energetic, they are being passed over or given the opportunity for early retirement.

LECTURE NOTES

I.   Chapter 21 concludes the discussion of change processes by focusing on career planning and development. The chapter addresses some important questions concerning people's careers in organizations, including the following: What forces impact on careers? How do people learn the expectations and requirements of their jobs?. What changes can occur in people's careers? How does a person's career develop? What key issues might people face in managing their careers? These questions, along with the answers provided by Chapter 21, are highlighted in Transparency 21.1.

TRANSPARENCY 21.1
(FROM TEXT MATERIAL IN THE TEXTBOOK)

KEY QUESTIONS AND ANSWERS ABOUT CAREER PLANNING AND DEVELOPMENT

II.   Overview of the forces impacting on careers.

     A.   As we have discussed in several previous chapters, the composition, needs, and values of the work force have changed in dramatic ways over the past two decades. These types of work force changes continue at a rapid pace.

     B.   The changing work force will influence careers in five ways (see Transparency 21.2).

TRANSPARENCY 21.2
(FROM TEXT MATERIAL IN THE TEXTBOOK)

HOW THE CHANGING WORK FORCE WILL INFLUENCE CAREERS

---

     1.   The new global economy requires people to be able to operate comfortably in various settings, including different cultures.

2.　More and more work will be performed as a member of a team working on projects that have a beginning and an end.

3.　Competition will be stiffer for fewer middle management positions, which means less and slower upward movement in the organizational hierarchy.

4.　People will not spend 30 years with the same employer.

5.　People will have to be self-reliant and assume responsibility for managing their own careers.

ENRICHMENT MODULE: PREPARING FOR THE FUTURE JOB MARKET

As a result of various factors, including global competition and corporate downsizing, many experts believe the world of work will be vastly different in the future than it has been in the past. How can people prepare for this future world? Here are some suggestions that the experts offer.

- Don't plan on spending your entire career with a big company.
- Look for employment opportunities at small and medium-sized companies.
- Be prepared to work for a foreign firm.
- Be prepared to work for a female.
- Obtain as much education and training as possible.
- Continually improve your skills.
- Be prepared to work independently or in small teams.

This enrichment module is based on:

Church, G.J. (1993, November 22). Jobs in an age of insecurity. *Time*, 32-39.

TRANSPARENCY 21.3
(The above list of suggestions is reproduced in the transparency package.)

III.　Organizational socialization: the process of joining up.

　　A.　Organizational socialization is the process by which employees learn about their new job and work environment.

　　B.　As shown in Transparency 21.4, organizational socialization occurs in three distinct—but related—stages: anticipatory socialization, encounter, and change and acquisition.

TRANSPARENCY 21.4
(FIGURE 21.1 IN THE TEXTBOOK)
STAGES IN EMPLOYEE SOCIALIZATION

1.　Anticipatory socialization stage.

　　a.　This stage of the socialization process occurs before a person actually joins an organization.

    b.   <u>Anticipatory socialization</u> is the process of accepting the beliefs and values of an organization before an individual actually joins it.

    c.   To provide realistic expectations regarding the organization and thereby avoid potential negative reactions of new employees, many organizations conduct realistic job previews. A <u>realistic job preview</u> provides applicants with an accurate description of the job they will perform and the department they will work in. At Nissan, for example, job applicants actually perform the job under the same conditions as they face if they join the company.

  2.   Encounter stage.

    a.   This stage of socialization begins when individuals actually start their new jobs. They learn the skills and roles—information, interpersonal, and decisional—required by their new job and become oriented to the practices, procedures, and culture of the organization.

  3.   Change and acquisition stage.

    a.   Sometime after joining an organization, people attain full member status by learning and practicing the attitudes and behaviors that are consistent with the organization's culture.

    b.   This stage of the socialization process involves individuals making adjustments in their personal lives and to their jobs.

IV.   Career changes.

  A.   A <u>career</u> is a sequence of work-related positions occupied by a person during a lifetime.

    1.   A career also involves the attitudes and behaviors associated with on-going work activities and experiences.

    2.   Some of the important aspects of the career concept are as follows (see Transparency 21.5):

TRANSPARENCY 21.5
(FROM TEXT MATERIAL IN THE TEXTBOOK)

IMPORTANT ASPECTS OF THE CAREER CONCEPT

---

    a.   Career success or failure is best determined by the individual, rather than by others.

    b.   Career success or failure is related to the concept of self-actualization in the need hierarchy.

    c.   An individual should examine a career both subjectively and objectively.

        d.   <u>Career development</u> involves making decisions about occupation and engaging in activities to attain career goals. The shape and direction of a person's career over time are influenced by many factors.

        e.   Cultural factors play a role in careers.

B.   Matching organizational and individual needs.

    1.   Effective career development requires a fit between the individual and the organization. To the extent that the matching process is done well, both the employee and the organization benefit.

    2.   Transparency 21.6 describes the organizational and individual issues that are associated with career planning and development.

TRANSPARENCY 21.6
(FIGURE 21.2 IN THE TEXTBOOK)

**MATCHING ORGANIZATIONAL AND INDIVIDUAL ISSUES IN
CAREER PLANNING AND DEVELOPMENT**

---

        a.   Organizational issues involve identifying human resource needs and making plans for meeting them.

        b.   Individual issues involve people committing themselves to a lifetime of learning, including the development of a career plan, A <u>career plan</u> is the individual's choice of occupation, organization, and career path.

        c.   The matching process concerns ways that an organization can attempt to match its human resource needs with its employees' career stages. People's needs, values, and goals change as they pass through different career stages. An organization's human resource needs also change over time.

C.   Successful organizations will give people career choices knowing that more and more people will make multiple career choices during their working lives.

    1.   Careers are affected by two major decisions: occupational choice and organizational choice.

    2.   Occupational choice seems to be related to personality and social background.

        a.   Personality, vocational behavior, and occupational interests.

            (1)   Transparency 21.7, which is self-explanatory, shows six personality types and their related problem-solving styles, personality traits, and representative congruent occupations.

TRANSPARENCY 21.7
(TABLE 21.1 IN THE TEXTBOOK)

HOLLAND'S PERSONALITY TYPE DESCRIPTIONS

---

b.   Self-esteem—another personality dimension—may strongly influence an individual's initial occupational choice.

c.   Social background—such as early childhood experiences, the socioeconomic status of the family, the educational level and occupations of parents, etc.—influence career choices by providing socialization experiences and setting practical constraints.

3.   A primary factor in organizational choice is the availability of opportunities at any given point in time.

a.   Transparency 21.8 identifies some of the questions an individual should ask in making an organizational choice.

TRANSPARENCY 21.8
(TABLE 21.2 IN THE TEXTBOOK)

QUESTIONS THAT YOU SHOULD ASK WHEN ASSESSING AN ORGANIZATION

V.   Career stages.

A.   A career stage in a person's life is a period of time characterized by distinctive and fairly predictable developmental tasks, concerns, needs, values, and activities.

B.   Career stages are examined from two perspectives:

1.   An individual's career movement within a specific organization.

2.   An individual's passage through career stages spanning an entire working life.

C.   Career movement within an organization.

1.   Transparency 21.9 identifies the three career movements—vertical, horizontal, and inclusion—that a person can have within an organization.

TRANSPARENCY 21.9
(FIGURE 21.3 IN THE TEXTBOOK)

A MODEL OF CAREER MOVEMENT IN ORGANIZATIONS

---

2.   A vertical career movement is a change up or down formal organizational levels.

a.   As organizations continue to downsize and outsource many functions, some individuals reach their final hierarchical level early in their careers.

3.   A horizontal career movement is a lateral change to another functional or technical area.

b.   By making a horizontal move, employees broaden their perspectives, learn new skills, and gain visibility to managers in other departments.

4.   An <u>inclusion career movement</u> is a movement toward the inner circle, or core, of the organization.

    a.   Inclusion occurs when a manager earns trust, develops greater understanding of the organization, takes on greater responsibility, and is consulted on important matters more frequently.

    b.   An inclusion career movement and a vertical career movement may or may not occur simultaneously.

    c.   Inclusion can be very subtle.

D.   Working-life career stages.

1.   Transparency 21.10 depicts the four distinct stages that people move through during their working lives. These stages are: establishment, advancement, maintenance, and withdrawal.

TRANSPARENCY 21.10
(FIGURE 21.4 IN THE TEXTBOOK)

WORKING-LIFE CAREER STAGES

---

    a.   While most people move through these stages at the ages shown, not everyone will. Some will progress through the stages more rapidly; others more slowly.

2.   Establishment career stage.

    a.   The <u>establishment career stage</u> involves fairly routine tasks which are parts of larger projects being directed by more senior employees or managers. In this stage, employees gain experience and learn how to effectively handle the superior-subordinate relationship as well as assigned tasks.

    b.   A mentor can be very helpful to a person in the establishment career stage. A <u>mentor</u> typically is an older and more experienced employee who will sponsor and speak to other's about the newcomer's accomplishments.

        (1)   Through mentoring, new employees become familiar with the organization's performance expectations and politics, as well as the ambiguous and complex nature of managerial work.

        (2)   Mentoring relationships are usually established as a result of one or more of the following events happening:

            (a)   A mentor usually is impressed with the person's performance.

            (b)   The mentor finds the employee easy and pleasant to be around.

            (c)   In some organizations new employees are encouraged to approach would-be mentors and actively ask for help or initiate a working relationship in other ways.

(3)   In return for helping a protégé, mentors expect:

(a)   The individual to work hard and complete assigned tasks satisfactorily.

(b)   The individual to be a loyal supporter within the organization and work the office politics to help ensure that certain projects sponsored by the mentor progress smoothly.

(c)   Recognition from others for helping bring along young talent and enhancement of their own standing by the younger employee's success.

(d)   To satisfy needs, such as self-esteem and self-actualization, for helping younger employees to learn the ropes.

(4)   Most successful managers have had one or more mentors during their careers.

(5)   Having a mentor seems to be more important for women than it is for men because of the glass ceiling that exists in some organizations. The glass ceiling refers to artificial, invisible barriers based on attitudes and organization folklore that women and members of minorities face that prevent them from rising above a certain level in an organization.

ENRICHMENT MODULE: GLASS WALLS AND STICKY FLOORS

Many people have heard about the glass ceiling that exists in some organizations. But have you heard about "glass walls" or a "sticky floor"? Both concepts are related to the glass ceiling. The glass wall concept refers to the situation where qualified women and minorities are occupationally segregated in jobs without any clear path to the top. People in this situation might advance, but not much—and certainly not into the upper managerial ranks. Instead, they will see people pass them by while they wonder how, if at all, they will ever be able to advance in organization.

The sticky floor concept means that qualified women and minorities can't progress beyond the entry level. People in the sticky floor situation have no legitimate hope for advancement—as long as they remain with the organization, they will be "stuck" in an entry level job. The only way for them to advance is to leave the organization.

This enrichment module is based on:

Kelly, P. (1993, October). Conduct a glass ceiling self-audit now. *HR Magazine, 38 (10),* 76-80.

---

(6)   The risks of having a mentor include the following:

(a)   Employees' careers may suffer if they rely on mentors with little power or who have fallen from power.

(b)   All the advice that mentors give is not necessarily infallible.

(c)   Young employees may become so dependent on mentors that the development of their own careers is slowed.

c.   Transparency 21.11 summarizes the concerns of employees at the establishment career stage.

TRANSPARENCY 21.11
(TABLE 21.3 IN THE TEXTBOOK)

CONCERNS OF EMPLOYEES AT THE ESTABLISHMENT STAGE—AGES 20-25

---

d.   Transparency 21.12 summarizes the characteristics of successful employees at the establishment career stage.

TRANSPARENCY 21.12
(TABLE 21.4 IN THE TEXTBOOK)

CHARACTERISTICS OF SUCCESSFUL EMPLOYEES AT THE ESTABLISHMENT STAGE

---

3.   Advancement career stage.

a.   The advancement career stage often involves new experiences: special assignments, transfers, promotions, offers from other organizations, and doing tasks that increase the employee's visibility to higher management.

b.   This stage involves:

(1)   Managing people, not just tasks.

(2)   Adjustment to the pressure-packed, hectic, and time-consuming realities of managerial life.

(3)   Managing conflicting demands on their time.

(4)   Holding subordinates accountable, yet tolerating mistakes and deficiencies, while also providing leadership to generate high performance.

c.   An important individual decision at this stage concerns specialization in a functional area. The individual must balance the potential career risks and rewards of becoming specialized.

d.   As they approach age 40, many employees have developed skills which make them attractive to other organizations. To retain valuable employees, organizations may use golden handcuffs—that is, salary, perks (*e.g.,* country club memberships, plush office, and company car), and fringe benefits (*e.g.,* deferred compensation plans and stock options) that organizations use to tie employees to them.

e.   At this career stage an individual relies less on a mentor and more on peer relationships for direction and advice.

f.   A person's struggles with decisions about work are compounded by struggles with personal decisions.

ENRICHMENT MODULE: ATTORNEYS WHO WORK AT HOME

Traditionally, success in the legal profession has involved working long hours, generating lots of client-billable hours, and becoming a law firm partner. Some attorneys, many of them women, have begun questioning whether the success is worth the sacrifice of their personal lives. They have decided that, at least for them, the answer is a resounding **NO**. Rather than follow a fast-track career path, some of these attorneys have begun practicing law out of their homes, often on a part-time basis. With this arrangement, they are able to balance more effectively the demands of their professional and personal lives.

This enrichment module is based on:

Keton, J.S. (1994, August 3). At-home attorneys. *The Dallas Morning News*, 2C & 17C.

---

g.   Transparency 21.13 summarizes the concerns of employees at the advancement career stage.

TRANSPARENCY 21.13
(TABLE 21.5 IN THE TEXTBOOK)

CONCERNS OF EMPLOYEES AT THE ADVANCEMENT STAGE—AGES 26-39

---

h.   Transparency 21.14 summarizes the characteristics of successful employees at the advancement career stage.

TRANSPARENCY 21.14
(TABLE 21.6 IN THE TEXTBOOK)

CHARACTERISTICS OF SUCCESSFUL EMPLOYEES AT THE ADVANCEMENT STAGE

---

4.   Maintenance career stage.

a.   The <u>maintenance career stage</u> is often associated with various personal changes, including changes in physical appearance and stamina and the possibility of experiencing a mid-life crisis.

(1)   A <u>mid-life crisis</u> results in radical changes in a person's behavior and usually occurs between the ages of 39 and 44.

ENRICHMENT MODULE: POTENTIAL RESPONSES TO A MID-LIFE CAREER CRISIS

What can individuals do when they face a mid-life career crisis? Employees cope with a mid-life career crisis in a variety of ways. Some employees move sideways to a more dynamic job but without a change in title or salary. Some employees may move down to a job with less responsibility but greater promise of growth. White-collar employees might take a blue-collar job for a period of time. Some employees simply adjust to a career situation that falls short of their earlier aspirations—they basically learn to tolerate the situation. Other employees seek satisfaction outside of their careers—they pursue hobbies or volunteer work. Still others forsake their current, and sometimes secure, jobs for a new career or to be entrepreneurs.

This enrichment module is based on:

Fierman, J. (1993, September 6). Beating the midlife career crisis. *Fortune*, 52-62.

b.   During the maintenance stage, an employee typically takes one of three career paths: star, solid citizen, or decliner.

    (1)   The path taken will depend largely on the direction of a person's career during the first two working-life career stages.

    (2)   Those employees who have been picked by top managers as <u>stars</u> will continue to receive promotions, new job assignments, greater responsibility, and higher status.

    (3)   Many employees become <u>solid citizens</u>. They are reliable and do good work but have little chance of promotion because they lack technical skills or interpersonal skills, have little desire for further promotions, or are too valuable in their present positions.

        (a)   Some solid citizens have reached a <u>career plateau</u>, a level at which the likelihood of promotions is very low. A plateau is reached in most cases simply because many more qualified people are available for higher level positions than there are positions.

    (4)   <u>Decliners</u> have little chance for promotion and are often given staff positions that top managers view as dead-end jobs. Their performance declines but they still do enough to avoid being fired. They have few relationships at work and little influence.

    (5)   Transparency 21.15 compares the career path characteristics of stars and decliners from the perspectives of the organizational features that influence careers, the jobs that people take, and the managers that people have worked for.

TRANSPARENCY 21.15
(TABLE 21.7 IN THE TEXTBOOK)

CAREER PATH CHARACTERISTICS OF STARS AND DECLINERS

c.   Transparency 21.16 summarizes the concerns of employees at the maintenance career stage.

TRANSPARENCY 21.16
(TABLE 21.8 IN THE TEXTBOOK)

CONCERNS OF EMPLOYEES AT THE MAINTENANCE STAGE—AGES 40-60

---

5.   Withdrawal career stage.

    a.   The <u>withdrawal career stage</u> occurs for most people when they reach about 60 years of age. Even though they ar still energetic, they are being passed over of given the opportunity for early retirement.

    b.   At this stage, senior employees may seek to mentor younger employees or devote time to establishing relationships outside their organizations and representing their organization to parties in the external environment.

VI.   Career planning issues.

A.   Career planning entails evaluating abilities and interests and considering alternative career development activities.

B.   Effects of career planning.

    1.   Positive effects of career planning.

        a.   It may reduce turnover, enhance the quality of working life, and improve job performance.

        b.   Stimulating realistic career aspirations is in the best interests of both the organization an its employees.

        c.   Horizontal career moves can be made attractive if career information focuses on personal development, work content, and job importance, rather than only on promotability.

    2.   Negative effects of career planning.

        a.   It may increase managers' work loads by requiring them to provide counseling and on-the-job development assistance.

        b.   It may lead to greater employee demand for career development resources.

        c.   Employees may request more information on job vacancies, pay practices, and career opportunities.

        d.   Employees may raise fundamental questions regarding individual strengths, weaknesses, and goals for the first time.

        e.   Greater expectations may increase employee anxiety.

f.   Unfulfilled expectations may lead to disappointment and reduce commitment.

C.   Four important career planning issues are dual-career couples, child care, women in management, and outplacement.

   1.   Dual-career couples.

      a.   <u>Dual careers</u> refers to both partners working outside the home.

      b.   Dual-career couples encounter a variety of stressors as they attempt to manage their careers and personal lives. Among these are family, work schedule, work role, and organizational stressors.

      c.   The increase in the number of dual-career couples poses problems for many companies when they try to relocate employees. When a relocation is overseas, the problems of dual-career couples can be especially challenging for both the organization and the couple.

ENRICHMENT MODULE: DUAL-CAREER COUPLES AND GLOBAL JOB ASSIGNMENTS

One of the challenges organizations face in making international job assignments is how to deal with the trailing spouse of dual-career couples. Sometimes organizations provide assistance to dual-career couples, sometimes not. When assistance is provided, it may take a variety of forms including:

- Career- and life-planning counseling to help the couple in clarifying and priortizing short- and long-term professional and personal goals, and in determining how those goals can be met through an international assignment.
- Intra-company employment opportunities if permitted by company policy and local labor conditions.
- Inter-company networking to identify job opportunities in other companies.

In the absence of assistance from the organization, trailing spouses may pursue volunteer activities or unpaid internships, change careers, consult, write or do research, continue their educations, change careers, or become entrepreneurs. A commuter marriage also may be an option for the dual-career couple.

This enrichment module is based on:

Reynolds, C., & Bennett, R. (1991, March). The career couple challenge. *Personnel Journal*, 46-48.

---

   2.   Child care.

      a.   Three major events have transformed child care as an issue for the working poor into an issue for the vast majority of working women, including female managers.

         (1)   The feminist movement encouraged homemakers to seek fulfillment in a career.

         (2)   Economic recession and inflation hit the family pocketbook hard.

(3)   The number of single-parent heads of household has skyrocketed.

b.   Child care concerns can weigh heavily on both mothers and fathers and can hurt productivity. Therefore, many organizations will need to deal with the problems faced by working parents, or risk losing valuable employees as the competition for good workers increases.

3.   Women in management.

a.   While women rarely occupy the top positions at the largest U.S. corporations, progress in women entering the executive ranks is being made at some corporations.

b.   Women in management positions face three types of pressures.

(1)   There is the pressure of the job itself.

(2)   There is the pressure of being in the minority and representing other women as a group.

(3)   Women are still expected to take major responsibility for maintaining a household, raising a family, and providing a caring and comforting environment at home.

c.   Transparency 21.17 compares six major success factors for female and male managers.

TRANSPARENCY 21.17
(TABLE 21.9 IN THE TEXTBOOK)

SUCCESS FACTORS FOR FEMALE AND MALE MANAGERS

---

d.   Many other cultures are even more restrictive than the U.S. in terms of women in management positions. For example, in Japan, almost no women hold managerial positions, and in Mexico very few women hold managerial jobs. However, in the Philippines, women from wealthy families can hold important managerial positions because of family connections.

ENRICHMENT MODULE: JAPANESE WOMEN LEAVE HOMELAND TO PURSUE CAREERS

In Japan, women usually are excluded from most managerial positions. Yet, increasing numbers of Japanese women aspire to be managers. So, what do they do? Often, they leave Japan for locations where their talents will be appreciated and utilized without regard to their gender.

Of the growing number of women leaving Japan, many go to Hong Kong despite a language barrier, lower wages, and exorbitant rents. These negative factors appear to be far outweighed by the opportunities for professional advancement.

This enrichment module is based on:

Cody, J. (1994, August 29). To forge ahead, career women are venturing out of Japan. *The Wall Street Journal*, B1 & B5.

ENRICHMENT MODULE: MYTHS ABOUT WOMEN MANAGERS AND INTERNATIONAL JOB ASSIGNMENTS

Research shows that reasons which managers often cite for not giving overseas job assignments to women are actually myths. One myth is that women don't want overseas management assignments. Research on MBAs indicates that the same proportion of women and men want international assignments. In addition, many women prepare themselves for the international arena but face corporate resistance to their global aspirations. A second myth is that women in dual-career marriages are not good candidates for international job assignments. However, research suggests that problems associated with dual-career marriages can be worked out, often with unexpected benefits such as household help. The third myth suggests that women will be ineffective international managers because of foreigners' unwillingness to accept them in managerial roles. Research shows that a higher percentage of women than men report successful international experiences. Moreover, in the international arena women have an advantage that men don't have—they aren't expected to act like the local women but men are expected to act like the local men.

This enrichment module is based on:

Adler, N.J. (1994, April). Women managers in a global economy. *Training & Development*, 30-36.

---

4.   Outplacement.

   a.   Because of downsizing, the number of attractive managerial positions has shrunk dramatically. These managerial ranks are expected to shrink even further.

   b.   Those most vulnerable to layoff are middle managers in the maintenance stage of their careers and whose contributions to the organization are difficult to measure.

   c.   Employers often use <u>outplacement firms</u> to assist laid-off managers in career planning and job hunting. However, nothing an outplacement firm can do compares to what displaced managers can do for themselves. In particular, displaced employees should:

(1)   Stay calm.

(2)   Save their network of contacts and friends until they are ready to move.

(3)   Be flexible.

(4)   Try to avoid emotional highs and lows.

(5)   Not pretend that they weren't fired.

(6)   Maintain a daily routine.

ENRICHMENT MODULE: RESPONSES TO BEING LAID OFF

People can be changed in dramatic ways when they lose their jobs. Usually, their beliefs about company loyalty, job security, and career development are changed permanently. When they become employed again, they adopt a new sense of realism, recognizing that if a layoff could happen once, it could happen again. Their focus in life may shift from career to family, even after re-employment. Some may strike out on their own, establishing business ventures where they are in control of their own destiny.

This enrichment module is based on:

Caminiti, S. (1994, June 13). What happens to laid-off managers. *Fortune*, 68-78.

VII.   Summing up: Why should managers care about people's careers?

A.   In one sense, a career is the totality of a person's experiences in the working world. If those experiences are positive, both the individual and the organizations for which that individual works will benefit.

B.   Mangers can be helpful to both their organization and to individual employees by providing career planning and development assistance which enables employees to meet their individual career goals while simultaneously meeting the organization's changing human resource needs.

C.   Because of the dynamic and highly competitive environment in which many, if not most, businesses operate, people cannot rely solely on their employers for career management. People must become more self-reliant in planning and developing their own careers so that their career goals are more likely to be met.

DISCUSSION QUESTIONS: SUGGESTED ANSWERS

1.   *Why should people be concerned about managing their careers? What can happen if people do not actively plan and manage their careers?*

A useful way to approach this question is from the perspective of the changing nature of the work force. Careers will be influenced by the changing work force in at least five ways:

- a. People must be able to operate comfortably in various settings, including different cultures.
- b. People must be able to function as effective team members.
- c. Competition will be stiffer for fewer middle management positions.
- d. People will not spend 30 years with the same employer.
- e. People will have to be self-reliant and assume responsibility for managing their own careers.

Being able to do these things requires, as an initial step, that people are concerned about adapting to the changing work environment. Moreover, in the complex, dynamic, and competitive environment facing people in the future, the failure of individuals to proactively manage their careers will increase the likelihood of career failure. People must decide what they want out of their careers, and then develop and actively pursue a plan to achieve those goals.

2. *How important will the amount and type of work be in your career? What makes you feel that way?*

This question encourages students to engage in some serious self-reflection. They should consider not only the amount and type of work that they desire, but also how work will be balanced against their personal needs and concerns.

3. *Do you plan to choose an occupation that matches your talents, values, and personality? What are some of the obstacles to finding such a match?*

This question provides students with an opportunity to reflect on their anticipated career choices. They should be encouraged to examine their key talents, values, and personality characteristics, and then consider the kinds of occupations to which these attributes might be related. In answering this question, the students might wish to draw on the text material concerning personality characteristics, occupational interests, social background, and occupational choice. In particular, they might wish to use Holland's theory of personality and vocational choice as presented in Table 21.1

Perhaps the biggest obstacle to pursuing an occupation that matches an individual's talents, values, and personality is the actual availability of such jobs. Other obstacles may include training and educational impediments, or competition from equally or better qualified individuals.

4. *Have your educational experiences in college given you a realistic picture of what being a new employee in an organization is like? Why or why not?*

A useful way to approach this question is to have the students reach a consensus view of what being a new employee in an organization is like. Then they can discuss the extent to which their own educational experiences are consistent with this consensus view.

5. *What are the advantages to organizations of utilizing realistic job previews? To prospective employees?*

A realistic job preview provides applicants with an accurate description of the job they will perform and the department they will work in. Employees tend to be more satisfied when they have realistic expectations regarding their jobs. Moreover, the organization will be less likely to experience substantial turnover from having disappointed and disgruntled employees. Because unnecessary turnover will be lessened, recruiting costs will be diminished.

6.   *Why are mentors important to people in the establishment career stage? How can mentors contribute to the development of protégés early in their careers?*

In the establishment career stage the concerns of employees focus on:

   a.   helping, learning, and following directions;
   b.   developing the subordinate relationship and finding a mentor; and
   c.   having a superior provide coaching, feedback, and visibility from senior management.

In short, people learn how to be effective subordinates in the establishment stage of their careers. Mentors can help people to be come effective subordinates by giving advice and counsel, helping them to avoid missteps and pitfalls, clarifying performance expectations, giving them special opportunities, providing visibility for their accomplishments, and, in general, helping them to develop as productive and valuable members of the organization. Performing these mentoring activities can be especially helpful to people early in their careers. Thus, if potential star performers are identified early enough, a mentor can have a substantial impact on the individual's development.

7.   *What are some of the problems that female managers face as they attempt to get promoted?*

Women managers are still a minority in most organizations and they face different pressures than men face. Not only do they face the pressure of the job itself, but there also is the pressure of being in the minority and representing other women as a group. They are often watched more closely than their male counterparts, and are not part of the "good old boy" network. Women also are the primary caretakers of their households and often are expected to assume major responsibility for raising a family and providing a comfortable home environment. Additionally, women may encounter a glass ceiling in the organization.

This question also could be approached from the perspective of the managerial success factors presented in Table 21.9. Certain factors are more crucial to the success of female managers, and therefore could be problematic. These critical success factors include getting help from above; having a solid track record; having a desire to succeed; being able to manage subordinates; being willing to take career risks; and having the ability to be tough, demanding, and decisive. To the extent that these success factors are absent, women would have some, if not a great deal of, difficulty in being promoted.

8.   *Describe the pressures facing dual career couples.*

Dual-career couples encounter a variety of family, work schedule, work role, and organizational stressors. Family stressors come into play in of terms balancing the amount and quality of family time with job demands. Work schedule stressors involve the demands for long hours, travel, and little vacation time that typically accompany advancement in an organization. Work role stressors concern role ambiguity, conflict, and overload. Organizational stressors include organizational politics and the lack of career progress. Additionally, dual-career couples can face pressures regarding child care and the impact of relocation on the trailing spouse.

9.   *What are some career issues facing employees during the maintenance stage of their careers?*

During the maintenance stage, employees' job concerns focus on training and directing others, developing mentoring relationships with others, and being granted autonomy and the opportunity to develop others. In short, employees typically become outwardly directed in terms of their job activities.

In addition, people at this career stage begin facing the aging process and the inevitability of their mortality. They may engage in serious self-reflection, pondering both met and unmet aspirations. For some, a midlife crisis results, perhaps providing the impetus for meaningful change or even enduring bitterness about unmet expectations. For others, acceptance sets in—some of these employees will merely go through the motions of being contributing members of the organization while others will remain contributing members but will also seek more gratification through outside personal interests.

10.   *What are some functions that outplacement firms perform for managers who have lost their jobs?*

Outplacement firms are organizations that assist laid-off managers in career planning and job search. Such assistance includes testing to uncover job preferences, extensive counseling, and the use of an office and support services. If nothing else, outplacement firms provide displaced employees with a place to go on a regular basis in order to maintain some structure in their lives and some sense of involvement with others.

11.   *Employees often say that success in a career, at least as measured by society's yardsticks of money and status, doesn't guarantee personal happiness. Do you agree? Why or why not?*

In responding to this question, the students could draw on the text material which describes the elusive concept of a career. The following ideas will be particularly helpful for this discussion:

   a.   Career success or failure is best determined by the individual, rather than by others.
   b.   Career success or failure is related to the concept of self-actualization in the need hierarchy.
   c.   An individual should examine a career both subjectively and objectively.

Career success should be gauged in the context of an individual's career goals and aspirations, not in terms of what society values as being important. The students should be encouraged to explore their own career aspirations, and then to describe success criteria that would reflect those aspirations. Also, have the students consider why they might be inclined to accept society's definition of career success even though money and status may be relatively unimportant to them personally.

12.   *Discuss the special problems that employees face when they relocate to a foreign country. Why might such an assignment be career ending?*

Adapting to the culture of the host country is probably the major problem that employees face when they relocate overseas. These employees may have to learn different norms, customs, and business practices in order to succeed in a foreign culture. If the relocated employee is part of a dual-career couple, an international assignment can pose special challenges for the trailing spouse. Trailing spouses may not be able to continue their careers or they may need to develop creative solutions—such as jobs in adjacent countries, consulting or writing, internships, pursuing further education, etc.—to the problem. Loss of spousal income is a related problem if the trailing spouse is unable to find work.

Success in an overseas assignment might not ensure career success. An overseas assignment might be career ending if the individual cannot successfully reintegrate into the culture of their home country.

DEVELOPING SKILLS—
SELF DIAGNOSIS: LIFE SUCCESS SCALE

Success means different things to different people. This instrument permits the students to determine what life success means to them personally. The students respond to the questionnaire by indicating the relative importance (1 = never important to 5 = always important) of 42 items regarding life success. Different measures of life success—status/wealth, contribution to society, family relationships, personal fulfillment, professional fulfillment, and security—are generated by averaging the scores in six subsets of the 42 items. Normative data from a sample of 439 women and 317 men are provided for comparative purposes.

DEVELOPING SKILLS—
A CASE IN POINT: TRADEOFFS

CASE OVERVIEW

After graduation from college, Martha Wilson became a management trainee at Comtec, a software manufacturer in Richardson, Texas. After only five months of training, Martha received her first supervisory assignment—managing a five-person customer service group—as part of a management reorganization. The supervisors were given considerable autonomy in running their units and Wilson saw this as an opportunity to institute team meetings and a training class. Wilson demonstrated her capability as a supervisor, producing substantial improvements in the unit's performance and earning a reputation as a rising star in the company.

After three years, Martha accepted an offer to head the marketing department at BanTec, a company located in Phoenix. The new job was exciting and challenging and required lots of travel. She developed her subordinates by giving them considerable autonomy and decision-making responsibility. To broaden her business horizons, she also entered an MBA program, where she met and developed a relationship with Art Cunningham.

Three years later, Martha had completed her MBA degree, had traveled overseas extensively, and had become engaged to Art. At this time, she was offered an assignment as vice-president for operations at BanTec's plant in Monterrey, Mexico. While the position would provide valuable experience, she would be reporting to Enrique Rangel, the plant manager. Wilson was unsure whether she would be able to adapt to Rangel's strict, task-oriented management style. Further, she would be the only woman manager at the Monterrey plant.

CASE QUESTIONS

1.   *What career stage is Martha in? What personal concerns is she facing?*

Martha is in the advancement stage of her career. See has already been recruited away from Comtec, and her subsequent success at BanTec has qualified her for consideration for further promotion. She has successfully dealt with the key activities of this stage, which include managing people, not just tasks; adjusting to the realities of managerial life; managing conflicting demands; and holding subordinates accountable, yet tolerating mistakes and deficiencies, while also providing leadership to generate high performance.

Martha appears to be facing three major personal concerns:

    a.   She is pondering whether to get the manufacturing experience—to generalize—or to remain a marketing specialist. The issue of specialization is characteristic of the advancement career stage.

    b.   She also is wondering about the potential conflict between her management style and that of Enrique Rangel, who would be her new boss.

    c.   Martha also may be pondering the balance between her work and nonwork lives. Her engagement to Art, who has his own career, raises issues associated with being a dual-career couple on an international assignment in a country where women are not frequently found in management positions.

2.   *Describe stressors that she will face if she and Art become a dual-career couple.*

Dual-career couples encounter a variety of family, work schedule, work role, and organizational stressors. Most likely, Martha will face work schedule, work role, and organizational stressors. There will probably be considerable demands on her time, leaving relatively little time for her personal life. Because Rangel is a task master, Martha might encounter the work role stressor of role overload. Since she would be the only female manager at the Monterrey plant, Martha would likely encounter organizational stressors in the form of office politics. Finally, family stressors could come into play, particularly if the couple would have children.

3.   *What decision would you make if you were Martha? What did you consider in making that decision?*

In answering this question, the students should consider what Martha's career goals might be. An evaluation of the decision then should occur in the context of those career goals.

The students can also be asked to identify what their career goals would be if they were Martha. Again, the appropriateness of a given decision should be weighed against the career goals.

COURSE ENHANCEMENT—
WEST'S ORGANIZATIONAL BEHAVIOR CUSTOM VIDEO SERIES

None of the videos from *West's Organizational Behavior Custom Video Series* are appropriate for use with this chapter.

APPENDIX
TOOLS AND TECHNIQUES FOR STUDYING ORGANIZATIONAL BEHAVIOR

APPENDIX OVERVIEW

This appendix exposes students to the tools and techniques that are used to investigate problems in organizational behavior. First, the scientific approach is described. Next, the basic nature and purpose of research design is explained. The nature of research hypotheses and the role of experimental design is also examined. Four types of research design—the case study, the field survey, the laboratory experiment, and the field experiment—and five data collection methods—interviews, questionnaires, observation, nonreactive methods, and qualitative methods—are discussed. For each type of research design and data collection method, we describe its basic nature and its advantages and disadvantages. Finally, three research-related ethics issues are explored. These issues concern misrepresentation and misuse of data, manipulation, and value and goal conflicts.

LECTURE NOTES

I.   By having a basic understanding of research methodology, managers are better equipped to analyze problems themselves, to evaluate the proposals and approaches of others who analyze problems on their behalf, and to be intelligent and appropriately critical consumers of others' research data and conclusions. Therefore, to assist students in developing their knowledge of basic research methodology, the appendix discusses the tools and techniques that are used to investigate problems in organizational behavior.

II. The scientific approach.

    A.   The scientific approach is a method for systematically collecting and analyzing information in an unbiased manner.

    B.   The three basic steps in the scientific approach are observation, measurement, and prediction. Each step leads to the next in a sequential fashion, and the entire process is circular such that prediction leads to further observation.

C.   The scientific approach also requires a systematic test of assumptions and guards against preconceptions or personal bias.

III.   Preparation of research designs.

A.   A *research design* is a plan, structure, and strategy of investigation intended to obtain answers to one or more questions.

1.   The *plan* is the researcher's overall program for the research.

a.   The plan should identify the types of data to be collected, sample populations, research instruments, methods of analysis, tentative target completion dates, etc.

2.   The *structure* is an outline of the specific variables to be measured.

3.   The *strategy* presents the methods to be used to validate the data, to achieve research objectives, and to resolve problems encountered during the research.

B.   A research design has two major purposes.

1.   To provide answers to questions.

2.   To control nonrelevant effects that could influence the results of the study.

a.   A *nonrelevant effect* is anything the investigator has little control over but that could affect study results.

C.   Rarely does a specific research design satisfy all the criteria associated with the scientific approach, but investigators should select a design that satisfies as many as possible.

D.   Hypothesis.

1.   A research design typically involves a stated hypothesis so that inferences of a causal relationship between an independent (causal) variable and a dependent (effect) variable can be tested.

2.   A *hypothesis* is a statement about the relationship between two or more variables.

3.   A hypothesis asserts that a characteristic or occurrence of the *independent* variable determines the characteristic or occurrence of the *dependent* variable.

4.   After a hypothesis is stated, data are collected and analyzed (usually statistically) to determine whether the data do or do not support the hypothesis.

E.   Experimental designs.

1.   Determining causality is a complex research issue, and a thorough discussion of it is beyond the scope of the appendix. However, we do provide a fundamental understanding of causality in relation to research design.

2.   An experiment should always have an experimental group and a control group.

    a.   Members of the *experimental group* are exposed to the treatment, or the independent variable.

    b.   Members of the *control group* are not exposed to the treatment.

3.   People can be selected to participate in the experiment on the basis of random selection or matching. Both selection methods are intended to control for the effects of extraneous influences and any preconceptions or biases the researcher might have.

    a.   *Random selection* occurs when each person has an equal chance of being chosen for either the experimental group or control group.

    b.   *Matching* involves choosing research participants who are alike in all aspects that are relevant to the experiment, and then assigning them (usually randomly) to the experimental group or the control group.

4.   Using a control group permits researchers to rule out explanations for the results other than the relationship specified by the research hypothesis.

5.   Some of the possible alternative explanations for research results include:

    a.   Natural maturing or development.

    b.   Influence of the measurement process itself.

    c.   Contemporaneous events other than the exposure of the employees to the research program.

IV.   Types of research designs.

A.   The adequacy of the research design (along with the adequacy of the data collection methods) influences the quality of the research that is performed.

B.   Of the many different research designs that exist, the investigator should select the best design for the research problem. The best design depends on:

1.   The types of information the design provides.

2.   The degree of confidence the investigator can have regarding inferences that are based on the findings.

3.   The amounts of time, money, and other resources required and available to perform the research.

C.   Four commonly used research designs are: the case study, the field survey, the laboratory experiment, and the field experiment.

D.   The case study.

1.   In a *case study* the investigator seeks detailed information about an individual or a group through records, interviews, questionnaires, and observations.

2.   Three features of a case study make it important for providing new insights into problems.

   a.   The researcher can adopt an attitude of seeking rather than testing.

   b.   The case study is intense.

   c.   The case study tests the researcher's ability to assemble many diverse bits of information and base a unified interpretation on them.

3.   Advantages of the case study.

   a.   It provides for substantial depth of understanding about the research problem.

   b.   It frequently provides many clues and insights for further investigation.

4.   Disadvantages of the case study.

   a.   Generalizing the results of one case study to other cases usually isn't practical or logical.

   b.   It usually doesn't permit systematic investigation of cause-and-effect relationships.

E.   The field survey.

1.   In a *field survey* data are collected through interviews or questionnaire from a sample of people selected to represent the group being studied.

2.   A field survey is used to gather information and not to change or influence the respondents, and it usually requires a large sample in order to reach valid conclusions.

3.   Advantages of the field survey.

   a.   It can be a convenient way to collect a large amount of data from a large number of people.

4.   Disadvantages of the field survey.

   a.   Its use is limited to collecting data about things of which the respondents are consciously aware.

   b.   Problems arise with the inference of cause-and-effect relationships, primarily because of the large number of unmeasured variables.

   c.   People don't return questionnaires. Only 25% of questionnaires usually get returned.

F.   The laboratory experiment.

1.   In a *laboratory experiment* the investigator uses an artificial setting to create and control the exact conditions desired, thereby improving the ability to establish cause-and-effect relationships.

2.   The essence of the laboratory experiment is to manipulate one or more independent variables and observe the effect on one or more dependent variables.

3.   Advantages of the laboratory experiment.

a.   It permits the researcher to control the conditions under which the experiment is conducted.

b.   It is most useful when the conditions required to test a hypothesis are not readily obtainable in natural situations or when the situations can be replicated under laboratory conditions.

4.   Disadvantages of the laboratory experiment.

a.   Because college students are the most common source of research subjects, the results of laboratory experiments may have questionable generalizability to other populations and treatment variables.

b.   Simulating many of the properties of organizational structure and process in the laboratory can be extremely difficult.

c.   Many behavioral problems in organizations can't be isolated to permit laboratory experimentation.

G.   The field experiment.

1.   The *field experiment* is an attempt to apply the laboratory method to ongoing real-life situations.

2.   In the field experiment the investigator manipulates one or more independent variables in an actual organization and then observes changes in one or more dependent variables. Cause-and-effect inferences can be made with a reasonable degree of confidence.

3.   Advantages of the field experiment.

a.   The field experiment avoids the artificiality of a laboratory experiment.

b.   It increases the generalizability of results.

4.   Disadvantages of the field experiment.

a.   Since subjects in a field experiment usually know they are being observed, the investigator must use procedures to minimize the likelihood that the subjects will change their behavior simply because they are being observed.

b.   The field experiment provides the investigator with fewer controls than the laboratory experiment.

H.   The case study, survey, laboratory experiment, and field experiment can be compared in terms of realism, scope, precision, control, and cost.

1.   Realism.

a.   Field research provides the realism that may be absent from the artificial conditions of the laboratory but it sacrifices the experimental control that is available in the laboratory.

2.   Scope.

a.   Case studies and field surveys are broader in scope than laboratory experiments and field experiments.

3.   Precision.

a.   Laboratory research is usually more precise than field research.

4.   Control.

a.   An experiment can be controlled so that the events being observed will be related to hypothesized causes, not to some unknown, unrelated events.

b.   The laboratory experiment permits easy replication.

c.   The laboratory experiment avoids many factors present in field studies over which the investigator has little control. However, the results obtained from ideal laboratory circumstances may not fit the real situation.

5.   Cost.

a.   The laboratory experiment has relatively low setup costs, requires relatively few other resources, and costs relatively little for additional subjects.

b.   Field experiments and surveys can be costly in terms of time, personnel, and acquisition of additional subjects or respondents.

6.   Effective investigators select the research design that is best for their purposes and circumstances at the time, use all the strengths of that design, and limit or offset its weaknesses whenever possible.

V.   Data collection methods.

A.   The adequacy of data collection methods (along with the adequacy of the research design) influences the quality of the research that is performed.

B.   Five commonly used data collection methods are: interviews, questionnaires, observation, nonreactive measures, and qualitative methods.

C.   Interviews.

1.   The interview involves direct questioning of a respondent. Its effectiveness relies on the willingness of people to communicate and the interviewer's ability to establish mutual trust and goodwill with the respondent.

2.   Advantages of interviews.

    a.   Asking someone a direct question can save considerable time and money.

    b.   The interview permits follow-up, in-depth probing of the respondent's answers.

3.   Disadvantages of interviews.

    a.   People may be unwilling to provide certain types of information to an interviewer face-to-face.

    b.   Interviews take time, which costs money.

    c.   To achieve reliability, interviewers must be well-trained, present questions in a way that ensures validity, and eliminate personal bias.

    d.   The questions asked by the interviewer limit the answers that respondents may freely give.

D.   Questionnaires.

1.   Questionnaires are sets of written items to which the subject is asked to respond. Typically, they are used to measure the respondent's attitudes, opinions, or demographic characteristics.

2.   Advantages of the questionnaire.

    a.   It provides a relatively inexpensive way to collect data.

    b.   It can be administered by relatively unskilled people.

    c.   It can be mailed to people individually or given to people in groups.

    d.   It provides the same stimulus to everyone surveyed.

    e.   It can be answered anonymously, which may lead to more truthful responses.

3.   Disadvantages of the questionnaire.

    a.   Missing data may be a problem if people do not answer all of the questions.

    b.   A low response rate may invalidate the results.

    c.   It cannot be used with individuals who have severe reading problems.

    d.   The respondent has no flexibility in answering, which limits the amount of information that can be obtained.

E.   Observation.

    1.   People observe the actions of others and, based on these observations, make inferences about others' motivations, feelings, and intentions.

    2.   Advantages of observation.

        a.   The observer actually can see the behavior of individuals rather than relying on verbal or written descriptions of it.

    3.   Disadvantages of observation.

        a.   Observers analyze and draw inference from their observations, and inferences are often incorrect.

F.   Nonreactive measures.

    1.   *Nonreactive measures,* such as company records, permit an investigator to collect data about people without requiring their cooperation.

    2.   Advantages of nonreactive measures.

        a.   They are inconspicuous because they are generated without people's knowledge of their use.

    3.   Disadvantages of nonreactive measures.

        a.   Their use can raise serious ethical issues, particularly regarding invasion of privacy.

G.   Qualitative methods.

    1.   *Qualitative methods* are open-ended and interpretative means of collecting data that rely on the experience and intuition of the researcher.

    2.   Qualitative methods require the researcher to become closely involved in the situation or problem being studied. For example, when applied to organizational behavior, *ethnography* requires the investigator to study the organization for long periods of time as a participant observer.

    3.   Advantages of qualitative methods.

        a.   It provides rich detail and depth of understanding about an organizational problem or situation.

        b.   It can lead to the development of insightful hypotheses.

    4.   Disadvantages of qualitative methods.

        a.   The investigator's objectivity may be compromised by being a participant observer.

        b.   It is time-consuming, and therefore costly.

H.   Criteria for assessing the different data-collection methods.

    1.   Data-collection methods should be evaluated in terms of reliability, validity, and practicality.

    2.   *Reliability* refers to the accuracy of measurement and the consistency of results.

    3.   *Validity* refers to the degree to which a data-collection method actually measures what it claims to measure.

    4.   *Practicality* refers to:

        a.   Acceptability of the data-collection method to the participants.

        b.   Accessibility of the method for participants and test administrators so as to save time and money and to minimize disruption of normal operations.

VI.   Ethics in research.

A.   Managers and investigators usually encounter three types of ethical issues in conducting research: misrepresentation and misuse of data, manipulation of the participant, and value and goal conflict.

B.   Misrepresentation and misuse of data.

    1.   The ethical issue for the investigator is the decision between fully disclosing all the information obtained or sharing just some of it.

    2.   Some examples of how this ethical issue arises in organizational research include the following:

        a.   *Computer monitoring* to collect detailed, minute-by-minute information on employee performance for management's use.

        b.   The presentation of false statements or the attribution of true statements to false sources as part of the design of a laboratory experiment.

C.   Manipulation.

    1.   Manipulation involves interfering with a person's exercise of free will. This occurs when the investigator requires employees to do something opposed to their personal values.

D.   Value and goal conflicts.

    1.   In conducting research, the investigator's values and goals should not violate federal, state, and local laws, especially a constitutionally protected right to privacy.

VII.   Summing up: Managers and the value of research methodology.

A.   The introductory lecture remarks are worth repeating to both summarize and reinforce the importance of managers being knowledgeable about research methods. By having a basic understanding of research methodology, managers are better equipped to analyze problems themselves, to evaluate the proposals and approaches of others who analyze problems on their behalf, and to be intelligent and appropriately critical consumers of others' research data and conclusions.

INTEGRATING CASES: TEACHING NOTES

CROSS-REFERENCING OF INTEGRATING CASES AND CHAPTERS

The following list identifies the chapters for which each of the integrating cases has the greatest relevance:

A Day in the Life of Yolanda Valdez	Chapter 1, 8, 12, and 18.
Bob Knowlton	Chapters 3, 4, 6, 9, and 11.
Conscience or the Competitive Edge	Chapters 3, 8, 14, 18, and 21.
The Shiftless Worker	Chapters 5, 6, 7, 9, 11, 13, 14, and 20.
The Road to Hell	Chapters 2, 3, and 12.
Resistance to Change	Chapters 13, 15, 17, 18, and 19.

A DAY IN THE LIFE OF YOLANDA VALDEZ

CASE OVERVIEW

This case describes the managerial activities of Yolanda Valdez, senior vice-president for marketing of ClearVision Optical Group, during what appears to be a typical working day from 7:25 a.m. to 5:45 p.m.. Her activities, in sequential order of occurrence, may be summarized as follows:

1. Yolanda started to work on developing a questionnaire for a customer survey regarding the firm's line of eyeglass frames. This was a high-priority item for the day's work.
2. Linda Brown, Yolanda's secretary, came in to review the day's scheduled activities.
3. Yolanda assigned Linda some work to complete during the day.
4. Yolanda returned to work on the questionnaire.
5. Yolanda met on the spur-of-the-moment with the vice-president of operations for the western division to discuss plans for marketing children's eyewear.
6. On the way back to her office, Yolanda was stopped by an optical lab worker who asked for advice on career opportunities in marketing.
7. Yolanda called the president of the company, seeking his opinion on a major new advertising campaign for children's eyewear.
8. Yolanda met with the contact lens group to hear their presentation and to set some goals to be accomplished prior to the next meeting.
9. Yolanda met with a group working on fall store displays and informed them about the

children's eyewear campaign.

10.   A display group employee talked to Yolanda about a conflict he was having with his team leader. Yolanda promised to look into the matter.

11.   She returned to her office, returned a couple of important phone calls, and put the other messages aside to answer later in the day.

12.   Yolanda met with an ad agency representative to discuss plans for their first-ever network TV advertising.

13.   She made routine calls to subordinates to check on progress on certain projects.

14.   She met with the vice-president for finance to discuss an acquisition of a chain of sunglass stores.

15.   Valdez discussed a new employee benefits program with the vice-president for human resources and the vice-president for finance.

16.   She returned phone calls.

17.   She met with the president about expansion strategy and an evaluation of the firm's frame supplier.

18.   Yolanda returned to her office to find an inventory control report on her desk, which she read and then discussed with the person who prepared it.

19.   She returned to working on the questionnaire.

20.   She signed letters.

21.   She worked on personnel evaluations.

22.   Yolanda took the questionnaire home so she could work on it with less likelihood of being interrupted.

CASE QUESTIONS

1.   What characteristics of managerial work did Valdez' day illustrate?

Effective performance of managerial work is based upon utilizing technical, interpersonal, conceptual, and communications skills. The following description summarizes how Yolanda used these skills in her own work:

Technical skills involve one's ability to apply the necessary methods, procedures, and techniques in a specialized field. Items 1, 4, 7, 12, 17, 19, 21, and 22 from the list in the case overview demonstrate Yolanda's use of technical skills.

Interpersonal skills involve one's abilities to deal with people as individuals or in groups. Items 2, 3, 4, 5, 6, 8, 9, 10, 12, 14, 15, 17, and 18 from the above list demonstrate Yolanda's use of interpersonal skills.

Conceptual skills involve one's abilities to think and plan, to see the "big picture" or overall organizational framework, and to relate variables to one another in the context of this big picture. Items 4, 7, 8, 9, 12, 14, 15, 17, and 18 from the above list demonstrate Yolanda's use of conceptual skills.

Communications skills include sending and receiving information in both oral and written forms, as well as being sensitive to and understanding of people's thoughts, feelings, and attitudes. All of the items from the above list demonstrate Yolanda's use of communications skills.

2.   What roles did Valdez play?

Yolanda Valdez played all but one of the ten managerial roles in one way or another. The following is a synopsis of the various interpersonal, informational, and decisional roles and how Yolanda did (or did not) play them.

Interpersonal Roles:

In the *figurehead role,* the manager performs various symbolic or ceremonial tasks for the organization. None of the items from the list in the case overview illustrate Yolanda's use of the figurehead role.

In the *leadership role,* the manager supervises and coordinates subordinates' work efforts in order to achieve organizational goals while satisfying employees' needs. Items 2, 3, 8, 13, 18, and 21 from the above list illustrate Yolanda's use of the leadership role.

In the *liaison role,* the manager develops information sources outside the organization or in other subunits within the organization. Items 1, 11, 12, 16, 18, 19, and 22 from the above list illustrate Yolanda's use of the liaison role.

Informational Roles:

In the *monitor role,* the manager searches for and gathers information that is relevant to the organization. Items 5, 8, 9, 13, and 18 from the above list illustrate Yolanda's use of the monitor role.

In the *disseminator role,* the manager distributes information to others within the organization. Items 6, 7, 9, and 21 from the above list illustrate Yolanda's use of the disseminator role.

In the *spokesperson role,* the manager distributes information to people outside the organization. Items 12 and 20 from the above list illustrate Yolanda's use of the spokesperson role.

Decisional Roles:

In the *entrepreneurial role,* the manager initiates projects or identifies changes in order to improve the organization or its subunits. Items 5, 7, 13, and 17 from the above list illustrate Yolanda's use of the entrepreneurial role.

In the *disturbance handler role,* the manager helps to resolve conflicts between organizational subunits or with outside organizations. Item 10 from the above list illustrate Yolanda's use of the disturbance handler role.

In the *resource allocator role,* the manager decides upon the type and amount of resources to be distributed to different organizational subunits. Items 7 and 15 from the above list illustrate Yolanda's use of the resource allocator role.

In the *negotiator role,* the manager represents the organization or one of its subunits in dealing with customers, vendors, unions, and governmental agencies. Item 12 from the above list illustrate Yolanda's use of the negotiator role.

3.   *How did she spend her day? Explain.*

Yolanda spent her day doing what mangers do with most of their time—communicating and making decisions. She communicated through a variety of conversations and formally scheduled meetings, both on an individual and group basis. She made decisions about goals to be pursued, problems to be solved, and operational actions to be taken. Additionally, Yolanda's day, while probably normal, was nonetheless hectic and perhaps somewhat stressful.

4.   *What fundamental concepts of the contingency approach are illustrated in this case?*

The contingency approach emphasizes the need to tailor managerial actions to the characteristics and demands of the situation. Throughout the case we see Yolanda Valdez engaging in a variety of activities, most, if not all, of which seem to be appropriately tailored to the problem situation or challenge she is currently dealing with.

BOB KNOWLTON

CASE OVERVIEW

Bob Knowlton, a recently appointed research project director at Simmons Laboratories, was reviewing the results of the initial test run on a new photon unit when a stranger, Simon Fester, appeared at his office door. Dr. Jerrold, Knowlton's boss, had Fester meet with Knowlton regarding Fester's interest in the work being done in the Photon Lab. Unknown to Knowlton, Fester was a candidate for a position at Simmons Laboratories. Knowlton and Fester discussed the photon project, and Fester revealed himself as a very knowledgeable, even brilliant, and seemingly arrogant individual.

Jerrold hired Fester, assigning him to Knowlton's project group. Fester immediately formed a relationship with Link, a mathematician in the Photon Lab, discussing an analytical method that Link had been working on for a month. Fester began studying progress reports on the photon project, even taking some home with him. After discovering a way of solving a photon problem, Fester insensitively called Knowlton in the middle of the night to discuss his solution. The following morning Knowlton, Fester, and Link reviewed Fester's work. For the next several days, Fester intensively reviewed all the progress reports that had been completed in the past six months.

The Photon Lab relied on a team approach in conducting its activities. At a regularly scheduled team meeting of all lab personnel, including secretaries, Knowlton resurrected a problem that had been discussed previously and judged by the team as unsolvable. This aroused Fester's interest, and he immediately began asking questions to understand the problem. Early on, the other team members discussed the problems, listing reasons why it had been abandoned. However, as they began to realize that Fester intended to disagree about the value of abandoning the project, they became less cooperative. Fester then proceeded to attack the value of a team approach to creatively solving problems. Knowlton defended the value of a team approach in terms of communication, coordination, and developing weaker members of the team.

Fester dominated subsequent team meetings, trying to demonstrate the superiority of his knowledge and ideas. Fester had a low opinion of every team members' abilities, except for Link. As a result of both factors, the team's cooperative spirit began to disintegrate and Knowlton felt his leadership of the team slip away.

Fester, however, did make several significant contributions to the development of the new photon unit. So when a progress meeting was scheduled with the project's sponsor, Fester presented the progress report. This was unusual, since such reports were normally presented by the project director and team members didn't attend the progress meetings. After learning that Jerrold expected Fester to attend the progress meeting, Knowlton suggested that Fester make the presentation since it would be a way of recognizing the outstanding work that Fester had done. In reality, however, Knowlton felt unsure of his ability to explain the part of the work Fester had done, or to answer questions on Fester's work. Fester's presentation was very successful, tending to dominate the meeting. Fester also attracted a great deal of attention at the banquet held that evening to which the entire laboratory was invited. Along with many others, Knowlton publicly congratulated Fester on his abilities and brilliance.

Without consulting anyone in the company, Knowlton began looking for a job elsewhere. He soon took a project director's job at another lab in a nearby city. Citing personal reasons, Knowlton sent a letter of resignation to Jerrold's home on a Friday evening. Jerrold was disturbed since he had decided to put Fester in charge of a new project and wanted Knowlton to continue heading up the photon project. However, Jerrold did not attempt to meet with Knowlton. Link was given the temporary leadership of the Photon Laboratory.

CASE QUESTIONS

1.   *What attributions did Bob Knowlton make?*

Bob attributed his lack of recognition from Jerrold after Fester arrived to Fester's success in making a great presentation to the sponsors of the photon project. This information caused Bob to perceive that Fester would be awarded the "fair-haired boy" status that Bob previously had enjoyed with Jerrold. Bob also attributed minor events, such as Jerrold having lunch with Fester when Fester joined the lab, as signals that Bob was not going to play a major role in the Photon Lab any more. That is, Bob focused on isolated events that enabled him to form an opinion about the relationship between Jerrold and Fester.

2.   *What team norms seemed to be operating in Bob Knowlton's team?*

A basic norm was team decision making. All members of the team shared the success or failure of a project. To establish and maintain this norm, Bob held weekly meetings in which everyone was invited to present his ideas and ask the group for assistance. The norm focused on task- and relations-oriented behaviors of the Photon Lab.

3.   *How do you characterize the decision-making styles of Dr. Jerrold, Bob Knowlton, and Simon Fester?*

Bob Knowlton uses a sensation-feeler style. He is a pragmatist who deals with problems in a methodical fashion. He works with his team and derives much satisfaction from working with them. He uses his team to explore new ideas and informally chat about problems in the lab. He pays attention to the details of running the lab and was even praised by Fester for his lab's precision and organization. A weakness in this style is an inability to understand and an impatience in dealing with abstract theories.

Simon Fester is an intuitive-thinker. He is the architect of new ideas and progress. He does not like group meetings, but prefers to be a "lone ranger." The reason why he quit his prior job was that he was bored. Fester demands a great deal of Bob, his fellow co-workers, and others in the lab. When he made his presentation to the sponsors of the project, he was rewarded for his individual efforts. A weakness of this style is ineffectiveness in dealing with others, notably Bob Knowlton, and viewing others as incompetent. Calling Bob at home during the wee hours of the morning to discuss a research report indicated Fester's lack of interpersonal skills.

Dr. Jerrold is probably an intuitive-thinker. Just like Fester, Jerrold is not aware of the interpersonal problems in the lab but reminds Bob that "The sky's the limit for those who can produce." He never introduced Fester to Knowlton and did not instruct Bob in what Fester's job duties would be. Jerrold figured that Bob would use Fester where needed.

4.   *What leadership style did Bob **need** from Dr. Jerrold after Simon arrived? Explain.*

Bob needed some initiating structure from Jerrold immediately after Simon's arrival. Jerrold did not explain to Bob what role(s) he envisioned Simon playing in the lab. This caused Bob to re-evaluate his own contributions. Since Jerrold did not clarify Simon's role and stopped displaying any affection toward Bob after Simon's arrival, Bob became frustrated and quit the lab.

5.   *What leadership style did Bob seem to get from Dr. Jerrold **before** and **after** Simon arrived? Explain.*

Prior to Simon's arrival, Bob received a considerate style of leadership from Jerrold. The considerate style was used in conjunction with the achievement-oriented style that made Bob feel like a major contributor in the company. Jerrold's vision of the lab enabled Bob to play a major role in the company. After Simon arrived, Jerrold used a style that could be characterized as low on initiating structure and low on consideration.

6.   *What leadership style did Bob use with his subordinates? Was it effective? Explain.*

Bob used a considerate style with his subordinates. This style generated job satisfaction for his subordinates, but did not foster a high drive for solving complex tasks. In fact, prior to Simon's arrival, the team concluded that a problem was unsolvable given the equipment and physical capacities of the lab; yet Fester solved the problem. Bob needed to exercise a greater degree of initiating structure or low LPC leadership in order to get the team to achieve higher performance. That is, when the task became unstructured, Bob needed to exercise a leadership style that was more focused on solving the task than on being considerate of the employees' feelings and satisfying their social needs.

7.   *What leadership style did Bob use with Simon? Was it effective? Explain.*

Bob used an achievement-oriented leadership style that permitted Simon to make decisions by himself. Simon was confronted with a nonroutine task. Bob's leadership style was appropriate for managing a person who acts as a solo contributor on projects. However, this style also reinforced Simon's independence from others in the group.

8.   *What would you have done with Simon if you were Bob?*

One of Bob's strengths is to build a highly cohesive team of people to solve problems. Bob should find out what Simon's needs are and attempt to satisfy these through working in a team atmosphere. For example, Simon should have made the major part of the presentation, but Bob could have delegated roles in the presentation to members of the lab. This way, the lab employees' esteem and social needs would have been fulfilled.

9.   *What would you have done to influence Dr. Jerrold if you were Bob?*

Bob needs to manage Jerrold. Jerrold's career is on the line to produce a product that will satisfy the lab's clients. The process of how Jerrold accomplished this result was not effective. By not consulting with Bob prior to Simon's appointment to the group, Jerrold undercut Bob's authority in the lab. Bob should have confronted Jerrold and tried to resolve the conflict as soon as he recognized that the situation was explosive. Bob should have clarified his role as director of the lab after Simon's appointment. Because Bob did not manage his boss, nor did Bob understand the pressures that were on Jerrold from the home office to produce a product to satisfy the client, Bob became frustrated and left the company.

CONSCIENCE OR THE COMPETITIVE EDGE?

CASE OVERVIEW

Olivia Jones, a buyer for a major European retailer, was on a four-day trip to Bombay, India to select cotton fabrics to be used in the following season's youthwear collection. On the last day of her trip, Jones asked to visit a factory. Despite attempts to dissuade her, she was determined to visit a factory. Her host took her to a typical factory which was located in a Bombay ghetto. The factory was located in an 800 square feet room (20 feet by 40 feet). In the room , "twenty men were sitting at treadle sewing machines, bent over yards of white cloth. Between them on the floor were rush mats, some occupied by sleeping workers awaiting their next shift." These men worked "a 24-hour rotation, 12 hours on and 12 hours off, every day for six months of the year." They were working on an order that Jones had placed a few weeks earlier in London. While she had been especially proud of the low price she had negotiated on the order, she later described her visit to the factory "as the most humbling experience of her life."

This is a classic social responsibility/personal values situation. An up-and-coming "western" manager is confronted head-on with how she is able to obtain a price/cost advantage in the European marketplace—*i.e.*, through the "supposed" exploitation of workers in lesser developed countries (LDCs) or newly industrialized countries (NICs) who are subjected to economic servitude in what some might consider degrading and inhuman working conditions. "What should Olivia Jones do?" is the action question which provides for a lively debate as the students wrestle with their "clinical and dispassionate advice to Jones" while confronting their own personal values on what they personally would do.

CASE QUESTIONS

1.   *What should Jones do?*

Generally, students agree that Jones' main options are:

- Demand a change in the working conditions for the workers in the factories that she does business with.
- Refuse to buy goods in India.
- Seek the advice of her superiors in this matter.
- Quit and look for a more socially active/responsible employer.

●   Do nothing/leave things as they are.

For the most part, the B case—which is included after question 2—addresses these options sufficiently. Therefore, they are not repeated here.

Some of the more interesting and varied arguments will come from those students who support "do nothing." In many ways, this represents the classic historical western economic viewpoint. Some students will try to sound noble in taking this perspective (*i.e.,* "We have no right to interfere in the affairs of a sovereign nation." "We have no right to interfere with the culture of another nation/people.") Some will put forth the old argument: "When in Rome, do as the Romans do." Then there are those who will take the economic perspective: "The workers suffering in the mills are still better off than 90 percent of the population." To be sure, there will be sufficient numbers of students who will have no part of such lines of thinking.

It is up to the instructor as to whether s/he wishes to distribute the B case in class. Because it is in Jones' own words, the B case may have an especially powerful impact on the class. Most students feel uneasy/disappointed with Jones' resolution of the case. It is here that the professor can force students to confront their personal values head-on with one question: "So what would you be prepared to do?"

2.   *What would you do if you were in her shoes?*

While the students may opt to sound noble, they need to be reminded about things like recessions, job mobility, lost career opportunities, and personal and family financial obligations as competing forces. Situations like Jones' forces everyone to determine "where they stand" and to confront the reality of their stated views.

The one option which students usually don't consider, however, is the "lobby group" or "political action committee" route. Perhaps Jones could persuade her firm to lobby the British government to ban/boycott Indian goods until local reforms are made. Other European firms might be persuaded to join in, as well. (Undoubtedly, this will take a lot of time and effort on her part—not to mention the company's—and may eventually interfere with her career!) This social activist approach, however, represents one of the best solutions because:

●   Olivia, her firm, and all other companies with a social conscience are spared the economic pain of and consequences of acting along.
●   They are protected from those whose social conscience is less sensitive and who would seek to take advantage of those trying to promote social change.
●   It creates a level economic playing field when successful.
●   It forces the Indian government to face its own problems directly.

To be sure, this will offend some who feel that this is a form of coercion and interference in the cultural matters of sovereign nations. There is, however, nothing preventing them from forming a "NO" political action committee. However, their advertising would probably be interesting to observe. (Would they really be prepared and willing to "defend exploitation"?) This would certainly force them to go public with their views and face their opponents squarely. That would be good for all parties concerned.

If Jones' firm is unprepared to act, Jones must decide:

●   Whether she feels comfortable working for such a firm.
●   Whether this is an issue over which she is prepared to fight the cause on her own.

To the extent that Jones attempts to take up the cause on her own, she must be prepared to be fired for taking a public stand on an issue which threatens probably one of her firms' largest and cheapest supply countries. Jones must, therefore, decide if this cause is worth that risk—as well as her ability to evoke social change.

In the end, Jones is right. Major social change occurs usually through the personal sacrifices of individuals. Jones clearly has been presented with such a challenge. For her own personal reasons, she states in the B case that she was not willing (or felt unable) to be a champion for change. Will your students feel the same? The answers you get in class are a harbinger for the future of our world!

CONSCIENCE OR THE COMPETITIVE EDGE? (PART B)

Olivia Jones described her subsequent decision as follows:

"The alternatives for me were perfectly clear, if somewhat unrealistic: I could stipulate a standard of working conditions to be reinforced at any factory employed, and offer to pay an inflated price for merchandise in an effort to fund the necessary improvements. This would mean having to increase the margins in other sections of the range and explaining to my controller exactly why prices had risen.

"There was, of course, no guarantee that the extra cash would make its way safely into the hands of the worker or improve his working conditions. Even exercising my greatest faith in human nature, I could see the wealthy factory owner getting increasingly fatter and some other keen and able buyer being promoted into my highly coveted position!

"I could refuse to buy from India. This would mean I would have to find alternative sources at equally low prices to justify my action. There was always Macau, where I knew conditions were worse if anything, or Hong Kong, where conditions were certainly better, from what I had seen, but prices were much higher. I had to ask myself if I would truly be improving the plight of the workers by denying them the enormous orders that I usually put through their factories. Or would I simply be salving my own conscious by righteously congratulating myself at not dealing in slave labor? Doubtless my production schedule would be snapped up eagerly by the next buyer who was hungry for cheap labour and fast turnaround.

"I would consider speaking to the powers that be and ask their advice. After all, the group was proud of its philanthropic reputation and had promoted its charity work and sponsorship of various causes, including Wimbledon Football Club and Miss World. This in mind, I approached my line manager, who laughed at my idealistic naivety and made it quite clear that I should hold my tongue if I knew what was good for me.

"It seemed I had but two choices. Either I quit the company and look for an employer which would be more responsible in its attitude towards sourcing merchandise, or I could continue to buy as before, but aware of the consequences and exercising a conscience wherever possible. I won't bother to list my excuses for opting for the latter choice.

"I believe that there is no solution, no generalization which can be used as a precedent in this type of scenario. I don't know to this day what action I could have taken to improve the lives of those individuals whom I felt I had compromised.

"Every day, in various work situations, employees, and specifically managers, come up against questions of conscience versus the **status quo**. It may be that you are encouraged to show prejudice against an individual or group of employees due to their race, colour or clique; maybe your boss asked you to lie to camouflage an embarrassing error and insinuate that the fault lies with someone else; maybe your employer's policy requires you to screw a client or a supplier to close a deal and maintain the bottom line.

"Each case is different and demands its own evaluation. Each man and woman must draw their own set of rules and regulations to suit their own situation and conscience.

"It takes brave individuals to jeopardize their careers for a cause but it is thanks to those who do take a stand that great feats of humanitarian work are successfully undertaken and completed. We should all evaluate the choices that are open to us and be true to ourselves. Let your conscience be your guide within the realms of reality.

"The most important lesson that I learned from the episode was that, above all, you have to learn to live with the choices that you make."

EPILOGUE

Jones writes, two years later, from San Francisco:

"The company that hired me spent thousands on my training and had me productive at a very high level within 18 months. Yet isn't it astounding that in all my courses on management techniques, negotiation skills, stress management, counseling staff, etc., there was no mention of issues of ethics, moral responsibility or conscience?

"Because of my firm's total lack of social responsibility and its unwavering focus on profits—at the expense of anything and anyone—I left the company within one year of my Indian trip. I went to work in business development for a smaller and more ethically minded company, which incidentally has nothing to do with the rag trade! I'm very happy."

Source: Adapted from the case and case teaching note prepared by Kate Button, journalist, and Dr. Christopher K. Bart, McMaster University, Canada. All events and individuals are real, but names have been disguised at the request of the principals involved. Copyright © 1993 by the *Case Research Journal* and Kate Button and Christopher K. Bart. The case appeared in the *Case Research Journal*, Winter 1994, 68-72. Used with permission.

THE SHIFTLESS WORKER?

CASE OVERVIEW

This case focuses on Lost River Processing, Inc., a processor of ore that is mined in the nearby mountains of Wyoming. Maintenance of high quality in processing the ore is essential to getting and retaining customers. The company operates 24 hours a day; crews and their supervisors switch shifts on a monthly basis. The key players in this case are: Charlie McManus, manager of department B; John Williams, a shift supervisor in area 7 of department B; and Mark Olson, an operator on Williams' crew.

With some exceptions, the work force at Lost River is generally hard-working, independent, and self-motivated. Thus, for the past couple of years, the company has eliminated layers of management and pushed decision making downward in its move toward operating on the basis of self-managed teams.

Most of the supervisors are experienced workers who have moved up within the plant. John Williams is one exception; he, along with three others, transferred from supervisory positions at a plant in South Carolina when the company closed it. The work force and organizational culture were much different at the South Carolina plant—the "workers were not highly trained and their supervisors tended to manage them quite closely."

Williams, and the other transferred supervisors, continued their close supervisory styles at Lost River, which upset many workers—most notably Mark Olson. Olson, a very capable individual and contrary to his prior performance record, began performing tasks poorly or not performing them at all. Williams complained to Charlie McManus about Olson's behavior, even asking for help in solving the problem. According to plant scuttlebutt, Olson's performance deficiencies were deliberately selected on a random basis to drive the supervisors crazy. While Olson's childish behavior was problematic, there were "grumblings" from other workers about the transferred supervisors (three of whom reported to Charlie McManus). For example, one worker commented: "They treat us like a bunch of slaves, don't let us make decisions, and treat us like we're stupid." Thus, as Charlie McManus pondered what to do about Williams' request for help with Olson, he also wondered whether the problem was much larger.

In essence, this case presents a middle manager with the immediate issues of what to do with a formerly excellent employee who has become careless in carrying out his job assignments and how to respond to the supervisor who has asked for assistance in dealing with the situation. The situation is somewhat ambiguous, however, with implications for larger issues beyond the immediate problem.

One larger issue is to ascertain the role the supervisor's style plays in fostering the problem behaviors. In addition, strategic issues are involved because the company, in beginning the process of delegating decision making downward and moving toward the creation of self-managed work teams, is encountering supervisors imported from a different corporate culture who are managing too tightly given the culture of this plant and its long-range goals.

Thus, the case raises issues of current importance to organizations attempting to move toward self-managed work teams, autonomous work groups, or leaderless teams. The issues raised are also relevant to the organizational integration issues raised by mergers, take-overs, buy-outs, expansions, etc. Issues can be discussed from the point of view of employee discipline, style of supervision, organizational culture and fit among all of these.

CASE QUESTIONS

1. *What is your analysis of the situation faced by Charlie McManus? What are the key issues facing him?*

    Charlie has been asked by one of his supervisors for help in dealing with a "problem" employee. In one sense, the request is probably legitimate since the employee apparently is behaving in an irresponsible manner. However, some clues indicate that the supervisory approaches used by some recently transferred supervisors may be fostering some of the employee reactions. Given that the company is moving toward an organization based on the concept of self-managed work teams, tight, highly controlling supervisory practices go counter to the culture being developed.

    Charlie is then faced with the problem of how to deal with the issue of supervisors who violate the desired cultural norms while still correcting the employee misbehavior.

2. *How do you explain the behavior of the operator in this situation? Why do you think he is performing the way he is?*

The operator, Mark Olson, is probably representative of the type of employees hired in this plant. They tend to be a hard-working, independent, and self-motivated work force in general. The plant has been moving toward self-management at lower levels, which is consistent with a work force exhibiting such qualities. The operator's reactions and resultant "grumblings" to the introduction of the new, and more controlling supervisors probably are understandable. We also know that Mark Olson is one of the brighter employees in this situation, so we are not extremely surprised by his development of clever, although ultimately probably self-defeating, ways of coping with the situation. The overcontrol implies to him that he is not responsible, and he reacts by becoming so or by failing to do parts of his job on a random basis to "drive them crazy."

3.   *What do you think charlie McManus should do? Explain in detail how you think he should proceed.*

Charlie can approach the situation in quite a number of ways, and may choose to use more than one approach simultaneously. The possibilities include the following:

●   He can deal with the immediate problem behavior by intervening as requested by the supervisor, John Williams, and meet with the problem employee, with the two together, or with each of them separately and then together.

In meeting directly with the employee, Charlie may be able to communicate more effectively with the employee than the employee's supervisor can. Charlie may be able to correct the behavior of a previously excellent employee who is quite bright and had shown much promise. In following this course, however, he may be undercutting the authority of the supervisor to deal with his people.

Meeting with the employee and his supervisor together may have the same effect on the supervisor's authority. Another danger here is that one never knows what may be said—the potential for surprise is high—and the presence of each may inhibit or otherwise affect what the other is willing to communicate.

If Charlie elects to meet with each separately, he is more likely to discover exactly what each is feeling about the situation. He can then decide whether he wants to meet with them together, and just what approach to take in such a meeting, or to take some other approach, such as giving the supervisor some coaching to handle the situation himself.

●   Another approach might be to meet with the supervisor with the goal of helping him see the contribution of his own actions to the problem behavior. These new supervisors are managing in ways that have proven successful for them in the past, and they probably don't understand and are upset by the reactions they are getting from their subordinates in the new setting.

Ultimately, these new supervisors, exhibiting a leadership style contrary to the expectations of current employees and to the culture being developed, must be more fully integrated into the culture of the plant. The movement to delegate and involve lower-level employees requires a more considerate leadership style.

If this approach is followed, the manager should intervene in a manner consistent with developing the supervisor to make his own decisions in line with the desired culture. That is, an educative strategy is necessary rather than an authoritarian approach ordering the supervisor to change his ways, thereby violating the desired cultural norms in the attempt to create culture.

This approach may be beneficial for the development of the new supervisor, and help him to achieve a successful resolution of the problem with his own employee. This strengthens his authority with his employees and most likely prevents any escalation of the kinds of employee reactions seen in this case.

●   The problem that has surfaced with the incidents presented in this case is part of a larger problem. In the present situation, one supervisor is having trouble with one employee. Yet we are aware that there are other employees who are at least "grumbling" and at least three other supervisors probably are contributing to similar feelings elsewhere in Charlie's department and in the plant. The manager may wish to discuss these issues with someone higher in the organization in order to initiate some program on a plant-wide scale to deal with the problem and prevent similar problems in the future.

The issue of how to socialize and acclimate new supervisors can also be raised. Of particular importance is how to socialize and train transferees from other locations with different organizational cultures. Perhaps some sort of training program for these new supervisors can be designed even at this point to prevent further deterioration of the situation.

4.   *What do you think the supervisor John should do? How do think the operator Mark will react to what you propose?*

The supervisor is in a problematic situation. He is probably incapable at this point in time of understanding his contribution to the problem behavior. Undoubtedly, his approach to dealing with subordinates, learned over many successful years of supervising in the plant back East and rewarded by the transfer to this plant, is deeply ingrained and natural to him.

If the situation is discussed with his manager, he may come to understand that employee expectations and the culture in which he must manage in this plant are different. If so, he may attempt to approach the problem employee in a different manner to see if he can rebuild their relationship and correct the inappropriate behavior. If he's a quick learner, he can essentially correct the immediate situation by himself, although this is an unlikely scenario. If he is willing to change, and realizes he could use some help, his manager, Charlie, can work with him.

5.   *What are the implications of the short-term, operational decisions in this situation for the long-range strategic goals of the plant?*

The plant has been eliminating layers of supervision and pushing decision making down in the organization, with the ultimate goal of operating on the basis of self-managed work teams. Given the hard-working, independent, and self-motivated nature of the work force, the history of positive employee relations in the plant, and the need in this highly competitive industry to continually reduce costs, this is probably a viable strategy.

The supervisory approaches and the culture being created in the plant are consistent with these goals. Given the importance of quality as well as cost in securing and keeping customers, it is important that disruptions to the productive process, including personnel problems, be minimized. The behaviors exhibited by Mark Olson, which are likely being duplicated to some extent by other operators in the plant, pose a real problem for management.

Plant management, and the company as a whole, should consider the implications of transferring supervisors from one location to another. The cultures of the plants involved should be explicitly considered, and perhaps some transfers advised against, or adequate training programs or other methods devised to acculturate the transferees to their new setting.

In the spirit of the self-managed culture being developed the plant, whatever approach Charlie takes to managing the immediate situation should contribute to the development of his supervisors for the long run. Thus, he must take a long-range, developmental approach to managing the situation, both with respect to how he handles his supervisor, John Williams, and how he or John proceeds to deal with the employee, Mark Olson.

6.   *In this specific situation, the issue was an inappropriate supervisory style and its impact on worker behavior. What other issues are likely to arise in the transition from a traditional hierarchically structured unit to a group-oriented, self-managed organization? What managerial practices might be considered in dealing with them?*

The incident described in the case may be merely symptomatic of what is taking place in the entire plant. If some layers of supervision have been eliminated and the process of pushing decisions downward in the organization has begun, then workers are expected to accept more responsibility for their own operating decisions. As they begin to make such decisions, they will inevitably make mistakes and may disagree with their supervisors on occasion. Supervisors, in turn, have seen whole layers of management excised from the organization structure and have seen a plant close down. Feeling threatened themselves, they are apt to be intolerant of worker mistakes and thus crack down on them.

To deal with and escape from the increased pressure felt by all, everyone may regress to a time when they felt secure. Supervisors retreat into authoritarian behavior to secure their world. Workers avoid responsibility through passive resistance or, in the case of Mark Olson, by regressing to childish behavior to drive them crazy while he waits for an opportunity to escape by transferring out.

Each of the individuals in the case is in the position of trying to understand his world and manage it alone. Each may be overwhelmed, frightened, and angry at what is happening to him. And it can't even be blamed on some evil or stupid higher management—the real cause of the pressures is the economic structure of the market and the pressures for achieving a low-cost producer status and securing single-source customers through quality assurance. The problem is systemic, yet the plant organization appears to be leaving resolution up to individuals at every level.

In making the transition from a traditional structure to a leaner one based on self-managed work teams with decision making pushed down to the lowest possible levels, some support system must be developed to help people at all levels through the change. Mechanisms must exist with the capacity to mange the dissent, anger, and stress that such a transition engenders. How are people at all levels in the plant, people like Charlie, John, and Mark, going to deal with the threats they each face and learn appropriate new ways to deal with their jobs and especially with each other?

From an organization development standpoint, these issues should be dealt with by collective rather than individual action. As decisions are being pushed down, it is appropriate to involve workers in addressing the problems they face. Some team building processes akin to role negotiation within and between groups and their supervisors or managers might be one approach. Such approaches combined with increased regular communication among all parties throughout the transition period have promise of creating a viable system.

Source: Adapted from the case and case teaching note prepared by William E. Stratton of Idaho State University. The names of the firm, individuals, and locations have been disguised to preserve the firm's anonymity. Presented to and accepted by the refereed Midwest Society for Case Research Workshop. All rights reserved to the authors. Copyright © 1990 by William E. Stratton. See R.A. Cook (ed.), *Annual Advances in Business Cases, 1990*. South Bend, Ind.: Midwest Society for Case Research, 1990, 610-623. Used with permission.

THE ROAD TO HELL

CASE OVERVIEW

In preparing to leave his position as chief engineer of the Caribbean Bauxite Company Limited of Barracania in the West Indies, for a promotion to production manager at another facility near Winnipeg, Canada, John Baker, an English expatriate, held a final interview with his successor, Matthew Rennalls. A Barracanian native, Rennalls had been groomed by Baker to take over as chief engineer. Development and promotion of citizens of the host country was part of the company's regionalization policy in its international operations.

As an expatriate manager, Baker preferred working in "developing countries" because he thought he had an innate talent for getting along with regional staff. Rennalls was very race conscious and was extremely sensitive to any sign of condescension from expatriate managers and employees. Baker and Rennalls seemed to have an amiable relationship, though an invisible, indefinable barrier always existed between them.

Baker began the interview by expressing his hope that Rennalls might be able to benefit from his advice because of his years of experience. Rennalls' nonverbal behavior indicated a lack of receptiveness to what Baker might have to say. Baker proceeded to describe what he perceived to be Baker's strengths and weaknesses. The crucial weakness, from Baker's viewpoint, concerned Rennall's behavior toward the European employees at the facility. As Baker said, "I have noticed that you are more friendly and get on better with your fellow Barracanians than you do with Europeans." Baker also mentioned the need for having Europeans in senior management positions until there were sufficiently trained Barracanians of Rennalls' caliber. Rennalls sat tensely and waited several moments before responding. Rennalls maintained that the description of his behavior toward the European staffers was inaccurate, but he recognized that he needed to correct the perception.

Baker was unconvinced by Rennalls' response so he pursued the prejudice issue via another avenue. Specifically, Baker complimented Rennalls' progress and accomplishments in the context of Rennalls' cultural heritage. In comparing Rennalls and himself, Baker said, "the situation is different, because you and your forebears have only had some fifty and not two or three hundred years. Again, Matt, let me congratulate you—and people like you—on having so successfully overcome this particular hurdle. It is for this very reason that I think the outlook for Barracania—and particularly Caribbean Bauxite—is so bright." Rennalls listened intently and thanked Baker for the compliment. The interview then ended with a few minutes of cheerful conversation unrelated to the purpose of the interview.

When Baker arrived at work late the following morning, he received a resignation letter that Rennalls had dictated to Baker's secretary earlier in the morning. The resignation letter contained a vitriolic attack on Baker for making comments that Rennalls perceived to be racially condescending.

CASE QUESTIONS

1.   *What were Baker's intentions in the conversation with Rennalls? Were they fulfilled or not, and why?*

At a conscious level, Baker appeared to have the intention of motivating Matthew Rennalls to do a good job as his replacement and to provide him with some pointers that would enhance his probability of success. These goals were obviously not achieved. One of the main problems with Baker's approach to Rennalls is that he used essentially a one-way communications approach. Baker served primarily in the role of "judge" by identifying the strengths and weaknesses of Rennalls—with little opportunity for Rennalls to identify his own strengths and weaknesses. Rennalls was never invited to really identify the problems or difficulties he perceived in working with others in the organization. Rennalls was put in a reactive posture, and Baker never really listened to Rennalls.

2.   *Was Baker alert to nonverbal signals? What did both Baker and Rennalls communicate to one another by nonverbal means?*

When Rennalls came into the room and sat down, Baker saw him stiffen slightly in his chair when Baker indicated that he was 10 years older and should be able to give Rennalls the benefit of his longer experience. While Baker was "aware" of the nonverbal message, it was not effectively interpreted. Rennalls also tensed up when Baker was speaking of the role of Europeans needing to occupy senior positions in Barracania. Baker nonverbally communicated to Rennalls that the things on **his** mind were those that count. Regardless of Rennalls' comments, Baker continued to return to the issues that he wanted to discuss. Moreover, it wasn't simply a matter of what he wanted to discuss: it was a question of what Baker wanted Rennalls to hear! Through Rennalls' nonverbal cues, he continued to communicate to Baker his **rejection** of Baker's feelings and thoughts.

3.   *How did Baker's view of himself affect the impression he formed of Rennalls?*

Baker apparently viewed himself as more seasoned and effective than Rennalls. As a result, Baker appeared to have an air of superiority and condescending attitude toward Rennalls. At a subconscious level, Baker may have been somewhat more racially conscious than he cared to admit to himself or others.

4.   *What kind of interpersonal relationship had existed between Baker and Rennalls prior to the conversation described in the case? Was the conversation consistent or inconsistent with that relationship?*

It appears that a self-protecting style existed for both Baker and Rennalls. They would both "give feedback" to the other. However, they seemed to "lack in openness to and from each other." This self-protecting pattern of communication seemed to be consistent with the conversation that took place.

5.   *What, if anything, could Baker or Rennalls have done before, during, or after the conversation to improve the situation?*

There are a variety of ideas and concepts that should have been implemented before, during, or after the conversation. In particular, the guidelines for giving effective feedback needed to be followed by both Baker and Rennalls. Of course, the primary responsibility for the failure to create the conditions for effective feedback falls on the shoulders of Baker, who is the superior. Much more time could have gone into thinking about the specific tangible issues to be discussed during this conversation. Baker presented too many generalities and tried to force his own conclusions about these generalities on Rennalls.

Rennalls was not given the opportunity prior to the meeting to identify those issues and questions he would like to bring up in the conversation. Baker should have given Rennalls an opportunity to "carry the ball" during the early part of the conversation by requesting that Rennalls think about questions, concerns, and issues that he would like to ask of or discuss with Baker.

Another major area of needed development concerns listening skills. Virtually all of the guidelines for increasing listening skills are relevant to the case. For example, good listeners tend to search for value and meaning in what is being said. Both Baker and Rennalls failed to exhibit good listening skills. Baker and Rennalls repeatedly assumed they understood what the other was saying. When the messages being transmitted are heavily emotionally laden, as in this case, the listeners should rephrase in their own words the content and feeling of what the sender appeared to be saying. The memorandum from Rennalls to Baker is an excellent example of an obvious misinterpretation and misunderstanding of Baker's real intentions. It is apparent that neither Baker nor Rennalls felt "good" about the conversation. Baker might have initiated a follow-up meeting the next day or possibly later that day if his schedule did not permit continuing the same conversation. On the other hand, Rennalls should have initiated a meeting with Baker to express his concerns and interpretations prior to submitting a formal memorandum that only served to increase the difficulty and tension in the situation.

6.   *How would you characterize the personality attributes of Baker and Rennalls?*

We recognize that it is always somewhat risky to characterize personality attributes based upon written accounts. The question should be interpreted in the spirit of encouraging students to develop their diagnostic skill in understanding individual differences rather than reaching hard conclusions. With these qualifications, we identify our interpretation of several personality attributes for Baker and Rennalls.

Baker	Rennalls
High self-esteem	High self-esteem
High assertiveness	High assertiveness
Internal locus of control	Internal locus of control
Extraversion	Extraversion
Moderate level of dogmatism	Moderate level of dogmatism

Our interpretation is that these personality profiles helped to create the conditions for the interpersonal difficulties experienced by Baker and Rennalls.

7.   *What perceptual errors and attributions are evident?*

Some of these errors and attributions include:

● Perceptual defense—the tendency for people to protect themselves against ideas, objects, or situations that are threatening. In a number of places in the case, both

Baker and Rennalls exhibited perceptual defense. The most dramatic example was the memo from Rennalls to Baker.

- Stereotyping—the tendency to assign attributes to someone solely on the basis of a category in which that person has been placed. A dramatic example is Baker's comment regarding Rennall's ancestors and the following statement: "Again, Matt, let me congratulate you—and the people like you—on having so successfully overcome this hurdle."
- Baker made attributions about Rennall's motives.
- Rennalls made major attributions about Baker's motives (especially in the memo).
- Baker assumes Rennalls has a "well repressed sense of race consciousness." Yet, the only negative "evidence" that Baker uses to attribute racial prejudice to Rennalls is that Baker has failed to establish as friendly a relationship with him as he would have wished and that a senior draftsman had recently complained about Rennalls' rudeness. But no concrete evidence is provided of this last incident.

RESISTANCE TO CHANGE

CASE OVERVIEW

As a result of rapid expansion, a desire to standardize operations, and for legal reasons, Forest Park Hotels, a division of Golden Horizons, Inc. adopted a centralized human resource policy. The centralization of the human resource activities was in line with the company's previous decisions to centralize the division's accounting, marketing, and purchasing functions.

A centralized human resource program was implemented under the direction of Cara Reynolds, division vice-president for human resources. Part of the centralized program included the development of operational guidelines with input from each hotel's general manager, human resource director, and other key members of the local management team. The guidelines were endorsed by the division vice-president, and everyone involved appeared to understand and accept them.

Approximately six months after their implementation, the Atlanta hotel requested an exception to the standardized job description and guidelines for hiring a sous chef to replace one who had resigned. Both Jim Evans, general manager of the Atlanta hotel (the most profitable operation in the division), and Joseph Langemier, the hotel's food and beverage director, contacted Reynolds to request an exception to the guidelines. Langemier emphasized that culinary experience was far more important than supervisory experience for the position of sous chef. He also recommended that Walter Steiner be flown from Baltimore to Atlanta to interview for the sous chef position. Steiner had the culinary experience but not the supervisory experience the position required. Plus Langemier suggested that Steiner be offered the maximum salary in the salary range guidelines for sous chefs. (Reynolds later discovered that Steiner probably was one of Langemier's "drinking buddies.")

Reynolds reviewed the standardized job description and salary range guidelines. She was aware that Atlanta was experiencing a hotel building boom in preparation for the 1996 Olympics, which in turn was creating an upward pressure on salaries and benefits for skilled hotel staff. Recently completed salary surveys indicated the Atlanta hotel was competitive in salary and benefits paid to sous chefs at comparable hotels. The three sous chefs currently on staff in the Atlanta hotel met the divisional guidelines. Moreover, two local individuals who met the guidelines had been referred to Langemier for interviews but had never been interviewed.

CASE QUESTIONS

1.   *Describe the change process, problems encountered with implementing the planned change, and techniques used to promote change.*

The change process begins with the change agent, Cara Reynolds, division vice-president of human resources. She has become the catalyst of the change process by instituting a centralized human resource program. By initially issuing a draft of new guidelines, she has begun the unfreezing process. Change begins to take place through the use of participation as the local hotel management groups review the new guidelines and make recommendations for additions, deletions, and modifications.

The availability of corporate support in meeting human resource needs also aids in the change process. In additional, coercion is presented since the vice-president of human resources can "veto" any decisions by local management that do not conform to the new program. As is typical in most situations where change is taking place, resistance is encountered. Not only does resistance occur because individuals are being asked to move away from the known patterns of accomplishing tasks, but also because they are concerned about their own personal loss of power in the decision-making process. After the new human resource program has been accepted by the local hotel management groups, it is necessary to refreeze the desired behaviors in order to eliminate pre-change behaviors.

Although political pressures will vary with each change situation, they will be present. Cara has utilized several strategies for implementing the planned changes. First, she developed and implemented the program with the full support of the division vice-president. Second, the program has been presented on the basis of its overall benefits of providing for future human resource needs while meeting Equal Employment Opportunity and other legally specified guidelines. Third, although it was not within Cara's control, the new human resource program is a continuation of the centralization process that began with the accounting, marketing, and purchasing functions.

2.   *If one of the most experienced managers with a consistently profitable operation is requesting an exception to the guidelines, are there other underlying problems, or is he simply not accepting the new centralized human resource system?*

Several subtle issues can be explored with this question. First, the general manager, Jim Evans, is apparently supporting his food and beverage service director, Joseph Langemier. He may have been allowing members of his management team to make their own human resource decisions in the past. Since his hotel has been quite successful, he may be resisting changes that could negatively impact the hotel's bottom line. Second, the apparent personal friendship between Joseph and Walter can be explored. Although many managers may desire to make decisions based on personal friendships, this may pose legal problems because of the inherent potential for discrimination. In addition, the potential for collusion and circumvention of controls is present along with potential "morale" problems if the friendship dissolves. Third, the fact that Jim is questioning the guidelines may indicate the new human resource program has not been properly designed and implemented. The importance of communication in the change process could be discussed at this point.

3.   *How should Cara Reynolds respond to Joseph and the local management team?*

Cara Reynolds must decide whether to:

a.   make an exception to the recently adopted human resource policies in considering Walter Steiner;
b.   modify the recently adopted policies;
c.   eliminate the policies completely; or
d.   let the policy stand as is.

Potentially divergent human resource needs among the geographically dispersed hotels in the division and the rapid growth of the hotel division may create unique problems in attempting to follow a centralized human resource policy.

On the surface, Forest Park Hotels appears to have completed the initial steps necessary to develop a strong program that will meet its present and future human resource needs. The corporate human resource department, with the assistance of other divisional managers and the general managers at each Forest Park Hotel, has analyzed the present and future staffing needs. Based on these analyses, exempt positions were identified and standardized job descriptions were prepared. The current human resource program has been adopted to achieve and maintain equity in hiring, training, developing, and compensating managerial and professional employees.

The newly centralized human resource program did not appear to cause any difficulties until it interfered with a local hotel's desires and autonomy. Jim Evans made several calls to Cara Reynolds seeking an exception to the newly adopted guidelines. Although the exception was not granted, Jim, relying on Joseph Langemeir's recommendation, instructed the local human resource manager to have Walter Steiner flown from Baltimore to Atlanta for an interview even though he was not "qualified" for the position.

The decision by the Atlanta hotel staff to unilaterally make an organizational change accommodating hiring Walter would seem to indicate that supervisory qualifications are not necessary and the position should no longer be considered exempt (an employee who is exempt from the overtime provisions of the Fair Labor Standards Act). If the position is changed to non-exempt, a new requisition should be initiated and recruitment activities should be redirected to include individuals currently working for the hotel as well as other potential external candidates. The potentially negative consequences of not promoting a qualified individual from within the organization must be considered.

Compensation may be a potential trouble spot for the Atlanta hotel, even though salaries appear to be competitive with the other hotels in the city. Employees should feel that their compensation is internally equitable relative to other employees in the organization and externally equitable relative to individuals doing similar work in other hotels. The availability of qualified, potential employees and local labor market conditions will influence both pay and benefits decisions.

Several potential alternatives are available to Cara Reynolds.

- Do not allow exceptions to the newly adopted guidelines. Walter Steiner should not be hired because he does not meet the standards set by the job specifications. There is no apparent need to hire a person from outside the organization who does not meet the minimum job specifications. Since final approval for the addition of an exempt employee to the payroll is retained by the divisional vice-president of human resources, permission for an exception should be denied along with the requests for interview expenses.
- Promote and/or transfer an individual from within the organization who meets the minimum job specifications. Expand the scope of the present recruiting program to develop an adequate pool of qualified talent.
- As an interim solution for meeting the immediate needs of the culinary department

at the Atlanta hotel, a sous chef from another hotel in the chain could be re-assigned on a temporary basis. If the Atlanta hotel were required to pay this individual's travel, maintenance, and salary while "on loan," it would probably speed up the selection process. In addition, a "fast track" training program could be instituted to develop and promote more people from within the organization.

- An exception to the present skill, experience, and compensation guidelines could be made while meeting legal requirements. Flexibility to modify the guidelines may need to be delegated to the general managers or human resource directors who are doing the actual hiring in situations where internal or external environmental conditions exist that cannot be controlled. An exception may need to be made in this situation so that Walter Steiner or a local individual with similar qualifications could be hired.

- The other Atlanta hotels should be surveyed to find out why they are able to lure away the hotel's key employees. A new salary survey could be conducted to insure equity between the current pay and benefit package of the hotel and its major competitors. Exit interviews should be reviewed to determine other potential reasons for their departures.

4.   *What should Cara Reynolds do to prevent situations similar to this from happening again?*

A training program should be established to inform all personnel involved in the hiring of exempt employees of the new human resource procedures. Although Jim Evans was well aware of the new procedures and had input during their development, he may not have adequately communicated these procedures to his subordinates. If the corporate human resource office were to develop and present the training program, it could receive valuable feedback to determine if the program was understood and could deal with specific issues that might foster resistance to the planned changes. The human resource manager at each hotel should be integrally involved in all the training activities to establish his/her credibility as a reliable source of information for interpreting and implementing the new program.

EPILOGUE

Cara Reynolds did not grant permission to hire Walter Steiner. The General Manager protested the decisions to the vice-president of the hotel division who concurred with the decision made by Cara Reynolds. However, the problem did not stop here. Jim Evans submitted the interview expenses for Walter Steiner's trip since he considered the situation to be a misunderstanding. Cara Reynolds did not authorize the reimbursement. After discussing the situation with the division vice-president, a training program was designed to answer questions, present the reasons for establishing the new human resource program, and iron out specific operational problems with the management staff at each hotel.

Source: Adapted from the case and case teaching note prepared by Roy A. Cook of Fort Lewis College and Jeryl L. Nelson of Wayne State College. The names of parties and all places in the case have been disguised. Presented to the Midwest Society for Case Research Workshop, 1989. All rights reserved to the authors. Copyright © 1989, Roy A. Cook and Jeryl L. Nelson. See L.L. Goulet (ed.), *Annual Advances in Business Cases, 1989*. South Bend, Ind.: Midwest Society for Case Research, 1989, 539-550. Used with permission.